Midwest Studies in Philosophy
Volume X

MIDWEST STUDIES IN PHILOSOPHY

EDITED BY PETER A. FRENCH, THEODORE E. UEHLING, JR.,
HOWARD K. WETTSTEIN

Many papers in MIDWEST STUDIES IN PHILOSOPHY are invited and all are previously unpublished. The editors will consider unsolicited manuscripts that are received by January of the year preceding the appearance of a volume. All manuscripts must be pertinent to the topic area of the volume for which they are submitted. Address manuscripts to MIDWEST STUDIES IN PHILOSOPHY, University of Minnesota, Morris, MN 56267, or Department of Philosophy, University of Notre Dame, Notre Dame, IN 46566, or Trinity University, San Antonio, TX 78284.

The articles in MIDWEST STUDIES IN PHILOSOPHY are indexed in THE PHILOSOPHER'S INDEX.

Forthcoming Volumes

Volume XI   Fall 1986 Studies in Essentialism
Volume XII   Fall 1987 Realism and Anti-Realism
Volume XIII   Fall 1988 Ethical Theory: Character and Virtue

Previously Published Volumes (All, but Volume I, are available.)

Volume I   1976 Studies in History of Philosophy
Volume II   1977 Studies in the Philosophy of Language
              Rev. Ed., Contemporary Perspectives in the Philosophy of Language
Volume III   1978 Studies in Ethical Theory
Volume IV   1979 Studies in Metaphysics
Volume V   1980 Studies in Epistemology
Volume VI   1981 Foundations of Analytic Philosophy
Volume VII   1982 Social and Political Philosophy
Volume VIII   1983 Contemporary Perspectives
              on the History of Philosophy
Volume IX   1984 Causation and Causal Theories

Midwest Studies in Philosophy Volume X
Studies in the Philosophy of Mind

Editors

PETER A. FRENCH
Trinity University
THEODORE E. UEHLING, JR.
University of Minnesota, Morris
HOWARD K. WETTSTEIN
University of Notre Dame

University of Minnesota Press ● Minneapolis

Published by the University of Minnesota Press,
2037 University Avenue Southeast, Minneapolis, MN 55414.
Published simultaneously in Canada
by Fitzhenry & Whiteside Limited, Markham.
Printed in the United States of America.

Library of Congress Cataloging-in-Publication Data
Main entry under title:

Studies in the philosophy of mind.

(Midwest studies in philosophy; v. 10)
1. Knowledge, Theory of—Addresses, essays, lectures.
2. Intellect—Addresses, essays, lectures.   3. Psychology
—Addresses, essays, lectures.   4. Consciousness—Ad-
dresses, essays, lectures.   5. Intention (Logic)—Ad-
dresses, essays, lectures.   6. Belief and doubt—Ad-
dresses, essays, lectures.   I. French, Peter A.
II. Uehling, Theodore Edward.   III. Wettstein, Howard K.
IV. Series.
BD161.S719   1986   128'.2   85-16488
ISBN 0-8166-1423-7
ISBN 0-8166-1424-5 (pbk.)

Midwest Studies in Philosophy
Volume X
Studies in the
Philosophy of Mind

Midwest Studies in Philosophy
Volume X

Why Paramecia Don't Have
Mental Representations

JERRY A. FODOR

. . . (Vamp till ready) . . . Oh: Birds do it/ Bees do it/ Even paramecia and fleas do it. And this consideration may occasion some embarrassment for the inquiring cognitive scientist.[1] Psychological theories purport to explain behavior by reference to the causal properties of mental states; but whereas behaving—at least in the sense of producing adaptive movements—is a pervasive achievement at all levels of the phylogenetic continuum, possessing mental states is presumably not. One might suppose, in particular, that the bag of tricks associated with the Representational Theory of Mind (hereinafter RTM) ought properly to be reserved for application to animals pretty much like us. It would, for example, be preposterous to attribute mental representations to paramecia; where would they keep them? Yet paramecia are negatively phototropic,[2] and tropisms are arguably behaviors in good standing. So, if our behaviors are to be explained by appeal to mental causes, *why shouldn't theirs be?*

Philosophers (and not only philosophers) have sometimes descried here the outlines of a challenge to the whole framework of intentionalistic psychological theorizing: Either show some principled difference in virtue of which intentional states and processes are warrantedly attributable to us but not to paramecia; or admit that consistent pursuit of the methods of RTM leads to preposterous conclusions, and hence that patterns of explanation in which appeals to mental representation figure can claim, at best, no more than a heuristic status. Here, for example, is D. C. Dennett (1978) commenting on some earlier work of mine:

> Fodor does not intend his argument to apply only to human beings, but how plausible is it that a mole or a chicken or a fish is capable of representing behavioral options of unbounded complexity. . . . We hardly

3

need a productive representation system to provide internal vehicles for them all, and the processes that lead to appropriate 'choice' ... would not often appear to be computational unless all processes are. ... Does a fish compute its proper depth of operation? Is there an important qualitative difference between the processes in the fish and the diving bell? .... Fodor has prepared a buttered slide for us and anyone who does not want to get on it might well dig in the heels at this point and ask for more details.

Notice two things: first, the worry is only *derivatively* about mental representations and operations because it arises about them only in case intentional states (beliefs, desires, thoughts, and so forth) are to be attributed to fish, chickens, moles, and the rest. If there *are* to be attributions of intentional states to lower organisms, then the appeal to RTM as a theory of such states would appear to be, in any event, no *more* implausible in their case than in our own. The point is that it's not just RTM but the whole apparatus of intentional ascription that Dennett's argument puts in jeopardy. Many philosophers who do not accept RTM are nevertheless prepared to believe that we do, and paramecia do not, act out of our beliefs and desires. (Contrapositively, many behaviorist—and especially Gibsonian—psychologists urge us to jettison the intentional explanation of human behavior on the grounds that consistency will otherwise require us to attribute mental states to creatures that patently do not have them.) In what follows, I shall take it for granted that RTM is the appropriate form for an intentional psychology. But it is worth bearing in mind that the slippery slope objection is one that *all* intentionalists in psychology must take equally seriously.

The second point is that, as Dennett sees, it's not just very small organisms that we have to worry about. Much the same slippery slope argument that gets you from us to paramecia can also be made to get you from computers to thermostats or, for that matter, from *us* to thermostats. It will not, in short, do to take Descartes's route and get off the slippery slope by postulating that lower organisms are machines. For one would then need an argument for not attributing mental representations to machines; and if to any machines, why not to all of them?

This consideration has sometimes been taken to warrant a very extreme 'chauvinism' (to borrow Ned Block's term) in the treatment of the mind/machine issue. It seems that, unless intentional states are attributed only to things *very* like us—perhaps only to things that have brains (see Searle 1980)—there can be nowhere to stop short of attributing them to thermostats and (who knows?) paper clips. There are those in artificial intelligence (see, for example, Dennett 1981, McCarthy 1979) who appear to be prepared to swallow the servomechanisms, maintaining, in effect, that Dennett's sort of argument shows thermostats to be much more our sort of chaps than had previously been supposed. But this really won't do; not, at least, on any reading of propositional attitude ascriptions that is other than blatantly instrumental. Perhaps there is *something* that would show that thermostats have nonfiguratively got beliefs and desires; some really world-shaking and spectacularly well-confirmed new sort of science might do it. But nothing of that sort is now in view. If, in the present theoretical context, we are forced to such wildly counterintuitive conclusions, then we have a reductio ad absurdum on our hands and the present theoretical context is seriously in jeopardy.

I'm not, of course, saying that we *are* so forced. It is, after all, perfectly reasonable to consider slippery slope arguments to be charges to which no answer is owing. For one thing, we know that arguments of (what seem to be) that form often lead from plausible premises to certainly false conclusions: as that acorns are oak trees; that zygotes are persons; that everybody is bald; that nobody is rich; and so forth. Moreover, what is (apparently) one of the premises of the argument looks to be either question-begging, or vague, or downright false. Presumably, the argument relies crucially on some such claim as that there is (to borrow Dennett's way of putting it) no "important qualitative difference" between the fish and the diving bell (hence, by iteration, between the paramecium and us) such as would justify attributing propositional attitudes to the one and witholding them from the other. But what does this amount to? There are plenty of what would *seem* to be *very* important qualitative differences between, say, me and a bug; for example, that it is a bug and I am not. If it's said that that sort of qualitative difference isn't important enough, one might well wonder what would possibly do. Why, in short, should one not take a slippery slope argument to be a reductio ad absurdum of its own 'no qualitative difference' premise?

One very well might; but I don't propose to continue in this vein. For, whether or not the slippery slope is impeccable as a *form* of argument — whether, even, it is precisely formulable — is really not the present issue. There is an unease that everybody feels about just what it is that an organism (or a system, or whatever) does or can do that makes it a plausible candidate for intentional ascription. The pain is not much relieved by wholesale adversion to argument to the best explanation (a tactic that friends of intentional ascription are often disposed to pursue). For though we do, no doubt, want to accept intentional theories just when they are the best explanations of what needs to be explained, it is perfectly reasonable to wonder what kind of phenomena it is that intentional theories are supposed to be the best explanations *of*. Dennett is quite right to "ask for more details," and I propose to approach the matter in just that spirit. The point is not so much to refute a prima facie sound objection to RTM; as just remarked, slippery slope arguments aren't sound even prima facie. The point is rather to get clear what it is about some sorts of creatures that makes it reasonable to hold that RTM is true of them.

More precisely, I propose to identify a certain (roughly behavioral) capacity and to claim that ascriptions of mental representations[3] to an organism are reasonable in virtue of the organism's possession of that capacity. By way of shorthand, I shall speak of a property P such that an organism has the capacity in question iff the organism has P. I hold that to identify P is to meet the challenge that the slippery slope argument against mental representation poses.

To get the ball rolling, I'm prepared to make certain concessions in favor of paramecia: to acknowledge certain similarities between them and us on which the case rests that if we have mental representations, so too must they. In particular, I'm prepared to grant the following.

(1) Some of a paramecium's movements count as 'behaviors' in some sense of that notion that brings them within the explanatory purview of psychological theory. This is to grant that they count as *responses* but not, of course, that they count as *actions*. I take it that only intentional systems can act.

(2) A paramecium can *see* in the minimal sense that its behaviors are affected by electromagnetic energy in what are, for us, the visible frequencies. I emphasize, however, that in conceding seeing in this minimal sense, I am conceding *only* photosensitivity. Thus, I am *not*, in general, prepared to admit claims about *what* paramecia can see; for example, about whether it can see *things*. (Perhaps all that a paramecium can see is light.) And I am not about to grant that a paramecium can see in the rich sense of the notion in which seeing is (or is a means to) the fixation of perceptual belief. On the contrary, my point is going to be that, although paramecia may see and behave, still, because they lack property P, there is no reason to attribute mental representations to them. Similarly, mutatis mutandis, for thermostats. I grant them thermal sensitivity, and I'm prepared to describe what they do as 'responding' to temperature change. But it won't follow from these concessions that they satisfy intentional ascriptions: that they want to keep the room at the temparature at which they're set . . . etc.

(3) I'm prepared to grant that, with paramecium as with us, the fact that they can see often plays a role in accounting for their behavior via a pattern of contingencies which define what I shall call a *primal scene*. The notion of a primal scence requires some discussion. It is central in much of what follows.

Anything counts as a primal scene in which:
(3a) An organism A sees something S.
(3b) S has some property O, such that:
(3c) A's behavior comes to exhibit some property C in consequence of (3a) and (3b).

I admit to not knowing what, precisely, the third of these conditions requires. Roughly, it's supposed to mean something like this: the fact that (3a) and (3b) are satisfied is part of the explantion of the behavioral effect; that fact is germane to explaining *why A's* behavior came to be *C*. But I don't, alas, know how to spell this out. Like many of the rest of you, I am unprepared to provide a general and adequate account of explanation. Lacking such, I shall rely upon intuitions about when the fact that *A* sees *S* and that *S* is *O* is germane to explaining the fact that *A's* behavior comes to be *C*, I *think,* however, that the intuitions I'll appeal to are untendentious except, perhaps, for those with axes to grind.

Notice that not every case of seeing constitutes a primal scene. For example, very often when *A* sees *S,* there will be no property that *A's behavior* comes to exhibit in consequence of *A's* having done so. We could, in fact, much reduce the artificiality of the notion of a primal scene by redefining it to admit cases where seeing *S* somehow affects *A's* mental states (e.g., *A's* beliefs and desires). But that won't do for present purposes because I want primal scenes of which paramecia can be the agents and, on my view, paramecia don't have propositional attitudes. For the sake of the argument, then, we shall have to pretend that the normal consequence of a perceptual encounter is a behavioral episode, not only in the paramecium's case but also in our own. Nothing central to what follows will rest on this, however.

Another reason why a case of seeing may fail to constitute a primal scene is that, although *A's* seeing *S* has some behavioral consequence *C,* still the fact that seeing the thing has that consequence is not, in any direct and straightforward way, attributable to properties of the thing that *A* saw. Suppose I see a house and foolishly take it to be a horse, with ensuing behavioral confusions. In such cases, it need not be primarily to properties of what I saw that the explanation of my behavior adverts. This is because what does explain the behavior is primarily certain (mistaken) beliefs that I came to have *about* the properties of what I saw. In such examples, *S's* properties explain *A's* behavior, if at all, only indirectly; via a story that says what it was about *S* that caused *A* to make the mistake he did.

The point is that entertaining a mistaken belief is an intentional state par excellence, so there is a short and well-traveled route from the contemplation of facts about perceptual errors, illusions, and the like to the postulation of mental representations and other cognitivist apparatus. I do not, however, propose to tread that path now because I want very much to avoid even the appearance of begging the main issues. Many psychologists think that the importance of misperception has been overestimated in the intentionalist tradition and that we ought to build our theories around cases where everything goes right.[4] Therefore, only cases of this latter sort are intended to count as primal scenes. For example, the case where I see a thing that is indeed a house and produce behaviors that are explained (inter alia) by its being so; such behaviors as, for example, uttering, "That's a house." Similarly, mutatis mutandis, where the organism at issue is a paramecium: primal scenes are intended to include only those of its putatively phototropic responses as are indeed elicited by the detection of light.

Having conceded all this to the lower organisms, I now propose to argue that there remains a critical difference between the sorts of primal scenes into which intentional systems can enter and those into which paramecia and such like can. The property P will be characterized in terms of this difference, and it will be seen that it is just the sort of difference that access to mental representations ought to make.

To begin with, consider the following question. It is true by stipulation that, when there is a primal scene, the fact that S has the property O enters into the explanation of the fact that A's behavior comes to be C, But now, how do such explanations go? It may help, in seeing the point of this question, to remember that not *every* property that S has is likely to be implicated in bringing about the behavioral consequences of perceptual encounters that organisms have with S. Consider such properties as being very, very far from the center of the Milky Way, or never having been thought of by Julius Caeser, or being furrier than a breadbox. These are, I suppose, all bona fide properties of my Siamese cat, Jerrold J. But it is wildly unlikely that any behavior consequent upon any sighting of my cat by any system, intentional or otherwise, ought to be explained by adversion to any of these of my cat's properties. Whereas, by contrast, being a cat, being cat shaped, being brownish, and being often underfoot, *are* properties of my cat in virtue of which perceptual encounters with her sometimes eventuate in behavioral consequences. What, then, is the difference between these two sorts of properties? Or, to put it more generally, what kind of link can there be between the fact that S is O and the fact that the behavior of A comes to be C, such that, in the primal scene, the former fact enters into the explanation of the latter?

Here is one kind of case: A's seeing S and S's being O explains A's behavior coming to be C in virtue of a *lawful relation among the properties involved.* This looks to be the natural thing to say about the phototropism of a paramecium, because it's plausible that the following expresses a lawful relation: When the light has a certain property (specificable, presumably, in terms of its frequency and intensity) and the appropriate 'psychophysical' conditions for the paramecium's detection of the light obtain (roughly, the light falls on the surface of the paramecium), then the paramecium moves in a certain way (say, in the direction of the least intense illumination). Similar remarks surely apply in the case of the thermostat since the explanation of its 'behavior' turns crucially upon a lawful relation between the ambient temperature that it detects and the length of the bimetallic strip that functions as its transducer.

In short, the thermostat's response to the temperature, like the paramecium's response to the light, constitutes what I shall now call a *primal scene of the first type*. The defining characteristic of a primal scene of the first type is that there is a lawful connection between a certain property of the 'stimulus' (viz, $S's$ property of being O) and a certain property of the ensuing behavioral response (viz, $A's$ behavior coming to be C).

I now want to indulge in some empirical speculation. In a certain sense it doesn't matter whether this speculation is *true,* but it maters very much whether it is *Plausible.* For, on my account, it is *because* this speculation is plausible that it seems clear that paramecium, thermostat, and the rest don't have representational states. Contrapositively, according to my account, if it were to turn out that this speculation is false, then we would indeed have learned something very surprising about paramecia and thermostats: at a minimum that they are intentional systems, at a maximum that they have minds.

The speculation is that, for paramecium, thermostat, and, generally, for *all* systems that are intuitively at the nonintentional end of Dennett's slippery slope, the *only* primal scenes that they enter into are primal scenes of the first type. To put it another way, what makes a paramecium a nonintentional system is that even if you are prepared to describe things that affect it as 'stimuli', and even if you are willing to describe the effects of the soi-disant stimuli as 'behavioral responses', and even if you are prepared to describe the causal interaction between stimulus and organism as involving the 'detection' of some property of the former by the later, *still,* all that happens when a nonintentional system gets involved in a primal scene is the lawful convariation of a property of the stimulus with a property of the response.

We're now very close to being able to say what property P is. To do so, I want to make a certain assumption about laws. Not all properties of things enter into lawful relations. There are, for example, laws that hold of things in virtue of their physical properties, and in virtue of their chemical properties, and in virtue of their hydrodynamical properties ... etc. But I doubt that there are laws that hold of things in virtue of, say, their astrological properties, or their distance from Eiffel tower, or their being grandmothers, or their being owned by grandmothers, or their being rumpled, or their being on the shelf just above the one where I keep my copy of *Word And Object,* or their being furrier than a breadbox. Which properties of things are the ones that enter into lawful relations is, in the largest sense, an empirical matter, not to be prejudiced by philosophical speculation here or elsewhere.

The metaphysical picture, in short, is that the world is filled with objects and that these objects are each possessed of indefinitely many properties. Laws are relations among properties; some properties are such that objects fall under laws in virtue of possessing them, and some properties are not. For convenience, I shall observe the following convention: if a property is such that objects fall under laws in virtue of possessing it, then that property is ipso facto *nomic*. All and only nomic properties enter into lawful relations; and, since not all properties enter into lawful relations, *not all properties are nomic.*

That's not much of a metaphysics, but, such as it is, I need it a lot, I therefore propose to digress just long enough to defend it against a plausible objection. Someone might say this: "You claim that not all properties are nomic; but I shall show you that there are, at a minimum, *laws about every empirical property.* For consider a case apparently to the contrary; consider, for example, the property of being a left shoe. It might *seem* that there are no laws about left shoes, but here's one: left shoes falling freely near the surface of the Earth accelerate at 32 ft/sec^2. Since this is a law, it follows by your stipulation that the property of being a left shoe is nomic. Similar examples will demonstrate the nomicness of any empirical property you choose; if being a left shoe is nomic, the rest are surely nomic too."

This argument is, however, ill advised; though all left shoes are subsumed by the laws of motion, nothing is subsumed by the laws of motion in virtue of being a left shoe. What shows this is the truth of the following counterfactual: Left shoes would *not* be subsumed by the laws of motion if they were not Newtonian masses (whereas anthing that is a Newtonian mass is subsumed by the laws of motion, whether it is a left shoe or not). Notice that this counterfactual is kosher; its antecedent expresses a logically possible state of affairs. For, of course, Newton might have been wrong (Aristotle might have been right), and then *nothing* would have been a Newtonian mass, left shoes included.

Well then, what's the property in virtue of which left shoes satisfy the laws of motion? It's the property of being a Newtonian mass, not the property of being a left shoe. It follows that the property of being a Newtonian mass is nomic, and that—at least so far as the present considerations are concerned—the property of being a left shoe is not.[5]

So much for deep issues in the philosophy of science; I return to the main track. If an object satisfies a law in virture of its possession of certain property, then that property is ipso facto nomic according to the present stipulation. It follows that, if all primal scenes in which the behavior of paramecium, thermostat, and other nonintentional systems are implicated are primal scenes of the first kind, then *only nomic properties of stimuli can elicit behavioral responses from such systems.*

I can now say quite succinctly what property P is: i.e., what the property is in virtue of our possession of which we are plausible candidates for intentional ascription and in virtue of their lack of which paramecia are *implausible candidates for intentional ascription. Unlike paramecia, we are frequently implicated in primal scenes in which the behaviorally efficacious stimulus property (the one that goes in for 'O' in the primal scene formula) is *nonnomic*. Or, as I shall sometimes put the point to achieve terminological heterogeneity: the difference between paramecia and us is that we can 'respond selectively' to nonnomic stimulus properties and they can't.[6] More generally, I claim that this distinction blocks Dennett's slippery slope: *any* system that can respond selectively to nonnomic properties is, intuitively speaking, a plausible candidate for the ascription of mental representations; and any system that can't, isn't.[7]

I seem to hear the following: "What about a 'system' consisting of a paramecium *and* a thermostat? This system 'responds selectively' to the *disjunctive* property of being either air at a certain temperature or light at a certain intensity. And this disjunctive property is nonnomic because, though there are laws about each of the disjuncts, there is surely nothing that satisfies a law in virtue of satisfying the disjunction. So then a thermostat-and-a-paramecium is an intentional system by you?"

There are two ways out of this. An obvious solution is simply to stipulate that the nomic properties are to be treated as closed under the Boolean operations; hence that being at a certain light intensity or a certain temperature is nomic after all. This is unnatural but it would do for the present polemical purposes. For, on any reasonable account of property identity, even this much too liberal notion of nomicness leaves us with scads of properties we can respond selectively to that are *not* nomic; hence with plenty of room for differences between paramecia and ourselves.

But I don't like it; it *is* unnatural, and it misses a deep point: viz, that not every system that responds whenever a stimulus is either F or G thereby responds to the property of being F or G.

If I say of an apple that I'm looking at 'red apple', then the property of the apple that I'm responding to is it's being red, not it's being red or a malted milk. If I build a gadget that's just a red filter and a buzzer, what the buzzer buzzes for is the redness of the input, not its redness or blueness. And if I have two such gadgets, one that's just a red filter and a buzzer and the other that's just a blue filter and a buzzer, then the whole thing buzzes for red and it buzzes for blue, but it doesn't—at least by my lights—buzz for red-or-blue. Similarly, mutatis mutandis, for the present case; a thermostat-and-a-paramecium responds to light at a certain intensity and it responds to some temperature or other, but it doesn't respond to the disjunctive property of being either-light-at-a-certain-intensity-or-some-temperature-or-other. (And, by the way, the laboratory subject who is trained to say 'blick' when the stimulus is either green or triangular *may* have learned a "disjunctive concept"; but the mere disjunctiveness of the response proclivities doesn't *show* that he has because it may be that he is just responding to green and responding to triangularity.)

I suppose that what *would* show that a disjunctive property is responded to would be behaviors mediated by patterns of inference like modus tollens: the system responds to the stimulus as an F because it takes the stimulus to have the property of being not G and the property of being G or F. But, of course, to describe a system as able to do all that *is* to describe it "from the intentional stance": to take some of its states as having content and some of its processes to be inferential. Considered as a criterion for selective response to a disjunctive property, this one would be question-begging. And, indeed, I have no such criterion; my point is just the negative one that mere disjunctiveness of response proclivities doesn't do it. Hence, the proposed objection to identifying intentional systems with ones that can respond selectively to nonnomic properties—viz., that the condition is trivially satisfiable—doesn't go through *even assuming that nomicness is not closed under Boolean functions.*

Back to business, P is the property a system has when it is able to respond selectively to nonnomic properties of its input. Not all organisms/ systems have this property, so P draws a line across the phylogenetic continuum. Just where the line falls depends, in two ways, upon empirical matters. It depends on which properties are nomic, and it depends on which psychological capacities given organisms actually have (which kinds of primal scenes they can enter into). Similarly, how thick the line is (whether there are intermediate cases) depends on such matters as whether nomicness is determinate for every property that organisms can respond to and whether the psychological capacities of organisms are determinate for every property that is nomic. I maintain, however, that wherever precisely the line is to be drawn, and however thick it may be, it is vastly plausible that we fall on one side and paramecium and thermostat fall on the other.

The argument for this last claim consists simply in pointing to relevant differences between our behavioral capacities and those of paramecia and thermostats. Paramecium/thermostat demonstrably respond selectively to such properties as, temperature and light intensity, and these properties are surely prime candidates for nomicness. On the other hand, I can't think of any case in which a paramecium/thermostat gives evidence of responding selectively to clear cases of nonnomic properties; hence the speculation, bruited above, that all the primal scenes they enter into are of the first type.

By contrast, it seems dead certain that among the primal scenes that *we* enter into are some where the relevant stimulus property (property O in the primal scene formula) is nonnomic, I would have thought, for example, that being a house is probably such a property, but perhaps not; perhaps Gibsonians would hold that there are "ecological" laws about houses. I'm prepared to grant the point *unless* it is being supposed that the mere fact that a property can go in for O in a primal scene is, in and of itself, sufficient for nomicness; that O *must* be nomic because, by assumption, there exist physical systems that respond selectively to O, I *don't,* of course, propose to grant *that,* because to do so would be to beg the question against the intentionalist

who, as we'll see, has a story of his own to tell about how *non*nomic properties can be the objects of selective response.

So, let's pick another case (remember that all blocking the slippery
slope requires is that there be *some* cases; that there be at least one case). Let's
pick being a crumpled shirt. Surely there are no laws, ecological or otherwise,
about crumpled shirts qua crumpled shirts. Yet, equally surely, this is a
property of things (viz., of crumpled shirts) to which we can respond selectively. That is, there are primal scenes that go like this: I see a thing that has
this property and respond to it in a way that is explained by reference to the
fact that the thing has the property and that I see it. For example, there is
the primal scene in which I see a crumpled shirt and, in consequence of doing
so, remark of the shirt that it is crumpled.

Various sorts of skepticism might now suggest themselves. One might,
for example, try denying:

  (a) that being a crumpled shirt is nonnomic;
  (b) that we ever really do see crumpled shirts;
  (c) that, even if we do see them, the fact that we see the shirts and that
        they're crumpled ever enters into the explanations of our behav-
        iors.

I won't scratch these itches here, though I'll return to related considerations further on. Suffice it, for the present, to remind the reader of a
consideration that one can loose sight of in the heat of philosophical polemic:
(a)-(c) are *truisms,* I proposed to defend the distinction between intentional
and nonintentional systems, but not against all comers; not, in particular,
against philosophers prepared to doubt any and every contingent truth that
the distinction presupposes. If, in short, the slippery slope argument can only
be run by denying one or more of (a)-(c), then it is, I think a challenge that
intentionalists can safely ignore. Slippery slope arguments yield *at most*
presumptive conclusions; and it seems to me that the presumption is now
on the other foot.

I do, however, need to meet a different sort of objection. Notice that
all I've done so far is to point to a property that, very plausibly, we have and
a paramecium does not. I have actually given no argument that the possession of that property is grounds for attributing mental representations to the
organisms that have it. Unlike the merely skeptical worries, this is a serious
objection; there are lots of ways of drawing a line across the phylogenetic
continuum. What is hard is to draw one that distinguishes the intentional
systems from the rest.

To see the connection between mental representation and the capacity
to respond selectively to nonnomic properties, let's return to the primal
scene. We have the fact that S is O being part of the explanation of the fact
that A's behavior comes to be C; and we have it that O is *non*nomic, hence

that there is no law that relates *S's* being *O* to *A's* behavior coming to be *C*. So there appears to be a puzzle: how does a property of a stimulus come to be implicated in the explanation of a property of a behavioral response if there is no law by which the two properties are connected? *It is largely this puzzle that motivates the representational theory of the mind.* Or, to put it less in the formal mode: selective response to nonnomic properties is, on the present view, the great evolutionary problem that mental representation was invented to solve. And the solution of that problem was perhaps *the* crucial achievement in the phylogeny of cognition. It was, I expect, on about the Tenth Day that God said: "Notice, I have made all these sorts of things that can respond selectively to instantiations of nomic properties in their environment: Iron filings to magnetic fields, paramecia to ambient light, thermostats to ambient temperature, and so forth, each to each. Now I shall make some sorts of things that can respond selectively to instantiations of *non* nomic properties in their environment as well. In aid of which: Let there be mental representation." And there was. There still is.

When the stimulus property in a primal scene is nonnomic, what connects *S*'s being *O* with *A*'s response coming to be *C* is that *O is a property that A represents S as having,*[8] and the relation between *A*'s representing *S* as *O* and *A*'s behavior coming to be *C is* lawlike (given mediation by other psychological states of *A*'s).[9] This requires to be done slowly. The idea is that the following must be the case if *S* is to affect the behavior of *A* in virtue of its possession of a nonnomic property:

(1) There must be a *psychophysical* relation between *A* and *S,* in virtue of which some of the *nomic* properties of *S* affect (nonbehavioral) states of *A*. Since *O* is, by assumption, nonnomic, it does not enter into such psychophysical relations.

(2) The detection of these psychophysical properties must eventuate in *A*'s coming to represent *S* as being *O*. The process involved is, in effect, the 'perceptual inference' of classical intentional psychology. Presumably such inferences exploit information from memory as well as information about the detected psychophysical properties of *S;* in the typical (though by no means exclusive) case, this would be information to the effect that the psychophysical properties cohabit with property *O,* so that the detection of the former provides a reliable index of the presence of the latter.

(3) There must be a lawful connection between *A*'s representing *S* as *O* and the appropriate behavioral consequence *C,* (However, see n. 9.) Figure 1 gives the gist.

In short, RTM attempts to answer the question how *S*'s being *O* can account for *A*'s behavior coming to be *C* in type two primal scenes, and it does so by introducing a *semantic* connection into the causal chain. *S*'s being

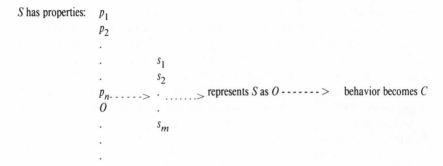

S has properties: p_1
p_2

represents *S* as *O* - - - - - - >   behavior becomes *C*

Figure 1

Figure 1. RTM explains how *nonnomic properties of the object of perception* can figure in determining the behavioral consequences of perceptual encounters: they occur as properties that the distal object both has *and is represented as having.* Thus *S* has psychophysical (hence nomic) properties $p_1 \ldots p_n$ as well as (nonnomic) property *O*. In virtue of psychophysical law, causal interaction between *S* and organism *A* eventuates in (nonbehavioral) psychological states $s_1 \ldots s_m$. In effect, states $s_1 \ldots s_m$ carry the information that *S* has $p_1 \ldots p_n$, and this information serves as the 'premise' of a perceptual inference of which the 'conclusion' is an attribution of *O* to *S*. Drawing this inference leads to behavioral consequences as illustrated. Roughly, horizontal connections indicated by dashed lines are nomologically necessary; those indicated by dotted lines are inferential.

O thus enters into the story twice; once in rerum natura, and once *as represented. Very* roughly, the first occurrence is required in order that the truth conditions of *A*'s perceptual belief should be satisfied ("see" is transparent to existential generalization; if *A* saw a crumpled shirt, then there was indeed a crumpled shirt that *A* saw). And the second occurrence is required in order that *S*'s being *O* should have consequences for *A*'s behavior, and in order that those consequences should be specific to the property *O* (as opposed, for example, to merely coextensive properties).

Another way to put the general proposal would be to say that the appeal to mental representation explains the possibility of perceiving properties that cannot be *detected,* where detecting a property requires, by stipulation, the activation of a *transducer* whose output is specific to that property. The idea is that what cannot be thus detected may nevertheless be *inferred* from (psychophysical) properties to which transducers *can* be tuned. Considered from this angle, the crucial difference between intentional systems and the rest would be that only the former can respond selectively to properties that are *not* transducer detectable.

Bob Matthews (among others) has often tried to convince me that this is the right way to see the matter; that the basic issue is not nomicness but transducibility. I'm inclined, however, to doubt that this is so. For, as far as I can see, the only difference between a transducer and anything else that responds selectively to proximal stimulation is that transducers are devices whose outputs, taken under their computationally relevant descriptions, are lawfully related to corresponding properties of their inputs; in short, the point about transducers is that they respond selectively only to nomic properties.[10] If there were a way of defining "transducer" independently of notions like nomicness, I would jump at it. But I don't know of any, and there's independent reason to suppose that nomicness is the more fundamental notion: unlike transduction, nomicness is a concept that we need outside the information sciences.[11]

Strictly speaking, I suppose I could stop here, I've done what I promised to do, which is to show a respect in which we are surely different from paramecia and in the explanation of which appeal to mental representation is plausibly involved. Having gotten this far, I can claim to have given presumptive grounds for disregarding Dennett's slippery slope even though I've said nothing at all about the epistemic question, "How do you tell when an organism has P?" There is, however, no reason to be disobliging, I now propose to provide a brief discussion of such epistemological matters, primarily because they throw some interesting cross-lighting upon the main issues; specifically, upon the origins of our intuitions about which sorts of creatures are *clear cases* of intentional systems.

We might start with what sounds like a skeptical objection of the epistemological kind. Someone could argue like this:

It's admitted on all hands that, whenever O is nonnomic and S's being O explains A's behavior coming to be C, there are bound to be *other* properties (specifically, $p_1 \ldots p_n$ of fig. 1) that *are* nomic and that are *also* involved in bringing about the behavioral consequences of A's perceiving S. If we think of a chain of states and events stretching between S's being O and A's behavior coming to be C, we can view S's being $p_1 \ldots p_n$ as a link in that chain; one that is, in fact, causally sufficient for producing the behavioral consequences. But since S's being $p_1 \ldots p_n$ *is* causally sufficient for A's behavior coming to be C, why should we think that S's being O comes into the story at all? Why shouldn't S's being $p_1 \ldots p_n$ bear the whole explanatory burden? This objection is crucial. Since $p_1 \ldots p_n$ are nomic by assumption, they are the sorts of properties that can be detected by transducers, mechanisms of a kind that we share with paramecia. So, perhaps we're not off the slippery slope after all.

Consider, for example, the case of the crumpled shirt. True, it *appears* to be the fact that Bill's shirt is crumpled that accounts for John's exclaiming: "Dear me, Bill, how crumpled your shirt is today." And, true again, being a crumpled shirt is a nonnomic property of crumpled shirts. However, there must be *some* nomic property that is immediately involved in the causal transaction that starts off with Bill's shirt being crumpled and ends up with John's exclamation. Following Gibson, we might say it's the property the shirt has of "structuring the light" in a certain way—a way such that an object which does structure the light that way can ipso facto be seen to be a crumpled shirt. By assumption, this property is psychophysical, hence transducer detectable; and, by assumption, its detection is causally sufficient for producing the appropriate behavioral response. So then, why not say that it is *this* property, and not the property of being a crumpled shirt per se, to which John's behavior is responsive? We could thus do without appeal to inference and mental representation in perceptual theory, and we could thus erase the line that intentionalists claim to have drawn between paramecia and higher creation.

I say this *seems* to be a skeptical objection; for one can imagine it uttered in the tone of voice: "Show me why I should suppose we ever see shirts at all; show me why I shouldn't suppose instead that what we always do is just detect light structures." I don't, however, propose to take the objection seriously in that form; we do see shirts, and it's loopy to deny that we do, and there's an end of it. There is, however, a *non*skeptical way of putting the matter, and it deserves sympathetic treatment. Someone might grant that we sometimes see things *via* (as it were) the light structures that we detect; and, granting this, might still want to know *which times those are.* Supposing, that is to say, that selective response to nonnomic properties is a real, not to say commonplace, phenomenon; and supposing too that, when it occurs, it is mediated by inference and mental representation, it is nevertheless reasonable to ask how bona fide occasions of selective response to nonnomic properties are to be distinguished from occasions on which *all* that happens is that some locally coextensive psychophysical property is detected.

I haven't any *criteria* for drawing this distinction, on account of there not being any. But I'll suggest some indexes: sorts of considerations that tend to tip the balance in favor of explanations that advert to S's being O (and not just to S's being $p_1 \ldots p_n$) in accounting for A's behavior becoming C. I don't mean to suggest that the considerations about to be reviewed are the only ones that can count in such decisions; on the contrary, the more we learn about mental representation, the more we learn about which sorts of phenomena it can be invoked to explain.

First, then, in the case of *verbal* organisms the decision is often easy. For the organism may *say* 'S is O' (rather than 'S is $p_1 \ldots p_n$') and this is a piece of behavior that is naturally accounted for by the assumption that it is the fact that S is O (and not the fact that S is $p_1 \ldots p_n$) that the organism is responding to. Notice, for example, that what John exclaimed was: "Dear me, Bill, how crumpled your shirt is today" and not, "Dear me, Bill, how crumple-shirtedly you structure the light today." We want a story about why John's seeing Bill eventuated in the former rather than the latter response; and the story that says that, in this case, detection of a light structure led to the perceptual inference that Bill's shirt was crumpled does the job nicely.[12]

It is, I think, for just this sort of reason that the apparatus of intentional ascription and mental representation seems securist in its application to verbal organisms. But for the fact that worries about circularity prohibit employing intentional idiom in the characterization of property *P*, the point till now could just as well have been put as: In type 2 primal scenes, *O* enters into the explanation of *C* as a property that *A sees S as having,* so that it is organisms that don't just see but also *see as* to which the representational account paradigmatically applies. And, of course, a verbal organism has resources for communicating, in considerable detail, not only *what* it sees, but also what it sees what it sees *as.* Roughly, the predicates of a natural language are sliced thin enough to correspond one-to-one with the properties to which we can respond selectively; the syntax of the language gives us, as it were, a distinct form of verbal behavior for each such property, and the semantics of the language gives us a mapping of each such form of behavior onto the property that it expresses.

This point is closely related to one of Donald Davidson's. He says that:

> without speech we cannot make the fine distinctions between thoughts that are essential to the explanations we can sometimes confidently supply. Our manner of attributing attitudes ensures that all the expressive power of language can be used to make such distinctions. One can believe that Scott is not the author of Waverly while not doubting that Scott is Scott; one can want to be the discoverer of a creature with a heart without wanting to be the discoverer of a creature with a kidney.... The intentionality we make so much of in the attribution of thoughts is very hard to make much of when speech is not present. The dog, we say, knows that its master is home. But does it know that Mr. Smith (who is its master), or that the president of the bank (who is that same master) is home? We have no real idea how to settle, or make sense of, these questions. (1975, 15-16)

There is, as I say, something to this point of Davidson's, but it oughtn't to be overplayed. In animal studies, we *can* very often deconfound locally coextensive stimulus properties; it's a matter of the appropriate application of the method of differences, and that is precisely what psychologists use 'split stimulus' paradigms to achieve. Nor is it really true, even in our own case, that we have terms corresponding to each stimulus property to which we can respond selectively. There are, for example, thousands of color distinctions we can make but that we can't encode. (I mean not just that we haven't single words for each of these colors, but that we can't reliably communicate, by purely verbal means, which color we intend.) And when we sail, or type, or paint, or tie our shoes, we respond reliably to subtle environmental properties that we are often quite unable to describe. Being able to produce the corresponding predicate is, in short, a useful index of a capacity for perceptual responses specific to O, but it's not a logically necessary condition; the connection between language and intentionality is pervasive but not deep. (Whereas, of course, the connection between *representation* and intentionality is the fixed point on which cognitive psychology turns; see Fodor 1975.)

We have a second, nonlinguistic, indicant of the involvement of O (and not just $p_1 \ldots p_n$) in the etiology of a behavioral response whenever it turns out that $p_1 \ldots p_n$ are *sufficient but not necessary* for the behavior coming to be C. This is, in fact, the *normal* relation between psychophysical properties and perceptual categories. The way a crumpled shirt structures the light (for example) changes from instant to instant depending on the state of illumination, the point of view that the perceiver assumes relative to the object of perception, and so forth. However, the *behavior* of the perceiver bent upon crumpled shirt identification will be largely insensitive to these sorts of variations; it will correlate *better* with the presence of O than with the presence of $p_1 \ldots p_n$. Indeed, as Fred Dretske has recently remarked (1981), the function of the perceptual constancies is precisely to ensure that this is so.

This sort of consideration has not, of course, been lost upon psychologists of Gibsonian persuasion. Their idea is that, where as the values of $p_1 \ldots p_n$ are likely to vary, literally from instant to instant, still there will be *higher order* nomic properties that are coextensive with being a crumpled shirt, at least when the circumstances are "ecologically valid." The burden of causal explanation in primal scenes can then be placed upon these higher order invariants, with whose detection the perception of crumpled shirts can be identified.

I have nothing to say about this proposal except that it is most unlikely to be true. Gibsonians require that for *each* nonnomic property to which we can respond selectively, there must be a coextensive, transducer-detectable, psychophysical invariant; eg., a light structure in the case of each such visual property. But, in fact, we haven't the slightest reason to believe that the set of light structures associated with, say, crumpled shirts is other than vastly and *open-endedly* disjunctive. To put it another way, we have no reason to believe that this set of structures constitutes a natural kind of explanatory purposes in *any* science (including psychology).[13]

A third and related index of the involvement of O—and not just of $p_1 \ldots p_n$—in the etiology of A's behavior is the *organism dependence* of the production of C in circumstances normally sufficient for seeing S. The point here is that what you can infer from the light structures you detect depends very much on *what you already know.* Since different organisms know different things at a given time (and the same organism knows different things at different times), whether you get *C* in primal scenes of the second type may depend extensively on *which* organism happens to be involved. Conspecifics, for example, can often produce quite different behaviors in type 2 primal scenes, whereas you'd expect all paramecia to be more or less interchangeable in respect of their phototropisms.

It is, I think, primarily the fact that inference depends upon the contents of the available knowledge base that underlies one's intuition that appeals to mental representation are most plausible in the case of explaining the behavior of relatively plastic organisms: organisms where 'individual differences' *make* a difference. Once again, though, this isn't a criterion. It's perfectly possible to imagine circumstances that would warrant attributing inferential/representational processes to account for very rigid (e.g., innate and reflexive) forms of behavior. All you need is that the stimulus property that elicits the behavior should independently prove to be nonnomic.

So much, then, for the epistemic issues. There would seem to be a variety of considerations that can support the intuition that appeals to nonpsychophysical (indeed, nonnomic) properties of an object may figure in explanations of the behaviors that perceptual encounters with the object engender. And, of course, this intuition is very strong. It is, quite generally, the 'perceptual' rather than the psychophysical properties of things that are psychologically (hence behaviorally) salient. It took science to tell us that there are light structures; but that shirts get crumpled one learns at mother's knee.

As for the larger questions, we now have several ways of marking the route that leads to Dennett's slippery slope. We can say that:

the relevant distinction between us and paramecia is that we can—and they can't—respond selectively to nonnomic stimulus properties:

or we can say that:

the relevant distinction between us and them is that they can't—and we can—respond selectively to stimulus properties that are not transducer detectable.

Or, since barring issues about consciousness, the notion of a *transducer-detectable property* plays approximately the same role in modern intentional theory that the notion of a *sensory* property did in more traditional accounts (see Fodor and Pylyshyn 1981), we could put it thus for those who prefer the older idiom:

What distinguishes intentional systems from the rest is that, whereas we've got perceptual categories, what they've got is, *at most,* sensory manifolds.

So ... even if ... Bugs do it/ And molds do it/ It's only 'cause their sensory mani-/Folds do it. And that's not good enough.

Notes

1. A lot of the conceptual groundwork for this paper was laid in Fodor and Pylyshyn (1981), from which I have borrowed extensively. I am indebted to my coauthor. I also want to thank the following: John Perry, Robert Shaw, and Michael Turvey for the late-night discussion that provoked these reflections; Tom Nagel for saving me, at the last possible moment, from protozoological solecism (see n. 2); and Georges Rey, Ned Block, and, especially, Michael Lipton for very helpful criticisms of earlier drafts.

2. Well, as a matter of strictest fact, they're not. But let's pretend they are.

3. Strictly speaking, I shall propose a condition whose satisfaction warrants the attribution of mental representation (rather than mental representations) to organisms. Less gnomically, I'm taking the issue to be: What justifies claiming that we do, and paramecia don't, have representational mental states. It takes further argument to show why the theory of representational mental states ought to quantify over mental representations (roughly, over mental symbols, sentences in the languages of thought). For discussion of this latter point, see Fodor 1975, 1980.

I should add that having representational states is a necessary, but not a sufficient, condition for having beliefs and desires; I take it that beliefs and desires are representational states *with characteristic functional roles*. To explain why ascriptions of mental representations may be justifiable in our case but not in that of a paramecium is thus only one step toward explaining why we have beliefs and desires and they don't. However, it's pretty clear that it's the crucial step.

4. See, for example, Gibson 1979, Neisser 1979, I am, in fact, not much moved by this. It is one thing to insist that veridical perception is, as it were, the unmarked case. It is quite another to embrace a theoretical apparatus that can make no sense of misperception at all. For discussion, see Fodor and Pylyshyn 1981.

5. Notice that this remains true even if one believes (as perhaps one does) that "all left shoes are Newtonian masses" is nomologically necessary. For, on the present account, not all nomologically necessary generalizations express laws; what is both nomologically necessary *and* a law is (not that all left shoes are Newtonian masses but) that all *physical objects* are Newtonian masses.

6. Any reply to the slippery slope argument that hopes to be more than question-begging must avoid appealing to intentional (with a 't') notions. It's thus worth emphasizing that "*A* responds selectively to property *P*" is transparent for the position that "*P*" occupies. Specifically, if expressions α and β designate the same property, then if "*A* responds selectively to α" is true so too is "A responds selectively to β."

7. In fact, this criterion concedes more than I really need to give away. Suppose that there are, after all, laws about left shoes: far away, on the planet Krypton, there is a special kind of geological stuff that glows in the ultraviolet when, and only when, in contact with a left shoe. And, as it turns out, this is a basic law, a physical postulate not further explainable even in an optimal physics. So then, the property of being a left shoe *is* nomic, contrary to what we had at first supposed.

Even on this assumption, however, it counts for our having mental representations that we can respond selectively to left shoes. This is because, though there is a law in which the property of being a left shoe is ineliminably involved, this law does not subsume *our* transactions with left shoes; specifically, *it doesn't enter into the explanation of our ability to respond selectively to left shoes.* This suggests a revised, less concessive version of the main principle: a system is intentional if it can respond selectively to a stimulus property even though no law connects the property it responds to and the selective property of its response.

Nothing in the text will turn on the difference between the weaker test and the stronger one, but it's worth bearing in mind that the latter is enforceable if you're hunting for counterexamples to the former.

8. Compare the "argument from illusion": How can reference to daggers figure in explanations of Macbeth's behavior, given that there was in fact no dagger there? Answer: the dagger comes in as the 'intentional object' of Macbeth's mental state, hence as the content of a mental representation.

9. The parenthetical provision is in light of the artificialty of primal scene talk. Strictly speaking, the effects of most stimuli impinging on intentional systems are *not* behavioral; they are effects on (e.g., nonperceptual) mental states of the system. You would thus expect laws to connect A's representing S as O with other A's mental states and thence, indirectly, to such overt events as A's behavior coming to be C.

10. And, conversely, if a property is nomic it is always possible—in principle at least—to build a transducer for it. Laws determine relations of co-instantiation among properties; whenever such relations hold, instantiations of one of the properties can be used to detect instantiations of the other. If there were some sort of geological stuff that glowed when exposed to left shoes (as per n. 7), then we could make a left-shoe-detector out of it; and this detector would be a transducer by the criterion given in the text.

11. This answers a question that I think Gibson was right to raise: viz., why can't we take the *whole organism* to be a transducer? The reply is that, by definition, transducers respond *only* to nomic properties of their inputs and at least *some* organisms—those that are intentional systems—can respond selectively to *non*nomic properties of their inputs as well.

12. I am, of course, now begging all sorts of skeptical worries about translation. Perhaps we can never know—perhaps there is no fact of the matter about—which of two locally coextensive properties a speaker is referring to. Perhaps it's not true that (perhaps we can't tell whether) 'your shirt is crumpled' means that your shirt is crumpled rather than that you structure the light crumple-shirtedly. I propose to continue to beg questions of this sort; skepticism bores me. And, anyhow, if the slippery slope argument requires these sorts of theses as ancillary premises, it is, to put it mildly, lacking in intuitive appeal.

13. This isn't, of course, Gibson's only problem. Either the property of structuring the light in a certain way is *identical* to the property of being a crumpled shirt, or else it is not. If it is, then contrary to previous assumption, being a crumpled shirt is transducer detectable after all and hence is nomic. Iterations of this argument lead to the (quite gratuitous) conclusion that *all* perceptual properties are ipso facto nomic; thus begs the question against intentionalist, besides outraging intuitions about which generalizations are laws.

So, let's suppose that the property of being a crumpled shirt is *not* identical to the property of structuring the light in a certain way. The question then becomes: by what process, if not by inference, could one get from the detection of the latter property to the perceptual identification of the former?

Much of the recent 'direct perception' literature amounts to an unedifying oscillation between the horns of this dilemma. (For discussion, see Fodor and Pylyshyn 1981.)

References

Davidson, D. 1975. "Thought And Talk." In *Mind and Language,* edited by S. Guttenplan. Oxford.

Dennett, D. C. 1978. "A Cure for the Common Code?" In *Brainstorms.* Cambridge, Mass.

Dennett, D. C. 1981. "True Believers. The Intentional Stance and Why It Works." In *Scientific Explanation.* The Herbert Spencer Lectures, edited by A. Heath. New York.

Dretske, F. 1981. *Knowledge and the Flow of Information.* Cambridge, Mass.

Fodor, J. 1975. *The Language of Thought.* New York.

Fodor, J. 1980. *Representations.* Cambridge, Mass.
Fodor, J., and Z. Pylyshyn. 1981. "How Direct Is Visual Perception?" *Cognition* 9:139 139-96.
Gibson, J. J. 1979. *The Ecological Approach to Visual Perception.* Boston.
McCarthy, J. 1979. "Ascribing Mental Qualities to Machines." In *Philosophical Perspectives in Artificial Intelligence,* edited by M. Ringle. Newark.
Neisser, U. 1979. *Cognition and Reality.* San Francisco.
Searle, J. 1980. "Minds, Brains, and Programs." *The Behavioral and Brain Sciences* 3: 417-24.

MIDWEST STUDIES IN PHILOSOPHY, X (1986)

Just What Do We Have In Mind?

LYNNE RUDDER BAKER

M any philosophers who otherwise have disparate views on the mind share a fundamental assumption. The assumption is that mental processes, or at least those that explain behavior, are wholly determined by properties of the individual whose processes they are.[1] As elaborated by Jerry Fodor, the assumption yields the widely held view called "methodological solipsism,"[2] a view developed from the plausible thought that whatever explains an individual's behavior must be "in the head" of the individual. Put this way, the assumption sounds innocent enough, perhaps even inevitable.

Nevertheless, I believe that, as it has been construed recently, the assumption is false. At the very least, it does not deserve the largely unquestioned status it enjoys, as I hope to show by a graduated series of thought experiments. I present the thought experiments as a series to expose a shared inadequacy in a variety of individualistic views, from type-type physicalism to the most sophisticated methodological solipsism; and I present them as graduated to suggest that having accepted the first relatively uncontroversial story, one has no principled place to demur later.

Although I shall discuss the thought experiments explicitly with regard to interpretations of Jerry Fodor's views, I believe that they have broad application. For example, I believe that they refute any physicalism that holds that for each distinct type of psychological state, there is a distinct type of internal, physical state; and that they refute any functionalism that holds that for each distinct type of psychological state, there is a distinct causal role.

1. METHODOLOGICAL SOLIPSISM

Fodor has developed the assumption that mental processes must be explained without reference to anything other than properties of the individual whose processes they are as a research strategy for cognitive psychology. Under the constraint of methodological solipsism, there are no psychological differences among molecularly similar individuals; relations between an organism and its environment can play no role in an explanatory psychology.[3] Fodor supports methodological solipsism by arguing that it is needed to secure intentional explanations of action—explanations in terms of an agent's beliefs, desires, intentions.

To the contrary, I shall show that methodological solipsism precludes intentional explanations, and that a solipsistic psychology, far from taking into account the way that the agent represents the world to herself, must deny that there is a fact of the matter as to whether an agent believes one thing rather than another in intuitively obvious cases.[4] The basic difficulty is that, contrary to the assumption of Fodor and other functionalists, classification of mental tokens by solipsistic computational features does not coincide with classification of mental tokens by "content," i.e., by what is expressed by 'that'-clauses of ascriptions, considered apart from truth or reference to individuals.

Mental states attributed by 'that'-clauses are individuated by the obliquely occurring expressions in the content clause. Obliquely occurring expressions are those for which substitution of coextensive expressions is impermissible. Thus, a belief that grass is green differs from a belief that snow is white in virtue of the obliquely occurring expressions in the embedded sentences. It will be useful to have a term for mental state tokens identified by obliquely occurring expressions in 'that'-clauses. Let us say that two tokens are of different *narrow semantic types* if there are semantic differences (other than truth or reference to individuals) in what is expressed by the obliquely occurring expressions in 'that'-clauses attributing them.[5]

More precisely, if 'A believes that p' and 'B believes that q' are true and 'A believes that q' is false and all the expressions in the 'that'-clauses occur obliquely, then tokens of A's believing that p and of B's believing that q are of different narrow semantic types. Because in the above 'p' abbreviates an English sentence S, to say that A believes that p is not to say that A would assent to the sentence S; A may not know English. Rather, for current purposes, a sufficient condition for A's believing that p is that there be some sentence S' in some language such that A would sincerely and comprehendingly assent to S' and S' has S as an adequate English translation. No ontological or theoretical commitment is intended; the idea of narrow semantic type that I employ can tolerate varying intuitions about, and theoretical positions on, for example, Kripke's puzzle about belief and Putnam's example of H_2O

on Earth and XYZ on Twin Earth.[6] The notion of a narrow semantic type is meant to provide an intuitive and pretheoretical means of referring to states individuated by obliquely occurring expressions in 'that'-clauses of ascriptions of those states.

Fodor has taken cognitive science to be defined by two theses:

The Content Condition. Mental states are relations to representations and mental processes are operations on representations, which are identified "opaquely" by 'that'-clauses.[7]

The Formality Condition. Mental processes are "formal" in that they apply to representations in virtue of their nonsemantic (e.g., syntactic, computational, functional, physical) properties.

Fodor's argument for the content condition is that attributions of beliefs, etc., via 'that'-clauses are required for explaining action. Fodor's main argument for the formality condition—which, he says, is tantamount to a sort of methodological solipsism (MS, 65)—is that it is "implicit in the computational model" of the mind (MS, 107), which he clearly regards as the only promising approach.[8]

Although the idea of formality must remain "intuitive and metaphoric" (MS, 64), formal properties are taken to be nonsemantic: "What makes syntactic operations a species of formal operations is that being syntactic is a way of *not* being semantic" (MS, 64). Formal operations "are the ones that are specified without reference to such semantic properties of representations as, for example, truth, reference and meaning" (MS, 64). Although representations are said to have semantic properties, it is only formal properties of representations—wholly dependent upon the "shapes" of the representations and independent of anything outside the subject—that are relevant to mental operations. Computational principles, which "apply in virtue of the form of entities in their domain,"[9] involve only formal properties. But any (contingent) properties of representations that entail anything about the external environment in which the subject is situated, or (contingent) properties that presuppose any actual relations between the subject and the environment are excluded by the formality condition as irrelevant to a scientific psychology.

The obvious examples of properties of representations that are thus irrelevant to explaining behavior are the semantic properties of truth and reference to individuals.[10] This much coincides wih pretheoretical intuitions: your child's desire to please Santa Claus may lead her to leave out cookies even though Santa Claus does not exist. Or your sister's belief that Fleet O'Foot is sure to win the Kentucky Derby may motivate her to cash in her certificate of deposit even though the belief turns out to be false. But, I shall try to show, the formality condition has much stronger consequences than such commonplace examples suggest. Indeed, it precludes the very sorts of explanations just offered. To see why, let us turn to the thought experiments.

I shall begin with an interpretation of Fodor's view that is probably too weak to be plausible, but that is suggested by his formulation at the beginning of his paper on methodological solipsism.[11] In any case, it will set the stage for more enriched interpretations. Moreover, the counterexample to this interpretation shows that many varieties of type-type physicalism are false.

2. AN ANTI-CARTESIAN MEDITATION

The first thought experiment is aimed at refuting the view that classification of mental state tokens by their actual causal relations coincides with classification of mental state tokens by narrow semantic type. Invoking non-singular, non *de re,* nonindexical attitudes, considered apart from truth, the first thought experiment will tell against the following thesis:

(A)   If two sequences of tokens cause two tokens of a single type of bodily movement, and if the tokens in the causal sequences are, pairwise, of the same physical types, then they are, pairwise, of the same narrow semantic types.

The thought experiments draw on several plausible assumptions. First, what a sentence says depends upon what language it is in. Second, people sometimes think in words. Third, which general belief a person expresses when sincerely and comprehendingly uttering a given sentence depends upon what language the person is speaking. Fourth, just as a single physical type of ink mark may have as tokens ink marks that have different meanings in different languages, so a single physical type of audible emission may have as tokens audible emissions that have different meanings in different languages.[12]

For example, in each of two languages, there may be meaningful expressions that are phonologically and even syntactically identical (insofar as syntax is independent of semantics), but whose correct English translations differ. A sentence from one of the languages may have "Life is short" as its closest English translation, whereas a phonologically and syntactically indistinguishable sentence from the second language may have "Art is long" as its closest English translation; in that case, native speakers of the first language would typically express different beliefs when using the phonologically and syntactically identical sentences.

Questions of indeterminacy of translation do not arise; for it does not matter whether there is a unique correct translation, just that some translations would be clearly incorrect. We need only imagine a case in which there are no plausible sets of analytical hypotheses relative to which the sentence translated into English as "Life is short," for example, could be translated into English as "Art is long." Nor do questions about the nontransitivity of translation bear upon anything I have to say.

A final preliminary: Some of the individualistic views I oppose—notably, Fodor's—draw explicitly on an analogy between minds and computers, according to which mental operations are to be treated as computations on formulas; and the only constraints on interpretation of the formulas are (to put it vaguely) coherence and consistency. Without endorsing the analogy, let me here enlist its aid. One feature of computers that should lead anyone impressed with the computer analogy to accept the thought experiments is that a given computer running a given program could be interpreted differently on different days. To cite an example of Georges Rey's:

> On Wednesday [a computer] deals with the intricacies of the SALT negotiations, on Thursday it plays chess with Bobby Fischer. Now it is perfectly possible in principle for the machine to pass through type identical computational and physical states on both days. All that would normally be needed is that on both occasions the input decks be themselves type identical, and that would occur should the two problem domains be construed, as it were, isomorphically. It's just that on Wednesday the punches in the cards are interpreted (say, by Carter) to refer to Brezhnev, Vienna, and 100-megaton bombs; and on Thursday the very same punches are interpreted (say, by Spassky) to refer to moves and pieces in chess. (MS, 91)

If minds are like computers in this central respect, then there is no conceptual bar to supposing that two minds could pass through the same types of physical and computational states and yet differ in certain of their types of mental states. The thought experiments are elaborations of this idea.[13]

It will be convenient to think of the following narrative as a movie, which we join midway and which we endure for only a few minutes.

The scene is upstate New York, where a man (who, as we know from reviews, is an unhappy lover considering making the first move to patch up his broken relationship) paces up and down in front of the building where his partner lives. We hear him mutter: "Should I give the familiar signal or not? Misunderstanding calls for reconciliation. I've been misunderstood and am ready for reconciliation. Giving the old familiar signal would be just the appropriate gesture of reconciliation." Several seconds later, he rings the doorbell in the distinctive way that is the familiar signal.

The scene changes to an unidentified frontier. Now a man (who, as we know from the reviews, is a soldier considering launching a retaliatory strike) paces up and down in front of his bunker (which bears a striking resemblance to the building in New York). Because the soldier speaks an obscure dialect (not Russian or any other well-known language), what he mutters is translated into English, in accordance with standard cinematic practice: "Should I launch the attack or not? Provocation invites retaliation. I've been provoked and am prepared to retaliate. Launching an attack would be an appropriate gesture of retaliation." Several seconds later, he presses a button in the particular code that launches an attack.

We leave the movie here, without waiting around to see what happens. On reflection, there seems no difficulty in supposing that the scenes described could occur in "real life." Suppose that they do. Then, the soldier does not believe what the lover believes, does not want what the lover wants, does not take into consideration what the lover takes into consideration. And the intuitive psychological differences between the two cannot be reduced to differences of objects of reference "outside the head." Their psychological differences extend to their general (nonsingular, nonindexical, non-*de-re*) beliefs. Surely the beliefs that provide the materials for their episodes of practical reasoning—for example, that misunderstanding calls for reconciliation and that provocation invites retaliation—are distinct general beliefs. Indeed, the lover, with complete mastery of his language and no slips of the tongue, emphatically denies that provocation invites retaliation. The lover's deliberation concludes with a decision to give the familiar signal; the soldier's deliberation concludes with a decision to launch the attack. Therefore, construed in terms of their opaque mental states, in terms of their *de dicto* attitudes, or in terms of the content clauses of ascriptions of attitudes, the intuitive psychological states of the lover and the soldier are radically dissimilar.

Suppose, however, that the way that the soldier launches the attack is by pushing a button with his left forefinger, and the way that the lover rings the doorbell is by pushing a button with his left forefinger. In fact, suppose that the soldier and the lover each flex the same muscles in the same way to the same degree. Considered as bodily movements, what each does is a token of the same physical type. And, considered physically, the proximate causes of their muscle flexings may be supposed to be tokens of the same physical type.

Suppose further that the portion of the soldier's dialect relevant to the story is phonologically indistinguishable from English. In fact, certain well-formed expressions in his dialect are acoustically and syntactically similar to well-formed expressions in English (though, of course, they differ semantically). Considered nonsemantically, nothing about these expressions distinguishes them from English expressions. When the real-life soldier utters aloud the sentence that is correctly translated into English as "Provocation invites retaliation," his utterance sounds just like an utterance of the English sentence "Misunderstanding calls for reconciliation."[14] There may be some play in what can be a correct translation from the dialect to English, but one thing is for sure: none of the soldier's current thoughts can correctly be translated into English as thoughts concerning reconciliation or familiar signals.

Because the bodily movements of the lover and the soldier are of the same physical types, and the proximate causes of the movements are of the same type, and their language have the odd relation just described, it is possible that, considered physically, the mental state tokens in their respective brains that constituted their episodes of practical reasoning are tokens of the same physical type.[15] For example, the physical operation that is the lover's tokening of "Should I give the familiar signal or not?" in the lover is of the same physical type as the operation that is the soldier's tokening that gets translated into English as "Should I launch the attack or not?" Of course, when the soldier scene in the movie occurs in real life, and the soldier asks his question in his dialect (not in translation), it *sounds* like a New Yorker's token of "Should I give the familiar signal or not?" The vibrations of the air waves are of the same type.

Because matters involving translation from one spoken language to another ar notoriously tricky, let me say a word more in defense of my description of the story. The key is that the soldier expresses his belief that provocation invites retaliation by uttering a sentence in his language that is syntactically and phonologically identical to the English sentence, "Misunderstanding invites reconciliation," but that is best translated into English as "Provocation invites retaliation."

We may assume that books from the soldier's dialect have been translated into English and have met all the standards of adequacy met by translations from, say, Swahili into English. In all these translations, every occurrence of what sounds like "Misunderstanding calls for reconciliation" gets translated as "Provocation invites retaliation." Since nothing is awry in the case of the soldier, and he is a native speaker of the dialect, it would be unreasonable to suppose that he uses the sentence in a nonstandard way. Moreover, there is independent evidence that "Provocation invites retaliation" is the best translation: the soldier does what one who had that belief would do in the circumstances—he launches the attack. A psychologist who knew the soldier's dialect and observed the soldier's behavior would not hesitate to attribute to him the belief that provocation invites retaliation. There is absolutely nothing fishy about such an attribution.[16]

The story depends upon no infelicity, linguistic or otherwise, on the part of either the lover or the soldier. Considered separately, there is nothing remarkable about either one or his situation. Each is a competent speaker of his language who is engaged in practical reasoning of the most straightforward sort; neither lacks any pertinent information nor makes a mistake in reasoning. There are no complications concerning tacit beliefs. There is no appeal to any intuitions about translation, other than that it is possible. There is nothing extraordinary or untoward about the situation of either party; it is only comparison of their situations in light of a certain theoretical standpoint that suggests a peculiarity.

The story of the lover and the soldier shows not only that two mental state tokens of the same kind (e.g., belief, desire, or intention) may be of distinct narrow semantic types without differing physically, but also that two *sequences* of mental state tokens, pairwise of the same kind, may be pairwise of distinct narrow semantic types without differing physically. We can represent the practical reasoning of each as an n-tuple of mental state tokens. Then we have two n-tuples of mental state tokens

$$<m_{11}, m_{12}, \ldots m_{1n}>$$

and

$$<m_{21}, m_{22}, \ldots m_{2n}>,$$

such that, taken pairwise (e.g., m_{11} and m_{21}, m_{12} and m_{22}, etc.), the members of each pair are of the same physical type, but of different narrow semantic types.

An immediate consequence is that many varieties of type-type physicalism, even relativized to species, are false. For two subjects may be in the same type of physical state (the brain state controlling emission of certain vocables, movement of one's finger in a certain way, etc.) without being in the same type of narrow semantic state (intending to launch an attack, as opposed to intending to give a familiar signal). Insofar as one takes such states, attributed by 'that'-clauses, to be typical psychological states, then psychological states are not wholly determined by physical states of the subject.[17] Thus, the first thought experiment, which shows that sequences of tokens of a single physical type need not be sequences of tokens of a single narrow semantic type, seems to refute type-type physicalism as set out by, for example, Kim and Armstrong.[18]

3. A SECOND ANTI-CARTESIAN MEDITATION

Someone may object that although the actual states of the lover and the soldier are of the same physical types, their dispositions regarding the button-pushing behavior seem to differ; causal role is determined, in part, by counterfactuals. Suppose, the objection goes, that just before the lover gave the familiar signal, his partner appeared at the door. The lover then would not give the signal, but, say, embrace his partner instead. But given the same physical type of stimulus, the soldier would not exhibit the same type of bodily movement; he would go ahead and push the button as before. Thus, the soldier and the lover seem to differ in disposition, in which case a more sophisticated Cartesian physicalism would not fall to the thought experiment.[19]

So let us enrich the thesis under attack by considering dispositional states as well as "occurrent" states. Suppose that the lover and the soldier not only are in the same sequences of physical states causing a bodily movement, but also that they have the same dispositions to make that bodily movement. The second thought experiment is aimed at showing the falsity of this thesis:

(B)   If two sequences of tokens cause two tokens of a single type of bodily movement, and if the tokens in the causal sequences are, pairwise, of the same physical types, and if two individuals in whom those sequences occur have the same dispositions with respect to that bodily movement, then the sequences of tokens are, pairwise, of the same narrow semantic types.

My response to the objection from dispositions is to augment the story in such a way that the soldier plausibly does have the same type of physical response as the lover to the same type of physical stimulus. For example, suppose that the soldier's sister looked just like the lover's partner and that the soldier had mistakenly believed that his sister had been killed in the provoking incident. Then, if she appeared at the door, the soldier would be so glad to see her alive, that, rather than launching the attack, he would rush up to embrace her.

Of course, the story can be extended to meet objections based upon other putative differences in dispositions regarding the (physically described) behavior in question; certainly all such putative differences proposed to me have been met in this way.

Now let us see how the thought experiments so far apply to Fodor's conjunction of the content condition and the formality condition in his paper on methodological solipsism.[20] My argument will be that tokens cannot be classified by narrow semantic type without violating the formality condition. Fodor does not consider this possibility because he supposes the content condition and the formality condition to be mutually supportive. Fodor holds—and I take this to be his central theoretical claim—that:

mental states are distinct in content only if they are relations to formally distinct mental representations; in effect, that aspects of content can be reconstructed as aspects of form, at least insofar as appeals to content figure in accounts of the mental causation of behavior. (MS, 68)[21]

Since the term 'content' has many uses, of more than one of which Fodor avails himself, let me reformulate Fodor's theoretical claim—that aspects of content can be reconstructed as aspects of form—like this:

(T)   Two mental state tokens of the same kind (belief, desire, etc.) are of distinct psychological types only if their representations differ formally.

Recall the story of the lover and the soldier. The only differences in their representations are narrow semantic differences, which are not

mirrored by any formal differences: the lover's representation concerns reconciliation; the soldier's, retaliation. So, we have:

(T')   Two mental state tokens of the same kind (belief, desire, etc.)
        may be of distinct narrow semantic types even if their represen-
        tations fail to differ formally.

From (T) and (T'), it follows that:

(T")   Two mental state tokens of the same kind (belief, desire, etc.)
        may be of distinct narrow semantic types, without being of dis-
        tinct psychological types.

That is, the formality condition allows no distinction between the lover's
belief token that misunderstanding calls for reconciliation and the soldier's
belief token that provocation invites retaliation. So, if (T) is true, then such
tokens are not of distinct psychological types. The lover's belief that misunderstanding calls for reconciliation is thus counted as being of the same
psychological type as the soldier's belief that provocation invites retaliation
(in accordance with [T]).[22] The general point suggested by the thought experiments is that, as long as these belief tokens are characterized nonsemantically
(in accordance with the formality condition), then the only difference between them is that they occur in different people; differences in narrow
semantic type elude anyone adhering to the formality condition.[23]

This result alone seems decisive reason to reject the formality condition; for it seems to me that there is a gross psychological difference between
believing that provocation invites retaliation and believing that misunderstanding calls for reconciliation; any theory that fails to countenance that
difference is inadequate as a psychological theory. Others may take a harder
line, however, and remind us that the price of a good theory is often to give
up certain intuitions. So suppose that, for the sake of the theory, we take the
lover and the soldier to be in the same psychological state. In that case, it
is unclear that there remains any purpose in attributing beliefs (or desires,
intentions) at all; such attributions would certainly be unsuitable candidates
for explaining anything.

Let me sharpen the point by imagining an alternative to the original
story. Suppose that just before the episodes of practical reasoning occurred,
the lover and the soldier were exchanged; so, in this alternative, unknown
to either of them, their respective environments are not what they believe
them to be. Since each is unaware of the switch, he reasons as before, in his
own language. But in the alternative version, the lover, believing that he is
giving the familiar signal, actually launches the attack. What is disconcerting
is that psychological explanations can not distinguish the soldier's (deliberate) launching of the attack in the first version from the lover's (unwitting)
launching of the attack in the alternative version, without violating the
formality condition.

Before showing why, let me emphasize that there is no incoherence at the level of intuitive intentional explanation.[24] From the alternative version of the story, we have this information ("data"): the lover does not believe that he is launching an attack; he is in the same physical states as the soldier who (in the first version) does believe that he is launching an attack. Both, in fact, launch attacks. Intuitively, without regard for the formality condition, it is fairly clear how to give an (adequate, to my mind) intentional explanation of each of the launchings; the explanation of the lover's (unwitting) launching of the attack would have two parts—an "intentional" part, including such attributions as that he believed that he was giving the familiar signal, and a "factual" part, including such information (unavailable to the lover) as that what he took to be a doorbell was actually a triggering device.[25] So, there is nothing particularly puzzling about the case as described. Now, however, let us subject the "data" to the theory that includes the formality condition.

Suppose that Fodor explained the soldier's launching the attack as satisfying this schema:

x believes that provocation invites retaliation.

x believes that he has been provoked and desires retaliation.

x believes that the most appropriate way to retaliate is to launch an attack.

Therefore, x launches an attack.

Within the strictures of methodological solipsism, there is no way to rule out explanation of the lover's (unwitting) launching of the attack by the very same schema. Since differences in psychological state, as we are currently considering them, require formal differences, and since there are no such formal differences between the soldier's belief that he is launching an attack and the lover's belief that he is giving a familiar signal, we attribute to the lover a single psychological state regardless of whether we characterize it as a belief that he is launching an attack or as a belief that he is giving the familiar signal. But if these are attributions of a single psychological state, they must have the same place in psychological explanations of his behavior.

This result is doubly unfortunate: First, *ex hypothesi,* the lover did not believe that he was launching the attack; therefore, such a belief cannot help explain his launching the attack. And since the formality condition does not permit a distinction between attributing to the lover the belief that he was launching the attack and attributing the belief that he was giving the familiar signal, the latter belief can be no more explanatory than the former. Thus, it is doubtful that beliefs, desires, or intentions can ever be explanatory if psychological explanations conform to the formality condition.

Second, an action performed deliberately should not receive the same psychological explanation as the same type of action (under the same description, in the same external circumstances) performed unwittingly. This suggests that the psychological explanations that do conform to the formality condition are defective; for without attributions of belief, such explanations must be blind to psychological differences between doing something deliberately and doing it unwittingly. From another angle: as long as the formality condition is honored, two *incompatible* intentional explanations are equally justified.[26] Thus, it appears that the formality condition and the requirement of methodological solipsism preclude intentional explanations of action, in which case the formality condition renders practical reasoning irrelevant to what one does.

To sum up the argument against Fodor's methodological solipsism: if we take psychological states in accordance with the formality condition, we cannot coherently ascribe content to them, in which case beliefs, desires, and intentions do not count as psychological states and do not figure in psychological explanations. On the other hand, if we take psychological states in accordance with the content condition, we can attribute beliefs, desires, and intentions, but only by violating the formality condition.[27]

More generally, the stories show that even very abstract beliefs—such as that misunderstanding calls for reconciliation—fail to conform to the strictures of methodological solipsism. The identity of such beliefs depends in part upon the language-using community of the believer; so even considered apart from semantic properties of truth and reference, such beliefs are not wholly "in the head."[28]

4. A FINAL ANTI-CARTESIAN MEDITATION

There is yet a further enrichment of the functionalist thesis available to the theorist who hopes to reconcile attribution of attitudes with the formality condition. It may be postulated that whether or not an individual has a certain belief, say, is a matter of total functional organization. Since the story of the lover and the soldier may have been just a local accident, the full machine table descriptions of the two may yet reveal differences in physical-functional state. A still more stringent functionalist view would require two individuals to share all their dispositional states in order to be in the same functional state. This suggests the following thesis:

(C)   If two sequences of tokens cause two tokens of a single type of bodily movement and if the tokens in the causal sequences are, pairwise, of the same physical types, and if two individuals in whom those sequences occur have the same dispositions with respect to all their bodily movements, then the sequences are, pairwise, of the same narrow semantic types.

To refute thesis (C), I shall propose a new thought experiment, one that will also refute the most stringent possible thesis, and with it a variety of versions of functionalist theories. The final thought experiment[29] is aimed at refuting not only (C) but also the following:

(D)   If two sequences of tokens cause two tokens of a single type of bodily movement and if the tokens in the causal sequences are, pairwise, of the same physical types, and if they occur in two individuals who are molecule-for-molecule duplicates, then the sequences are, pairwise, of the same narrow semantic types.

I would venture to guess that most philosophers of mind today take it as a constraint on psychological theories that molecule-for-molecule duplicates must be psychological duplicates.[30] Under such a constraint, I hope to show, psychology would have nothing to do with beliefs, desires, or intentions.

Suppose that hidden in the Andes is an isolated culture—call it *Unique* —whose language and customs are very different from ours; a casual English-speaking observer would immediately be struck by the cultural differences and would not understand the language. Even so, it happens that a small fragment of the Uniques' language is acoustically indistinguishable from grammatical English. When a Unique utters what sounds like 'Jet planes are faster than trains', she is not talking about jet planes at all—nobody in Unique has the slightest idea of what a jet plane is; the Uniques are too remote even for electricity. (The Unique sentence 'Silicon chips are useful' is best rendered in English as 'Coca leaves are good to chew'.)

Now, for reasons of their own, one rather eccentric family raises their daughter in seclusion, isolated even from much of the communal life of the village. It also happens that, unlike other Uniques, the isolated daughter becomes acquainted only with that part of the Unique language that is acoustically indistinguishable from grammatical English; so, every sentence she utters in Unique has an acoustic and syntactic twin in English, which, of course, would not be a correct translation of its Unique counterpart. For example, when the isolated daughter utters what sounds like 'Berries are more abundant than bananas', she is not talking about berries and bananas, but rather about goats and chickens.

Since the Uniques are physiologically similar to us (and, of course, subject to the same physical laws), there is no difficulty in supposing that the isolated daughter has an anatomical duplicate, a molecule-for-molecule replica, in North America. The North American duplicate also has eccentric parents, who keep their daughter not only in seclusion but also on an unusual diet. Both daughters learn their languages without normal contact with the external physical and social world.[31]

At every moment throughout their short lives, the isolated daughter and her North American duplicate are in the same types of physical states.

But the Unique daughter and her North American duplicate do not share the same *de dicto* beliefs in this sense: if objects of belief are taken to be sentence-like entities in the head, the Unique daughter and her North American counterpart each have tokens of the same formal (syntactic, causal, functional, physical) type, but of distinct narrow semantic types. The argument does not require that they differ in all of their narrow semantic states, only that they differ in at least one narrow semantic state without differing in functional organization.

Consider, for example, a belief whose only physical or behavioral manifestations are verbal dispositions. (E.g., "Love means never having to say you're sorry.") Suppose that the Unique daughter complains to her mother that the rainy season, during which she has little to entertain her, is awfully long, and her mother cheers her with the thought that she should be grateful that it does not last a century, which is a much longer period of time, longer than anyone lives. In this conversation, the Unique daughter comes to believe that centuries are long, but to express her belief in Unique, she says what sounds like the English sentence, "Good ideas are rare."

At the same time, the North American daughter and her mother are having a phonologically similar conversation about the difficulty of staving off boredom when one cannot go outside. The North American mother cheers her daughter with the thought that she should be grateful that she ever has any interesting ideas about what to do, since good ideas are hard to come by. In this way, the North American comes to believe that good ideas are rare. Both the Unique daughter and the North American daughter assent when presented with the sounds, 'Good ideas are rare', but in doing so, they do not assent to the same thing. Since both beliefs—that centuries are long and that good ideas are rare—are abstract and relatively isolated from other attitudes and from nonverbal behavior, it is not difficult to suppose that with the same machine table descriptions (and hence with the same dispositions regarding their bodily movements), the girls could differ in these narrow semantic states.[32]

Although I believe that this example suffices to show that molecular duplicates may have different beliefs (considered apart from truth and reference to individuals), it should be noted that the differences in narrow semantic type need not be confined to attitudes so removed from observation of nonverbal behavior. For example, when it occurs to the North American duplicate that berries are more abundant than bananas, it occurs to the Unique daughter that goats are larger than chickens—although to assert that goats are larger than chickens in Unique, one would utter what sounds just like the English sentence, "Berries are more abundant than bananas."

Suppose that each daughter were presented with drawings of goats, chickens, berries, and bananas and were issued instructions that sound like "Pick out the berries." The North American daughter would point to the picture of the berries. The Unique daughter would interpret the instructions to concern goats. Would she point to the picture of a goat? No. The sounds "Pick out" do not mean in Unique what they mean in English; they should be translated as "Point to the left of." So the Unique daughter, interpreting the instructions (which sound like "Pick out the berries") as "Point to the left of the goat," also points to the picture of the berries, just like her North American counterpart.

Now suppose that the drawings are presented again, but that this time the picture of the berries is to the right of the picture of the goat. On being issued the same instructions, the North American daughter again points to the berries. Again, the Unique daughter interprets the instructions as "Point to the left of the goat." Would the Unique daughter in this case fail to point to the berries—and thus diverge in her physical movements from her North American counterpart? Again, no. Small children are apt to confuse left and right, especially if they are ambidextrous as the daughters are. The Unique daughter does not yet have an adequate grasp of the concepts of left and right and so she points to the right of the goat—i.e., to the berries.

Just luck, one may reply: If the Unique daughter is presented with enough instructions, sooner or later, her bodily movements will differ from those of her North American counterpart. This consideration is not to the point, however. Since she does not yet have the same dispositions concerning spatial directions that we do, as far as her current dispositions are concerned, there are no grounds for supposing that her bodily movements will ever differ from those of the North American daughter.[33] All that is claimed is that they are molecule-for-molecule duplicates throughout their short lives; had they lived longer, they might have developed molecular differences.

One day the Unique daughter and her North American duplicate are in forests on their respective continents. Each sees an orange mushroom. Although neither has seen such a plant before, each has been told things that lead her to have certain beliefs. The Unique daughter believes that the plant has magical properties, and is curious to experience its effects; so she eats the mushroom. The North American duplicate, undergoing the same types of functional and physical states as the Unique daughter, believes that the plant is poisonous, and is curious (as children seem to be) to know what a poisonous plant tastes like; so she, too, eats the mushroom. Of course, the North American duplicate goes through the same types of physical states as the Unique daughter. Since the mushrooms are poisonous, unfortunately, the little girls both die—in exactly the same way at exactly the same time.

Because the girls had different beliefs and desires, intentional explanations of their eating the lethal mushrooms should differ. Perhaps we would trace the Unique daughter's eating the mushroom to her false belief about magical powers and the North American daughter's action to her reckless desire to know how a poisonous plant tastes. No such explanations are allowed by the formality condition, of course. For on the formality condition, there is no psychological difference between the Unique daughter's wanting to experience magical effects and the North American duplicate's finding out how a poisonous plant tastes; nor does the formality condition permit any psychological difference between the Unique's belief that the plant has magical powers and the North American's belief that the plant is poisonous. Typed nonsemantically, the belief and desire tokens are of the same types.

On a computational psychology guided by the formality condition, the intentional explanations invoking the girls' beliefs and desires are interchangeable; but it would be clearly unacceptable to explain the Unique's eating the mushroom by reference, say, to a desire to see how a poisonous plant tastes—a desire that she did not have.

So, in terms of the physical states they instantiate and in terms of their machine table descriptions, the Unique daughter and her North American duplicate lead parallel lives; but their beliefs, desires, and intentions diverge. Therefore, molecule-for-molecule replicas can differ in their *de dicto* beliefs.

The case of the molecular replicas, I believe, refutes any view that supposes, as functionalist views typically do, that psychological states identified by narrow semantic type coincide with functional states identified by causal role. No matter how causal role is described, molecule-for-molecule duplicates have the same causal history.[34]

5. BROADER IMPLICATIONS

The upshot is that the functionalist hope of giving an account of propositional attitudes in terms of computational states is doomed.[35] Fodor remarks, "I shall simply take it for granted that you cannot save the cognitive science program by going syntactic. Either mental representations are going to honest-to-God represent, or we are going to have to find an alternative to [the representational theory of the mind]."[36] But as we have seen, given the formality condition, they cannot represent. If psychological states are construed as computational states, then beliefs, desires, intentions, and other states attributed by 'that'-clauses fail to qualify as psychological states.[37]

Let me conclude by recapitulating some of the consequences of accepting the computational view of the mind as governed by the formality condition, or for that matter, by Stich's autonomy principle.[38]

1. A computational view of the mind allows believing that *misunderstanding calls for reconciliation* and that *provocation invites retaliation* to be tokens of a single psychological type.
2. A computational view of the mind thus precludes any *intentional* explanations of action.

3. A computational view of the mind permits no explanations of any sort of actions as ordinarily described, for example, 'launching an attack', 'giving a familiar signal'. Such commonplace actions could receive no psychological explanation at all. For without recourse to beliefs, desires, and intentions, nothing remains that is capable of explaining such actions under those descriptions.

4. A computational view of the mind cannot handle the ways that action can go wrong. Without invoking beliefs and desires, there is no distinction between the lover's accidentally launching the attack and the soldier's intentionally launching the attack, nor between the Unique's eating the mushroom in the (mistaken) belief that it has magical properties, and the duplicate's eating the mushroom in the (true) belief that it is poisonous.

5. A computational view of the mind makes the whole legal process unintelligible. The determination of intentions, beliefs, and desires is integral to many legal proceedings; on the formality condition, there are no correct determinations of such attitudes.

6. A computational view of the mind allows no way to assess action as to its rationality or irrationality: Without access to what an agent believes that she is doing, there are no grounds for determining the rational merits of what she does.

7. A computational view of the mind makes moral judgments false or senseless. If there is no psychological difference between believing that one is doing A and not so believing, it is inappropriate to praise or blame a person for doing A.

All these unsavory consequences of a psychology constrained by the formality condition are aspects of what is perhaps the most fundamental consequence: A computational view of the mind severs psychological explanation from practical reasoning; since the lover's and the soldier's episodes of practical reasoning are of formally indistinguishable types, the formality condition makes a mystery of how practical reasoning can be connected to action. The deliberations of the soldier that lead up to his launching the attack cannot figure in the true psychological explanation of what he did (which could only be described in such terms as 'muscle-flexing in left forefinger'). It would thus become totally unclear how action can be connected with, for example, satisfaction of desires.

These consequences seem to me to be sufficiently devastating to make the formality condition (and with it, methodological solipsism and the computational view of the mind) utterly implausible. A computational psychology would seem useless for the aims of prediction and control as usually conceived: the only descriptions under which behavior could be predicted would be ones that hold no psychological or ethical or social or legal interest.

Such a psychology may be able to predict that a person will contract certain muscles, but not that he will write bad checks.[39]

Fodor applauds the Cartesian point that one's mental states are entirely independent of how the world actually is. But he stops too soon. For computational psychology governed by the formality condition, not only would it be true that one's mental states are independent of how the world actually is, but much more radically, it would also be true that one's mental states are independent of how the world *seems*. For how the world seems to one is a matter of one's beliefs and other attitudes attributed by 'that'-clauses. But on a theory about mental processes that conforms to the formality condition (and to methodological solipsism), such attributions become unintelligible.[40]

Notes

1. Those who share this assumption include functionalists, who take mental states to be capable of multiple physical realizations; type-type physicalists, who take types of mental states to be nothing other than types of physical states; (some) Cartesian interactionists, who take changes in mental state to cause changes in brain states; epiphenomenalists, who take changes in mental states to be caused by changes in brain states; (some) token-token physicalists, who take tokens (i.e., datable occurrences) of mental states to be identical with tokens of brain states. Although I aim to cast doubt on all these positions, there is one sort of token-token physicalism that is compatible with everything I say here: Every occurrence of a mental event may be identical with the occurrence of a physical event, as long as what counts as physical includes features of the individual's social environment. Call this position, with which I am not taking issue here, 'social supervenience', to indicate that if the mental supervenes on anything, it supervenes on the physical-cum-social, and not on states of the individual considered in isolation. Thus, methodological solipsism is appropriate as a general target of my argument.

2. The term 'methodological solipsism' in its current use originates with Putnam. See Hilary Putnam, "The Meaning of 'Meaning', in *Mind, Language and Reality: Philosophical Papers,* vol. 2 (Cambridge, 1975, 215-71. There is an ambiguity in formulations of methodological solipsism. In Putnam's original formulation, methodological solipsism is the assumption that "no psychological state, properly so called, presupposes the existence of any individual other than the subject to whom that state is ascribed" (220). Subsequent formulations, according to which, for example, narrow states are what molecular duplicates share, require that narrow states must be specifiable independently of any facts about the world "outside the head." The second formulation of methodological solipsism would be violated by presupposing that there exists anything other than the individual whose mental processes are being explained; the first formulation would be violated only by presupposing the existence of a particular entity outside the head. Formulating methodological solipsism as the requirement that mental states be explained without presupposing the existence of anything outside the head is ambiguous between the two readings. Although there may be (narrow) psychological states interestingly describable without presupposing the existence of any particular entity other than the subject, my arguments will suggest that there are no (even narrower) psychological states interestingly describable without presupposing that there exists anything other than the subject. For a discussion of ambiguity of methodological solipsism from another angle, see Kent Bach, "*De Re* Belief and Methodological Solipsism," in *Thought and Object: Essays on Intentionality,* edited by Andrew Woodfield (Oxford, 1982), 121-52, esp. 123-29.

Fodor develops his position in "Methodological Solipsism Considered as a Research Strategy in Cognitive Psychology," *The Behavioral and Brain Sciences* 3 (1980): 63-109. Hereafter, this article will be referred to as "MS," and subsequent citations to MS will be made in the text.

3. Stephen P. Stich's principle of autonomy is another, more precise formulation of a solipsistic restriction, according to which "any differences between organisms which do not manifest themselves as differences in their current, internal, physical states ought to be ignored by a psychological theory." *From Folk Psychology to Cognitive Science: The Case against Belief* (Cambridge, Mass., 1983), 164.

4. The consequence is that Fodor's program, in effect, collapses into Stich's. Stich adopts a "syntactic" view of the mind, according to which putative states, individuated by "content," such as believing that *p,* are not genuine psychological states. They do not figure in explanations of behavior described "autonomously," where an autonomous behavioral description is one such that "if it applies to an organism in a given setting, then it would also apply to any replica of the organism in that setting." (*From Folk Psychology to Cognitive Science,* 167.)

5. What I am calling 'narrow semantic type' is in line with at least one of Fodor's uses of 'content': In "Propositional Attitudes" (in *Representations: Philosophical Essays on the Foundations of Cognitive Science* [Cambridge, Mass., 1981], 183), Fodor takes the " 'content' of a propositional attitude, informally, to be whatever it is that the complement of the corresponding [propositional attitude]-ascribing sentence expresses." Fodor's "opaque" taxonomy of attributions of attitudes yields attitudes identified by narrow semantic type.

6. Since Putnam's Twin Earth case may be pressed as an immediate counterexample to methodological solipsism, and since Fodor seeks to rebut such a use ("Cognitive Science and the Twin-Earth Problem," *Notre Dame Journal of Formal Logic* 23 [1982], 98-118), I shall give Fodor the benefit of the doubt here; successful defense against Putnam is irrelevant to my arguments, which raise different issues.

7. 'Content condition' is my term, but it is clear that the significance of the representational theory of the mind lies in its recourse to content. To think that Marvin is melancholy, for example, is to be in a relation "to a representation the content of which is *that* Marvin is melancholy." Or again, "mental states are distinguished by the *content* of the associated representations, so we can allow for the difference between thinking that Marvin is melancholy and thinking that Sam is . . ." (MS, 63; emphases his).

8. Fodor's argument for the content condition is that "opaque" attributions of attitudes (i.e., identified by narrow semantic type) are required to explain action: "In doing our psychology, we want to attribute mental states fully opaquely because it's the fully opaque reading which tells us what the agent has in mind, and it's what the agent has in mind that causes his behavior" (MS, 67). Or again, Fodor proposes the thesis that "when we articulate the generalizations in virtue of which behavior is contingent upon mental states, it is typically an opaque construal of the mental state attributions that does the work" (MS, 66). Finally: "Nontransparent taxonomies respect the way that the organism represents the object of its propositional attitudes *to itself,* and it is this representation which functions in the causation of behavior" (MS, abstract, 63). Fodor takes transparent and opaque taxonomies of attributions of attitudes to be associated with "naturalistic" and solipsistic psychologies, respectively. The only alternative that Fodor sees to solipsistic psychology is a "naturalistic" psychology that considers subjects as embedded in their environments. Fodor regards naturalistic psychology as unfeasible because, he claims, it would have to wait upon the completion of all the other sciences to get canonical descriptions of environments, in the absence of which the project of explaining organism/environment relations is hopeless. My arguments show that opaque taxonomies of attributions of attitudes (i.e., attitudes identified by narrow semantic type) are not solipsistic.

9. Fodor, "Propositional Attitudes," 201.

10. There are other grounds, independent of the formality condition, for supposing that the truth and reference of an agent's beliefs are irrelevant to explaining behavior. See, for example, John Perry, "The Problem of the Essential Indexical," *Nous* 13 (1979): 3-22; and William G. Lycan, "Toward a Homuncular Theory of Believing," *Cognition and Brain Theory* 4, (1981): 139-59.

11. MS, 64. There is no suggestion that dispositions are required to identify a token as being of a particular semantic type. Also see Dennett ("A Cure for the Common Code?" *Brainstorms: Philosophical Essays on Mind and Psychology* [Cambridge, Mass., 1978], 104), who raises questions about Fodor's apparent commitment to "the impossible view that ... nothing can be believed, thought about or learned without being explicitly represented." Note, however, that my arguments strike at a different point: in the case envisaged, all the beliefs are explicitly represented. Also, I have no quarrel (unlike the Churchlands, for example) with the functionalists' contention that the objects of belief are (in some sense) linguistic entities. Rather, assuming that beliefs are explicitly represented and dependent upon language, the difficulty lies in the solipsistic presuppositions about language.

12. If we add to the four assumptions a fifth—that what language one speaks is not determined solely by what's in one's head—we are close to a valid argument for the conclusion that some *de dicto* beliefs are not in the head. But rather than focus on such an abstract argument, it seems more illuminating to approach the issues more concretely through an example.

13. In "Tom Swift and His Procedural Grandmother" (*Representations: Philosophical Essays on the Foundations of Cognitive Science* [Cambridge, Mass., 1981], 204-24), Fodor considers an example of programs simulating, on the one hand, the Six-Day War and, on the other hand, a chess game: "It's a possible (though, of course, unlikely) accident that these programs should be *indistinguishable when compiled;* viz. that the [machine language] counterparts of these programs should be identical, so that the internal career of a machine running one program would be identical, step by step, to that of a machine running the other" (207; emphasis his). Also, "machines typically don't know (or care) what the programs that they run are about; all they know (or care about) is how to run their programs. This may sound cryptical or even mystical. It's not. It's merely banal" (207). Banal or not, the possibility seems to have substantial and unforeseen implications.

14. Indeed, a more contrived example would have the lover and the soldier physically overlap in such a way that a single token expresses the two beliefs. This possibility indicates that the issue is how to characterize differences between the uses of a token. David Austin made this point to me.

15. Burge's important articles make my description of the story all the more plausible. See Tyler Burge, "Individualism and the Mental," *Midwest Studies in Philosophy* 4 (1979): 73-122; "Other Bodies," in *Thought and Object: Essays on Intentionality,* edited by Andrew Woodfield (Oxford, 1982), 97-120.

16. As Arthur Danto has pointed out, there could be two languages that are phonologically similar in this way: A token of one of the languages could be acoustically indistinguishable from a token of the second, yet the best translation of the first into English is "Motherhood is sacred," and the best translation of the second is "Beans are high in protein." ("The Last Work of Art: Artworks and Real Things," reprinted from *Theoria* 39 in *Aesthetics: A Critical Anthology,* edited by George Dickie and R. J. Sclafani (New York, 1977), 551-62). The stories here are extensions of Danto's insight into the context of practical reasoning.

17. It may not be apparent that these thought experiments also refute a common brand of Cartesian interactionism. If it were supposed that the relevant mental states were "occurrent" and dispositional states of immaterial souls, rather than of brains, a similar conclusion would follow: two individuals may be in the same type of soul state without being in the same type of narrow semantic state as long as soul states are individuated without presupposing that anything exists other than the individual whose states they are. The issue of what makes the lover's soul token a token of a particular narrow semantic state is just as problematic as what makes his brain token a token of a particular narrow semantic state. In the case imagined, which narrow semantic state the lover is in is a matter of what language he speaks; but what language one speaks cannot be determined by an individual brain or soul, considered as if nothing else existed. Since invoking putative soul states does not solve the difficulty I am raising, for the

remainder of this paper, I shall not assume that there are immaterial souls. These points emerged from a conversation with Bob Hambourger.

18. The story is applicable to numerous views. See, for example, D. M. Armstrong, *A Materialist Theory of the Mind* (New York, 1968); also Jaegwon Kim, "Physicalism and the Multiple Realizability of Mental States," reprinted in *Readings in the Philosophy of Psychology,* vol. 1, edited by Ned Block (Cambridge, Mass., 1980), 234-36; David Lewis, "An Argument for the Identity Theory," reprinted in *Materialism and the Mind-Body Problem,* edited by David Rosenthal (Englewood Cliffs, N.J.; 1971), 162-71; J. J. C. Smart, *Philosophy and Scientific Realism* (New York, 1963). At times, Dennett also seems to assume that a robot that "models" a person's internal processes must have the same beliefs as the person ("A Cure for the Common Code?" 105). Igal Kvart emphasized this objection to my original example.

20. It may be objected that we should only speak of functional states *within an individual,* and hence that examples considering states in different individuals are not to the point. The objection is not to the point. (1) We could just as well consider a single individual at two times. (2) The notion of functional equivalence across individuals must make sense for Fodor since he proposes methodological solipsism as research strategy for cognitive science. (3) The example concerns sequences of physically similar *tokens* that have causally similar relations; the notion of function would make no sense if it did not follow that such sequences may be functionally equivalent.

21. Fodor qualifies this somewhat by saying, "That taxonomy in respect of content *is* compatible with the formality condition, plus or minus a bit, is perhaps *the* basic idea of modern cognitive theory" (MS, 68). I do not believe that the "plus or minus a bit" affects my argument; nor do I see a better way to try to reconcile the content condition and the formality condition than the way I suggest here.

22. This result seems to undermine *any* intentional psychology that conforms to the formality condition. In particular, it refutes Fodor's conception of propositional attitudes and, with it, his view of cognitive science:

> That is, one might think of cognitive theories as filling in explanation schema of, roughly, the form: *having the attitude R to proposition P is contingently identical to being in computational relation C to the formula (or sequence of formulae) E. (The Language of Thought* [Cambridge, Mass., 1979], 77.)

If to have an attitude were to be in a certain computational state, then having the belief that provocation invites retaliation would be "contingently identical" to having the belief that misunderstanding calls for reconciliation. Although it is unclear what contingent identity comes to in this context, there is surely no possible world in which those are the same beliefs. Although this alone does not force abandonment of (T), retention of (T) (and of the formality condition) becomes quite costly. What must be given up is the view that individuation by sentence believed coincides with individuation by psychological type.

23. Dennett makes a similar point. See his "Three Kinds of Intentional Psychology," in *Reduction, Time and Reality,* edited by Richard Healey (Cambridge, 1981), 37-61, esp. 56; and "Beyond Belief," in *Thought and Object: Essays on Intentionality,* edited by Andrew Woodfield (Oxford, 1982), 1-95.

24. It is sometimes noted that explanations are pragmatic, in that what counts as an explanation of an event for one purpose may not be a suitable explanation of the same event for another purpose. Such pragmatic differences are irrelevant here. The purpose throughout will be to exhibit the connection between mental processes and behavior.

25. In *"De Re* Belief in Action" (*Philosophical Review 91,* [1982]: 363-87), I proposed such a two-stage approach to explaining intentional action; the result of the argument of the current paper is that even the first stage, in terms of the agent's point of view, is not available to the methodological solipsist. In "Why Computers Can't Act" (*American Philosophical Quarterly 18* [1981]: 157-63), I alluded to the fact that the first-person perspective is not private.

26. In addition, Fodor's account does not seem to meet his own conditions. In "Propositional Attitudes," Fodor proposes a set of conditions of adequacy on views of propositional attitudes. Of the five "a priori conditions, which, on my view, a theory of propositional attitudes ... ought to meet," (177), I believe that the theory that Fodor actually proposes in "Methodological Solipsism Considered" fails to meet at least three. The only condition clearly fulfilled by the conjunction of the content condition and the formality condition is that propositional attitudes are analyzed as relations.

27. David Austin has pointed out that my stories may be seen as an extension of inverted-spectrum objections to belief states, states that are thought most susceptible to a functionalist account. Vis-à-vis Block's examples against functionalism, David Sanford has noted that my stories are analogous to comparing China's pain to India's tickle. Cf. Shoemaker's remark that the inverted spectrum problem for functionalism is one of a class of 'qualia inversion' problems for that view. Sidney Shoemaker, "Inverted Spectrum," *Journal of Philosophy* 79 (1982.): 368, n. 10.

28. William G. Lycan has noted that a proponent of referential semantics would hold that the difference between the soldier and the lover is merely a difference of reference; if so, the solipsist may be safe because he excludes differences of reference along with truth as irrelevant to determining psychological states. I believe that I can accommodate this objection. The reason to introduce a term like 'narrow semantic type' is to have a convenient way to refer to attitudes individuated by 'that'-clauses, as they ordinarily and pretheoretically are attributed; if attitudes cannot be thus individuated without reference to individuals, I should adjust the characterization of 'narrow semantic type' accordingly. My position would not thereby be threatened. Suppose that semantics is exhausted by truth and reference; then my claim would be that what is "in the head" cannot be coherently characterized as belief that such-and-such. This is so because what is in the head does not suffice to distinguish between belief that p and belief that q, where p and q are logically nonequivalent propositions. I need not claim (nor deny) that there is a *tertium quid*—a difference in narrow semantic type that outruns sameness of physical constitution but is not merely a difference in referential semantics. But the *tertium quid* is the solipsist's best shot if he wants an intentional psychology; for without it, it is obvious that classification by 'that'-clauses violates the formality condition—a point that I am at pains to argue below. The point that I want to establish is this: no matter how narrowly one construes belief, as long as it is still recognizably belief (i.e., attributable by 'that'-clauses), it cannot be understood wholly in terms of properties of the individual whose belief it is; therefore, if behavior is to be explained only by what's in the head, it is not to be explained by belief. To put it another way, intentional psychology that aims to explain behavior cannot be solipsistic.

29. The upcoming case of the Unique daughter takes care of objections from the language of thought. It would be to no avail, for example, to claim (implausibly) that we *never* think in a natural language, and hence that the soldier's and lover's thoughts may be encoded in different Mentalese representations. I do not see how Fodor could take this route; he says: "Presumably *which* proposition an internal representation expresses—what content it has—would be complexly determined by its functional role in the organism's mental life, including, especially, the way it is connected to stimulations and responses. Functional identity of internal representations would then be criterial for their intertranslatability" ("Propositional Attitudes," 203). In any case, there are independent arguments against the possibility of a language of thought. See Patricia Churchland, "A Perspective on Mind-Brain Research," *Journal of Philosophy* 78 (1980): 185-207, especially 189, for some arguments. Also see Dennett, "A Cure for the Common Code?" 90-108, and Gilbert Harman, "Language Learning," in *Readings in the Philosophy of Psychology*, vol. 2, edited by Ned Block (Cambridge, Mass., 1981), 38-44. Moreover, to deny the possibility of molecular duplicates (as in the Unique daughter case) would be, in an important way, to give up the machine analogy.

30. Stich explicitly invokes a "replacement argument" to justify his principle of autonomy. *From Folk Psychology to Cognitive Science*, 165.

31. The supposition that one could learn a language in such circumstances is not alien to the methodological solipsist, who must assume either that one could acquire a substantial fragment of a language—enough to be said to speak a language—if one were a brain in a vat, or that learning a language lies outside the purview of psychology.

32. From the point of view of methodological solipsism, the history of the acquisition of beliefs is irrelevant. We may as well simply stipulate that each daughter has the belief attributed; evidence that each does is provided by sincere and comprehending assent to appropriate sentences. The solipsist's concern is confined to *current* internal states, the identities of which are independent of facts about their acquisition. Telling these stories is part of the general strategy throughout: to employ unexceptional, ordinary descriptions of ordinary phenomena without the strictures of solipsism, and then to see what descriptions and explanations are available to the solipsist.

33. Igal Kvart has pressed such counterfactual cases; however, he would agree, I think, that the only counterfactuals that need concern me are those grounded in the girls' actual dispositions, not in dispositions that they would have if, say, they had had wider experience or a fuller grasp of their respective languages.

34. At the Chapel Hill Philosophy Colloquium at the University of North Carolina in 1983, Fodor argued for a reinstatement of the observation/inference distinction. Certain beliefs are said to be theory-neutral in that, given similar stimulations, individuals come to have similar beliefs regardless of differences among their theoretical commitments. I do not believe that such a move would affect my arguments for several reasons. (1) It is implausible to suppose that behavior-explaining beliefs could be construed wholly in such observation terms. 'Retaliation' is a long way from observation, and it is implausible to suppose either that all those who understand the concept of retaliation "connect" it to observation in the same way, or that such general concepts fail to function in explanations. (2) Terms that could be observation terms in Fodor's sense would not be ordinary English words like 'drinkable'. At the very least, the Unique daughter case shows that there is a gap between environmental stimulus and solipsistic stimulus. (Cf. "Point to the berries.") David Sanford suggested that the observation language project begins to resemble Husserl's attempt to isolate a purely phenomenological language; what connection would such a "language" have to ones we speak?

35. Indeed, I believe that a contradiction may be formally derived from assumptions that seem central to the enterprise of using computer models to account for propositional attitudes. See my "A Farewell to Functionalism," in preparation. Patricia Kitcher remarks: "Support for the 'computer model' . . . derives largely from the belief that the software-hardware relation is a prototype for the correct model of the relation between contentful psychological states and physiological states." ("In Defense of Intentional Psychology," *Journal of Philosophy* 81 [1984]: 103.) My arguments are intended, in part, to raise questions about the machine analogy. Thus, I would side with Searle in his denial that an individual has intentional states by virtue of instantiating a program, though, of course, I am less sanguine about Searle's positive view of intentionality as a purely biological phenonomenon. See, for example, John Searle, "Minds, Brains and Programs," *Behavioral and Brain Sciences* 3 (1980): 417-57.

36. Fodor, "Cognitive Science and the Twin-Earth Problem," 102.

37. If we stipulate that psychological states are whatever states cause behavior, it may be supposed that, say, 'signing one's name' may be a canonical description of behavior conforming to the formality condition, and 'intending to sign one's name' a psychological state. (Contrast 'making a contract' and 'intending to make a contract'.) What I have tried to show is that even 'signing one's name' is not a narrow enough description to conform to solipsism. The risk of proprietary uses of terms like 'behavior' is that what emerges may have no interest for anybody.

38. In my forthcoming book, I shall develop these issues more fully. Also, by setting out a view according to which the mind is, in an important sense, social, I hope to avoid relativism as well as solipsism and foundationalism. David Austin has observed that if my examples work against solipsistic views of the mental, it is not clear how adding more people would help: Why

couldn't one raise the same objections against a "social functionalism?" I shall try to address such issues in the book.

39. Of course, one may hold, with Barbara von Eckardt, for example, that cognitive psychology does not aim to provide explanations of action so much as explanations of cognitive capacities—such as the capacity to understand stories, read, reason deductively, recall common facts and so on. ("Cognitive Psychology and Principled Skepticism," *Journal of Philosophy* 81 [1984]: 67-88.) But this line is hardly satisfactory: practical reasoning is a cognitive capacity, and one that is intimately connected with intentional action. Thus, there is no begging off explanation of action by confining attention to cognitive capacities.

40. I am especially grateful to David F. Austin, William G. Lycan, and Igal Kvart for criticisms and suggestions; also helpful were Jonathan Malino, David Sanford, and Robert Hambourger. This work was supported by the National Endowment for the Humanities, the National Humanities Center, and Middlebury College. I read earlier versions of this paper at the National Humanities Center and at the University of North Carolina at Chapel Hill.

Consciousness

BRIAN O'SHAUGHNESSY

What is consciousness? Clearly, as its verbal roots suggest, it must have intimate links with *knowledge*. Thus, one supposes that it must be a psychological state that puts one in a position to know about the environment, and in the self-conscious to know about one's own mind as well under the widest possible headings. But exactly what does consciousness do for its owner? And what is its relation to sleep, anesthesia, coma, hypnotic trance, and so forth? How does it relate to the psychological phenomena that occur in one who is conscious; in particular, how does it relate to that centrally important psychological phenomenon, thinking? And what are we to say about that very special phenomenon, self-consciousness? For example, what is the relation between self-consciousness and the consciousness that obtains in nonrational animals? What is the link between consciousness itself and what might be called *particular* consciousnesses or awarenesses?

These are some of the questions I hope to consider in the course of providing an account of the nature of consciousness. One important constraint I recognize in arriving at such an account is that we want a theory that will be adequate for rational and nonrational animals alike. Intuitively, it seems clear to me that they are conscious in the very same sense; after all, "stunned" seems to have the same sense for man and beast. But I also believe that a correct theory should necessarily entail that some measure of rationality in the prevailing mental state is, in rational beings, a logically necessary and sufficient condition of consciousness. Is it not clear that consciousness in humans is not merely *a* rational state but that it is *the* one and only rational state? Despite formidable difficulties posed by the existence of consciousness in the insane, it seems certain that even there, beliefs are formed largely on the basis of good reasons. It is precisely because such a state of affairs is absent in the dream, that those states of consciousness that permit dreaming must be accounted nonrational states.

A natural model for consciousness is the canvas upon which a painting appears. It is a faulty model because an empty canvas is an unproblematic possibility, whereas an empty consciousness is at least a difficult concept to wrap the mind around. Yet the model is a natural one: although a canvas in and of itself presents nothing to view representationally, it makes possible and is a physically necessary condition for the configurations of paint that do present something to view. Thus, it is natural and perhaps also correct to conceive of consciousness as the necessary ground for those of the mind's episodes that enable us to relate in the way that we normally wakefully relate to the environment—even, perhaps, as the necessary ground for absolutely *any* of its phenomena. This last, however, cannot possibly be true. After all, consciousness must be the state that creatures lose when chloroformed, and yet this latter state is consistent with dreaming. So consciousness cannot be a necessary condition of psychological phenomena. It cannot even be a necessary condition of that important brand of psychological phenomenon that we single out under the general but precise concept of the *experience* (which ranges across imagings, thought events, perceptual episodes, and dreams, but excludes phenomena like onsets of belief and fadings of memory). There is also reason for thinking that consciousness must be a necessary condition for what one might call an awareness of *reality* (or something such). This, at any rate, will condition my approach. I shall attempt to characterize consciousness by listing those of its necessary properties that are causal powers of such a kind as to make possible whatever it is that we think consciousness typically achieves. In particular, something like awareness of the world or environment in general; and in addition, in the self-conscious, awareness of the inner world and (as a direct result) the possibility of self-direction and hence of freedom itself.

A further preliminary question: we speak of particular consciousnesses, but also of consciousness itself. Why? Well, what do we mean in speaking of "particular consciousnesses"? The expression "awareness" is ambiguous as between knowing and noticing, and only the latter is an experiential sense. After all, neither knowing nor coming-to-know, unlike hearing or seeing, is an experience. Should we then understand "particular consciousness" merely as being synonymous with noticing, and therefore as an experience that is an awareness of some distinct *something?* The trouble with this is that it leaves out imagings and emotings and hallucinatings, all of which can be classified as "particular consciousnesses."

I think it best to assume that "particular consciousness" or "awareness" might be taken in the nonexperiential sense (A) of knowing or coming-to-know, or in one of the two experiential senses of (B) attentive or noticing experience; or (C) simply to conclude that "particular consciousness" is synonymous with "particular experience." All of these states could very naturally be described as "particular awarenesses" or "particular consciousnesses," the object of such awarenesses being (respectively) (A) propositional object, (B) material object, and (C) intentional object. Then I can see no reason for restricting "particular consciousness" to one rather than another sense. Now in the sense in which waking or sleep rate as "states of consciousness," no one of these "particular consciousnesses" can possibly be characterized as a "state of consciousness." Rather, particular consciousnesses occur *in* states of consciousness, as when we say that a particular dream image occurs *in* the state of consciousness, sleep. Then why allow the word "consciousness" to span these three particular usages, and simultaneously to occur on its own simply as "consciousness"? What is the link between that state of consciousness that we simply dub "consciousness" and such particular consciousnesses? The relation between them can tentatively be summed up in the following statement: Consciousness is a state that both makes possible and actually necessitates a continuous array of experiences, among which characteristically occur attentive experiences that characteristically generate particular cognizant awarenesses of the state of the physical environment at that time. The fundamental bond between consciousness and an attentive knowledge of the world finds recognition in this formulation.

What is the object of consciousness? What is the object of that psychological state that is lost when concussion occurs? Or is it that there simply is *no* object? Or might it be that there are a multitude of separate objects? Or is the state of consciousness directed instead to one highly general object?—somewhat as the state of hunger is directed to nothing more specific than food, or even merely to something to eat, before it crystallizes onto one specific food object? Consciousness is a psychological state. Indeed, in some sense it is the preeminent psychological state—not in being a necessary condition of all psychological states (which it is not), but in that the real possibility of consciousness is a necessary condition of absolutely any psychological state. After all, whereas philosophers might disagree over *what* psychological phenomena necessarily exist in whatever is animal, no one could suppose consciousness to be absent from their number. Then, because it is a psychological state, might it be that consciousness (like much else that is psychological) is intentionally directed? That seems unlikely, if only because the concept of *aspect* seems inapplicable to the phenomenon: What is an aspect of the environment? Then, does consciousness take a material object? If so, it would either be one general thing like The World or The Environment or else many distinct, simultaneous perceptual objects. But we know that consciousness can persist when absolutely all of the senses are masked and when the environment and even the body are imperceivable. Thus, it can hardly be that we *redescribe* a certain state of consciousness as "consciousness" in the light of the consideration that it finds its required external object.

In short, the state of consciousness is not a perception, and unlike sense perception does not qualify for being "consciousness" in virtue of standing in certain (doubtless causal) relations to some external object. At the very most, consciousness may be putatively and perhaps intentionally directed towards some highly general object such as Reality. But such a view faces serious difficulties. Of what is a conscious, nonrational animal aware or even putatively aware if absolutely all of its senses are masked? Although its desires may point towards realities like food, wakefulness apparently has no internal object. This psychological state seems to be undirected, let alone directed under an aspect. In a word, consciousness seems not to exhibit *intentionality.* Consciousness is not a perception of something, not a putative awareness of something, not even a directed phenomenon. The model of the empty canvas seems not all that far from the truth.

An important preliminary task in this discussion is the sheer delineation or individuation of the phenomenon whose character we shall subsequently describe. In short, I wish to determine which phenomenon *is,* and which neighboring phenomena *are not,* the phenomenon of consciousness. Waking is one state and sleep another. How do these two states relate to one another? Clearly, nothing can simultaneously support both; equally, something capable of both need support neither, for a person under a general anesthetic is neither asleep nor awake. Thus, these several states look as if they must be contraries rather than contradictories. We seem to have three distinct, nonoverlapping states here: waking, sleep, and a third state that I somewhat loosely refer to as "anesthesia" or as "unconsciousness" but that I for the moment shall call "insensibility" (to avoid premature theoretical commitments). These three states are such that if any creature is in any one of them, then logically and necessarily it is not in any of the other two.

The questions that arise at this point will occupy my attention for a considerable part of this paper. First, do waking, sleep, and that third state (which for the moment we are calling "insensibility") cover *all* logical possibilities? That is, do all and any seemingly different states of consciousness prove on investigation to be no more than—possibly untypical—forms of these three primary states? Second, do these questions of classification or terminology rest upon the existence of real, distinct objective states? That is, might there not exist several equally good principles of classification of states of consciousness, no one more valid than the other? Third, are "conscious" and "unconscious" really contraries, as we have suggested, or are they instead contradictories? In particular, is waking the state that is consciousness itself and are all other states (including sleep!) states of unconsciousness? Or is unconsciousness instead that special state that is induced by chloroform or concussion or refrigeration, and are all other states of consciousness instances of the state of consciousness? Or might it be that the state induced by chloroform (etc.) is the state of unconsciousness, that waking is the state of consciousness, and that all other states of consciousness are neither of these? Finally, of what general type are all these states? That is, what do we mean in speaking of "a state of consciousness"? I shall begin with this last question first.

David Pears has said of dreaming that it is a "mode of consciousness."[1] Did he mean that the dream is a "state of consciousness"? I believe that all Pears could properly have meant is that the dream is an *experience* and that experiences necessarily and exclusively go to constitute the special process that we call "the stream of consciousness." I think that this is undeniable. But if waking rates as one state of consciousness, and if that into which chloroform and concussion plunge us rates as another state of consciousness, then dreaming cannot itself *be* a state of consciousness. After all, it is precisely because of that specific state of consciousness into which chloroform and concussion precipitate us—it is because that state obtains in a person—that dreaming is at that moment a real possibility. Were the person awake, dreaming would be impossible; but because a specific state of consciousness obtains that permits the dreaming mode of experience, dreaming can happen.

Dreaming is an experience that, like any other kind of experience, requires a state of consciousness that permits its occurrence; it is in this sense that dreaming, although not itself a state of consciousness, depends upon a prior state of consciousness that supports it without ensuring it. So what do we mean by "a state of consciousness"? Not an experience or "particular consciousness," and not even something that permits experiences or "particular consciousnesses." I believe we use the expression "state of consciousness" in such a way that it is a logical necessity that any living animal is at any particular moment in a specific state of consciousness and in only one such. Thus, a refrigerated though living animal, even an animal refrigerated to such a degree that absolutely all vital and a fortiori all psychological phenomena have come to a complete halt, would nonetheless be in a certain state of consciousness, viz., that of *deep unconsciousness;* indeed, in the state of deepest possible unconsciousness: an Absolute Zero of Consciousness. This nadir is consistent with no psychological phenomena and a fortiori with no particular consciousness or experience.

In this way we have managed to separate "state of consciousness" from "particular consciousness" or "experience" or (to use Pears's expression) "mode of consciousness." To be sure, one tends to think of unconsciousness as a kind of psychological *black:* as the analogue in consciousness of a black and empty visual field; that is, as somehow an empty experience of emptiness—and in any case, as a special experience. Of course, this is an error: unconsciousness is consistent with the impossibility of experience. In making the claim that it is a logical necessity that any living animal is at any instant in one and only one determinate state of consciousness, we at least imply that logically and necessarily a state prevails that is such that a real or empirical possibility of experience, even the possibility value of Absolute

Zero (which can after all change!), exists in this being. This draws a significant contrast with plants and minerals, in whose case this possibility is conceptually disallowed.

So much for the distinction between particular consciousness or experience and state of consciousness, of which sleep and wakefulness are in all probability two distinct varieties. The next question I wish to consider is whether waking and sleep and the state that we are referring to as "insensibility," exhaust the field. In particular, do bizarre states like hypnotic trance constitute yet another category, or are they instead to count as special forms of one of these three supposedly primary types? One might wish to characterize hypnotic trance as a mode of waking in which the world of which a wakeful person is normally aware has shrunk to the mind of another, or as a mode of sleep in which one is responsive to one voice only, and so on. So let us take the hypnotic trance as a case in point.

Hypnotic trance is a variety of trance and (for reasons that I shall shortly advance) almost certainly *not* a variety of waking. Is it a kind of sleep, or a variety of what we are calling "insensibility," or is it some other state altogether? The hypnotic trance depends precisely for its existence on the fact that almost all experiences and novel beliefs depend in this state upon the mind of another. Thus, this state can hardly be consistent with the phenomenon of *thinking,* for the course of the thinking process depends to a degree upon our own will or choice, and for that reason alone the hypnotic trance can hardly count as a form of waking. Waking is surely a state that at least permits thinking. For the same sort of reason, it cannot be a form of sleep, since sleep is necessarily consistent with dreaming. How can one whose experiences and novel beliefs depend directly on the mind of another be capable of engaging in the free floating of the imagination that is dreaming? It seems unlikely. But there are several more decisive reasons for refusing to class hypnotic trance as a mode of sleep. These reasons are causal and appertain both to origin-conditions and to removal-conditions. Of these two causal conditions, the latter is the more dramatic. We know that the hypnotic trance, unlike sleep, is usually brought to an end not just by any old sensation, not by merely intense sensation, and not by turbulent emotion or great anxiety, but by means of an order that is conveyed by meaningfully arrayed sensation—howsoever soft. Equally, it is caused neither by drugs nor by fatigue but by the establishing of a certain psychological situation, a kind of psychological division of labor, between two people. Thus, it has a properly mental and meaningful eraser, (viz., a belief that a determinate order has been given), and an interpersonal psychic cause; and these causal considerations very strongly militate against classifying it as a mode of sleep—which by contrast is more or less necessarily erasable by intense sensation. Similar causal considerations argue strongly against classifying hypnotic trance as a mode of waking. Both of these theoretical positions accord nicely with the necessary lack of interiority in the state, with the necessary dearth of thinking or imaginative phenomena in a person in an hypnotic trance.

What of the suggestion that the hypnotic trance is to be classed with the states we are bringing under the term "insensibility"? I take these latter states of consciousness to range across the following: the state resulting when a general anesthetic is administered; the state produced by concussion; and, rightly or wrongly, the state of consciousness produced by a deep refrigeration that does not kill. Like sleep, this state, which we normally describe as a state of unconsciousness, is capable not of intensity but of depth—whatever precisely that connotes; in this regard, both states contrast with waking. Prima facie there is much to be said in favor of classifying hypnotic trance with those states of "unconsciousness" or "insensibility." After all, the subject is not asleep and seems to be completely unaware of the surroundings. But is this really unawareness? Is the person not acutely aware of the sounds that issue from the mouth of the hypnotist? And must the person not therefore also be selectively indifferent to, and so in some sense actually aware of, all other sounds? This seems to be a very powerful reason for not describing the person as "insensible" *simpliciter.*

Other considerations, now of a causal kind, back up this account of the matter. Of what ontological status is the cause of the several varieties of "insensibility" that we have instanced? All the examples so far mentioned, (anesthetic chemical, physical trauma to the brain, cooling of the brain), are physical, nonmental. The only cures for such physically induced "insensibility" are changes of precisely the same kind, though in reverse (dispersal of anesthetic chemicals from the brain, healing of traumatized brain tissue, warming of the brain). By contrast, the cause and cure of the hypnotic trance are psychological phenomena: the setting up by experiential means (like repetitive speech), of a specific type of psychological relation between two people, and the removal of that relation and state by the mental means of a special utterance. These causal considerations seem to me to be of decisive importance. They argue strongly in favor of our separating the state of consciousness of hypnotic trance from those states that I have termed conditions of "insensibility."

One other consideration—the type of *inner life* that is open to a person in this state—points strongly in the same direction. Because the novel beliefs and so presumably also the thoughts and much of the experience of this person seem to be determined by the mind and free choices of another, how can the hypnotized person engage in that free floating of the imagination that is dreaming? Dreaming occurs in sleep, but it also occurs in the light condition of "unconsciousness," or "insensibility," induced by nitrous oxide. Of course, dreaming is not possible in a refrigerated being in whom all mental life has come to a halt; however, this is not because a state of "insensibility" (or "unconsciousness") obtains, but because *all mental life has stopped.*

Dreaming is impossible because the depth of unconsciousness is total: the next thing to death, as it were. The impossibility derives from the depth of the state of unconsciousness rather than from the unconsciousness of the state of unconsciousness. Therefore, if a state of consciousness that obtains in a person is inconsistent with the phenomenon of dreaming, not because of its depth or intensity or quantity or whatever but because of the very type of that state, then the prevailing state cannot be one of sleep nor of either "insensibility" or "unconsciousness."

For these reasons, I feel confident in saying of the state of hypnotic trance that it is neither a state of waking nor a state of sleep; nor is it an example of the state I have been calling "insensibility." It is instead a quite distinct and nonoverlapping fourth state. The three states of waking, sleep, and "insensibility" thus do not exhaust the field of logical possibilities. All of these states are contraries rather than contradictories; like colors and even tastes, it looks as if they might proliferate. The hypnotic trance does not seem to be an aberrant or wayward form of sleep, waking, or "insensibility."

This brings me to the second in the earlier list of four questions. Do these questions relating to classification rest upon our managing to distinguish *real, distinct states?* Might there not exist several equally good principles of classification, which could yield different answers to these questions? Might it not be, for example, that in and of itself the hypnotic trance is no different from certain aberrant states of waking and that we then redescribe that state in the light of its cause and cure? In that case, we would have made a mistake in taking these causal properties of the hypnotic trance as seriously as we have done: the state proves instead to fall under the heading of "waking" and the whole issue of whether or not these states exhaust the field is once more open. Indeed, the situation may be worse than that. Might it not be that there exist several systems of classification of states of consciousness and that one is as good as the other, with no one system having any right to claim that it is the true system?

These are the criteria I have appealed to in distinguishing one state from another: the ontological type of their origin and removal conditions, the inner life that is consistent with the state of consciousness, and the psychological phenomena that are consistent and inconsistent with it. These necessities are logical, and they tend to go in packets. Yet, it is clear that some psychological phenomena can span diverse states of consciousness. For example, pain is consistent with both sleep and waking but it is inconsistent with "unconsciousness" or "insensibility." Equally, dreaming is consistent both with sleep and with the type of light unconsciousness induced by nitrous oxide. Why not say, then, that sleep and unconsciousness are distinct varieties of the one broad state of consciousness? Is it not just a matter of playing one logical necessity off against the other? How else do we individuate these states, which are not in any case experiences themselves, than by assembling their properties and comparing them? Is it not after all just a matter of counting properties? I admit that this conclusion does not sound too good, but what else can we do? We can scarcely regard it as a matter of convention that there exists a state with the required necessary properties of waking. Is not waking as bona fide a psychological phenomenon as any other? To return to the suggestion that sleep and unconsciousness might be subvarieties of the one broad state of consciousness, we should note that the deepest possible sleep is not a condition of unconsciousness, even though deep sleep can be replaced by unconsciousness. By contrast, the lightest of light unconsciousness does not overlap with the deepest of deep sleeps. The gap between these states cannot be bridged by manipulating their depth or intensity, nor by inducing anesthesia, for sleep is consistent with a universal local anesthesia. Indeed, the anesthesia of unconsciousness owes its existence not to a series of particular local causes but to the prevailing state of consciousness.

For these reasons, it seems to me that although sleep and unconsciousness share certain properties, they are distinct as states—though I admit this conclusion is somewhat tentative. By "state of consciousness," I must emphasize, we do not mean a type of phenomenon that can occur *in* that particular state of consciousness, not even the type of the thinking process or stream of consciousness that is possible with such a state. Psychologically speaking, states of consciousness are unanalyzable simples, and they are what they are and not another thing. I mention this matter because one is inclined to say that, because dreaming can occur both in sleep and nitrous oxide unconsciousness, the two states of consciousness must be experientially indistinguishable and therefore identical. What is in fact the same, however, is the *type of experience* permitted at a certain instant by the prevailing state of consciousness. Neither sleep nor unconsciousness are experiences, and both are consistent with a total absence of experience.

I now move on to the third of the questions posed earlier. Are "conscious" and "unconscious" contraries or contradictories? Is waking the state of consciousness, and are all other states (including sleep!) conditions of unconsciousness? That is, is waking one state of consciousness, and are all other states of consciousness logically and necessarily subvarieties of the only other logically possible state of consciousness? Or is unconsciousness the special state that is induced by chloroform or concussion, and are all other states of consciousness logically and necessarily subvarieties of the only other logically possible state of consciousness—a type whose most noteworthy and perhaps most characteristic variety is waking? Or is the state that is produced by chloroform and concussion the state of unconsciousness, with waking another distinct state that is consciousness? Are states like sleep and hypnotic trance distinct from both of these?

These questions have more or less been answered by now. Rightly or wrongly, we have wished to separate out as distinct and contrary the states of waking, sleep, "insensibility" or "unconsciousness," hypnotic trance, and so forth. Simultaneously, we have come across no grounds for unifying two or more of these states as subvarieties of the one type. For example, the fact that waking and sleep are normal or healthy, whereas "insensibility" is either pathological or abnormal, constitutes no grounds for unifying the former two states of consciousness as subvarieties of one broad-spanning state of consciousness. Health or normality is an insufficient ground. We thus seem to have a set of distinct states that resist further classification under the heading "state of consciousness." From this point, the issue seems to be little more than stipulative. Thus, if we decide to dub the distinct waking state "consciousness" and to treat "unconscious" as a contradictory, we would find that it singled out no one determinate type of state—spanning, as it does, at least three distinct states of consciousness. Such a move would seem to run counter to usage, and in any case to embody a confusion insofar as these supposedly contradictory terms cannot really be in the same line of business, consciousness being a state of consciousness and unconsciousness either a something else or a nothing. So we shall treat "conscious" and "unconscious" as contraries, using the former term to stand for waking and the later for the state induced by chloroform or concussion. This implies that we are not free to characterize sleep as a form of unconsciousness. But neither are we free to treat it as a form of consciousness. Maybe this runs counter to usage, again for what that's worth. It seems natural enough to say that a patient has "regained consciousness and is sleeping soundly," without implying that the patient actually woke up in the interim. Such an utterance depends on the idea that to be conscious is not to be in the state induced by concussion and chloroform; it seems a stipulative matter, and of no great consequence. Accordingly, I suggest that we dub waking "consciousness," leave sleep and hypnotic trance as contrary states of consciousness, replace the artificial term "insensibility" by "unconsciousness," and leave the matter at that. No substantive issues of type seem to have been neglected.

Let me at this point pass on to the task of characterizing the various states of consciousness, finishing with the most important of all, waking. And let us accomplish this, as we have so far, simply by listing necessary properties.

We have said enough about *hypnotic trance*. Its causal characteristics have been spelled out in some detail; in particular, the fact that cause and cure are mental and meaningful, maybe necessarily but at the very least usually. We have noted that it is inconsistent with thinking and dreaming, probably necessarily so, and that auditory and tactile perception tend to persist in this state.

What about "insensibility," or as I shall hereafter term it, "unconsciousness"? Consider its causal properties to begin with. I cannot really imagine what it would be like for this state to have an immediate mental or meaningful cause or cure. After all, a necessary though hardly a sufficient condition of unconsciousness is the state of anesthesia or incapacity to support sensations of any kind. How could that be effected by anything but a physical, nonpsychological cause? But that question raises a difficulty that throws some of our previous conclusions in doubt: how are we to accommodate the fact that a whole set of sensations can be extinguished by a dose of chloroform? Either this causal transaction is mediated by the state of unconsciousness or sleep and unconsciousness may well be two subvarieties of the one state of consciousness. If the causal transaction were not mediated by unconsciousness, what causal properties would distinguish sleep from unconsciousness? A person could remain awake even though anesthetised all over, so presumably a person could be asleep though anesthetised all over. Now what would distinguish this latter state from the state of unconsciousness? Not experiences, but rather causal properties. Then the cause of anesthesia in the right hand of the sleeper is distinct from the cause of anesthesia in the left hand, and both are distinct from the cause of sleep; whereas the cause of unconsciousness is chloroform and the cause of anesthesia in the hands is the state of unconsciousness itself. Tentatively, I shall hang onto the theory that sleep and unconsciousness are distinct states of consciousness, but at the cost of abandoning the theory that all sensations have immediate nonpsychological causes.

I return then to the characterization of unconsciousness via its causal properties. Among those causal properties is the fact that unconsciousness makes sensation impossible. This lack of sensation has important consequences: it means that sense-perceptual awareness, whether of the environment in general or single items in the environment, is not a possibility; and a fortiori it also means that the subject cannot be roused out of the state by intensity of sensation, say by sticking with a pin or making a loud noise nearby. Yet we know that unconsciousness is consistent with what might be termed *interiority,* provided the unconsciousness is not too deep, for it is consistent with (though does not require) the properly inward phenomenon of dreaming. Note that the absence of all sensation is insufficient to plunge a person into unconsciousness. The reason is, apart from the fact that all thinking must be dreaming in unconsciousness, that the attention would still be awake or "on the ready" (as one might say); such a person would be aware of the darkness and emptiness of the visual field and of the seeming prevailing silence. The person would seemingly still be aware of the physical state of the world as one devoid of light or sound, which is after all a possible state for the environment to be in. But the attention, both in sleep and most of all in unconsciousness, is simply not there to be courted: it has withdrawn into its shell, and it does not even deliver zero readings. If it is like an ammeter, then it is like an ammeter no longer engaged with the circuit. It is unclear to me why such a state of affairs should go hand in hand with the possibility either of a complete cessation of all experience or of dream experience. Nevertheless, it seems to be so. Unconsciousness is marked by several necessary traits: the absence of all sensation and hence of any intuitional awareness of any physical items, the possibility of no experience, and the complete unavailability of the attention. Of the two possibilities, that of dreaming and that of no experience, it is the latter that is in some sense primary. We have seen that the depths of unconsciousness, which are such as to necessitate no experience, are precisely for that reason inconsistent with dreaming. The possibility of dreaming can lapse, whereas the possibility of no experience can never lapse. It is in this sense that the latter possibility is primary for the state of unconsciousness.

Let me now try to offer a characterization of the state of sleep by trying (as I have done with hypnotic trance and unconsciousness) to list the logically necessary and sufficient conditions of the state. Its causal properties are very interesting and a little perplexing. Of what type are the cause and cure of sleep? Why do people sleep and why do they wake? I do not know the answer to these questions. But one thing is certain: They can and must be able to wake because of psychological "stimuli" like intense pain or intense auditory sensation or nightmare. A "passed out" drunk is generally rousable, and, if not, unconscious. On the other hand, people normally wake up when, as we rather fatuously say, they have *had enough* sleep or are no longer "sleepy." Just what is the state of sleepiness? Is it a feeling, an inclination, or a merely physical state that induces such feelings or inclinations? Or is it a disposition to sleep? Can a person *feel* sleepy but not *be* sleepy? Can a person feel tired but not be tired? As a person can feel tired but yet march on at top speed for miles, so one who feels fantastically sleepy can lie awake all night. Then what causes sleep—sleepiness or feeling so? I suppose one has circularly to plump for sleepiness, aided and abetted by the intentional actions of the putative sleeper; for, as Merleau-Ponty observed, we generally fall asleep by pretending to ourselves to be going to sleep. So far as I can tell, this account implies that the cause of sleep is for the most part nonpsychological, even though it is generally assisted into existence by the chosen abstention from deeds of the putative sleeper. In sum, although sleep must always be capable of being terminated by purely psychological phenomena, it generally comes into being as a result of factors that are partly psychological but primarily nonpsychological.

What of the possibility of sensation? There can be no doubt that sensations can survive the state of sleep. Indeed, the psychological phenomenon that is the usual psychological terminator of sleep is intense or disturbing sensation—such as toothache, or the auditory sensation caused by an exploding gun. It is not a meaning-laden hearing that causes waking, it is rather what one might call the shock-value of sheer auditory sensation. When toothache wakes a person it is the ache itself, not some mere material cause or condition, that achieves this result. People do not just surface out of sleep *to* toothache: they surface out of sleep to *knowledge* of the toothache that precipitated them out of sleep. There is thus reason for supposing that sensation persists all the way through sleep, so that sleep cannot be a condition in which sensations abate and a universal anesthesia reigns. Rather, one of the most important features of sleep is the unavailability of the attention, which retires like its owner for the night, even though it is here and there available for stray tasks. Thus, a sleeper scratches a light tickle on the cheek, and although this probably necessitates that the sleep be light, it fails to necessitate that the sleeper has actually woken. The attention, although generally withdrawing its services, is sufficiently available for the performing of stray tasks that help to perpetuate sleep. It spares its owner thereby, who has no need of self-consciously recording such deeds.

Here we have a number of significant differences between the states of unconsciousness and sleep, thus strengthening the case for construing them as contraries. Although the attention is for the most part knocked out in sleep, in unconsciousness that knockout is total and absolute; and whereas in sleep the possible objects of the attention (mainly sensations) persist for the most part unremarked, in unconsciousness all these sensory objects are destroyed; and whereas the causes of sleep are in part psychological, and the causes of its termination can be completely psychological, the cause and cure of unconsciousness is and has to be nothing but physical nonpsychological in type. Sleep then is a state of consciousness in which the attention is for the most part unengaged or simply failing to give readings, whether of positive or zero content (such as silence); in which any thinking that occurs has instead to take the imagination-form of dreaming; and in which the subject is rousable to waking by intensity of sensation. Perhaps this suffices to delimit the state.

One final comment on sleep: although the attention generally takes a rest like its owner, it can on occasion be fully engaged and coordinated with meaningful, intentional physical action. This is evident in the following sort of case. A person can not only talk while sleeping but can actually answer questions that are put by another. Here we have a situation in which veridical auditory sense perception occurs and in which the sense perception leads to and is coordinated with intentional physical action—and I say "intentional" for the reason that, because there is a correct and incorrect way of interpreting an ambiguous sentence uttered by the sleeper, that sentence must have been intended in one rather than another sense, which surely requires that it give expression to an intention. Of course, such a situation is far from typical of sleep, but it reminds us of the very great difference between a sleeper and an unconscious person and in particular the dissimilarity in the relation holding between the subject and physical objects in general and the person's own body in particular. In unconsciousness, it is as if these last did not exist; in sleep, it is otherwise. It is to be expected that a person will stir during sleep; in unconsciousness, it is not.

Note

1. David Pears, review of Professor Norman Malcolm: *Dreaming, Mind* 70 (1961): 145-63.

Consciousness and Self-Identity

PETER UNGER

If I am anything at all, then I am a *conscious being.* Now, it seems certain that there are times when I exist but am not conscious. Even so, at those times at least I have the *capacity* for consciousness, in some appropriately central sense of those terms. When my capacity is exercised, then I am conscious. I might have existed, it seems, without ever having been conscious; perhaps by being killed in my mother's womb or shortly after birth, or perhaps by living a long enough life but always, even in the womb, in some sort of drug-induced state of unremitting unconsciousness. In the latter case, as I am imagining it, I always *could have* been brought to consciousness, and not with any enormous difficulty, but in fact I never was. In a world where I only have the capacity for consciousness and never am in fact conscious, things are extremely unfortunate for me. In a world where there is nothing that is my capacity for consciousness, I do not exist at all.

Suppose that the foregoing remarks are not strictly or completely true. If so, then they are at least nearly true. Suppose that they are only nearly true. Even so, they would strongly indicate this: any discussion of self-identity had best concern itself with the phenomenon of consciousness, whatever other phenomena it may also consider.

What is consciousness? Unhelpfully, it is what a being has just when that being is conscious. When is a being conscious? Both roughly and unhelpfully, a being is conscious when that being has some conscious thought or experience. Perhaps others can be much more helpful in this matter. I hope so. For now, let us trust to an intuitive, and perhaps somewhat naive, understanding of consciousness. Without meaning to be doctrinaire, we might very roughly express our working stance like this: if you are (sometimes) conscious, then you already know what consciousness is, even if you cannot say much about what you thus know; if an entity is never conscious, then there is nothing useful to be said to that entity in this matter. Taking consciousness as both appreciated and undefined, I want to bring us to think about it, much more than seems recently to have been done, in connection with self-identity, the nature of selves or conscious beings, and related topics. Toward this end, I will try to present, clearly enough for our consideration, some new and troublesome examples. The trouble from the examples is this: most people have *conflicting* intuitions, or make conflicting responses, to the examples. Moreover, if we accept the prevalent methodology for treating examples, many of the responses go against what is now the most standard philosophical treatment of the area.

My own methodology for treating responses to examples is much more broadly psychological than that employed by most philosophers.[1] Using a broadly psychological approach, I will try to explain these puzzling responses along the following lines: each person in our culture holds two radically disparate and conflicting views about the nature of selves, or of conscious beings, one appropriately called the *objective view of the self* and the other suitably called the *subjective view of the self*.[2] Whether noticed by us or not, these two views are in constant tension. In the great majority of contexts, we much favor the objective view. Perhaps for that reason, and understandably enough, it is such a view that, in one form or another, is standardly favored in most of the recent literature on personal identity. But suitable cases will make consciousness a most salient consideration. When presented with those cases, we will tend to favor, at least more than otherwise, the conflicting subjective view.

After clarifying and arguing for the hypothesis that we hold these two self-views, I will make some comments concerning the implications of this psychological situation for the philosophy of the self and, thus, for the philosophy of mind. My tentative conclusions will be that our subjective self-view is substantially inadequate and, in any case, is inferior to our objective view. The former cannot be modified so as to alter this disparity, nor can it be mined for material to form an acceptable hybrid or compromise view—one that would incorporate main features from the objective view as well. The latter view, however, is not similarly inadequate. So we should, at least in our more reflective thinking, abandon only our subjective view of the self.

When we do this, then we become freer to develop our objective view. For we may then discount intuitions we have that, on the one hand, seem constraining for an objective view and, on the other, are traceable (mainly) to our implicitly holding a conflicting subjective view. These intuitions might well include our idea that matters of self-identity are always (fully) determinate, our idea that their determinate status does not depend (heavily) on our linguistic conventions, and our intuition that the relations involved in these matters must be intrinsic and never are heavily relational. If we rationally discount such intuitions as these, then we may develop our objective self-view along lines that otherwise would seem too radical, perhaps even quite bizarre. For example, we might accept much of the thinking of Derek Parfit in this area.[3] I will suggest, rather tentatively, that we do that, allowing that other main aspects of his thinking about persons might well be questioned or even rejected.[4]

1. DISEMBODIED CONSCIOUSNESS AND PERSONAL IDENTITY

Let me present an example with you as the central character. I will try to describe the case in a way that is both intriguing and coherent.

Suppose that you have taken a very special drug. This drug is, in its effects, a lot more complex than a powerful anesthetic. True, it does put your body in a very deep sleep and, in particular, makes your brain quite inactive. So, as with a mere anesthetic, none of your physical parts supports any consciousness. But with this drug a lot more also happens.

One thing that happens is that you never lose consciousness; there is a continuous flow of your conscious experience even while your body and brain "get left behind." Although strange effects may be supposed to occur for your longer term memory, your very-short-term memory is in no way impaired and may even be heightened. Perhaps this assumption helps to clarify what may be involved in the presumed continuity, or flow, of your conscious experience.

Suppose, for the sake of vividness, that there is a shift of your perspective (within your experience). This shift may be supposed itself to be gradual, or it may be abrupt. The mode of experience involved here will be, we may presume, primarily the visual mode, but that is inessential. At any rate, let's suppose that the shift occurs in such a way that eventually your original body is viewed from the outside, say, from the ceiling overhead. We are supposing, indeed, that you not only lose your original body, including your brain, but that you come to have no body at all or even any spatial extension. (We may still suppose, if we like, that you always have a *location* in space, at a pure *point,* and a *perspective from* the point where you are.)

Suppose that, after a period of time, the body on the floor seems to awaken and to act. Suppose the explanation of this is straightforward: there is now, once again, consciousness intimately associated with that body, just as the brain patterns indicate and just as we would be given to believe. Then there was an *interruption* of consciousness with respect to the body, as seems often to happen in the lives of actual human beings. At any rate, when the body awakens, and for a goodly period thereafter, there are two conscious beings in the situation, one with a human form and one with no spatial extension at all. You are the being with no extension now; you are not the being whose body and brain are those that used to be yours.

Is the example just presented an intelligible, coherent one? Whatever is the correct answer to this question, my dominant *response,* apparently not eccentric, is that the case *is* perfectly coherent, even if wildly hypothetical. And for the elicitation of further response to a candidate case, *appearance* of coherence is all we need. Indeed, aside from the appearance it tends to promote in us, actual coherence is quite irrelevant to this properly psychological matter.

This indicates, though it does not establish, that we have a view of ourselves on which continuity of brain and body are not essential and on which, perhaps, no physical continuity of any sort is very important for our personal identity over time. This view need not be correct, of course, and nothing so far noted does much to indicate that it is. And this view may not be the only view of ourselves that we hold. There may be another view, or views, that we also hold on which some such physical continuity is essential for survival, or is at least very important. But these are further matters, and the facts about them, whatever they are, will be consistent with our noted indication.

Let me amplify or further specify the example. Suppose that, even while your conscious experience continued and you left your body and brain behind, you suddenly underwent great changes as regards all the major aspects of your dispositional psychology: you suddenly suffered a very substantial loss of (more than short-term) personal memory, and even apparent personal memory; you suddenly underwent a great change of personality and character traits, and so on. At the same time, whatever being might have then been most intimately associated with your brain and body underwent no such changes. So the being who wakes up with or in the body on the floor, in your original body, is psychologically much more like you were before the drug-taking than is the person who has been viewing that body (as though from above) and whose consciousness is continuous with your own. Indeed, of the two conscious beings around at the example's end, only the person near the floor has not only great physical or bodily continuity with the drug-taker, but also much psychological continuity apart from the continuous flow of conscious thought and experience. But you are the being whose consciousness is continuous with your original consciousness; you are not the being who realizes all those other continuities.

Is this more finely specified, more radical example still one that is coherent, that has been consistently described? My *dominant* response is that it is. There is some conflict in my response pattern now, for I have some feeling that too much has been placed on the other side for the disembodied being to be you. So mainly I respond that the example is coherent, and that you will survive (only) as a being that does continue consciousness, even while all sorts of other factors concerning you are better continued by someone else, who you will never be. But I also have response tendencies that go against this main response of mine here, that push me in the direction of denying coherence to our example as so described.

Now it may well be that you respond differently to this example from the way that I respond to it. Suppose that this is so. Then in what might the difference consist? Well, I have a dominant response in favor of the conscious viewer along with conflicting, thus dominated, responses in other directions: I have a weak response that you will survive only as the finally awakened human being. And I have a weak response, perhaps even weaker, that you will not survive in the case at all (but will have two intimate descendants, neither of them you). We might differ because you have one of these other responses as dominant, or yet still some other one, and have as a sensed dominated response an impulse toward favoring only the conscious viewer. If so, then there is almost as much of a problem, if not just as much, of explaining your response pattern as that of explaining mine. Indeed, I can think of only one way for you to respond here that leaves your response pattern looking even relatively unproblematic: you have a strong response that you will survive only as the human being, not as the continuously conscious viewer, and have *no other response to the case in any conflict with that one.* In my admittedly limited experience with this example, I have found few, if any, who make just that response. So there is an explanatory problem here for virtually all respondents, not just those with my pattern.

A similar point will apply to other examples we will consider, indeed to most cases pertaining to the topic area. I won't bother to articulate the point much elsewhere; but, as seems more appropriate, will ask you to bear it in mind.

2. CONTINUOUS CONSCIOUSNESS AND PHYSICAL DIVISION

The case just presented, following Descartes, featured a disembodied consciousness or self with no spatial extension. Some find this idea itself to be incoherent, or so they say, and for that reason alone might repress any response tendency toward taking the example as a whole to be coherent. Now, I think that this sort of thinking is misplaced. But as our task here is largely psychological, we should try to accommodate this "objection."

We may accommodate the objection in two ways. In one way, the continuous consciousness can be embodied in some special sort of ghostly stuff or, alternatively, in one atom from the original brain. My dominant reaction is the same: you survive only as the continuous consciousness. Just as much as before, *any* reaction along these lines, even a weaker one, is difficult to explain on the most standard accounts of personal identity. What is more troublesome, I still have conflicting responses.

But there is, I think, a more direct and more interesting way of accommodating this objection—a way that does more to show how misplaced it is.

Cases of surgical division have figured prominently in the recent literature on personal identity. I would like to consider a new case of this general type. In our example, an anesthetic is applied to the major portion of someone's brain, say, an appropriate two-thirds. As a result, there seems to be continuous consciousness intimately associated with, or bound up with, only a third of the patient's brain, but with none of the rest of the brain or body. The apparently continuously conscious one-third is severed from the rest of the brain and surgically removed from the body. Still conscious, or supporting some consciousness, it is kept viable elsewhere, perhaps in a vat, perhaps, better, in a donor body whose entire brain has been previously removed and destroyed. After all of this, the anesthetic wears off in the major portion, and consciousness is again intimately associated with what is there, too. At the end of the procedure there are *two* people, both of them conscious; there are no more direct mental connections between them at that time than there now are between, say, you and me.

Suppose that you undergo such an operation. Now, the resultant person with the third of your original brain will be, we naturally enough suppose, only moderately like you were at the start as regards relevant dispositional psychology. There will be only a moderate overlap of ostensible memories— many will be lost; there will be only moderate similarity of personality, and so on. These great changes will have occurred suddenly, the immediate result of a quick surgical slicing.

We are explicit in our supposition regarding the dispositional psychology of the person (eventually emerging or continuous) on the other side. That person, with two-thirds of your original brain and all the rest of your original body, we specify, will be in all these psychological respects *exactly like* you were at the start. This is, of course, somewhat unrealistic, but I do not think excessively or harmfully so. At any rate, those are the essential details of our example of surgical division.

For vividness, let me add some inessential details as well. Suppose that after the selective anesthetic has been applied, but before any surgical division has occurred, the conscious part is hooked up temporarily with an excellent artificial sensory device. In consequence, that part will, both then and later, seem to see the rest of the operation and subsequent proceedings, and also seem to hear what is going on. It seems to see itself being severed from the major portion of the brain and then moved to a new body, while the major portion remains in the original body. It seems to hear the surgeons' discussion of what is going on and seems to think about these proceedings. Later on, it seems to notice the original body to be animated and, indeed, to be the body of an incredibly familiar person.

Will you survive such an operation? And, if so, who will you be?

Though there is some conflict, my dominant response is, first, that you *will* survive and, moreover, that you will be the patient who was conscious throughout and nobody else. (Also, as I dominantly respond, you will have an intimate descendant, one who is, both physically and psychologically, more like you were before the operation than you yourself will be. And that descendant will have, I respond, much more of your original matter and body and brain than you will have.)

This appears to be not only my own dominant response, but a typical one. It seems to reinforce the result we obtained with the previous, more ethereal example: in judgments about our own survival, (what we take to be) the continuity of consciousness tends to outweigh so many other factors all weighted together against it. So (what we judge to be) the continuity of consciousness, or where we suppose there to be the locus or seat of such continuity, has great weight in our thinking about our existence over time.

3. ALTERATIONS THAT ACCENTUATE THE POSITIVE

Although many respondents seem to react to these two examples as I dominantly do, a fair number do not. What are we to make of this discrepancy? In that we are doing informal psychology here, whatever else we may be doing at the same time, some individual differences are only to be expected. So our finding some is not disconcerting. Nonetheless, some attempt at explanation is called for.

I will not try to do very much explaining now. For there are several factors at work, no doubt, and an attempt to be even remotely complete would detain us too long at this stage of our study, a stage where explanation is largely to be postponed. It is enough for now to spot one plausible factor.

In both of the cases considered, as well as in several yet to come up, the continuously conscious person seems less desirable, less the way you want to be, than the person with consciousness interrupted but with so much else intact. For example, the continuously conscious person has a poorer remembrance of your past. For example, such a one has, in the second case, a body unfamiliar to you now or, in the first case, no body at all. Who wants any of that? Not me or you.

As I hypothesize, people tend to *identify* more, or more readily, with candidate selves that are more the way they want to be, or would like to be. With regard to the cases in question, this tendency can help promote a response in favor of the side with interrupted consciousness.

There are people whose traits I envy; there are those who, in many ways, I think to be better than me. I sometimes fantasize pleasantly that I am more like them. But I do not really want to be so much like them in so many ways. On the whole, I want to be pretty much the way I am, and to have such changes as do befall my person to occur gradually and in the normal course of events, not suddenly and bizarrely. So the factor of desirability cannot be fully discounted. Still and all, we might hope to discount it to a considerable degree and then observe the results of our discounting.

Contrary to the usual suppositions, we may redescribe our physical division case as follows. First of all, the continuously conscious one-third brain will be housed in a very desirable body that it operates perfectly well. Many male readers may think of themselves, for example, as getting the donor body of Burt Reynolds, a pretty fair athlete as well as a man of obvious physical attractions. Many female readers may assume themselves to get the body of Jane Fonda. Since you're being asked to leave your familiar home, so to say, we let you pick whatever new one you like best.

As far as psychological aspects go, we also make ourselves accentuate the positive. For example, it is natural to suppose that the person who at the end has only one-third of a brain will be less intelligent, and generally duller, than the person with two-thirds, who is exactly like you are at the start. Contravening what we usually take to be principles of biology, let us suppose just the reverse: slicing off that one-third was like cutting a diamond from the rough. Amazingly, the person with one-third is far *more* intelligent than the person with two-thirds, far *more* charming and witty and hospitable than the already gracious person you are at the outset. In a phrase, the person with the physically smaller brain is the self of your fondest dreams.

With quite a few respondents, this accentuation of the positive gets them to favor continuity of consciousness at least somewhat more than they did before. Then we may presume that, all along, they had a strong tendency to favor it masked by the obvious depressing factor. Please notice that by accentuating the positive we are not loading one side overwhelmingly in its favor. On the contrary, given the choice, I would prefer to stay just as I am, whether or not that preference is rational, than to be so radically and positively altered. We do not want to take our fantasies all that seriously in *any* case; but if we must, then we prefer a fantasy that seems better than one that seems so depressing.

4. CONTINUITY OF CONSCIOUSNESS THROUGH RADICAL CHANGE

The two cases so far considered each appear to present a kind of "branching": continuous consciousness seems to go along one of the branches, and almost everything else goes along the other. As I dominantly respond, the person in question seems to go along the first branch, the branch with continuous consciousness. At the same time, I make conflicting responses.

Let's look for examples that show the importance of consciousness but have no apparent branching. If we are successful, then the intuitive weight of consciousness for judgments of personal identity will seem quite general, to be present both with branching and without, even in a most liberal sense of this somewhat technical term.

By developing a suggestion of Mark Johnston, we can get a helpful nonbranching example. First, while my brain remains most active and continues to support consciousness, the rest of my body is painlessly scrapped and replaced by an appropriate bionic body; instead of protoplasm, the body surrounding my brain is made of metal and silicon and other unusual materials in appropriate combination. Though this new body is so basically different, it *seems* to be quite human, unless microscopic means of examination are employed. Let us say that, to the casual observer, it seems to be just like the body of Senator Bill Bradley.

While consciousness is kept continuous still, an appropriate half of my brain is removed and destroyed, being replaced by an appropriate bionic construction, one that suddenly gives me a dispositional psychology about halfway between my original one and that of Albert Einstein at age forty.

Then a powerful anesthetic is applied to the remaining protoplasm so that, for the first time in the case, no part of my original brain (or body) supports any consciousness. But consciousness seems to be continuous anyway. And now my dispositional psychology is suddenly very much like, or even exactly like, that of Einstein and quite unlike my original one. The sleeping half-brain is, while totally without consciousness, suddenly removed and destroyed. Though there is only a purely bionic being now in the case, consciousness seems, and presumably is, continuous throughout the episode. At the end, there is a bionic being with a dispositional psychology just like that of Einstein, and very unlike that of Unger.

Will I survive such a procedure? My dominant response is that I will survive. I will become a wholly bionic man who is in almost all gross physical respects like Bill Bradley, and in all relevant psychological respects just like Albert Einstein.

The natural way for me to think of the case is that there not only seems to be, but actually is, continuity of consciousness here, though very little in the way of any other sort of interesting continuity. Despite the great and sudden breaks along relevant physical and psychological dimensions, the continuity of consciousness means continued existence for me in the case, or so I dominantly respond.

Compare this response with that to the following close variation on the case. A powerful anesthetic is first applied to me so that no relevant matter supports any consciousness for any person in focus until the very end of the scenario. At that point, there awakens into consciousness a bionic version of Bradley combined with Einstein, with only half a bionic brain as before but of course one that is relevantly, and very powerfully, productive of conscious thought and experience. In all other respects, the variation is just like the original example.

Will I survive the bionic procedure in such a case, where consciousness is emphatically interrupted? My strong response is that I will *not* survive, but will cease to be; at the end, there will only be somebody else, a bionic person who is no more me than he is Bradley or than he is Einstein.

Continuous consciousness appears to be, and is judged to be, present in the first of the two cases; it is absent in the second. Everything else about the two cases is assumed to be the same. I judge that in the first case I survive, continuous consciousness overriding so much sudden and radical change. In the second case this continuity is absent. As I intuitively judge the matter this time, there is no question but that I do not survive.

We have just considered, as I said, an example based on a suggestion from Mark Johnston. Johnston's suggestion was, in fact, a closely related example. For certain purposes, his example may be more helpful than the one just considered. Let us consider it now.

Instead of making a few striking bionic replacements, we make a series of many innocuous ones. We replace a few of my cells by certain microminiature silicon devices, then a few more by some others, and so on. Though done in gradual sequence, this can be done rather rapidly, say, in less than eight hours. At the end there is a bionic man with, say, the body of Bradley and the brain of Einstein. Again, there are two alternatives: on one, consciousness is kept continuous throughout; on the other, a powerful anesthetic is first applied so that there is no consciousness intimately associated with anything being operated upon until after the whole operation is completed. Only at that point do we have a being, indeed a bionic being, that is conscious.

My responses to these gradual, or sorites, alternatives parallel my response pattern just before. With conflict, my dominant response is that I survive in the case where consciousness is kept continuous; without any conflict, I think that I cease entirely in the case where the anesthetic is applied. My response patterns to these two versions confirm each other.[5]

There are some respondents who always dominantly respond that the original person doesn't survive the operation, even when consciousness is, or seems to be, continuous throughout. But even with most of these people there is a telling discrepancy: there is a (stronger) *dominated* response in favor of survival with consciousness (apparently) kept flowing than in the cases where there is clear and substantial interruption. This difference needs explanation, as much as does the more obvious discrepancy more typically found.

5. THE CAPACITY FOR CONSCIOUSNESS AND THE CAPACITY FOR A DISTINCTIVE MENTAL LIFE

Let me devote this next section to an example that, perhaps more than any other, indicates the nature and the extent of the complexity of our thought about ourselves. My hope is that, at least sooner or later, we might be moved to explore this complexity in a manner that is, at least roughly, adequate to it.

To present this case, let me first provide some background assumptions. My brain is the most direct (physical) causal ground of my distinctive psychological features: my personality traits, my (putative) memory as of a certain past life, my penchant for protracted skeptical inquiry, and so on. My brain is also the most direct (physical) causal ground of my (sometimes) being conscious, a condition that does not distinguish me from you. The same is true for other human beings. At least, let's suppose this to be so.

I am told that the brain stem, along with just a small bit of the cortex, is enough to support consciousness. But without attachment to a healthy active brain stem, no amount of cortex will support a state of being conscious. On the other hand, with the brain stem appropriately inactive, a lot of complex *unconscious* thinking may go on, as in deep sleep. For example, in such sleep, a philosopher may finally plot the difficult concluding chapter of his main work. But that author, though feverishly creative psychologically, and engaged in highly distinctive mental activity, will not then be conscious at all. Whether this is in fact true or not, let us suppose all of it to be true.

Let me make some explicit causal assumptions, as further background, that are at a remove from our accepted belief. First, the brain stem and, say, a tenth of my cortex can be removed from the rest of me and kept conscious all the while. As soon as it is severed, the rest of me will support no consciousness. But the rest, unlike the brain stem, will continue to support a lot of unconscious mental activity that is interesting and that is distinctive of just me among all actual human beings. In these considerations, we will do nothing to "accentuate the positive."

Here is the case itself. Before anything fancy takes place, I am first put under a very powerful anesthetic so that there is *no state of consciousness* intimately associated with me or with any of my parts. Only then is my brain stem and a tenth of my cortex severed from the rest of me. Both the severed minor portion and the remaining major one are kept alive and functioning. But, as the anesthetic is kept in force for the brain stem and company, there is still no consciousness anywhere intimately associated with me or any part of mine. This state of affairs is maintained for a long period. Now, by hypothesis, *were* the anesthetic lifted from the brain-stem grouping at any time during this period, consciousness would occur over there. But, it is supposed, this does not happen. (Were the anesthetic removed from the major portion, as our background assumptions have it, there would not be consciousness supported there anyway.)

Would I survive such a procedure and, if so, where would I be? Toward this case, my intuitions are in so much conflict that I can report no stable pattern. In some moods, I mainly think I survive only as a person consisting largely of a brain stem. Then I think of myself as becoming a *very* dull person who, nonetheless, could wake up at any moment if only they'd remove the drug. In other moods, I mainly think of myself surviving as the person with so much of my old body and cerebral cortex. Then I'm rather more interesting psychologically, at least potentially so, but I could become conscious only under much more special circumstances, to put it very mildly. And there are still other moods when I think I will not survive at all here, perhaps even that the question of my future identity will have no determinate answer in this case.

As far as I can tell, my messy response pattern is reasonably representative. On most accounts of the self, or of personal identity, the fact of this mess is quite troublesome. Everything that is psychologically distinctive about me is on one side, and that is the side with almost all of my bodily continuity and brain continuity. The other side doesn't even have continuity of consciousness here. All that it has is the most direct (physical) causal ground of my consciousness; perhaps a continuity of my *capacity* for consciousness (or much more of such a continuity). Why isn't this continuity easily outweighed by all the rest? It is puzzling, at least, that we give it anywhere near the weight that we do. Better, it is puzzling on anything like the most standard contemporary accounts of our thinking about ourselves. What I would like to explore, then, is the possibility of providing a better account of our thinking about ourselves, one on which our responses to examples are allowed as complex and on which much of this complexity is at least partially explained. However good or poor my own efforts in the matter may prove to be, the exploratory task itself seems very worthwhile.

6. HOW WE MIGHT EXPLAIN OUR RESPONSES TO THESE EXAMPLES

A most conspicuous feature of the response patterns to cases involving consciousness and self-identity is that of *conflict* of response. It is a rare respondent, it seems, who consistently replies to any of these cases along just one coherent line of reply. In trying to account for the response patterns, we must, above all, account for this fact of conflict.

No approach that is only moderately complex will account for this conflict fully. Indeed, even for any approach to make much headway, various auxiliary hypotheses must often be employed. But perhaps there is an approach, not too complex, where the auxiliary hypotheses required will be plausible propositions and each appropriate to the occasions on which it is used.

Here are the main lines of an approach that seems promising. Each person in our culture ordinarily has two views of himself or herself, and so of other selves. Although your two self-views may differ from mine, the differences are relatively slight. Although each of your two views may be internally consistent, there are certain inconsistencies between them. In responding to our puzzle cases about self-identity, allegiance to one view often pulls us in one direction while the other view pulls us in another direction. Thus we have tendencies toward conflicting responses to the examples.

It may be that most of us have a greater allegiance to, more confidence in, just one of our two views. Other things equal, the dictates of that view will do more to determine our responses than do those of the other. But often other things will not be equal. For one thing, a certain sort of example, even the way that the example is presented, might make one of the views more salient and more accessible temporarily. Then we might respond mainly in line with the dictates of the view less believed overall, thus going against the view that we generally prefer.

As I conjecture, there is one view of ourselves that is believed most strongly by most in our culture and that may appropriately be called the *objective view of the self.* On this view, I am always an object in the world, though perhaps a very special and complex objective entity. The conflicting view of ourselves, less strongly believed by most of us, may appropriately be called the *subjective view of the self.* On this other view, I am never an object in the world; but I am, in some appropriate sense or way, always a subject of conscious thought or experience.

What do I mean by 'view' here? I cannot be very precise. But, roughly, a view of something can be regarded as a body of beliefs about that thing. And a body of beliefs about something can be regarded, well enough, as a group of beliefs about the thing among whose members there is considerable coherence and harmony. This is quite compatible, of course, with there also being some incoherence among some of those beliefs; the notion of an incoherent view is itself a coherent notion. But too much incoherence means no view at all. As far as coherence and incoherence go, then, having a view of something is a matter of degree. Indeed, there will generally be a good deal of vagueness involved in the attribution of views to people and in the individuation of a person's several views. But we can tolerate this vagueness and make some judgments in the domain it concerns.

What do I mean by 'self' here? Roughly, I mean what, at the outset, I meant by "conscious being." This is also quite vague, as I then suggested, but I cannot see that this vagueness means any insuperable problem or harm.

The terms 'subjective' and 'objective,' as roughly opposite adjectives, have been used by philosophers in a variety of ways. Almost always they are used unclearly, but that is not much of a drawback. Almost always, too, they are used uninterestingly, so that no stimulating new approaches are suggested by their use for us. That is a serious drawback, and one most difficult to avoid. But recently Thomas Nagel has had some success along these lines.[6]

Encouraged by Nagel's vague but stimulating usage, I will try to use these terms, although rather vaguely, in a way that might suggest some new lines of conjecture and inquiry.

With these hopes and disclaimers, I hypothesize that, as part of our ordinary implicit psychology, each of us holds a (shared) subjective view of the self as well as a conflicting, generally more influential objective view of the self. Do we implicitly also hold a third view of the self, significantly different from these two, and perhaps a fourth? Perhaps we do. But at least for reasons of intellectual economy, I will hypothesize that just two substantially differing self-views will be enough to posit for us; any further candidate is, if not a mild variant of one of these two, without adequate basis for postulation in our responsive behavior.

So much for the general lines of my hypothesis. Let's try to get some sense of the views I am hypothesizing for us.

7. THE OBJECTIVE VIEW OF THE SELF

In our culture, we try to understand all of concrete reality as belonging to a single system of things. According to our ordinary thinking, each of us is part of concrete reality, in no wise a mere abstraction. In particular, then, we try to understand ourselves as each belonging to that system of things.

The system we are ordinarily inclined to find available, and at least reasonably suitable, is a system of things in objective time and (many of them at least) in objective space as well. By some route through space and time, everything in the system is related, apparently clearly enough, to everything else in the system. Here is a box, for example, an object in the system that is (fairly) substantial spatially and that has existed for a moderate period of time. This box, as it is now, is related in the system, in the objective world, to Julius Caesar's token thinking of his crossing the Rubicon at that long ago time when he was crossing the Rubicon. Indeed, as we ordinarily conceive of these matters, the relation is uniquely appropriate, so that it takes us from this present box through space and time to just that ancient thought. First we go from the box here and now to the there and then of Caesar's body and brain. Further, as we presume, there is a single Caesarian thought with the appropriate content that is then most intimately associated with that organism. And the inverse relation takes us, we presume, from that particular thought to just this box now. So the thought, like the box, finds its own unique place in the system that is our objective order—a space-time system well able to accommodate them both. In our natural sciences, we strive to gain an understanding of everything concrete in terms of this unifying objective system. In these terms, we strive for as deep an understanding as is possible for us to achieve.[7]

Much as is a box, or a tree, so also is a person understood in this way.

Informed by scientific inquiry, we form a view of ourselves as living human beings, each of us in fact a somewhat distinctive member of our biological species. It is characteristic of members of this species that each can think and experience, both consciously and unconsciously, and that this capacity is realized mainly in the appropriate configuration and functioning of the brains of its members. As compared with other species with which we are familiar, ours is best at thinking and at achieving a higher level, or a greater degree, of consciousness. Given all this, we take our brains as those (salient) parts of us that realize our most conspicuously distinctive capacities. So we take our brains to be, in fact, much more important parts of ourselves than any other parts we have external to our brains; they are more central to our existence, indeed, than all of those other parts taken together.

We treat other conscious beings along the same general lines to the extent that it seems appropriate. Because the analogous capacities of a dog are most directly realized in its brain, we take this organ of the dog as more central to its existence than all the rest of the dog, external to the brain, taken together. Consider a worm that is brilliantly intelligent and highly conscious, if such there be, but whose capacities thereof are not centered in any of its parts. Then we consider that worm as a whole, no part favored over any other as regards its existence, much as with a presumably nonconscious rock. Treated somewhat variously but always here objectively, the human, the dog, and the worm may each be called an *objective self*.

The objective self is studied not only by physics, chemistry, and biology but also by psychology and other softer, more humane sciences or disciplines. Each of us comes to accept that one's distinctive (ostensible) memories are centered in the brain along with distinctive personality traits, emotional and intellectual dispositions. This further adds to the brain's importance in our objective conception of ourselves, at least in terms of (almost all) ordinary cases or situations.

But then we may imagine that these psychological capacities, so complex and individual, can be reduplicated while the originally supporting, or realizing, brain is left behind and possibly destroyed. Now, we all place great importance on our capacities and dispositions, on our personality, character, intellect, and so on. So the realization of them by whatever route or means, in whatever medium or material, can take on much weight for us in judgments about ourselves and others. Also, each of us places great importance on our (sometimes) being in, and on our capacity to be in, a state of consciousness. So the realization of such a state in us, and of the capacity for that state, by whatever route or means, medium or material, can also take on much weight for us in judgments as to self-identity. As a matter of fact, both sorts of capacity are most directly realized in our brains. But the shared capacity for consciousness is mainly realized in the brain stem, where as the (more) distinctive dispositional capacities are most directly realized in the cortex.

At all events, when we think about ourselves in terms of our objective self-view, we are apt to balance or weigh certain physical continuities and discontinuities, on the one side, against continuities and interruptions of the noted psychological states and capacities, however realized, on the other. All the continuities we balance are, in general terms, of a causal (or quasi-causal) sort. Our shared objective view itself, it is reasonable to hypothesize, is sufficiently vague as to leave room for different weightings of these continuities. One respondent can favor certain psychological continuities more; another can favor continuity of normal (brain) physical realization of that psychology instead; the objective view might have neither respondent be correct at the expense of the other.

8. THE SUBJECTIVE VIEW OF THE SELF

Few contemporary philosophers would deny that we employ what I call the objective view of the self.[8] On the contrary, many accept that we do have and ordinarily employ some such self-view. And many of these thinkers believe that this view of the self is *correct,* and thus that we have and employ the (only) correct and comprehensive view of ourselves.[9] For them, then, any quite different, comprehensive view of the self, conflicting with the objective view, is incorrect.

The subjective view of the self is just such a conflicting, comprehensive view. As most contemporary philosophers doubt that we hold a severely incorrect view of ourselves, hold it even implicitly, few would allow that we subscribe to the (incorrect) subjective view. But then, I believe, they will be missing out on a good deal of the truth regarding our ordinary psychological attitudes. For whatever the correct view of the self may be, our conflictful response patterns make it plausible to posit for ourselves an adherence, not only to the objective self-view, but also to a radically different and conflicting subjective view of the self.

As I hypothesize, our subjective view of the self will have each of us be subjects of consciousness *as opposed to* objects in the world. This statement is suggestive. But we must try to go beyond the suggestion. So what does our subjective self-view amount to; what are its main implications?

The view has major implications regarding the self in relation both to space and to time, the two (main) dimensions of the objective order (as such an order is ordinarily conceived by us). First, we consider space. As I hypothesize it, the subjective view clearly requires that the self not occupy any finite or infinite volume of space; a conscious being must have *no spatial extension.* Why do I think this to be such a clear requirement? As I see it, the subjective view does not allow any self to be in any way divisible, not even in principle, and spatial extension for a self would allow for at least some such divisibility. But the subjective view goes beyond this. Even though it would not affect the question of the self's divisibility, on this view a self *cannot be* at a pure *point in objective space.* For even that much involvement with space would make the self at least something of an object in the world. At the very most, on the subjective view, a self can be *intimately related* to (some) points in space (but need never be so related to any).

Let us consider time. The subjective view is just as insistently isolationist: a self or conscious being cannot exist in objective time, neither for a substantial period nor for a moment. Rather, each self has its own subjective time, which is the only appropriate temporal framework for considerations of its existence. At the very most, a self can be intimately related to (some) points or periods of objective time. Now, this idea of (a self's) *subjective time* is, admittedly, a vague and unclear one. But then our subjective view of the self may also be, and very likely is, vague and unclear.

On both the subjective view and the ordinary objective view, the self is utterly concrete, a token, if you will, rather than any sort of type. On our implicitly held objective view, a self is distinct from other selves *in virtue of* its position, or positions, in objective space and time (and certain causal relations involving this). On the subjective view, in contrast, although each self is utterly distinct from all of the others (and from everything else), no self is distinct from anything in virtue of anything at all. So, on this view, two utterly distinct selves may each be intimately associated, in qualitatively identical ways, with just the same points of objective space and objective time. This can obtain even should the selves, numerically distinct, be qualitatively identical, each having precisely the same (sort of) conscious thought and experience in its own subjective (parallel) time.

On both implicit views of the self, mental states—notably, thoughts and experiences—are individuated in terms of the selves that have them, and certainly not the other way around. So *this* (token) experience is *mine because I have it;* it is not that I have it because it is mine, or because it has any property, such as the property of being mine.[10] Whether or not a being must have some mental states in order to exist, the matter of which ones the being has is quite clearly left entirely open, on both of our posited self-views.

On our purely subjective self-view, someone must not merely have the capacity for consciousness at every moment but actually be conscious at every moment of existence. But then the moments in question are all instants of the person's own subjective time, not of objective time, for that is the only time appropriate to consider. That is why the subjective view can make this strict demand: in terms of one's own subjective time, *one's existence is temporally continuous, uninterrupted by any (relevant) moment or period.* In contrast, the objective view has our relevant time be objective time. But, as we believe, there are periods of such time when we are not conscious. Now, if the objective view required consciousness itself, it would declare that a person ceased to exist when, say, undergoing the effect of a powerful anesthetic. As far as I can discern, we have no tendency at all to believe that. So on the objective view there is no such requirement. At the very most, perhaps there is a weaker parallel requirement of the objective view: in objective time, any given self must uninterruptedly have the *capacity* for consciousness; but at any objective time the capacity may not be exercised, the self then existing but having no conscious experience or thought. This idea of (a self's) *capacity for consciousness* is somewhat vague and unclear. But then our objective view of the self may be, and very likely is, itself somewhat vague and unclear. (That does not mean, of course, that it is as deeply vague and unclear as our subjective view might be.)

Because we employ the subjective view, not only the objective one, we can readily understand many speculations about ourselves that otherwise would seem more troublesome. For example, I can easily think along these lines: while my body is asleep, I go back to the time of the ancient Greeks and overhear a conversation between Plato and Aristotle. What does this involve? My subjective time breaks off intimate relation with current objective time and assumes, instead, such association with the objective period of ancient Greece. I break off my intimate relation with my current body, with its points of objective space, and assume some such relation with some points in the area of ancient Greece. I then have experiences that arise from, or at least are reflective of, the behavior of Plato and Aristotle. Their behavior in turn arises from, or is reflective of, thoughts and experiences of Plato and Aristotle themselves, many of these mental states being conscious ones. For each of these people is, in the case in question, intimately related to certain points in the objective space and time of ancient Greece and, thus, to suitably behaving bodies. Further details can be supplied in terms of our subjective view.

After overhearing that conversation, I can return to my body here and now. Such a return will involve my breaking off relations with ancient objective time and spatial points then near the bodies of Plato and Aristotle. And it will involve my entering into appropriate relations with current objective time and spatial points now occupied by (parts of) my body. Now, largely because our subjective view of the self is very vague and incomplete, especially as regards its notion of a self's subjective time, there is a lot of vagueness and incompleteness in any such speculation. But, as far as it goes, this present speculation appears to be not only intelligible enough but even coherent.

Because we hold the subjective self-view, we can think with great freedom about time travel for ourselves. Perhaps we can think about time travel also for objects about which we hold no subjective view, for rocks perhaps, or certain machines. But we do not seem *quite so free* to do this, or to achieve coherence with such thoughts so readily and over such an unrestricted domain. So, at least psychologically, there is a difference here between ourselves and time, on the one hand, and such objects and time, on the other. This difference can be best explained, I hypothesize, by the supposition that we hold a subjective view of ourselves but not of such objects.

Because we can think in terms of such a subjective view, as well as an objective view of self, many religious and metaphysical speculations not always treated as such are, I believe, intelligible. Perhaps those speculations, or the great majority of them, get little credence from us, which is probably about what they deserve. But this matter of belief is a further matter. As a psychological phenomenon, the main matter here can be reasonably well understood providing that there is posited for ourselves both an objective view of the self and also a (conflicting) subjective view. To handle the matter of belief, or disbelief, we need only add to our postulation that we subscribe much more *strongly,* overall, to the objective self-view, not the subjective one. But this is something that most of us are very ready to accept in any case.

These points remain even if there is, as I suspect there may well be, some *deep* incoherence or inconsistency in the posited subjective view.[11] So long as the incoherence of a view is sufficiently unobvious, as deep inconsistencies often are, there is no bar to the view being relevantly intelligible, nor to our understanding it at least moderately well and accepting it as thus understood. Perhaps this point is itself very obvious, but I think it worth emphasizing now.

These considerations of free time travel and of the quasi-religious speculations provide, I believe, important, if somewhat obvious, support for our psychological hypothesis. In particular, they provide support for the conjecture of a purely subjective self-view implicitly held by us all. The explanation of our response patterns to our somewhat novel examples concerning consciousness and self-identity provide further support that is not so easy to notice. We will examine this additional support shortly. But first it will be useful to say a few words about our possible motivation for holding these two conflicting views of ourselves.

9. ON OUR MOTIVATION FOR OUR SELF-VIEWS: SOME SPECULATIONS

How have we come to hold these two self-views? What keeps them with us, once they've been generated? Even without a hint of an answer to these questions, I believe our hypothesis of two self-views can be made deserving of serious consideration. To do that, we just need show its usefulness in explaining our cognitive responses. But at least a hint of an answer to the questions will make our hypothesis more plausible than it would otherwise be. Although I can give no more than a hint, an attempt in this direction seems appropriate now. With no systematically gathered empirical data, my attempt must be speculative. But perhaps my speculations will be plausible ones.

We each come into the world with no view of ourselves at all, nor of anything else. As time goes on, we form some views of some things; we acquire beliefs and they are grouped and patterned. So we form a view of ourselves and others, a single view that is such a mess that it is barely a view at all. We are moved to understand the world around us and also to understand ourselves. We are apt to understand things as *systematically* as we can. Indeed, we form a view of the world, of concrete reality, as a system of connectedly related things; many of these connected things are smaller things, about which we have smaller views. We think of ourselves as such parts of the world. Thus, from our *very* messy view of ourselves, there emerges a *somewhat less* messy view of ourselves: the objective view of the self or, at least, a view that is the embryo of that.

What is left behind and is still in our heads? It is the rest of the original messy view; the part or aspect not readily incorporated into our systematic view of the world. That is the embryo of our subjective view of the self.

As our systematic, objective understanding develops, we neglect facts and features not readily seen to be part of the system. Sensuous qualities, and the experiences thereof, present a problem. (Illusions and hallucinations and dreams present a more obvious problem). Where are we to understand these things to be? Perhaps better, how can we understand them as occurring at all? The embryo of the subjective view is allowed to grow so that we have an appropriately encompassing view of the self as pure subject, distinct from the world of our system, of objective space and time. Then the recalcitrant items and aspects of concrete reality can be viewed as existing in or *occurring to* at least one self or subject, not in (the system that is) the world.[12]

Incomplete as it is, that is a sketch of our intellectual motivation for having two views of the self, an objective and subjective view. But once the objective view gets any headway, there is also a more emotional motivation for a subjective view of the self.

Each of us wants more consciousness; better pleasurable than painful, better veridical than illusory, better this way than that. But those are all modifications of the basic theme: other things equal, we want more and more conscious experience and thought; there is never enough to satisfy us *fully*. Each of us fears the end of all of his conscious thought and experience, even if resignedly so. We want to hope, however mild and "irrational" be the hope, that there will be more experience for us, not no more at all.

The evidence of our senses, and our powerful objective view of ourselves as living things, tend to thwart any hope: ashes to ashes, and dust to dust. We just cannot believe, with any real confidence, that such a self, a mere organism, has any hope of no end to its consciousness. A self not part of the objective order, however, is a self for whom this hope can make more sense. For such a self, such a hope can be maintained. So, owing to our deep wish for evermore consciousness, we are moved to promote and maintain our subjective view of the self. Our allegiance to this view may not be very great, as our fears testify, but it is not nonexistent, as our hopes serve to indicate.

10. HOW THE HYPOTHESIS OF TWO VIEWS GIVES US EXPLANATIONS

Early on, we considered four examples that elicited conflicting patterns of response. In each case, one of the responses was to be expected, according to the most prevalent philosophical theory in the area; but the opposite response was not. For me at least, that opposite response, favoring (apparently) continuous consciousness, was often the dominant reaction. With our hypothesis of two self-views now in hand, and with the aid of plausible auxiliary hypotheses, let us now essay explanations of these patterns of response.

In the case first considered, conscious experience seemed to flow on only "in one direction" while physical and other psychological continuity was all "on the other side." We responded, whether strongly or weakly, that a subject would survive in the case and do so only as a disembodied conscious being. What prompted this response?

By the very nature of the case described, consciousness would be a most salient feature for a typical respondent. We may hypothesize, plausibly enough I think, that when consciousness is salient we will be quite prone to think in terms of our subjective self-view. Indeed, many of us then will be more inclined to think in terms of this view than in terms of our objective view, which is generally by far the more dominant view for most of us.

It is very natural for us to think of the at least apparent flow of consciousness as a genuine continuity of conscious experience. True enough, we think of experiences as individuated via their subjects, via the selves that have the experiences. But on the subjective view, now so accessible, there is nothing in the way of having the disembodied self be there for the wanted individuation. We can think of this self as intimately associated with certain points of objective space and time, and we seem to do just that. At the case's start, it was so associated with spatial points of the relevant body, and the temporal points of the body's history then. When the peculiar anesthetic was applied, the self broke off this association with those spatial points and, perhaps, started to be so associated with other points in space. It need not, and we tend to think it did not, break off any close temporal relation to the objective order. Now with this implicit reasoning, we have an (apparently) coherent view applied to the case that has experience be genuinely continuous, that has the experiences all be those of one subject who is conscious throughout. This is our subjective view of the self. Because we have this view all along, and becaue it is made so accessible by this example, we are prone to respond to the case as one where we do survive, and survive as a being who is conscious throughout the entire example.

We have no *sensed* tendency to think of the case as one where there were two people all along, one surviving as continuously conscious and the other surviving through a continuity of brain and body and so on. Though David Lewis might propose a judgment of such "overlap," the judgment would appear to be derived from a largely invented systematic metaphysics, not part of any view (of the self) that we ordinarily have, not even an implicit one.[13] Rather, we feel forced to choose among these alternatives: (1) we survive as the one; (2) we survive as the other; or (3) we do not survive at all, but only have some very intimate descendants. Along the lines just indicated, our subjective self-view urges the first alternative; our generally powerful objective self-view urges the second; and the sensed clash between them, with the thought of no clear winner, urges the third. Though there are plenty of details that might still be added helpfully, and certain general modifications might be of some use as well, we have sketched, I believe, most of the explanation of our conflictful response pattern to our first case.

Our second case was rather similar to our first as regards essential features. So our explanation of the conflictful response pattern to it will be rather similar as well. Salient consciousness makes most accessible our subjective view of the self. There is, as before, our tendency to take apparent conscious flow as more than merely apparent. We can go with this tendency by way of the following implicit reasoning: the original self, as subjectively viewed, breaks off spatial relations with most of the brain and all of the rest of the body; it retains such close relations only with the one-third of the brain not anesthetized. Thinking along subjective lines, we judge there to be a sole survivor, one who was conscious throughout. As we also think along the generally powerful objective lines, we judge otherwise as well. Thus there is our sensed conflict of response.

Third, we considered a contrasting pair of examples (in two versions). In the first example of the pair, there was continuity of consciousness. But there was very little relevant continuity of anything else we consider important for self-identity. We responded, with sensed conflict, that one would survive in the case: one would *become* a bionic being, a conscious entity that was, both physically and psychologically, very different from how one used to be. Why do we make this dominant response? Again, consciousness is salient in the case. So we tap into our subjective view of the self, there in our heads all along, and bring it to bear. Along lines of implicit reasoning lately indicated, we arrive at (what is for me) the dominant response: one survives all those radical changes. Our conflicting response of no survival is prompted by our generally potent objective self-view, displaced once again to the psychological background.

In the second case of the pair, consciousness was thoroughly interrupted (by an assumed anesthetic). Consciousness was not, then, so salient for contemplation. That is why we respond to this contrasting case completely in terms of our more powerful self-view, the objective view of the self. That is why our response to that case is, without sensed conflict, that one does not survive.

These explanations raise questions, some of them via the auxiliary hypothesis they contain. For example, why have we the tendency, apparently real enough, to regard apparently continuous consciousness as actually continuous? Why do we tend to individuate conscious experience (and other mental phenomena) via their possessors and, moreover, in such a way that they cannot be shared? But, of course, all explanations that are in any way incomplete will raise questions for contemplation and, at least generally, for further explanation. The questions ours raise here are, then, only to be expected and, on the face of it at least, mean no damage to our psychological account.

We turn to our fourth case now, the most difficult to treat for any account. My brain-stem-plus goes one way, the rest of my brain and body go another. Do I survive this splitting? If so, where will I be? As noted, our responses are a confused mess here. So, what promotes the confusion?

By speaking of the brain-stem-plus as so involved with *consciousness,* we make consciousness at least a *fairly* salient consideration. We thus call upon our subjective self-view, giving this generally weak view somewhat more chance for influence than it would otherwise have. But it cannot influence us very directly for response to the case. That is because, in the case, the brain-stem-plus is not actually conscious or supporting consciousness but is rendered always dormant by the assumed anesthetic. Still, we do feel some pull here toward favoring the brain-stem-plus; otherwise our response pattern wouldn't be the mess it is. So it is plausible to think that our subjective view is having some influence anyway, the influence being, of course, somewhat indirect.

We take the brain-stem-plus, I conjecture, to be an approximation to what is wanted by our subjective self-view. On that view, what is wanted is a particular *seat of consciousness,* indeed, the one that I am. Such a seat will, on the view, always be conscious (in its own time). The case does not give us that. But it does give us a seat of consciousness in an attenuated sense or way: my brain-stem-plus can be treated as the seat of my *capacity* for consciousness (in objective time). That *seems to us* a reasonably good approximation to what is wanted by our subjective view, a view made somewhat salient by the indirect reference to consciousness. So we take that view to direct us to think we go with our brain-stem-plus. In other words, we reach this response, perhaps for many a rather weak one, by way of a *compromise* between the demands of the (temporarily salient) subjective view, on the one hand, and the features of the case itself on the other. Our powerful objective view urges us in the other direction. But its dictates do not seem as clear as might be expected: they are messed up, I hypothesize, in the manner just indicated.

My psychological hypotheses are not, of course, the only way of explaining our conflictful patterns of response to these examples. Nor are they the only way of giving such explanations that, at the same time, make appropriate sense of our quasi-religious speculations. With various alternative explanatory frameworks, auxiliary hypotheses may be piled on freely so that a tailored fabric will, eventually, display our noted reactions as only to be expected. Trite though it is to say so in these Quinean times, it is mainly a matter of comparative complexity and plausibility. I suggest that the approach adopted here is at least as plausible and uncomplicated as any competitor; it is probably better off than any diverging from it significantly.

11. THE PHILOSOPHY OF THE SELF: FOUR ALTERNATIVE APPROACHES

Suppose that I am right about our psychology and that we do hold these two views of ourselves, the subjective view and the more powerful, conflicting objective view. It is unsatisfactory simply to continue to maintain them both. Indeed, that would be a block to the advancement of philosophy.

There are four alternatives to such unsatisfactory inactivity. First, we might try to develop a view of the self that has some elements from the objective view combined with some from the subjective view and that discounts as illusory some elements from each view. This will give us a compromise view, or a hybrid, between the two conflicting views we now implicitly hold. We want a hybrid that is internally consistent, of course, but also one that is reasonably compelling for our belief and explanatory of our phenomena.

Second, we might discount the subjective view of the self as being deeply false and illusory and feel free to develop the objective view. Unconstrained by intuitions attributable to our holding the subjective view, we might develop the objective approach in what would now seem quite a radical direction. This might yield us an objective view that was, not only internally consistent, but credible and adequately explanatory.

Third, we might instead discount the objective view as being deeply false and illusory and feel free to develop the subjective view. Unconstrained by the powerful intuitions attributable to our holding the powerful objective view, we might then develop the subjective approach in what would now seem a highly radical direction. Eventually, this could yield us a purely subjective view of the self that, from our present mainly objective perspective, would seem radical in the extreme. But perhaps some such view might be, nonetheless, internally consistent, at least barely credible for us, and highly explanatory of the relevant phenomena.

Finally, we may abandon both of our views entirely and attempt to construct a new view of the self, or of something relevantly like the self, out of propositions (most of which) we do not now accept at all. This fourth option is an extremely radical last resort.

At least in the present paper, I do not want to be highly pessimistic. Partly for this reason, I will ignore the fourth alternative, that of abandoning our implicit self-views entirely. In that I have already advocated such a terribly radical option elsewhere, this represents no closed-minded dogmatism on my part.[14] Rather, my ignoring that option now allows, I believe, for a more fruitful focusing of our effort and attention.

We turn, then, to discuss the three of our four alternatives that are not quite so radical or pessimistic. I present a brief discussion of each of the three.

12. SHOULD WE ATTEMPT A COMPROMISE VIEW?

The first alternative, that of compromise, may strike many as being our most reasonable one. But although compromise is productive in many areas, I do not think it will work well here. I cannot prove this, of course, so I will try to make my distrust of this alternative seem reasonable.

In the history of philosophy, as I see it, some hybrid views have been explicitly espoused. They were not offered, of course, as compromises between views implicitly held because there was no recognition of people holding conflicting self-views implicitly. But, we may conjecture, part of the motivation for the offering of these views was an attempt by the philosopher making the offering to advance a consistent position that derived something from both of his own implicit bodies of belief. Whatever the motivation, the most notable hybrids arise, it seems to me, by taking the self to exist in objective time (not in its own subjective time). Despite a look to some historical figures in my search for interesting hybrids here, I intend no serious, scholarly contribution to the history of philosophy.

Writings that compellingly invite one to take the first-person point of view to examples, and to objects of thought generally, make salient for one the subjective view of the self. When we consider the first-person perspective in relation to the history of philosophy, we are apt to think of Descartes. In large measure, the most compelling parts of Descartes's *Meditations* owe their power to their leading the reader to adopt this perspective while pushing to the background the alternative third-person point of view. Then Descartes exploits the first-person perspective to a remarkable degree.

We are moved to inquire, then, at least a bit into Descartes's philosophical view of the self. First, Descartes did not allow any self, or conscious being, any spatial extension. And it is plausible enough to understand him as denying for any self as well any spatial location even at a point. At most, a self could be intimately related with certain points of objective space and, so, with whatever (matter) was properly at those points. As regards *spatial* questions, we may agree, Descartes drew quite completely from our posited *subjective* view of the self.

Descartes also drew from the *subjective* view as regards the relation between *consciousness and self-identity.* For Descartes, a self is, as it must be, conscious at every moment of its existence. Moreover, a self must exist uninterruptedly with respect to the time in which it exists, as a self is an utterly concrete entity. But about the question of the self and *time,* Descartes drew from our *objective* view of the self, not from our subjective view. For Descartes, a self existed in objective time, not in its own subjective time.

Descartes's view of the self is, then, a hybrid view. It draws a good deal from our subjective view but also something substantial from our objective view of the self. Because any hybrid view draws on views to which we subscribe, any such position will have some appeal for us, as Descartes's view certainly does. But hybrid views are mixtures of elements that more naturally, for us, go in combination with other aspects of the views from which they were drawn, not those of the hybrid. So any hybrid or compromise will have some unattractive features, too. In any attempt at compromise, there will be a result with certain aspects that we find counterintuitive. In particular, so it is with Descartes's view of the self.

For Descartes, nobody can endure any gap of consciousness with respect to objective time. That is because everyone must exist in this time (his objective requirement) and also everyone must be conscious at every moment of existence in whatever is the time in which that person exists (a requirement at least partly drawn from the subjective view). So, for Descartes, we cannot be unconscious in a period of deep sleep, or under very powerful general anesthetic (and possibly survive the objective episode). Now, we all believe we do survive some such episodes, a belief Descartes wished to respect and maintain. To do this, he required an auxiliary hypothesis. In objective periods of deep sleep and so on, though it *appears* that there is no consciousness, one really is conscious nonetheless; each of us just *completely forgets* all of the conscious thoughts and experiences almost directly upon having them.[15]

Right off, this hypothesis strikes one as highly implausible. This is a sign that Descartes's view of the self is not a view we ordinarily hold, not even one we hold only implicitly. But it is a rather uncertain sign of this. For a somewhat surer sign, let us look with some vigor in the direction in which this first sign points.

Suppose we were confronted with scientific findings that strongly suggested that Descartes was actually *right* about the self in this matter. There is discovered certain esoteric brain activity that is associated with near-immediate forgetting under all sorts of circumstances. And it is found that this (sort of) activity is most intense and is continuously present whenever we are in periods of deepest sleep, under powerful general anesthetic, and so on. Moreover, another sort of esoteric brain activity is discovered to correlate positively with intensity of consciousness, whatever exactly we take the latter to involve. This activity is found to be present, at least to some degree, in every human brain until death, whatever death may exactly involve. Pointedly, such activity is found often to obtain to a fairly high degree when we are in deepest natural sleep and when we are under very powerful general anesthetic. Thinking of (the possibility of) them now, what is your reaction to such supposed findings?

My own main reaction is that such findings would indeed (help) confirm Descartes's view and that, thus, they would be most surprising and interesting. But I do not sense them to involve any matter that I am urgently concerned about. Now, if I implicitly held a self-view like Descartes's, held it with even a moderate degree of strength, then I should feel a kind of relief to be associated with contemplation of such findings. But I do not feel such relief. This is a further sign, I think, that Descartes's view of the self is not one that I hold ordinarily or even implicitly, at least not with any significant degree of strength or confidence. Supposing that I am not eccentric in this reaction pattern, the implication is clear enough for the self-views of others.

None of this shows that Descartes's view is false or otherwise inadequate. But as things now appear, there is little reason for us to adopt his (radical) compromise, and more reason for us to reject it. Few, at any rate, will accept this philosopher's hybrid view of the self; many of us will not accept it. We will not be unreasonable, I submit, in taking that position.

Let us look quite briefly at some related compromise views, offered by less luminous thinkers than Descartes but by philosophers who are very able. As I read them, Joseph Butler and Thomas Reid offer a (shared) philosophical view of the self that is in some ways like Descartes's but differs in such a way as to avoid the unnatural Cartesian consequence just discussed.[16] Like Descartes, these thinkers draw from our subjective view regarding the self and matters spatial: a self has no spatial extension and, presumably, not even location at a point in objective space. And, like Descartes, their view is a hybrid in that they also draw from our objective view regarding the self and temporal matters: the self exists in objective time. As must any utterly concrete entity, a self must exist uninterruptedly in whatever time it does exist. Thus, a self must exist in objective time without any interruption.

Butler and Reid avoided Descartes's "problem of the apparent gap" by requiring a less stringent, and less pure, relation between the self and consciousness. The self need not actually be conscious at every moment, but need only have the *capacity* for consciousness at every moment it exists; a self's capacity need not always be exercised. With this vague but motivated alteration, these thinkers give up a second key element of the subjective view, thus offering a hybrid rather closer to our shared objective view than is Descartes's position.

With this second step toward our psychologically powerful objective self-view, these philosophers can offer us a hybrid position that has no very glaring appearance of unnaturalness. But the decrease in discomfort is dearly bought. For this position, we feel, is not a view of which we can make much sense. When the self is *not* exercising its capacity for consciousness, *what*, in any positive terms, is this nonspatial self supposed to be? No plausible answers come to mind. So this hybrid view, also, doesn't seem to make any very great contact with a view of the self that we ordinarily hold, whether explicitly or only implicitly. Moreover, there seems little reason now to adopt this apparently mysterious compromise position, and more to leave it alone. In point of fact, few will adopt this view, I take it, and many of us will not. In doing that, it seems to me, we will not be unreasonable.

In a recent book that is quite excellent in several respects, *The Identity of the Self,* Geoffrey Madell claims to understand well the apparently obscure view of Butler and Reid.[17] And Madell claims to be defending their view, which he takes to be a purely subjective view of the self and which he takes to be only marginally different from the view of J. M. E. McTaggart. Leaving to the side the question of McTaggart's position in these matters, it seems to me that Madell's own view is, first, a hybrid rather than a purely subjective position and, moreover, a compromise that is rather closer to Descartes's view than it is to the view of Reid and Butler.

I will not discuss the basic tenets of Madell's position, which are a bit obscure but very stimulating. Rather, I will take note of his position on the matters we have been discussing, a position he thinks, whether rightly or wrongly, to be most harmonious with his basic tenets. As I understand these philosophers, for both Madell and Descartes, but not Reid or Butler, the self must be conscious at every moment of its existence; no mere (unexercised) capacity for consciousness will suffice.

As his three discussed predecessors do, Madell has the self exist in objective time, not in its own subjective time. This is an objective element in Madell's view.[18] So Madell's view, too, is a compromise position and, as noted, one interestingly similar to Descartes's view. But there is an interesting difference between Madell and Descartes as well, the latter being in this respect quite the same as Reid and Butler. For Madell, but not for any of these three other philosophers, the self can have temporally interrupted existence (with respect to whatever is the time in which it exists). Although utterly (or highly) concrete and conscious at every moment of its existence, a self, according to Madell, can exist at one objective time, then not exist for a long while during a later objective time interval, and then at a still later objective time exist once again.[19] This idea about the self strikes us as highly counterintuitive. Intuitively, such great temporal gaps seem compatible with the existence of "more abstract" entities like social organizations (which are never proper subjects of consciousness), but wildly out of place when it comes to the existence of you or me. So this hybrid doesn't seem to be much in harmony with any view of the self that we ordinarily hold. And there seems no more reason for us to adopt this compromise than we saw with the earlier compromise positions. Few will adopt this unusual view, I trust; we will not be unreasonable this time, either.

Each of these views is interesting philosophically; given their implausibility, each is surprisingly well argued by its advocates, as a reading of the relevant works will show. But it is hard to see any of them argued, or developed, to a point where they should receive widespread acceptance. As far as I can see, none of these views will do very much to be, or even to form an integral part of, a satisfactory understanding of what we are. Perhaps this only reflects a failure on my part, no inadequacy in at least one of these (mutually conflicting) views itself. For all I know, that is possible; but I do not think that it is so. Nor, I suppose, does the reader think that it is.

Supposing that we are right in this, then these particular compromises should not be adopted. But perhaps there is some other hybrid that is much more satisfactory than any of these. Perhaps so, but I cannot see that to be a very likely prospect. If I am right about this more general point, then we should take some approach other than compromise. Although I do so quite tentatively, I suggest that that is what we should do. This suggestion, I trust, will not be an unreasonable one.

13. SHOULD WE TRY TO EXTEND THE SUBJECTIVE VIEW?

Forsaking attempts at compromise, we are left with two at least somewhat appealing alternatives. Of the two, I feel almost compelled to believe that the more promising is to discount our subjective view and, having done this, freely but judiciously extend our objective view of the self. But let us not rush into this apparently compelling position. That requires some discussion of our subjective view.

The subjective view is not entirely silly. If we reflect on our discussion of compromise positions, we can be moved to this realization: so long as we do not require that for a self, as for an object in the world, the appropriate time for its existence is objective time, we need not confront any of those implausible hybrid views. Instead of objective time, we may consider as most appropriate to the question of the self and time, a subjective time that each self has for itself. With respect to its own subjective time, each self will always be conscious. Then we are back with our purely subjective view of the self, perhaps always implicitly held by each of us, perhaps now somewhat better appreciated.

Moreover, it is worth exploring the question of whether some notable philosophers actually endorsed just such a purely subjective view. McTaggart appears to have found the very notion of objective time to be inherently perplexing.[20] Avoiding such time as a standard for existence, perhaps he faced no barrier to embracing our subjective self-view.[21] Berkeley, I am told, may have espoused such a purely subjective view of the self.[22] This would seem a fertile area for historical research and interpretation (by scholars far better qualified than I).

But after having made these favorable gestures toward our subjective view, we must come to grips with the question of how much understanding of ourselves it can (help to) provide us. The prospects look bleak. For one thing, the required notion of a self's own subjective time, distinct from any (physical or) objective time, seems irrevocably obscure. Now, if we take the notion as quite a limited one, then, it is true, much of the obscurity can be dispelled. When we are bored, objective time seems to pass slowly. We might then say that we go through a lot of our subjective time while living through only a little objective time. And when an extremely interesting entity or event captures our attention, we might speak in the opposite way. But any such relatively clear notion of subjective time as is here employed will be far weaker than what is needed by our subjective self-view. For one thing, this relatively clear notion at least allows, if it does not indeed require, that a self that is involved in its subjective time does exist in objective time.

For another thing, if we suppose that we are not in (any) objective space and have no objective spatial extension, then it is very hard to see what could possibly be involved in our supposedly *intimate relations* with certain spatial things or points. At the very least, we become embroiled with all of the difficulties of traditional mind-body dualism as regards causation. And the difficulties for understanding compound where there is no objective time in which the mental and physical can exist, in terms of which they can be suitably related. Indeed, what are we to make of our supposedly intimate relations with certain objective times? This underscores the limitations of the required notion of subjective time.

I cannot prove beyond any doubt, of course, that the development of our subjective self-view is not the approach that would eventually work out best. But given such understanding as we presently have, which is all we have to go by, that seems to be a rather unpromising option. Few, I trust, would disagree with me here. I do not think we will be unreasonable if, in the not very distant future, we expend little intellectual effort in trying to extend or develop our implicitly held subjective view of the self.

14. LIBERATION FROM THE METAPHYSICALLY INDEPENDENT SELF

On the subjective view, each of us is utterly distinct from anyone else, and from anything else. On this view, this distinctness is a brute, fundamental fact of reality. We are *not* distinct *in virture of* any *other* facts, or in virtue of anything at all. The differences between us people are metaphysically basic. So these differences loom large in our thought about ourselves and others; they appear greatly important.

I am myself alone, and anyone else is utterly distinct and separate, on this view. We may share all of the same objective properties and relations, but that will be relevantly trivial: we may both be intimately related with just the same points of objective space and objective time. We may both have exactly the same (sorts of) objective properties, in particular, the same (sorts of) thought and experience. For any *third* person, there will be no conceivable *indication* of any difference or distinction between us. Yet there will be an absolute and fundamental separateness between me and the other or others.

This deep and basic separateness can engender a feeling akin to loneliness. And, of course, that is a negative response. Nonetheless, the emotional responses to this line of thinking are, for me at least, on the whole rather positive. In the main, I feel a certain dignity and autonomy when I am made aware of this implicit view and think consciously in terms of it. And I savor the possible freedom from the death of my body, from the cessation of any objective entity, that it seems to allow. Concerning the emotions in me that it tends to excite, our subjective self-view is, on balance, just fine. But intellectually it is stifling.

Given the very character of this view, there is nothing for us to develop in the way of any understanding of our true nature, or even an understanding of anything approximating to our nature. Indeed, all that there is for us to do is to detail, and perhaps to systematize, the various accidental relations in which one or another of us may be involved. Insofar as we seek to understand much about ourselves and about each other, the subjective view is, on reflection, bound to produce (feelings of) dissatisfaction.

On balance, our intellectual wants and needs are not so strong as to wholly override others that are more heavily emotional. So the subjective view will have an appeal for us no matter how dim we judge its prospects for truth, or for anything approximating to truth. Few, if any of us, are all that concerned about science, philosophy, or any advancement of understanding. But it is these latter concerns that, though not overwhelmingly strong, should dominate our development of perspective and, to the extent that it is psychologically possible for us, our choice of belief. In this light, our discounting our subjective view will mean freedom that we value. In this context, abandoning the idea of people as so completely independent and autonomous will be a liberating intellectual act.

Now I do not say that the only motivation we have for the idea of the metaphysically independent self comes from our attachment to the subjective view of the self. Indeed, our psychology is so complex that that is unlikely to be the case. Nor do I say that the only source of intuitions to be discounted, on the way toward developing a more adequate objective self-view, is our adherence to the subjective view. That, too, is unlikely. But I do conjecture, not unreasonably I think, that our adherence to the subjective view is the main motivation we have for that unrealistic idea and that it is the main source of those illusory intuitions. So, by discounting the deliverances of our implicit subjective view, we may, to a very large degree, enable ourselves to develop, freely but carefully, our objective view of the self. Having brought this admittedly valid point to our notice now—the point that the relevant factors are matters of degree—I will not always continue to speak in terms of these acknowledged complexities. For purposes of ready exposition, we may speak more simply and categorically.

Liberation from the independent self will attach to any approach that discounts as illusory the deliverances of our subjective view of the self. In particular, it will attach to certain attempts to develop our objective view, those that proceed without (much) concern for those deliverances. (This liberation will also attach to the alternative of last resort, where we abandon both of our accepted views of the self, [almost] all of our intuitions in the area, and start [almost] from scratch to rethink the entire area. Having noted this point, we will not press it.)

This intellectually welcome liberation will not attach to any approach that refuses to do much of that discounting. Thus it will not attach to attempts at compromise between our two implicit self-views. Most obviously, this liberation is foregone by attempts to extend our subjective view of the self. That is a powerful consideration, I believe, against our making attempts in either of those two alternative directions.

15. ON EXTENDING OUR OBJECTIVE VIEW

The ideas we have presented and examined suggest, however tentatively, that the most promising alternative for us is to develop and extend our objective view of the self. These ideas suggest that we may now reasonably assume a certain freedom in such an endeavor that, heretofore, we may have felt constrained from enjoying. And they suggest, as well, a somewhat detailed strategy for exercising this freedom.

We have certain intuitions about our own existence and identity and about the existence and identity of other *conscious beings* that are very pronounced. These intuitions are more pronounced than parallel intuitions of ours concerning entities that we take to be natural entities, like ourselves, but assume not to be conscious beings, such as rocks and, for most of us, even oak trees. These parallel feelings are weak enough and in conflict with enough other feelings we also have that we are often prepared to discount them. The ideas we have been developing here suggest that we should be just as well prepared, or nearly as well prepared, to discount our intuitions on the other side of the parallel, our more pronounced intuitions about ourselves and other conscious beings. What I have just said is very general, so I will amplify.

We have the intuition, along with a weaker conflicting intuition, that matters concerning the existence and identity of *any natural object,* such as a tree, or even a rock, are *metaphysically determinate.* But we have a stronger intuition, perhaps with no sensed conflict, that matters of our own existence and identity, and of other conscious beings, are metaphysically determinate. About a rock, we are prepared to allow, even if somewhat reluctantly, that there are cases in which nature, or the objective facts or whatever, *do not yield a decision* as to whether or not the rock (still) exists. About conscious beings, notably ourselves, we are not so ready to allow any such thing. Thus we are ready to develop and accept an objective view of rocks that allows for indeterminacy, but not so ready to adopt a view of conscious beings that allows for that. Perhaps we should be just as ready, or very nearly as ready, to develop such a view in the latter case as in the former.

Why is there the difference in the strength of our intuitions about the two sorts of cases, leading to such a difference in our readiness to develop such a more lenient objective view of conscious beings? No doubt, our psychology is so complex that there is no single answer here that is anything like being both simple and complete. But our inquiries suggest that *most* of the answer may well be this: we have a *subjective view of conscious beings* (as well as an objective view). On that subjective view, questions of our existence and identity are always metaphysically independent; thus, they are *independent of all matters of degree.* So, on this view, there is *no room* for considerations to arise that might engender some indeterminacy concerning those central questions about ourselves. So our subjective view insists that questions of our existence and identity are fully determinate matters. Because we are not much prone, in contrast, to view rocks, or even trees, as conscious beings, we have little, if anything, of a subjective view of them. So our intuition that matters of their existence are metaphysically determinate receives no extra strength from such a source.

Our inquiries have led us to discount such intuitive factors as are traceable to our holding a subjective view (to the extent that this source is influential). It seems that, as regards the difference in our feelings about conscious beings and about nonconscious entities, our holding such a view is very influential; it is, indeed, the main reason for the difference in strength of the intuitions noted. Accordingly, we should be reasonably well disposed, perhaps more than most of us are in fact disposed, toward a view that allows metaphysical indeterminacy regarding our existence. For we are well enough disposed toward a view of rocks that allows that for them. And there is, it appears, little to block the former disposition, but not the latter, that is reliable or sound.

The same considerations can apply, I suggest, to other intuitions we have about ourselves that are stronger than parallel feelings we have about rocks and trees: that matters of our existence and identity are *not conventional,* or not decided largely in terms of conventions we have adopted implicitly; that these matters are importantly *intrinsic,* rather than being largely relational and extrinsic matters. And, of course, there are other such feelings that we have. Let us forgo the details of the applications.

If we apply this reasoning to these intuitions, we become freer to adopt a view of ourselves that would at first appear somewhat radical and counterintuitive. We can, for example, adopt a version of the so-called Complex Theory importantly similar to that developed, and being further developed, by Derek Parfit.[23] On such a view, the importance of self-identity is derivative rather than fundamental. Thus there will be cases where (almost) everything that is important (for us) to our survival is present to a high degree, but where we do not literally survive. The rational attitude toward these cases will be that they are as good (for us) or nearly as good as are related cases where we do survive, not that they are as bad (for us) as are typical cases of human death. At bottom, most of what blocks us from taking this attitude is, I believe, our allegiance to the subjective view of the self. Perhaps by convincing ourselves of this, and by discounting the deliverances of this false, implicitly held view of the self, we will be more able to see that attitude as being the rational one and to adopt it on at least one level of our thinking.

As we become progressively more open to extending our objective self-view, we may even take seriously the idea that we are not utterly concrete entities. Part of why we usually think ourselves to be so utterly concrete is that this is part of our implicitly held subjective self-view. However, that is only part of the story. For as we ordinarily hold it, this is part of our objective self-view as well. So more needs to be said.

The idea that we are utterly concrete is, as I see it, *essential* to the subjective view. On that view, each of us is both a concrete entity and also a *metaphysically basic* entity. There is no way for the view to accommodate any degree of abstractness for us, or for beings like ourselves. Any move in that direction requires abandoning the view absolutely. Now, although this idea that we are so concrete is also part of our shared objective view, it is not an essential part of this quite different approach. For on the objective view, we *need not* be metaphysically basic entities, but can be complexes of metaphysically more basic, simpler entities. Because we can be complex, on this view, the view can be extended or modified so that we might be somewhat abstract. The metaphysically more basic constituents of ourselves may be more concrete, or more nearly absolutely concrete, than we are. As regards the notion of concreteness, then, there is an important difference between our two implicitly held self-views, along with the noted point of similarity.[24]

Parfit offers an analogy between people and nations. He recognizes that there are limits to this analogy, and I think the limits are quite considerable. Nonetheless the analogy may have some validity, and I think we may more readily accept it as such by recognizing, and by discounting, the force of our subjective view. Just as nations are complex in such a way as to be somewhat abstract, so people may be complex in another way but also in a way as to be somewhat abstract. Now, we might be a good deal less abstract than nations, and I believe that we are; but we may be somewhat abstract, somewhat less than utterly concrete, all the same.

To avoid misunderstanding, let me interject that, in my judgment, there are central matters concerning both the nature of personal identity and also the importance of the underlying relations and continuities involved therein where Parfit's views are wrong.[25] But as we may separate his views on those matters from the points now being discussed, we need not treat them now. My own point here is simply that we might reasonably adopt a good deal of Parfit's approach to questions of the self even while rejecting, or at least doubting, various substantial aspects of his position. One idea to be adopted, I suggest, is the thought that each of us is somewhat abstract, not utterly and absolutely concrete.

Thinking in terms of degrees of abstractness, and of degrees of (closeness to complete) concreteness, is somewhat unnatural and even uncomfortable for us to do. Thinking in this way in regards to the existence and identity of conscious beings, including our own case, is extremely difficult for us. But especially in light of our work on the subjective view, this should not be impossible.

How far should we go in this direction? I do not know. In unpublished recent work, Arnold Zuboff has developed, and is further developing, a view of consciousness on which the self is something like an Aristotelian universal.[26] On this view, there is *only one self,* one subject of consciousness, in the entire universe. The one self is *realized completely* in *any* objective (and at least moderately) concrete entity or process that appropriately promotes conscious experience, or is appropriately associated with such experience, or whatever. No concrete thing, then, exclusively realizes the single self, which (somewhat) abstract entity is adequately realized, in fact, many times over.

That is, of course, only the crudest outline of Zuboff's view. But it suffices to show that his view is an objective self-view, one that has little or nothing in common either with our subjective view of the self or even with our ordinary objective self-view. Rather, Zuboff's view is an enormously radical extension of that ordinary objective position.

I suggest that this extension, though very possibly the most original and interesting endeavor in all of contemporary philosophy of mind, goes much too far in the way of extension. At least I cannot believe that this extended view is true, or even that there is very much truth in it. Nonetheless, it must be highly instructive to watch the development of Zuboff's approach if only better to appreciate those less ambitious extensions of our objective view that seem more acceptable. But why am I, as indeed I am, so disinclined to accept such a view as Zuboff's? Although I don't (yet) see how it could be so, perhaps this propensity itself is promoted, not exclusively but far too much, by my implicit adherence to our shared, but false, subjective view of the self.[27]

Notes

1. This psychological approach is presented in my papers "Toward A Psychology of Common Sense," *American Philosophical Quarterly* 19 (1982) and "The Causal Theory of Reference," *Philosophical Studies* 43 (1983) and in my book, *Philosophical Relativity* (Minneapolis, Minn., 1984). I am aware that the approach is not only informal but quite programmatic and incomplete, as its application in the present work will show.

2. My use of these terms was suggested mainly by Thomas Nagel's paper "Subjective and Objective," in his *Mortal Questions* (Cambridge, 1979). Despite certain affinities between them, there are significant differences between our uses: briefly and roughly, Nagel's employment is more epistemological than mine; mine is a more metaphysical usage.

3. See his seminal early paper "Personal Identity," *Philosophical Review* 80 (1971) and his recent book *Reasons and Persons* (Oxford, 1984).

4. I have substantial disagreements with Parfit as well as substantial areas of agreement. In the present work, I want to emphasize the latter and neglect the former, hoping to do the reverse in a future study of these issues.

5. In *Reasons and Persons,* Parfit presents a less extreme sort of case of this sorites variety. Individual cells (or other small organic parts of me) are replaced by cells that are duplicates of, say, Einstein's at age forty. Parfit implicitly assumes that the procedure is done on a wholly unconscious patient. Unsurprisingly, he responds that I would not survive this process, a strong and unrivaled response for almost anyone. If the patient were kept conscious throughout, however, the response pattern is more messy. This fits well with our response pattern to the cases discussed in the text, and it can be explained by the sorts of considerations to be presented in section 10.

6. See note 2.

7. There are, I think, significant points of contact between my discussion here and the "descriptive metaphysics" discussed by Peter Strawson in part I of his *Individuals* (London, 1959).

8. Perhaps there are some that would. Perhaps the best example is Geoffrey Madell in his fine recent book, *The Identity of the Self* (Edinburgh, 1981). Some might class here such philosophers as Roderick Chisholm, as in his *Person and Object* (Lasalle, Ill., 1976) and Richard Swinburne, as in his "Personal Identity," *Proceedings of the Aristotelian Society* 74 (1974). But Chisholm and Swinburne do not, I think, have us holding no objective view at all, just none of a type now philosophically most fashionable. Indeed, I think that Madell's denial of an objective view for us, though a genuine denial, is based in part on his failure to distinguish adequately among subjective views, objective views, and *hybrid* views of the self. I will discuss Madell further in section 12.

9. This would include both those many philosophers who hold a so-called complex view and those, apparently fewer in number, who hold the so-called simple view of the self. Among the former are H. P. Grice, "Personal Identity," *Mind* 50 (1936); David Lewis; "Survival and Identity," in *The Identities of Persons,* edited by A. Rorty (Berkeley, 1975); Robert Nozick, *Philosophical Explanations* (Cambridge, Mass., 1981); Derek Parfit, *Reasons and Persons* (Oxford, 1984); John Perry, "Can the Self Divide?" *Journal of Philosophy* 69 (1972) and "The Importance of Being Identical," in *The Identities of Persons;* and Sydney Shoemaker, "Persons

and Their Pasts," *American Philosophical Quarterly* 7 (1970). As mentioned in note 8, the latter would include Roderick Chisholm and Richard Swinburne.

10. In *The Identity of the Self,* Madell seems to advocate the latter view (137-38). Even if the correct metaphysics is that an experience is one that *I* have *because* it has the *property of being mine,* which I doubt, it is very unlikely that this is part of a view that we ordinarily employ.

11. In section 13, I indicate what I take to be some insuperable difficulties for the subjective view.

12. In a book-length manuscript that greatly expands on the themes of his "Subjective and Objective," Nagel says some interesting things that might lend support to these remarks. At any rate, I am well aware that my ideas here are merely suggestive, not well substantiated.

13. See Lewis, "Survival and Identity," which is reprinted with a new postscript in his *Philosophical Papers,* vol. 1 (New York, 1983). Such a metaphysics may, for all I know, be correct, though I am inclined to think that it is not correct. But correct or not, it has no very close connection to our psychological responses to examples in the area. In the present work, we need only be concerned with this latter, more directly psychological issue.

14. See my papers "I Do Not Exist," in *Perception and Identity,* edited by G. Macdonald (London, 1979), "Why There Are No People," *Midwest Studies in Philosophy* 4 (1979) and "The Problem of the Many," *Midwest Studies in Philosophy* 5 (1980). Although never very confident of those arguments for radical nihilism, I am less moved by them now than when they were formulated. But I am quite unsure *what* is wrong with those reasonings or what would be a *philosophically* adequate response to them. Many philosophers have made responses to the arguments, perhaps the most prominent being W. V. Quine's "What Price Bivalence?" *Journal of Philosophy* 77 (1981) and reprinted in his *Theories and Things* (Cambridge, Mass., 1981). But I have not found any of these responses, at least none of which I am aware, to be sufficiently illuminating or convincing. Perhaps my change of mind here, or change of attitude, has little to do with rational inquiry. As I say in the text, then, an open-minded approach seems appropriate to me.

15. Descartes presents his position on this matter in his *Reply to the Fifth Set of Objections.* This is conveniently available in the Dover edition of Haldane and Ross's *Philosophical Works of Descartes,* vol. 2 (New York, 1955), 210. For my previous points about Descartes's view, perhaps a sympathetic reading of the *Meditations* alone will suffice. But, in any case, I trust that, as Cartesian scholarship goes, my remarks are not only not very controversial but not even terribly interesting.

16. My understanding of Butler and Reid is based on the short selections from their work found in John Perry's anthology, *Personal Identity* (Berkeley, 1975) and on recent discussions of them by philosophers more concerned with questions of personal identity themselves than with scholarly contribution to the history of philosophy. Accordingly, I claim no great scholarly accuracy in my treatment of these thinkers. But if the view I attribute to them was not theirs and is only my own invention, we should discuss it now anyway.

17. See notes 8 and 10.

18. Moreover, as I understand him, Madell allows that a self can exist in objective space and even occupy significant portions of it, having objective spatial size and shape as well as spatial location. This is a second objective element of his view (perhaps not properly derived from his basic tenets) and one not present, as I understand them, in the views of his noted predecessors.

19. The semantics of 'continuous' leaves the same room for debate and perhaps for indeterminacy as do words I have called *absolute terms,* such as 'straight'. If so, then it will not be the only philosophically conspicuous term where such (apparent) controversy will arise: the terms 'know', 'certain', 'free', 'can', 'cause', and 'explain' are all of this sort. This is the main theme of my *Philosophical Relativity;* questions of continuity and perhaps even of identity, like those of knowledge and freedom, present variations on this pervasive theme.

But suppose that 'continuous' is both contextually sensitive and indicates a salient matter of degree; that is, suppose the worst for the point I am about to make. Then while we might allow continuous existence for entities that, on some absolute scale, only flicker in and out of existence, we would still not allow it for an entity that exists for a few minutes now and next exists some centuries hence, while everything else is as normal as can be. Nor would we allow that it was one and the same entity, personal or otherwise, that exists at those widely separated times. So any issue of a relativity in continuity bypasses Madell's view here, as well as any point I'm making in the text about his view.

20. A prominent recent discussion of McTaggart on time is Michael Dummett's "A Defense of McTaggart's Proof of the Unreality of Time," in *Truth and Other Enigmas* (Cambridge, Mass., 1978).

21. In his interpretation and defense of McTaggart on the self, Madell cites McTaggart's *The Nature of Existence*, vol. 2 (Cambridge, 1927), chap. 36.

22. As George Pitcher has pointed out to me, there is reason to think that Berkeley held that there were only subjective times, no objective time (in my sense), and so that he held a purely subjective view of the self. See Berkeley's *A Treatise Concerning the Principles of Human Knowledge,* part I, section 98. For a discussion of Berkeley on this matter, see Pitcher's *Berkeley* (London, 1977), 206-11.

23. As in his *Reasons and Persons.* As I understand it, professional, rather than intellectual, considerations determined the time of this work's publication, even while its author meant to alter it in several ways. But, as I am also given to understand, the intended and unrealized alterations are relatively minor. If so, then the text we have gives all of the essentials of the view.

24. It would be useful to have at least something like a definition of 'concrete' or 'abstract' or both. But I can't provide anything much good in this connection, and so trust to intuitive understanding and sympathetic readers.

There has been little thought given to *degrees* of concreteness, and not much more to degrees of abstractness. Recently, Laverne Shelton has done some work on the topic, though I don't know how her work might apply to questions of the self and personal identity. This would seem a good area for exploration.

25. For Parfit, any sufficiently reliable cause that continues enough of one's character traits and ostensible memories, and perhaps preserves enough physical similarity, will give us all we (rationally) care about, or pretty nearly all, in the neighborhood of personal identity. So, for example, Parfit would hold that a Startrek-like beamer would indeed be a transportation device, as the story has it, and would not be a machine that kills people and creates (unique) duplicates of them elsewhere. On my view, which I cannot develop here, this is misguided or worse. But this is not a very *distinctive,* or very interesting, aspect of Parfit's view, even if it is a quite substantial aspect. Many philosophers who are otherwise much more conventional than Parfit, or much less radical than he, *agree* with him on this point, somewhat to my stupefaction. For a conspicuous example of such more orthodox work, see Robert Nozick's *Philosophical Explanations* (Cambridge, Mass., 1981), chap. 1, part I, especially 37-43.

26. Zuboff has kindly sent me some fifteen cassette tapes of lectures he gave at University College, London, in 1983-84 on the individuation of consciousness and related matters. It is a great hope of mine that this material, or a suitable descendant of it, find its way into print. But I do not know how to bring this to pass, or even how to much increase its probability. If any reader has a suggestion about this, please contact me.

27. Thomas Nagel had an enormous influence on this paper with insightful criticisms, suggestions for development, and general encouragement. I am extremely grateful to him. Mark Johnston was of great help to me at many points, for which I am very thankful. Among the others who gave me good advice, I should mention, with thanks, Gerald Cohen, David Lewis, and John Richardson.

Introspection and the Self

SYDNEY SHOEMAKER

Few passages in philosophy are better known than David Hume's denial that there is introspective awareness of a self or mental subject: "For my part, when I enter most intimately into what I call *myself,* I always stumble on some particular perception or other, of heat or cold, light or shade, love or hatred, pain or pleasure. I never can catch myself at any time without a perception, and never can observe anything but the perception."[1] Hume's denial has been repeated by philosophers as different as Kant and Wittgenstein and has commanded the assent of the majority of subsequent philosophers who have addressed the issue. And it has been widely seen as having important implications concerning the nature of the self and the nature of self-knowledge and self-reference. Some have followed Hume in concluding that a self is "no more than a bundle or collection of different perceptions," or, in more recent versions of the view, that it is a "logical construction" out of experiences and other mental particulars. Some have taken the Humean denial to support the Lichtenbergian view, which has had the endorsement of Wittgenstein and more recently of Elizabeth Anscombe, that the word "I" does not refer. And many have taken it to undermine Cartesian dualism. A recent expression of this last assessment is Saul Kripke's observation in *Naming and Necessity* that "Descartes' notion seems to me to have been rendered dubious ever since Hume's critique of a Cartesian self."[2] In a more recent work, Kripke has argued that the Humean denial is one of the things that underlies Wittgenstein's rejection of the idea that we imagine the sensations of others on the model of our own.[3]

But despite the intuitive appeal of Hume's denial, it is far from clear what its basis is, what exactly it means, or what its philosophical implications are. On the face of it, the basis is empirical; Hume looks within for a self and finds only particular perceptions. But Hume's denial that he is aware of a self can hardly have the same basis as my present well-founded denial that I see a teakettle. The latter denial is well founded only on the assumption that I have some idea of what it would be like to see a teakettle. Hume, on the other hand, is quite emphatic on the point that he has no idea of "self" (*qua* subject of experiences) and so, presumably, no idea of what it would be like to introspect one. And while many who find Hume's denial credible would not agree with his claim that we have no idea of "self," I think that most of them would admit no more than he would to a conception of what it would be like to confront a self as an object of introspection. First appearances notwithstanding, the basis of the Humean denial can hardly be empirical.

If the basis of the Humean denial is less than clear, so also is its meaning. Sometimes it is put by saying that we are not "acquainted" with a self or that we are not, in introspection, presented with a self "as an object." But what is it to be acquainted with something in the required sense? Adapting the answer to this once suggested by Paul Grice, we might say that "I am acquainted with X," where X is a particular, means "(a) I have direct (noninferential) knowledge of some facts about X, and (b) X is not a logical construction."[4] I think this captures one meaning that might reasonably be given to talk about acquaintance with, or awareness of, objects. But it can hardly be the meaning it commonly has in the Humean denial that there is introspective acquaintance or awareness of the self. On Grice's construal of the denial that there is acquaintance with the self, this denial presupposes that the self is a logical construction, i.e., that something like the Humean bundle theory is true—it presupposes this on the reasonable assumption (which those who make this denial are committed to) that we do have some direct knowledge of facts about ourselves. And in that case, as Grice points out, the denial cannot be offered as *grounds* for the view that the self is a logical construction. But one of the reasons why the Humean denial has been philosophically interesting and disturbing is that it has seemed to provide prima facie grounds for that view. Moreover, many philosophers who have accepted Hume's denial, or at any rate found it plausible, have believed both that persons do have direct knowledge of facts about themselves and that persons (selves) are *not* logical constructions. And unless these philosophers have been very confused indeed, they cannot have meant by Hume's denial what it means on Grice's construal—for on that construal they are committed to its rejection.

A natural suggestion is that what Hume and others have meant to deny is that we have in introspection anything like a *perceptual* awareness of a self; that we perceive a self by an "inner sense." Perception is in the first instance a relation to *non*factual objects; we perceive facts by perceiving objects that they are facts about—e.g., we perceive that the branch is bent by perceiving the branch.[5] The Humean denial, on this suggestion, is that in having introspective knowledge one stands in a perceptual or quasi-perceptual relation to a self. This seems to me right, but it raises the question of what it is to stand in a perceptual relation to something; or, more to the point, it raises the question of how those who have accepted Hume's denial, or taken it seriously, have conceived the perceptual relationship. It is initially tempting to give some such account as the following of what it is to perceive a thing: S perceives O just in case S stands to O in a relation R such that, for any x and y, x's standing in R to y is apt for the production in x of (direct) knowledge of y. Examples of the relation R would be the relation a person stands in to a tree when she is conscious, in good light, and has well-functioning eyes that are open and directed towards a tree, and the relation a person has to a cat when he is stroking it. But no one who accepts the Humean denial, or thinks that it is even possibly true, can accept this definition. For on this definition it is beyond dispute that in introspection we *do* perceive a self; here R can be the relation x has to y just in case x is a conscious subject and identical to y. So this definition of perception shares with the Gricean definition of acquaintance (which it resembles) the defect that it does not permit the Humean denial to get off the ground. On the other hand, we do not want to trivialize the Humean denial by giving an account of what it is to perceive that is tailored to fit the five senses and nothing else. Obvious though it may seem, the Humean denial is a striking and (on first hearing) startling claim, and it is certainly not the truism that introspective awareness is not by means of sight, touch, hearing, smell, or taste. The Humean denial requires a conception of perception somewhere in between the narrow conception that would trivialize it and the broad conception that would trivialize its rejection.

A philosopher who seems to accept something like the broad conception of perception just considered is David Armstrong; and Armstrong is a staunch supporter of the view that introspection is "inner sense," i.e., is to be conceived on the model of perception. He writes: "Eccentric cases apart, perception, considered as a mental event, is the acquiring of information or misinformation about our environment. It is not an 'acquaintance' with objects, or a 'searchlight' that makes contact with them, but is simply the getting of beliefs. Exactly the same must be said of introspection. It is the getting of information or misinformation about the current state of our mind.[6] Given this view, one might expect that Armstrong would hold that in introspection one perceives a self (or mind, or mental subject). But Armstrong apparently thinks of himself as accepting the Humean denial. He says that:

> we must . . . grant Hume that the existence of the mind is not something that is given to unaided introspection. All that 'inner sense' reveals is the occurrence of individual mental happenings. . . . I suggest that the solution is that the notion of 'a mind' is a *theoretical* concept:

something that is *postulated* to link together all the individual happenings of which introspection makes us aware. In speaking of minds, perhaps even in using the word 'I' in the course of introspective reports, we go beyond what is introspectively observed. Ordinary language here embodies a certain theory.[7]

Here it looks as though Armstrong is endorsing the view, to be considered later, that accepts a perceptual model of introspection but denies that the self is among the objects perceived by this "inner sense." Of course, what Armstrong explicitly denies here is not that the self is perceived but that its existence is "given to unaided introspection." Perhaps he could hold that one perceives what is in fact a self, but that the fact that it is a self—indeed that there are such things as selves—is not something "given" but rather something one comes to believe as the result of accepting a theory (rather as one might see what is in fact a supernova and only later, after learning some astronomy, realize that there are such things). But if he did mean to deny that one perceives a self, this denial is at least in prima facie conflict with his apparent acceptance of the broad conception of perception.

It might seem that the task of interpreting and evaluating the Humean denial is essentially that of giving a satisfactory account of perception—one that enables us to see whether perception, or something strongly analogous to it, is involved in our introspective awareness of our mental states. But I think that what matters here is not so much what the true nature of perception is (supposing indeed that there is something common to all of those things that are counted as modes of perception) as what is involved in the conception of it that underlies the thinking of those philosophers who have accepted, or been tempted or disturbed by, the Humean denial. It seems a good bet that there is a noncontrived conception that makes the Humean denial true; and it seems likely that we can learn something of importance about the nature of self-knowledge (and not just about philosophers' conceptions of it) by trying to see what this conception is.

I now want to begin considering the sources of the Humean denial. I will start with a consideration that I think must have been operating in the case of Hume himself and that I feel sure has been an influence on others as well. I should perhaps insert a warning here that this paper is not primarily an exercise in Humean exegesis; any sources of the Humean denial that are *peculiarly* Humean, and cannot plausibly be supposed to be at work in the thinking of many of the philosophers who have seconded Hume's denial, are of no interest to me here.

Earlier in the *Treatise,* Hume wrote: "To hate, to love, to think, to feel, to see; all this is nothing but to perceive."[8] In this passage there is no hint that Hume thinks that there is no subject that does the perceiving. And what is suggested by this passage, and consonant with much else that Hume says, is that all mental states are relational—that having a mental state always consists in having a certain relation, namely perceiving, to a perception (impression or idea) of one sort or another. This cannot have been Hume's official position in the end, given his denial that there is anything that could be the subject of such relational states. But I think that we can say that Hume took it for granted that if there were a mental subject, a self which is something over and above particular perceptions, its mental properties would all have to be relational properties of this sort. Given that mental states are the only states of which one can be introspectively aware, and given that on this conception all mental states of selves would be relational rather than intrinsic, it would follow that a self could not have any intrinsic states at all that could be accessible to introspective awareness. But surely it makes no sense to speak of being aware of something, by a certain kind of perception, if the thing has no intrinsic properties whatever that it could be perceived as having by that kind of perception. I suggest, then, that Hume had a conception of what a mental subject would have to be—namely, something whose mental states are all relational—which implies that such a thing could not be introspectively perceived.[9]

No doubt it is also the case that Hume was enough of a dualist to take it for granted that a *mental* subject could have no intrinsic properties that are not mental—e.g., that what we would ordinarily think of as the bodily properties of a person could not count as intrinsic properties of a self. From this, and the conception just mentioned, it would follow not only that mental subjects lack introspectable intrinsic properties but that they lack intrinsic properties altogether. And from this it is natural to conclude that no such thing could exist. On the other hand, someone who thinks that selves have some intrinsic physical properties, but agrees with the idea that all mental states are relational, could hold that a self could be perceived in virtue of its physical properties, and even that it could be so perceived by itself—as when one sees oneself in a mirror, or in foreshortened view. But it would still be ruled out that the self could be an object of *introspective* perception.

An important ingredient in this line of thought is what is sometimes called the "act-object conception" of sensations and other mental states. Feeling pain, for example, is taken to consist in standing in a certain relation to a mental particular of a certain sort, namely a pain; and visualizing a tree is taken to consist in standing in a certain relation to a mental particular of another sort, namely an image of a tree. And if we ask what the relation is, the answer is "perceiving," "apprehending," "being acquainted with," or the like. As I have already indicated, it cannot be said that Hume's official position incorporates the act-object conception, if the act is taken to require an actor, a mental subject. But I think it is fair to say that this conception is what he starts from. Humean perceptions are precisely the sorts of entities the act-object conception calls for on the object side.

The act-object conception of mental states goes naturally with, and may be said to incorporate, what I have called the perceptual model of introspection—the idea that our access to our own minds is to be conceived on the model of sense-perception, differing from other sorts of perception only in being, in Kantian terminology, "inner sense" rather than "outer sense." If Humean perceptions are, as I have said, just the sort of entities the act-object conception calls for on the object side, they are also just the sort of entities the perceptual model of introspection calls for, if there are to be mental particulars other than the self to serve as objects of introspective awareness. What we have just seen is that the very conception of mental facts that provides us with a stock of mental particulars to serve as objects of introspective awareness tends to make it appear that the self, or mental subject, cannot itself be an object of introspective awareness. The more widely the act-object conception is applied, the greater is the number of mental states that are construed as relational—and if all are conceived as relational, it will make no more sense to speak of perceiving a self introspectively than it does to speak of seeing or feeling a point in empty space.

The attitude of contemporary philosophers towards the act-object conception seems to me somewhat equivocal. When they face the issue squarely, I think, most of them reject the conception as mistaken. J. J. C. Smart noted some time ago that in order to maintain that experiencing a roundish, yellowy-orange afterimage is identical to a state of the brain he had to reject the idea that having this state is a matter of standing in a certain relation to a roundish, yellowy-orange particular.[10] Although it is possible to be a materialist without accepting Smart's sort of identity theory, it does not appear that any version of materialism can plausibly allow that what is called having a roundish, yellowy-orange afterimage involves being related to something actually roundish and yellow orange. Materialism aside, moreover, the grounds philosophers have given for rejecting the sense-datum theory of perception are precisely gounds for rejecting the act-object conception as applied to sense experiences. I think it is widely accepted that the act-object conception ought also to be rejected in its application to sensations like pain. Yet when we are not addressing this specific issue, most of us tend to slide back into this conception in our thinking about the mental. Nothing is more natural than to speak of pains that we feel and images we see and to think of the feeling and seeing as our perceptual access to mental particulars. I think it is partly because of this that the Humean denial is so striking. If we did not take it for granted that we do perceive *something* by introspection, and that this introspective perception is the source of our introspective knowledge, it would not be so likely to strike us as significant or disturbing that we do not introspectively perceive any self or mental subject.[11]

Suppose that the act-object conception is rejected for all mental states; will there then be any mental particulars suited for being the objects of introspective awareness, conceived as a kind of perception? Well, even if we refuse to allow that there are such things as yellowy-orange afterimages, we will allow that there are such things as experiencings of yellowy-orange afterimages or (in another idiom) states of being appeared yellowy orange to; and surely these will be mental particulars of a sort. But an experiencing is something whose existence is "adjectival on" a subject of experience. The ontological status of an experiencing, or an episode of being appeared to, is similar to that of a bending of a branch or a rising of the sun. One perceives a rising of the sun by observing the sun rising; here the primary nonfactual object of perception is the sun. Likewise, one perceives a bending of a branch by observing a branch bending; and here the primary nonfactual object of perception is a branch. It hardly makes sense to suppose that there could be a mode of perception that has as its objects bendings of branches and risings of the sun, but never branches or the sun. And it makes equally little sense to suppose that there might be a mode of perception that had as its objects experiencings but never experiencers—never subjects of experience. Experiencings and the like seem as ill-suited as sun-risings and branch-bendings for being the primary nonfactual objects of a mode of perception.[12] I am of course taking it as an obvious conceptual truth that an experiencing is necessarily an experiencing by a subject of experience, and involves that subject as intimately as a branch-bending involves a branch.

Where does this leave us? Since the time of Hume, it has been widely held that we do have introspective perception of many sorts of mental particulars, but never of a self or mental subject. But what I have just inferred from the rejection of the act-object conception is that if we have introspective perception of anything, we have it of the self, and that only the self could be the primary nonfactual object of introspective perception, if such a mode of perception exists. Earlier I sketched a line of argument against the possibility of introspective perception of the self that was grounded on the act-object conception, and so on the view that there is a multitude of possible nonfactual objects for introspective perception. This was the argument that if the act-object conception is applied universally, all mental states will be relational and the self will lack the sorts of intrinsic properties it would have to have to be an object of introspective perception. Let us now see what reasons there might be for rejecting introspective perception of the self if we assume that the act-object conception is mistaken, or at least is not to be applied universally. Notice that if what I have said is right, such reasons would be, if combined with the reasons for rejecting the act-object conception, grounds for holding that there is no such thing as introspective perception at all—that is, they would be grounds for rejecting altogether the perceptual model of introspective self-knowledge.

Ordinary modes of perception admit of our perceiving, successively or simultaneously, a multiplicity of different objects, all of which are on a par as nonfactual objects of perception. There is such a thing as singling out one from a multiplicity of perceived objects, distinguishing it from the others (which may be of the same kind as it) by its perceived properties and its position in a space of perceived objects. Perceived objects are candidates for several sorts of perceptually based identification. One can identify one of them, or misidentify it, as being of this or that sort—call this sortal identification. And one can identify one of them, or misidentify it, as being a certain particular thing—call this particular identification. Where the perceived object is a continuant, it will also be a candidate for what Strawson has called "reidentification," the identification of something observed at one time with something perceived at another time. This will be on the basis of resemblances and other relationships between the observed properties manifested at different times; and, in the most favorable case, where there has been continuous observation of a thing over a period of time, it will be grounded on a sort of perceptual "tracking" that presents the observer with an observed continuity of properties of a kind that constitutes the most direct evidence of identity, for things of that sort, that perception can provide.

Now none of this seems to apply in the case of one's introspective awareness of oneself. If this is a mode of perception, then either there is for each person exactly one (nonadjectival) object, namely himself, that is perceived by that person in this way (this will be so if the act-object conception is mistaken across the board and selves are the only basic objects of introspective perception); or, at least, there is exactly one self that the person can perceive in this way. In the latter case there can be no such thing as picking out a self and distinguishing it from other selves by its introspectively perceived properties; and in the former case there can be no such thing as picking out a self and distinguishing it from other perceived things, of any sort whatever, by its perceived properties. It would seem to go with this that there could be no question of one's having to identify this self as oneself by its perceived properties, or of one's having to identify selves perceived at different times as one and the same. Moreover, it seems that if such identification were possible, it ought to be possible for one to misidentify an introspected self as oneself, or to misidentify a presently introspected self as the same as one introspected previously. But in fact no such possibility of misidentification seems to exist. Similarly, if sortal identification of an introspected self were possible, it seems as if sortal misidentification ought to be possible, analogous to the case in which I misidentify a mole as a mouse. And again it seems that in fact no such possibility of misidentification exists— there is no such thing as introspective misidentification of nonselves with selves.[13]

Faced with these claims, the proponent of the perceptual model of introspection must either deny that these differences really exist or deny that they matter. If he takes the latter line, he can be expected to say that it was clear from the start that there are some differences between introspective awareness and standard sorts of perception. No one supposes, for example, that there is an *organ* of introspection—yet most philosophers have not regarded that as an insuperable obstacle to conceiving introspection on the model of sense perception. What we now find, he might say, is that there is a further difference, which we might sum up by saying that introspective perception does not play the role of providing us with "identification information" about the perceived objects, namely ourselves. But unless we can show that this role is essential to perception, this leaves his view untouched.

Rather than attempting immediately to meet this response head on, I want to go on to a different point that eventually I will link up with the point that the self is not presented in introspection as a candidate for identification and that introspection does not play the role of providing identification information. I hope that this point will help to make plausible the claim that this role is essential to perception (on at least one central conception of it).

Presumably it will be pointless, at best, to suppose that there is introspective perception of a self unless this perception plays some role in explaining our introspective self-knowledge—our knowledge of our own mental states. The most straightforward account would be this: I know that I have thus and such a mental state—that I am angry, in pain, or desirous of a drink—because I introspectively observe myself having it.[14] Obviously, however, the introspective observation of a self being angry is not going to yield the knowledge that *I* am angry unless I know that that self is myself. How am I supposed to know this? If the answer is that I identify it as myself by its perceived properties, we have to point out that this requires that I already know that I have those properties. Indeed, it requires that I know that I am the unique possessor of that set of properties, because otherwise the observation that the perceived self has them would not suffice to identify it as me. So I would already have to have some self-knowledge, namely the knowledge that I have certain identifying properties, in order to acquire any self-knowledge by self-observation. If it is supposed that this self-knowledge is in turn acquired by self-observation, then still other self-knowledge is required: namely, the knowledge that one has whatever identifying properties one used to identify as oneself the self that one observed to have the first set of identifying properties. And so on. On pain of infinite regress, it must be allowed that somewhere along the line I have some self-knowledge that is not gotten by observing something to be true of myself.

It may be objected that I am overlooking the point that only one self could be the object of my introspective perception; there is no need to identify the observed self as myself by its perceived properties, since, given that I perceive it introspectively, there is no other self it could be. But this amounts to saying that I can infallibly identify the observed self as myself by the fact that it is introspectively observed by me. That requires that I know that I introspectively observe it. And that is a piece of self-knowledge I could not get by introspective observation; for unless I already know that this self is myself, observing that it perceives itself is not going to tell me that I observe it. So it remains true that if I am to get self-knowledge by introspective perception I must have some that I have not gotten by introspective perception. But if to explain our introspective self-knowledge we have to posit some self-knowledge that is not observational, in the sense that it is not gotten by perceiving what one knows to be oneself and observing something to be true of it, why shouldn't we suppose that all of our introspective self-knowledge is of this nonobservational character? At best, the hypothesis that there is introspective self-perception seems to explain nothing that cannot be equally well explained without it.[15]

I think that the only way around this for a proponent of introspective self-perception is to hold that "I" is synonymous with "this self," where "this" functions as a logically proper name in Russell's sense.[16] Obviously, "this" could not be here the ordinary demonstrative pronoun, for the latter can be used to refer to selves (persons) other than the speaker. But if we think of it as a special sort of demonstrative pronoun that can be used to refer only to objects of introspective perception, then the proposal finesses the problem of how one is to identify an observed self as oneself. We were, in effect, imagining our introspective perceiver asking himself "Is this self me?" and attempting to answer this on the basis of facts he observes about it together with facts he knows about himself. But on the present proposal, the question "Is this self me?" is equivalent to "Is this self this self?"—which answers itself.

Bizarre and farfetched though this suggestion may seem, there is a certain appropriateness about it, given the view that we have introspective perception of a self and that this is the source of our self-knowledge. Perception and demonstrative reference are intimately related; to perceive something is, among other things, to be in a position to refer to that thing demonstratively, and it is a necessary condition of the primary sort of demonstrative reference that the speaker perceive (or remember recently perceiving) the object referred to. It is quite natural that a view that construes self-knowledge as based on self-perception should attempt to assimilate self-reference to demonstrative reference.

But can such an assimilation be correct? If we focus only on present tense judgments, the assimilation of first-person judgments to demonstrative judgments may seem promising. It is characteristic of both sorts of judgments that they are "identification free" and "immune to error through misidentification."[17] It is not the case that I say "I am angry" because I find that someone is angry and identify that person as myself; and normally it is not the case that I say "This is red" because I find that something is red and identify that thing as "this." But when we turn to the past-tense versions of these judgments, the situation seems different. Briefly, and omitting necessary qualifications, the immunity to error through misidentification of first-person judgments is preserved in memory, whereas that of demonstrative judgments is not. If I say, pointing, "This *was* red then," meaning to express the knowledge I previously expressed with "This is red," then my judgment involves an identification that could be mistaken; it could be that the thing I see now is not the thing I remember seeing earlier. By contrast, and still omitting the qualifications, if I say "I was angry then," meaning to express the knowledge I previously expressed by saying "I am angry," then a mistake of identification is impossible. It goes with this that the past-tense demonstrative judgment rests on an observationally based reidentification of the thing referred to with "this," whereas the past-tense, first-person judgment does not rest on an observationally based reidentification of the person referred to with "I." "This was red" might be grounded in part on an observed similarity between the thing one sees now and the thing one remembers seeing to be red in the past, or it might be grounded in part on a series of phenomena one observed in perceptually tracking an object over time. "I was angry," if said on the basis of memory in the ordinary way, could not be grounded either on an introspectively observed resemblance between a past self and a present self, or on an introspective tracking of a self over time. This is the point, familiar from discussions of personal identity, that first-person memory judgments are not grounded on criteria of personal identity.[18]

The qualification I have mentioned has to do with the possibility, which I have discussed elsewhere, that one might "quasi-remember" past experiences or actions that are not one's own.[19] For example, this could happen if it were possible for someone to undergo "fission" and split into two people, both of whom remember (or quasi-remember) "from the inside" the actions and experiences of the original person. To allow that this is possible is to allow that in a certain sense first-person memory judgments are subject to error through misidentification. But this does not really affect the point I am making. It remains true that first-person memory judgments do not involve identifications of oneself that are grounded on observed similarities between selves observed at different times, or on a perceptual tracking of a self over time. Assuming that quasi-remembering of the experiences and actions of persons other than oneself is a logical possibility, what entitles us to think that it has not occurred in our own case is not that the contents of our memories provide us with direct evidence that one and the same person was involved in the various actions and experiences we remember "from the inside" (for in general they provide us with no such evidence), but rather the fact that our general knowledge of the world supports a presumption that "fission" and the like do not in fact occur. Given the truth of this presumption, my awareness that I remember (or quasi-remember) from the inside a past action is decisive evidence that I did that action—but it is not the sort of evidence that grounds observationally based identifications.

There is an additional reason for declining to assimilate self-reference to demonstrative reference, and this is that such an assimilation makes inexplicable one of the constitutive features of self-reference. As recent writers have noted, one of the distinctive features of first-person belief is the role it plays in the explanation of behavior. Having a genuine first-person belief, of the sort one expresses by saying "I," is not merely a matter of believing something of what is in fact oneself. To use David Kaplan's example, if I merely believe of the person I in fact am that his pants are on fire (I see someone in a mirror with his pants on fire, but do not realize that it is me), this will not influence my behavior in the way that the belief I would express by saying "My pants are on fire!" would.[20] It seems reasonable to hold that part of what makes a belief a belief about the person who has it (in the way beliefs expressed by first-person sentences are about the speaker) is the fact that it plays this distinctive role in the determination of action. It is a consequence of this, I believe, that the reference of "I" in the idiolect of a particular speaker is determined very differently than is the reference of other expressions, including demonstratives. Roughly, whereas the reference of other expressions is determined by facts about the causal etiology of their use, the reference of "I," when used as first-person pronoun, is determined by the causal role of the beliefs it is used to express. To suppose that "I" is just a special sort of demonstrative pronoun, one used to refer to introspectively perceived selves, and that its reference is determined in the way that of demonstratives in general is determined, leaves totally unexplained the role of "I"-beliefs in the determination of behavior. Why should the belief that *this self's* pants are on fire, together with the desire not to be burnt, gird me into fire-dousing behavior? It will, of course, if I know that this self is myself; but given what turns on it, knowing that cannot be just a matter of knowing that this self is this self. The way in which a belief is about oneself is utterly different from the way in which a belief is about a perceived object *qua* observed object.

We have seen, I think, that introspective knowledge of ourselves cannot legitimately be assimilated to either of two paradigms of perceptual knowledge of an object—that in which the knowledge involves an observationally based identification of the object, and that in which the object is designated demonstratively. This seems to me to provide a strong reason for denying that introspective awareness should be conceived on the model of sense perception. But this plainly links up with my earlier point that in introspection we are not presented, and do not need to be presented, with "identification information" about ourselves: the sort of information we would need to have to identify a self as oneself, to reidentify a self, or to "track" a self perceptually over an interval of time. For the assimilation to either of these paradigms would require that introspection be a source of identification information in a way that in fact it is not.

It is worth asking, in connection with this, why it has been so commonly assumed that if we were aware of a self in introspection, the self would have to be something nonbodily. It is of course assumed to be obvious that in fact we are not presented with ourselves in introspection *as* bodily entities. But why is it assumed that if the self were something bodily, and were perceived introspectively, it would have to be perceived *as* something bodily? What underlies this assumption, I suspect, is the idea that a way of perceiving a thing of a certain sort must be a source of identifying information about things of that sort, and so must reveal the sorts of properties by which things of that sort are individuated. Bodily entities are individuated in part by their bodily properties and by their spatial relations to other things, and for this reason perception of them ought to provide information about such properties and relationships. Given that introspection does not provide such information, either it is not perception at all or it is perception of something nonbodily. Wittgenstein says in the *Blue Book:* "We feel . . . that in cases in which 'I' is used as subject, we don't use it because we recognize a person by his bodily characteristics; and this creates the illusion that we use this word to refer to something bodiless, which, however, has its seat in our body. In fact, *this* seems to be the real ego, the one of which it was said 'Cogito, ergo sum'."[21] The tacit assumption underlying this diagnosis of the attractions of dualism is that we assume that we must be provided in introspective perception with identifying facts about ourselves; and therefore that since we are not presented with identifying facts of the sort appropriate to bodily entities, we are not bodily entities. I have argued that we are not presented with identifying facts of any sort and therefore that the proper conclusion is that introspection is not a mode of perception (a conclusion with which Wittgenstein would have agreed). Here it is worth quoting Kant's observation that "in what we entitle 'soul' everything is in continual flux and there is nothing abiding except (if we must so express ourselves) the 'I,' which is simple solely because its representation has no content, and therefore no manifold [of intuitions], and for this reason seems to represent, or (to use a more correct word) denote, a simple object."[22] Patricia Kitcher glosses this by saying, "The Rational Psychologists go astray because they expect to find intuition of the self and so mistake the absence of any intuition for the intuition of something with remarkable properties."[23] I suggest that the lack of content, or of a manifold of intuition, is basically the lack of introspectively provided identification information; and that this is a large part of what lies behind the denial that there is introspective perception of a self.

I now want to give what seems on the face of it to be a very different objection to the idea that there is introspective perception of a self. This will be, in fact, an objection to the idea that there is introspective perception of anything whatever. But I think this objection turns out to be closely related to the objection just given, that which rests on the claim that perception ought to be a source of identification information about the objects of perception and that introspection is not a source of such information about the self.

It is characteristic of sense perception, of all of the familiar kinds, that perceiving something involves its appearing in a certain way to one, a way that may or may not correspond to the actual nature of the thing perceived. An object's appearing a certain way to someone involves that person's being in a subjective state, call it a sense impression, having a certain phenomenal character; and how the object appears will be a function of the phenomenal character of the sense impression. There is (in the phrase made current by Thomas Nagel) "something it is like" to perceive something, and we can equate what this is like on a given occasion with the phenomenal character of the sense impression. Having a sense impression with a certain phenomenal character is not just a matter of having certain beliefs, or certain inclinations to believe, about the properties of the object of perception. For one thing, one sometimes has to learn to interpret the phenomenal character of one's sense impressions; and prior to one's learning this, the phenomenal features of the sense impressions will not be associated with features of the perceived objects.

Now some of the states we are aware of in introspection are themselves sensory states having a phenomenal character. And in the case of these, it is natural to say that there is "something it is like" to be aware of them. But it seems plain that this "something it is like" is just the phenomenal character of the states themselves, and not the phenomenal character of still other states that are sense impressions of them. There is something it is like to be in pain. And because being in pain and feeling pain are one and the same thing, there is something it is like to feel pain. If one holds the act-object conception of sensation, one may be tempted to equate the introspective awareness of the pain with the feeling of the pain: adopting the perceptual model of introspection, one thinks of "feeling" as the mode of perception by which one has introspective awareness of pain. But that has to be a mistake, whether or not one adopts the act-object conception. Feeling pain and being in pain are, to repeat, the same thing; and the introspective knowledge that I am in pain is at the same time the introspective knowledge that I feel pain. And it is certainly not the case that I feel my self feeling pain; there is not a feeling of the feeling that is something over and above the feeling of pain. There is something it is like to be in pain, or to feel pain, but there is nothing additional it is like to be aware of pain, or of feeling pain; and the same goes for other sensory states. And so there is no such thing as a sense impression of a sensory state, having a phenomenal character of its own.

If being aware of being in pain does not involve having something analogous to a sense impression of the pain, it can scarcely involve having a sense impression (or quasi-sense-impression) of the self. If one perceives the self at all in introspection, one perceives it as having various states, like being in pain; so one could not have sense impressions of it without having sense impressions of its various states, which I have just denied that we have. And I think that there is not the slightest plausibility in the idea that in introspection we have quasi-sensory states that relate to the self as our sense impressions of a tree relate to the tree. The self does not appear in any way to itself in introspection. One does, of course, have beliefs about oneself in introspection. And no doubt it is possible for some of these beliefs to be mistaken. But having a mistaken introspective belief cannot be said to constitute the self's appearing to itself other than it is; for as I said earlier, something's appearing (perceptually) a certain way to one is not just a matter of one's believing, or being inclined to believe, certain things about it.

But what is the status of this denial that the self appears in a certain way to itself in introspection? Is it itself a deliverance of introspection. If it were that, or only that, then the use of this denial as a basis for the denial that there is introspective self-perception would not be much of an advance on Hume's claim that when he looks within himself he finds no self over and above his particular perceptions. But I believe that we can find another basis for this denial by reflecting on the function in ordinary sense perception of the phenomenal character of sense impressions. What I suggest is that the informational content of a sense impression is embodied in its phenomenal character and that a crucial part of this informational content consists of what I have been calling identification information. As I walk around the table, its appearance changes without there being any corresponding change in my beliefs about its intrinsic properties. What do change are my beliefs about its spatial relations to myself; and facts about these spatial relations are an important part of the identification information provided me by ordinary sense perception. If there were introspective sense impressions of the self, they could not play any such role in providing us with identification information about the self, given that introspection does not provide such information at all. The only other role they could play is that of providing information about the intrinsic features of the self, such as that it is in pain. But for there to be (quasi) sense impressions that do this would be for there to be sense impressions of such states as pain—and it seems quite obvious that there are no such things. The conclusion seems to be that there is no such thing as an introspective sense impression of the self, just as there is no such thing as a sense impression of a pain or other mental state and (assuming that sense impressions are essential to perception) that there is no such thing as introspective perception of the self, or indeed of anything else.

I expect that what I have just said will meet some resistance. Indeed, it does so even in me. It is natural to object that there is such a thing as picking out one afterimage from others, and also such a thing as introspectively tracking an afterimage over time. If so, our introspective awareness of afterimages does involve the provision of identification information. But it should be remembered that in this part of my discussion I am assuming that the act-object conception of sensation is false. To reject the act-object conception is to hold that although there is such a thing as experiencing-an-afterimage, there is no such thing as an afterimage *qua* colored patch that hovers in front of one when one closes one's eyes after looking at a bright light. Experiencing an afterimage is merely *seeming* to see such a colored patch. And just as the seeing of afterimages is only seeming-as-if-one-were-seeing, the picking out of afterimages is only seeming-as-if-one-were-picking-out and the tracking of afterimages is only seeming-as-if-one-were-tracking. It is indeed true that when one is experiencing an afterimage it is *as if* identification information about perceived objects were being provided; this is part of what constitutes its being as if one were seeing something. But its being as if something is so, from the subject's point of view, is not the same thing as its actually being so.

This is not the place for an attempt to refute the act-object conception. I will only record my conviction that if I am mistaken in thinking that this conception is wrong as applied to experiencing afterimages and the like, then the whole philosophical establishment has been mistaken in its rejection of the sense-datum theory of perception. For there is this much truth in the "argument from illusion": *if* it is right to give an act-object analysis of such phenomena as "seeing afterimages," "seeing double," etc., and thus to posit sense data (images) that are seen in such cases, there is no justification for refusing to give such an analysis of the sensory experiences that occur in normal perception—i.e., there is no justification for refusing to accept the claim that in all perception, "veridical" as well as "illusory," we directly perceive sense data. Those who wish to reject the sense-datum theory, as I think nearly all philosophers nowadays do, will be well advised to deny the antecedent of this conditional rather than denying the conditional itself.

I now return to my main theme. Earlier I sketched a broad conception of perception on which it seemed obviously true that we do have introspective perception of a self and also obviously true that we have introspective perception of individual mental states and events. This raised the question of what we must add to that conception, by way of narrowing it, to get the conception implicit in the thinking of those who have accepted, or at any rate taken seriously, the Humean denial that there is introspective perception of the self. I suggest that what must be added is something like the following: a mode of perception must be such that someone's perceiving something in that way can enter into the explanation of how it is that the person has knowledge of that thing, where part of the explanation is that perceiving the thing provides the person with identification information about it, which it does by producing in the person sense impressions of the thing. This seems to me a plausible way of narrowing the broad conception, and one that justifies the Humean denial without trivializing it.

Let me now return briefly to the view of David Armstrong, according to which what is "given" in introspection is "the occurrence of individual mental happenings" and according to which the mind or self is something postulated to "link together all the individual happenings of which introspection makes us aware," the postulation involving a theory that is embodied in ordinary language.[24] The most natural reading of Armstrong is one according to which we have introspective perception of individual mental happenings but not of a mind or self. This will not be defensible on the conception of perception just sketched, because on that conception we do not have introspective perception even of particular mental happenings (and I suggested earlier that if we reject the act-object conception, which a materialist like Armstrong seems to be committed to doing, then we cannot have introspective perception of mental particulars without having introspective perception of a self, or mental subject, on which they are "adjectival"). Is the view perhaps defensible on the broad conception of perception? I have said that on that conception it is obviously true that we do have introspective perception of the self; but that was on the assumption that in introspection we have "direct" knowledge of facts about ourselves, and Armstrong may be denying this assumption in claiming that the self (he says "mind") is something "postulated" in accordance with a theory. But it is hard to see why Armstrong should think that the notion of the mind is any more theoretical than notions of particular mental happenings like thoughts and pains (especially given his view that the latter have rather complex causal definitions).[25] And if he does think that first-person beliefs are the results of theory-mediated inferences from more primitive beliefs in which the notion of a self or mind does not figure, he owes us an account of how such beliefs might be formulated (obviously they cannot refer to pains, desires, and beliefs *qua* states, since the notion of a state is correlative with the notion of a subject of states) and of how the inference would go (in particular, of how "I" would make its appearance). In any case, such a view is thoroughly implausible on the naturalistic approach to epistemology of which Armstrong himself has been a champion. If we were wired by evolution (or, for that matter, by God) so that our being in various mental states directly produces in us beliefs about them, then the job was hopelessly botched unless the beliefs thus produced are beliefs to the effect that we ourselves are in those states—and only a philosophical picture (probably one involving the act-object conception) could make it plausible to suppose that they are anything else.

It seems to me, then, that whether we interpret "perceive" in the broad sense or in the narrow sense, the view that we have introspective perceptions of individual mental happenings but not of a self is indefensible. If we interpret it in the broad sense, we have introspective perception of both; if we interpret it in the narrow sense, we have introspective perception of neither. In the latter sense, indeed, introspective awareness does not involve perception of anything at all. And I think that this puts the Humean denial in an interesting new light. For it completely undermines the view, which motivates "bundle," "logical construction," and "no subject" theories of the self, that from an empiricist standpoint the status of the self (the subject of experience) is suspect compared with that of such things as sensations, feelings, images, and the like. What of the bearing of the Humean denial on Cartesian dualism? Although I think that there are lots of good reasons for rejecting Cartesian dualism, I do not think that the truth of the Humean denial is one of them. For I see no reason to think that the Cartesian dualist is committed to there being self-perception in the narrow, as opposed to the broad, sense. What does seem to be true, however, is the suggestion, implicit in the passages quoted earlier from Kant and Wittgenstein, that the Humean denial undercuts one argument in favor of Cartesian dualism, namely the argument from the fact that we do not in introspection perceive the self as having bodily properties; for that argument goes through only on the assumption that in introspection we do perceive the self in the narrow sense.[26]

Notes

1. David Hume, *Treatise of Human Nature,* edited by L. A. Selby-Bigge (Oxford, 1888), 252.

2. Saul Kripke, *Naming and Necessity* (Cambridge, Mass., 1980), 155, n. 77.

3. Saul Kripke, "Postscript: Wittgenstein and Other Minds," in *Wittgenstein on Rules and Private Language* (Cambridge, Mass., 1982).

4. H. P. Grice, "Personal Identity," *Mind* 50 (1941): 330-50, reprinted in *Personal Identity,* edited by John Perry (Berkeley, 1975). In Grice's own formulation (on p. 82 in Perry), (a) read simply "I know some facts about *X.*" On most people's intuitions about knowledge, this would force one to choose between saying (1) that I (who have never been to India) am acquainted with the Taj Mahal and (2) that the Taj Mahal is a logical construction. My wording of (a) avoids this.

5. "Nonfactual" is not meant to connote "false" or "erroneous"; by nonfactual objects I simply mean objects, of which tables and chairs are examples, that are not themselves facts or factlike entities.

6. David Armstrong, *A Materialist Theory of the Mind* (London, 1968), 326.

7. Ibid., 337. There are similar remarks in Armstrong's more recent essay, "What is Consciousness?" in *The Nature of Mind and Other Essays* (Ithaca, N.Y., 1981); see especially 64-65.

8. Hume, *Treatise,* 67.

9. If this is right, Hume had some conception of what a self or mental subject would have to be, despite his denial that he had any idea of such a thing.

10. J. J. C. Smart, "Sensations and Brain Processes," *Philosophical Review* 68 (1959): 141-56.

11. As William Alston has pointed out to me, one could not say that on the act-object conception one has introspective perception of mental *states* but not of a mental subject. For a state, on the act-object conception, will be not an object of the sort Hume thinks he finds when

he looks within but rather a relational state of affairs consisting in a subject's being aware of such an object—and this, presumably, will not be perceivable if the subject is not. But if we characterize introspection as awareness of mental particulars of whatever kind, rather than as just awareness of mental states, then it will still be true on such a view that there is something that is an object of introspective perception, even though the self is not such an object.

12. Here sun-risings should be distinguished from sunrises. One can perhaps see a sunrise without seeing the sun—maybe seeing a glow in the east is sufficient. But this is not to see a sun-rising, i.e., is not seeing the sun to rise.

13. See my "Self-Reference and Self-Awareness," *Journal of Philosophy* 65 (1968): 555-67.

14. Bertrand Russell seems to have held such a view at one time; see *The Problems of Philosophy* (London, 1950), 51.

15. This argument was given in my "Self-Reference and Self-Awareness," 563. It might be objected (and has been by William Alston) that the argument proves too much. Won't the same reasoning lead to the false conclusion that all of my knowledge of your house might be nonobservational? It will prove (and it is true, not false) that if I am to identify your house by its observed characteristics, I must have knowledge that is not observational in the sense (call it the narrow sense) that it is gotten by observing your house and observing something to be true of it. Here, of course, I might acquire knowledge of the identifying characteristics by observing other things—e.g., by hearing you describe your house. I would then be relying on knowledge of the past and background knowledge of various sorts (e.g., about the tendency of houses to retain certain sorts of characteristic) my acquisition of which was, in a broad sense, observational. But it is agreed on all sides that reports of immediate experience containing "I" are minimally dependent on background knowledge and knowledge of the past; total amnesia would presumably impair my ability to identify someone's house perceptually but would not impair my ability to make "I" statements. The philosopher who is the target of my argument is someone who thinks that "I" statements are simply "read off" from the contents of immediate experience, and such a philosopher could not allow that anything comparable to what might enable me to know the identifying characteristics of someone's house could explain my ability to identify an introspectively perceived self as my self. Once such a philosopher sees that my knowledge of identifying characteristics of myself could not be observational in the narrow sense, I think that he has no recourse but to allow that it is not observational at all. And then, I think, he has no principled way of justifying the requirement that other introspective self-knowledge be observationally (or perceptually) based.

16. I have the hazy recollection that Russell somewhere makes this suggestion but cannot find any place where he did so. After he abandoned the view that there is acquaintance with a self, Russell did in various places advance the suggestion that "I" means something like "the subject of this," where "this" names some object of immediate experience—but that of course is a different view.

17. For these notions, see Gareth Evans, "The Varieties of Reference" (Oxford, 1982), chap. 6 and 7, and my "Self-Reference and Self-Awareness."

18. See my *Self-Knowledge and Self-Identity* (Ithaca, N.Y., 1963), chap. 4, and P. F. Strawson, *The Bounds of Sense* (London, 1966), 165.

19. See my "Persons and Their Pasts," *American Philosophical Quarterly* 7 (1970): 269-85.

20. The example is cited in David Lewis, "Attitudes De Dicto and De Se," *Philosophical Review* 88 (1979): 513-43, and attributed to Kaplan's unpublished manuscript *Demonstratives.* See also John Perry's papers "Frege on Demonstratives," *Philosophical Review* 86 (1977): 474-97, and "The Problem of the Essential Indexical," *Nous* 13 (1979): 3-21.

21. Ludwig Wittgenstein, *The Blue and Brown Books* (Oxford, 1958), 69.

22. Immanual Kant, *Critique of Pure Reason,* translated by Norman Kemp Smith (London, 1953), 353 [A381-2]. The bracketed addition to Kemp Smith's translation is Patricia Kitcher's (see n. 23).

23. Patricia Kitcher, "Kant's Paralogisms," *Philosophical Review* 91 (1982): 515-48.

24. Armstrong, *Materialist Theory of the Mind,* 337.

25. Indeed, it is arguable that a satisfactory causal, or functional, definition of particular mental states must invoke a relation of "copersonality" and so (implicitly) the notion of a self. See my "Identity, Properties and Causality," *Midwest Studies in Philosophy* 4 (1979): 321-42, and my essay in S. Shoemaker and R. Swinburne, *Personal Identity* (Oxford, 1984).

26. I am grateful to William Alston for perceptive comments on the penultimate draft of this paper.

Unconscious Mind or
Conscious Minds?

EDDY ZEMACH

I

"The concept of there being unconscious mental processes," writes James Strachey, "is of course one that is fundamental to psycho-analytic theory. Freud was never tired of insisting upon the arguments in support of it and combating the objections to it."[1] But, in fact, there is only one serious argument that Freud has employed, in various forms, to defend his theory that some mental processes are unconscious, and this is none other than the old philosophical argument from analogy. Freud claims that in several interesting cases (his choice examples are posthypnotic suggestion and hysterical symptoms), the subject's behavior is of a kind that normally makes us attribute a certain mental state (say, a desire or an intention) to the person as its cause. Now if this move is generally justified—if a piece of behavior of some kind, *bk,* justifies the ascription of a certain mental state, *mk,* to the subject who manifests *bk*—then ascription of *mk* ought to be justified in those cases, too.

> The assumption of an unconscious is, moreover, a perfectly *legitimate* one, inasmuch as in postulating it we are not departing a single step from our customary and generally accepted mode of thinking. Consciousness makes each of us aware only of his own states of mind; that other people, too, possess a consciousness is an inference which we draw by analogy from their observable utterances and actions, in order to make this behavior of theirs intelligible to us. . . . Psycho-analysis demands nothing more than that we should apply this process of inference to ourselves also. (SE 14:169)

121

Behavior, says Freud, can justify an inference to the best explanation as to what causes it; and if that is a mental state, so be it. An introspective confirmation of that ascription is not necessary, or else the psychologist were debarred from ascribing mental states to anyone but himself. Freud could have also pointed out that, in general, an avowal of being in some state cannot be a necessary condition for ascribing that state to a person. The reason is that if we are to say that sincere avowals (as distinct from mere avowal *behavior*) ever occur, we must *assume* the said inference from behavior to mental states; in this case, from avowal behavior to the conclusion that a genuine avowal took place.

I find the argument compelling. But does it show that some mental states are unconscious, i.e., are such that *no* subject is aware of them? Freud himself saw that the answer is negative. The analogy argument does not show that I may ascribe a mental state to someone who is not conscious of it; what it shows is that I may ascribe a mental state to someone when I am not conscious of it. The difference is absolutely crucial. Instead of indicating the existence of unconscious mental states, it indicates, as in the case of other minds, the existence of a subject who is quite conscious of his or her mental states but does not avow them (perhaps, because of being unable to speak). Indeed, Freud honestly admits that his argument indicates a case of dissociation, not unconsciousness:

> This process of inference ... does not, however, lead to the disclosure of an unconscious; it leads logically to the assumption of another, second consciousness which is united in one's self with the consciousness one knows. (SE 14:170)

The conclusion then is not that the same subject is in mental state *mk* and, being unaware of it, sincerely disavows being in that state. Rather, it is that several distinct subjects have some control over the same body (e.g., at different times, or with respect to different functions). The one who consciously experiences *mk* manifests *bk;* the other, who does not experience *mk,* sincerely disavows it.

This theory, the view that the same human person is composed of several *conscious* selves, was well known to Freud and enjoyed a wide influence at the time, especially in France. Freud refers to it as the *multiple consciousness theory* (I shall refer to it as MCT). Myers, in England, writes in 1892 that a single organism may be operated by more than one consciousness. William James, who in *The Principles of Psychology* (1890) vehemently rejects the notion of *unconscious* mental processes, writes in *The Varieties of Religious Experience* (1902) that Myers's work is the greatest discovery ever made in psychology. A couple of years later, Morton Prince writes:[2]

> The synthesis of the original consciousness is broken up, so to speak, and ... certain conscious states, which are rejected in the synthesis of

the new personality, may remain outside the consciousness of the latter, synthesised among themselves, and thus form a second *simultaneously* acting consciousness. This is called a subconsciousness. (P. 3)

or, even more explicitly:

By a subconscious self I mean simply a limited second, coexisting, extra series of 'thoughts', feelings, sensations, etc., which are largely differentiated from those of the normal waking mind of the individual. In abnormal conditions these secondary 'thoughts' may be sufficiently organized to have a perception of personality, in which case they may be regarded as constituting a second self. (P. 18)

But Freud rejects this view, which most of his teachers (e.g., Ribot, Binet, Janet) tended to accept. Instead, he opted for the Leibnizian idea of unconscious mental events that was advocated during the nineteenth century by such writers as Herbart (*Psychologie als Wissenschaft,* 1824), Edward von Hartmann (*Philosophy of the Unconscious,* 1868), Wundt (*Grundzüge der Physiologischen Psychologie,* 1874), E. Closenet (*La vie inconsciente de l'esprit,* 1880), and others. Their model of the mind included, instead of the several semi-independent conscious systems, a bifurcation of the mind into a conscious and an unconscious mental system. It was the latter theory, the unconscious mind theory (I shall refer to it as UMT) that Freud had adhered to and that, through his enormous influence, became so famous that its rival, the MCT, soon became extinct and almost entirely forgotten.

Freud gives four arguments that, supposedly, conclusively show that MCT ought to be abandoned and that, despite the fact that the argument from analogy tends to favor it, we should instead prefer UMT as a model of the human mind. To evaluate the cogency of Freud's reasoning, let us follow him and reproduce his four arguments, assessing them one by one.

II

A. In the first place, a consciousness of which its own possessor knows nothing is something very different from a consciousness belonging to another person, and it is questionable whether such a consciousness, lacking, as it does, its most important characteristic, deserves any discussion at all. Those who have resisted the assumption of an unconscious *psychical* are not likely to be ready to exchange it for an unconscious *consciousness.* (SE 14:170)

The argument is clearly fallacious. It is not true that, on the MCT, a possessor of some mental state is unaware of it. Rather, the conscious possessor of that state is a different subject from the one who denies any knowledge of it. Likewise, the fact that Jones knows nothing of Smith's mental states does not prove that Smith's mental states are unconscious; it only shows that Smith and Jones are distinct subjects.[3] The argument goes like that: (1) Body b manifests behavior bk, which, by our criteria, is sufficient for attributing mental state mk, to a subject x that we associate with b. (2) Body b manifests denial behavior, which, by our criteria, is sufficient for attributing sincere denial of being in state mk to a subject y that we associate with b. (3) On general grounds, we maintain that a mental state is a state of which its subject must be conscious. (4) Thus y who sincerely denies being in mk is not the subject of mk. (5) Therefore, $x \neq y$. (6) Therefore body b has more than one subject associated with it. The alleged contradiction that Freud seemed to find—that the same mental state both is and is not conscious—does not follow.

> B. In the second place, analysis shows that the different latent mental processes inferred by us enjoy a high degree of mutual independence, as though they had no connection with one another, and knew nothing of one another. We must be prepared, if so, to assume the existence in us not only of a second consciousness, but of a third, fourth, perhaps of an unlimited number of states of consciousness, all unknown to us and to one another. (SE14:170)

But why should the number of subjects of experience associated with the same body be limited to two? Freud himself, we may recall, found it necessary later on to increase the number of independent *un*conscious systems from two (Ucs, the Unconscious, and Pcs, the Preconscious) to three (Id, most of Ego, and Superego). In cases of dissociation we often find more than two subjects associated with the same body: such cases were extensively discussed by Freud's French predecessors.[4] Freud was also familiar with many of the numerous multiple-soul theories, from Egypt and Greece to the medieval notion of possession. The feigned ignorance of the very possibility of such models seems suspicious. The last phrase of this argument is again wrong. First, the existence of several subjects "in" a given body may be know to *us*, even when it is not known to any of these subjects. Second, the different subjects need not be ignorant of each other's existence. To take the most famous example, although Eve White knew nothing of Eve Black, the latter was (contemptuously) aware of the former. Freud's own work can be used by MCT against this argument: it may be said that his greatest achievement is alerting the dominant subject to the existence of rich mental life of which it knew nothing before.

Finally, this very question (how many subjects per person?) is quite meaningless when no principle of individuation for subjects is offered. Later on I shall argue that MCT is in no way committed to assign a definite number to the subjects it recognizes per person, because subjects may partially overlap. It is a matter of degree, and therefore of linguistic convenience, whether to speak of *one,* albeit severely disrupted and discontinuous, subject, or else of two (or more) distinct subjects that yet have some parts in common.

C. In the third place—and this is the most weighty argument of all—we have to take into account the fact that analytic investigation reveals some of these latent processes as having characteristics and peculiarities which seem alien to us, or even incredible, and which run directly counter to the attributes of consciousness with which we are familiar. Thus we have grounds for modifying our inference about ourselves and saying that what is proved is not the existence of a second consciousness in us, but the existence of psychical acts which lack consciousness. (SE 14:170)

What Freud must have in mind is that the great differences between logical thinking (secondary processes) and the atemporal, symbolic, condensing, displacing mode of operation attributed by him to processes in the Ucs, make the attribution of the term 'consciousness' to both inappropriate. But the reasoning behind this statement is most obscure. A cat, a dolphin, a frog, or a bee can be conscious although it is certainly not rational and its manner of handling data is surely quite different from that of the human. Why, then, can there not be a conscious subject whose thinking and emoting processes are those that were called by Freud "primary processes"? Freud has never attempted to show that such processes cannot be conscious. People in alien cultures think in ways "alien to us, or even incredible," yet they are surely conscious. Last but not least, the odd way of thinking (including modes of reasoning, ways of feeling, and motivations) that takes place in dreams (I refer here to what Freud called "the dream surface," which he has hardly ever touched, dismissing it as a hasty put-up job, done by Pcs to hide the real dream content) is at least *akin* to the kind of illogical, primary data processing that occurs in Freud's Ucs or Id. Freud's "most weighty argument" is therefore a total failure. So far, then, we are given no reason at all not to adopt MCT.

D. The well-known cases of *'double conscience'* prove nothing against our view. We may most aptly describe them as cases of a splitting of the mental activities into two groups, and the same consciousness turns to one or the other of these groups alternately. (SE 14:170-71)

This last argument has a Kantian flavor; to see how Freud uses it against MCT, however, we have to flesh it out. MCT is a Humean position: it takes a subject to be a highly cohesive set of mental processes. When the mental life engendered by a given human body falls into two (or more) such sets, MCT holds that there are two (or more) subjects "in" the same person. Freud takes the more Kantian position: mental contents belong to the same subject not if they form a cohesive set, but rather if they are present to the same consciousness. What a single consciousness represents (its *Vorstellungen)* may, but need not, be very cohesive. Thus in cases of hysteria, for example, where the same person seems to have conflicting overall attitudes (and beliefs) at the same time, MCT attributes these attitudes to different subjects; whereas Freud, who holds that there can be only one consciousness (subject) per person, has to postulate the existence of the Unconscious, saying that one of the said attitudes is conscious, the other not.

But Freud has a problem here. In cases of dissociation, both conflicting attitudes (and beliefs) are conscious. Does it not prove that there can be more than one consciousness (subject) per person? Freud's answer is that, in such cases, the conflicting attitudes (and beliefs) do no exist simultaneously. Thus he may still maintain that even in cases of dissociation it is the same consciousness (subject) that at one time turns to one set of contents, which includes one overall attitude and set of beliefs; and at another time turns to another set, which includes the opposite overall attitude and set of beliefs.

To rebut this argument, one has only to remember that in some cases of dissociation both subjects report being conscious at the same time. Some such subjects (e.g., Eve Black) tell us that they were "listening in" or "looking on" when the other subject (e.g., Eve White) was in control of their common body. Eve Black hated what Eve White enjoyed *while* Eve White was enjoying it. Thus *if* conflicting sets of attitudes-cum-beliefs cannot be consciously maintained by the same subject simultaneously, we may, as indeed we do in dissociation, infer the simultaneous existence of several conscious subjects. That conflict need not imply, as Freud held, that at least one of the conflicting sets of attitudes-cum-beliefs must be unconscious. Both may be conscious; if they also control behavior at the same time, then what results is the typical symptoms of neurotic behavior. The conflict itself, however, *need* not lead to neurosis: these subjects, *together,* causally interacting over long periods of time, constitute the normal human *person.*

Thus the MCT model of the mind comes out absolutely unscathed by Freud's attack. There is no need to suppose that the subconscious is unconscious.

III

Freud's attempt to prove the existence of unconscious mental processes has failed. Are there other arguments for this thesis? It is widely held among psychologists that a proof exists in some findings of cognitive psychology and the psychology of perception. In the perceptual process, for example, we discover some highly complex interpretations, generalizations, and inferences of which the perceiver is entirely unaware. Perceptual cues (of whose existence, too, one need not be conscious) are used to derive and apply a perceptual "hypothesis" concerning the *real* properties of the stimulus object (e.g., its relative location, its size, its motion, its value, its identity); and this hypothesis determines what one will find oneself seeing. Hence, unconscious mental processes do exist.[5]

I agree that there is no reason to believe that these processes, too, are consciously performed by some secretive, yet hyperintelligent, homunculus. Such a theory will have to go on and attribute consciousness to any complex apparatus (and which apparatus is not complex?) whatsoever. There is, however, a much better ploy for MCT: why should one take the said processes to be mental? Typical unminded devices may have a scanning mechanism attached and a set of instructions on how to use the scanned data for choosing among several methods of processing the said data. The choice can be revised by additional data, or even randomly by using lower-probability hypotheses (methods of processing) after higher-probability ones were aborted. Indeed, if such a mechanism is attached to a conscious subject, it will determine what that subject consciously perceives: it will determine whether the stimulus object is seen as near or as far, for example. But the mechanism itself does not perceive, nor does it entertain any hypothesis. One cannot show that the mental need not be conscious by calling complex processes that determine conscious experiences "mental." The motion of a falling apple is incredibly complex (try to give a detailed account of it, down to the elementary particle level!) but this is no reason to call it mental. A thermostat that scans the room's temperature does not feel the cold *unconsciously;* it does not feel it at all.

A detailed argument against metaphysical functionalism falls outside the scope of the present article. At any rate, if the proof of the existence of the unconscious depends on the truth of functionalism, then psychoanalysis is much worse off than its advocates, even in their gloomiest moments, believe. Suffice it for me to say that no one has ever shown how any phenomenological description (e.g., 'I am cold') can be recast, without loss of information, in the vocabulary of either physics or sociology. Until such an account is given, or even crudely intimated, one has no right, without begging the question, to call processes that determine conscious mental processes "mental processes."

The crucial difference between the unconscious that Freud talks about and the "hypotheses" and "inferences" of cognitive psychology is that there is a first-person experience of *recognition* only of the former, and never of the latter, states and events. The psychoanalyst's patient, unlike the student in the cognitive psychology lab, often describes her experience by saying that she now recognizes the event or desire attributed to her by the analyst; she now remembers what she has experienced and "blocked" in the past. I am not ignoring the difficulties: the said avowal may be illusory, a result of intensive indoctrination, of transfer, or of a desire to please. But, with all that, it is undeniable that the avowal constitutes *some* ground for believing that the now avowed experience or desire is truly remembered.

Both UMT and MCT try to account for this phenomenon. UMT gave it three models. On the first, the change from consciousness to unconsciousness (or vice versa) is a change of *location*—a representation can "go" from Ucs to Pcs and back. But this metaphor has no explanatory power; it just repeats what was said (that the representation became conscious) in another way (that the representation moved into consciousness); it tells us nothing about the nature of the change. Now Freud himself regarded this "topographic" model as "cruder" than the others (SE 14:175) and "easily defeated" by them (SE 14:180). Let us then turn to the second model, which uses the notion of psychical energy. A representation becomes conscious, on this model, when it is hypercathected by Pcs, and it becomes unconscious (repressed) when that energy is withdrawn.

But what is this energy? Freud sometimes says it comes from the Id and identifies it with the libido. If so, the second model is self-contradictory. How can the withdrawing of cathexis be identified with being unconscious, when unconscious ideas are said to be throbbing with psychic energy? This view is probably a residuum of the early *Project,* where a conscious state was identified with higher motility and an unconscious state with the lower motility of neurons. But it seems to me that such an account is no more cogent than saying that by tossing a ball you can make it into a prime number: how can an accelerated particle *be* an experience? On other occasions Freud recognizes several kinds of psychic energy, and that energy with which the presentation is cathected to become conscious is the special Pcs energy. But here we have an empty metaphor again, for "cathecting x with conscious energy" is nothing but a cumbersome way of saying, "making x conscious." The model explains nothing. It is totally vacuous. Freud's preferred explanation of becoming conscious and losing consciousness is the third model, with which I shall deal in the next section; it is that you make a presentation conscious by associating it with a word. Let me just say briefly that this is *clearly* wrong. Having a word for an item is neither a necessary, nor a sufficient, condition for one to become conscious of it.

Turning now to the MCT model I admit that it is highly speculative and may please only hardened dualists, but it is, at least, not patently absurd. How can an experience be owned up to by someone who had previously sincerely disavowed it? I think we ought to believe her on both occasions. The experience has never been hers when she denied ever having had it. It was an experience of the other self [6] who shares the same body with her and has thus helped to shape the behavior of the person they both constitute. But barriers between selves are not insurmountable, as we know from the case of telepathy where one subject may share another's experience. That condition is probably easier to achieve between subjects who share the same body. Thus it is possible that some method, such as the psychoanalytic one, can put the dominant subject in touch with the mental life of the repressed subject. Note that the insight in question is not an intellectual acknowledgment by the patient that the therapist's interpretation is plausible (although this also happens), but a paradoxical kind of remembering. Patients say that a veil has been lifted, that a faulty connection (between half-independent, half-symbiotic selves) is restored. But how can something that was never known to one yet be remembered by one? Freud sought to explain this bizarre experience by splitting the *known* in two: the consciously and the unconsciously known. The MCT explains it by splitting the *knower* instead. What is, and yet was not, known to one is what is known to someone who is not entirely distinct, but yet not entirely identical, with one. That is, what is revealed to the dominant self in analysis is not an unconscious, submerged part of one's own self, but rather a conscious part of another, submerged self of the same person. We saw that selves may overlap. Now we see that they may also merge and diverge, by gaining (and losing) epistemic access to each others' experiences. I shall say more about this in the last section.

A clear case of that phenomenon is found in hypnosis. A hypnotist may give the subject some posthypnotic suggestion, e.g., "open the window after the fifth time you say 'and'." Complying with the suggestion, the subject tries to rationalize this behavior when asked to explain it ("I just needed some fresh air"). Hypnotized again, the right answer is given as a matter of course, sometimes with a complaint about how difficult it is to count words when someone else it talking! Thus, the presence of two distinct subjects, who were both conscious at the same time, is clearly indicated. Finally, the hypnotist may let the subject remember the order, and help to bring about a reunification of the two selves into one subject who has noninferential access to all the above experiences. Nothing even remotely similar happens in the cases discussed by cognitive psychology. There is little reason, therefore, to refer to the events discussed by it as 'mental', since we have no indication that they *might have been* conscious experiences.

IV

So far, I have attempted to show that Freud's reasons for rejecting the MCT are *obviously* fallacious. This, however, raises a question. How could Freud be persuaded by such worthless arguments? The first and foremost explanation I shall offer is philosophical. I shall argue that Freud's Kantian-Husserlian (henceforth, K-H) convictions made UMT look cogent to him. The philosophical background is given immediately after the arguments quoted above. In fact, it was already *assumed* in the last argument where Freud likens consciousness to a searchlight that being distinct from the contents it "illuminates," can be trained on one, and then on another, group of mental phenomena.

> In psycho-analysis there is no choice for us but to assert that mental processes are in themselves unconscious, and to liken the perception of them by means of consciousness to the perception of the external world by means of the sense organs. . . . The psycho-analytic assumption of unconscious mental activity appears to us . . . as an extension of the corrections undertaken by Kant of our views on external perception. Just as Kant warned us not to overlook the fact that our perceptions are subjectively conditioned and must not be regarded as identical with what is perceived though unknowable, so psycho-analysis warns us not to equate perceptions by means of consciousness with the unconscious mental processes which are their object. (SE 14:171)

On a Humean model of the mind, mental contents (ideas) are bits of self-conscious consciousness. Each idea is an awareness, and what it is immediately aware of is itself. This model has no need for a transcendental ego to be aware of those ideas. On the K-H model, however, phenomena (ideas) *as such* are not conscious: they become conscious when they are present *to* something, which Husserl calls "the transcendental ego" and Kant, who would not let us reify it, describes functionally as "the transcendental unity of the apperception." Freud fully subscribed to this transcendental model. Therefore, in his theory, the role of consciousness is

> *only that of a sense-organ for the perception of psychical qualities . . .* being susceptible to excitation by qualities . . . The psychical apparatus, which is turned towards the external world with its sense-organ of the Pcpt. systems, is itself the external world in relation to the sense-organ of the Cs. (SE 5:615-16) (Freud's italics)

At the bottom of Freud's theory of consciousness we find, therefore, transcendental metaphysics, with an interesting twist. To avoid the Husserlian gambit of making consciousness into a transcendental entity, Freud makes it into an internal sense organ, an equivalent of the traditional Inner Sense. But this combination has disastrous consequences. Perception (the system Pcpt), for Freud, is a mechanism that, when stimulated by external objects, has an output of certain internal objects, the phenomena. These objects are *not* known: they are, as Freud says, unconscious. Now consciousness, we are told, is just another mechanism, Cs, similar to Pcpt, except that instead of being trained on external objects, it has internal ones as its objects. Consciousness is then, for Freud, the perception of perception. If the perceptual model is followed through, however, the output of this mechanism can only be the production of yet another set of phenomenal objects, this time internal to system Cs. But on Freud's K-H view, mere perceiving does not render the stimulus object known, nor is the newly produced phenomenal object self-conscious. Thus the new set of objects in the Cs will be just as unconscious and unknown as the two previous sets of objects—the noumenal (external objects) and the phenomenal (internal objects). If the perception of an unknown object *is* the production of another, internal, object that is also unknown, then nothing can ever be known.

Freud's rejection of the empiricist's identification of the mental with the self-conscious, and his adopting, instead, the K-H model minus its transcendental element, led him quite naturally to the concept of the phenomenal unconscious. But it also made him unable to account for consciousness or find any place for it. Quite rightly, I think, he refuses to make it a transpsychological (i.e., transcendental) agency. But the price he pays is that the entire model is incoherent, fading away, so to speak, in an infinite regress of perceptions of perceptions of perceptions, all unconscious and unknown.

Freud was not happy with this view of consciousness as Inner Sense, and five years later he offered another model for it, the most incredible and inadequate theory he has ever promulgated.:

> We now seem to know all at once what the difference is between a conscious and an unconscious presentation . . . the conscious presentation comprises the presentation of the thing plus the presentation of the word belonging to it, while the unconscious presentation is the presentation of the thing alone. . . . Now, too, we are in a position to state precisely what it is that repression denies to the rejected presentation in the transference neuroses: what it denies to the presentation is translation into words which shall remain attached to the object. A presentation which is not put into words . . . remains thereafter in the Ucs. in a state of repression. (SE 14:201-2)

This is a terrible howler. A nonverbal presentation of a thing may be conscious; creatures lacking language can be aware of their surroundings; they are not automata. On the other hand, there is no reason why a word, like any other presentation or symbol, can not be unconscious. Finally, repression is clearly *not* forgetting or not forming the correct word for what one can otherwise (e.g., by a drawing) accurately represent. Freud knew this better than anyone else because he, himself, gave examples of repressed *words*. The whole concept of the unconscious is now in danger, and Freud uses the most inadequate scaffolding to prop it up.

The amazing thing is that Freud could have taken the other way out, and instead of trying a truncated transcendental model he could have used the empiricist model. The result would have been the replacement of UMT by MCT. Freud, as we saw, had no valid argument against MCT, and it fits all his empirical findings at least as well as any of the models he actually adopted. Moreover, the work of Binet and Janet should have inclined him in this direction. Most important of all, in *Preliminary Communication,* written jointly with Breuer, Freud actually endorses MCT!

We have become convinced that *the splitting of consciousness* which is
so striking in the well known classical cases under the form of *double
conscience* is present to a rudimentary degree in every hysteria, and that
a tendency to such a dissociation, and with it the emergence of abnormal states of consciousness (which we shall bring together under the
term 'hypnoid') is the basic phenomenon of neurosis. . . . These hypnoid states share with one another and with hypnosis . . . one common
feature: the ideas which emerge in them are very intense but are cut off
from associative communication with the rest of the content of consciousness. . . . Moreover, the nature of these states and the extent to
which they are cut off from the remaining conscious processes must be
supposed to vary just as happens in hypnosis . . . from complete recollection to total amnesia. (SE 2:12)

This, and similar passages, are truly sensational. They prove beyond
doubt that in 1893 Freud still held that the mental experiences that occur in
hypnoid states are conscious, and not unconscious. They are only cut off, to
a larger or smaller degree, from "the *rest* of the content of consciousness,"
i.e., "from the *remaining* conscious processes." At this stage, the theory is

that in hysteria groups of ideas originating in hypnoid states are present
and that they are cut off from associative connection with the other
ideas, but can be associated among themselves, and thus form the more
or less highly organized rudiment of a second consciousness, a *condition seconde*. . . . During the attack, control over the whole of the so-
matic innervation passes over to the hypnoid consciousness. (SE 2:15)

There is no unconsciousness; rather Freud holds that the subconscious is a
second consciousness. The direction, however, is soon reversed. Two years
later, in *Studies on Hysteria,* Freud and Breuer introduce the concept of the
unconscious mental state, entirely divorcing it from the case of *double consciousness* ("split personality"). Indeed, one cannot but wonder how Freud
could have neglected the phenomenon so completely, and how little thought
he gave to cases of dissociation, which are certainly striking and which
seemed to him, at the beginning of his career, to hold the key to the mysteries
of the mind. Even at those places where Freud does mention double consciousness, he treats it like a hot potato, anxious to get rid of it and forget
all about it as quickly as possible:

Depersonalization leads us to the extraordinary condition of *double
conscience*, which is more correctly described as split personality. But
all of this is so obscure and has been so little mastered scientifically that
I must refrain from talking about it any more to you. (SE 22:245)

Freud's avoidance of this line of explanation and his reluctance to deal with
this "obscure" issue call, perhaps, for a psychoanalytic interpretation. What

could have caused this extraordinary reaction? E. Berman, who raises this question,[7] offers three answers. The first is the one offered by Luborsky: that "Freud often took a stand against explanations in terms of consciousness."[8] This is no doubt true, but it does not answer our question of *why* he took such a stand?

The second answer given by Berman is that the earlier concept of defense evolved into that of repression; and the latter took the form of "horizontal split" (to use Kohut's term), which is substantially different from the "vertical split" (Kohut's term for multiple consciousness).[9] Thus dissociation cases and those of hysteria could no longer be accommodated in the same framework, and Freud had to move away from MCT. This answer, which is basically Pruyser's,[10] seems reasonable but insufficient. Granting that the said differences exist, it would still be much more natural for Freud to use MCT as an overall theory, distinguishing between horizontal and vertical splits within consciousness. The fact that he did not do so, constructing instead a new model that left the previously discussed cases of vertical splits completely unaccounted for, calls for explanation. If Pruyser were right, the hypnoid state theory would have been expanded by introducing a developmental element into it so that it could, so to speak, fit both Anna O. and Frau Emmy von N. What actually happened was entirely different: dissociation was simply ignored. This, I think, must be because there is no doubt that in dissociation we deal with several conscious subjects (selves) associated with the same person, and this possibility was precisely the one that Freud did not wish to be reminded of. The question of the reason why Freud refused to use and develop MCT is freshly posed, rather than answered, by this purported explanation.

The third answer given by Berman is that "Janet's pretence . . . angered Freud" and that Morton Prince's anti-Freudian position strengthened Freud's reluctance to use their MCT model. But it seems highly unlikely that for this reason Freud would discard an otherwise serviceable explanatory model that was available to him. It seems implausible that Freud went through all this trouble just because someone angered him. Were Freud to have foresworn every area of research entered by a colleague who angered him, he would not have written a single book nor seen a single patient.

Earlier I outlined what, in my opinion, was Freud's main philosophical reason for rejecting MCT. But there is, I think, a psychological reason, too. In *Studies on Hysteria,* Freud and Breuer offer a general theory of human nature; it applies not to mentally ill persons only, but to all human beings. Now, how could an "enlightened" person at the turn of the century claim that all human bodies are possessed by several semi-independent, conscious selves, some of which are beastly and irrational? He would have been dismissed as a reactionary who speaks, in the age of reason, about demonic possession, evil spirits, and exorcism. Janet and Binet could get away with their MCT because it never occurred to them that it applies to *normal* people; it was a "degeneration." But this, precisely, was the conclusion suggested to Freud by his work on hysteria: that repression is a universal phenomenon and that submerged processes were ubiquitous. To save his discovery, Freud had to find a mechanical, nonsentient model for it, and thus to obliterate the striking similarity between the Janets' "vertical" and his own "horizontal" split. This is why Breuer, in the theoretical part of *Studies on Hysteria*, repeatedly insists that the so-called subconsciousness is not conscious. This is, I think, how the concept of the Unconscious was born. It all seems to be a classical case of a traumatic discovery, leading to fear, guilt, and repression.

V

Freud, then, need not have chosen UMT as his metapsychological (i.e., philosophical) framework. But is there also independent, nonpsychoanalytic evidence *for* MCT? I believe we have three such sources of evidence: from ordinary psychology, from current brain research, and from contemporary philosophy of mind. In the present section I shall take one case from the first source, the case of dreams.

Dreams are a part of ordinary experience, yet they differ from all other, nondream, experiences in several ways. First, they are almost entirely forgotten as soon as they are over. Except for a few sequences, especially those occurring right before waking up, the awake subject does not know what the dreamer's experiences were. There is no doubt that the dream experiences are conscious; it is just the case that, as with other people's experiences, we do not know what they are. Yet (unlike other people's experiences) we do remember *some* dreams; there are some cases when we do have first-hand knowledge, from the experiencer's point of view, of some dream experiences. But is this sufficient for saying that the dreamer and the waking subject are strictly identical and that their experiences are segments in the life history of the same person?

It is clear to me that a set of experiences, any one of which is not epistemically accessible from this present experience of mine, nor from any experience epistemically accessible from this present experience of mine, and so on and so forth ad infinitum, cannot possibly be considered *my* experiences. But this is not the case with dreams: some of them are remembered. Thus, through this bottleneck of a few remembered dreams that, presumably, are in turn epistemically integrated with the rest of the dream life (not ever remembered after waking up) I am at present not entirely cut off epistemically from "my" dreams. But since this bottleneck is so narrow, is it not more realistic to speak here of two distinct subjects who overlap in that bottleneck area, epistemically accessible by both? These subjects, of course, causally interact, but this is not a good enough reason for considering them as a single subject.

In a previous article I suggested, half jokingly, the following test.[11] A person would normally be willing to undergo an operation and/or spend a great amount of money so that *he himself* will be spared an intense, chronic pain. Now suppose that you have it on the best authority that, in dreams, which you never do and never shall remember, you suffer, every night, a dire, excruciating pain. Will you consent to have an extremely costly and fairly complicated operation for the sole purpose of eliminating that pain? Probably not. Yet surely had that daily pain occurred during waking hours, you would have taken the operation. How can we account for this striking disparity if not by saying that the subject of the dream experiences, although not quite distinct from you, is yet not plainly and simply identical with you, either? But if this is the case, then we have already conceded one important contention to MCT: that it is more illuminating to describe our mental life by referring to several semi-independent subjects (selves) associated with the same human body.

The second great difference between the dream consciousness and the consciousness of a normal, rational, adult is in desires, intentions, and kind of reasoning used. The dream's logic and the dreamer's goals (on the dream's *surface*) are different from those of the waking subject. On the other hand, there are close similarities between dream and waking experiences and goals. Some are obvious, as with one's own name, social identity, and the set of encountered persons and places. If Freud's contribution is taken into account, the similarity, causal and otherwise, becomes even more evident. Yet it is undeniable that an awake, rational subject is more similar to any other awake, rational subject (with whom he is clearly not identical) than he is similar to the dreaming subject that constitutes the same person with him. Take any well-known criterion of same-personhood based on memory and similarity (e.g., Locke's, Hume's, or Grice's)[12]: it is clear that most of the conditions in it are not met in this case, even though some highly indicative conditions *are* fulfilled, such as causal dependence on the same body and recall from the experiencer's point of view. Again it seems that, as in classical dissociation cases, we would best describe the situation by referring to the dreaming and to the awake subjects as two distinct but overlapping subjects, between which there exist some intimate, causal, and contentual relations. Again, it is precisely this complex system of relations to which the *person* owes his identity and course of development.

It is a central contention of the psychoanalytic doctrine that what appears in dreams (the dream's surface) is *not* what goes on in the Id. The Id., like Kant's *Ding an Sich,* is "inaccessible to consciousness." Dreams consist of conscious images edited by the Pcs (later, the Ego), which attempts, in this way, to reduce the pressure of the Id while not upsetting Cs too much.

The dream story is entirely unimportant, as it is a rough-and-ready yarn edited by the Pcs which tries in this way to give some measure of respectability and order to the substitute images it has concocted to hide the true contents of the Id.

Even if we accept everything Freud has to say about the interpretation of dreams, there is still no reason to accept this theoretical framework as well. It is "chauvinistically" biased in favor of Cs: there is no reason for denying that dreams *are* the Id's stream of consciousness. *This,* we may say, is precisely how the Id feels and how it sees the world. Using its own ("primary") categories of sentience, feeling, and thought, this is how it perceives, feels, desires. The world appears to it not as it appears to us (the dominant subject, i.e., the Cs) but after its own manner. If the world as it appears to us, the Kantian phenomena, is the translation of the external world (the *Ding an Sich*) into our language, then Freud should have said that the dream is a translation of the external world into the Id's language, using its modes of world construction.

Freud may have answered that the symbolic dream-language is so hard to understand that, in a sense, the thoughts and desires thus expressed can still be called "unconscious." But this is plainly wrong. It would be the same as an Englishperson saying that all Germans are unconscious because the language they use to express their thoughts is so hard to understand and that it takes such an effort to understand it! If primary processes are indeed the "cognitive style" of the Id, then is it not natural for it to express itself in this mode—in the language of dreams? To assume that the content of the Id is really what we find through the interpretation of the dream and not what appears on the dream surface is like saying that a German person who wants to talk about a table first says the English word 'table' in her heart, and then, to hide it, perversely says 'Tisch' out loud; when we decode it, we restore the original occurrence of the word 'table' in her heart! This description is surely preposterous. But then I think it is equally bizarre to say that dreams are codes for what the Id *really* wants to say in the Pcs language. Instead, why not simply say that dreams are the Id saying what it has to say in its own language? Dreams are the conscious experiences of the Id, just as our thoughts and sense experience are the ongoing mental life of the dominant self. Freud, who studied Frazer and read Cassirer, knew that his "primary" processes can be used as categories for sensing and conceptualizing; yet he did not come to see dreams as the MCT does, as another symbolic form in action.

The third and most obvious difference between dreaming and waking experiences is, of course, that dreams are "not true"; the events that the dreamer believes to take place at the time of dreaming do not in fact take place at that time. Why is this so? Freud, I think, was right in holding that dreaming is a goal-directed, purposive activity. But then why is it so utterly unsuited to overt action? Ordinary sense experience is just one of the many possible ways of the organism to respond profitably to its environment. We represent the world, if science is to be believed, very inaccurately (think, e.g., of phenomenal color) but in a way that is highly sensitive to some of our needs. Sense experience reflects certain changes having a survival value for us, and it is uniquely suited for immediate reactions to such changes. If a dream, too, represents the real world, in a way that is relevant to some other needs of ours, why is it so "wrong" or impossible to act on that these experiences are mercifully confined (in normal people) to periods when the body is paralyzed in sleep and cannot move? Freud says the operative principle governing dreams is the pleasure principle only. Why is the reality principle excluded?

MCT has an explanation. If we assume that "the Id" is conscious and aware of the external world but normally has no control of the motor, speech, and other important centers of the organism's brain, we can predict (using experimental results from studies dealing with the paralytic) how it will sense and conceptualize the world that it cannot manipulate or modify. We should expect some similarity between the Id, as characterized by Freud, and the personality of the radically paralyzed. Now this is precisely what we do find.[13]

Consider the status of the Id: where mental occurrences have little or no impact on the external world, the reality principle naturally tends to play a very minor role in world construction. If I do not have to see the world aright so that I can change it, why not indulge in fantasy and see the world as I please, or governed by the pleasure principle alone? Where responsible intentions and actions are not rewarded and where wanton, asocial ones not punished, I can indulge in wild desires to my heart's content. Since prompt timing of reaction to external stimuli is of no use, the flow of time can be ignored. As Freud puts it, the Id is atemporal. Thus, lack of motor control makes the Id what we know it to be: highly imaginative and creative but childish, aggressive, and autistic. Once more, Freud's clinical data confirm MCT, which predicts them.

Finally, I would like to mention the following near-dream experience. When one is drowsy, momentarily losing contact with what one is doing, some people report not feeling the beginning of a very short reverie, but, rather, feeling as if one is joining in the middle of a train of thought already in progress. Some people I have spoken to never had this experience, whereas others were quite familiar with it. "It feels as if I have been there all the time", they say. For a brief second, one thinks "in a completely crazy way," seeming to know things one does not know. Obviously, this near-dream experience is nicely explained by MCT: like remembering a dream, it is a glimpse into the mental life of a sibling self.

VI

The most important philosophical lesson to be drawn from the experiments with commissurotomized patients (patients whose corpus callosum, the bundle of nerves linking the left and the right cerebral hemispheres, has been cut) is, in my opinion, the proof positive it supplies that two *simultaneous, independent* streams of consciousness (subjects or selves) can "exist in" (or, as a dualist should say, be causally connected to) the same organism.

By speaking of proof positive, I do not mean to say that this conclusion has not been denied: it has, by one of the leading authorities on the brain (and a fellow dualist), Sir John Eccles. But I think the denial can be shown to be highly implausible. Eccles (for religious reasons, I think) feels very uncomfortable about the possibility of there being (at least) two subjects of experiences associated with the same human body. He admits:[14]

> On this hypothesis we can regard the minor hemisphere as having a status superior to the non-human primate brain. It displays intelligent reactions, even after delays of many minutes, and learning responses; and it has many skills, particularly in the spatial and auditory domain, that are far superior to the anthropoid brain. (P. 328)

Yet Eccles goes on to deny that this system is conscious:

> But it gives no conscious experience to the subject, being in this respect in complete contrast to the dominant hemisphere. Moreover, there is no evidence that this brain has some residual consciousness of its own. (Ibid.)

The position is surprisingly similar to Freud's denial of consciousness to the Id and, I think, as erroneous. One may notice here, as with Freud, the long shadow of the K-H philosophy. Unlike Freud, however, Eccles adopts its transcendental consequences, too. Both Freud and Eccles reject the empiricist's identification of the subject with a set of experiences. They both consider the subject to be a substance that is distinct from its experiences. For Freud, this substance is the brain; for Eccles, the brain can "give" experiences to a separate entity, the Mind: it *causes* experiences to occur in it. Both, however, deny that there is more than one mind per person.

What happens when the dominant brain hemisphere is removed or deactivated? Eccles says that the remaining part is not conscious. Thus he is committed to the amazing view that a human being who functions in most ways almost normally, and whose intelligence is, by Eccles's own admission, superior to that of the anthropoid primates, still lacks consciousness. The said person behaves as if he had feelings, emotions, intentions, and thoughts. Is he faking it all? And why? Does Eccles wish to infer that chimpanzees, gorillas, and other primates who are less intelligent than our subject are, a forteriori, mindless automata, having no feelings, sensations, or desires?

About such a view I can only say that a person whose dog's behavior does not convince him that it is conscious should be equally skeptical about his next-door neighbor; the ability to mouth phonemes can hardly be the *sole* indication of the presence of consciousness.

Eccles does quote Sperry's opposing view that the minor hemisphere constitutes

a conscious system in its own right, perceiving, thinking, remembering, reasoning, willing and emoting, all at a characteristically human level, and that both the left and the right hemisphere may be conscious simultaneously in different, even in mutually conflicting, mental experiences that run along in parallel. (P. 325)

But he refuses to accept the conclusion suggested by Sperry, Bogen, Puccetti, Zangwill, and others that the minor hemisphere is conscious, on the ground that the minor, separated hemisphere can hardly express itself verbally. He would rather deny consciousness to all nonhumans:

The minor hemisphere resembles the brain of a non-human primate, though its performance is superior to that of the brains of the highest anthropoids. In both of these cases we lack communication in a rich linguistic level, so it is not possible to test for the possibility of some consciously experiencing being. (P. 328)

Yet a few sentences later Eccles is willing to reconsider. Although the dominant hemisphere is "exclusively in liaison with the self-conscious mind" (329), he says, the subordinate hemisphere may be in touch with another, lesser mind, which is also conscious. We must therefore distinguish between

the self-consciousness associated with the dominant hemisphere, as reported by the conscious subject, and the consciousness that is assumed to be associated with the minor hemisphere because of its skilled responses that display insight and intelligence. (P. 329)

For a dualist like Eccles, however, this concession is fatal. Once he admits (albeit halfheartedly) that the minor hemisphere is conscious, he ought to say that it is a minded subject. Perhaps this subject is quite different in tendencies and capacities from the one associated with the dominant hemisphere — MCT is not disputing this — but the main claim of MCT has been granted.

By the way, one should note that Eccles exaggerates the impossibility of communicating verbally with the subordinate hemisphere subject. Because the subject can understand spoken language, all we need is ask, "Are you conscious now?" "Do you remember who you are?" and so on. The same procedure can be carried out (if needed) in cases of left hemispherectomy. If a clear affirmative nod is not enough, it is hard to see what will be.

But if both hemispheres are conscious subjects (or, as I would put it, give rise to tightly connected sets of experiences, volitions, and beliefs that constitute a human subject), do we noncommissurotomized people host (at least) two subjects, the left-brain one and the right-brain one? Such a conclusion is indeed drawn by Puccetti,[15] but it seems highly implausible. Because the left hemisphere usually controls speech and the right hemisphere usually controls manual skills, a person whose right- and left-brain parts are (or, for the dualist, are controlled by) different subjects with different goals and beliefs is surely in a very awkward position, very different from the normal level of efficiency of normal persons. Here indeed there is a clear difference between Freud's case and Puccetti's: Freud does have behavioral evidence that the Id exists even "in" normal people, arguing that some items of normal behavior that we all recognize are best explained by the assumption of its existence. On the other hand, Puccetti's argument that each brain half senses separately even in noncommissurotomized persons is rather flimsy.[16]

Another explanation would be that in normal persons the right brain is an automaton, giving rise to no conscious experience. This assumption, however, is entirely without merit. How could a dumb machine be "awakened into life" and become a conscious subject because it is no more connected to a human subject? A lesion of healthy, functioning tissue is hardly likely to bring into existence, because of a stroke of the knife, so to speak, the highest achievement of organic life—consciousness.

What is indicated by the commissurotomy experiments is therefore that in normal persons both left and right hemispheres give rise to conscious experiences that are so well integrated and closely related that they can be said to form a single subject. Apparently, it is the constant flow of information between the brain's parts that allows these experiences to be considered as parts of the same stream of consciousness (i.e., the same subject). The major impediment to the flow of information in the human brain caused by commissurotomy thus results in the formation of two parallel, conscious streams. These two selves are still connected to each other and they mostly overlap; under laboratory conditions, however, it is possible to highlight the nonoverlapping areas, discovering some experiences, goals, and beliefs that are *not* shared by the entire person but are peculiar to one of these selves only.

The neocommissures, says Sperry, are not, in this respect, so special: several parallel streams of consciousness can develop as a result of lesions in, or by depressing the function of, other groups of nerves other than the commissural ones:[17]

> The fiber systems uniting right and left hemispheres are viewed as being not essentially different in their relation to consciousness from those uniting front and back or other areas within the same hemisphere. I know no evidence as yet that says we must exclude white matter neural events from consciousness, or, in other words, that conscious effects are confined to grey-matter dynamics. (P. 161)

To summarize: it was experimentally established that by depressing the function of certain connecting fibers in the brain, several independently conscious subjects were allowed to develop where before only one, superior system existed. It was also empirically established that such subjects can have very different skills, desires, goals, sensations, emotions, and cognitive styles. Now, let us speculate a bit. Is it plausible that at present, normal human brain is such that there exists, between all its consciousness-producing parts, a maximal degree of unity and commerce? I do not think so. It is much more reasonable to assume that not all brain information-transmitting devices are as effective as the formidable corpus callosum. In that case, "in" a normal human brain several loosely connected, conscious systems (i.e., subjects) may develop. These subjects would differ from each other a lot more than would the two mostly overlapping subjects who are artificially produced through commissurotomy. If the connections between certain brain systems may be few and far between, then, although they would exert causal influence on each other, there is no reason why these subjects need be epistemically accessible to each other or even be aware of each other's existence. Thus I, the conscious subject in control of the speech and motor centers of this brain, need not be aware of the existence of another conscious system that is also causally dependent on this ("my") brain. The system Freud has called 'Id' may then be such a system.

Thus, according to MCT, it is possible that the various selves or systems that comprise the person are associated with certain combinations of brain parts. We may then interpret Freud anachronistically as having shown that even with no artificial lesion, the flow of information in the brain may be such that it gives rise to several systems, causally interrelated but epistemically opaque to each other. In split personality and related cases, no clear pattern of dominance between the subjects is achieved and the speech center (for example) may be alternatively programmed by either system. In normal people, the dominant system apparently commands all speech and motor centers. The other systems adapt, developing the more self-sufficient primary processes as their mode of operation.

If this is our model of the brain-mind relation, it is obvious that the question "how many minds per brain?" becomes nonsensical. Mental contents can exist in various *degrees* of integration, both causal and epistemic. These degrees of integration are reflected in (degrees of) causal interaction between brain parts and functions. As Sperry says:

> Already it makes little sense, employing past definitions, to argue about how many "minds" or "persons" are present in the bisected brain. What is needed is better understanding of the functional relationships between the neural mechanisms that are divided and those that are not, and their respective roles in the generation of conscious experience. (P. 172)

One of the most striking features in the behavior of commissurotomized patients during the experiments is their attempt to *rationalize* the behavior that was effected (as we know, but the left-brain subject does not) by the right-brain subject in response to instructions given by the experimenter. The left brain (or its subject) tries to make sense of the obviously purposeful behavior of *its own* body, which otherwise would seem to take place without its willing or intending it. Those lame rationalizations are, to my mind, dramatically and remarkably reminiscent of the attempts of various mental patients (especially hysterics and cases of neurotic obsession) to rationalize the compulsive behavior they manifest. These attempts to fit a behavior into an alien context and account for it by using sometimes ingenious, sometimes ridiculous excuses are, of course, pathetic and the epitome of irony. What Freud tried to do is to discover the correct explanation and purpose of that behavior. The subject's own feeble rationalizations, he says, are but defenses of a subject who is afraid to admit that one's body is a vehicle of the unconscious mind. But perhaps we are now in a position to say that the Freudian explanation is itself a feeble rationalization, a pathetic attempt to cover up and avert one's eyes from the frightening truth. It is one of the deepest and oldest fears of human beings that the body that one is accustomed to regard as one's own, nay, as one's very self, may be snatched away from one's control and made to obey an alien will. This is precisely what happens in hypnosis and, more dramatically, in obeying posthypnotic suggestions. On such occasions, too, the frightened subject is usually trying to rationalize away the strange behavior that the body manifests, to find some (generally, again, quite pathetic and comic) internal reason for the said behavior. This is why Breuer's term "hypnoid state" is, I think, so adequate: not because hysteria is a state in which one's unconscious mind expresses its past traumas, but because it is a state in which a conscious, purposeful, but (almost entirely) alien subject gets hold of the brain's reins and controls one's body.

We now know, as Breuer did not, that not only hypnosis but other kinds of hypnoid states exhibit not only a distinctive pattern of desires, character, and manner of processing data but also a set of memories that are reaccessible at these states only. Indeed, Breuer should have consented to speak about our semi-independent selves or subjects, instead of about mere hypnoid *states* of a person. It is, after all, part of what we mean by saying that Smith and Jones are distinct subjects that we do not expect Jones to know things that Smith has learned; and it is part of what we mean by saying that Smith is one and the same subject that we expect Smith to know at a later time things that Smith has learned at an earlier time. But this feature was found in many independent researches to characterize hypnoid states (or, perhaps, we should say, 'hypnoid selves'), in humans and animals alike.

Girden and Culler (1937) taught curarized dogs to respond to a certain stimulus by bending their knees.[18] The dogs did not respond to that stimulus at all when not on that particular drug, but as soon as they were in that state again they remembered what they had learned under that drug. Overton (1964) taught drugged rats to negotiate a certain maze, and they were able to perform successfully again only under that drug. Otis (1964) tried the same experiment with two different groups of rats, each taught under the influence of a different drug. But learning was evident only under the same drug, or, as we may say, when the same hypnoid self was examined. Bliss (1974) conducted the two-drug experiment with monkeys. The results were stunning: almost perfect recall when examined under the influence of the drug under the influence of which the behavior was learned, almost zero knowledge when examined under the influence of the other drug or when not drugged.

Many more such experiments were done with humans. That a person may recall, when hypnotized again, what went on in a previous hypnotic session (but be completely unaware of that when wide awake) is well known, and was mentioned by Breuer and by Prince. But more recent experiments produced the same effect with different hypnoid states. Evans (1972) made suggestions to people in rapid eye movement (REM) sleep that were followed by the people only when in REM sleep (in one case, for months after the original suggestion was made).[19] Goodwin et al. (1969) taught some of his subjects when inebriated, the rest of the class being sober. Again, those who learned while drunk, unlike the others, performed better while drunk. Eich et al. (1975) used marijuana to the same effect, and Thompson and Neely (1970) used electric shocks on rats with similar results.

It is not a mere semantic question to ask whether we are allowed, as a result of these and similar experiments, to talk about several selves constituting the same person, each with partially independent character, intentions, beliefs, capacities, and preferences. This model is an explanatory one: it accounts for facts that we would otherwise find incomprehensible.

VII

During the last few decades, an all-out search has been going on in philosophical circles for a criterion of personal identity. What are the necessary and sufficient conditions for saying that x, identified at t, and y, identified at t', $t \neq t'$, are segments in the life history of the same person? Some suggested bodily continuity, and others suggested mental continuity; but a third view, expressed (among others) by Derek Parfit and myself, is that the very assumption that any two human temporal segments must either be segments of the *same* person, or else segments of *distinct* persons, is misguided because persons may, can, and do overlap.[20] Parfit proposed several thought experiments to show that this is the case; the following story is a variation on one of them. A person, x, enters a cell-splitter, which divides each cell in his body in two. Each half is then made to restore itself. Thus out of the splitter come two entirely similar people, $x1$ and $x2$, each claiming to be x, on the usual criteria of personal identity. It is absurd to say that neither one is x, i.e., that x is dead. Had part of the splitter malfunctioned and either $x1$ or $x2$ alone came out of the splitter, we would have had no doubt that x came out of the splitter. As Parfit puts it, double success cannot amount to total failure. But then it is equally absurd to say that $x1$ and $x2$, who sue each other and probably engage in fistfights, are both identical with x and hence also with each other. The only reasonable model for this situation is a Y-shaped diagram: until x entered the splitter $x1$ and $x2$ were best considered as being the same person, x. From that moment on, they are better considered as distinct. Thus, it is possible for people to overlap, merge, and bifurcate.

All the criteria of personal identity we use admit of degrees. The human body consists of many parts that are constantly substituted for new ones, which are more or less qualitatively similar to those they eventually replace. How many parts can be replaced at one time, how similar to the original must a replacement be, and how often can such replacements take place, all without jeopardizing the person's identity? The answer can only be a rough-and-ready one, leaving wide, fuzzy margins for overlap. The same picture holds, even more obviously, for the criteria of memory continuity and similarity (in consecutive moments) of beliefs and intentions. How strong should the similarity be for us to say that it is the career of the *same* person? Worse yet, our problems multiply when, in this brave new world of ours, the two sorts of criteria part ways. What are we to say about personal identity in a world where memory traces can be transplanted from person to person, or copied directly brain to brain? When a new edition of one's body can be cloned at will (e.g., upon the old body's demise)? When a person can have additional bodies manufactured and moved about by one's own will, sentient and transmitting, say, a reduced version of their sensations to the original person? Similar puzzle cases abound in current philosophical literature. These cases are puzzling, however, only for those who believe that *person* is a natural kind and therefore that the question "are x and y stages of the same person, or else of different persons?" *must* have a definite answer. On the present view, however, no answer to such questions need be made. A person is a system of several mental items, and there may be no sharp boundary between one such system and other systems. Because mental and physical connectedness is a matter of degree, it is quite possible for there to be a whole set of past, present, and future people who are, to some degree, the same person.

In other articles from 1966 on, I argued that the concept of a person can be used as a counting sortal in our culture due to the contingent fact that the various criteria for same-personhood, until very recently, happened to agree.

This gives the wrong impression that 'person' is a count-noun (a sortal) under all circumstances. Actually, when certain technological difficulties (e.g., in storage and transmission of information, or, in replacing defective body parts) are overcome, it will be impossible to *count* persons. It is therefore perfectly possible for x to be the same α-person (using one kind of criteria, e.g., those based on information retrieval) as y, but not the same β-person (using another kind of criteria, e.g., those based on matter identity) as y. Therefore, persons distinguished according to different criteria of personal identity such as α and β above may overlap. It is hard to imagine two person-states, x and y, for which we cannot find some criterion of personal identity, γ, on which they are stages of the same person; and another criterion of personal identity, δ, on which they are stages of different persons.

Moreover, even persons falling under the same person concept (i.e., the same *kind* of criterion for person identity) may overlap. To use Austin's term, being a person is an *institutional* fact: to say that x and y are stages in the career of the same person is to be committed to many ethical and legal implications—for example, that y may be justly rewarded or punished for what x did. Now a society identical with ours in all noninstitutional facts may still apply our concept of a person in a much wider, or in a much narrower, way. For an example of the narrower use, imagine a society where the puberty rite is considered as the demise of one person, the child, and the birth of a new person who inherits the deceased's body and other belongings. For an example of the wider use, imagine a society where what we regard as a father and a son is considered as the same person in two bodies. Instead of saying, "My child is now in pain," what we call 'the father' would rather say, "I am now in pain in *that* body" and would regard the lack of noninferential information about that pain as we regard a lapse of memory: both result from poor information flow between one's various spatiotemporal parts. Why should these wider and narrower entities not be considered as persons, too? But if they are persons, then all persons overlap and we need the ontology of MCT.

Although developmental psychologists habitually speak of the *construction* of the self, most (non-Humean) philosophers regard this expression as metaphorical. What is gradually constructed, they say, is my self-*image*, and not my very self. This, they say, must be the case, because for a certain experience or desire that I feel to be or not to be integrated into my emerging personality it must already be felt by me. Hence the existence of the self is presupposed by the psychological ego-constructing process and does not result from it. Without this self *to* which the experiences are present, we cannot explain (they say) the close bond between two sensations that are simultaneously present to the same consciousness. This, for many philosophers, is the root of the ego.[21]

As a Humean, however, I can take the developmental psychologist quite literally. The human brain, I believe, can produce (I know not how) mental contents, such as sensations and volitions. We may suppose that those contents are initially connected to each other and to outside reality only very tenuously. Then, perhaps, larger groupings of those mental contents emerge and are selected Darwinianly for having a positive survival value. How is this selection possible? My explanation is interactionistic. Some mental contents are causally efficacious; they can (and again, I do not know how) effect motions of matter. They can cause a certain center in this brain to make this hand go up. Crudely, we may thus envisage clusters of mental entities vying with each other for control of experience-producing and motor-controlling brain centers. The more realistic and integrated the mental grouping is, the better its chances are for perpetuating itself through the success of the organism it directs. Integration, however, also spells exclusion. Mental contents that cannot be incorporated into the dominant grouping are repressed. This does not mean that they become unconscious. Repression, rather, is exclusion from the dominant set (a subject) that, in normal cases, gains exclusive control over its brain's speech and motor centers and that can perpetuate itself by ensuring that the said brain produces mostly such mental contents that are more or less compatible with it.

How should we characterize the relations between these mental items that constitute a single subject? We have already mentioned the three major traits of such sets: falling into integrated patterns (Hume's *similarity*), causal dependence on earlier items in the set, and epistemic accessibility. The last relation can also be stronger or weaker, like the two others. Minimal epistemic accessibility is a mental item including a symbolic representation of other items of this set. The representation can be more of less informative, as evidenced (roughly speaking) by memory.[22] The strongest accessibility is when a mental item merges with another to form with it a continous whole. For want of a better term, we may say that such items are copresent: for example, there is a strong relation of copresence between sound and color sensations simultaneously present to one and a weaker copresence relation between a current sensation and a sensation that was present to one a second ago.

Because some degree of content integration, epistemic accessibility, and causal connection exists between any two mental contents in the world, the boundaries between subjects are indicated by a sharp decline in the degree of such connectedness. The degree of connectedness also determines the usefulness and predictive power of psychological generalizations, that is, when it is profitable to talk about long-term tendencies, intentions, emotions, traits of character, nonoccurrent beliefs and values. Obviously, where connectedness is low, predictive and explanatory power is minimal. MCT can thus be developed into a useful tool for psychologists and can give philosophers a coherent model of the mind.

My last argument showing how MCT and contemporary philosophy support each other and give new meaning to the practice of psychoanalysis is one that I owe to a very important philosopher of psychology and psychoanalysis, R. Wollheim.[23] Although Wollheim does not subscribe to MCT, I think he produced an excellent argument for holding it.

It is commonly believed that (A1) for any two events, x and y, either they do or else they do not happen to the same person: i.e., it is not a matter of degree whether X, who experiences x, and Y, who experiences y, are or are not the same person. It is also believed that (A2) there is nothing X can *do* to become identical with Y (and thus become the experiencer of y). On the other hand, it is commonly believed that (B1) whether X's life is of a piece, i.e., whether x constitutes an interconnected whole with the rest of X's experiences, *is* a matter of degree. It is also believed that (B2) there is a lot X can do to make x of a piece with the rest of X's life.

Wollheim claims, however, with an admirable insight, that the (A) cases and the (B) cases are not mutually independent and hence cannot be treated in such radically different ways. Similarly, I have argued that whether x and y are or are not segments of the same person's life is a matter of degree of connectedness. Now, because one *can* strive to make one's life more unified, more of a piece, then, by doing so, one determines whether or not y is or is not going to be one's own experience; i.e., whether the person who undergoes x will or will not be the same person who undergoes y. If the degree of relevant unity between x and y is considerable and of high psychological interest, we ought to assign them to the same person; if it is even higher, we ought to assign them to the same subject (self). Thus viewed, personal identity is an *achievement* that can exist to a larger or smaller degree, among larger or smaller sets of experiences and volitions, depending on what one *does* with one's life. A person can to a large extent determine whether a certain future self shall, or shall not be *oneself;* also, how *much* of a person one is going to be.

Psychotherapy is now seen to have a central role in this new philosophy of mind. Unifying one's life, gaining wider epistemic access to it, making its experiences more copresent, and owning up to it—in short, making it really one's own—is what psychotherapy is all about. But then it is a mistake to regard this process as one of tinkering within, as if what is and what is not oneself in no way depends on the therapeutic process. The integration process does not happen *to* the person but, rather, is creative *of* the person.

This idea has far-reaching sociological and political implications. We can regard the history of humankind as a series of improvements in communication: language, then writing, then the media made human experience more tightly knit, more interconnected and coherent. Today, one person can inform the other about personal experiences by using language; tomorrow, the experiences may literally be shared. Thus if therapy is a process of creating a person out of sundry conflicting, stupid, ignorant, savage, and miserable selves, then civilization can be seen as a process of creating a rich, intelligent, highly integrated, and happy superperson, an *anima mundi,* out of our world of warring persons. Strife and war between persons are not, on this philosophy of mind, any different in kind than strife and war inside persons or between selves. Thus, MCT gives an additional, cosmic meaning to Freud's art.

Notes

1. *The Standard Edition of the Complete Psychological Works of Sigmund Freud,* edited by James Strachey (London, 1953) (henceforth, SE). Vol. 14, 161-62.

2. Morton Prince, *The Dissociation of A Personality* [1904] (London, 1930).

3. This error was discerned by Thomas Nagel, who writes: "But of course if the Unconscious were conscious of *itself,* then it would have a "possessor" distinct from the subject of ordinary consciousness in the same person, and it would be only the latter who was unconscious of these conscious states of the Unconscious." "Freud's Anthropomorphism," in *Freud,* edited by R. Wollheim (New York, 1974), 16, note 11.

4. Cf., e.g., A Binet, *Les Alterations de la Personalité* (Paris, 1892): "In a large number of people, placed in the most diverse conditions, the normal unity of consciousness is disintegrated. Several distinct consciousnesses arise, each of which may have perceptions, a memory, and even a moral character of its own" (8).

5. D. Dennett, who, in his introduction to his (and D. R. Hofstadter's) *The Mind's I* (New York, 1981) erroneously attributes MCT to Freud (12), cites the presence of such cognitive processes as proving the existence of the unconscious (12-15).

6. I use the terms 'self' and 'subject' (or 'subject of consciousness') interchangeably. A *person* may include several interacting selves, which may or may not be aware of each other's existence.

7. E. Berman, "Multiple Personality: Psychoanalytic Perspectives," *International Journal of Psycho-Analysis* (1981) 62:283-300.

8. L. Luborsky, "Momentary Forgetting during Psychotherapy and Psychoanalysis," in *Motives and Thought,* edited by R. R. Holt (New York, 1967), 175-217. See also 204.

9. Heinz Kohut, *The Analysis of the Self* (New York, 1971), 185ff.

10. P. W. Pruyser, "What Splits in 'Splitting'?" *Bulletin of the Menninger Clinic* 39 (1975) 1-46.

11. E. Zemach, "The Unity and Indivisibility of the Self," *International Philosophical Quarterly,* 10 (1970): 542-55.

12. J. Locke, *An Essay concerning Human Understanding,* book 2, chap. 27; D. Hume, *Treatise of Human Nature,* book 1, sec. 6; H. P. Grice, "Personal Identity," *Mind* 50 (1941): 330-50.

13. There is a vast literature on the psychology of the disabled. To limit citations to a minimum, let me only mention J. W. Daniel, *Physical Disability and Human Behavior* (Elmsford, NY., 1976), 56-124. Daniel's comparison of the psychology of the disabled with that of subjects in sensory deprivation experiments (the work of, e.g., Heron or Fuller) is important for our purposes. See also H. H. Nielsen, *A Psychological Study of Cerebral Palsied Children* (Copenhagen, 1966), 166-209; and L. C. Rustad, *An Investigation of the Relationship between Imaginational Processes and Motor Inhibitions: The Fantasy Life of Paraplegics and Quadraplegics* (Doctoral dissertation, Case Western Reserve University, 1975). I shall note one older book that connects disability and madness: P. Schilder, *Studien zur Psychologie und Symptomalogie der Progressiven Paralyse* (Berlin, 1930). About the relation between motoric control and per-

ception, see esp. W. H. Werner and S. Wepner, "Toward a General Theory of Perception," *Psychological Review* 59 (1952): 324-38.

14. K. R. Popper and J. C. Eccles, *The Self and Its Brain* (New York, 1977). See 328.

15. R. Puccetti, "The Case for Mental Duality: Evidence from Split Brain Data and Other Considerations," *Behavioral and Brain Sciences* 4 (1981): 93-99.

16. Ibid., Open Peer Commentary, 99-116.

17. R.W. Sperry, "Mental Phenomena as Causal Determinants in Brain Function," *Consciousness and the Brain,* edited by G. G. Globus et al. (New York, 1976). See 161.

18. E. Girden and E. A. Culler, "Conditioned Responses in Curarized Striate Muscle in Dogs," *Journal of Comparative Psychology* 23, part 2: (1937) 261-74; D. A. Overtone, "State-Independent or 'Dissociated' Learning Produced with Pentobarbitol," *Journal of Comparative and Physiological Psychology* 57 (1964):3-12; L. S. Otis, "Dissociation and Recovery of a Response Learned under the Influence of Clorpromazine or Saline," *Science* 143 (1964):1347-48; D. K. Bliss, "Theoretical Explanations of Drug-Dissociated Behavior," Federation Proceedings 33, part 7 (1974):1787-96.

19. F. Y. Evans, "Hypnosis and Sleep: Techniques for Exploring Cognitive Activity during Sleep," in *Hypnosis,* edited by E. Fromm and R. E. Shor (London, 1972); D. W. Goodwin et al., "Alcohol and Recall: State Dependent Effects in Man," *Science* 163 (1969):1358-60; J. E. Eich et al., "State-Dependent Accessibility of Retrieval Cues in the Retention of a Categorized List," *Journal of Verbal Learning and Verbal Behavior* 14, part 4 (1975):408-17; C. J. Thompson and J. E. Neely, "Dissociated Learning in Rats Produced by Electroconvulsive Shock," *Physiology and Behavior* 5 (1970):783-86.

20. Derek Parfit, "Personal Identity," *Philosophical Review,* 80 (1971): 3-27; E. Zemach, "Sensations, Raw Feels, and Other Minds," *Review of Metaphysics* 20 (1966):317-40; E. Zemach, "The Reference of 'I'," *Philosophical Studies* 23 (1972):65-75.

21. Cf., e.g., R. Chisholm, *Person and Object* (LaSalle, Ill., 1976), 15-21; R. Chisholm, *The First Person* (Minneapolis, Minn., 1981), 75-91; G. Madell, *The Identity of the Self* (Edinburgh, 1981).

22. For a more accurate statement, see my "Memory: What It Is, and What It Cannot Possibly Be," *Philosophy and Phenomenological Research* 44 (1983):31-44; and "*De Se* and Descartes," *Nous* 19 (1985):181-204.

23. R. Wollheim, "On Persons and Their Lives," in *Explaining Emotions,* edited by A. Rorty (Berkeley, 1981), 299-331.

Intentionality

DAVID M. ROSENTHAL

1. INTRODUCTION

Thought and speech are intimately connected, in ways that make the study of each shed light on the other. But the nature of that connection, and of the illumination it casts, are vexed issues that are the subject of considerable controversy.

At the level of our platitudinous background knowledge about things, speech is the expression of thought. And understanding what such expressing involves is central to understanding the relation between thinking and speaking. Part of what it is for a speech act to express a mental state is that the speech act accurately captures the mental state and can convey to others what mental state it is. And for this to occur, the speech act at least must have propositional content that somehow reflects that of the mental state, and perhaps must have other such properties as well.

Speech acts must not only resemble the thoughts they express; they must also differ in important ways. Speech plainly cannot occur without thought, but thought unexpressed in speech can and often does occur. A satisfactory account of the relation between speech and thinking must, accordingly, do justice both to the resemblance between speech and thought and to this difference between them.

This asymmetry between thinking and speech may appear to imply that the study of speech must be based on the study of thought. Thus, one might argue, if thought can occur without speech but not conversely, thought must somehow be more basic than speech. Moreover, if speech is at bottom the expression of thought, perhaps we cannot understand the nature of speech without knowing what it is for something to express thought. And we cannot understand that unless we know what thought is. On this view, thought is prior to speech, and the primacy of thought implies that to understand speech we must first understand the nature of thinking.

But, if the asymmetry of the expressing relation suggests that we cannot understand speech without understanding thought, the way speech acts must correspond to the thoughts they express suggests that we can proceed in either direction. Since speech and thinking share their most important properties, we should be able to learn equally about each by studying the other. If so, we need not follow the Cartesian suggestion that the study of thought must precede the study of speech.

In what follows, I defend an account of the relation between speech and thought according to which the priority that thinking does have implies nothing about how we must study them. We need not understand speech only by appeal to the nature of thought. I begin by discussing, in section 2, how speech acts must resemble, in crucial respects, the mental states they express. In section 3, then, I advance a strictly causal explanation of what it is for a speech act to express a thought. On this suggestion, a speech act expresses a thought just in case the thought causes the speech act, and the two have the same or corresponding intentional properties, in the manner sketched in section 2. If this causal account proves to be defensible, we will have no reason to suppose we must study thinking before we can understand speech. Thought is only causally prior to speech, and causal priorities do not, by themselves, dictate how we should study things.

To sustain this conclusion, I take up, in section 4, claims by various authors that thought is prior to speech in a way that we cannot explain in causal terms. On these claims, the basis for this priority is that the intentionality of thought is intrinsic, whereas the intentionality of speech is not. I argue that these claims about intrinsic intentionality, and the noncausal primacy of thinking, are both unfounded. Section 5 examines insincere speech, which is a useful test case for a theory of the relation between speech and thought. For, if we hold that insincere speech acts express thoughts the speaker does not have, it is difficult to see how such expressing can be a causal matter. Section 6, then, considers the question of whether a causal account suffices to give a satisfactory explanation of intentionality, or whether we need, in addition, some thesis about intrinsic intentionality and the noncausal primacy of thought. In section 7, finally, I urge that we can best understand the force of the idea that thought is noncausally prior to speech if we appeal to the way we are automatically aware of our own thoughts and speech acts. And I conclude by arguing that this suggestion is compatible with an account of such primacy cast in strictly causal terms.

2. THE CORRESPONDENCE OF THOUGHT AND SPEECH

One way that thinking and speech resemble each other pertains to their propositional content. Whenever I think something, I can express what I think by saying it. My speech act then has the very same content as my mental state.[1] And whenever I perform a speech act, what I say expresses something that I am thinking, at least if I speak sincerely. To sincerely say it's raining, I must also think it is; and again my speech act expresses my thought. For a speech act to express a mental state, the two must have the same propositional content.

But the expression of thought by speech goes beyond just expressing content. To see this, it is important to distinguish two ways we put words to our mental states, and convey those thoughts to others. For example, I can express my belief that it's raining by asserting that it's raining. But if, instead, I only expect it to rain, I can express my expectation as well, by saying it will probably rain. And, in general, I can express in words the whole range of propositional attitudes that I can hold. If I say something you did was nice, I express my gratitude. If I say that something is nice, I express my admiration or pleasure; if I say it would be nice to have, I express my desire. In each such case, my speech act not only conveys the content of my mental state; it also captures my mental attitude.

When I convey the content and mental attitude of my thoughts in the ways just illustrated, I do not explicitly mention those thoughts. Sometimes, my speech act simply has the same content, and has an illocutionary force parallel to my mental attitude. Other times, I may modify the content of my mental state so as to capture my mental attitude, as when I say that something would be nice to have, rather than that it just is nice. I can also, however, put words to my mental states by explicitly describing them. I can convey my expectation of rain by making a prediction that expresses my expectation; I can say, for example, that rain is likely. But another way to convey that expectation is just to say, straight-out, that I expect rain. These two kinds of speech act are not equivalent. The truth conditions of 'Rain is likely' differ from those of 'I expect it to rain', and either can be true without the others also being true. But the two speech acts both convey the same mental state. Consequently, the conditions in which one can correctly perform the two speech acts are the same. Similar remarks hold of other kinds of mental state. I can convey my gratitude either by saying 'Thank you' or by telling you that I am grateful. I can express admiration of something either by saying that it is nice or by saying that I admire it. The conditions under which we can appropriately perform such pairs of speech acts will always be the same.

This divergence of truth conditions from performance conditions emerges particularly vividly in connection with what Wittgenstein called Moore's paradox (Wittgenstein 1953, 2:190; see Moore 1944, 204). As Moore noted, even though the sentence 'It's raining but I don't believe it is' is not an actual contradiction, we cannot use it to make a coherent assertion. There are circumstances in which the sentence would be true, but none in which anybody could use it to say so. Its truth conditions thus differ from its conditions for coherent assertibility. Such sentences resemble 'I do not exist', which I cannot assert even though it can be, and indeed has been, true.[2] Parallel considerations affect other mental attitudes and the illocutionary acts that express them. I cannot coherently say 'Thank you but I feel no gratitude', or 'Rain is likely, but I don't expect it'. If someone were to produce such forms of words, we would automatically try to interpret those words nonliterally, or as having been used ironically or with some other oblique force. Only thus can we regard the speaker as having performed any speech act at all.

It is important to stress that there are grammatical forms of words that one can utter and yet perform no speech act. Otherwise, we could not explain what goes wrong with sentences such as 'It's raining but I don't believe it' and 'I do not exist' by saying that the literal meanings of these sentences prevent us from using them to say anything. But indisputable examples of this phenomenon are easy to come by. If somebody assertively utters a blatant contradiction, such as 'It's raining and it isn't raining', that utterance does not, on its face, constitute the comprehensible asserting of anything. If such a case actually occurred, we might try to take the person to be saying something that goes beyond those words; for example, that it is raining in one place but not another. But if the speaker insisted that we take those words literally and rejected any helping reconstrual, we would be unable to understand what illocutionary act was being performed.

Things are different, of course, with a covert contradiction. People can, and do, say contradictory things without explicitly realizing that that is what they are doing. But if a contradiction is so blatant that its falsehood cannot be missed, we cannot use it, at least not in any literal way, to make an assertion. The impossibility of using a blatant contradiction to say anything explains the commonsense reaction people typically have to such cases. People do not normally say that contradictory assertions are false, or even necessarily false; they say, instead, that they are meaningless. This is not the crude error it is often supposed to be, but only the result of focusing on speech acts rather than on sentence types. Contradictory sentence types are plainly false, but the speech acts that result when one tries to assert them literally are meaningless. There is no way to understand the speech act, and thus no meaning we can give it. These considerations are, in effect, a commonsense counterpart of W. V. Quine's observation that no translation can be acceptable if it results in our rendering as elementary contradictions sentences that people actually assert (1960, 58-59). The point is unexceptionable once we note that translations must, in part, tell us how to construe people's speech acts. Since there is no way to regard the assertion of a blatant contradiction as a coherent speech act, any translation that leads us to construe utterances this way must be in error.

Manifest contradictions are not the only cases of meaningful, grammatical sentences whose literal meaning blocks the performance of any coherent speech act. Any time we cannot construe the content of a person's speech act as a literal match of the sentence in question, the conditions for the coherent performance of a speech act cannot be met. Part of what distinguishes such cases is that hearers automatically try to reconstrue the speech act as having some content or illocutionary force different from those which the grammatical and lexical properties of the sentence indicate. This desire to reconstrue, however, occurs in other kinds of cases as well. But when the sentence is perfectly grammatical, and there is nothing about the context of its being uttered that explains the hearers' tendency to reconstrue, then no speech act is possible that has the literal content and force of the sentence in question. The sentences that exemplify Moore's paradox are prime examples of this phenomenon. If somebody actually uttered 'It's raining, but I don't believe it', we would very likely try to reconstrue the speech act. Perhaps, for example, the speaker wants to say only how very surprising it is. Perhaps somebody who utters 'Thank you but I feel no gratitude' means not to thank anybody, but only to produce, albeit grudgingly, the proper formula. Unless we reconstrue these examples in some such way, one cannot understand the person as performing any speech act whatever.

To explain the divergence manifest in Moore's paradox between truth conditions and conditions for the coherent performance of speech acts, we must distinguish expressing mental states from reporting that one is in them. 'It's raining' expresses, but does not report, one's belief that it's raining. By contrast, 'I believe it's raining' reports that belief, but does not express it. One cannot therefore assert 'It's raining but I don't believe it is', since the second conjunct denies that I have the very belief that the first conjunct purports to express. If expressing were not distinct from reporting, the first conjunct would both express and report one's belief, whereas the second conjunct would still deny that any such belief exists. So on this construal the sentence would be contradictory, which is plainly is not. Accordingly, a correct explanation of Moore's paradox is impossible unless we recognize that reporting a mental state is distinct from expressing it.

We tend to use verbs of illocutionary act in a way that may blur the difference between expressing and reporting one's mental states. Rather than say that rain is likely or that something you did was good, I can make my illocutionary force explicitly by saying 'I predict rain' or 'I commend what you did', perhaps with the formulaic 'hereby' inserted where appropriate. But 'I predict rain' and 'Rain is likely' not only make the same prediction; they also express the same mental state, namely, my expectation of rain. Similarly, saying that something is good and that I commend it both express the same mental state, namely, my approval.

These considerations may tempt one to hold that the phrase 'I predict' is something like an optional variant of 'is likely', and 'I commend' a variant of 'is good'. One might then go on to infer that 'I expect' and 'I approve' are just other such variants, and that when predictive illocutionary force is already present, both 'I expect' and 'I predict', like 'I commend' and 'I approve', are merely ornamental pleonasms. It would follow that 'I expect rain' does not report my expectation, but rather expresses it, by making a prediction. Similarly, we would conclude that 'I approve of this' expresses, rather than reports, my approval.

Some such reasoning appears to have influenced Wittgenstein's assessment of such cases. According to Wittgenstein (1953, 2:190,192), "the statement 'I believe it's going to rain' has a meaning like, that is to say a use like, 'It's going to rain'." He concludes: " 'I say' , . . . in 'I say it will rain today' , . . . simply comes to the same thing as the assertion 'It will . . . . ' " If we take the use of linguistic expressions as central to their semantic character, it will be difficult not to assimilate reporting mental states to expressing them.[3]

But the considerations raised earlier are still decisive. Whatever we may think about meaning and use, the use of a sentence is plainly distinct from its truth conditions. The sentences 'I hereby predict rain', 'Rain is likely', and 'I expect rain' are all three alike with respect to conditions of appropriate use. But their truth conditions indisputably diverge. Indeed, we can construct Moore's paradox using any pair from among this triad of sentences. We can assert neither 'I hereby predict rain but rain isn't likely' nor 'I expect rain but I predict it won't rain', though neither sentence is contradictory.

The identity of conditions of correct use despite divergence of truth conditions not only shows that expressing mental states differs from reporting them. It also confirms that for a speech act to express a mental state the speech act must, in addition to sharing its propositional content with the mental state, have an illocutionary force that reflects the attitude of that mental state. For the paradox will arise using any mental attitude together with the corresponding illocutionary force. Only if expressing a mental state implies that the illocutionary force of the speech act reflects the attitude of the mental state is it open to us to explain Moore's paradox as due to the denial in one conjunct of a mental state that the other conjunct purports to express. No alternative explanation is available that is equally compelling.

That illocutionary force expresses mental attitude is also shown by impressive parallels that hold between verbs of illocutionary act and those of propositional attitude, and the grammatical complements that various verbs of each kind require. These syntactic and semantic parallels, and their importance, have recently between articulated in elegant and illuminating detail by Zeno Vendler and John R. Searle.[4]

The parallelism between mental attitude and illocutionary force strongly supports the view that satisfactory accounts of speech acts and mental states must proceed hand in hand. We can learn about either by appeal to the other. Traditional arguments for the interdependence of such accounts have generally stressed the impossibility of explaining what it is for either mental states or speech acts to have propositional content without presupposing a notion of propositional content common to both. The difficulty resembles that which Quine finds in breaking out of the family of terms that ascribe synonymy and analyticity.[5] The parallelism of mental attitude and illocutionary force complements traditional appeals to propositional content in supporting the claim that speech acts and mental states together form a family whose members cannot be explained except by appeal to other members of that family.

Indeed, parallels of illocutionary force and mental attitude tell us more about thought and speech, and the way they are connected, than can parallels that involve propositional content. For one thing, the way we classify mental states is a function of differences in mental attitudes, and we also classify speech acts into kinds on the basis of differences in illocutionary force. Propositional content tells us relatively little about how the various sorts of mental state and speech act differ from one another. More important, as Moore's paradox shows, a match between illocutionary force and mental attitude is necessary for a speech act to express a mental state. That match is central to the tie between thought and speech.

3. THE PRIMACY OF THOUGHT

The claim that thought and speech are interdependent is unexceptionable. And, since speech acts have properties that correspond to those of the mental states they express, knowing about either will help us understand the other. But a compelling intuition exists that, whatever parallels there are between the properties of speech and thought, the nature of speech is dependent on thought, but not conversely. When a speech act expresses a mental state, the two do indeed have corresponding properties. But the speech act, on this intuition, somehow owes its properties to the mental state. We can understand speech only as the expression of thought. So we can explain speech by reference to thought, but we cannot explain thinking by appeal to speech.

The idea that thinking is, in some such way, more basic than speech has been formulated with particular force and clarity by Roderick M. Chisholm (1958). According to Chisholm, "nothing would be intentional were it not for the fact that thoughts are intentional," although "[t]houghts would be intentional even if there were no linguistic entities." So "[t]houghts are a 'source of intentionality'," whereas speech acts are not (533). Accordingly, we cannot "explicate the intentional character of believing and other psychological attitudes by reference to certain features of language." Rather, we must "explicate the intentional characteristics of language by reference to believing and to other psychological attitudes" (521).

The view that thought has primacy over speech is not new: It is of course present in Descartes, and can be found in Aristotle.[6] And more recently, such primacy has been championed by Vendler and by Searle. Both Vendler and Searle concede that, because speech has a physical realization that is readily observable, speech is intersubjectively more accessible than thought (Vendler 1972, 3; Searle, 5). But greater epistemic accessibility does not always indicate a more fundamental nature. And Searle and Vendler both insist, with Chisholm, that thinking is more basic than speech in some way that reflects the nature of both processes.

That thinking is in some way prior to speech seems plain, and it is natural to try to explain this priority by appeal to the asymmetry of the expressing relation. Speech expresses thoughts, but thoughts do not express speech. Indeed, nothing whatever expresses speech, and thinking itself does not express anything, at least not in the way in which speech expresses mental states. Thoughts can therefore exist unaccompanied by any other sorts of intentional items, whereas speech is parasitic on thinking. In this spirit, Searle maintains that the intentionality of thinking is intrinsic, as opposed to the derived intentionality of speech. For a person's meaning something cannot "stand on its own in the way that [a person's] believing" something, for example, can (29).

By itself, however, this appeal to expressing raises more questions than it resolves. We cannot explain the primacy of thought over speech simply by saying that speech acts express thoughts unless we know what such expressing consists in, and why it exhibits the asymmetry it does. Parallels between verbs of propositional attitude and illocutionary act help little here. Without some actual account of what the relation of expressing involves, 'expressing' is hardly more than a label for whatever it is that explains and underlies that parallelism.

Moreover, a satisfactory explanation of expressing, for these purposes, must show how the expression of mental states by speech results in the primacy of thought. Not every asymmetric relation implies that one of the relata is somehow more fundamental than the other. And the primacy that such expressing implies must square both with the interdependence of thought and talk, and with the greater intersubjective accessibility of speech. An account of expressing which met these conditions would be able to explain satisfactorily the kind of primacy thought has, and why it has it.

The account that immediately suggests itself relies on causal connections. On this proposal, a speech act expresses a mental state just if, in addition to having the right propositional content and illocutionary force, the mental state is causally necessary for the speech act to occur. If thought does cause speech, speech cannot occur without thought. So thought is causally prior to speech. This suggestion fits nicely with our having better inter-subjective access to speech. Effects are often more readily observable than their causes, and we often learn much about the nature of causes by studying effects. The direction of epistemic primacy is often opposite to that of causation.

A causal account of expressing also squares well with the interdependence of thought and speech. For one thing, we not only learn about causes from examining their effects, but also about effects from looking at their causes. More important, however, that interdependence is due chiefly to the impossibility of breaking out of the family of illocutionary acts and propositional attitudes when we explain any of its members. The explanations that tie us to that family, however, are not causal, but conceptual explanations. They are explanations of what it is to be this sort of illocutionary act or that kind of propositional attitude. The situation is similar with many natural processes and properties—for example, with colors. We cannot explain what it is, phenomenally, to be some particular color except by reference to other colors. But this is a limitation on what we can explain conceptually, not causally. Causal explanations of color are of course possible that do not themselves refer to color. Similarly, the conceptual interdependence of thought and speech has no bearing on what causal links may connect them.

But an even stronger case can be made for a causal account of expressing. There are features of our commonsense views about the relation between thinking and speech that it is hard to see how to explain except by reference to the idea that speech acts causally depend on the mental states they express. Mental states often go unexpressed, and utterances occur that express no mental state, for example, when they consist in words that someone merely recites without thought. And a person may think two distinct things, each expressible by the same words, and yet use those words to express only one of the two mental states. So mere accompaniment of a thought by a corresponding speech act does not suffice for the speech act to express that very thought. Expressing is not like resembling. A speech act does not express a mental state just by having the right properties. There must also be some specific tie between the two.

Moreover, we must explain a person's performance of a speech act by appeal, in part, to that person's being in that particular mental state. Indeed, genuine speech acts, as opposed to mindlessly recited utterances, presumably cannot even occur in the absence of mental states that have the same content and a corresponding mental attitude. If mental states do not cause the speech acts that express them, these features of the relation between thought and speech must remain puzzling.

Sometimes we speak of a speech act's expressing a belief without meaning to talk about any particular mental state that the speech act expresses. Instead, we may mean only that the speech act has the propositional content that such a belief would have. To describe a statement as expressing the belief that it's raining may be just a way of describing it in terms of its propositional content, and not by reference to some particular state of believing. In such cases, we do not speak of any particular state of believing: Rather, we mention a type of mental state, some token of which the speech act presumably expresses.[7]

Similar remarks hold for other kinds of illocutionary force. We can describe a speech act as expressing the expectation that it will rain, for example, without meaning to describe it in terms of any relation it bears to a specific mental state. We may, instead, only mean to specify the content and force of the speech act. That is, we may mean to say no more than that it is the kind of speech act that expresses mental states that are, in turn, instances of expecting it to rain. We can, in general, say that a speech act expresses something in order to describe its relation to a mental state, or just simply to say what kind of speech act it is.

An example of the second way of speaking occurs when we say that a speech act expresses a proposition. Here it is plain that we mean only to be talking about the speech act and its content, and not also about any mental state. Typically when we mean to be specifying the character of the speech act, we say what kind of force it has as well, as when we say the speech act expresses the belief that it's raining or the expectation that it will. But it will be convenient, and help us avoid ambiguity, to speak of expressing a proposition when what we mean is not to speak of a particular mental state that the speech act expresses, but to say what its force and content are.

The distinction between expressing mental states and expressing propositions will assume special importance in subsequent sections. For now it is enough to note that the distinction can help dispel whatever doubts we may have about whether speech acts are caused by the mental states they express. These doubts stem from the correct observation that we can describe a speech act as expressing beliefs, expectations, and the like without implying anything about a causal tie with some particular mental state. But to so describe a speech act is to do no more than specify, somewhat obliquely, its propositional content and illocutionary force. By contrast, when we actually do say that a speech act expresses some particular mental state, we cannot explain the tie to an individual mental state unless we presuppose a causal connection.

An illustration of how this distinction can help us understand the relation between speech and thought arises in connection with the point, just noted, that mere accompaniment is not enough for a speech act to express a mental state. Suppose I speak the words 'It's raining' and, at the same time, have the thought that it's raining. It may seem impossible not to conclude that my words express my thought. In ordinary cases, of course, my words do just that. But this is not always the case. All that we can be certain of, in the case under consideration, is that my words have the same propositional content as my mental state, that is, that my words express the proposition that my thought expresses. We cannot conclude that my words also express that very act of thinking. It is possible to use 'thought' in such cases to refer either to the act of thinking or to its propositional content, and confusion can result.

Once again, Moore's paradox helps out. In section 2, we used Moore's paradox to show that expressing a mental state is distinct from reporting that one is in it. Only if the two kinds of speech acts are distinct can we avoid construing sentences like 'It's raining but I don't believe it is' as contradictions. But, if speech acts could occur in the absence of corresponding mental states, the opposite difficulty would arise in trying to explain Moore's paradox. For then not only would Moore's-paradox sentences not be contradictory; we would be unable to construe them even as being in any way problematic. If speech acts need not be accompanied by corresponding mental states, there would be no difficulty about one's simply asserting that it's raining, but that one has no corresponding belief.

Accordingly, to explain Moore's paradox we must suppose that speech acts cannot occur in the absence of corresponding mental states. And, as noted above, the best explanation of this regularity is that speech acts are causally dependent on such mental states. So the best explanation of Moore's paradox will imply a causal connection between speech acts and the mental states they express. This should not be surprising. If the connection between the two conjuncts of Moore's paradox were conceptual or analytic, we would once again have difficulty in explaining why such sentences are not contradictions. Indeed, we would have difficulty even in explaining why parallel problems do not affect sentences like 'George says that it's raining, but he doesn't believe it is'. Such sentences are slightly odd, but we can explain such oddity as due not to any analytic connection between speech and thinking, but to our background knowledge that speech always does express mental states. Our background knowledge about speech and thought is so well entrenched as to be taken for granted. And any sentence that offends against such a well-entrenched piece of background knowledge will strike us as somewhat odd.[8]

One might insist, however, that Moore's paradox, and the regularity that speech acts cannot occur without corresponding mental states, both reflect the very way we think about mental states and speech acts. And if so, one might object, causal connections could not underlie or help explain either the paradox or that regularity. Causal connections are empirical, and so could have gone unknown by us. Thus they cannot, on this objection, underlie our conceptions about things.

But it is hard to imagine that the causal ties that bind speech to thought could escape our notice. And causal connections often do influence the ways we conceive of things. Indeed, if there were any area in which causal ties would be likely to shape our conceptions, it would presumably have to do with our conceptions about the mental. For our introspective awareness of our own mental states very likely detects, or at least is somehow responsive to, such causal ties. And our introspective sense that such causal ties obtain will doubtless affect how we think about speech and thought.

Accordingly, it is arguable that a causal account of the expression of thought by speech does all one could ask to explain the primacy of thought. In particular, it seems to do justice to Chisholm's point that, although thinking would be intentional without speech, speech without thought would not be. It is natural to take subjunctive and counterfactual conditionals to express causal connections. So we can understand Chisholm to be claiming that, whereas speech is causally dependent on thought, no opposite dependence obtains. Similarly, we can offer a causal construal of Searle's observation that "I couldn't make a statement without expressing a belief or a promise without expressing an intention" (28), and Vendler's (1972) insistence that speech involves "putting thought into words" (44).

But one can concede that thought causes speech without also accepting that this causal tie is all there is to the primacy of thought. And all three authors insist that thought is primary in a way that is not at all causal. Thus Chisholm (1958) maintains that "[t]he meaning [i.e., content] of thoughts is to be analyzed in terms of the meaning of language, and not conversely" (529). Vendler echoes this claim when he writes that "the full analysis of the [notion] of saying something . . . inevitably involves a concept which . . . essentially corresponds to the Cartesian idea of thought" (4). Searle too endorses this asymmetry with respect to analyzability: "the direction of logical analysis is to explain language in terms of [the] Intentionality [of the mental]." We can, Searle concedes, use language heuristically to explain the intentionality of mental states, but "the relation of logical dependence is precisely the reverse" (5). Thus "speakers' meaning should be entirely definable in terms of . . . forms of Intentionality that are not intrinsically linguistic" (160). These claims suggest that, though thought and speech may belong to the same conceptual family, within that family thought has pride of place. If so, the primacy of thought will not be solely causal, but conceptual as well. And if thinking is conceptually prior to speech, perhaps we can understand the nature of speech only by reference to thought.

An initial response to these claims would be that what looks like conceptual priority is actually just a causal connection that is so much a part of our lives that we tend to take it for granted. Truths so ordinary as to be axiomatic often seem conceptual. Such conflation of causal with conceptual matters occurs in more mundane areas. It may seem to be a conceptual truth that the sky is blue simply because its terrestrial color figures so centrally in our everyday picture of how things are. Similarly, we so take it for granted

that thought causally underlies speech that this primacy can seem conceptual. Any causal connection that we take to be partially constitutive of our
picture of reality will seem to us, as Hume observed, to be grounded in our
concepts.

4. INTRINSIC INTENTIONALITY

We may fairly regard the foregoing considerations as placing upon advocates
of conceptual primacy the burden of showing that the priority they champion
is actually conceptual, and not due simply to causal connections. But it is
arguably precipitous to convict the advocates of conceptual primacy of
conflating platitudinous truths with conceptual connections. Even if such
confusion does underlie claims of conceptual priority, we must address directly the reasons these authors have given for such primacy. To sustain a
claim of conceptual primacy one must show that there is some feature of
thought or speech we cannot explain or do justice to if the priority of thought
is only causal. So we must see whether any such feature exists. The insistence
on conceptual priority seems to be based largely on the idea that the intentionality of thinking, unlike that of speech, is in some way intrinsic. If
thinking is intrinsically intentional and speech is not, then perhaps some
conceptual connection exists between thinking and intentionality that does
not hold between intentionality and speech.

The idea that thoughts, unlike speech acts, are intrinsically intentional
has considerable intuitive appeal. But, to evaluate the force of that intuition,
we must first specify what it means for intentionality to be intrinsic. One way
to articulate the idea of intrinsic intentionality is by appeal to an apparent
disparity between speech and thought with respect to physical realization.
Speech acts cannot occur except by virtue of the production of specific
sentences, which have determinate phonetic features. And sentences can
occur parrotingly, as when one mouths words without meaning anything by
them. So words with determinate phonetic features can occur without exhib-
iting any intentionality, whereas the opposite is impossible. Words cannot
manifest intentionality without having phonetic properties, or other equivalent observable properties.

By contrast, there may seem to be no properties that thinking must
manifest in order to be intentional. Indeed, introspection suggests that, aside
from causal or temporal properties, thoughts have no properties whatever
except for their mental attitudes and propositional contents. As Vendler puts
it, there is no "mental 'medium' " (44), in the way words are the medium of
speech. So it may be tempting to conclude that thought, unlike speech, is
intrinsically intentional.

Perhaps Vendler is right that thinking involves nothing we would call
a "mental 'medium'." But the intentional character of thoughts no more

exhausts their nature than the intentionality of speech acts exhausts theirs. Thoughts have a multitude of causal ties, some to mental events and others to nonmental, physical events. The best explanation of these causal connections is that thoughts themselves have certain nonmental, physical properties. For even if one regarded the intentionality of thoughts as some sort of nonphysical property, it would be mysterious how thoughts could be connected causally with physical states and events unless thoughts also have physical properties that enable these connections to hold. There is presumably nothing about the intentional properties themselves that explains these causal connections. So thoughts must have some nonintentional properties that make the connections possible. And, if thoughts must have nonintentional properties, physical properties that pertain to the central nervous system are easily the most likely candidates. Indeed, it is reasonable to insist, with Searle (160, and chap. 10; see also Searle 1980), that the mental as we know it has a biological basis. We can most readily explain how biological processes could issue in thinking if we suppose that thoughts themselves have suitable physical characteristics.

Like Donald Davidson's (1970) well-known argument for anomalous monism, the foregoing argument infers to what we must assume if we are to explain causal interactions between mental and bodily events. But the present argument circumvents Davidson's difficult thesis about the impossibility of psychophysical laws. It may seem that the use of this thesis as a premise enables Davidson to establish a conclusion stronger than the foregoing argument can reach. Anomalous monism is the claim that intentional mental events are actually physical events, whereas the conclusion reached here, that intentional mental states have physical properties, may seem to be weaker. But the difference is illusory. The bodily events that Davidson holds are identical with mental events are physical only because they have physical properties that enable them to have causal ties with various physical events that are not also mental events. And that is exactly the conclusion reached here about mental states that interact causally with nonmental, bodily events. No reductive materialist thesis is at issue here, any more than in Davidson's argument. And, in the absence of independent argument to the contrary, there is no reason why events cannot be both mental and physical.[9]

Thoughts need not, of course, have the same physical character or embodiment in order to have the same content and mental attitude, any more than speech acts must use the same words to mean the same things. In both cases, physical properties determine intentional character only in the context of a larger systematic structure. Patterns of sounds are speech acts only relative to a language. Similarly, it is reasonable to expect that individual neural events have specific intentional properties only relative to the overall operation of the central nervous system. So, even if it is wrong to regard the physical characteristics of thinking as a "mental 'medium'," there is no significant disanalogy on this score between thought and speech. Both have nonintentional, physical characteristics. We must therefore look elsewhere for justification of the idea that the intentionality of thought, unlike that of speech, is in some way intrinsic.

Searle explicitly notes that thinking resembles speech in having physical "forms of realization." He also points out that no one-to-one correspondence exists between those forms of realization and the intentional character of particular speech acts (15). Nonetheless, he holds that the intentionality of thought is "*intrinsic*," as opposed to the "*derived*" intentionality of speech acts (27). And, since he speaks of thought as being prior to speech in respect of logical dependence and definability, we must see whether his distinction between being intrinsic and derived supports a view that thought has a kind of primacy that goes beyond mere causal priority.

The intentionality of mental states is intrinsic, according to Searle, because "[t]o characterize them as [mental states] is already to ascribe Intentionality to them." By contrast,

> speech acts have a physical level of realization, *qua* speech acts, that is not intrinsically intentional. There is nothing intrinsically Intentional about the products of the utterance act, that is, the noises that come out of my mouth or the marks I make on paper.

Speech acts, on Searle's view, are "entities such as marks and sounds that are, construed in one way, just physical phenomena . . . like any other" (27). The intentionality of mental states is intrinsic because to describe them as mental states is to describe them as intentional. The intentionality of speech acts is derived because a description in terms of their physical realization implies nothing about intentionality.

But, as Searle concedes, intentional mental states, no less than speech acts, have some physical realization or other. So we could use that physical realization to refer to those states if only we knew enough neurology. And, even knowing no neurology, we can describe mental states in terms that imply nothing about intentionality. We can, for example, describe them as states that cause particular pieces of behavior. Searle is right that we seldom talk about our thoughts except in terms of their intentional character, whereas we do have occasion to describe illocutionary acts in nonintentional terms. But to sustain his distinction between intrinsic and derived intentionality, it is not enough that physical realization should sometimes figure in characterizations of speech, but seldom if ever in descriptions of thinking. Searle must present some way in which physical realization matters to the very nature of speech, but not to that of thought.

We can, of course, describe speech acts in terms of their intentional character, rather than their physical realization. Indeed, that is our standard practice. To specify a speech act in *oratio obliqua* is to characterize it solely by reference to its illocutionary force and propositional content. Moreover, direct discourse describes speech acts not just in terms of their physical realization, but by way of intentional character as well. A direct quotation tells us not only the exact words, but the content and illocutionary force as well.

So to evoke his intuition about the derived intentionality of speech, Searle must get us to abstract from the intentionality of speech, and focus only on its physical realization. Accordingly, he puts his point in terms of "the products of the utterance act[s]" (27), rather than in terms of illocutionary acts. The marks and sounds we produce when we use language can also occur in the absence of any intentional speech act. And, even when we produce marks and sounds by way of performing such speech acts, it is implausible to regard the marks and sounds on their own as bearers of intentionality. But the actual speech acts, by contrast, are intentional. For speech acts all have propositional content and illocutionary force. Indeed, no nonintentional utterance would count as an illocutionary act. The disparity Searle sees between the intentionality of thought and that of speech is illusory.

If we focus on speech acts simply as marks and sounds, we need to explain how those physical phenomena could have intentional character. Since marks and sounds are not always intentional, those which are must somehow derive their intentionality. The "problem of meaning," Searle suggests, is the question of how they do so. But Searle also holds that no parallel problem obtains for thinking (27; cf. 167ff. and Chisholm 1958, 524). This is puzzling, since, as Searle concedes, thinking also has physical realization. So the question will also arise about how neural states of the relevant kind can have intentional character. The explanation of how speech acts derive intentionality from mental states cannot help support the idea that the intentionality of thought is different in status from that of speech.

It is important here to distinguish two problems. Some marks and sounds are intentional and others are not. So the question arises of what it is about those marks and sounds which are intentional in virtue of which they differ from those which are not. But there is a second, distinct question about how it is possible for such things as marks and sounds to have intentional character at all.

The two questions are sometimes run together, perhaps in part because it is tempting to try to answer both by appeal to intrinsic intentionality or the primacy of thought. But the two questions are plainly distinct. One cannot even pose the question about what it is that makes intentional marks and sounds intentional unless one brackets the other question, about how it is that sounds and marks can have intentional character in the first place.

Even if one believed that we can satisfactorily resolve the question of how sounds and marks can be intentional by appeal to some connection that those marks and sounds have with mental states, a parallel problem automatically arises all over again with the mental states themselves. If marks and sounds can be intentional because of their causal tie with mental states, what is it that can explain how neural events themselves can be intentional? Unless there is some way to block this question, the appeal to mental states only postpones the problem; it does not resolve it.

Moreover, the question about how marks and sounds can be intentional is not the only problem about speech acts that has a parallel for mental states. Once we see that a question arises about how neural events can be intentional, the question will also arise of what makes intentional neural events intentional. The two parallel problems that apply to mental states are arguably more pressing, since there is no move we can make, analogous to the move from speech to thinking, that can help out here. The existence of these problems may make it tempting to postulate that the intentionality of mental states is, after all, intrinsic. If we can see no place that such intentionality could come from, must we not conclude that it is intrinsic, rather than derived? But without some independent reason to hold that the intentionality of mental states is intrinsic, and an explanation of what being intrinsic amounts to here, such a claim is merely the label for the problem, and cannot provide a solution.

This line of reasoning does illustrate, however, how we may be misled by not taking account of the difference between expressing mental states and expressing propositions. Suppose we set out to explain how marks and sounds can be intentional by appeal to their expressing mental states. We may then seek to make an analogous move for the case of mental states themselves, and propose to explain how neural events can be intentional on the basis of their expressing propositions. But the analogy here is unfounded. To say that some event, whether neural or linguistic, expresses a proposition is just to say that it has propositional content. To explain how neural events can be intentional by reference to their expressing of propositions is viciously circular.

Again, if we focus on speech acts simply as marks and sounds, one might claim that sentences are relevantly unlike thoughts. For we can individuate sentences without reference to intentionality, but we cannot do so with thoughts. When we do individuate a sentence independently of its intentional character, however, we leave open what speech act the sentence realizes, just as we presumably would have to be noncommital about what mental properties a mental state has if we were to specify the state in solely neural or causal terms. No disanalogy occurs here that can sustain Searle's claims about intrinsic and derived intentionality. And, in the absence of some other way to substantiate such claims, we cannot use them to support the thesis that thought is conceptually prior to speech, and not just prior causally.

One can occasionally get the impression from what Searle writes that he believes the derived intentionality of speech acts not to be genuine intentionality at all. If one focuses on mere sounds and marks, rather than on actual speech acts, it is understandable that one might reach that conclusion. But genuine speech, as Searle himself explicitly insists (e.g., 169), is more than simply sounds. Speech is the producing of sounds in those cases in which the very acts of producing have propositional content and illocutionary force.

Similarly, by saying that the intentionality is intrinsic, Searle may mean only to say that its intentionality is not a relational property. Thinking is intrinsically intentional because, on this construal, its having some propositional content and mental attitude does not consist in its bearing some relation to something else. Speech would thus have derived intentionality, presumably because, on Searle's account, its having any sort of intentional character consists in its bearing a certain relation to the thoughts it expresses. On this suggestion, derived intentionality is relational, or extrinsic, intentionality.

But there is a difference between what it is for something to have a particular characteristic and what causes it to have that characteristic. Mental states cause speech acts to be intentional; without those causes, speech acts would not be intentional at all. But it does not follow that the intentionality that speech acts do have consists in a relation they bear to those causes, any more than the movement of a billiard ball consists of a relation that billiard ball bears to the cause of that motion. Indeed, many thoughts are caused either by other thoughts or by nonmental, bodily states such as perceptual stimulations. But we do not conclude that the intentionality of these mental states consists in their bearing some relation to their causes.

As noted in section 3, Searle holds that a person's meaning something cannot "stand on its own in the way that [a person's] believing" something can (28). For

> John couldn't mean that p unless he was saying or doing something *by way of which* he meant that p, whereas John can simply believe that p without doing anything.... In order to mean that p, there must be some overt action. (P. 29)

But these considerations do not help show that thinking exhibits a kind of intentionality different either in kind or in status from the intentionality of illocutionary acts. To explain these observations, all we need is the causal tie between speech and thought. Meaning something cannot "stand on its own" because meaningful performances depend causally on the mental states those performances express.

5. INSINCERE SPEECH

Insincere speech provides a pivotal test case for any account of the relation between speech and thought. When we speak insincerely, the connection between what we say and what we think is not the same as it is when our speech acts are sincere. So to give an account of the intentional character of insincere speech requires that we examine our commonsense, presystematic intuitions about the connection between thought and speech, and the justification we have for holding them.

According to Searle, "a lie or other insincere speech act consists in performing a speech act, and thereby expressing an Intentional state, where one does not have the Intentional state that one expresses" (10). Vendler makes a similar claim. Insincere speech, he holds, expresses thoughts that the speaker does not have (1972, 37).

These remarks, if correct, cast doubt on our being able to give a causal explanation of what it is for a speech act to express a mental state. If speech acts express mental states even when we speak insincerely, no causal relation can, in general, connect speech acts with the mental states they express. Speaking insincerely is just saying something we do not think. So when we speak insincerely, there is no corresponding mental state to cause our speech. Moreover, if we cannot construe expressing causally, we must find some other way to explain what it is for speech to express thought. And the most inviting alternative may very likely seem to be an explanation that postulates some conceptual relation that ties speech acts to the mental states they express. Having to appeal to this sort of conceptual tie would, in turn, lend support to the idea that thought is conceptually prior to speech, rather than causally prior. So how we account for insincere speech has an important bearing on whether a causal explanation of expressing can succeed. We must therefore examine Searle's and Vendler's claims about insincere speech acts in some detail.

At first sight, the view that insincere speech expresses thoughts that the speaker does not have may seem intuitively compelling. Some such view is roughly what most people would say, if asked to explain insincerity. But on closer scrutiny it is unclear that we can make clear sense of that idea. For one thing, if a person who lies lacks the mental state that the lie is supposed to express, how can the lie express it? One person's lie cannot express another's mental state. So it is no help that somebody else may have the relevant thought. The claim that insincere speech acts express mental states that the speaker is not in implies that such speech acts express mental states that do not even exist. How this can happen is a mystery. And it is a mystery whatever one's view may be about what it is for speech to express thinking. 'Expresses', in 'This speech act expresses that mental state', does not generate a referentially opaque context.

This puzzle becomes particularly acute if one holds, with Chisholm, Vendler, and Searle, that speech acts derive their intentionality from the mental states they express. If no such mental state exists, an insincere speech act will, in Chisholm's phrase, have no source of intentionality. The speech act will therefore end up having no intentional character. Searle and Vendler both explicitly reject this conclusion. As Searle puts it, an "insincere speech act . . . express[es] an Intentional state" (10). But it is hard to see how, on their view, one can avoid it. Nor, it will emerge, should we want to.

Searle notes that "it is possible to perform a statement while lying." To think otherwise is simply to "confuse the intention to make a statement with the intention to make a true statement" (168). For to make a statement, Searle tells us, is to represent things in a certain way. And one can readily choose to represent things as being different from the way one takes them to be. These sensible observations seem to capture accurately the way we ordinarily talk about stating, asserting, and the like. But Searle also holds that one cannot "make a statement without expressing a belief" (28). And this claim lands us back with the problem about how speech acts can express nonexistent mental states.

A satisfactory account of intentionality must somehow resolve these opposing pressures. It must explain our inclination to regard insincere speech as having intentional character, and thereby explain Searle's observation that, at least in casual usage, we speak of the telling of lies as cases of making statements. But it must also recognize the oddness of insisting that insincere speech acts derive their intentionality by expressing mental states that do not exist.

As noted earlier, we sometimes use such terms as 'thought' and 'belief' not to speak of mental states, but to describe the propositional content of a mental state, at least as long as the mental attitude or illocutionary force is appropriate. This ambiguity will help explain the force of the intuition that lies express beliefs that the speaker does not have, while enabling us to avoid puzzles about nonexistent mental states. For we need not interpret that intuition to mean anything about the expressing of mental states by insincere speech acts. Rather, the intuition may amount just to the idea that even insincere speech acts have propositional content. There is no problem about attributing to an insincere speech act propositional content that is shared by none of the speaker's mental states. To say such a speech act has propositional content is simply to talk about the semantic character of the sentence in question. Propositional content in such cases results not from any connection the speech act has with any mental state, but from the way people typically use the relevant form of words in the language in question. In the case of insincere speech, one's speech act does, indeed, express a belief, but only in the sense of expressing a proposition. It does not express a mental state. So the intuition that even lies express beliefs tells us nothing about the relation of thinking to speech.

Insincere speech is intentional, therefore, only in an attenuated way, by virtue of the role other tokens of the relevant sentence types play in the language. Indeed, although sincere speech is intentional in just the way mental states are, insincere speech exemplifies something we can reasonably think of as derived, as opposed to intrinsic, intentionality. Insincere speech acts count as intentional only because they are token of a type of utterance, other tokens of which are intentional directly.

When somebody lies, we tend to describe that person as stating something, albeit insincerely. And, as argued in section 2, all speech acts express mental states. These natural observations seem to imply, once again, that insincere speech expresses nonexistent mental states. But when one tells a lie, one states something only in the somewhat attenuated sense that the sentence that one utters is a token of a type we ordinarily use to make statements. The sentence token itself is not used, in such a case, with the illocutionary force of a statement. Only thus can we avoid the conclusion that we always believe the content of our lies. Parallel remarks hold for insincere speech acts that seem to exhibit other types of illocutionary force.

The foregoing considerations suggest that a promising account of insincere speech would model it not on the making of statements at all, but on the rehearsed speech of actors. Actors are not typically in the mental states of their characters, and so the utterances of actors do not normally express those mental states. Rather, actors in effect pretend to perform illocutionary acts of stating, requesting, commanding, and the like, in accordance with the demands of their parts. Actors may even pretend to think the thoughts of their characters. But pretending to think something is not the same as actually thinking it, any more than pretending to say something is the same as actually saying it. If an actor does happen to think something that corresponds to the lines of a character, it is incidental to the actor's uttering those lines. When an actor playing Macbeth utters 'I have done the deed', he does not believe he has killed Duncan. Nor does the actor, himself, actually say he has. If an actor did not merely pretend to say and think the things the character is supposed to think and say, but actually said and thought those things, we would very likely question the actor's sanity.

Similarly, when we speak insincerely, we simulate illocutionary acts. Pretense in this case is not the real thing. When one lies, one intends to deceive. Moreover, we intend our lies to deceive not just about whether our utterances are true, but also about what we actually believe. We try to get our audience to accept that we believe our utterances are true, when we really believe they are not. Thus we hope to deceive our audience into thinking that we are trying to tell them something, and to keep from them that we are, instead, trying to deceive them. It is at best a misleading ellipsis to say in such a situation that the speaker has made a statement. To insincerely make a statement is to pretend to make a statement.

It is convenient to use the words for ordinary illocutionary acts to describe what happens when we speak insincerely. For, except in special cases such as lying, there is simply no term for the insincere counterpart of an illocutionary act. So, when context makes it clear what we are saying, it is an innocuous shorthand to speak of an insincere simulation of a prediction or question, for example, as a prediction or question, without qualification. But it hardly follows that insincere speech consists of the actual performance of illocutionary acts. We also use such language to describe the speech of actors, without meaning thereby to elide the difference, in that case, between pretense and the real thing. Indeed, we even speak as though the fictional character an actor plays were a real person. Similarly, we describe, by an equally innocuous courtesy, both insincere utterances and lines recited in playacting as though they were genuine illocutionary acts.

One reason why insincere speech acts may seem more like actual illocutionary acts than like the speech of actors is that an actor's goal is just the simulation itself. When we speak insincerely, our goal is not primarily to simulate, but to deceive. And it may seem natural to describe speech as simulated only when the speaker's goal is simply to simulate. But this difference in how we ordinarily describe things is not telling. Even if the aim of insincere speech is primarily to deceive, simulation is a means to that end. We simulate ordinary illocutionary acts, hoping, in part, to get our audience to think that we have performed the real thing.

Sometimes insincere speech acts have much the same effects as their sincere counterparts. As Austin (1962) observed, we tend to count an insincere promise as a case of promising, though we also regard it as infelicitous (16). But we do not count such cases as promising because the sincere and insincere cases are the same kinds of speech act. Partly we do so because, as just noted, we have no special word for insincere promises. But we also do so because we hold people responsible the same way, whether they speak sincerely or not. If I try to deceive you in thinking that I am sincerely promising something, I am responsible for my speech act just as though I had been sincere. The same holds for lying. You will hold me responsible for my lie just as if it had been a sincere statement. But responsibility is not a reliable guide to how we classify things, and insincere lies and promises are not genuine statements and promises.

We can reinforce this conclusion by turning again to the comparison between insincere speech and the rehearsed speech of actors. Though we hold each other responsible for our insincere speech acts, nobody would think of holding actors responsible for the illocutionary acts of their characters. We cannot explain this difference as due to the simulated nature of actors' speech, since we do hold people responsible for simulations. The difference here is rather that actors have no intention to deceive, and context makes it unlikely that their utterances would fool anybody. We peg responsibility to considerations of intention and probable outcome, not to types of speech act.

It might appear that insincere speech acts are genuine speech acts because the insincerity, properly understood, attaches not to the speech act but to the speaker. If I insincerely tell you something, the insincerity is a matter of my state of mind in speaking to you. My act of telling you something is perfectly genuine, one might urge. In telling you what I believe is false, however, I myself am not being genuine. But this objection trades on a false dichotomy about how adverbs operate. If I do something carelessly or willfully or generously, both my action and I are careless or willful or generous. Similarly with my saying something insincerely. Nor, of course, can we infer from my saying something insincerely that I say it, *tout court.* Adverbs do not, in general, detach.

One might maintain, however, that whatever the case about insincere speech, genuine speech acts can occur unaccompanied by corresponding mental states. And if this is so, the causal account of expressing will not do justice even to sincere speech acts. Thus one might urge that, in general, we can choose to say whatever we please, regardless of what our mental states may be. One can, for example, say "The moon is made of green cheese," or even "2 + 2 = 5," if one so chooses. And plainly there is no question of one's believing these things. But saying such things would not be genuine speech acts. Rather, if one uttered such things, they would simply be cases, once more, of simulated assertion. If somebody were to produce these words, we would automatically assume either that the person somehow misspoke, or that no real illocutionary act was in question. We would either try to construe the utterance nonliterally or ironically, so as to allow us to attribute to the speaker some genuine speech act, or we would simply dismiss the person's words as not worth taking seriously. As Vendler (1972) stresses, saying something, in such cases, is the saying of words and sentences, and "none of these 'sayings' will carry an illocutionary force" (25; cf. 93).

When one speaks sincerely, what one says corresponds to some mental state that one is in. Indeed, this is what it is for a speech act to be sincere. We can only understand a speech act to be sincere if we suppose that the speaker is in a corresponding mental state. But in section 2 we argued that all speech acts express corresponding mental states. Moreover, the argument there did not hinge on whether or not the speech act is sincere. It was simply that if speech acts did not invariably express corresponding mental states, we could not explain why we cannot coherently assert, for example, 'It's raining but I don't believe it is'. Thus, suppose that not all speech acts do express corresponding mental states. Then there should be no difficulty about my saying that it's raining, albeit perhaps insincerely, and immediately going on to say that I don't believe it. But I cannot do so. Accordingly, the conditions for a speech act's being sincere coincide, in this respect, with the conditions for something to be a genuine speech act at all. In both cases, one's speech must express a corresponding mental state. As Vendler and Searle both note, for something to be a genuine speech act, "one must mean what one says" (Vendler 1972, 26; see Searle, 69).

If I say that it's raining and go on to say also that I don't believe it, I simply betray my insincerity. That, one might object, is all that goes wrong in Moore's paradox. Indeed, Moore himself seems, at one point, to offer such a diagnosis (1942, 542-43). But this suggestion cannot be correct. There is nothing problematic about one's speaking insincerely in ways that betray one's insincerity. The difficulty with Moore's paradox is not just that one avows one's own insincerity. If I say it's raining and go on to say I don't believe it, I tell you that I did not mean what I said, that is, that I did not actually perform the illocutionary act that I purported to. Only if sincerity is presupposed in the performing of genuine illocutionary acts can we explain why this is so.

These considerations may seem to provide the basis, after all, for insisting on a conceptual connection between thinking and speaking. It is part of our conception of genuine speech acts that they express actual mental states that the speaker is in. We do not count any utterance that does not do this as an actual speech act. But how we conceive of things and how we classify them often does not reflect any analytic connections among our concepts, but only well-entrenched background knowledge about those things. We do not count as water anything that is not H_2O, nor anything as gold whose atomic number is not 79, though no analytic or conceptual truths underlie our refusal to do so. And, as noted in section 3, there are strong theoretical reasons to conclude that no conceptual or analytic truth explains the connection between thought and speech, either. If it did, we could not explain why 'George says it's raining but does not believe it is' is not a contradiction.

Once again, focusing on speech as simply marks and sounds misleads. If speech acts were merely utterance acts, the kind of simulation that occurs both when actors recite lines and when we speak insincerely would not make the resulting utterance a case of simulated speech. Whatever simulation there is in such cases, genuine uttering does occur. But mere uttering does not suffice for the performance of an illocutionary act. Uttering can and indisputably does occur unaccompanied by any illocutionary force.

6. EXPLAINING INTENTIONALITY

The foregoing discussion of insincere speech not only helps sustain a causal account of expressing and of the primacy of thinking over speech. It also has a useful implication about the status of the distinction between expressing mental states and expressing propositions. Unless we invoke that distinction, we cannot explain our commonsense, presystematic intuition that insincere speech expresses thoughts we do not have. The distinction between expressing mental states and expressing propositions is therefore not the product of abstruse considerations of limited application. Rather, our double use of words for mental states, to refer to mental states or to their propositional content, emerges in the course of the very attempt to understand the ways we ordinarily describe thinking and speaking.

We may expect, therefore, that the distinction between expressing mental states and expressing propositions will be central to any satisfactory explanation of the relation between thinking and talking. This turns out to be so. In particular, once we see that thoughts, beliefs, and the like may be either mental states or propositions, we are in a position to explain the powerful temptation we have to subscribe to claims about the intrinsic intentionality of thinking, and the noncausal priority of thought over speech.

Propositional content is simply intentional content. Such content cannot, presumably, occur on its own, since it is only a characteristic of concrete mental states or speech acts. We conceive of such content by abstracting from particular mental states or speech acts that have that content. Since we conceive of propositional content in abstraction from particular mental states and speech acts, it is independent of any other aspect of speech or thinking. So a thought, in the sense of a propositional content, is no more than some intentional property or other. Thoughts, understood as propositional contents, are therefore as intrinsically intentional as anything could be.

Conflating thoughts in the sense of mental states with thoughts in the sense of propositions can therefore lead us, albeit tacitly, from the unexceptionable but unexciting claim that propositions are intrinsically intentional to the interesting but indefensible claim that mental states are. We saw in section 5 that the only way to explain Searle's and Vendler's views about insincere speech is to appeal to such a conflation. It is therefore a natural speculation that this conflation also underlies their insistence on the intrinsic intentionality of mental states.

The same ambiguity also helps explain the pull of the idea that thought is prior to speech in some noncausal way. Thoughts in the sense of propositional contents are, indeed, conceptually prior to speech. We cannot understand what it is for something to be a genuine speech act unless we understand what it is to have propositional content. But mental states are, in this respect, no different from speech. We can understand what it is for something to be an intentional mental state only if we grasp what it is to have propositional content. If one fails to notice that 'thought', 'belief', and the like can refer either to mental states or to propositional contents, one might conclude, wrongly, that thoughts in the sense of intentional mental states are also conceptually prior to speech acts.

One might question, however, whether a causal account of expressing, and of the primacy of thought, enables us to deal satisfactorily with all the questions we have about the relation of speech to thinking. In particular, a causal account might seem not to do justice to our sense that we must in some way make reference to thinking in order to explain the intentionality of speech. And if it does not, perhaps we must appeal to some sort of noncausal primacy of thought or to intrinsic intentionality.

In section 4 we distinguished two questions about intentionality. One was the problem of how such things as marks and sounds can have intentional character at all. A parallel problem arises, as we saw, for mental states if those states have physical characteristics. But we can bracket that concern and ask the more limited question of how those sounds and marks which are intentional differ from those which are not. What is it that accounts for the intentionality of those speech events that do have intentional character? Again, we can pose a parallel problem about thoughts, if thoughts have physical realization. What is it in virtue of which those neural events which are intentional differ from those which are not?

These various questions are not entirely independent. How we answer each will influence, to some extent, the way we can answer the others. But it is tempting to try to answer the question of how intentional marks and sounds differ from those which are not intentional in strictly causal terms. The intentional cases are caused by mental states that have the same content and a corresponding mental attitude, whereas the nonintentional cases are not. Indeed, not only do mental states cause corresponding speech acts; they presumably also cause those speech acts to have whatever properties they have that enable them to be intentional. So mental states actually cause those performances to be intentional. Mental states are thus a causal source of intentionality.

Mental states not only cause speech acts and other behavior. They also cause other mental states. Indeed, we can introspectively discern that this is so. We are often aware that thinking one thing causes us to think another. And, introspection aside, it would be strange if mental states had such a multitude of causal connections with various bodily events but not with one another. Suppose, then, that the mental states that cause speech acts also cause them to have the intentional character they have. There is no reason to think that the way mental states cause speech acts differs from the way they cause other mental states. So it will be equally natural to suppose that when one mental state causes another it also causes that other mental state to have the particular intentional character it has.

These considerations have consequences about intrinsic and derived intentionality. We cannot reasonably hold that the intentionality of thoughts is intrinsic if those thoughts are causes of other thoughts, but derived if they are effects. For one thing, many mental states are both causes and effects of other mental states. Moreover, the distinction between intrinsic and derived intentionality does not, intuitively, fit with any difference we know to hold between those mental states which cause other mental states and those which are caused. But mental states are sources of intentionality for speech acts in just the way they are sources of intentionality for other mental states. In each case, they confer intentionality by causing the speech act or other mental state to have whatever properties it has in virtue of which it has its intentional character. So we cannot sustain a distinction between intrinsic and derived intentionality by appeal to the idea that thinking is the source of the intentionality of speech.

The causes of speech acts are not themselves speech acts. And this may seem to provide a disanalogy between thought and speech that would allow us to characterize as intrinsic even the intentionality of those thoughts which are caused by other thoughts. Thus we might urge that something has derived intentionality only when it is different in kind from the source of its intentionality. Speech acts have derived intentionality, on this suggestion, but those mental states whose intentionality is caused by other mental states would nonetheless have intentionality that is intrinsic. But there is no reason to think that whether something differs in kind from the source of its intentionality matters to whether the intentionality of that thing is intrinsic or derived. Indeed, to determine whether it does matter, we would need some independent grasp of the distinction between intrinsic and derived, which we lack.

In any case, there are other reasons to reject the idea that something is intrinsically intentional if it causes something different in kind to be intentional. Some mental states are caused by other mental states. But some are caused by nonmental, bodily events, such as perceptual stimulations of various kinds. We cannot conclude that such causes of mental states have intrinsic intentionality, since these causes are not even intentional. The distinction between intrinsic and derived intentionality cannot, therefore, enable us to explain anything about the intentionality of speech that we cannot explain by the causal theory of expressing.

Even if we can give a satisfactory causal explanation of how those sounds and marks which are intentional differ from those which are not, there is also the problem about how such things can have intentional properties at all. As already noted, this problem arises equally for thoughts. Since we can, in principle, describe mental states in neurological terms, we must explain how such things as neural events can be intentional.

If mental states had no nonintentional, physical features, no such problem would arise for them. There would be nothing to being a mental state other than being intentional. To ask how it is possible for mental states to be intentional would then be just to ask how intentional states can be intentional. We can sensibly formulate the problem of how mental states can be intentional only if we can describe such states in nonintentional terms.

Accordingly, if mental states had no nonintentional, physical features, the status of the intentionality of thought would differ from that of the intentionality of speech. For speech acts plainly do have nonintentional, physical features. So the question about how such things can be intentional would still arise for speech, though not for thought. This disparity would justify our thinking of the intentionality of thought as intrinsic. We could maintain that something is intrinsically intentional just if the question about how it can be intentional does not arise. Intentionality is intrinsic, on this suggestion, when it is pure—unaccompanied and undiluted by nonintentional properties other than causal connections and spatiotemporal location.

But, if mental states with no nonintentional features did exist, we would need to explain how such states are possible. And we would have the additional burden of explaining how such states can interact with nonintentional bodily states. So, even though no question would arise about how mental states can be intentional, we would have to explain at least as much if the intentionality of mental states were pure, in the foregoing sense, as we would if mental states have properties other than their intentionality. The idea that we need not explain something's being a certain way if its being that way is all there is to it is an unfortunate legacy of Aristotle's unmoved mover, adapted with disastrous results in Descartes's postulation of a substance whose sole nature is thinking. And the idea of thoughts that have no characteristics other than their intentionality is no more than a further adaptation from substances to states.

Indeed, the difficulties we encountered above in discussing the question of how speech acts come to be intentional suggests that there may well be something misconceived about that question. There is no difficulty about how speech acts get to be intentional if that question is simply the question of how speech acts come to exist. But if, instead, it is the question of how intentionality can come to belong to states or events that also have physical properties, the situation is less clear. But the correct answer here must, in any case, depend on what it is for something, whether speech act or mental state, to be intentional.

Insofar as we want to explain how such things as speech acts and mental states can be intentional at all, and what it is for them to be so, we should expect that whatever understanding we gain about the intentionality of one will help us explain the intentionality of the other. We can come to understand why intentional performances occur at all, and why particular ones do, by appeal to the mental states that cause them. But there is no reason to expect more help from mental states than from speech acts about what it is for something to be intentional, or how it is possible for particular kinds of states and events to be so. A satisfactory explanation of intentionality must accordingly stress the interdependence of thinking and speech, rather than rely on the causal asymmetry between them.

Indeed, it is arguable that speech acts inherit their intentionality from mental states by being part of an overall causal network that involves those mental states. If so, mental states would be responsible for the intentionality of speech acts in a way that goes beyond merely causing their occurrence. But even this line of argument cannot help establish any priority of thought over speech. Whatever considerations might go to show that the intentionality of speech acts derives from their having suitable causal connections with other intentional states and events would also apply to the mental states themselves. Moreover, it is arguable that what makes something a mental state is its causal connections with other mental states and with behavior and sensory stimulation. (See David Lewis [1966 and 1972] for an especially effective defense of this view.) If so, then not only is the intentionality of speech acts due to their causal connections with thoughts; the intentionality of mental states themselves consists, in part, in the causal relations those states bear to speech acts. Accordingly, the causal network containing both mental states and speech acts will yield no priority for either thought or speech beyond the circumstance that mental states cause speech acts.

7. INTENTIONALITY AND SELF-AWARENESS

If the preceding argument is correct, we have no reason to suppose that our ability to explain intentionality will be impaired if we forgo claims about intrinsic intentionality and the noncausal primacy of thinking. There is, however, a difference between speech and thought which does support a kind of primacy for thinking, and which also helps explain the force of the intuition that thoughts are intrinsically intentional. We are ordinarily aware, without having to infer or observe anything, of what we say and of much of what we think. This awareness, moreover, is not couched in terms of the physical features of either our mental states or our speech acts. We are, of course, ignorant of the physical realizations of our thoughts. And our automatic awareness of what we say typically involves no conscious attention to the words we use. We are often fully aware of what we have said, but either cannot recall our actual words or must concentrate to do so. And, even when we do know what words we spoke, we rarely determine what we have said on the basis of our knowing those words.

Now insincere speech aside, whenever we say anything we are in a mental state with the same propositional content and some corresponding mental attitude. Since we do not normally determine what we say by inferring it from our words, the best explanation of our effortless awareness of what we say is that we are aware of what we think, and aware that we gave expression to that mental state in speech. Accordingly, our automatic awareness of what we think is less direct, by two steps, than our awareness of what we think.

A number of factors nicely corroborate this account. Notoriously, we have comparative difficulty remembering the content of our lies. We more often make mistakes about our lies than we do about our sincere statements, and they sometimes slip our mind altogether. Our account predicts this. When we lie, we get no help from any automatic awareness of the mental state our speech expresses, as we do with sincere speech acts. For no such mental state exists. Accordingly, our awareness of our lies is more studied than our awareness of sincere speech, and we would therefore expect, correctly, that we would have a harder time accurately recalling them.

Moreover, although others must sometimes tell us how to take their words, we need never to do this for ourselves. We know automatically what construction to place on our own words. The best explanation of this knowledge is, again, that we come to be aware of what we say by being aware of what mental state our words express. We may, of course, occasionally have to do something like figure out what our own words amount to. If my thought is confused, I may have to sort out what, as we might put it, I really meant by my words. (I am grateful to Richard Mendelsohn for insisting on this point.) But even then I do not so much figure out what it was I said as figure out what I should have said. And, if I am inarticulate, or misspeak, then my words may be confused even though the thought itself is not. Indeed, I can presumably distinguish cases in which my thought is confused from those in which only my words are, precisely because my awareness of my mental state makes me aware of how to take my words.

Cases of misspeaking and confusion aside, the match between thinking and speech typically seems flawless. Our words make clear the content of our thoughts, and illocutionary verbs indicate our mental attitudes. Nonverbal behavior, by contrast, seems unable to keep up with the detailed and subtle accuracy with which speech conveys thought.[10] We tend even to attribute to our thoughts the syntactic structure of the speech acts that express them, though it is plain on reflection that we have no reason to suppose that thoughts have much of the complex compositional structure that sentences exhibit.

The best explanation of this sense of seamless match between thought and speech is, once again, that we know what we say because we know in the first instance what we think, and know also that our speech expresses those thoughts. The situation is analogous with nonverbal behavior. We are also automatically aware of our nonverbal actions; we do not have to watch ourselves, or infer from anything, to know what actions we perform (see Searle, 88-89). This awareness results from our knowing what we intend, and knowing that our actions have given expression to those intentions.

If our awareness of what we say derives in this way from our awareness of what we think, we can understand why thought should seem to be prior to speech in a way that goes beyond the fact that mental states cause speech acts. This additional primacy of thought is due to our deriving our awareness of what we say from our awareness of what we think. Such primacy is basically an epistemic matter. But it also has to do with the nature of thinking itself. Our automatic awareness of our own mental states is presumably possible, in part, because of the nature of mental states themselves. And our ability to rely on that awareness to know our own speech acts doubtless tells us something, in addition, about the connection between thinking and speech.

These considerations can also help explain the appeal of the idea that the intentionality of thought is intrinsic. There are two ways we learn about what we say: by our awareness of the thought expressed, and by our words. But, without neurological knowledge far beyond anything we now have, we can have no such double access to our own thoughts. So, for practical purposes, we can regard the intentionality of mental states as if it were intrinsic. For, given our current knowledge, our thoughts have no nontrivial properties other than those we apprehend introspectively.

Since our automatic awareness of what we say relies on our automatic awareness of what we think, but not conversely, we can sustain an epistemic version of the primacy of thought, and a pragmatic version of something resembling the intrinsic intentionality of thought. But things would be different if intentional mental states were necessarily conscious, as some have urged. On the present suggestion, the primacy of thought and the intrinsic character of its intentionality stem from the way we are conscious of our own intentional states. So, if that consciousness is a necessary feature of our intentional states, then the primacy of thought and the intrinsic character of its intentionality would arguably be necessary as well. Indeed, if intentional states are necessarily conscious, it is reasonable to suppose that such consciousness would be a necessary consequence of the intentionality of such states. Such intentionality would then itself arguably be a necessary feature of the states that have it.

These considerations provide one more way to explain the appeal that such primacy, and intrinsic intentionality, have for us. One who holds with Descartes that thinking is necessarily conscious[11] will very likely also insist on the primacy of thought, and the intrinsic intentionality, which seem both to follow from such necessary consciousness. Indeed, the idea that intentional states are invariably conscious plays a pivotal role in Vendler's (1972) discussion (50, 155, 161, 191-93), though Searle equally explicit disavows that idea (2).

Searle's disavowal is undoubtedly correct. Many, indeed probably most, of our intentional mental states occur outside our stream of consciousness. Nor is there any reason to suppose that any necessary connection does hold between a mental state's being intentional and its being conscious. It is arguable, instead, that a mental state's being a conscious state is just a matter of its causing a roughly contemporaneous, second-order thought to the effect that one is in that very mental state.[12] Indeed, this account of what it is for a mental state to be a conscious state is intuitively most compelling in the case of intentional mental states. On this view, the consciousness of intentional states is indeed the result of intentionality. But although such consciousness is a result of intentionality, it is not a result of the intentionality of the states that are conscious. Rather such consciousness is due to the intentionality of the second-order thoughts about such states. Moreover, although neither thought nor speech is conceptually prior to the other, on this view, those thoughts which are conscious do have a primacy that is doubly causal. For that primacy consists in those thoughts' causing both the speech acts that express them and the higher-order thoughts that make them conscious.

Notes

1. In what follows I use 'mental state' to refer only to intentional mental states, thereby excluding nonintentional mental states such as bodily sensations. I also frequently use 'thought' not to refer just to beliefs and similar mental states, but as a generic term for intentional mental states of any sort, regardless of the kind of propositional attitude they exemplify.

2. Since the problem about these sentences is assertibility, and assertion is an expression of thought, these considerations suggest an inviting way to explain Descartes's insistence that "this statement, 'I am, I exist' is necessarily true every time it is produced by me, or mentally conceived" (Adam and Tannery edition [1964-75], 7:25; cf. Haldane and Ross translation [1931], 1:150). I argue for such an account of the *cogito* at the end of "Will and the Theory of Judgment" (1985) and, more extensively, in "Will, Mind, and Method in Descartes" (1983, sec. 4).

3. This view suggests a way to help clarify Wittgenstein's (1953) well-known but puzzling suggestion that we construe such sentences as 'I am in pain' not as straightforward assertions that one is in pain but as expressions of that pain, on a continuum with such natural expressions as crying (part 1, sec. 244). Whatever reasons we have to hold that 'I believe it's raining' expresses my belief rather than reporting it should equally help to show that 'I am in pain' expresses, rather than reports, my pain. But see Wittgenstein's distrust of this analogy at part 1, sec. 317.

4. Vendler (1972, chaps. 2 and 3) and Searle (1983, 166, 175; 1975, passim). Unless otherwise indicated, page references to Searle are to the 1983 work.

5. On analyticity and synonymy, see *From a Logical Point of View* (1980), chap. 2. Quine formulates the analogous difficulty about intentional mental states in *Word and Object* (1960), 221.

   In "Talking about Thinking" (1973) I argue that the difficulty about intentional mental states is insuperable. See also Davidson, "Thought and Talk" (1975), on the interdependence between speech and thinking.

6. Descartes: *Discourse* V (Adam and Tannery edition [1964-75], 6:56-59; Haldane and Ross translation [1931], 1:116-18) and Correspondence (Adam and Tannery edition [1964-75], 4:573-76, 5:275-79; Kenny translation [1970], 206-8, 243-45). Aristotle (1984): *de Interpretatione*, 16a3-8.

7. On this distinction, see Sellars, "Notes on Intentionality" (1964) and *Science and Metaphysics* (1968, chap. 3). See also Sellars's *Science, Perception and Reality* (1963), esp. chaps. 2, 5, and 11.

   It will be evident throughout that the present discussion has been strongly influenced by Sellars's important and penetrating work on these topics.

8. Searle also appeals to Moore's paradox to show that all speech acts must express mental states. He writes: "It is logically odd, though not self-contradictory, to perform the speech act and deny the presence of the corresponding Intentional state" (9). But he leaves unexplained

what this logical oddity consists in and how, if it is logical, it differs from analyticity. In any case, since Searle takes the oddity to be logical and not a feature of the relation between thinking and speech, it is unclear why, on his account, there is no difficulty with third-person counterparts.

9. The difference Davidson's denial of the possibility of psychophysical laws does make is that it enables him to claim a priori status for his conclusion about mental events. On there being no difficulty about events being both mental and physical, see my "Mentality and Neutrality" (1976).

It may be worth noting that, since the present argument makes no appeal to laws or regularities that causally connected events must fall under, it is compatible with Searle's contention that causal connections involving intentional states can obtain in the absence of a corresponding universal regularity (135; see 117 and chap. 4, passim).

10. Compare Wittgenstein's observation: "Suppose we think while we talk or write—I mean, as we normally do—we shall not in general say that we think quicker than we talk, but the thought seems *not to be separate* from the expression" (part 1, sec. 318; emphasis in original).

11. For example: "it is not possible for there to be in us any thought of which, at the moment it is in us, we are not conscious" (*Fourth Replies:* Adam and Tannery edition [1964-75], 7:246; cf. Haldane and Ross translation [1931], 2:115).

12. I have defended this view in detail in "Two Concepts of Consciousness" (forthcoming) and "Thinking That One Thinks" (1980).

References

Austin, J. L. 1962. *How To Do Things with Words.* Cambridge, Mass.

Aristotle. 1984. *The Complete Works of Aristotle,* edited by Jonathan Barnes. Princeton.

Chisholm, Roderick M. 1958. "Intentionality and the Mental." In *Minnesota Studies in the Philosophy of Science,* vol. 2, edited by Herbert Feigl, Michael Scriven, and Grover Maxwell, 507-39 [in part, correspondence with Wilfrid Sellars]. Minneapolis, Minn.

Davidson, Donald. 1970. "Mental Events." In *Experience and Theory,* edited by Lawrence Foster and J. W. Swanson, 79-101. Amherst, Mass.

Davidson, Donald. 1975. "Thought and Talk." In *Mind and Language,* edited by Samuel Guttenplan, 7-23. Oxford.

Descartes, Rene. 1931. *The Philosophical Works of Descartes,* translated by Elizabeth S. Haldane and G. R. T. Ross. Cambridge.

Descartes, Rene. 1964-75. *Oeuvres de Descartes,* edited by Charles Adam and Paul Tannery. Paris.

Descartes, Rene. 1970. *Descartes' Philosophical Letters,* translated by Anthony Kenny. Oxford.

Lewis, David. 1966. "An Argument for the Identity Theory." *Journal of Philosophy,* 63:17-25.

Lewis, David. 1972. "Psychophysical and Theoretical Identifications." *Australasian Journal of Philosophy,* 50:249-58.

Moore, G. E. 1942. "A Reply to My Critics." In *The Philosophy of G. E. Moore,* edited by Paul Arthur Schilpp, 533-677. LaSalle, Ill.

Moore, G. E. 1944. "Russell's 'Theory of Descriptions'." In *The Philosophy of Bertrand Russell,* edited by Paul Arthur Schilpp, 177-225. New York.

Quine, W. V. 1960. *Word and Object.* Cambridge, Mass.

Quine, W. V. 1980. *From a Logical Point of View.* Cambridge, Mass.

Rosenthal, David M. 1973. "Talking about Thinking." *Philosophical Studies* 24:283-313.

Rosenthal, David M. 1976. "Mentality and Neutrality." *Journal of Philosophy* 73:386-415.

Rosenthal, David M. 1980. "Thinking That One Thinks." Typescript.

Rosenthal, Daivd M. 1983. "Will, Mind, and Method in Descartes." Typescript.

Rosenthal, David M. "Two Concepts of Consciousness." Forthcoming.

Rosenthal, David M. 1985. "Will and the Theory of Judgment. In *Essays on Descartes' Meditations,* edited by Amelie O. Rorty. Los Angeles.

Searle, John R. 1975. "A Taxonomy of Illocutionary Acts." In *Minnesota Studies in the Philosophy of Science,* vol. 7, edited by Keith Gunderson, 344-69. Minneapolis, Minn.

Searle, John R. 1980. "Mind, Brains, and Programs." *Behavioral and Brain Sciences* 3:417-57 [with commentaries and response].

Searle, John R. 1983. *Intentionality: An Essay in the Philosophy of Mind.* Cambridge.

Sellars, Wilfrid. 1963. *Science, Perception and Reality.* London.

Sellars, Wilfrid. 1964. "Notes on Intentionality." *Journal of Philosophy* 61:655-65 [reprinted with minor changes in Wilfrid Sellars, *Philosophical Perspectives,* Springfield, Ill., 1967, 308-20].

Sellars, Wilfrid. 1968. *Science and Metaphysics.* London.

Vendler, Zeno. 1972. *Res Cogitans.* Ithaca, N.Y.

Wittgenstein, Ludwig. 1953. *Philosophical Investigations.* New York.

Intention and Evaluation

MICHAEL BRATMAN

I form the intention this morning to go to a symphony concert tonight, though I leave till later a decision as to which symphony concert, how to get there, and so on.[1] What can we say about the conditions under which such an intention is rational?

A natural and common view is that I must think so acting best, or at least better than other considered alternatives, or—if I have taken account of probabilistic considerations in the way systematized by decision theory— that so acting would "maximize expected utility" or something similar. On this view, there is a certain kind of positive evaluation of an option, A, that settles the question of whether to A, and that is always present (at least implicitly) when one rationally intends to A.[2]

This view is grounded in a plausible, though highly idealized model of rational intention formation. On this model, I form an intention to act in response to some practical question as to what to do in a certain situation. To resolve this practical question, I consider those alternatives I think will be open in the situation and assess their comparative pros and cons. This involves determining what features my performance of the different alternatives may have and assessing, to the extent possible, both the merits of these different features and their likelihood, given that I so act. In this way I *evaluate* these different options, in a broad sense of 'evaluate' that allows for reference to moral, prudential, aesthetic, and other values and norms. I thereby arrive at a positive evaluation in favor of one of the options, an evaluation that settles what to do. I judge that so acting would be best, would maximize expected utility, or something similar, and so form an intention so to act.

We thus have a plausible model of intention formation that supports an equally plausible condition on rational intention. Nevertheless, this view—

that a rational intention to A requires such a positive evaluation of A—is threatened by a basic difference in the logic of intention and evaluation.

Recall my intention this morning to go to a symphony concert tonight. It seems evident that by virtue of having this intention I also intend to go to a concert tonight. Of course, I do not *merely* intend to go to a concert tonight; and it might be misleading for me *just* to tell you that I intend to go to a concert. Still, it seems clear that I *do* intend to go to a concert: by virtue of having the more specific intention to go to a symphony concert, I also have the more general intention to go to a concert.

There is a general principle at work here. Though my argument does not require an airtight formulation of this principle, it will be useful to have a rough-and-ready version in hand. Let us distinguish the *act types* of going to a symphony concert and going to a concert from a *particular act* of going to a symphony concert. Let us further assume some version of Davidson's conception of the individuation of particular acts,[3] so that a particular act will generally be an instance of many act types. A particular act may be an instance of going to a symphony concert, going to a concert, and going somewhere. Let us say that an *act type* A *is a more specific version of act type* B just in case it is necessary that any act of type A also be an act of type B, but not vice versa. Going to a symphony concert, then, is a more specific version of going to a concert, since any act of going to a symphony concert will be an act of going to a concert, but not vice versa.

Now, something like the following seems true:

> *Principle of Derived Intention:* If I intend to A, and I know that act type A is a more specific version of act type B, then I intend to B.

To illustrate with a different example, if I intend to speak loudly to you then I intend to speak to you, since I know that speaking loudly to you is a more specific version of speaking to you.

We can be confident that some version of this principle—perhaps refined in ways not relevant here[4]—is correct, because there is a clear sense in which an intention to go to a concert tonight is *weaker than* an intention to go to a symphony concert tonight. My intention to go to a symphony concert shares with a mere intention to go to a concert a commitment to going to a concert, but adds to this the *further* commitment to going to a *symphony* concert. In being more determinate, the more specific intention is stronger than the more general intention.

With the principle of derived intention in hand, let us turn to the evaluation that is supposed to accompany rational intention. My rational intention to go to a symphony concert requires a judgment that going to a symphony concert would be best (would maximize expected utility). By the principle of derived intention, my intention to go to a symphony concert brings with it an intention—which we may presume also to be rational—to go to a concert. So, on the theory, I must also judge that going to a concert would be best (would maximize expected utility).

The problem is that there is no guarantee that by virtue of accepting the former evaluation (in favor of going to a symphony concert) I will be in a position to accept the latter evaluation (in favor of going to a concert). To see this, recall the sorts of considerations that, according to the model, shape the evaluations required for rational intention. Begin with going to a symphony concert. I know there are various cases of my going to a symphony concert tonight that are compatible with my beliefs. In some the concerts are better, in some I get rained on in transit, and so on. In judging that going to a symphony concert would be better than, say, going to a movie, I assess, to the extent possible, both the likelihoods and the merits of these various different cases of symphony concert-going.

Now consider going to a concert. Again, I know there are various different cases of concert going that are compatible with what I believe. So I try to assess both the likelihoods and the merits of these different cases. But now the crucial point is clear: *as the type of action being assessed becomes more general, the scope of the evaluation gets larger.* The assessment of my going to a symphony concert is concerned with versions of symphony concert-going that are compatible with my beliefs. The assessment of my going to a concert will *in addition* concern versions of concert going that are not versions of symphony concert-going. So there is no general guarantee that if I think that going to a symphony concert would be best (would maximize expected utility) I will be in a position to conclude that going to a concert would be best (maximize expected utility). If there are versions of *non*-symphony concert-going that are compatible with my beliefs, and that I dislike, I might well be in the position of accepting the former evaluation but rejecting the latter.

Suppose, for example, I am in a country with whose language I am unfamiliar. I know there is a real chance that I will stumble into a rock concert while trying to go to a symphony concert, given the difficulty of reading the posters. Because I dread rock concerts, this possibility leads me to assign a lower expected utility to going to a concert than to going to a symphony concert. So though I think that going to a symphony concert would maximize expected utility, I do not think the same of going to a concert.

Nevertheless, if I rationally intend to go to a symphony concert, I intend—presumably, rationally—to go to a concert. This follows from the principle of derived intention and the obvious assumption about my knowledge. So I have a rational intention—to go to a concert—that need not be accompanied by a judgment that so acting would be best (maximize expected utility).

It is clear what has gone wrong. An intention to act in the more general way is a weaker commitment to action than an intention to act in the more specific way. But, on the model, the evaluation of the more general type of action concerns a wider range of cases than does the evaluation of the more specific type of action. So the move from the more specific to the more general evaluation is not guaranteed. Such evaluations do not mirror the logic of intentions; so we cannot expect rational intention always to be accompanied by such evaluations in favor of what is intended.[5]

We could block this problem if we could assume that rationally to intend to go to a symphony concert I must believe that if I go to a concert it will be a symphony concert. Given this belief, versions of concert going that are not versions of symphony concert-going would be incompatible with my beliefs. So my dislike for such non-symphony concert-goings would not block a positive assessment of my going to a concert. So we would no longer be in danger of violating the principle of derived intention.

This reply depends, however, on a strong assumption about the beliefs required for rational intention, an assumption that I find questionable. It seems to me that I may rationally intend to go to a symphony concert even when I suspect that I might stumble into a rock concert by mistake. Further, this strong belief assumption seems to go beyond what is initially suggested by the model of intention formation that led to the evaluative condition on rational intention being examined here. That model does require me to see my A-ing as a real possibility for me rationally to intend to A. But that does not mean that I must suppose that I will A. So it would be at least a surprise if it turned out that only by embracing such a strong belief condition could one defend this evaluative condition.[6]

Still, some philosophers[7] have argued that an intention to A always involves a belief that one will A. If this were so, then we could assume that my rational intention to go to a symphony concert involves the belief that if I go to a concert it will be a symphony concert, and thereby avoid conflict with the principle of derived intention. As I have indicated, I am skeptical of such a belief condition on intention. However, rather than try to settle the matter here, let me just state my conclusion as follows: so long as we do not accept some such strong belief condition on rational intention, we cannot suppose that rationally to intend to A I must think that A-ing would be best, would maximize expected utility, or something similar.[8] The relation between rational intention and evaluation is more complex than this.[9]

Notes

1. This paper has been influenced by comments from John Dupre, John Etchemendy, John Fischer, David Hilbert, Julius Moravcsik, Christopher Peacocke, John Perry, Kwong-loi Shun, and Holly Smith. I want to thank them for their help. Work on this paper was partially supported by the Center for the Study of Language and Information.

2. Donald Davidson holds a version of this view in "How Is Weakness of the Will Possible?" and "Intending," both in *Essays on Actions and Events* (New York, 1980). Davidson

goes on to *identify* intention with such an evaluation. (See esp. "Intending," 99.) The criticism I will offer here of the cited evaluative condition on rational intention also applies to this identification of intention and evaluation. See below, note 8. I discuss these papers of Davidson's in further detail in my "Davidson's Theory of Intention." *Essays on Davidson: Actions and Events,* edited by Bruce Vermazen and Merrill Hintikka (New York, 1985).

3. See many of the papers in Davidon, *Essays on Actions and Events,* in particular "Agency," "The Logical Form of Action Sentences," and "The Individuation of Events."

4. For example, we may want to add to the antecedent the further condition that I know that it is under my control whether or not I *B*. This would help avoid the problem posed by an example of Gilbert Harman's: knowing I am about to sneeze, I might intend to sneeze softly, without intending to sneeze.

5. Perhaps at this point it will be suggested that the evaluative judgment that must accompany my rational intention to *A* is the judgment that there is a highly specific version of *A*—one that is determinate in all respects that must be decided upon for me to *A*—that is optimal. Such a view would not be threatened by the principle of derived intention; for a highly specific version of going to a symphony concert will be a highly specific version of going to a concert. The problem, however, is that such an existential judgment does not settle the question of whether to *A*. If I have this existential judgment but despair of finding out, in the available time, *which* highly specific version of *A* makes my judgment true, I still might rationally decide to refrain from *A*. In such a case, my rational intention to refrain from *A* would not be accompanied by the cited existential judgment.

6. It would certainly surprise Davidson, who emphatically rejects such a belief condition. See "Intending," 94-95.

Note that one might develop the model of deliberation by stipulating that options evaluated be ones whose successful performance the agent thinks can be guaranteed just by deciding so to act. (This is roughly what David Lewis does in "Causal Decision Theory." *Australasian Journal of Philosophy* 59 (1981): 5-30, esp. 7.) But then we cannot suppose that rational intentions are limited to the options evaluated in such deliberation; we cannot, that is, unless we accept a strong belief condition on rational intention.

7. Notably, H. P. Grice, "Intention and Uncertainty," *Proceedings of the British Academy* 57 (1971):263-79; and Gilbert Harman, "Practical Reasoning," *Review of Metaphysics* 29 (1976):431-63. See also Harman's useful, further reflections on this issue in "Willing and Intending," forthcoming in *Philosophical Grounds of Rationality,* edited by R. Grandy and R. Warner.

8. An important consequence of this is that we must reject at least one major component of Davidson's theory of intention. We cannot accept *both* his rejection of a strong belief condition on intention, *and* his identification of an intention to *A* with an "all-out" judgment that *A*-ing would be best.

9. A conjecture worth examining—though I shall not do so here—is that this more complex relation is roughly as follows: If I rationally intend to *A* then either I judge *A* best or there is some more specific version of *A* such that I judge *it* best. Note that such a conjecture gives up the idea that there is a single type of evaluative judgment in favor of *A*-ing that settles the question as to whether to *A* and that always accompanies a rational intention to *A*.

I hope it is clear that I do not take myself to have argued against more complex accounts along such lines. My target has been only the simpler view that a rational intention to *A* requires the judgment that *A* would be best, as well as the further (Davidsonian) attempt to identify an intention to *A* with such an evaluation. The problem raise by the principle of derived intention may not block other, more complex views. But it is a problem that should be taken into account in the defense of such views.

Rationality and the Range of Intention

HUGH J. McCANN

One of the guiding principles of nearly all recent action theory has been that all human action is in some way founded upon intentional action. For despite the truism that many of the things we do are unintentional, it does seem to be the case that when we perform unintentional actions, we characteristically also perform some act that is both intentional and ontologically related to the act that is unintentional. If, for example, I fail to notice a stop sign while driving and unintentionally go through it, I will still have driven through the intersection intentionally. And while it might be unintentional on someone's part to poison the dinner guests, one might intentionally serve them fresh mushrooms that turn out to be poisonous. How one interprets these cases depends in part, of course, on what one takes the ontological relation between the pairs of actions to be. If with Davidson we believe that driving through the intersection and going through the stop sign are in fact identical, then we might claim, as Davidson has, that an event counts as an action just in case there is some description under which it is intentional.[1] If, on the other hand, we adopt Goldman's fine-grained view of action, we might try treating unintentional actions as arising only out of intentional ones. Poisoning the guests would be seen as generated by the more basic, intentional act of serving them fresh mushrooms, and similarly for running the stop sign and driving through the intersection.[2] On either approach, however, the study of intention—what it is, and what is involved in our having an intention—becomes a paramount concern of action theory. For the presence of an intention of some kind would seem to be required for a person to perform an action at all, even where much of what is done is not intentional.

Now if, as I believe, this is a correct understanding of the matter, one thing that is needed is a way of distinguishing those things done in a particular episode of action that are intentional from those that are not. And I think we get at least the beginning of a correct distinction if we claim that for an action A to be intentional, the agent must intend to A at the time of the action. Indeed, such a point might appear too obvious to bear mentioning: surely to say a person A'd intentionally is to say that the person undertook the act in question either for its own sake, or as a means to another act that was intended. And either way, it would appear that the person intended to A. Thus intending to A appears to be a necessary condition of A-ing intentionally. But however obvious this may appear, it has been denied. For some theories of intention restrict intentions to actions that one believes one will perform, or at least to actions that one does not believe one will not perform. Unfortunately, however, we sometimes succeeed in performing actions that, at the time they are undertaken, are at best doubtful of success. Such actions appear to be intentional, but by the theories in question they cannot be intended. If such theories are correct, therefore, it is not a necessary condition of an action's being intentional that the agent intend to perform it. I think they are incorrect, and that is what I shall argue in what follows. If the argument is successful, we shall have gained in two ways. First, we shall have avoided what promises to be a most intractable problem: namely, how to distinguish between actions none of which are intended, but some of which are intentional and some not. Secondly, we shall have learned more about what is required in order that it be rational for an agent to have an intention.

I

One way in which belief requirements come to be imposed on intending is through theories that treat intending as itself consisting partly in a state of belief. A number of now classic treatments of intention are at least implicitly reductionistic in this way. Rather than viewing intention as a unique kind of state or event that precedes or accompanies action, they hold an action to be intentional provided just that it is appropriately caused. As a first approximation, the cause may be viewed as a desire to do A, together with a belief that one will do A if one does B, the means.[3] On this kind of view, there is really nothing to the state of intending to A other than the presence of the cognitive and conative states that are held to cause the action. Intention simply consists in the desire and belief in question. Now to be sure, the conditional belief that one will do A if certain means are employed, even though required for intending on this account, is not yet an unconditioned belief that one will A, or even that there is a likelihood that one will. A stronger requirement can, however, be generated, as will be seen if we consider some objections against the view just described and how the reductive analysis of intention might best be shored up to meet them.

The main problem with this view is simply that to try to reduce intention to a mere desire, together with a belief as to the means by which it might be fulfilled, is to capture none of the sense of resolve and purpose usually associated with intention. Consider this: it is doubtless true that most every philosopher alive believes that if he or she were to shoot any other philosopher right between the eyes, that philosopher would die. Should we conclude, however, that in the present state of philosophy, half the conditions are met for every philosopher to intend to kill all the others? Not on this basis, at least. Suppose moreover that I, who have the above belief, also have a philosophical rival I would dearly love to kill. Do I thereby intend to kill that rival? No. Such desires are cause for regret, but not for alarm. Indeed, I would suspect that the vast majority of actions people would very much like to perform are actions means for which are known and are readily available. But we simply don't have intentions that correspond to the vast majority of our desires, even the strong ones.

If this is correct, then the attempt to reduce intention to a pair of cognitive and conative states will not work unless one or the other side of the analysis is strengthened. Which side should it be? It might be thought that the conative side is the likeliest candidate. Perhaps it should be claimed that the desire involved in intention is the agent's strongest or "definitive" desire, what he or she desires to do all things considered—or, switching gears a bit, what the agent judges to be best overall. There are, however, a number of reasons for rejecting this alternative. For one thing, to the extent that it appeals to ordinary or commonsense concepts of desire and the like, it relies on notions that simply won't bear this kind of weight. It is just not the case that when a person tells us she thinks a certain action would be best, we can conclude that she intends to do it: she might intend to do what she wants. On the other hand, if she tells us a certain action is the one she most wants to perform, she might not intent that either: she might intend to do what she thinks is best.[4] Now of course people who say things like this without the relevant intentions might be deceived about themselves. But there really is no evidence of that, and until it is forthcoming we should not bend the facts to fit the theory. If this is right, then the only way we can introduce terms like "definitive desire" is to treat them as technical terms and explicate them in such a way as to make clear that they cannot be cashed out in terms of ordinary notions like strongest desire, or judgment as to what is best overall. The problem then, however, is that we are apt not to produce a reductive account of intention at all, but rather one that simply reintroduces the unanalyzed notion covertly, under the guise of a technical term.

A second difficulty with seeking to strengthen the desire component alleged to belong to intention has to do with the possibility of incompatible desires. It is well known that people can have incompatible desire, even strong ones. Thus I might strongly desire to go to Europe next summer, and also strongly desire to go to the Rockies. There is nothing irrational in this, nor need I even bother to do anything about it, especially if I don't think I have time to take a vacation anyway. I might, however, address myself to the matter, and adjudicate between the desires. Indeed, that is precisely one of the things intention formation is for. I can decide which desire I will follow by forming the intention, say, to go to Europe. But then having an intention seems to go beyond having a desire. Note, moreover, that in deciding to go to Europe I do not *relinquish* my desire to go to the Rockies. That desire may persist just as strongly after my deliberation as before. There is, then, nothing irrational about having conflicting desires, nor is adjudicating between them a matter of relinquishing one or the other.

Contrast this situation to that with regard to intention. It is hard in ordinary circumstances even to imagine someone having conflicting intentions and knowing about it. To be sure, one could have such intentions and not know it: I might intend to go to my daughter's graduation on the third Wednesday in June, and also intend to join my brother on a fishing trip he has planned for June 16th, not realizing that the third Wednesday is the 16th. Once I do realize this, however, it is almost as though a sort of mental paralysis sets in. For if I have these intentions I should be planning how to carry them out; yet, because they conflict, any planning I do in one direction undercuts my planning in the other direction. My intentions, which ought to guide my behavior, provide no guide because they push me in opposite ways. Unlike the situation with conflicting desires, this is an irrational one. If I am to be rational, I must adjudicate between these intentions: I must decide which of the two to carry out. And in this case, to adjudicate *is* to relinquish one of the intentions. If, say, I decide to attend the graduation and abandon the fishing trip, then I no longer intend to go fishing.

To have conflicting intentions, then, is in normal circumstances to be in a state that is irrational, a state one is rationally bound to adjudicate. We shall have to consider below whether there can be exceptions to this rule, but certainly it holds in most cases. The same, however, is not true of desires: conflicting desires are never irrational, no matter what their strength.[5] Moreover, to adjudicate between conflicting intentions is to abandon one of them, but to adjudicate between conflicting desires is not. Prospects for saving the reductive analysis of intention by strengthening the desire component are, then, not bright. Intention is something much more strongly bound by strictures of rationality than desire. What about prospects for strengthening the belief component? In fact, they are somewhat brighter, at least on the surface. For one thing, certainly most cases of intending are cases where the agent believes that he or she will perform the intended act. Moreover, conflicting beliefs, like conflicting intentions, are irrational. People who discover that they are in a state of conflicting belief are apt to be in just as much a quandary as people who find they have conflicting intentions—the more so, perhaps, if the beliefs in question are about themselves and what they will do. If, then, the belief component in the analysis of intending to A can be strengthened to a categorical one—a belief that one will A, rather that just that one will A if certain means are employed—the sense of resolve associated with intention might be more closely approximated and the irrationality of conflicting intentions accounted for.

There is a natural way of strengthening the belief requirement in just the manner these considerations would suggest. The sort of belief cited earlier, that one will A if one performs some action B as a means, is in order only if A, the intended action, is the sort of act that requires a means to begin with. But not all actions are this way. Action theorists are widely agreed that for us to be able to act at all, there have to be basic actions, actions that are not done *by* doing anything else. Thus, someone who intends to A must also intend to perform some basic action, which will initiate the sequence of events A requires. And surely the appropriate belief to ascribe to the agent about this basic action is simply that he *will* perform it.[6] No *if*-clause is needed, for there is no means he need adopt. But then we can see that it is reasonable to require that he believe that he will do A as well. For if he believes that he will perform whatever action is basic in his plan to do A, and also that if he does perform this act, he will perform those further acts he seeks to accomplish *by* performing it, then it is only natural for him to believe he will do A as well. If, then, intention is to be understood as reducing to a pair of states one of which is a state of believing, there is reason to think that anyone who intends to A is in a mental state that includes as one component a belief on his part that he will do A.

The problem is, however, that if such a view is adopted, there are going to be cases in which a person performs an action intentionally, but in which by the theory he cannot have intended to perform it. Thus, to give a more or less standard sort of example, suppose that a sheriff spies an escaping outlaw. The sheriff knows that he is at best an average marksman, and that the outlaw is nearly out of range. He thinks there is only one chance in a thousand that he can shoot him. Nevertheless, he *tries* to shoot him: he aims carefully, and fires at the outlaw. To his surprise, the attempt succeeds, and the outlaw is brought down. Now in such a case, it is correct to say the sheriff shot the outlaw intentionally; that is exactly what he meant to do when he fired, and should it turn out that the fellow was not an outlaw after all, the sheriff would not be able to disown responsibility for shooting him on the ground that it was unintentional. Yet it is not reasonable to say the sheriff believed he would shoot the outlaw. Indeed, given his estimate of the odds, and his surprise at his success, the only reasonable thing to expect is that he believed he would *not* shoot him. Thus, given the reductive account of intending, he could not have intended to shoot him. Robert Audi, who defends one such account, says that at best people in situations like this only hope to do what they accomplish; they do not intend to do it.[7] If this is correct, then the sheriff's act was intentional, but not intended.

II

To some ears, such a claim will sound flatly self-contradictory. Thus, in view of this outcome, one might be deeply skeptical about reductive analyses of intending, and it will be seen eventually that such skepticism is well founded. But reductive treatments of intending are far from being the only ones that restrict intention to accord with the agent's beliefs about what he will do. Philosophers on both sides of the reduction issue often find it simply incorrect to speak of intending in cases where one does not believe that one will perform the action in question. Thus Audi, who prefers a reductive analysis, holds that it would be odd to say, "I intend to go to your paper, though it is not likely that I will make it."[8] Gilbert Harman, who explicitly disavows the reductionist approach, concurs. As he sees it, we can intend to do only those things that are up to us, that we can do "at will." According to Harman, " . . . if one concludes one will not be able to do what one has been intending to do, that conclusion must change one's intention."[9] A similar claim has been made by Michael Bratman, who says in one place that it would be irrational for a person both to intend to finish an essay, and to believe that he will not.[10] If this is right, then quite apart from the matter of reduction, considerations of rationality alone might require that intentions be restricted in some way to accord with one's beliefs as to what one will do.

It has to be admitted, I think, that there is something right about these claims. There is indeed something odd about avowing an intention while in the same breath disavowing a belief that one will carry it out or, still worse, avowing a belief that one will not. A good theory of intention needs to account for this oddity. A way to do so would be to restrict intentions to accord with some principles of rationality. Moreover, as Bratman points out,[11] such a principle need not go as far as the reductionist analysis does in requiring that one believe one will do whatever one intends to do. Rationality in intentions may require only that the agent who intends to A not believe that he or she will not do A. I believe the case of the sheriff still violates this weaker requirement, but such a requirement might at least minimize such odd cases; or it might deal with them by allowing that the sheriff intends to shoot the outlaw, but declaring his intention to be irrational. Perhaps, then, rational intentions should be consistent with the agent's beliefs, in that a person cannot rationally intend to do things he believes he will not do.

The basis for such a requirement would appear to be twofold. In part, it has to do with what might be viewed as the overarching reason why we form intentions to begin with. The whole point of intentions, after all, is to guide our actions in bringing about changes in the world. When intentions are carried out, the world is brought more into accordance with our will than otherwise it would be. But then, the argument would run, surely if we are rational we would not waste the time and incur the frustration of pursuing intentions we believe we cannot fulfill. For in the vast majority of such cases, the world will not be changed, or at least not changed in the way the intention requires. This is, at least in part, why it seems unreasonable to announce an intention—an expression of one's will for the world—together with a belief that it will not be carried out. If the point of intentions is to guide us in changing the world so that it will suit us, then intentions of this kind would seem to lose their point.

Second, as Bratman has emphasized in several places, intentions are supposed to play a coordinating role with regard to our planning for the future.[12] Carrying out one intention often requires forming further ones, as to means that must be employed and preparations that must be made. It also requires that we not form conflicting intentions whose pursuit would endanger our fulfilling those intentions we already have. But how can an intention coordinate our planning if we do not believe we can carry it out? There seems little point in selecting a means to a goal if in fact we believe that no means will achieve it, and little point in retaining purposes we cannot achieve, when they can easily be abandoned in favor of intentions embodying other, more realistic goals.

On both these grounds, then, one might wish to require that intentions conform to belief, at least to the extent that a rational person could not intend to do something he believes he will not do. Moreover, adopting such a restriction would provide a way of explaining what is irrational about conflicting intentions. As we have seen, a person with conflicting intentions need be in no state of dismay if he does not recognize the conflict. My perplexity about intending both to go to my daughter's graduation and to accompany my brother fishing begins only when I realize these intentions are opposed to one another. But to say this is to say the problem begins when I come to have a certain belief: namely, that I cannot carry out both intentions. Because of this belief, the coordinating role of the intentions is destroyed. I cannot plan on jumping into my car and heading off on a fishing trip if, at the same time, I know I have an intention that would require me to drive to my daughter's graduation that very morning. Perhaps, then, the reason why conflicting intentions are irrational is that, when one's beliefs are correct, they violate a requirement all rational intentions must observe—that one not intend to do things one believes one will not do.

In essence, this is the approach to conflicting intentions taken by Michael Bratman. On his view, intentions can fulfill their coordinating role only if they, together with one's beliefs, form a consistent background against which further planning can take place. In one place, Bratman articulates this requirement of consistency in a principle of what he calls "agglomerativity" for rational intentions: if at one and the same time a person both rationally intends to do A and rationally intends to do B, then it ought to be possible and rational for that person to intend to do both A and B.[13] The effect of this principle is to require that the content of all the intentions one has at any given time should be capable of being conjoined in one collective intention, embodying all one's purposes at that moment. And of course, the conjunction must be rational; it cannot be in conflict with one's beliefs as to what will be accomplished. If one's beliefs in this regard are correct, conflicting intentions cannot rationally be agglomerated: I cannot rationally intend both to attend my daughter's graduation and to go fishing once I realize the dates of these events are the same, for the agglomerated intention would run directly counter to my belief that I cannot do both. The principle of agglomerativity might also be interpreted to cover the example of the sheriff, as a kind of limiting case. If he believes he will not hit the outlaw, then any intention on his part to do so would be irrational, for that intention alone would be in violation of his beliefs.

In fairness to Bratman, it does not always appear in his writings that he would treat principles like that of agglomerativity as blanket requirements for rational intentions; in other places he is prepared to allow for exceptions.[14] This caution is certainly warranted, for the principle of agglomerativity is of a type that is unusual for mental attitudes, most of which are not agglomerative. To take one important example, no general principle of this kind appears to apply to belief: it is perfectly rational for me to believe of each of a thousand ticket holders in a raffle that he or she will not win. Yet it would not be rational of me to hold that none of them will win, which I would have to if I agglomerated those beliefs.[15] Nor does agglomerativity apply to desire, as Bratman himself points out.[16] I might desire to go to Europe for my vacation and also desire to go to the Rockies, yet not desire to do both: enough vacation is enough. So there is at least something of the unusual about requiring agglomerativity of the attitudes of rational subjects. Moreover, although this requirement does provide *one* account of what is wrong with conflicting intentions, it is hardly necessary to providing such an account. For whether they are intended separately or in conjunction, my goals of going to my daughter's graduation and going fishing with my brother are equally incompatible with my belief that I cannot do both. Here again, the comparison with believing is instructive. I need not believe the conjunction "Smith will win the raffle and Jones will win the raffle" in order to be inconsistent with my belief that only one person can win the raffle. Separate beliefs about Smith and Jones will suffice to produce an inconsistent triad. In the same way, separate but incompatible intentions on my part, once recognized, will hamstring my planning every bit as much as they would if agglomerated. Combining them into one intention would produce no increase in my perplexity, nor would it generate any problem I did not have before they were combined.

All the same, it might be thought that Bratman's principle should be accepted as applying to all rational intentions. Whether they are intended separately or together, incompatible goals will never all be achieved; thus they seem to violate the rationale for having intentions at all, which is to bring the world closer into conformity with one's will. It might be more easy to recognize when our intentions are incompatible if the principle of ag- glomerativity is followed, and following such a principle would in general be an asset to planning for the future. The problem with this, however, is that if we make the principle of agglomerativity a blanket requirement for ratio- nal intentions, we will again encounter cases in which it appears a person performs an action intentionally, but where our theory says that the person cannot, rationally at least, have intended to perform it. All one needs is a case in which someone correctly finds it rational to pursue two goals simulta- neously, but where they are not both capable of fulfillment.

Here is such a case.[17] Let us suppose that instead of one escaping outlaw, there are two. Although they are escaping quickly, both are still within reasonable range and present fair targets. Instead of a sheriff, let us have a marshal who is an excellent shot with either hand and carries two guns. He has only one problem: he had just begun to clean his guns when he heard that a holdup was in progress, and he had already unloaded one of them. Upon news of the holdup, the marshal sprang to his duty, grabbing both guns as he went and shoving them into his holsters. The trouble is, he does not remember which gun is loaded and which is empty, and he will lose valuable seconds if he looks to see. The marshal calculates that his best course of action is simply to draw both guns, aim each at one of the outlaws, and pull the triggers simultaneously. This will maximize his chances of bringing down one of the outlaws, even though if he shoots either one he will fail to shoot the other. He proceeds to try simultaneously to shoot each outlaw. Now if the marshal succeeds in shooting either outlaw, he will have shot him intentionally: he will have had shooting the outlaw as his goal, and he will have succeeded because of his excellent marksmanship. But by the principle of agglomerativity, the marshal could not intend to shoot either outlaw. For that principle requires that if he intends to shoot outlaw 1 and intends to shoot outlaw 2, then he must be able rationally to intend to shoot both outlaws. This agglomerated intention runs directly counter to the mar- shal's knowledge that he cannot hit both, and so is irrational. Rationally, therefore, he could not intend separately to shoot the outlaws, either; such a pair of intentions could at best be irrational. Yet, given both his skill and the interpretation he has of his chances of bringing down one of the outlaws if he tries to shoot both, his conduct in this case seems completely rational. And there is no reason to believe he only intended to hit outlaw 1, or only intended to hit outlaw 2, for his attitude toward both outlaws is the same. Seemingly, then, the marshal has no intention whatever of shooting either outlaw, even though if he does so, he will have done so intentionally.

We have now seen two ways in which theories of intention can impose belief requirements on intending. If one pursues a reductive analysis, one might require that an agent actually believe that he *will* do anything he intends to do. But even without seeking such an analysis it is possible to impose the weaker requirement that one cannot rationally intend to do what he believes he will *not* do, on the ground that such intentions thwart the purposes for which we have intentions at all. Bratman's principle of agglomerativity derives from this second sort of requirement: it forbids incompatible intentions on the ground that they will conflict with beliefs. It is, however, of special interest because taken universally it imposes a requirement on intentions that is unusual for psychological attitudes, yet for which a prima facie case can be made. As we have seen, however, all such restrictions lead to there being cases where it is plausible to say of an agent that he performed an action *A* intentionally, yet where our theory would say he could not, at least rationally, have intended to do *A* when he acted. Thus all such requirements endanger the principle that anyone who *A*'s intentionally intends to *A*. Must we then surrender that principle? I think not: rather, it seems to me, all of these restrictions are too strong.

III

To see that this is so, we need to consider what happens in cases where a person tries to perform an action. The interesting thing is that all the cases that, by the foregoing accounts, would count as cases of *A*-ing intentionally without intending to *A,* are cases where it is correct to say that the agent tries to perform the act in question. The sheriff tries to shoot the fleeing outlaw and succeeds, thus shooting him intentionally; the marshal tries to shoot each outlaw, and if he succeeds in hitting either one, shoots him intentionally. Thus the acceptability of these accounts rests on the plausibility of the claim that in at least some cases where a person tries and succeeds, he performs the attempted action intentionally, yet without intending to perform it. Note that this need not be claimed for every case where it is correct to say someone tries, nor would such a claim succeed if made. For in many cases, talk of an agent trying is justified not by considerations having to do with the agent's frame of mind, but rather by doubts entertained by the speaker. If, for example, our sheriff did not realize how far away his outlaw was, he might have been optimistic about his chances of bringing him down and thus have sincerely believed he would shoot him. If so, we would have no reason to say the sheriff lacked the intention of shooting the outlaw, or that his intention was rationally inconsistent with his beliefs. Even so, if *we* know he is aiming at a difficult target, *we* can correctly say he is trying to shoot the outlaw. That statement would be true even if, as it turns out, he is successful, and even if, from the sheriff's point of view, this is simply a normal case of intentional action. The same lesson can be gotten from cases where an agent unexpectedly fails to do something he sets out to do, even though at the time *no one* would have doubted he would succeed. Here too we say the agent tried, and there is no reason to suppose that in such cases the agent does not, in trying to *A,* act with the intention of *A*-ing.

There can, then, be no general claim that people who try do not intend to do what they try to do. Rather, the most that can be claimed is that in certain cases—namely, those in which the agent himself has strong enough doubts that he does not believe he will succeed, or believes he will fail—the agent both tries to *A* and, if he succeeds, *A*'s intentionally, yet never intends to *A* and never acts with that intention. But this is not plausible at all. Indeed, on some accounts of trying it would be rejected immediately. For in those accounts, the word "trying" tends to go proxy for what others, including myself, have called "volition" or "willing."[18] Trying thus becomes the standard way of carrying out our intentions, in which case it would seem that trying to *A* would automatically involve intending to *A*. Now it does not seem to me that these accounts are quite correct. As I have argued elsewhere,[19] "trying" is not the name of a particular species of action, as I think "volition" or "willing" is. Rather, "trying" is a word that is general in meaning: it signifies the business of going about the performance of an action, and it is used when we have occasion to distinguish this enterprise from that of actually carrying the action off. Usually, what occasions the distinction is failure on the agent's part to do what he sets out to do, or doubt that he will succeed. Thus, when a person tries, his attempt will consist not necessarily just in willing, but in whatever actions he undertakes in pursuit of what he is trying to do. Nevertheless, the approach of the views just mentioned is on the right track as regards the present problem. For there is ample reason to think that those actions that do constitute attempts would not do so unless they were undertaken by the agent with the precise intention of accomplishing what he is said to try to do.

To see this, let us concentrate on the case of the sheriff. First, it should be noted that trying itself is always intentional. No one ever unintentionally or inadvertently or accidentally tries to do anything. And there is at least a prima facie reason for believing that this is because to try is precisely to act with the intention of doing what one tries to do. For in one use at least, "What are you trying to do?" simply *means:* What are your intentions in acting this way? Second, the actions that constitute a person's attempt, those he performs by way of trying, have to be allowed to be intended at the time of their performance, no matter what the agent's beliefs are about ultimate success. The sheriff aims, pulls the trigger, fires the gun, and indeed fires *at* the outlaw, all intentionally. Surely this must in the end signify that there was *some* intention he had at the time, an intention with which these things were done. For he had no doubt that he would do these things. Moreover, to say these acts were not intended would ultimately be to imply not only that the sheriff shot the outlaw intentionally without intending to shoot him, but also that he shot him intentionally without, at the time, intending to do anything whatever. And surely it is preposterous to say a person can do *A* intentionally yet have no intention of any kind, for then the word "intentionally" would fail to signify anything to do with intention. What, then, is the intention with which the sheriff fires at the outlaw? The answer I wish to defend is the obvious one: he fires at the outlaw with the intention of shooting him, notwithstanding the fact that he believes he will not succeed. I can think of three alternatives to this view, and none of them seems to me to be correct.

The first is simply that the sheriff fires at the outlaw more or less for its own sake: good sheriffs fire at outlaws whether they think they can hit them or not; it has symbolic value, if nothing else. Well, a good sheriff might on occasion do something like this, but leave that aside for the moment. The problem here is that if the only intention the sheriff has in firing at the outlaw is to make a symbolic gesture, then firing does *not* count as an attempt to shoot the outlaw for, so far at least, the sheriff is not *trying* to shoot him at all. At best, he is trying only to behave as a good sheriff would. Indeed, in one sense he is not even firing *at* the outlaw; he is only firing *toward* him. Even though, as it turns out, he hits the outlaw, the right thing for him to say would be, "I was not really trying to shoot him; I was only trying to make a point." This is another indication of what was suggested above—namely, that in acting, the boundaries of what we intend are precisely those of what we are trying to do.[20]

A second alternative would be to argue that in firing at the outlaw, the sheriff has a conditional intention—namely, the intention to shoot the outlaw if he can.[21] But this view mistakes what a conditional intention is. The sheriff would have a conditional intention if, for example, he intended to fire if no one else was likely to be hit. He would then check to see that the field was clear before proceeding to fire. This is because conditional intentions cite in their *if*-clauses conditions that the agent needs to have some assurance obtain *before* he acts. Moreover, when the agent gets this assurance, he typically proceeds from having a conditional intention to having an unconditioned one. Thus, if the sheriff intended to fire if no one was in the way, he would, upon noting that the field was clear, come to intend simply to fire. The situation where he intends to shoot the outlaw if he can is nothing like this. There, the *if*-clause cites no condition the agent must believe or suspect is satisfied before he acts. Indeed, it cites no condition on the intention at all. Rather, for the sheriff to intend to shoot the outlaw if he can is for him to intend to shoot the outlaw, period. The *if*-clause here is one of J. L. Austin's nonconditional ones.[22] It serves not to cite a condition on the intention, but rather to record the sheriff's awareness that success is not likely. I would agree, then, that the sheriff intends to shoot the outlaw if he can. But to say this is simply to say in part that he intends to shoot the outlaw: it is not to describe an alternative independent of having that intention.

There is one other possible account of the sheriff's intention in firing at the outlaw, which might at first appear more hopeful. It might be thought that the intention with which the sheriff fires is precisely that of trying to shoot the outlaw. After all, he does believe he can try to shoot him, even though he does not believe he can succeed. Moreover, it is not at all unusual for people who have such doubts to say things like, "I may not succeed, but in any case I intend to try." Perhaps, then, the intention with which the sheriff fires at the outlaw is not that of shooting him, but that of trying to shoot him. But this will not work either. I would agree that in trying to shoot the outlaw the sheriff intends to try. But unless the intention to try is supplemented by a more substantive intention, it becomes totally vacuous. The reason for this is the fact mentioned earlier, that trying is not a species of action. Unlike the case with acts like moving a finger or pulling a trigger, which consist in bringing about a specific sort of change in the world, there is no one sort of change that counts as a "try." Rather, any action might, if the circumstances are right, be described as an attempt. What we must ask, therefore, is this: what is it about the sheriff's act of firing at the outlaw that makes it count as fulfilling his intention to try to shoot the outlaw, rather than simply being done for its own sake, or out of a desire to look like a good sheriff?

Clearly, the answer to this question has to have something to do with the sheriff's frame of mind. He has to view the action of firing in a certain way, to undertake it out of considerations that are such that it will count as an attempt to shoot the outlaw. And we cannot settle just for saying he must view it as an attempt. That is true enough, but unless we can spell out what it means we will still have only a vacuous account of what goes on here. Rather, the question is: what enables the sheriff to view the action as an attempt? The answer, I think, is not far to seek. For the sheriff to see the action as an attempt, it has to be tied to a project of his—one that, however remote its chances of success, he nevertheless sees as worth pursuing. And that project is clearly the project of stopping the outlaw by shooting him. That is to say, the sheriff has to view the act of firing at the outlaw as fitting into a plan, the object of which is to stop the outlaw; and he has to undertake it precisely for this reason. If he does not, then he has no reason to consider it an attempt to shoot the outlaw, and neither do we. It is the planning aspect that is crucial: it is not enough that the act be merely accompanied by a desire to shoot the outlaw, or a hope that he will. Rather, the act has to be undertaken as a means of fulfilling the hope, or there will be no attempt at all to shoot the outlaw.

But now if all of this is true, then it seems to me that in fact, the sheriff *does* intend to shoot the outlaw, and he fires at him with that intention. Thus, what I am claiming is that the option of saying the intention with which the sheriff fires at the outlaw is to try to shoot him reduces to the claim I wish to defend: that he fires at him with the intention of shooting him. For he cannot carry out his intention to try unless he does something he conceives as a means to shooting the outlaw, and does it because he so conceives it. But to do this is precisely to intend to shoot the outlaw. Shooting the outlaw is the sheriff's purpose in firing, the goal of his act; if it were not so, he would as yet have no reason to fire, and no reason to consider his firing an attempt to shoot the outlaw. I see no difference between saying a person has a purpose out of which he acts and saying he has an intention with which he acts. I suppose someone might at this point simply insist that in the absence of belief in success, we still cannot speak of intent here; but rather must say only that the sheriff hopes to shoot the outlaw, or the like. But the trouble then is that we still have no intention with which the sheriff fired the gun, and he surely intended to do that. Moreover, the dispute at this point is becoming hopelessly verbal: one insists on finding another word to describe action that, as far as its purposiveness is concerned, is clearly no different from any full-fledged intentional action. Yet surely it is purposiveness that is crucial to acting with an intention. Indeed, we seem to admit as much when we grant that, given the sheriff's success, his act of shooting the outlaw is, after all, intentional. The idea that this can be so without his ever intending to shoot the outlaw or carrying out such an intention seems to me completely mistaken. To appeal to his acting with the hope of achieving the sought-after goal, as though this fell short of intending, is to overlook the obvious fact that when we seek to fulfill our hopes, we do so precisely by acting with the intention of fulfilling them—with the intention of doing what we hope to do.

As nearly as I am able to tell, then, there is no such thing as trying to do something without intending to do so, and acting with that intention. The sheriff's action of aiming and firing as he does counts as an attempt to shoot the outlaw precisely in that he acts with the intention of shooting him. The same goes for the marshal. In trying to hit each outlaw, he performs certain actions—namely, aiming each gun and pulling each trigger—that he has no doubt he will perform and that constitute his attempts to hit his targets. But no action on his part could count as an attempt to shoot an outlaw unless it was undertaken with the intention of so doing. If this is not his intention, then whatever else he may be trying to do, he is not trying to shoot either outlaw. Thus, I would claim that neither of the cases we have seen counts as one in which, given success, the agent A's intentionally but does not intend to A. Nor do I see any reason for calling the agent's intention in these cases irrational. After all, if it is rational for these agents to try, and it certainly seems to be, then it is rational for them to have the intention trying requires—namely, the intention of doing what they try to do.

IV

If this is correct, then the belief requirements cited earlier do not in fact apply to intention. This is most obvious in the case of the strong belief requirement associated with reductive analyses of intention—that intending to A requires believing that one will A. For the sheriff clearly does not believe that he will shoot his outlaw, yet he intends to do so. This being the case, the chances for a reductive analysis of intending seem to me to be quite slim. We have already seen that intention does not approximate to strong desire because it is subject to constraints of rationality that desire is not. And the sense of resolve associated with intending cannot be captured by requiring that the agent believe he will do what he intends to do, for as the case of the sheriff shows, intending requires no such belief. Indeed, even the presence of such a belief would not suffice to assure us that intention was present. I could strongly desire to go to Europe next summer, and firmly believe I will, and yet still not intend to go. My belief might only be a speculative one about what I will decide when I eventually get around to considering the matter. And this, I think, points to the real problem with reductive accounts— namely, that they overlook phenomena such as decision. However strongly one desires to perform an action, or believes that it would be best, and however firm the belief that it will be performed, one may simply not have formed the intention to do so, never have made up one's mind to do so. If not, then one does not have the *purpose* of performing the action in question; and in contrast to desire and belief, intention requires purpose. It is, then, unlikely that intention can be reduced to other mental states.

As for the weaker requirement supposed to apply to rational inten- tions—namely, that the agent cannot believe he will not do what he in- tends—it too, I would claim, is violated in the case of the sheriff. For if he believes he has only one chance in a thousand of hitting the single outlaw, then his dominant expectation by far *has* to be that he will *not* hit him, and I think a dominant expectation has to count as a belief. Indeed, I would suggest that any case of trying in which the agent is genuinely surprised at his own success is probably one in which he believed he would not succeed, and there are clearly many such cases. Yet there is nothing irrational in the sheriff's behavior, given that he is the sheriff and the other fellow is the outlaw. It makes perfectly good sense for him to take careful aim and fire at the outlaw, thus trying to shoot him, despite the remote chances of success. Now if it is rational for him to *act* in this way, it has to be rational for him to *intend* so to act. And we have seen that if his actions are to count as an attempt to shoot the outlaw, he must intend to shoot him. There is, then, something wrong with this requirement for rational intentions.

It will be remembered that in part, the rationale for this requirement stemmed from the role intention plays in coordinating our plans for the future. This seemed to require not only that our intentions be consistent with one another, but that they be consistent with our beliefs about what we will do. It is at best difficult to select actions as means to our goals if we believe no means will succeed. It is not, however, impossible; and this role of intention can be fulfilled in the sheriff's case despite his belief that he will not hit the outlaw. For he can still select means designed to exploit whatever remote chances may exist: he can, for example, fire at the outlaw, rather than in the opposite direction. The oddity of the sheriff's case is rather that, on the surface at least, it appears to violate the other part of the rationale for requiring that intentions not run counter to beliefs. That part involved the overriding reason for having intentions at all, which is to effect changes in the world, thereby bringing it more into conformity with our preferences. And indeed this is the more important aspect of the role of intentions. The coordinating role is subordinate to it, for there would be no point in worrying about coordinating our plans except for the sake of changing the world. But if the main point of having intentions is to effect changes in the world, then people like the sheriff appear to act irrationally by forming intentions that, as least according to their own beliefs, will not lead to the very changes in the world that they are intentions to bring about. How can this be rational, if the point of having intentions is as described?

In fact, there are at least two ways for the sheriff's intention to be rational. First, he knows he might get lucky: that is, he knows he *might* hit the outlaw, even though he believes he will not. For even in cases where the chances are judged to be one in a thousand, we sometimes succeed. And the sheriff could easily judge that the changes he will effect in the world if he should succeed are desirable enough to make it worth incurring the risk of failure. After all, he has next to nothing to lose by trying: cartridges are cheap. Why not, then, incur the high risk of failure, in which case the cost of a cartridge is lost, in the interest of achieving a world in which the vastly greater value of an outlaw apprehended is made a fact? If the sheriff views things in this way, he is perfectly justified in adopting and acting upon the intention to shoot the outlaw, even though he believes he will not. The point of this kind of justification is that our beliefs, however strongly held or justified, do not always constitute knowledge. They are sometimes false. Yet it is our beliefs in terms of which we have to plan. Thus, because the only basis we have for planning is inevitably infirm, it cannot be allowed to override the desirability of achieving certain goals when that desirability is great and the cost of failure is small. Even extremely high risks of failure are worth incurring on certain occasions. It is wrong to think, then, that intentions are irrational whenever they have little or no chance of being carried out. They will be rational provided only that a world in which success is achieved is deemed by us to be preferable enough to worlds in which we fail or never try.

There is another consideration that makes it rational for the sheriff to intend to shoot the outlaw, and this one could make it rational even if he thought he had no chance whatever of hitting him. When we think of intentions as being for the sake of effecting changes in the world, we should not make the mistake of supposing that "the world" in this context includes only those changes wrought by our actions, and not those actions themselves. Rather, the world includes ourselves, the things we do, and the states of intending out of which we do them. Thus in evaluating the kind of world that will be ours if a certain intention is adopted and acted upon, we have to remember that one difference between that world and worlds in which the intention in question is omitted will be the very fact that this intention gets pursued in the one but not the others. And even in a case where the goal embodied in an intention is not achieved, we may well deem the world to be better than it would be were the goal not even pursued. Thus, quite apart from any considerations having to do with likelihood of success, a world in which the sheriff adopts and pursues the intention of shooting the outlaw might well be deemed by him to be better than one in which he does not even try, and better precisely *in* that he follows that intention.

Upon consideration, I think we can see a lot of things about such a world that might appeal to the sheriff. It is a world in which an example is set, in which duty is pursued, in which sheriffs do not give up no matter what the odds. It is a world in which an outlaw may have fear struck in his heart by the fact that yet another sheriff is shooting at him, and take this as signifying that he is but a fugitive from justice, who must ultimately be either apprehended or hounded to his grave. For all of these reasons, the sheriff might well conclude that a world in which he adopts and acts upon the intention to shoot the outlaw will be better than one in which he does not. Moreover, he might conclude this even if he estimated his chances of success at zero. Nor should it be thought that in such a case he would not really intend to shoot the outlaw, but rather only intend to achieve the other goals described. He would, of course, intend to achieve those goals; but what would be necessary for him to do so in his estimation would be that he try to shoot the outlaw, which we have seen requires intending to shoot him. His goal is not a world of haphazard shots and empty shows of duty, but of duty taken to heart and bullets aimed with all the skill he can muster. Thus he might well intend to shoot the outlaw, even though he believes he has no chance.

What emerges from consideration of this case is that intentions are *not* to be judged as rational or irrational simply on the basis of whether they conform to our beliefs. To impose this requirement is to say in effect that intentions must conform to our best judgment as to the way the world is. But this kind of criterion of rationality belongs, if anywhere, only in the epistemological realm; it is too impoverished for the realm of intention and action.

Rather, if the overriding purpose of having intentions is to effect changes in the world, then the overriding criterion for rationality in intentions has to be that they conform to our values—to our best judgment as to the way the world ought to be. Now to be sure, this will usually involve an epistemic criterion as well. A world in which our intentions were constantly frustrated would be of little value. And there will be many cases in which the effort it takes to pursue goals we think we will not achieve will not be counterbalanced by the potential gain should a remote chance of success come to fruition. It is, then, reasonable to expect that people will not often intend to do things they believe they will not do. That is why it is odd to avow an intention in the same breath with a belief that one will not carry it out. But this epistemic criterion of rationality is only of secondary importance, as the example of the sheriff shows. His intention does not conform to his beliefs about the way the world is, but it does conform to the overall context of his beliefs taken together with his judgments about the kind of world we ought to have. It is this overall context that has to be taken into account in judging the rationality of intentions.

Considerations of the same kind apply to conflicting intentions, as in the case of the marshal. There, the problem is that whereas it is rational for the marshal to act as he does in trying to shoot both outlaw 1 and outlaw 2, it appears not to be rational for him to intend to shoot outlaw 1 and intend to shoot outlaw 2. The problem arises from the claim that rational intentions must always be agglomerative, and it would be irrational for the marshal to intend to hit both outlaws 1 and 2 when he knows he cannot. Thus we seem forced to the conclusion that the marshal acts without intending to do those things that, if he does them, he will have done intentionally. But if the analysis of trying presented above is correct, then the marshal must intend to shoot outlaw 1 and intend to shoot outlaw 2. If he did not, then the actions he performs by way of trying to hit them could not constitute attempts to do so. Moreover, these intentions are rational ones for the marshal to have. As with the case of the sheriff, it makes no sense whatever to say it is rational for the marshal to act as he does, yet not rational for him to intend so to act.

If this is correct, there are two lessons to be drawn. The first is that it is not always irrational for a person to have conflicting intentions. The reason for this is in part that, as in the marshal's case, it is sometimes possible to *pursue* conflicting intentions simultaneously, even though both cannot be achieved. All that is needed, then, is for the circumstances to be such that the potential gain to be gotten by pursuing them be great enough to outweigh the risks and disappointments of so doing. That is exactly what obtains in the case of the marshal. He sees the greater likelihood of his shooting one or the other outlaw if he acts in the way he does as outweighing the risk of getting neither fugitive if he delays to see which gun is loaded. But to say this is clearly to say that overall, a world in which he makes an effort to shoot each outlaw is likely to be better, in his view, than one in which he does otherwise. And this is precisely the sort of situation in which, if what has been said above is correct, an intention to shoot each outlaw is called for. Far from being irrational in having conflicting intentions, then, the marshal would be irrational if he did not have them!

The second lesson to be drawn from this case is that the principle of agglomerativity does not always apply to rational intentions. Although it is rational for the marshal to intend to shoot outlaw 1 and intend to shoot outlaw 2, it is not rational for him to intend to shoot both. As long as he only intends separately to shoot them, he has a pair of intentions both of which can effectively be acted upon, and neither of which he need believe he will not carry out. The agglomeration of these intentions cannot effectively be acted upon, for there is no means to shoot both outlaws, and the marshal knows this. Other things being equal, therefore, he should not form the intention to shoot both. And other things are equal: there is nothing whatever to be gained by forming the agglomerated intention, and hence it would be irrational for him to do so. At most, these intentions combine for the marshal only disjunctively: he intends to shoot one outlaw or the other, thereby apprehending one of them.

This is not meant to imply that it would not usually be rational to follow the principle of agglomerativity in forming intentions. Consolidating intentions into single, overall plans might often be useful for purposes of planning. But rational intentions do not always observe this principle; rather, they follow it only when it is rational to agglomerate them, which the marshal's case shows is not always so. As intimated earlier, therefore, it turns out that intending is just like other mental attitudes in this respect. If I desire A and desire B, I might desire both; but I will not do so if the combination displeases me, as the case of the two vacations shows. If I believe A and believe B, I will often believe their conjunction; but not if I know their conjunction is false, as in the raffle case. Similarly, if I intend to do A and intend to do B, I need not intend to do both. That will be in order only if the joint intention represents or involves something to be *gained*. This is, first and foremost, what rational intentions have to do, and epistemic restrictions are always subordinate to it.

V

There are two general conclusions that can be drawn from this discussion. The first is that we need not abandon the principle that a necessary condition for an action to be intentional is that it be intended by the agent when it is performed, either for its own sake or as a means to some other act that the agent intends to perform. We have as yet seen no examples in which this principle fails to hold. Rather, what are thought to be counterexamples to it arise only because unreasonable belief constraints are placed on intentions. There is no intrinsic plausibility in the idea that a person who does something intentionally could fail to intend to do it, and analysis of cases where this is alleged to be so only underscores the implausibility.

Second, if the above discussion is correct, we have learned more about what the proper strictures on rational intentions should be. It is not that the notions that intentions should conform to our beliefs as to what we will do, and should be agglomerative, are of no value. Rather, most intentions that are rational will conform to these principles, for the simple reason that by and large, there is little to be gained if they are ignored. But these principles are at times overridden by a larger consideration, embodying the reason why we have intentions at all: to be rational, intentions must above all conform to the principle that having and pursuing them offers a reasonable chance of bringing the world more into conformity with out best judgment as to the way it ought to be. Because this usually requires that our intentions conform to our opportunities, it is odd for a person to express an intention together with a belief that he or she will fail to carry it out. Pragmatically, to speak in this way is to suggest that one has failed to obeserve this requirement. But all this shows is that the speaker has some explaining to do. It does not yet show that the speaker is being irrational, for at times the most rational course is precisely to adopt and act upon intentions that, alone or in combination, we know we cannot fulfill.[23]

Notes

1. D. Davidson, "Agency," in *Essays on Actions and Events* (Oxford, 1980), 46.

2. A. I. Goldman, *A Theory of Human Action* (Princeton, 1976), 56-63. On Goldman's account, the basic actions that generate all others are always intentional.

3. This was Davidson's view in "Actions, Reasons, and Causes," in *Essays on Actions and Events;* see also Goldman, *Theory of Human Action,* 54f.

4. The phrase "what she thinks is best" is ambiguous. It could refer to a moral judgment, or to a prudential one, or to a judgment that might be held to occur at the end of a process of deliberation in which all relevant considerations have been taken into account. But I would maintain that the above points hold regardless of the sense in which the phrase is taken.

5. Cf. Lawrence Davis, "What It Is Like to Be an Agent," *Erkenntnis* 18 (1982): 195-213, esp. 205.

6. Cf. R. Audi, "Intending," *Journal of Philosophy* 70 (1973): 387-403, esp. 395.

7. Ibid., 388.

8. Ibid.

9. G. Harman, "Practical Reasoning," *Review of Metaphysics* 29 (1976): 431-63, esp. 435.

10. M. Bratman, "Castaneda's Theory of Thought and Action," in *Agent, Language, and the Structure of the World,* edited by J. E. Tomberlin (Indianapolis, 1983), 159.

11. Ibid.

12. "Castaneda's Theory of Thought," 159. See also M. Bratman's "Davidson's Theory of Intention" in *Essays on Davidson: Actions and Events,* edited by Merrill Hintikka and Bruce Vermazen (New York, 1985); "Intention and Means-End Reasoning," *Philosophical Review* 90 (1981): 252-65; and "Two Faces of Intention," *Philosophical Review* 93 (1984): 375-405.

13. "Davidson's Theory of Intention."

14. For example, in "Intention and Means-End Reasoning," 259, Bratman also holds that intentions should be consistent to be rational, but here he clearly attaches a *certeris paribus* clause.

15. The importance of cases like this was pointed out to me by Jonathan Kvanvig.

16. "Two Faces of Intention," 380-81.

17. The case is modeled after one of Bratman's own, which I first heard him describe at the University of Dayton Conference on Practical Reason, March 1983. Bratman's treatment of that example can be found in "Two Faces of Intention," 382-83.

18. See especially J. Hornsby, *Actions* (London, 1980), chap. 3; and B. O'Shaughnessy, *The Will: A Dual Aspect Theory* (Cambridge, 1980), chap. 11.

19. "Trying, Paralysis, and Volition," *Review of Metaphysics* 28 (1975): 423-42.

20. There may be a secondary sense in which the sheriff could still be said to "try" to shoot the outlaw in this case. Sometimes one is said to "try" to do something when one's real purpose is to do something else. Thus if my purpose is simply to jump as high as I can, I might "try" to touch a ceiling eight feet above my head even though I know I cannot and in fact have no purpose of doing so. This use of "try" is, however, deceptive: it arises from the fact that even though, in the primary sense, I am *not* trying to touch the ceiling, my action consists in precisely what I would do if I *were* to try, in that sense, to touch it. Now under the interpretation considered above, the sheriff's action might count as "trying" to shoot the outlaw in the secondary sense, for he does just what he would do if he were really trying to shoot the outlaw, rather than simply to act like a good sheriff. This point, however, does no damage to the argument of this paper. For even if one succeeds in doing what, in this secondary sense, one "tries" to do, one does not do it intentionally. If I do touch the ceiling, my doing so will have been unintentional, for I will not have meant to do so; nor will the sheriff have meant to hit the outlaw if his only intention in firing was to appear to be a good sheriff. Thus we still would not have a case of an act that was intentional but not intended.

21. This is suggested in H. P. Grice, "Intention and Uncertainty," *Proceedings of the British Academy* 57 (1971): 263-79.

22. J. L. Austin, "Ifs and Cans," in *Philosophical Papers,* editied by J. O. Urmson and G. J. Warnock (Oxford, 1961), 158-60.

23. My thanks go to Michael Bratman for several helpful and encouraging conversations on the subjects of this paper. An earlier version of it was read at the University of Texas, and I benefited from the comments received. I am also indebted to Robert Audi, Myles Brand, Robert Kane, and Jonathan Kvanvig for useful suggestions.

Intentional Actions and Plans

MYLES BRAND

My basic thesis is that intentional action is action performed in following a plan. An intentional action can be a momentous occasion in one's life, such as marrying, or it can be a mundane occurrence, such as showering in the morning; but in all cases, the agent is following his plan when acting. He has before his mind, as it were, a pattern of activity to which he brings his actions into conformity. In this paper I will articulate, defend, and, where necessary, qualify this basic thesis.[1]

1. INTENTIONAL ACTION AS PLANNED ACTION

I do not know of any conclusive argument for—or against—taking intentional action to be planned action, but several supporting reasons can be adduced in favor of this thesis. The first reason is that intentional action is coextensive with planned action. Consider the well-worn case of intentionally raising one's arm in order to ask a question. The subject has a preconception of a pattern of activity that includes asking a question by raising his arm. This preconception is his plan. Or consider a complex action, say changing a flat tire. Here too the subject has a conception of a future pattern of activity that he is to undertake. Indeed, this is more obvious in the case of a complex action. The more complex the action, the clearer it is that the subject has a mental 'picture' or representation of what he is to do.

Nonintentional actions are not performed when following a plan. Purely automatic actions, for instance, are not intentional. When falling forward, a normal person under normal conditions will automatically extend his arms. Observe that extending one's arms is an action, something done, and not something that happens to one. It is different from moving one's leg because of a blow to the patellar tendon. The latter is a reflex movement over which a person could not gain direct control; the former is a movement over which a person does not normally have control but over which he or she *could* gain direct control. Extending one's arms when falling, in normal circumstances, is not preplanned. Immediately before performing it, the subject lacks a conscious representation of a pattern of activity into which he or she fits the action.

Actions reach into the world. That is, some effects of our bodily movements are parts of our actions. The *reach* of such actions is marked by the extent to which these effects are planned. Suppose that I moved my arm, thereby signed my name, thereby wrote a check, thereby purchased a car, and thereby made Shady Sam Salesman-of-the-month. Suppose also that I knew nothing of Sam's candidacy for Salesman-of-the-month but otherwise knew what I was doing. Here I intentionally moved my arm, signed my name, wrote a check, and purchased the car; but I did not intentionally make Sam Salesman-of-the-month. The intentionality of the effects of my bodily movements extends as far, and no farther, than my prior plan. If, contrary to the supposed facts, I had known about Sam's candidacy and had made it part of my plan that he become Salesman-of-the-month, then I would have intentionally made him Salesman-of-the-month. The relevant difference between this counterfactual situation and the supposed actual one is that of preconceiving Sam's becoming Salesman-of-the-month. My bodily movements and their effects remain the same in both cases. (More on effects and consequences later.)

The second reason for my basic thesis, put succinctly, is this. To follow a plan is to realize a solution to a problem. To realize a solution to a problem is to act intentionally. Hence, plan following is intentional action.

There are two sorts of problems: practical problems and theoretical problems. Practical problems are those whose solutions can be realized only through physical activity; theoretical problems do not essentially involve physical activity. (Of course, many actual problems are complex in that they contain both practical and theoretical subproblems.) Suppose that I am confronted with a list of shopping chores and my problem is to complete this list most efficiently. The solution to this problem is realized by my physically completing the chores in a specified time. By contrast, deriving a theorem does not involve overt physical activity. If the deduction is relatively complicated, I might use memory crutches, such as transcribing the steps; but in principle this deduction can be carried out in my head.

Plan following is a type of problem solving. For practical problems, plan following consists in acting on a prior selection and organization of physical activities. When I mentally construct my shopping route and act on it, I am following a plan. Similarly, plans are followed in realizing solutions to theoretical problems. In deriving the theorem 'in my head', I use preconceived strategies.

To realize a solution to a problem is to act intentionally. In intentional action, a goal is set and activity is undertaken as a means of achieving this goal. The goal is the solution to the problem and the means is the method of achieving this goal. Consider practical problems. My goal in the shopping case is to complete these chores in the allocated time. I realize this goal by performing actions in a preplanned order. These actions are my means for achieving the goal and are performed intentionally. Similarly, to realize a solution to a theoretical problem is to set a goal and to achieve this goal by intentionally performing those actions, none of which must be physical, that are a means to the goal.

Intentional action is not the same as deliberative action: all deliberative action is intentional, but not conversely. Deliberative action is action in which the agent consciously deliberates about what to do prior to undertaking that activity. Shall I attend the lecture or the film this evening? On the one hand, the lecture will likely be boring and the film has received good reviews; but, on the other hand, I have an obligation to attend the lecture. In making this decision, I compare the advantages and disadvantages of each course of action. It is plausible to model this process decision theoretically, assigning utilities and subjective probabilities to each possible outcome. But the issue here is not that of the best formal model for deliberation. It is, rather, the simple point that all deliberative action involves prior comparison among alternatives, whereas not all intentional action does. My showering this morning was intentional. It was part of my routine for going to the university. But I did not consciously consider the alternatives to showering, nor their comparative advantages and disadvantages. I have a well-established routine that I follow on weekday mornings when I go to the university that includes showering. Although at one time I might have considered the comparative advantages of showering or not in the morning and made a conscious decision to do so, I now follow a well-rehearsed routine and do not in fact consider these alternatives.

Like acting intentionally, plan following can either involve prior deliberation or it can proceed routinely. A plan is followed routinely when it is well learned and the environmental conditions are normal. That intentional action and plan following can be deliberative or not is consistent with their being realizations of solutions to problems, since not all problem solving is deliberative. My finding an ordering for my shopping chores by consciously comparing alternative routes is deliberative. But my solving simple mathematical problems is not, since for these problems I do not deliberate about strategy or tactics.

The third reason for thinking that intentional action is planned action is this. We have common beliefs that persons act intentionally and that, as we descend in the order of life forms, the likelihood of intentional action decreases. Chimpanzees, it would seem, act intentionally, and perhaps also dogs and maybe—though doubtfully—white rats and pigeons. Our intuitions are quite clear that sponges and slugs do not act intentionally. One plausible explanation for these intuitions is that intentional action requires a level of cognitive capacity that is present in higher life forms but absent in lower ones. In particular, higher life forms have the capacity to form plans and to follow them. Sponges and slugs have cognitive capacities; they sense environmental changes and guide their bodily movements accordingly. But sponges and slugs lack the capacity for forming and following plans. In general, the more likely we think it is that members of a species are capable of forming and following plans, the more likely we also think it is that members of that species act intentionally.

Can computerized robots act intentionally? The answer depends on whether robots can be in states duplicative of persons with respect to representing patterns of goal-directed activity and whether they can bring their movements into conformity with these patterns. I will not enter here into the debate about whether computational devices in principle are capable of having such representations. My point is only that our answer to the question of whether computerized robots can act intentionally is dependent on our answer to the question of whether they can represent and follow plans. And that, again, speaks to the identity between intentional action and planned action.

Consider one more supporting reason for my basic thesis. There is a connection between intentional action and the attribution of moral responsibility: indeed, it is this connection that has led many philosophers to attend to the analysis of intentional action. But the connection is not a simple one. Intentional action is not a necessary condition for the attribution of moral responsibility. Persons can be morally responsible for omittings, such as not taking precautions in a potentially dangerous situation. (Omittings are to be distinguished from refrainings; the latter are intentional not doings, whereas the former are not actions at all.)[2] Persons can also sometimes be morally responsible for the intentional actions of others to whom they bear a special relationship, such as parent to child or military commander to soldier. Nor is intentional action a sufficient condition for the attribution of moral responsibility. I can perform intentional actions alone in my room, such as adjusting my glasses, that have no moral significance. The connection between intentional action and moral responsibility, rather, seems to be something like this: if a person acts intentionally and if this action is performed in a social situation affecting more than one person, then the agent can be held morally responsible for what he or she does. That is, a precondition for the ascription of moral responsibility is that the agent acts intentionally within a social setting.

Let us restrict attention to those intentional actions performed in the appropriate social situations. In these cases, intentional action is sufficient for the possibility of the attribution of moral responsibility. But now someone can be held morally responsible for what he does only if he can reasonably be expected to foresee the outcome of his bodily actions. To be in a position to foresee the outcome of one's bodily actions is to perform these actions while conforming to a mental representation into which these bodily actions and their outcomes fit. And to act on a mental representation of this type is to follow a plan. So, in social settings, someone acts intentionally only if he follows a plan.

2. PLANS

So much for plausibility arguments. Let me turn to articulating the thesis that intentional action is planned action. In this section I will deal with the status of plans and in the next one with the issue of following a plan.

What is a plan? There are two main competing answers: (i) a plan is a psychological state; or, (ii) a plan is an abstract object. To many, the first answer is attractive.[3] The nature of abstract objects is somewhat obscure, or at least there are lingering doubts about intelligibility whenever they are introduced. Those with strong nominalistic inclinations would like to restrict reference to spatiotemporal objects. Moreover, ordinary talk about plans often seems to be talk about psychological states. We often seem to refer to plans as mental representations of future courses of action (as I did at times in the previous section).

However, it does not appear that the first answer can be sustained. If plans are psychological states, then all true statements about plans can be understood without reference to abstract objects. But there are some true statements about plans that make sense only if plans are abstract.

Consider the following meaningful and (let us suppose) true sentence:

(1) Richard and Pat have the same plan.

A natural rendering of (1) is that it talks about types of plans: namely,

(2) There is a plan-type such that Richard and Pat each have a token of it.

Plan-types are abstract objects; they are not psychological states. Plan-types would exist even if there were no persons or other organisms or machines that token them. A person *has* a token of a plan-type. The having of that token, presumably, would be a pychological state. But the plan itself, *what is tokened*, is abstract.

It might be supposed that (1) can be reinterpreted without quantifying over plan-types, or any other abstract object. One such suggestion is:

(3) Richard is in a certain psychological state $\emptyset$' and Pat is in a certain psychological state $\emptyset$'' and $\emptyset$' and $\emptyset$'' are relevantly similar states.

This rendition of (1), however, is not without difficulty. To say that psychological states ∅' and ∅'' are relevantly similar in this context is to say that they have certain abstract properties characteristic of plans in common. Suppose that the plan Richard and Pat share is to visit Spiro during the holidays. According to (3), Pat and Richard are in psychological states in which they each represent to themselves performing certain action types in a certain sequence. This sequence of action types, common to each one's psychological state but abstracted from each agent, is the plan and is not itself a psychological state.

The epistemological issue of *attributing* a plan to someone must be distinguished from the ontological one of the nature of plans. For the purposes of plan attribution, it is sufficient to refer only to psychological states. How do we tell whether Richard and Pat have plans, and under what conditions can we attribute to them the same plan? We ascribe the having of plans to people the same way we ascribe to them any psychological state—on the basis of their behavior, especially their verbal reports. We ascribe to them the same plan when, given the specificity demanded by the context, their predicted actions are relevantly similar. Pat and Richard both pack for the trip; but some of Pat's actions, such as putting the hairdryer in her overnight case, are not duplicated by Richard, nor conversely. In an everyday context, we attribute to persons the same plan for taking a trip if their destination and purpose is the same, their mode of transportation is the same, and so on; it is not normally required that all their minute actions be the same. In short, judgments about sameness of plans depends on context and availability of behavioral evidence. But none of this speaks to plans *being* psychological states. A criterion for *telling* or *judging,* for *attributing* or *ascribing,* sameness of plans does not say what a plan is. Such a criterion does not give the existential commitments necessary for the truth of statements like (1).[4]

Taking plans to be abstract objects permits straightforward interpretation of sentences like the following:

(4)   There is a plan for world peace but no one has thought of it and no one will.

This sentence is most naturally read as construing plans to be person-independent. If plans are psychological states, and nothing more than that, it is difficult to see how it is that (4) and its kin can be literally true.

It might be suggested that (4) can be reinterpreted in terms of possibility. One such rendering is:

(5)   In the actual world no one will ever have a plan for world peace; but there is a possible world just like the actual one, except that someone has a plan for world peace in it.

Variations of (5) can be constructed that quantify not over possible worlds but possible plans held by possible people. But in all these reinterpretations, no progress has been made toward eliminating reference to abstract ojects. By opting for (5) or some variant of it, rather than a literal reading of (4), we would be trading abstract plans for abstract possible worlds, thoughts, and people. I, for one, am less uncomfortable with abstract plans than these other sorts of nonspatiotemporal objects. In any case, unless some viable reductive renderings of sentences like (1) and (4) are found, we should take them at face value and quantify over plans as abstract objects.

Simple plans have only a few steps and are linearly ordered. The goal of a simple plan is the event (or state) brought about by the terminal step in the plan. But not all plans are simple. Sometimes plans have many steps; sometimes these steps are ordered nonlinearly, often with branching and 'tangled' structures; and sometimes plans have several goals, or subgoals, that are not associated with the terminal actions in a squence. In general, a plan can be modeled by the triple

$$\wp = <A, h, g>,$$

where A is a set of action types, h is a function that order members of A on the basis of dependency relations, and g is a function that designates which events (or states) brought about by members of A are goals (or subgoals). Plans, then, are ordered triples consisting of a set of action types, a schema for ordering these action types, and one or more designated event types.

Function h sequences the set of action types $A\text{-}\{A_1, A_2, \ldots, A_n\}$ in terms of their dependency relations. A good start on characterizing this function has been made by Goldman, and I shall not pursue that issue here.[5] Observe that g, the goal-designating function, is a necessary part of this model. Two plans can be exactly the same with respect to the set of action types and their interdependencies, but differ with respect to goals. You and I might follow the same recipe in baking a cake, yet act on different plans. The goal of your plan might be to produce a finished cake, whereas the goal of my plan might be to test the recipe; nevertheless, we both performed the same types of actions in the same order. As I mentioned, goals are events (or states) brought about by planned actions. Suppose my plan is to run a 5:00 minute mile. This plan includes a training regimen and a timed run at the end. My goal is not the action of running the timed trial, which is the terminal action in the sequence, but rather the event (or state) of having completed that run within 5:00 minutes. For some complex plans, furthermore, the goal is not associated with the terminal action. A plan for robbing the First National Bank might have as its goal the obtaining of the money; but the plan continues past this goal to the escape and eventual division of the loot.

Although highly general, $\wp$ is restrictive in one way. It models only the single-agent case. In addition to single-agent plans, there are plans for groups.

Football coaches construct plans for playing games that involve the coopera-tive actions of several dozen players, not to mention coaches and water boys. Surgical teams utilize plans that involve intricate cooperation and interac-tion. On a grand scale, there are plans for armies and even for entire nations.

Plans, in short, are abstract objects. But they are no more mysterious or obscure than properties and set-theoretic objects. Although plans are person-independent, they bear relations to persons (and perhaps other spe-cies and machines). In particular, a person *has* a plan when the content of his psychological state is a plan relativized to himself. Plans are the contents of thought; but these contents must be relativized to the subject. A plan itself is a schemata of action types and does not include a specification of the person who is to perform it. Agent specification must be first-person; some-one has a plan only when he is aware that it is he who is to perform these actions. In general, where P can be modeled by $\wp$,

(6) Subject S has a plan to P iff S entertains that he, himself will P.

The 'he, himself' in (6) is used to mark the fact that this thought is first person.[6]

To have a plan is to be in a certain cognitive state. I have characterized this state neutrally in (6) by saying that the subject entertains the plan. Perhaps it would be better to say that he considers undertaking the plan, or 'pictures' himself carrying out the plan, or conceives of the plan, or some such. The main point is that in having a plan the subject need not *believe* that he will carry out the plan. Some people have precautionary plans for what to do in emergency situations (pilots I imagine have such plans), without believing that in fact they will ever act on these plans.

Plans need not reflect the nomological structure of the actual world; they need only have the formal structure $\wp$. Thus, there are plans that cannot be successfully completed and persons can have such plans. Indeed, persons can — and do — have plans that are highly unrealistic, even silly. These plans, nevertheless, can guide activity. Richard might have a plan to square a circle. This plan then guides his actions of picking up a pencil and protractor, drawing lines on paper, and so on. Of course, Richard cannot successfully complete this plan; he can only successfully undertake its initial steps.

To have a plan is to have a cognitive representation of a possible future course of action. This type of mental representation has no motivational force; it does not impel us to do anything. It is a projection of a course of activity on which the subject will act when, and if, he is moved to do so. A person might come to have a plan to rob the First National Bank. This plan might be extraordinarily detailed and complete. Yet, he may never be moved to rob the bank. It is not that he has other motives, such as a fear of being apprehended, that override a motive generated by the plan; it is, rather, that merely having the plan provides no motive for acting on it. The subject could have constructed the plan as an intellectual exercise, without having any desire to carry it out. For the most part, persons develop plans because they have some reason to achieve the plan's goal. This reason to achieve the goal is a motive to undertake the plan. But the reason to achieve the plan's goal is not itself part of the having of the plan.

Sometimes ordinary talk appears to assign motivational force to the having of a plan. If Richard did not make a plane reservation to New York and did not rearrange his appointments, then, despite his claims to the contrary, we would say that he did not have a plan to visit New York. However, this ordinary talk can be explained without supposing that the psychological state of having a plan is itself motivational. For such ordinary talk can be the result of our expectation that plans are often coupled with motives.

In general, motivational states cannot be assimilated to cognitive ones. Suppose, purely for the sake of argument and only for the moment, that desires plus beliefs cause actions. On this view, desire is the motivational component and belief the cognitive component of the cause. Belief alone does not cause action. One way to think about having plans is that they play the same role for a pattern of activity that belief plays for individual actions. Having a plan is the antecedent cognitive event that guides a sequence of actions; but it does not, by itself, initiate action.

3. INTENTIONAL ACTION: A FIRST APPROXIMATION

A first approximation for an adequate definition of 'intentional action' is:

> (D1) S As intentionally during t iff (i) S's Aing during t is an action and (ii) during t, S follows a plan that includes his Aing,

where S ranges over subjects, A over action types, and t over temporal durations. This definition will have to be modified later to take into account some actions that are not—explicitly, at least—plan following, but are nevertheless intentional. That modification will leave intact several noteworthy features of (D1).

Definition (D1) presupposes another definition for 'action'. I have argued elsewhere for a causal analysis of action.[7] A person performs an action just in case what that person does is proximately caused by a specific type of mental event. In a sense, this is a functional theory. An action, whether bodily or not, is whatever is proximately caused by this type of mental event. I contend that this mental event is an intending, an event that has both cognitive and conative components but is nevertheless distinct from a belief and desire complex. Beliefs and desires are *intention-formers*. Intention, however, is not my target here; and I shall assume that clause (i) can be cashed out.

Definition (D1) says that subject *S follows* a plan. Following a plan is to be distinguished from acting according to a plan. It is sufficient to act according to a plan that the subject's actions conform to that plan; but conformity to a plan is not sufficient for following that plan. Suppose that an aborigine fiddles with a combination lock and, as luck would have it, opens the lock. On the assumption that he does not know the combination, nor that he knows anything at all about combination locks, he would not have followed a plan to open the lock. Nevertheless, his actions are in accordance with a plan for opening the lock. There is an abstract structure of the form $\wp$, whose designated goal is the lock's being open, such that the aborigine's actions exemplify this structure.

Acting according to a plan is a weak notion. Given that there are indefinitely many patterns of activity that exemplify structures of the form $\wp$, it is likely that we act according to a great many plans, no doubt some of them simultaneously. Acting according to a plan does not require awareness of the plan or any cognitive attitude about the plan on the part of the subject. It requires only conformity of action to the plan. Following a plan, by contrast, requires more than conformity to a plan.

A person can have a plan without following it. Someone can have a plan for robbing the First National Bank without acting on that plan, and hence, without following it. Richard can have a plan for running for governmental office without his acting on this plan. His plan could be as detailed as any plan he has had for any activity; nevertheless, he might never bring this plan to fruition. A person has a plan when he or she has a neutral cognitive attitude whose content is that plan. Having a plan is like having a road map with a route drawn on it. But, as we do not follow every marked road map that comes our way, we do not follow every plan we have.

Having a plan and achieving the goal state of the plan, clearly, are not sufficient for following the plan. Cases of causal waywardness illustrate this point. To alter a well-known example for our purposes, suppose that a dastardly nephew planned to kill his rich uncle by stabbing him in his sleep. The nephew sets out for his uncle's house; and as luck would have it, he hits and kills a pedestrian who is his uncle. The nephew had a plan for killing his uncle and he in fact killed him; but he did not do so intentionally. The nephew's actions did not conform to the plan he had. His plan included killing his uncle by stabbing him, not by running him down. Note incidentally that some of the actions performed by the nephew were intentional, namely, those that conformed to the initial stages of his plan. His getting into his car and driving toward his uncle's house were both intentional, since they were included in his plan to kill his uncle at his home. But intentionality stops when the plan goes awry; the mere achievement of the goal state (goal event) is otiose.

Having a plan and acting in accordance with it are necessary, but not sufficient, for following that plan. I have a plan for driving to the university: I drive north on Houghton Road, then west on I-10, and so on. Driving to the university by this route is something I have done many, many times. Sometimes, however, I have performed actions that conform to this plan without following it. I have wanted to go to the east side, the side of town opposite that of the university, but have found myself, unhappily and unexpectedly, enroute to the university. I acted in conformity with a plan I have; but I did not follow it.

At this point it is natural to suggest that the cognitive attitude toward a plan when following it must be stronger than neutral. That is, we follow a plan when we act in conformity with a plan that we have and, say, to which we attend. The reason why I did not follow my plan for going to the university is that I did not attend to my plan; if I had attended to my plan when I was acting in conformity with it, I would have been following that plan to go to the university. However, this view of plan following is too strong. Sometimes a person follows a plan without attending to it. Good athletes think ahead. A centerfielder might devise a plan that includes throwing directly to third base on a short fly. A short fly is hit and he throws directly to third without further thought and without attending to this plan. Indeed, he would not be able to succeed in his plan if he attended to it, since his plan calls for fast action in the circumstances, without time for reflection or focusing of attention on the plan.

Plan following without attention is, in fact, commonplace. Often we follow plans routinely and without attending to what we are doing at the time we are doing it. When I wake in the morning, I routinely wash and dress without attending to this sequence of actions. I might be thinking about any number of things. My activity in the morning is well practiced and proceeds without conscious rehearsal. This routine is habitual. From the viewpoint of efficiency, it is important that persons be able to follow plans without attending to them. Given that we have limited capacity for attention, we would have little opportunity to think and plan ahead if our attention was always directed toward contemporaneous activity. Similar problems arise for other attempts to explain plan following by strengthening the cognitive attitude involved in having a plan. Plan following can proceed without reflection, conscious review, and so on.

A subject follows a plan, I submit, just in case he has this plan, acts in accordance with it, and is moved to achieve the goal of the plan. Active attention or reflection is not necessary for plan following. We need only represent the plan to ourselves when following it; a plan is, as it were, a cognitive map through the maze of future possible action. Plan following requires activity that conforms to the plan; we follow a plan only if our actions fit the sequence of action types constituting the plan. The third necessary ingredient in plan following is that the activity be initiated by a conative, or motivational, attitude directed toward the achievement of the plan's goal-state. The reason why someone could have a plan to rob the First National Bank but not follow it is because he is not moved to achieve the goal of the plan. Similarly, during my absentminded drive to the university, I did not follow my plan because I lacked the motive to be at the university.

Good evidence for someone's being moved to achieve the goal of a plan is that he or she exhibits commitment to the plan. Commitment to a plan, in turn, can be unpacked as a bundle of behavioral tendencies. It involves at least the following: a tendency to respond correctly to questions about the plan, and especially its goal; a tendency to return to action in conformity with the plan if interrupted or sidetracked, and so on. It is possible that a person follow a plan without any of these tendencies becoming manifest; for it is possible that a person follow a plan without being asked questions about it, without being sidetracked, and so on. Moreover, even if some or all of these tendencies are manifest, it is not necessary that a person be moved to follow that plan. There could be ulterior motives on the subject's part to manifest these tendencies; one might, for instance, try to intentionally mislead one's audience. To think that this collection of tendencies is identical with the attitude of being moved toward the goal of a plan is to fall into logical behaviorism. Commitment to a plan, understood as a collection of behavioral tendencies, is only *evidence* that a subject has the conative attitude requisite for following the plan.

4. INTENTIONAL ACTION: A SECOND APPROXIMATION

Definition (D1) is not quite right. It serves to delineate the reach of intentional action, but not its extent. Recall the example about Shady Sam, the used-car salesman. When I bought the car from Sam, there were actions I performed that were not preconceived or preplanned, yet were intentional. For example, adjusting the mirror and seat before test-driving one of Sam's cars was not explicitly preconceived, but it was something I did intentionally. When I constructed my plan to buy a used car, I thought of the highlights—the major actions—of that activity. I preconceived going to the car lot, looking at a number of cars, test driving some of them, and so on. My plan was relatively complicated; but it did not include thinking of every action I would perform. To suppose that I explicitly preconceived every minute action is to attribute to me extraordinary mental capabilities. Definition (D1), in short, is too narrow; it excludes actions that are intentional.

It might be replied that these minute intermediate actions are not intentional and that (D1) in this regard is correct. However, these intermediate actions have all the marks of intentional action. They are actions for which one can be held responsible in appropriate circumstances. They require high-level cognitive abilities to perform. They are not accidental or reflexive. Adjusting the mirror and seat before test driving Sam's car is an action for which I could be held responsible, under certain conditions; it is not accidental or reflexive; and it demands high-level cognitive capacities to complete successfully.

The intentionality of intermediate actions is inherited from the intentionality of the major actions of a plan. Actions are intentional even though not explicitly preconceived when they fall within a pattern of activity that is planned. Normally, only the main steps of a plan are explicitly preconceived. The intermediate actions are performed in the process of performing the main steps. Adjusting the mirror and seat were not explicitly preconceived; but they were undertaken in performing a major action, test-driving the car, that was explicitly preconceived.

Definition (D1) should be replaced by the following:

(D2) S As intentionally during t *iff* (i) S's Aing during t is an action and (ii) during t, S follows a plan that has subroutines $R_1, \ldots, R_n$ ($n \geq 1$) and his Aing is contained in at least one of $R_1, \ldots, R_n$,

where the range of the variables remains the same. A subroutine is a chunk of activity. Some plans are composed of a single chunk; that is, for some plans, the plan is identical with a single subroutine. Most plans, however, are made up of a series of chunks.

To see how (D2) works, consider my plan for going to the university in the morning. This plan consists of a number of subroutines: getting out of bed, showering and grooming, dressing, eating breakfast, driving to the university, parking, and walking to my office. On a normal Monday morning, let us suppose, I follow my plan for going to the university. My showering, according to (D2), is intentional because it is explicitly included in my plan. But my taking the soap from the tray is also intentional, despite my not explicitly preconceiving this action. For my taking the soap from the tray is contained in the subroutine of showering. If I were to articulate every minute action of the subroutine of showering, it would include taking the soap. But when I normally think of my plan to go to the university, I organize my plan in terms of subroutines. I do not explicitly think of the actions contained within these subroutines. According to (D2), these intermediate actions are intentional in virtue of being contained within explicitly preconceived chunks of the plan. These actions fall within the preplanned pattern of activity.

Suppose that on my way to the university, I find the road blocked and must detour. I travel along this new road, and then return to my original route. Is my driving on this new road intentional, even though it was not contained in any subroutine of my original plan? And is the remainder of my trip to the university intentional, despite the disruption of my plan?

To begin with the second question—whether interruption affects intentionality—definition (D2) rules that plan interruption is otiose. According to the definition, all actions performed while following a plan are intentional, independent of whether the plan is interrupted. After the interruption the subject reverts to the original plan; and since what the subject then does is to be explained by reference to the original plan, those actions are intentional. (A technical point: the dependency relations among action types, function h of $\wp$, must be formulated so as to reflect the possibility of interruption.)

The first question concerned the status of the interrupting actions. It is consistent with (D2) that interrupting actions are themselves intentional: they are intentional if they are included in another one of the subject's plans. There is no minimum time, other than the speed of thought, required for plan formation. It is not necessary that we ponder our plans; plans can be formed rapidly. Rapid plan formation often proceeds by combining well-rehearsed subroutines. As I see the detour sign, I quickly form a new, ad hoc plan. This plan utilizes well-rehearsed subroutines for safe driving. Of course, some interrupting actions are not intentional. Suppose that, as I am walking to my office, I trip and automatically thrust my hands forward. My thrusting my hands forward is a nonintentional, interrupting action. It is an automatic response to an emergency situation; it is not part of any plan I have, not even a plan hastily constructed for the occasion.

Plans can interrupt plans, and these ad hoc plans can themselves be interrupted. Nesting of plans can be considerable. But it cannot go on indefinitely. The subject must be capable of returning to the original plan. To return to the original plan involves remembering that plan and the points of nested interruption. The limit of plan nesting, then, depends on the subject's memory capabilities. Infraspecies are capable of little or no nesting. Future robots, *if* they perform actions and follow plans, should be capable of enormous plan nesting.

Plans can be disjunctive. Suppose I form a plan to scale Mt. Wrightson. From the ground I see several possible routes to the summit. I reserve my decision about the route until I get partway up the mountain. My plan to scale Mt. Wrightson has several tracks, each preconceived, and a choice point. If decisions are actions, then these too are intentional.[8] Note that it is not necessary to preconceive each track prior to the decision point. A subject's plan can be open-ended. That is, his plan could be determinate to a decision point and then include a procedure for completing the plan. The final steps in the plan must be conceived prior to performing those steps, but not before beginning the plan.

5. FORESEEN CONSEQUENCES AND INTENTIONAL ACTION

A critic might argue that there are foreseen but unintentional consequences and that this view of intentional action leaves no room for them. For being foreseen is sufficient for being part of a subject's plan; and being part of his plan is sufficient for intentionality.[9]

On the contrary, however, this view does not preclude foreseen consequences of intentional actions. A consequence of a subject's action is foreseen by him just in case he believes with good reason that this future effect of his actions will occur. Being foreseen is *not* sufficient for being part of the subject's plan. A foreseen consequence differs from a future planned action in regard to both the source of the belief about the future event and the role that the belief plays in the subject's conduct. Typically, the belief about a foreseen consequence arises from an inferential process involving common-sense generalizations and other beliefs about the circumstances. But also typically, the source of one's cognitive attitude about a future planned action is not acquired by this type of inferential process. Rather, a plan is formed on the basis of one's goals and a recollection that such goals can be achieved using certain subroutines in one's repertoire.

A person's cognitive attitude toward future planned action is embedded in a network of goals and attitudes about related subroutines; a belief about a future consequence is not embedded in this type of network but rather within a complex of beliefs about the causal structure of the world. The cognitive attitude toward a planned action plays a crucial causal role in the subject's conduct, whereas a belief about a foreseen consequence need not. Beliefs about future consequences do not guide activity; they are predictions about how the world will come to be and ordinarily do not affect activity. The cognitive attitude associated with a planned action does affect future activity. Although such attitudes are not motivational, they do play a causal role in that they provide a guide—or 'map'—of a future course of action. The difference between foreseeing a consequence of one's actions and having planned one's future actions can be summarized as the difference between a cognitive attitude acquired by theoretical reasoning and one acquired by practical reasoning.

A man might form a plan to take a long hike and simultaneously come to believe that his hike will result in painful blisters. Gaining blisters is a foreseen but unplanned consequence of his future activity. He comes to believe that he will have blisters because of an inference about the terrain and his knowledge that certain processes produce blisters. His belief that he will gain blisters as a result of this hike does not guide his activity. Indeed, he acts in spite of this foreseen consequence.

Foreseen side effects are like foreseen consequences, except that side effects occur concurrently with the plan. Consider again my going to the university in the morning. One of the side effects of this activity is wearing down my tires. Wearing down the tire rubber occurs at the same time I carry out my plan to go to the university, though it is (or, can be) foreseen prior to its occurrence. Wearing down the tire rubber is not part of my plan. If I were to come to have the belief that the tire rubber is being worn, I would typically have it in virtue of an inference from my knowledge about tires and road trips, not in virtue of my goals and the subroutines normally used to achieve these goals. My belief that tire rubber is being worn would play no role in the guidance of my ongoing activity.[10]

Suppose, instead, that I were a member of the Goodyear Research Team and that I had the assignment of evaluating tire wear for my automobile under normal use. In that case wearing down my tires would not be a side effect but part of my plan. Photographically, no difference in physical activity would be apparent between this case and my normal drive to the university. But my cognitive attitudes would be different. When employed by the Goodyear Research Team, my belief that tire rubber is being worn plays a role in guiding my activity. This belief is situated within my network of goals and subroutines. In the normal case in which I am not affiliated with Goodyear, the belief that tire rubber is being worn is isolated from my network of goals and subroutines.

As a way of highlighting these points, consider briefly the Catholic doctrine of double effect. This doctrine presupposes a distinction between intentional actions and foreseen consequences. Some intentional actions are absolutely forbidden. However, if the event brought about is only a foreseen consequence of an intentional action, and not part of the action itself, then it may not be forbidden. Suppose that a physician performs an operation to save a woman's life and thereby kills the fetus she is carrying. For the sake of argument, let us agree that killing an innocent person is absolutely forbidden and that the fetus is an innocent person. According to the doctrine of double effect, then, the physician did not do something absolutely forbidden, since killing the fetus was not an intentional action but only a foreseen side effect.[11]

Intentional actions are included within a subject's plan; consequences and side effects, foreseen or otherwise, are not. In essence, the status of an event the subject brings about depends on his prior cognitive attitude. If the physician's plan included killing the fetus, then he did it intentionally; but if killing the fetus was not part of his plan, he did not do it intentionally.

Suppose that it is well known in the medical community that killing the fetus is a necessary means to successfully completing this type of operation. In that case, it is difficult to imagine that killing the fetus would not be part of the physician's plan. If the physician were to recite his plan for saving the woman, it would include killing the fetus. This case is different from my taking a long hike and predicting that I will get blisters. In it, I come to believe that I will get blisters from generalizations about the past. Acquiring blisters is not part of my plan. In the case of the physician, no such theoretical deduction is made. Killing the fetus is a means to saving the woman. This thought is contained within his network of goals and subroutines. We can suppose that the physician does not want to kill the fetus. Still, that is not sufficient for excluding if from his plan. Sometimes our plans include means with which we are unhappy.

It is possible that some physician, despite being well informed, suppresses the thought that killing the fetus is a necessary means to successfully completing the operation. That physician would not have killed the fetus intentionally. And thus, according to the doctrine of double effect, he would not have done what is absolutely forbidden. However, this physician would be irrational, perhaps even pathological. He would have totally suppressed normal practical reasoning patterns because of their unpleasantness.

6. SUMMARY AND PROSPECTUS

Intentional action, I have argued, is action performed when following a plan. A plan is an abstract structure. To have a plan is to represent this abstract structure to oneself. And to follow a plan is to act according to a plan that one has and to be moved to achieve the goal of the plan. Having a plan is a purely cognitive attitude; following a plan involves both cognitive and conative attitudes.

An action can be intentional even if not explicitly preconceived, provided that it is part of a preplanned pattern of activity. A pattern of activity is a series of 'chunks'; these chunks, or subroutines, must be preplanned, but the minute actions within them need not be.

Some things we bring about are not part of any plan we undertake. These events are consequences and side effects of our intentional actions, some of which can be foreseen on the basis of our general, theoretical knowledge about the world.

This entire discussion has been an exercise in descriptive philosophy of mind. Strawson began his well-known book *Individuals* with the lines:

Metaphysics has been often revisionary, and less often descriptive. Descriptive metaphysics is content to describe the actual structure of our thought about the world, revisionary metaphysics is concerned to produce a better structure.[12]

An analogous distinction can be made between descriptive philosophy of mind and revisionary philosophy of mind. Descriptive philosophy of mind is concerned with the conceptual framework of folk or commonsense psychology. It is not so clear what is the subject matter of revisionary philosophy of mind. A highly plausible candidate is the conceptual framework of scientific psychology.

If revisionary philosophy of mind deals with the conceptual framework of scientific psychology, then the interesting question about the relationship between folk and scientific psychology arises. My guess is that, to a significant degree, they are continuous. Folk psychology provides gross explanations; scientific psychology refines these explanations, altering the underlying conceptual framework when necessary. Scientific psychology, as a consequence, is constrained by folk psychology. Now if this conjecture about the relationship between descriptive and revisionary philosophy of mind is correct, then this discussion of the folk psychological concept of intentional action is a prolegomena for a discussion of the underlying conceptual framework for a scientific psychological explanation of such action.[13]

Notes

1. The view that intentional action is also planned action is advanced by Alvin Goldman, *A Theory of Human Action* (Englewood Cliffs, N. J., 1970), esp. chap. 3. Goldman's position on intentional action is discussed by Raimo Toumela, *Human Action and Its Explanation* (Dordrecht, 1977) and Hector-Neri Castaneda, "Intentionality and Identity in Human Action and Philosophical Method," *Nous* 13 (1979): 235-60. I discuss the view that intentional action is planned action in *Intending and Acting* (Cambridge, Mass., 1984).

2. See my "The Language of Not Doing," *American Philosophical Quarterly* 8 (1971): 45-53. Cf. Douglas Walton, "Omitting, Refraining and Letting Happen," *American Philosophical Quarterly* 17 (1980): 319-26.

3. Michael Bratman, for example, adopts the view that plans are psychological states in "Taking Plans Seriously," *Social Theory and Practice* 9 (1983): 271-87.

4. In "On the Ascription of Content" (in *Thought and Object,* edited by A. Woodfield [Oxford, 1982], 153-206), Stephen Stich formulates careful and useful criteria for the attribution of sameness of psychological content. Unfortunately, he fails to distinguish carefully between this epistemological project and the ontological one of stating the existential commitments necessary for the truth of statements of psychological content. Matters are somewhat improved in Stich's *From Folk Psychology to Cognitive Science* (Cambridge, Mass., 1983).

5. Goldman, *Theory of Human Action.* Cf. Jaegwon Kim, "Noncausal Connections," *Nous* 8 (1974): 41-52.

6. Hector-Neri Castaneda has argued convincingly that first-person thoughts are irreducibly so. See his *Thinking and Doing* (Dordrecht, 1975). See also *Agent, Language, and the Structure of the World,* edited by J. Tombelin (Indianapolis, 1983), for discussion of Castaneda's views about first-person reference.

7. See *Intending and Acting.*

8. In "Choosing and Doing," *Ratio* 12 (1970): 85-92, I argue that choices are actional.

9. Cf. Gilbert Harman, "Rational Action and the Extent of Intentions," *Social Theory and Practice* 9 (1983): 123-41.

10. For simplicity, I leave out cases of coming to know about side effects or consequences by means other than one's own theoretical reason. Sometimes, for example, we come to know about consequences of our actions by learning about them from reports of others.

11. Cf. Harman, "Rational Action," and Philippa Foot, "The Problem of Abortion and the Doctrine of Double Effect," *Oxford Review* 5 (1967).

12. P. F. Strawson, *Individuals* (London, 1959), xiii.

13. I profited from comments by Hugh McCann and by "dry runs" of this paper at SMU and Robert Audi's NEH Action Theory Institute at the University of Nebraska, where Audi's and Margaret Coyne's remarks were especially helpful.

The Logical Status of Mind

GEORGE BEALER

Much work in contemporary psychology and philosophy of mind proceeds reductionistically by likening, or by equating, the mind to something that is believed to be better understood: a system of behavioral dispositions, the nervous system, or a computational device.[1] To liken a puzzling kind of entity to something we better understand is often a wise explanatory strategy, and to identify one type of entity with another often yields considerable economy of theory. However, advocates of the prevalent reductionistic approaches to the mind have not at an earlier stage tried to do something that is always appropriate in theoretical inquiry. Namely, they have not early on tried to define what intuitively the subject at hand is supposed to be; they have not tried to give a definition of mind whose immediate purpose is simply to fit the clear-cut, intuitive examples of mental phenomena. This is the primary purpose of the present paper. When surveying these examples, one finds right on the surface purely logical features that are jointly necessary and sufficient for mentality. In this way, the clearcut, intuitive examples reveal that the distinction between the mental and the nonmental—unlike, say, the distinction between sugar and salt—is not naturalistic or empirical in character; rather, the distinction is so basic that it is logical in character. If correct, this is the sort of proposition that can be established before any empirical theorizing. And those who do not make use of this proposition lose the ability to demarcate clearly and precisely the very subject matter of psychology, namely, the mind.

With these bold claims before us, some conciliatory remarks are in order. When I suggest that it is appropriate early on in an inquiry to try to define basic notions of the subject at hand, I am not assuming that success is always possible. Many would hold that definitions of such things as heat, plant, or animal simply could not be given until thermodynamics, botany, or zoology has reached a relatively advanced stage of development. However, at least provisional definitions of fairly basic notions are possible early on in some areas of natural science. For example, we have seen this rather often in mathematical physics: consider the classical Newtonian definition of acceleration as rate of change in velocity; this did not turn on particularly advanced developments elsewhere in the theory. And successful definitions of basic notions are commonplace at the outset of investigations in logic and mathematics. Only a philosophical dogma would exclude out of hand the corresponding definitional possibilities in psychological theory. The general point, then, is not that definitions are always possible early on; rather, the point is that, if such definitions are possible, surely they are desirable; therefore, it is always appropriate to try to find them. Psychological theory should be no exception.

The thesis that the distinction between the mental and the nonmental is logical in character is at odds with the philosophical naturalism so popular nowadays. An assumption of contemporary naturalism is that the natural sciences—physics, chemistry, biology—provide the immediate theoretical framework for psychological theory. But given the special affinity that reason has to logic, there is at least some plausibility in the thesis that it is logic that provides the immediate framework for characterizing certain basic mental notions. Again, it would be dogmatic simply to rule out this prospect.

The thesis that some interesting features of the mind might be discovered by purely a priori means is also out of step with the prevalent empiricism of our time. Yet the goal of psychology is not limited to the prediction and explanation of thought, experience, and behavior. Any acceptable psychological theory must also account for—or at least allow for—the fact that the psychologist has engaged in a psychological process: specifically, that the psychologist has arrived at his or her theory by rational means and, therefore, that it has epistemic merit.[2] To provide for this inevitable rational dimension, psychological theory must contain certain logically distinctive formal features. It should not be surprising that such formal features can be isolated a priori without the aid of empirical research. Reasonable empiricists should be able to admit that such transcendental loops might ensure a priori elements in their otherwise empirical theories. We shall see that such formal features are the ingredients needed for our purely logical analysis of mind.

Despite these conciliatory remarks, this sort of approach to the analysis of mind is unlikely to receive much support from the contemporary cognitive science community. In the present intellectual climate, the effort may be counted a success if others were simply to recognize in it a coherent alternative should their favorite approaches to the mind encounter difficulties.

1. INTENSIONAL LOGIC

When I say that the distinction between the mental and the nonmental is logical in character, I mean that the analysis of it can be stated entirely in terms belonging to logic; specifically, in terms belonging to intensional logic. In extensional logic, expressions having the same extension may be substituted for one another *salva veritate*. Intensional logic is that part of logic in which such a principle of substitutivity is not valid, at least prima facie. Consider a familiar example:

> It is possible that some creature with a kidney is not a creature with a heart.
> Every creature with a kidney is a creature with a heart, and conversely.

∴   It is possible that some creature with a kidney is not a creature with a kidney.

The premises are both true; the second premise ensures that 'creature with a kidney' and 'creature with a heart' have the same extension, and the conclusion arises from the first premise by substituting the first of these expressions for the second. Yet the conclusion is false. Hence, a prima facie counterexample to the substitutivity principle of extensional logic.

Working in the tradition of Gottlob Frege and Bertrand Russell, we may account for intensionality in logic by means of intensional entities. Intensional entities are the kind of extralinguistic entity that can be distinct from one another even when they are equivalent. Properties, relations, propositions, concepts, ideas, etc., are examples. In the above argument, the 'that'-clauses

> that some creature with a kidney is not a creature with a heart

and

> that some creature with a kidney is not a creature with a kidney

are singular terms denoting propositions. Because these propositions are both false, they have the same truth value and, hence, are equivalent. Nevertheless, they are distinct and can therefore have different properties. In particular, because the former proposition would have been true had biological evolution taken an appropriately different course, it has the property of being possible; because the latter proposition actually contradicts a law of logic, it does not have the property of being possible. Thus, the argument is invalid. Here, then, is a typical example of how intensionality in logic can be explained by means of intensional entities. Of course, various logicians and philosophers have tried to explain intensionality in logic without appealing to intensional entities. However, the known attempts to do so, including "syntactic" attempts like that of Carnap, have all run into one difficulty or another. I submit that every attempt will upon critical examination be seen either to fail outright or to appeal covertly to intensional entities.[3]

There have been two prevalent conceptions of intensional entities in the history of logic and philosophy. On the first conception, intensional entities are taken to be identical if and only if they are *necessarily equivalent.* Thus, beyond the requirement of necessary equivalence, this conception just on its own imposes no further requirements on what it takes for a definition of an intensional entity to be correct. For example, each of the following candidate definitions taken from contemporary philosophy could be a correct definition as far as this conception of intensional entities is concerned:

(a) x is grue if and only if x is green if examined before t and blue otherwise.

(b) x is green if and only if x is grue if examined before t and bleen otherwise.[4]

The second conception of intensional entities imposes far stricter conditions on what it takes for a definition to be correct. On this conception, when an intensional entity is defined completely, the result is *unique* and *noncircular.* In this example, (a) is certainly a correct definition in view of its stipulative character. Therefore, on the assumption that complete definitions are unique, green must show up somewhere in the definition of grue either as a defined or as an undefined term. However, on the assumption that complete definitions are never circular, green cannot in turn be defined in terms of grue. Therefore, even though (b) provides us with a necessary equivalence, it cannot be a correct definition. Necessary equivalence is a necessary condition but not a sufficient condition for the identity of intensional entities.

The first conception underlies the currently popular possible-worlds treatment of intensional entities, and it also underlies Alonzo Church's "Alternative (2)" formulation of Frege's theory of senses.[5] This conception is particularly well suited to the treatment of the modalities (necessity, possibility, etc.), probability statements, counterfactuals, and so forth. The second conception has a rather livelier history. It underlies Leibniz's doctrine of simple and complex properties and Russell's doctrine of logical atomism. And when intensional entities are identified with ideas (concepts, thoughts), we see that this conception was adopted at least implicitly by nearly all modern philosophers from Descartes and Locke through Kant. For example, it is evident in the distinction made by Descartes and Locke between simple and complex ideas, and it underlies Kant's original definition of analyticity. Finally, this conception underlies Alonzo Church's "Alternative (0)" formulation of Frege's theory of senses.[6]

Some people who are friendly to the first conception of intensional entities might doubt the legitimacy of the second conception. However, just as the first conception matches the intensionality present in the logic for the modalities, probability statements, and counterfactuals, the second conception matches the intensionality present in the logic for intentional matters—belief, desire, decision, assertion—and the intensionality present in the logic for logical truth and validity, provability, natural language semantics, and epistemic appraisal. Consider a sample argument involving logical truth:

> It is logically true that all triangles are triangles.
> It is necessarily true that all and only triangles are trilaterals.

∴   It is logically true that all triangles are trilaterals.

Given the first conception of intensional entities, the second premise of this argument would entail that being a triangle is identical to being a trilateral and, in turn, that the proposition that all triangles are triangles and the proposition that all triangles are trilaterals are identical. And if this is true, the conclusion of the argument would follow logically from the two premises. But intuitively the conclusion does not follow, for the proposition that all triangles are trilaterals is only a truth of geometry, not a truth of logic. The type of intensional entities that are the primary bearers of the property of logical truth are more finely distinguished than those provided by the first conception. The finely distinguished intensional entities provided by the second conception fill the bill. To see fine-grained intensions at work in natural language semantics, notice that

> 'All triangles are trilaterals' means in English that all triangles are trilaterals.

is true, whereas

> 'All triangles are trilaterals' means in English that all triangles are triangles.

is false. To see the call for fine-grained intensions in epistemic appraisal, notice that

> The proposition that all triangles are triangles requires no epistemic justification.

is true, whereas

> The proposition that all triangles are closed figures whose internal angles sum to 180° requires no epistemic justification.

is false. And for an example involving provability: it is provable in elementary logic that all triangles are triangles but not that all triangles are trilaterals.

Now there exist other conceptions providing intensional entities that, though more finely distinguished than those provided by the first conception, are not as finely distinguished as those provided by the second conception. Virtually all of what I have to say below would hold if one of these intermediate conceptions were to serve the logical functions I have ascribed to the second conception. However, I submit that a consideration of the full range of examples inevitably forces one to this conception. Alonzo Church arrived at this conception by consideration of examples from intentional logic.[7] Nonintentional examples would also suffice for this purpose. Consider purely logical examples such as the following taken from the logic for the relation of logical validity (consequence):

> (1) Given that everything is self-identical, it follows validly by exactly one application of the principle of double negation that everything is not not self-identical.

It will not do to treat this example "syntactically":

> (2) Given the English sentence 'Everything is self-identical', the English sentence 'Everything is not not self-identical' follows validly by exactly one application of the principle of double negation.

because syntactic treatments fail the Langford-Church translation test.[8] Thus, translating (1) and (2) into a foreign language, say, German, we obtain two sentences that patently report quite different information:

> (1′) Gegeben, dass alles selbstidentisch ist, folgt es stichhaltig durch genau eine Anwendung des Doppeltnegationprinzips, dass alles nicht nicht selbstidentisch ist.
> (2′) Gegeben den englischen Satz 'Everything is self-identical', folgt der englische Satz 'Everything is not not self-identical' stichhaltig durch genau eine Anwendung des Doppeltnegationprinzips.

For example, whereas (1′) reports something known by every German logic student, (2′) reports something known only by people with knowledge both of some elementary logic and of the English language. Purely logical examples like (1) thus cannot be plausibly treated by means of syntactic entities. But their treatment requires extralinguistic "semantic" entities that nevertheless have a structure (or logical form) very much like that of syntactic entities. The fine-grained intensions provided by the second conception answer perfectly to this requirement.

Intensional entities play an ultimate role in the objective, nonarbitrary categorization and identification of objects; in the objective description and theoretical explanation of change; and in the constitution of experience. But not just any intensional entities can play these important roles; the ones that can are said to be *qualities* and *connections*. Among the myriad intensional entities it is qualities and connections that determine the logical, causal, and phenomenal order in reality.[9] Now when qualities and connections are combined by means of appropriate fundamental logical operations, sooner or later one comes to *conditions*. Conditions are the sorts of things that can be said to obtain or to be so.

Intensional entities that are neither qualities, connections, nor conditions are ones that pertain primarily not to the world but instead to thinking and to reason, taken broadly. Such intensional entities are called *concepts* and *thoughts*. Consider the example of green and grue mentioned earlier. Whereas green is a genuine quality (specifically, a sensible quality), grue is only a concept (i.e., the concept expressed in English by the complex expression 'green if examined before *t* and blue otherwise'). As such, grue plays no ultimate role in the objective, nonarbitrary categorization and identification of objects; nor does it play an ultimate role in the description and theoretical explanation of change; nor does it play an ultimate role in the constitution of experience. Nevertheless, like other concepts, grue can play a role in matters of thinking and of reason. Now, from a purely logical point of view, the difference between qualities, connections, and conditions on the one hand and concepts and thoughts on the other is that qualities, connections, and conditions conform to the first traditional conception; i.e., qualities, connections, and conditions are identical if and only if they are necessarily equivalent. However, though necessary equivalence is a necessary condition for the identity of concepts and thoughts, it is not a sufficient condition. For concepts and thoughts conform to the second traditional conception.[10]

Consider an example involving shape. Take the following figure:

(α)

What shape is (α)? In answer to this question, one might say that (α) is a triangle. Or one could equally well say that (α) is a trilateral. Each of these answers suffices to inform us of its shape. The reason for this is that, intuitively, the quality of triangularity and the quality of trilaterality are the very same quality. They are how it is with (α) in regard to shape. Though the concept of being a triangle and the concept of being a trilateral are distinct, they correspond to the same quality of things in the world. The reason is that qualities, unlike concepts, are identical if there is no possibility of an object having one of them but not the other. Qualities (and connections) are what fix the actual conditions in the world, and they do not exhibit distinctions finer than necessary equivalents. Concepts, on the other hand, pertain to thinking and to reason; it is here that finer intensional distinctions show up. Thus, we arrive at the accompanying picture of the types of intensional entities.

	0-ary intensions	1-ary intensions	2-ary intensions	...
conception 2 (ideas)	thoughts	1-ary concepts	2-ary concepts	...
conception 1	conditions (states of affairs)	qualities	2-ary connections	...

Given this two-tier picture, it remains to account for how conception 2 intensions are related to conception 1 intensions. On realistic accounts, conception 2 intensions are contructed ultimately from qualities and connections (plus perhaps subjects of singular predication) by means of certain fundamental logical operations—singular predication, conjunction, negation, existential generalization, and so forth. So, for example, the thought that x spins is the outcome of predicating the quality of spinning of the object x. [That is, the thought that x spins = Pred(spinning,x).] A primary advantage of this account is that it includes a solution to the problem of representation: ideas succeed in representing things in the world because they actually are constructed from things in the world; nothing is needed in the account of how thoughts and concepts represent except the fundamental thought-building operations (like singular predication, conjunction, etc.) and objects in the world, including qualities and connections.[11] Notice that according to this theory, qualities and connections are not radically different from thoughts and concepts; indeed, they are just the limiting case. That is to say, they are those intensions that cannot be analyzed (defined) in terms of the fundamental thought-building operations plus other intensions. More precisely, they are in the range of none of these operations, and accordingly, they have no (complex) logical form.

But why should someone accept this full two-tier logical theory? Besides answering to a large family of logical and conceptual intuitions, the full theory is required for a long list of important theoretical tasks.[12] Suppose, however, we encounter someone (e.g., a nominalistically inclined, naturalistic empiricist) who resists this sort of logical theory on two counts: first, logical and conceptual intuitions do not qualify as legitimate data (evidence) because sense experience is the only legitimate source of data; and, second, in this person's own theoretical work there is no need to accomplish those special tasks that require this rich formulation of intensional logic. I believe that these two claims can be overturned by means of certain "transcendental" arguments. Although it is not feasible to present these arguments in detail here, I will sketch them in broad outline.

Concerning the first claim, what is it that makes our opponent's extreme empiricist theory of data a rational one? Why is it not a mere expression of preference or a mere biohistorical episode that someone pursuing knowledge need not take seriously? Any response that falls back on the same empiricist theory of data only invites the same question. For example, suppose the response invokes a "total" theory that is generated by and that includes the empiricist theory of data. Why accept this total theory rather than some (perhaps simpler) alternate total theory that is generated by and that includes some alternate theory of data? Is the empiricist's choice more than an expression of preference or a biohistorical accident? One way for the empiricist to try to escape this circle would be to assert something like, "By definition, an item is a datum iff . . . " or " 'data' is definitionally equivalent in English to ' . . . '. " But how is any such definitional assertion to be defended? If our opponent again attempts an exclusively empirical justification (say, in the guise of an empirically defended behavioral or causal theory of meaning), the same sort of question may be asked once more; no significant progress will have been made out of the circle. Why is the thus-enlarged collection of (allegedly empirical) assertions more than a biohistorical episode having no special epistemic merit? Why not accept some (possibly simpler) collection of assertions that affirms some alternate definition of data? At this ultimate stage of epistemological dialectic, our opponent has no alternative left but to invoke as data logical and conceptual intuitions concerning the nature of data (or the meaning of 'data') and the application of the concept to actual and hypothetical cases. But if the empiricist must admit these logical and conceptual intuitions as data, it follows that the original empiricist theory of data cannot be consistently maintained. Further, if the empiricist must admit these intuitions as data, it would be arbitrary to exclude as data other logical and conceptual intuitions including, in particular, those that support our logical theory.

Next consider our opponent's second claim. (Here I will extend a line of argument developed by George Myro in "Aspects of Acceptability.") To justify their scientific and philosophical theories and to criticize those of their opponents, naturalistic empiricists must inevitably invoke a principle of epistemic appraisal or acceptability. The following, which is extrapolated from the writing of W. V. O. Quine, captures what is at the heart of these principles: a theory is acceptable if and only if it is (or belongs to) the simplest overall theory that explains the data.[13] A second basic principle of naturalistic empiricism is that, when taken together, the natural sciences (plus perhaps extensional mathematics) comprise the simplest overall theory that explains the data. It follows from these two principles that a theory is acceptable if and only if it is (or belongs to) the overall theory that consists of the natural sciences (plus perhaps extensional mathematics). Notice, however, that the expressions 'acceptable', 'simplest', 'explain', and 'data' do not belong to the primitive vocabulary of this overall theory. Let us suppose that these expressions are not definable in terms of that primitive vocabulary. In this case, the two basic principles of naturalistic empiricism—and all the powerful conclusions that depend on them—would not belong to the overall theory and, therefore, would not be acceptable according to naturalistic empiricism. This self-defeating consequence can be avoided only if the key expressions 'acceptable', 'simplicity', 'explanation', and 'data' are, contrary to our supposition, definable within the overall theory. (We allow that some of these expressions and their definitions might have to be ramified à la type theory to avoid certain logical difficulties.) For this reason, naturalistic empiricism is forced to accept the thesis that these expressions are indeed so definable. But this thesis entails that the overall naturalistic theory must possess an apparatus for representing definitional relationships. Now this apparatus either would or would not be metalinguistic. If it were not metalinguistic, it would have to be (something like) one of the following:

By definition, Fx iff ... x ....
It is definitionally true that Fx iff ... x ....
The concept of being an x such that Fx = the concept of being an x such that ... x ....
F-ness = the property of being an x such that ... x ....

(Mere material biconditionals would not suffice, for they lack the force of definitions.) But the logic for constructions of this type is clearly intensional, and the simplest explanation of intensional constructions is in terms of intensional entities. So on this option, naturalistic empiricists would be forced to invoke an ontology that, by their very own principles, is unacceptable. On the other hand, if the apparatus for representing definitional relationships were metalinguistic, it would have to involve a strong semantical term like 'synonymous in L', 'definitionally equivalent in L', 'analytic in L', or some kindred term. But once again strict naturalistic empiricism would be thwarted. For generalized Quinean indeterminacy considerations show that strong semantical terms like 'synonymous in L' cannot be defined using only terms belonging to the natural sciences and extensional mathematics. (See section 5 for more on this.) So on this metalinguistic option, naturalistic empiricists would again be committed to a definitional apparatus that, according to the central principles of their philosophy, is unacceptable. This is not to say that strong semantical notions like synonymy cannot be defined. They can be, but only in terms of intentional notions—along Gricean lines, for example. But considerations rather analogous to those leading to Quine's indeterminacy thesis (see section 5 below) show that these intentional notions cannot be defined using only terms belonging to the natural sciences and extensional mathematics. At the core of these considerations is the fact that the logic for intentional matters is intensional (indeed, "hyperintensional"). However, as we have seen, the simplest explanation for intensionality in logic is in terms of intensional entities. So as in the case of a nonmetalinguistic apparatus, a metalinguistic apparatus for representing definitional relationships produces an ontological commitment to such entities.

Our conclusions so far are the following. Naturalistic empiricists are forced by their own basic principles to avail themselves of some apparatus for representing definitional relationships. But any such apparatus— metalinguistic or nonmetalinguistic—turns out to be unacceptable according to these very same principles. Thus, naturalistic empiricism in its strict form is a self-defeating philosophy and, hence, is unacceptable. Further, because any apparatus adequate for representing definitional relationships presupposes a logical theory that is ontologically committed to intensional entities, naturalistic empiricists have no choice but to weaken their basic principles to make room for this inevitable intensional ontology.

This line of argument indicates that a logical theory with an intensional ontology is inevitable, but can we go on to show that our full logical theory— with its ontology of qualities, connections, conditions, concepts, and thoughts— is inevitable? Do naturalistic empiricists have specific theoretical tasks to perform that force them to accept the full intensional logic? To show that they do, we must look to the specific notions they employ in the basic principles of their philosophy—in particular, the notions of simplicity and explanation. (At the close of the paper I will indicate how the full two-tier intensional ontology is also needed in an account of the notion of data.) Consider simplicity first. The only way to assess the simplicity of a theory is to express the theory using just primitive constants for qualities and connections; failing this, the simplicity of a superficial syntax can mask the true complexity of a theory.[14] Thus, in the defense of their second basic principle (stated earlier), naturalistic empiricists must invoke the ontology of qualities and connections. Next, consider explanation. Naturalistic empiricists hope to define this notion by means of a hypothetico-deductive account, which employs notions of logical validity and causal law. But how are these notions to be defined? Consider logical validity. A language-neutral, extralinguistic notion is what is needed for a *general* formulation of the hypothetico-deductive account of explanation. Such a notion may be defined along the following lines: a thought is logically valid iff$_{df}$ every thought having the same logical form corresponds to a condition that is necessary. And the notions of logical form, correspondence, and necessity are definable in the full intensional logic.[15] Finally, consider the notion of causal law. A standard regularity account is inadequate because it is unable to accommodate such phenomena as the antisymmetry of the explanation relation (vis-à-vis causal laws that are biconditional in form). Either the notion of causal connection (causal connections being inherently antisymmetric) or, at least, the general notions of quality and connection are required to accommodate such phenomena.[16] Once again, these notions are definable in the full intensional logic.[17] In the above ways, then, the full intensional logic proves useful for dealing with the naturalistic empiricist notions of simplicity and explanation. At the same time, no essentially weaker theoretical framework appears to be adequate for all these purposes. In view of this, naturalistic empiricists appear to have no alternative but to modify the basic principles of their philosophy to make room for the full intensional logic.

Although these remarks have been highly schematic, they should at least make it credible that anyone inclined to espouse naturalistic empiricism—or, more generally, anyone with aspirations to theories comprehensive enough to account for their own acceptability or epistemic virtue—is forced eventually to incorporate the sort of intensional logic I have been advocating. It is this sort of logical theory that provides a framework rich enough for analyzing intentionality and mind.

2. INTENTIONALITY

An intentional phenomenon, according to Franz Brentano, is one that makes reference to, is directed upon, or is about other objects, perhaps even objects that do not exist. Brentano used this concept of intentionality to formulate his two-part thesis of intentionality:

(1) All and only mental phenomena are intentional.
(2) No purely physical phenomenon is intentional.

I will return to Brentano's thesis later. My goal now is to analyze intentionality—this special phenomenon of *aboutness*—without resorting to linguistic or spatial metaphors as Brentano did.

In the history of philosophy, the prevailing theories of intentional phenomena have been nonpropositional/nonrelational. On Brentano's theory, for example, when one judges that there exists a man, one does not stand in a relation to the proposition that there exists a man. Rather, one affirms or accepts men. Evidence of such nonpropositional/nonrelational theories are found in works ranging from Plato's *Sophist* and *Theatetus* to Russell's introduction for the first edition of *Principia Mathematica* and to his *The Problems of Philosophy*. These theories all suffer from a central shortcoming that is *logical* in nature: namely, they are unable to handle *general* statements concerning intentional phenomena.[18] For example, they are unable to account systematically and without circularity for intuitively valid inferences such as the following:

Whatever x judges y judges.
Whatever y judges z judges.
_____
∴   Whatever x judges z judges.

Whatever x judges is true.
x judges that A.

∴   It is true that A.

However, if we treat 'judges' as a two-place predicate and 'that A' as a singular term, then such arguments are easily represented within the framework of quantifier logic:

$(\forall u)(xJu \rightarrow yJu)$
$(\forall u)(yJu \rightarrow zJu)$

$(\forall u)(xJu \rightarrow zJu)$

$(\forall u)(xJu \rightarrow Tu)$
$xJ[A]$

$T[A]$

However, in adopting this treatment we are led inevitably to the conclusion that 'judges' expresses a binary relation and that the range of this relation is made up of the sort of thing characteristically denoted by 'that'-clauses, namely, propositions.[19] And so it is that we arrive at the relational/propositional theory of judgment.

Nowadays, the adverbial treatment is perhaps the most popular non-relational treatment of judgment. On this treatment, 'x judges that A' is rendered '$(A(J))x$'. Here '$(A(J))$' is a compound monadic predicate, and the formula A functions as an adverbial phrase that modifies the monadic predicate J by fixing a relevant "way of judging" (intuitively, the way one judges when one judges that A). On this treatment, a general sentence such as 'Whatever x judges y judges' must then be rendered '$(\forall\phi)((\phi(J))x \rightarrow (\phi(J))y)$'. Here the variable ϕ takes formulas as substituends, and it functions as an adverbial phrase whose semantical values range over "ways of judging." Notice, however, that the construction '$(\phi(J))x$' requires the adverbial theorist to admit that singular-judgment statements are true only if there is a relation—namely, $[(\phi(J))x]_{x\phi}$—that holds between individuals and "ways of judging." Further, since '$(\phi(F))$' and '$(A(F))$' are unfamiliar idioms, we are owed an account of their semantics. This can be done but only if the adverbial theorist in effect reintroduces the relational/propositional treatment in the metatheory. (For example, adverbial occurrences of ϕ may be treated as fixing partial functions that take a certain kind of relational property to another kind of relational property: if $F = [(\exists q)xR^2q]_x$ for some relation R^2 and if $p = $ the proposition expressed by ϕ when it functions as a formula, then the partial function fixed by an adverbial occurrence of ϕ takes F to $[xR^2p]_x$. Accordingly, $[(A(J))x] = [xJ[A]]$.) Consequently, nothing is gained by the adverbial approach, and hence, the essentially simpler relational/propositional approach is superior.[20]

Now each expression in the family 'thought', 'belief', 'judgment', and so forth, has at least three related uses. Each can be used to mean (1) a kind of intentional act, (2) the propositional object of the intentional act, or (3) a relation holding between persons performing the intentional act and the propositional object of the act. The nonrelation/nonpropositional theory acknowledges only the first of these three uses, the one for intentional acts. This forces the theory to give its account of intentionality in the inevitably opaque terms of intentional acts, making metaphor and circularity unavoidable. By contrast, the relational/propositional theory acknowledges all three uses and thus is free to analyze intentional acts in terms of the associated relations and their propositional objects. The following is an illustration of how easy these analyses can be: x performs the intentional act of thinking that A if and only if x stands in the relation of thinking to the thought that A.

However, I have said nothing yet concerning the intentionality of intentional acts, their directedness or aboutness. How does that arise? The answer is that it arises from the intensional entities, (e.g., from the thoughts) to which the person stands in the relation thought, belief, judgment, and so forth. After all, thoughts in the propositional sense are themselves things that are characteristically said to be about other objects; indeed, they are often said to be about objects that do not exist. The same thing holds not just for thoughts but for all ideas, concepts as well as thoughts. On this account, an intentional act can be said to be about other things for one reason only; namely, the intentional act consists in standing in a certain relation to an idea—a thought or concept—that can be said to be about things. (Intentional acts of the kind described with objectival constructions might seem to be an exception; section 3.3 shows why this is not so even if these constructions are taken at face value.) This is to say, an intentional act can be said to be about other things only secondarily through the idea that is the immediate object of the act. Ideas—the type of intensional entities provided by the second traditional conception—are the objects that can in a primary way be said to be about other things. (Qualities, connections, and conditions are not like this. They simply qualify, connect, or obtain; they are not *about* anything.)

With the intensional logic described earlier, we are able to catalogue the ways in which ideas—thoughts and concepts—can be about other objects, even nonexistent ones. And we can do this entirely in terms of fundamental logical operations on intensional entities: namely, singular predication, conjunction, negation, existential generalization, etc. For example, the most direct way in which a thought can be about an object occurs when the thought is the outcome of a singular predication and the object is its subject (i.e., the thought that $Fx = \text{Pred}(F,x)$, where x is the object, F is a 1-ary intension, and Pred is the logical operation of singular predication).

So far, then, we have the following conclusions. First, there are independent logical grounds supporting the relational/propositional theory of thinking. Second, using the relational/propositional theory, we are able to analyze intentional acts in terms of the associated relations and propositional or conceptual objects. Third, the intentionality (i.e., the aboutness) of an intentional act can be accounted for by the fact that the intentional act consists in standing in an appropriate relation to an idea—either a thought or a concept—that, given the right context, can be said to be about other objects, even objects that do not exist. Fourth, using the logic for thoughts and concepts, we can identify all the formal features that are at work in determining what in a given context an idea can be said to be about.

Yet the story is not complete, for there is an unsolved problem. Standing in just any relation to a thought or concept does not constitute an intentional act. Only certain very distinctive relations will do—relations such as thinking, believing, judging, remembering, perceiving, desiring, deciding, intending, etc. These relations, naturally enough, are called intentional relations. The problem is to give a noncircular definition of what an intentional relation is. If this problem can be solved, then the analysis of intentionality will be complete.

What makes this problem seem difficult initially is that there are many ad hoc relations (i.e., grue-like relations, which are not genuine connections) whose logical behavior is very much like that of genuine intentional connections. (Recall that connections are those special relations that, together with genuine qualities, fix the logical, causal, and phenomenal order of the world.) The key to the problem is to proceed in two stages. The first stage is to define what an intentional connection is. In the second stage, we then state what it takes for an ad hoc relation to be intentional; it is one whose analysis depends in a logically essential way on intentional connections. Naturally, there are many forms this kind of dependence can take, so there are many ways in which an ad hoc intentional relation can be said to be intentional. But this is a technical point not important to the central concerns in philosophy of mind. The core of our problem comes down to the problem of discovering what is logically distinctive about intentional connections.[21]

Given what I have already said, we know that intentional connections can connect individuals to ideas—thoughts or concepts. However, there are certain nonintentional logical connections that are like this too. Consider an example that arose earlier, namely, the operation of singular predication. This basic logical relation connects individual objects x and 1-ary intensions F to thoughts that Fx. Notice, however, that whenever this relation holds among three such items, it does so necessarily, not contingently. Thus, when this relation holds, we do not have what we may call a real phenomenon; we have instead a logically necessary condition. Intentional connections, by contrast, are typically not like this: when an intentional connection holds, typically it does so contingently, not necessarily. This is why intentional connections give rise to genuine phenomena. Thus, in our definition we should require of intentional connections that they be able contingently to connect individuals to ideas—concepts or thoughts. I call this the *contingency requirement*.

For a second example of a nonintentional relation that can connect individuals to ideas, consider the relation of falling under a concept. This relation meets the contingency requirement: it can contingently relate an individual to a concept. (For example, it is contingent that Socrates falls under the concept of being more than five feet tall.) But notice that, whenever this relation holds between an individual and a concept, it must also hold between the individual and all necessarily equivalent concepts. Intentional connections, by contrast, are not like this. An intentional connection can contingently connect an individual to a concept independently of whether it connects the individual to necessarily equivalent concepts. Analogously, an intentional connection can contingently connect an individual to a thought independently of whether it connects the individual to necessarily equivalent thoughts. I call this feature *hyperintensionality*.[22]

There are a number of nonintentional, naturalistic relations that can contingently relate individuals to ideas. None of them, however, is a connection with the special additional feature of hyperintensionality. Consider an example.[23] Suppose that we come across what appears to be a rabbit's footprint in the snow. We might say of this little depression in the otherwise smooth surface that it makes it probable that a rabbit was here. But notice that, necessarily, if a particular x makes a thought y probable and y is necessarily equivalent to another thought z, then x also makes z probable. (That is, for each argument x, x's image under the rendering probable relation is closed under necessary equivalence.) However, nothing analogous is true of intentional connections. To see this, consider an example taken from Quine.[24] The thought that a rabbit was here is necessarily equivalent to the thought that an undetached rabbit part was here. Thus, necessarily, if a depression in the snow renders it probable that a rabbit was here, then the depression also renders it probable that an undetached rabbit part was here. However, a person can think (remember, desire, etc.) that a rabbit was here and yet fail to think (remember, desire, etc.) that an undetached rabbit part was here. Indeed, the person might at the moment be quite unable to grasp the latter thought. Now the broader philosophical point is this. The nonintentional, naturalistic relation of rendering probable does not have the capacity to cut those fine-grained intensional distinctions characteristic of conception 2: standing in this relation to one thought requires standing indiscriminately in it to all necessarily equivalent thoughts. Thus, in effect, this relation relates individuals not to thoughts singly but instead to equivalence classes of necessarily equivalent thoughts. Now there is a one-one map that takes each such equivalence class to the condition to which the thoughts in the class correspond. Thus, in effect, this relation of rendering probable does little more than relate individuals to conditions. Intentional relations, by contrast, make discriminations finer than necessary equivalence, opening up the possibility of beings whose states are indistinguishable from the point of view of naturalistic (i.e., probabilistic) information flow but who nevertheless are in distinct states. (Of course, there might be hyperintensional naturalistic relations that are not real connections; some candidate examples are discussed in section 3.4.)

There are traditional philosophical views that intentional connections need not display both contingency and hypertensionality with respect to *every* individual and *every* idea. For example, on certain views God necessarily thinks all and only true thoughts, and certain inanimate objects (e.g., stones) necessarily think no thoughts. Further, some philosophers hold that anyone who thinks at all must think certain thoughts; for example, if I think at all, perhaps I must think I exist (at least as a transcendental unity of apperception). And other philosophers maintain that there are logically degenerate thoughts such that, if we think one of them, we must also think at least some other thought that is necessarily equivalent to it; for example, if we think that A and $A,$ then we must also think that $A.$ Finally, on some views, there are some thoughts that are impossible for any one person to think. For example, suppose that p is the first-person thought someone thinks when asserting 'I am thinking', that q is the first-person thought someone else thinks when asserting 'I am thinking', and that r is the result of conjoining p and $q.$ Then, perhaps the privacy of a person's first-person thoughts makes it impossible for anyone to think r directly (i.e., without the aid of any intervening descriptive concepts). Now many people will wish to question some of these views. (For example, some will doubt any view implying that God's thoughts are necessarily determined and, hence, that He is unfree, and others will doubt the limitation on what is logically possible implicit in the metaphysical essentialism concerning stones.) In any event, even if each of these views is correct, it is clear that intentional connections can be contingent and hyperintensional for *some* individuals and *some* ideas.

The resulting logical picture is this. The family of genuine connections that can hold between an individual and some other item is quite distinctive to begin with. And the connections that can hold between an individual and an idea are particularly distinctive. Of the latter connections, all and only those that are intentional can be both contingent and hyperintensional.

Assembling the foregoing ideas, we arrive at the following analysis:

A connection is intentional if and only if it can contingently connect an individual to a thought or a concept independently of whether it connects the individual to a necessarily equivalent thought or concept.[25]

In symbols, a connection c is intentional iff$_{df}$

$$\Diamond(\exists xyz)(\text{Ind}(x)\ \&\ \text{Idea}(y)\ \&\ y\approx_N z\ \&\ \Diamond(x,y\ \Delta\ c\ \&\ x,z\ \cancel{\Delta}\ c)\ \&\ \Diamond x,y\cancel{\Delta}\ c).$$

What is most distinctive about this analysis is that it is given entirely in terms of logic, specifically, the intensional logic I described earlier. (The ultimate primitive terms of the analysis are just those for intensional abstraction and the copula Δ.) The view that emerges is that the intentional/ nonintentional distinction is so basic that it is neither naturalistic nor empirical in character; rather, it is purely logical. The claim here is that all and only intentional connections have the indicated logical character; what is distinctive about us intentional beings is that we can stand in contingent connections to ideas independently of the necessarily equivalent ideas to which we might be connected. Within the tide of naturalistic information, we intentional beings exercise our capacity to be connected to subtly distinct aspects of that brute flow and, indeed, pursue our lives in these terms. It is thus that the phenomenon of intentionality emerges into the less subtle world of nature.

3. POTENTIAL COUNTEREXAMPLES

There are a number of potential counterexamples to this analysis of the concept of intentional connection. Although many appear promising at first, they can all be dealt with. Still, some of them are of philosophical interest in their own right. For this reason, as well as to impart a better feel for the analysis, I will explain why the best of these counterexamples fail.

(1) Ad hoc relations

There are countless ad hoc nonintentional relations that can be defined by tricks of elementary logic so that they have the properties of contingency and hyperintensionality. For example, let Rxy iff$_{df}$ x is more than five feet tall and $y =$ the proposition that there are nine planets. Then the relation expressed by 'Rxy' holds between anyone more than five feet tall and the proposition that there are nine planets, and it does so contingently and without holding between such people and any necessarily equivalent propositions. Obviously this relation is not intentional, but just as obviously it is ad hoc and not a genuine connection. So it is not a counterexample to the proposed definition of intentional connection.

   Naturally, there also are ad hoc intentional relations that lack contingency, hyperintensionality, or both. However, the second stage of our two-stage strategy takes care of intentional relations of this sort. In each case, the definition of the relation involves intentional connections in some logically essential way. For example, the relation holding between x and y such that x believes something that is necessarily equivalent to y does not have hyperintensionality. However, the definition of this nonbasic relation involves an intentional connection—namely, belief—in a logically essential way. So it qualifies as intentional at the second stage of the proposed analysis.

For a somewhat more interesting family of nonbasic relations, let us consider physical measure functions. These functions are nonintentional relations that contingently correlate individuals with numbers. For example, the relation holding between a parent and the number of his children, the relation holding between a physical object and the number of grams in it (i.e., the number of disjoint one-gram parcels in an exhaustive decomposition of it), the relation holding between a physical object and the number of ounces in it, and so forth. For these relations to be even prima facie counterexamples to our analysis, numbers would have to be identified with concepts. In this case, we should ask to what sort of things these number concepts apply. A broadly Fregean answer is surely the best: numbers are not concepts of *single* individuals (e.g., this parent or that piece of gold); rather, they are concepts of the abstract items (sets, concepts) that we employ for the purpose of thinking about individuals *collectively*. When we say that three is the number of x's children, we are not suggesting that each (or any) of x's children is three or three-ish. Rather, the set (or concept) of x's children is three or three-ish; the set (or concept) falls under the numerical concept of being a set (concept) with three individuals in it. Now the details of this kind of approach are not important here; and, as is well known, there are many alternative analyses that differ from Frege's own in one way or another. What is important is that on any broadly Fregean analysis, physical measure functions turn out to be nonbasic relations defined exclusively in terms of fundamental formal relations (such as the logical relation of falling under a concept) and physical relations that hold exclusively among individuals (such as the parent relation or the relation of weighing the same).[26] Therefore, even though physical measure functions might have a superficial resemblance to genuine intentional connections (by virtue of the fact that they can contingently correlate individuals and intensions), they are significantly different. Upon closer examination they are revealed to be nonbasic relations definable in terms of underlying physical and formal relations that are not even in prima facie conflict with the proposed analysis of intentional connections.[27]

For a final example of nonbasic relations that bear a superficial resemblance to genuine intentional connections, consider *utterance-token meaning*—as in the relation holding between utterance tokens and what they mean in a community. This is a contingent hyperintensional relation: it can contingently relate a particular (namely, an utterance token) to an idea (namely, the meaning of the utterance token in the community) without relating the particular to any necessarily equivalent ideas. Is utterance-token meaning truly a connection? It hardly seems so. An utterance token and the relevant idea are not related to one another just on their own; the active intervention of a third element is required, namely, the intentional activity of the thinking beings in the community. Not unless these beings make utterances with appropriate intentions and beliefs do utterance tokens become related to the relevant ideas. Intending and believing are the genuine intentional connections; the relation between the utterance token and the idea that comes to be its meaning is entirely derivative. Unlike intending and believing, it plays no role in the primary causal and phenomenal order of the world. Indeed, on a broadly Gricean approach, utterance-token meaning is explicitly definable in terms of these underlying intentional connections.[28]

The reader may ask how in a given case one can determine that a relation is ad hoc and not a genuine connection. There are two related procedures. First, we do, as a matter of fact, have quite firm intuitions about these matters generally. The following familiar criterion often helps to bring out these intuitions: predicates that are not just syntactically primitive but semantically primitive as well always express qualities and connections. Since traditional philosophical analysis strives to systematize our conceptual intuitions within an ordered framework of definitions, it can often settle questions regarding semantical primitiveness and, in turn, questions of whether or not a relation is basic. This sort of procedure was just illustrated in our application of a broadly Fregean philosophical analysis of numerical measure functions and in our application of a broadly Gricean philosophical analysis of utterance-token meaning. Second, this sort of procedure meshes with another procedure that one can follow to help settle problematic examples that arise in the context of empirical inquiry. This second procedure, which is built upon the first, is this. Given the special role that qualities and connections play in phenomenal description—and in the constitution of experience itself—we may look to our experience to identify certain genuine qualities and connections, namely, phenomenal qualities and mental connections. (For example, we can experience green but not grue. If we were unable to identify phenomenal qualities and mental connections in this way, we could not notice change or constancy in our experience.) Having identified these, we may then seek causal explanations of why we experience them when we do. Among the competing explanations, consider those that posit theoretical qualities and connections described solely in terms of known phenomenal qualities and mental connections, the notion of causation, the general notions of quality and connection, and any other basic notions isolated by our best system of philosophical analysis. Since the explanations are all formulated with the same terms, one can straightforwardly compare their complexity without running into the relativist's worry that ad hoc properties and relations might sneak in under the veil of a superficially simple syntax of primitive theoretical terms. After doing this, one would be justified in identifying the simplest of these explanations as correct. Then, from this explanation one can extract a provisional list of theoretical qualities and connections. Suppose, however, that this procedure should fail to isolate a unique causal explanation—and, hence, a unique list of theoretical qualities and connections. The resulting situation would not be revolutionary; it would be just one more instance of the familiar problem of the underdetermination of theory by the data.

(2) Infinitive and gerundive constructions

Philosophers with an interest in intentionality have focused recently on those intentional phenomena that are naturally reported in language by means of 'that'-clause constructions: for example, 'x believes that A', 'x doubts that A', 'it appears to x that A'. Less attention has been paid to those intentional phenomena that are naturally reported in language by means of infinitive and gerundive constructions: for example, 'x intends to F', 'x decides to F', 'x wants to F' 'x fears F-ing', 'x imagines y F-ing', etc. We have seen that the proposed analysis fits nicely those intentional relations associated with 'that'-clause constructions, as in the relations of believing, doubting, being appeared to. For example, 'x believes that A' is parsed as:

$$\underline{x} \text{ believes that } A.$$

And the singular term 'that A' denotes an intensional entity belonging to the second traditional conception, for the occurrence of A in 'that A' has the type of fine-grained intensionality characteristic of that conception. Accordingly, 'believes' expresses a relation that characteristically holds between an individual and a conception 2 intension. Further, this relation holds between these items as a contingent fact independently of whether it holds between the individual and necessarily equivalent intensions. Thus, it fits the analysis. And the same thing goes for the relations of doubting, being appeared to, etc. But does the analysis fit those intentional relations associated with gerundive and infinitive constructions—the relations of intending, fearing, etc? The answer is that it does.

Let us suppose that these infinitive and gerundive constructions should be taken at face value syntactically. Then, for example, 'x intends to F' and 'x fears F-ing' would be parsed respectively as follows:

$$\underline{x} \text{ intends to } F.$$
$$\underline{x} \text{ fears } F\text{-ing.}$$

Given this parsing, the singular terms 'to F' and 'F-ing' would in at least some cases denote intensional entities belonging to the second traditional conception, for in at least some cases the occurrences of F in these singular terms have the type of intensionality characteristic of the second conception. (For example, it is possible for someone to intend to build something whose top surface forms a trilateral and yet not to intend to build something whose top surface forms a triangle. And it is possible for someone to fear riding a cycle with fewer than three wheels and yet not to fear riding a cycle with fewer than $\sqrt[3]{27}$ wheels.) Accordingly, 'intend' and 'fear' would express relations that can contingently hold between an individual and a conception 2 intension and can do so independently of whether they hold between the individual and necessarily equivalent conception 2 intensions. Thus, if these infinitive and gerundive constructions are taken at face value, the associated intentional relations straightforwardly satisfy the proposed analysis. The same thing goes for the other relations in this family—deciding, wanting, etc.

It should be noted, incidentally, that each of the verbs 'intend', 'decide', 'want', 'fear', etc., can take 'that'-clauses as well as infinitives and gerundives: for example, 'x intends that x himself will F', 'x decides that x himself will F', 'x fears that x himself Fs'. Since such 'that'-clauses straightforwardly denote conception 2 intensions, the associated intentional relations—intending, deciding, fearing—satisfy the analysis quite independently of the matter of infinitive and gerundive constructions. Indeed, someone might try treating these infinitive and gerundive constructions not at face value but as transformations from certain underlying 'that'-clause constructions. For example, someone might try treating 'x intends to F' as a transformation from 'x intends that x himself will F'. If this works, the issue of infinitive and gerundive constructions would not even arise.

(3) Objectival constructions

Constructions of the following kind are frequently used to report intentional phenomena: 'x looks for y', 'x wants y', 'x thinks of y', 'x is interested in y', 'x sees y', 'x loves y'. Yet on the surface, such constructions hardly seem to be stating that an individual stands in an intentional relation to a conception 2 intension.

There are two ways to deal with this family of examples. First, following Church, Quine, and others, we might treat objectival constructions as transformations from logically prior constructions that require right on their surface that an individual stand in an intentional relation to an intervening conception 2 intension. For example, 'x looks for y' and 'x wants y' might be treated as transformations from 'x strives to find y' and 'x wants to have y', respectively. And we have just seen that intentional connections associated with such infinitive constructions straightforwardly mesh with the proposed analysis of intentionality. The other objectival constructions can be dealt with in analogous ways.

Although the transformational treatment might seem a bit forced, there is good reason to take it seriously. Suppose we were instead to treat objectival constructions as ordinary relational formulas. Then, because a sentence like 'Ponce de Leon looks for the Fountain of Youth' seems true, we would seem to be forced to hold that Ponce de Leon actually stands in some relation to the Fountain of Youth. But since the Fountain of Youth does not exist, we would be forced to hold, as Meinong did, that there literally are objects that do not exist, that there literally are unreal things. When fully generalized, this unrealism might be more than ontologically excessive; it might produce insuperable logical difficulties.[29] However, if we were to adopt the transformational approach, the offending occurrences of vacuous names and vacuous descriptions would give way to occurrences within intensional contexts, occurrences free of problematic ontological commitments. Indeed, even the thorniest instances of the problem of intentional identity could be resolved without recourse to nonexistent objects.[30]

The second way to deal with objectival constructions is to take them at face value. After all, each of the relations expressed by these objectival constructions either is identical to—or is necessarily included in—a relation that can contingently hold between an individual and an idea independently of whether it holds between the individual and necessarily equivalent ideas. For example, not only do individuals think of other individuals, but also they think of ideas; not only do individuals look for other individuals, they look for new ideas (new theorems, new concepts); not only do individuals want other individuals, they want new ideas (new strategies, new scenarios). And this is often so independently of whether they stand in these relations to necessarily equivalent ideas. Thus, if objectival constructions are to be taken at face value, the associated mental relations satisfy the proposed analysis straight off. In this case, however, I must add a bit more to the account of the aboutness of intentional phenomena.

According to that account, fine-grained intensions are the items that are in the primary sense about other objects. An intentional act is about objects only secondarily, inasmuch as it involves standing in an intentional relation to an intension that is about those objects. However, if objectival constructions are to be taken at face value, then a person will perform an intentional act if he stands in one of the associated objectival relations, not to an intervening intension, but directly to the object the act is about. For example, I perform an intentional act of looking for this pen if I stand in the looking-for relation, not to an intension that is about this pen, but to the pen itself. Would this show that the proposed account of the aboutness of intentional phenomena needs revision? Not clearly.

To see why, consider the following thesis: for each of the problematic objectival connections d, there is an intentional connection c such that, necessarily, d connects an individual x to an object y if and only if c connects x to an intension that is about y. (For example, necessarily, x looks for y if and only if x endeavors to find y; endeavoring is an intentional connection, and that which x is endeavoring, namely, to find y, is an intension that is about y.) Suppose that this thesis is correct. It follows that the condition that d connects x to y is the same as the condition that c connects x to an intension about y. Therefore, since phenomena are just contingent conditions, the phenomenon of x's standing in relation d to y *is* just the phenomenon of x's standing in relation c to an intension about y. Given this, my account of the aboutness of intentional phenomena remains intact even if objectival constructions are taken at face value.

Is the above thesis correct? It, or some variant of it, certainly seems to hold for most of the objectival relations in question. However, for the sake of argument let us explore the possibility that there are exceptions, perhaps the relations of loving and attending. Is it really true that someone can genuinely love something without, in the very act, loving to know it or loving to have it? And can someone genuinely attend to something without, in the very act, realizing that it participates in a figure/ground relation or that he himself is aware of it? These possibilities certainly may be doubted. However, it would be good for us to have waiting in the wings an account that does not turn on these issues. I will suggest one that is based upon a distinction between directedness and aboutness.

Let us suppose that the above possibilities of loving and attending are genuine, that it is truly possible to love an object or to attend to it without the indicated sort of conceptual mediation. In this case, although it would still be quite appropriate to say that the phenomenon of loving the object and the phenomenon of attending to the object are *directed toward* the object, we could not say that these phenomena are *about* it. Aboutness arises only via conceptual mediation; that is, aboutness enters just at the point when an individual stands in an appropriate intentional connection to a concept or thought that is about the object.

To spell out this account precisely, we will make use of the notion of a determinate intentional connection. Some intentional connections are species of others in the sense that they are necessarily included in them. For example, attending is a species of awareness because it is necessary that, if x attends to y, then x is aware of y. An intentional connection is *determinate* if and only if no other intentional connection is a species of it, i.e., no other intentional connection is necessarily included in it in this fashion. We need this notion for the following reason. Suppose that a traditional empiricist theory of pure, nonintentional experience is correct. For example, suppose that a pure experience of a fragrance or of undirected anxiety is possible. If so, such a phenomenon would be neither about anything nor directed toward anything; it merely occurs. Or so the traditional empiricist would have it. (On our analysis, the reason that the empiricist's relation of pure experience does not qualify as intentional is that thoughts and concepts are necessarily excluded from its range. See the next section for a fuller discussion of the empiricist's theory.) Notice that, necessarily, if x has a pure experience of y, then x is (in some sense) aware of y. In such a case, the phenomenon of x's being aware of y (say, the feeling of undirected anxiety) would not be directed toward or be about anything. Now the relation of awareness satisfies our analysis of intentional connection because (on other occasions) thoughts and concepts can occur hyperintensionally in its range. So merely standing in just any intentional connection (say, awareness) to an object is not sufficient for being directed toward the object. However, unlike general intentional con-nections like awareness, determinate intentional connections always guarantee directedness. (For example, if I am actually attending to the feeling of anxiety, the phenomenon of my doing so is of necessity directed toward this feeling.) Indeed, the restricted notion of a determinate intentional connection leads immediately to an analysis of directedness.

With this explanation in mind, I suggest the following as a first approximation: (elementary) phenomenon p is *directed toward* an object y if and only if, for some individual x and some determinate intentional connection c, p is the phenomenon of x's standing in relation c to y. But how, on this approach, does aboutness arise? The answer is very much in the spirit of our original analysis. Aboutness is a species of directedness, namely, one that involves conceptual mediation: (elementary) phenomenon p is *about* an object if and only if p is directed at a thought or concept that is about the object. Minor adjustments might be called for in this account of directedness and aboutness,[31] but it seems safe to say that a fully satisfactory analysis of intentional phenomena is at hand even if, as we have been doing, problematic objectival constructions are taken at face value.

(4) Nonintentional relations to ideas

There is a family of relations that can contingently relate individuals to ideas and that give an initial appearance of being basic. When we examine them, however, most or all lose that appearance. In any event, each of these relations can be disqualified as a counterexample on another ground: most of them do not appear even superficially to be hyperintensional. Consider the sentence 'a is disposed to F'. Suppose we parse it this way:

$$\underline{a} \text{ is } \underline{\text{disposed}} \text{ to } \underline{F}.$$

And suppose the infinitive phrase 'to F' denotes the concept of being something x such that Fx. Then, the relation of being disposed would be able to relate contingently an individual to a concept. But this relation would not be a counterexample to our analysis, for clearly it is not hyperintensional. For example, it is necessary that, if one is disposed to be depressed, then one is disposed to be not not depressed. Likewise for any other infinitive phrase necessarily equivalent to 'to F'. Other relations like being disposed include tending, approaching (as a limit), needing, and even the ought relation: a person tends to be depressed, an electron approaches (moving at) the speed of light, Sister Teresa resembles (being) an angel, the plant needs to have more water, the soup ought to have more salt. As with the relation of being disposed, each of these fails to be hyperintensional.[32]

There are, nevertheless, four kindred relations that some people might deem hyperintensional and that are not intentional connections: (1) a certain relation of efficient causation, (2) organismic striving, (3) final causation, and (4) natural meaning. (For example, it might be said that the car *causes* the boy to fall, the liquid *strives* to be in a state of equilibrium and the plant *strives* to be in the sunlight, the kidney *functions* [so as] to remove wastes from the blood, the red spots *mean* that the child has measles.) Because some or all of these relations might be hyperintensional, it would be good to be able to show on other grounds that they do not qualify as counterexamples. I will indicate briefly why most philosophers today would agree that there indeed are such grounds.

First, to most philosophers the above causal relation should be counted as ad hoc on the ground that, as a categorial fact, a causal connection can only connect phenomena (or events) to phenomena (events). That is, only phenomena (events) can be true efficient causes or effects; concrete particulars (e.g., cars), in contradistinction to phenomena involving them, can be neither efficient causes nor effects.[33] Second, most philosophers would doubt that there is any genuine nonintentional connection answering to our casual talk about striving: anything that literally strives for ends has a mind; all other uses of 'strive' are only metaphorical and do not express the sort of relation that serves to fix the fundamental order of the world. Third, concerning final causes, the leading view is that our use of 'function' divides into two distinct types—intentional and natural. The former type is reducible to more fundamental intentional notions such as desiring, intending, trying, etc; the latter type, to more basic, purely mechanistic notions (plus perhaps certain normative notions such as fitness, health, or well-being).[34]

Finally, if natural meaning does not just boil down to the relation of rendering probable, which we dealt with earlier, it seems in any case not to be basic. After all, it is highly doubtful that any genuinely basic relation of natural meaning can ever really hold between an individual just on its own and an idea. For an individual to mean naturally, a third parameter certainly is required—namely, (i) a person or group of persons with a system of background beliefs or (ii) a background theory or context, where these items are treated as systems of propositions considered in abstraction from the intentional fact that they are believed by the person or group of persons in question. However, if these suppressed third parameters are brought in, the resulting explicitly ternary relations mesh smoothly with our analysis. For the first ternary relation is intentional and, hence, is not even a candidate counterexample in the first place. Although the second ternary relation is nonintentional, it fails to be a counterexample on the grounds that it does not meet the contingency requirement: whenever it holds, it holds necessarily.[35] [For example, suppose that (a) these spots on the child mean (b) that the child has measles given (c) the proposition that, if the child has spots like these, the child (in all probability) has measles. Then this ternary meaning relation holds among these three items necessarily.] Furthermore, these two ternary relations are nonbasic: (i) the relation of x's naturally meaning y to person(s) z is a definable intentional relation more or less equivalent to the relation of x's making y evident to z, and (ii) the relation of x's naturally meaning y given proposition(s) z is a logical relation no doubt definable in terms of the notion of logical consequence together with other purely logical notions.

These and analogous considerations will, I hope, convince most people that these four relations pose no threat to our analysis. But if there is residual doubt, the analysis can easily be tightened up so as to rule them out explicitly.[36]

Since I have been unable to find better candidate counterexamples than the foregoing, I am inclined to hold that the analysis is indeed free of all counterexamples. At most, minor adjustments would be called for to deal with one controversial philosophical theory or another.

4. NONINTENTIONAL MENTAL PHENOMENA

According to the first half of Brentano's thesis of intentionality, all and only mental phenomena are intentional. Is it really true that intentionality is the mark of the mental? The counterexample that springs to mind is that of pure, uninterpreted experience—pure sensation or pure inner feeling—as posited by traditional British empiricists. Any such experience would certainly be a mental phenomenon, but it would not be *about* or *directed toward* anything. Brentano and other intentionalists of course want to deny that there is any such thing as pure experience. However, Brentano puts forward the first half of his thesis as analytic, or at least as necessary. Therefore, this half of the thesis would be undermined if pure experience were *merely possible* for some beings or other, not necessarily human beings. In the face of this threat, we would be wise to have an analysis of the mental that is neutral with respect to the possibility of pure experience.

Just as in the case of judgment, so in the case of pure experience there are both relational and nonrelational theories. We saw that nonrelational theories of judgment ran into difficulties over the matter of generality. It is predictable, therefore, that nonrelational theories of experience (for example, so-called adverbial theories) also run into difficulty over this issue. Briefly, natural language has an apparatus for comparing experiences in infinitely many general ways: for example, 'the sense experience of creature u is qualitatively exactly like that of creature v', 'the sense experience of u is qualitatively exactly like that of v except for some colors', 'the sense experience of u is qualitatively exactly like that of v except that their color spectra are inverted', etc. Nonrelational theories are unable to capture the full expressive power of this idiom except by resorting to constructions that are at least implicitly relational, and the semantical properties of these constructions evidently cannot be spelled out without reintroducing our familiar relational constructions in the metalanguage. (See section 2 for corresponding difficulties in the adverbial theory's attempt to avoid the relational treatment of judgment.) Therefore, it is simpler and more natural to adopt the relational theory of pure experience right from the start.

If one adopts a relational theory, one encounters a striking parallelism between the relation of pure experience and the familiar intentional connections, except that now qualities and conditions play the role that concepts and thoughts played before. Specifically, the pure experience relation can contingently connect an individual to a quality or condition independently of whether it connects the individual to any necessarily equivalent concept or thought. For example, in "raw" sense experience I can be connected to a sensible quality (say, a taste or a smell) and I can do so even if I am connected to no concept that is necessarily equivalent to it. And in "raw" sense experience I can be connected to a condition (say, that something red is surrounded by blue) independently of whether I am connected to any necessarily equivalent thought.[37] Likewise for inner feelings: I can be connected to a pure feeling (say, the quality of sadness or pain or anxiety) independently of whether I am connected to any concept that is necessarily equivalent to the quality. Or so a theory of pure experience goes.

According to this account, then, the difference between pure and interpreted experience lies in the intensional objects: in pure experience the intensional objects are conception 1 intensions—qualities and conditions—whereas in interpreted experience the intensional objects are conception 2 intensions—concepts and thoughts. This suggests that pure experience and interpreted experience are mere modes or species of a single underlying relation of experience. Like pure experience, this general relation can contingently connect an individual to a quality or condition independently of whether it connects the individual to any necessarily equivalent idea. And like interpreted experience, the general relation can contingently connect an individual to a concept or thought independently of whether it connects the individual to any necessarily equivalent idea. But notice that the latter fact shows that this general relation satisfies the analysis of intentional connection.

On the picture that is emerging, pure experience is a species of this general relation, namely, the species with conception 2 intensions excluded from its range. And interpreted experience is a species of the general relation that arises via some other, perhaps rather more complex, operation (see the discussion of directedness and aboutness in section 3.3 for an indication of what might be involved here). In either case, the species is necessarily included in the general relation: that is, necessarily, if x has a pure experience of y, then x experiences y, and if x has an interpreted experience of y, then x experiences y. This, together with the fact that the general relation satisfies the analysis of intentional connection, suggests that we may obtain an analysis of the full notion of a mental connection simply by extending the previous analysis so as to bring in all connections that are necessarily included in intentional connections.

We thus arrive at the following definition:

A connection is mental if and only if it is necessarily included in an intentional connection.

In symbols, c is a mental connection iff$_{df}$

($\exists d$)(d is an intentional connection & $\Box(\forall uv)(u,v \mathbin{\Delta} c \rightarrow u,v \mathbin{\Delta} d)$).

All the intentional connections are of course mental according to the definition, for a connection is always necessarily included in itself as a limiting case.

With this definition in hand we may go on to the second stage of our approach. Using the definition of mental connection, we can define what a nonbasic mental relation is. Putting the two definitions together, we will have succeeded in characterizing what a mental relation is in general. Furthermore, the objections to this general analysis all seem to be variants of those facing the analysis of intentionality, and they can be disqualified for corresponding reasons.

On the view of the mind we now have, a descendant of the first half of Brentano's thesis of intentionality is vindicated, for intentional connections are the key to the analysis of mind. Nevertheless, we allow for the prospect of nonintentional experience as a special mode of experience. We are able to allow for this so easily just because the relation of pure experience is a species of the general relation of experience, which admits complex intensions into its range. In all cases, however, mental connections possess a contingent hyperintensionality, and this distinguishes them from all purely physical, naturalistic connections. Although beings without minds are connected to intensions in various ways, they can never be connected to them in this highly discriminating way. Indeed, the fact that no purely physical connection is mental may be viewed as the essence of the second half of Brentano's thesis of intentionality: given certain reasonable criteria for classifying phenomena, this fact implies Brentano's original claim that no purely physical phenomenon is mental. Suspended in a world of physical phenomena, the mind is a prism diffracting nature's stream of cause and effect into the colorful discriminations of thought and experience.

5. THE EXISTENCE OF MENTAL CONNECTIONS AND MIND

Our strategy for defining mental relations is two-staged. First, we say what it takes for a relation to be a mental connection. Then we use this notion to characterize the remaining, nonbasic mental relations: the relations whose definitions involve mental connections in some logically essential way. This strategy is based on the plausible premise that there are indeed mental connections. But critics might challenge this, alleging that all mental relations are nonbasic and, indeed, definable ultimately in terms of purely physical qualities and connections. According to these critics, the structure of the world would be fundamentally physical and formal.[38] In these closing pages, I will briefly sketch the ways in which I believe these critics can be answered.

One way to meet this criticism is phenomenological: regardless of its causal underpinnings, consciousness has a structure of its own that can be investigated phenomenologically, independently of the physical sciences. Such investigation reveals that familiar phenomenal properties are basic determinants of that structure and, analogously, that (at least some) familiar conscious relations are too. For example, the presence or absence in consciousness of nonbasic intensions can produce two types of detectable alteration: an alteration in the intentional contents of what one is thinking or a gestalt shift in how one is perceiving things. But unlike the presence or absence of such intensions, the presence or absence in consciousness of phenomenal properties can produce, not just these types of alteration, but a third type as well; namely, it can produce a shift in the "preinterpretive stuff" of consciousness. Phenomenal properties can thus be "in" consciousness in a particularly basic way. Similar considerations indicate that (at least some) familiar conscious relations can be "in" consciousness in an analogously basic way.

Another way to meet our critics' challenge is epistemological. There are two points to be made. First, let an ad hoc grue-like relation experiencing* be defined so that the following hold: x experiences* green iff x experiences green, and x experiences* blue iff (x has not just experienced green and x experiences blue now) or (x has just experienced green and x continues to experience green now). Assume what we suspect is false, namely, that the familiar relation of experiencing is on a par with this grue-like relation experiencing*. Then, 'x experiences* green at t_1 and x experiences* blue at t_2' and 'x experiences green at t_1 and x experiences blue at t_2' would be on a par too. But the change reported in the former sentence is a mere "Cambridge change"; only the second reports a real change. So experiencing is not on a par with the grue-like relation experiencing* after all. Generalizing on this, we are led to the conclusion that, if experiencing (and other conscious relations) were not among the genuine connections, there would be no plausible explanation of how it is that we successfully identify change or constancy in our conscious mental lives. The second epistemological point is this. The fact that we take phenomenal properties as qualities and the familiar mental relations as connections evidently plays a role in how ideally we should actually determine our list of theoretical qualities and connections in empirical science. (See section 3.1 for more on this procedure.) Failure to follow this procedure would seem to invite relativism on the matter of theoretical qualities and connections in science. But in this case, our physicalist critics might well lose the theoretical backing they thought they had for their thesis that no mental relation is a genuine connection and that physical qualities and connections suffice for the definition of all mental relations.

The third way to meet our critics is to refute straight off their physicalistic definability thesis. Physicalists have three strategies for attempting their definitions of the standard mental relations, strategies motivated by behaviorism, the mind-body identity thesis, or functionalism. When properly formulated (in some cases this requires considerable care), cerain well-known arguments are, I believe, successful against these definitional strategies. I will briefly review some of them with an eye toward setting up a new argument, one purely logical in nature.

Behavioral definitions can be attacked by means of a "perfect pretender" argument: it is in principle possible for someone (to be disposed) to display the behavior typically associated with thinking p when, in fact, the person only pretends to think p out of a desire to deceive.[39] They can also be attacked by adapting W. V. O. Quine's argument for the thesis of the indeterminacy of radical translation: a speaker of a radically foreign language could share all our behavioral dispositions and yet think, e.g., that rabbithood is manifest on those occasions when we instead think that there exists a rabbit.[40] By either argument, it follows that behavioral dispositions do not pair up with a person's thoughts in the way required for behavioral definability of the thinking relation.

We come next to physicalistic definitions motivated by the mind-body identity thesis. These definitions can be attacked by a straightforward modal argument: even if it is a causal law that all and only creatures who think p have the neurophysiological property P, it is metaphysically possible for a being to think p and not to have P (or to have P and not to think p); thus, the property of thinking $p \neq P$. And there is an epistemological argument: using nothing but introspection and pure reason, I cannot know that I have [neurophysiological property] P, yet using nothing but introspection and pure reason, I can know that I have the property of thinking something; so the property of thinking something $\neq P$.[41] Finally, there is the multiple-realization argument: the number of metaphysically possible physiological bases for thought is infinite, and it is impossible to give a finite specification in first-order physiological terms of what is common to them.[42]

As I indicated, I think there are sound formulations of all these arguments. However, suppose we come across some physicalists who simply deny some or all of the premises used in these arguments; for example, they might hold that, as a matter of *metaphysical necessity,* the mental supervenes on the physical (behavioral histories, physiological states, or even total physical worlds). And suppose, moreover, that they insist that there is no ontological significance in being able in principle to state a definition by finite means. For them, infinitary "definitions," though unstatable, are quite acceptable: if a mental relation is necessarily equivalent to, say, an infinite disjunction of physical properties and relations, this shows that the relation is physically definable and that it is not in a new category of nonphysical connections.

By careful argumentation we can, I think, refute the doctrines of modality and definition advocated by these physicalists. But for the sake of argument, suppose we were to allow these doctrines. We can construct a new, purely logical argument against the physicalistic conclusion. The key to our opponents' downfall is the failure to allow for the phenomenon of self-embedding. Consider the proposition that x thinks that everyone thinks many things. Is it the very same relation of thinking that "occurs" twice in this proposition? Contrary to ramified type theories, there are extremely compelling arguments that, in fact, it is the same relation. For example, how else are we to explain the important family of everyday "cross referential" dialogues like the following:

A: I think many things.

B: So do I; in fact, what you have just asserted is one of them [i.e., one of the things I think].

Here A asserts a proposition "involving" the relation of thinking, namely, the proposition that he thinks many things. Then B affirms the corresponding proposition about himself, namely, that he [i.e., B] thinks many things too. And then B goes on to provide an example of one of the things to which he stands in this relation of thinking, namely, the original proposition A asserted, which, as we saw, is a proposition "involving" this very relation of thinking. Everyday dialogues like this would make no sense if thinking could not "occur" in propositions that fall within its very own range.[43]

Now our opponents posit an infinitary definition of the form:

x thinks y iff$_{df}$ (x has P_1 & $y =$ the proposition that Fa) or (x has P_2 & $y =$ the proposition that Fb) or . . . .

where *ex hypothesi* P_1 is a physical property that is metaphysically necessary and sufficient for thinking the proposition that Fa; P_2, for thinking the proposition that Fb; etc. Here is the problem. What happens when we come to a proposition about thinking itself, such as the proposition that someone thinks something? Let it be granted that there is a physical property P_i that is metaphysically necessary and sufficient for thinking this proposition. What does the associated disjunct in the infinitary definition look like? It cannot be this:

x has P_i & y = the proposition that someone thinks something,

for then the definition would appeal explicitly to *the very relation being defined.* Alternatively, our opponents might try to offer the following candidate disjunct:

x has P_i & y = the proposition that, for some u and v, either u has P_1 & v = the proposition that *Fa* or u has P_2 & v = the proposition that *Fb* or ... or u has P_i & v = the proposition that someone *thinks* something or ....

In symbols,

$$P_i x \text{ \& } y = [(\exists uv)((P_1 u \text{ \& } v = [Fa]) \text{ v } \ldots \text{ v } (P_i u \text{ \& } v = [(\exists wz)w \text{ thinks } z]) \text{ v } \ldots)].$$

But plainly this does no good, for the same problem just recurs: the psychological relation being defined has not been eliminated in favor of physical terms, but instead it occurs explicitly in the definiens one level down.

There are sophisticated logical techniques for avoiding this explicit circularity. However, if our opponents base their case on such techniques, it can be shown that the resulting overall physicalistic theory suffers new defects that make it unacceptable in comparison to a theory that treats the standard mental relations as connections.[44] So this hope for physicalistic definitions inspired by the mind-body identity thesis appears to be thwarted.

The only remaining strategy open to the physicalist is the functionalist one. The central premise of functionalism—and the premise upon which functional definitions are based—is that the standard mental relations are uniquely determined by their causal roles in functioning organisms. Therefore, the most direct way to undermine the prospect of functional definitions is to show that there exists a system of deviant relations that are demonstrably different from the standard mental relations and yet are causally and functionally indistinguishable from them. It turns out that we can construct just such a system of deviant relations by means of a certain generalization of a Quinean indeterminacy argument.[45] Thus, functional definitions are in vain, and the final strategy of the physicalist proves barren. It is important to note, moreover, that the possibility of this anti-functionalist argument is tied to the hyperintensionality of the standard intentional relations and, therefore, can be adapted to undercut the prospect of defining these relations in (naturalistic) information-theoretic terms.[46]

Ironically, nothing prohibits one from attempting a dualist theory of the standard mental relations that is akin to the old functionalism. Specifically, one could revise the old functionalist definitions by explicitly requiring that the key relations over which the predicate variables range be genuine connections, not deviant relations. But if the resulting definitions were correct, they would have as a consequence the thesis of the present section, namely, that the standard mental relations are indeed genuine connections.

On the basis of the arguments reviewed in this section I believe that the overall definitional strategy of this paper is immune to physicalist attack. But there is one more question to ask. Must our theories posit mentality in the first place? According to eliminative materialism, the answer is negative: the standard mental notions are just unscientific; with the progress of science these notions will be seen to be on a par with those of alchemy and astrology. Even if this radical claim is granted for a moment, it would hardly show that the proposed analysis of intentionality and mind is without philosophical value, for in philosophy the value of an analysis does not ride on the utility a notion plays in science. Consider an analogy. Even if it turns out that we have no free will, philosophers will continue to be interested in defining the notion. For they will want to know what it is we lack, and indeed, they can use a precise analysis to improve their arguments that we truly are not free. Furthermore, even if eliminative materialism—at least as it is usually formulated—were true, that would not call into question the correctness of the proposed analysis of intentionality and mind. To be correct, an analysis is required to fit neither more nor less than the actual and hypothetical cases to which our mental notions are applicable. Eliminativism implies at most that there are no actual cases. But since our analysis takes no stand on the existence of actual cases, it is strictly independent of eliminativism. There would be trouble for the analysis only if it were impossible in principle for any mental relation ever to be realized in any being whatsoever. However, eliminativism hardly implies this highly counterintuitive thesis. In any event, this worry would be dissolved automatically if we could show the eliminativist that every acceptable comprehensive theory must posit actual cases of mentality. Let us in closing give a brief sketch of how we might try to show this.

The goal of theory is not restricted to the prediction and explanation of what we observe. Any acceptable comprehensive theory of the world (and indeed any acceptable comprehensive psychological theory) must also account for the fact that the theory itself has been arrived at by rational means, that it has epistemic merit—in short, that it is acceptable.[47] Because terms for acceptability, epistemic merit, rationality, etc., do not presently belong to physical theory, something like the following theoretical statement must be adjoined to the theory to obtain the requisite account:

A theory is acceptable for a person if and only if it is (or belongs to) the simplest overall theory that explains the person's data.

But as we saw in section 1, this statement exceeds the resources of nominalist and extensionalist physical theories. At a minimum, an apparatus for representing definitional relationships and for dealing with the notions of simplicity and explanation is required, and our rich intensional logic for qualities and concepts is (part of) the simplest theory that fills the bill. But so far this need only be Platonistic, not mentalistic. To discover the inevitable mentalist ingredient in any acceptable comprehensive theory, we must look to the matter of data.

After years of searching, philosophers have learned that there is no faintly plausible definition of the notion of data that does not directly or indirectly bring in some mentalist notion or other—observation, experience, pure experience, sensation, etc.[48] In the notion of data, therefore, we find the mentalist ingredient we are seeking.

Nevertheless, moderate eliminative materialists still have available an intermediate position that poses a threat to the full intentionalist picture of ourselves that we have been developing. According to this intermediate position, (1) all mental notions are eliminable except the notion of data; (2) the notion of data is definable in terms of pure experience without appeal to any intentional notions (for example, p is a datum for a person x iff$_{df}$ p = the proposition that x has a pure experience of y, where y is some sensible quality or condition, and p is true);[49] (3) the notion of pure experience is really materialistic because, unlike intentional notions, it has a first-order physiological definition.

Now I believe that the modal argument, the epistemological argument, and the multiple-realization argument can be formulated to show that physiological definitions of pure experience are either mistaken or unworkable for the epistemological purposes at hand. But even without resorting to these arguments, we can fault this moderate anti-intentionalist position. For there are two closely related vicious circles in which the resulting theory of acceptability is caught. The first we encountered in section 1: since our opponent's theory disallows logical and conceptual intuitions as data, how are the definitions in this theory to be justified? Why not adopt different definitions of data, explanation, and acceptability itself? Is the preference for the anti-intentionalist's definitions more than a bias or historical accident? It does the anti-intentionalist no good to appeal to the resulting simplicity of the overall theory, for there exist alternative definitions that yield even simpler, albeit *intuitively* unacceptable, overall theories. The second difficulty arises when one attempts to apply the anti-intentionalist theory in actual empirical situations. How can a theoretician x tell whether to accept into his overall theory a proposition p to the effect that he has a pure experience of some sensible quality or condition y? On what basis does x accept propositions like p into his overall theory? It will do x no good to answer that p is data, for on what basis can he say that? According to his definition of data, p is data for x if and only if p is an elementary proposition about x's pure experience and p is true. So to show that p is data, x must already be able to show that p is true. No progress at all will have been made. At the same time, it does not help x to appeal to the simplicity of his overall theory, for its identity is fixed by the very propositions, like p, that he initially accepts into the theory as data. But that is what is in question: on what basis does x accept propositions like p into his theory in the first place? After all, by not accepting *any* propositions like p, x could have a very simple theory indeed. It appears that x has no choice but boldly to accept p and dogmatically to decline to give any further justification for it. Now this move might be acceptable; however, if x's theory of acceptability is comprehensive, it certainly must include the proposition that not just any proposition is acceptable straightaway without further justification. Given this, x's theory, if comprehensive, must also include an explanation of what it is about propositions like p that makes them acceptable straightaway without further justification. However, x's anti-intentionalist, purely physiological theory of data and sense experience seems quite incapable of providing such an explanation.

As far as I can tell, the only way out of these difficulties is to accept an explicitly intentionalist theory of acceptability. Such a theory might go as follows (with suitable qualifications): to accept a proposition or a theory is just to believe it; and for any elementary conceptual or logical proposition that is clearly and distinctly understood and for any elementary proposition about one's own present conscious states (including one's own conscious intentional states), one's mere belief in the proposition entails that the proposition is true. (Or more cautiously: it is necessary that *most* of the propositions like these that one believes must be true.) It is for this reason that such propositions are acceptable to the person without any further justification. If a theory of this general sort provides the only solution to the difficulties confronting the anti-intentionalist theory, then any acceptable comprehensive theory must posit intentionality at least in the theoretician himself.[50] And if the proposed analysis of intentionality is correct, such intentionality has a special logical status that necessarily distinguishes it from the physical. It would follow that any pure materialist is unable to reach the conclusion that his is an acceptable theory. An intentionalist can, but only by acknowledging the logically distinctive status of his own mind.

Notes

1. I have dealt with this topic in lectures at several philosophy departments and also in chapter 10 of *Quality and Concept* (Oxford, 1982). The purpose of returning to the topic at this time is to give a revised analysis, together with an extended defense, that responds to the long list of provocative comments I have received. The following are only some of the people whose comments have helped me: Bruce Aune, Mark Bedau, Jose Benardete, Jonathan Bennett, Romane Clark, Crawford Elder, Kit Fine, Jaegwon Kim, Keith Lehrer, Michael Loux, Bill Lycan, Warren Quinn, David Smith, Chris Wagner, and Peter Woodruff. I am particularly grateful to Carol Voeller, whose probing comments on each draft were essential, and to George Myro, for numerous rewarding conversations on epistemic appraisal and acceptability. Finally, I thank the National Endowment for the Humanities for its generous support.

2. Here I am adapting an argument from George Myro's important paper "Aspects of Acceptability," *Pacific Philosophical Quarterly* 62 (1981): 107-17.

3. See chapter 1, *Quality and Concept,* and "New Foundations for Intensional Logic," *Handbook of Philosophical Logic* (Dordrecht, in press) for a detailed defense of this assertion.

4. See Nelson Goodman, *Fact, Fiction, and Forecast* (Cambridge, Mass., 1955), 75ff.

5. "A Formulation of the Logic of Sense and Denotation," *Structure, Method, and Meaning: Essays in Honor of Henry M. Scheffer,* edited by P. Henle, H. M. Kallen, and S. K. Langer (New York, 1951), 3-24.

6. Ibid.

7. For example, "Intensional Isomorphism and Identity of Belief," *Philosophical Studies* 5 (1954): 65-73.

8. See Alonzo Church, "On Carnap's Analysis of Statements of Assertion and Belief," *Analysis* 10 (1950): 97-99.

9. Hilary Putnam's "fundamental magnitudes," David Armstrong's "universals," Sydney Shoemaker's "properties," and David Lewis's "natural properties" are examples of qualities and connections. See Putnam, "On Properties," *Essays in Honor of Carl G. Hempel,* edited by N. Rescher, et al. (Dordrecht, 1970), 235-54; Armstrong, *Universals and Scientific Realism,* 2 vols. (Cambridge, 1978); Shoemaker, "Causality and Properties," *Time and Cause,* edited by P. van Inwagen (Dordrecht, 1980), 109-35; Lewis, "New Work for a Theory of Universals," *Australasian Journal of Philosophy* 61 (1983): 343-77.

10. Thoughts (i.e., 0-ary conception 2 intensions) appear to be what John Searle calls "propositional contents," and, taken together, thoughts and concepts appear to be what he calls "intentional contents" (see *Intentionality* [Cambridge, 1983]). Moreover, conditions (i.e., 0-ary conception 1 intensions) appear to be what he calls "conditions of satisfaction." However, Searle has not tried to treat these types of entities within a systematic logical theory, and he seems to think that the relation holding between a propositional content and its condition of satisfaction is an unanalyzable representationalist primitive. On the approach I advocate, this relation is just the relation of correspondence from the traditional correspondence theory of truth, and it is definable within the sort of intensional logic I have been sketching. Furthermore, Searle defines intentionality as aboutness or directedness, but he treats the latter notions as unanalyzable representationalist primitives belonging to what he calls "the circle of intentional concepts." On my approach, aboutness and directedness can be defined without circularity in terms provided by intensional logic. Finally, Searle invokes a basic distinction between intrinsic and derived intentionality, but no definition is offered. On my view, the intrinsic/derived distinction can be defined, but only within the framework of an intensional logic that is realistic about qualities and connections (i.e., our distinguished categories of conception 1 intensional entities).

11. In *Quality and Concept,* I do not state general definitions of the notions of fundamental logical operation, thought-building operation, etc.; I simply give lists that are adequate for my purposes there. However, general definitions are possible in the language $\mathcal{L}_\omega$ with Δ. Though

certain details are omitted, the following should make clear the overall strategy behind these definitions:

v is a condition iff$_{df}$ $(\exists z)|(\exists u)u \, \Delta \, z| = v$.

v is a quality iff$_{df}$ $|u \, \Delta \, v|_u = v$.

v is an n-ary connection iff$_{df}$ $|<u_1, \ldots, u_n> \Delta \, v|_{u_1 \ldots u_n} = v$.

$\Box A$ iff$_{df}$ $|A| = ||A| = |A||$.

v is n-ary L-determinate iff$_{df}$

$$\Box (\forall u_1 \ldots u_n)(<u_1, \ldots, u_n> \Delta \, v \rightarrow \Box \, <u_1, \ldots, u_n> \Delta \, v).$$

v is an n-ary fundamental logical operation iff$_{df}$ v is an univocal $n+1$-ary L-determinate connection whose range consists exclusively of intensions.

v is an n-ary thought-building operation iff$_{df}$ v is an n-ary fundamental logical operation not having conditions, qualities, or connections in its range.

Notice that intensional abstracts $| \ldots |_\alpha$ are used in these definitions; however, we could get along without them by using instead one of our standard notions of singular predication, namely, the one according to which predicating one thing of another sometimes results in one of the original things itself (i.e., $\text{Pred}(u, v) = v$ for some u, v). This of course is the standard condition-building operation of singular predication. Circularity does not result if we use this notion in our definitions, for the goal here is to define the *general* notions of fundamental logical operation, etc. None of these notions are used in the definitions; rather, a standard notion of singular predication is used.

Incidentally, some commentators have asked what it takes for a thought-building operation f to "correspond" to or to be "associated" with a condition-building operation g. The answer, which is given in *Quality and Concept* (note 18, p. 276), is that f and g must be *equivalent*, i.e., $(\forall \alpha \beta)(\alpha \, \Delta \, f(\beta) \equiv \alpha \, \Delta \, g(\beta))$. This answer makes it clear that there is no circularity in the definition given in the book (p. 196) of the key relation of correspondence that holds between conception 2 and conception 1 intensions and that provides the basis for the traditional correspondence theory of truth.

12. See chapters 8 and 9 in *Quality and Concept* for a partial survey of these theoretical tasks; see also David Lewis's elegant paper "New Work for a Theory of Universals" for a forceful defense of a kindred point of view.

The primary differences between Lewis's theory and mine lies not so much in the applications as in the foundations. Whereas Lewis posits possible individuals (both actual and nonactual) plus sets thereof, I prefer actual individuals, qualities, and connections plus logical combinations thereof. Beyond its inherent naturalness and ontological realism, this traditional Platonistic approach has several other advantages. For example, whereas the set-theoretical possibilist approach evidently must take the notion of a "natural property" as primitive, it is definable on the Platonistic approach. And because some relations (e.g., belief) can be "constituents" of propositions falling in their very own range, an apparently severe formal problem of ill-foundedness arises for the set-theoretical possibilist when trying to construct these relations out of sets and possible individuals. (See section 5 of this paper for discussion of an analogous ill-foundedness that produces difficulties for first-order physicalistic definitions of belief inspired by the mind-body identity thesis.) A unique feature of the logic for qualities and concepts is that the theory for these important "self-embeddable" relations is already worked out. Of course, what makes this possible is that these relations are taken as primitive entities rather than as set-theoretic constructs. Incidentally, to accommodate fine-grained intensionality, set-theoretical possibilism appears to have no alternative but to identify thoughts and concepts with ad hoc entities such as sequences of "intensions" (i.e., sets of sets of sets of possible individuals). However, it is highly unintuitive that such ad hoc entities *really* are the sort of thing we believe.

13. This way of phrasing the principle invites a kind of self-application, reminiscent of the self-application involved in the Montague-Kaplan paradox of the knower, that might lead to conflict with Gödel's second incompleteness theorem. (For an accessible and illuminating study of the Montague-Kaplan paradox, see C. Anthony Anderson's "The Paradox of the Knower," *Journal of Philosophy* 80 [1983]: 338-55.) We may assume that this sort of difficulty can be avoided by adapting some device or other developed for resolving the logical paradoxes.

14. See *Quality and Concept,* 180f., and David Lewis, "New Work," 167f.

15. See *Quality and Concept,* section 47, for a detailed defense of this approach to logical validity. See also note 11 above.

16. See David Lewis, "New Work," 365-70, for a nice defense of this thesis.

17. Although he uses a different terminology, David Armstrong gives an appealing analysis of what is in effect the notion of a causal connection. See *Universals,* vol. 2, 148-57, and *What Is a Law of Nature?* (Cambridge, 1983). I advocate a similar approach; on my account, however, phenomena (and not qualities) are typically the relata of causal connections. (A phenomenon is a contingent condition wherein either a single item has a nonlogical quality or a number of items are connected by a nonlogical connection.) Incidentally, despite the affinities between Armstrong's theory and mine, the only intensions Armstrong acknowledges are causal and formal qualities and connections, whereas for me there are further intensions: for example, those constituting the contents of experience and thinking (i.e., phenomenal qualities, mental connections, and the full range of concepts and thoughts). I believe that these further intensions are unavoidable in epistemology and the theory of mind.

18. For a detailed defense, see *Quality and Concept,* chap. 1, and "New Foundations for Intensional Logic." General sentences about intentional phenomena (e.g., 'Self-aware people think of all and only things that they think that they think of'; 'for all x and y, if x has y, it is possible that someone knows that x has y'; etc.) also appear to be a problem for the self-ascription theories of belief recently developed by Roderick Chisholm (*The First Person,* Minneapolis, Minn., 1981) and David Lewis ("Attitudes *De Dicto* and *De Se,"* *Philosophical Review* 88 [1979]: 513-43). Section 39 in *Quality and Concept* suggests a solution to the Castaneda-Perry puzzles that prompted the theories of Chisholm and Lewis, a solution that leaves intact the usual apparatus for making general intentional statements.

19. Some people might try to avoid this conclusion by adopting a substitutional treatment of quantifiers and by treating 'that'-clauses as vacuous singular terms. There are significant problems with this maneuver, however. See *Quality and Concept,* 252, note 5, and "New Foundations for Intensional Logic."

20. See "New Foundations for Intensional Logic" for a more complete critique of the adverbial approach and other nonrelational approaches.

21. This strategy would be undercut if there simply were no intentional connections or if there were ad hoc intentional relations whose analyses depended in no logically essential way upon intentional connections. In section 5, I will argue that these worries are unfounded.

The analysis of intentional connection I will give here differs from that given in *Quality and Concept.* Although I believe that (some version of) the original analysis is correct, the present analysis is perhaps easier to defend. Of course, nothing would prevent one from combining the two analyses. This might be the safest strategy in the end; see note 33.

22. I borrow this term from Peter Woodruff, who uses it more broadly as a term for any form of conception 2 intensionality.

23. I discuss this relation largely for heuristic reasons, for it hardly seems to be a genuine connection, the sort of relation that fixes the logical, causal, or phenomenal order of the world. Indeed, it is doubtful that this relation can ever really hold just on its own. Individuals do not seem to belong to a category of things that can just on their own render thoughts probable; an entire condition or thought (perhaps involving an individual) is the only sort of thing that might entirely on its own be able to do so. By the way, I assume an objectivist doctrine of probability in the text. If probability is ultimately a subjectivist notion, then probability relations would

be defined (partly) in terms of intentional notions. They would not, however, be basic psychological connections. (See note 28 for the definition of the notion of a psychological connection.)

Incidentally, some philosophers (e.g., Peter Achinstein, Elliott Sober) believe that there is hyperintensionality in nature. To see why these views do not threaten my account of intentionality, see section 3.4 and note 33.

24. See *Word and Object* (Cambridge, Mass., 1960), section 12. It is no coincidence that Quine believes that "Brentano's thesis of the irreducibility of intentional idioms is of a piece with the thesis of indeterminacy of translation" (p. 221).

25. Notice that the analysis in no way restricts the possible range of the connection *c*. As far as the analysis is concerned, items from any metaphysical category can be in *c*'s range. Notice also that the analysis is given for binary connections only; however, it can be generalized. Finally, for expository purposes I have stated the hyperintensionality condition in its simplest and weakest form. There are stronger versions available. For example, '$y \approx_N z$' might be replaced with '*x* and *y* are analytically equivalent' or '*y* and *z* are relevantly equivalent'. Or we might use the following substitute analysis:

$$\lozenge (\exists xy)(\text{Ind}(x) \ \& \ \text{Idea}(y) \ \& \ (\forall z)((y \neq z \ \& \ y \approx_N z) \rightarrow \lozenge(x,y \ \Delta \ c \ \& \ x,z \ \cancel{\Delta} c)) \ \& \ \lozenge x,y \ \cancel{\Delta} \ c).$$

Further alternatives also come to mind. Nevertheless, the ensuing discussion will, I believe, show that the present version suffices.

26. These definitions of physical measure functions might also need to appeal to relations that hold between individuals and certain abstract entities known as *physical amounts* (1 ounce, 5 liters, 2 feet, etc.). Physical amounts, however, belong to the Aristotelian category of quantity and are not concepts at all. They certainly should not be confused with number concepts as the following equations make clear: 2 ounces = 56.7 grams and the concept of being (or weighing) 2 ounces ≠ the concept of being (or weighing) 56.7 grams. (See C. D. C. Reeve, *Mass, Quantity, and Amount* [unpublished dissertation, Cornell University, 1980], for a careful discussion of these distinctions.) Now the primary relation(s) holding between an individual and its amounts might be purely physical (the piece of gold *weighs* 3 grams); on the other hand, the primary relation here might be purely logical, namely, a relation of predication (e.g., the piece of gold *is* 3 grams). Either way, measure functions that correlate individuals with number concepts (such as the relation holding between a physical thing and the number of grams in it) still would be plainly derivative.

I should mention that there is a rather different approach to the theory of measurement than the one sketched in the text. According to this approach, the derivative character of measure functions is explained by means of various representation and uniqueness theorems: given a sufficiently rich characterization of physical objects in terms of physical relations among them (e.g., in terms of equality of weight, equality of length), one can actually derive the existence of the usual numerical measure functions. Advocates of this approach think of these functions as nonbasic just because they are "extrinsic" to the underlying "intrinsic" physical relations that ensure their existence and fix their identity (up to multiplication by a positive real number). Whether or not this explanation is fully correct, the approach does draw attention to a feature of numerical measure functions that clearly is ad hoc. None of the functions in the infinite class of functions equivalent up to multiplication by a positive real number is more basic than any other; the decision to use one over another depends on an arbitrary choice of standard unit. For an elegant philosophical introduction to, and extension of, this approach to the theory of measurement, see Hartry Field's *Science without Numbers* (Princeton, N.J., 1980).

27. Anyone still in doubt about this conclusion could always add to the proposed analysis the further requirement that intentional connections must possess independent veracity, that is, that they can contingently connect some individual to some thought or concept independently of whether or not the thought is true or the concept has any instances. This move would explicitly block numerical measure functions as counterexamples, for a number concept must

have instances if it is the value of a measure function. (On some analyses, zero is a concept having no instances; however, it would be impossible for a thing to be related to zero with independent veracity since, on these analyses, zero *necessarily* has no instances.)

28. The relation of speaker meaning—i.e., the relation holding between a speaker x and an idea y such that x means y by uttering something—would not be a counterexample to our analysis since it is an intentional relation; of course, on a broadly Gricean analysis, speaker meaning is definable in terms of more basic intentional relations—intending, believing, etc. Now, like speaker meaning, utterance-token meaning fails to be a counterexample to our analysis simply on the grounds that it too is an intentional relation. But if, contrary to what I say in the text, utterance-token meaning were truly a connection, we should not be happy to leave things here. A goal of the analysis is to isolate those connections simply in virtue of which a creature (as opposed to an utterance token produced by a creature) is intentional, and utterance-token meaning would not be such a connection. Thus, if we were to agree that utterance-token meaning is a connection, we should want to implement the following routine. A plurality of intentional connections is deemed *minimal* if and only if all intentional connections can be defined in terms of them, where no smaller number of them suffices for this purpose. Then, an intentional connection is defined to be *psychological* if and only if it is necessarily included in the union of the connections in such a minimal plurality. These psychological connections are those in virtue of which a creature is intentional. Because utterance-token meaning is not psychological in this sense, this routine would solve our problem. However, I do not implement this routine, for, after all, utterance-token meaning is disqualified as a connection in the first place.

When I speak of utterance-token meaning in the text, I am referring to meaning relations that hold contingently between utterance tokens and intensions in virtue of appropriate utterers' intentions. What is the relationship between these intentional meaning relations and the abstract meaning functions that arise in formal semantics? The answer is roughly this. To establish a given language as their own, the members of a speech community institute a convention to produce tokens of utterance types in the language only if the meaning (as specified by an abstract meaning function) of the utterance type is the intension that the speaker (intentionally) means by producing the token. Because an abstract meaning function is an antecedently given, purely abstract pairing of utterance types and intensions, it does not qualify as a counterexample to the analysis of intentionality. First, these functions pair utterance types (universals) and intensions, but to be a counterexample they would have to pair particulars and intensions. Secondly, these functions violate the contingency requirement since they are L-determinate. Thirdly, because these functions are arbitrary pairings of utterance types and intensions, there is no reason to think that they are genuine connections.

29. For an indication of some of the logical difficulties that might arise, see my review of Terence Parsons's *Nonexistent Objects (Journal of Symbolic Logic* 49 [1984]: 652-55).

30. See, for example, the technique sketched at the end of section 39, *Quality and Concept.*

31. Here is an illustration. It seems possible for someone to be thinking of a concept and not to be thinking of any object that the concept is about. For example, since I have a special theoretical interest in singular concepts, perhaps I am able to think of the concept of being identical to the color red without thinking of the color red itself. If this is possible, it would seem odd to say that this phenomenon of my thinking of the concept is *about* the color itself. Thus, if we assume that thinking of is a determinate intentional connection (of course, this is doubtful), then we should want to adjust the analysis of aboutness just given in the text. The following would suffice: (elementary) phenomenon p is *about* an object y iff p is directed toward a thought or concept that is about y and the occurrence of this phenomenon entails the occurrence of an associated phenomenon that is directed toward the object y itself (that is, for some individual x, some determinate intentional connections c and d, and some thought or concept z that is about y, p is the phenomenon that x stands in relation c to z and, necessarily, if x stands in relation c to z and z is about y, then x stands in d to y). This adjusted analysis solves the above

problem as follows. *Ex hypothesi* my thinking of the concept of being identical to the color red does not entail that I am thinking of the color red itself. Likewise for any other determinate intentional connection: my thinking of the concept does not on its own entail that I am connected by such a connection to the color itself. Therefore, according to the analysis, merely standing in the thinking-of relation to the concept does not qualify as a phenomenon that is about the color. And this is the outcome we are seeking. At the same time, other phenomena that are actually about objects are correctly counted as such by the analysis. For example, the phenomenon of my doubting that this (i.e., the color red) is a dispositional property is about this color, and our analysis counts it as such: the proposition that this is a dispositional property is about this color; my doubting that this is a dispositional property entails that I am thinking of this color, and the phenomenon of my thinking of this color is directed toward this color.

32. Although these relations do not pose a threat to our analysis, they do bring out some interesting points of difference between intentional and nonintentional relations. Recall the relation of falling under a concept, which we examined earlier. Whenever this relation holds between an individual and a concept, the concept *must* always have *that very individual* as an instance. Let us call this feature *dependent instantiation*. Intentional connections typically do not have dependent instantiations: if an intentional connection can connect an individual to a concept, typically it can do so independently of whether the concept has that individual (or indeed any individual) as an instance. Now unlike the relation of falling under a concept—and like intentional connections—the relations just discussed in the text do not have dependent instantiations. Nevertheless, there is an important logical affinity these relations have to the relation of falling under a concept, an affinity that intentional connections all lack. Take the ought relation as an example, and consider how we treat the modals 'must' and 'might'. 'A body must have a location' is best treated as a transformation from 'It is necessary that a body have a location', which ascribes the modal property necessity to the proposition that a body has a location; likewise, 'Socrates might philosophize until dawn' is best treated as a transformation from 'It is possible that Socrates will philosophize until dawn', which ascribes the modal property possibility to the proposition that Socrates will philosophize until dawn. Uniformity would seem to demand that we treat the modal 'ought' analogously. If so, '*a* ought to *F*' would be a transformation from 'It ought to be that *Fa*', which ascribes the modal property of what ought to be (i.e., what is good) to the proposition that *Fa*. If so, it would follow that the proposition that *a* ought to *F* is necessarily equivalent to the proposition that it ought to be that *a* falls under the concept of being *F*. Generalizing, we obtain the following necessary equivalence: *x* ought *y* iff it ought to be that *x* falls under *y*. Put metaphorically, ought is a relation that acquires a dependent instantiation *in the ideal,* as the world approaches what ought to be (what is good). Indeed, each relation in the cluster just discussed in the text has this special logical feature: it acquires a dependent instantiation in a relevant modal ideal. Intentional connections are never like this.

This observation is rather vague, and there is more than one way to make it more precise. Here is one. We saw that ought is a relation R that necessarily satisfied the following scheme for a basic modal property Q: xRy iff $Q[x$ falls under $y]$. And tending seems like this too; just let Q be probability or likelihood. After all, it is necessary that x tends to F iff it is probable (likely) that Fx. Needing is not exactly like ought and tending in this respect, but it is similar. For it necessarily satisfies the following scheme for a basic modal property Q and a basic normative property G: xRy iff $Q[Gx \rightarrow x$ falls under $y]$. Just let Q be natural necessity and G be well-being or flourishing; necessarily, x needs to F iff it is a natural necessity that x has well-being (flourishes) only if Fx. And the other nonintentional relations in our cluster all satisfy these or similar modal schemes. Intentional connections, by contrast, are never tied to underlying basic modal properties in any of these ways.

33. This categorial fact also protects our analysis of intentionality from the worry voiced in the closing section of Elliott Sober's "Why Logically Equivalent Predicates May Pick Out Different Properties," *American Philosophical Quarterly* 19 (1982): 183-89. In this article Sober

constructs an example of a triangle-selecting device whose description allegedly involves fine-grained intensionality. Then in his closing section Sober asks whether examples like this might not threaten analyses of intentionality that depend upon fine-grained intensionality. The answer is that such examples do not threaten our analysis: intentional connections must be able to connect individuals to fine-grained intensions; causal connections, by contrast, can hold only between phenomena and phenomena (or between events and events). Indeed, Sober himself seems tacitly to accept this categorial fact, for he writes as though "*a*'s having *F* causes *b*'s having *G*" is the canonical form for statements of singular causation. Suppose, however, that someone were to deny this categorial fact and to insist instead that particulars really can cause fine-grained intensions or that fine-grained intensions really can cause particulars. And suppose, moreover, that this person alleges that the envisaged causal connections are hyperintensional. Now we could mount persuasive counterarguments. But we could also deal with this person simply by tightening our analysis. For example, we could require intentional connections to have not only contingency and hyperintensionality but also independent veracity. (The latter notion is characterized in note 27 above and in section 48 of *Quality and Concept*.) Then the envisaged causal connections would not qualify as intentional because they do not have independent veracity. After all, the car does not cause the boy to fall unless the boy *in fact* falls, and triangularity does not cause Sober's triangle-selecting device to select an object unless something *actually* is triangular.

34. Incidentally, according to an Aristotelian theory of final causes, if the function of, say, a kidney is to remove wastes from the blood, then, necessarily, this is the function of the kidney. Hence, this Aristotelian notion of function would violate the contingency requirement and, therefore, would not be an intentional connection according to our analysis. This is the desired outcome because the Aristotelian notion is not intentional.

35. The meaning relation envisaged by John Perry and Jon Barwise in their system of situation semantics is a somewhat similar ternary relation holding between a particular token, a meaning, and a system of constraints. This relation would not be a counterexample to our analysis, however; for in their system, whenever this relation holds, evidently it holds necessarily, hence violating the contingency requirement. If not, one could disqualify this relation as a counterexample by suitably adapting the strategy sketched for utterance-token meaning in note 28.

36. The following revised analysis would suffice for this purpose:

A connection is intentional iff it is identical to—or it is necessarily included in—a connection that can contingently connect an individual to an L-determinate idea independently of whether it connects the individual to any necessarily equivalent idea.

None of the problematic relations under consideration in the text can connect an individual to any L-determinate idea. Incidentally, since the consciousness relation satisfies this analysis and since the relations of pure and interpreted experience are necessarily included in the consciousness relation, this analysis could be adopted for use in the full analysis of mental connection given in the next section.

37. On the standard nominalist relational theory of sense experience, the range of the pure experience relation does not include sensible qualities and sensible conditions, but instead it includes mental particulars (sensa, sense data, phantasms, subjective spaces, etc.). However, no ontological economy is gained by adopting this theory, for such private mental particulars cannot be compared with one another in all the ways we ordinarily compare sense experiences except by invoking the full apparatus of sensible qualities at some level or other. So one is ontologically better off adopting the Platonistic relational theory described in the text. In any case, the definition of mental connection offered in the text is designed to handle the pure experience relation regardless which of these two theories is correct; for as far as the definition is concerned, items from any metaphysical category could be in the range of any mental connection. As a result, the analysis is compatible with the nominalist theory that every object of pure experience is a private mental particular.

38. For example, this is David Armstrong's position in *Universals and Scientific Realism.*

39. See, for example, Hilary Putnam, "Brains and Behavior," *Analytical Philosophy,* 2nd ser., edited by R. J. Butler (Oxford, 1963), 1-19.

40. See *Word and Object,* chapter 2 and section 45.

41. See, for example, Frank Jackson, "Epiphenomenal Qualia," *Philosophical Quarterly* 32 (1982): 127-36; Thomas Nagel, "What Is It Like to Be a Bat?" *Philosophical Review* 83 (1974): 435-50; Richard Warner, "In Defense of Dualism," unpublished manuscript. See also Saul Kripke, "Naming and Necessity," *Semantics of Natural Language,* edited by Gilbert Harman and Donald Davidson (Dordrecht, 1972), 253-355, 763-69, especially 335.

42. See, for example, Hilary Putnam, "Psychological Predicates," *Art, Mind and Religion: Proceedings of the 1965 Oberlin Colloquium in Philosophy,* edited by W. H. Capitan and D. D. Merrill (Detroit, 1967), 37-48.

43. See "New Foundations for Intensional Logic" for an extended defense of the thesis that the standard psychological relations are self-embeddable. A wealth of further arguments can be extrapolated from those Saul Kripke gives aginst Tarski's infinite hierarchy of distinct truth concepts for English; see "Outline of a Theory of Truth," *Journal of Philosophy* 72 (1975): 690-716, sections 1 and 2. A principal aim of *Quality and Concept* is to provide an intensional logic able to treat self-embeddable psychological relations without invoking the implausible, artificial distinctions posited in ramified type theories.

44. I give the argument in full in "A Disproof of the Mind-Body Identity Thesis from Self-embedded Attitudes" (forthcoming).

45. See my "Mind and Anti-Mind: Why Thinking Has No Functional Definition," *Midwest Studies in Philosophy* 9 (1984): 283-328. It is worth noting that the argument of this paper is not tied to the use of Quinean transformations that concern ontology (e.g., the universal/particular transformation); elementary logical transformations also suffice (e.g., a transformation that maps fine-grained propositions $[((A \ \& \ B) \ v \ C) \ \& \ D]$ to fine-grained propositions $[D \ \& \ (C \ v \ (B \ \& \ A))]$).

Incidentally, functionalism also runs into fatal difficulties regarding self-embeddable attitudes; see "A Disproof of the Mind-Body Identity Thesis."

46. This result thus contradicts the central thesis of Fred Dretske's book, *Knowledge and the Flow of Information* (Cambridge, Mass., 1981).

47. Here again I am adapting the line of argument developed by George Myro, "Aspects of Acceptability."

48. For example, the eliminative materialist Paul Churchland is unable to state his account of scientific progress without making repeated use of the mentalist terms 'sensation' and 'intrinsic qualitative identity of . . . sensations'. See chapter 2, *Scientific Realism and the Plasticity of Mind* (Cambridge, 1979).

49. A moderate eliminativist might initially be drawn to the following alternate definition:

p is a datum for x iff$_{df}$ p = the proposition that x has a pure experience of y, where y is some sensible quality or condition, and x accepts p.

The problem with this definition for the moderate eliminativist is that the term 'accept' is prima facie intentional. The advantage of the definition in the text is that it avoids intentional terms.

50. Because such a theory must appeal to self-embedded intentional relations (acceptance, belief), we have a transcendental justification for the starting point of our purely logical argument (sketched earlier) against the possibility of physicalistic definitions of intentional relations. With this in mind, we might consider building self-embeddability right into our analysis of intentionality.

MIDWEST STUDIES IN PHILOSOPHY, X (1986)

Bodily Movements, Actions, and Mental Epistemology

JENNIFER HORNSBY

I

In philosophy we find reasons for recognizing events that fall under the generalized description 'a person's body's moving' or 'bodily movement'.[1]

One reason that might be offered for talking about such events—about movements of fingers, or legs, or whatever—is that in doing so we talk about what is overt or in the public and observable realm. If knowledge of people's minds needs to be built upon observable features of people, and if movings of peoples' bodies are all that can be observed, then we should have to focus attention on bodies' movings to understand how people can learn what they do learn about one another. But I shall suggest that we make a mistake if we think that people's bodies' movings must have the special status of being visible alike to a psychologically quite ignorant and a psychologically informed spectator, so that they can serve as a neutral basis for knowledge of mind.

Another reason for concern with people's bodily movements has nothing directly to do with epistemology: we want to understand the relations between the things that happen when there are human actions. Where so-called physical action is in question, it is a necessary condition of someone's doing something that a movement of her body occur;[2] and we can have a clearer picture of what goes on if we are able to say how the event that is her body's moving is related to her doing what she does.

I take the view that the relation between an action of someone's moving her body and her body's moving is a causal one and that a person's body's moving is no part of her action of moving her body. It has been objected that this view has the consequence that we do not see actions and that this consequence is problematic. I hope to fend off this objection in this paper. I shall start by sketching and discussing various views in the philosophy of action; to begin with, I shall avoid any epistemological matters.

II

Three claims about human physical action will have to be taken for granted here. First when a person intentionally does anything, that person's doing that thing is an action, and this action is her moving her body.[3] Second, if a person moves a part of her body, that part of her body moves. And third, typically at least, when a person intentionally does something, she tries to do that thing.[4] If these three claims are true, then when someone does something and intentionally moves her body,[5] there are events of three sorts: there is an event of that person's moving her body, which is her action; there is an event of her body's moving; and there is an event of her trying to move her body.

These claims are controversial. But even when they are accepted, there is still disagreement about what relations obtain between particular events of the three sorts. (Note that to say that there are events of these three sorts is not yet to say whether there are three events.)

Let us focus on a particular occasion of an action—someone wiggles her finger to attract someone else's attention, say. Call the event of her wiggling her finger *the action,* the event of her finger's wiggling *the movement,* and the event of her trying to wiggle her finger *the attempt.* Then I claim that the action causes the movement; but others claim that the movement is a (proper) part of the action; and others that the movement is the same as the action. Claims about the relation between the action and the movement are not independent of claims about the relation between the action and the attempt. I claim that the attempt is the same as the action. But some of those who hold that the movement is a part of the action or that the movement is the same as the action will deny that. Those who hold that the movement is a part of the action and deny the identity of attempt with action think that the attempt is a part of the action: their picture is one in which actions are "ontologically and conceptually hybrid," composed from events of trying on the one hand and movements of the body on the other.[6] Those who hold that the movement is the same as the action and deny the identity of attempt with action think that the attempt causes the movement: their picture is one in which actions are those movements of the body that are caused by events of trying.

There are so many possible views here (including ones not sketched above) that one must hope to rule out some with a general argument. It is often supposed that we are more or less free to choose whether actions are to be identified with attempts and that we have only to compare the pictures we get of action according as we assume the identity or not.[7] But in fact it is possible to argue in a general way against any view that denies the identity of actions with events of trying (or attempts). For it seems that someone who accepts the account of the individuation of actions presupposed here (which is summed up in the first of the three claims that I said would be taken for granted) must already have an argument for such identities. To argue for this account of individuation is to argue for the following schema:[8]

If x ϕ-s by ψ-ing, then x's ϕ-ing is the same as x's ψ-ing.

Clearly this yields statements of identity relating actions. But if we can write as an instance of 'ϕ' or of 'ψ' here 'tries to——', then we shall reach a statement of identity linking action with attempt. And we can sometimes instantiate 'ϕ' or 'ψ' with 'tries to——'. (We can truly say such things as 'He upset Mary by trying to pacify John' or 'She managed to trill moderately well by trying to move her fingers in the way her teacher had shown her'.) It seems then that whatever leads one to say that Jones's killing Smith was the same as his moving his finger (on the gun) will lead one to say that Jones's *trying to* kill Smith was the same as his moving his finger on the gun and (if Jones tried to move his finger) was the same as his *trying to* move his finger.[9] If this is right, the identity of action with attempt may be assumed in determining whether the relationship between movement and action is *part/whole* or *identity* or *cause/effect*.

One motive there has been for thinking that movements and actions are related as *parts to wholes* is that it enables us to give a particular literal sense to the idea that actions are psychophysical.[10] But this motive seems to lapse when we assume the identity of the action with the attempt; then we cannot say that actions are composed both from events that we recognize as psychological (viz. attempts) and events that we recognize as physical (viz. movements). Given the identity of action with attempt, someone who thinks that movements are parts of actions, when he is asked what it is that along with the movement constitutes the action, apparently has no way to answer except by saying 'that which is left over when the movement is subtracted from the action'. Of course, someone might find plenty to say about the event that is action-minus-movement residue even though no psychological term straightforwardly latches onto it. But he would now do well to offer an argument specifically for the view that movements are parts of actions.[11]

If the thesis that the movement *is the same as* the action were correct, then the three sorts of events we began from would prove to be such that a single event is of all these three sorts: the action is itself movement and attempt. If we favor a certain uniform account of the nature of trying, however, we have a reason to think that the movement is distinct from the attempt.[12] The difference, we may want to say, between a successful and unsuccessful attempt to do something (no matter what that something is) is that a successful attempt, but not an unsuccessful one, results in an event whose occurrence then suffices for the thing's having been done. The difference between a successful and unsuccessful attempt to turn on a light, for instance, is that the former but not the latter results in an event—a light's going on—whose occurrence then suffices for the light's having been turned on.[13] Applying the account to the case of trying to move the body, we find ourselves saying that successful but not unsuccessful attempts to move the body result in bodily movements.[14]

This last argument purports to demonstrate not only that the relation between action and movement is not identity, but also that the relation is in fact a causal one. Doubtless the argument is not definitive.[15] But perhaps it can be allowed that nothing in the sorts of consideration so far adduced suggests that a view of movements as parts of actions, or as the same as actions, is obviously correct if set against a view of movements as caused by actions.[16] At this point, then, I turn to something thought to be definitive against this view: it is said that it has the absurd consequence that actions are invisible.[17]

III

Actions are events. So we might suppose that a question about their visibility would have to be answered by reference to some general account of what it is to see events. Notice that the usual discussions of the perceptual relation do not supply such an account. We are accustomed to think of vision as relating persons (or other animals) to things that can be described as being opaque, say, or as having some particular surface facing an observer. Applying this conception of vision in an automatic way to the case of events would appear to have the consequence that all events are strictly invisible. For events presumably do not have the light-reflecting properties that the objects of vision are now conceived as having.

Perhaps something could be learned from a general account of what it is to see an event, as opposed to a material object. But we shall find that there is no need to seek such an account here if we pause to consider the source of our confidence that we see actions. It might be that we felt so confident because we are sometimes so sure of the truth of such simple relational visual claims connecting persons with actions as 'She saw his moving of his finger' (or, generally, 'She saw his doing something'). But this seems unlikely: claims like this are so seldom made that they are unlikely to ground our confidence.[18] It is much more plausible that it is claims such as 'She saw him move his finger' (or, generally, 'She saw him do something'[19] that convince us of the belief expressed when we proclaim the visibility of actions: 'Why are you so sure that actions are visible?' 'Well of course we see people acting'.

What is at issue, then, when it is asked whether some thesis allows for or precludes the visibility of actions, is only whether that thesis accommodates the fact that people see one another doing things. It seems that the visibility of actions can hardly be the crux in determining whether bodily movements are caused by, or partially comprise, or are the same as, actions: the obtaining of any of these relations would presumably present no obstacle to the idea that people can be seen doing things.

IV

"This is all very well as far as it goes", it may be said, "but one leaves something out of account if one is prepared only to address questions about what people can be seen doing. If we want an understanding of how knowledge of others is gained, then we need to be told *how* it is that people can be seen doing the things they intentionally do. After all, it can perfectly well be said that we see people try to do things. ('I saw him trying to catch the chairman's attention.') But in this case, if we assume that events of trying are hidden from view, we surely want to know what sort of thing we directly see, in virtue of which it can be said that we see someone try to do something."

The objector maintains that literal questions about the direct visibility of particular events have to be pressed. So let us for the moment take him on his own terms and see what might come of pressing such questions. (In section V, we shall consider what his terms are.)

Let us adopt a picture of attempts causing movements. But let us resolve to leave it an open question where actions fit into this picture. (If any conclusions were reached in section II, they are to be ignored here.) We can raise a question now about visibility in respect of certain events that we may call attempt-plus-movements; these we stipulate have as parts an attempt and a movement and nothing else.

Someone who was convinced that attempts themselves are hidden might have his doubts whether an attempt-plus-movement is visible; but perhaps the overtness of movements can somehow persuade even him of the visibility of attempt-plus-movements.[20] So let us take it that our question might be settled in the affirmative: attempt-plus-movements can be seen. Would this be a useful result?

Well, if we thought that our knowledge of other people had to be got from seeing their attempt-plus-movements, then no doubt it would be as well to be sure that these things are indeed visible. But if the visibility of these things were the issue, then the needed result could be secured (if it could) while setting to one side the question whether actions are visible. For we have not said which of the events in the picture the term 'action' applies to. And if someone now introduces the claim that actions are attempt-plus-movements, his claim appears idle when it comes to the questions about other minds which were supposed to turn on issues of visibility.

A similar point may be made in relation to the thesis that actions are movements simply: someone's stand on that thesis apparently need not affect his view about what it is upon whose visibility we rely for our knowledge of other people.

It seems, then, that if we do insist upon raising questions in miniature about what is and is not visible among the events that occur when there is an action, then nothing of moment has to revolve around the specific question whether, among these events, *actions* are visible. And it is arguable that we have no firm intuition on this specific question which is not dependent on some prior view of what actions are.

V

Our objector had some definite ideas about why we should need to determine what is and what is not literally visible among attempts, movements, and actions. He thought that when we look at people, only some of their features—or only some of the events that go on where they are—are open to view, whereas others are hidden; and knowledge of others needs to be based on what is open to view.

It is easy to suppose that these ideas stem from a certain traditional epistemology of "other minds," which makes joint use of a division between physical and mental and a division between what can be present to another's senses and what can be known by another at best less directly.[21] The view is sometimes expressed using a distinction between bodies and persons: only other bodies are unproblematic objects of sense experience; experience of other bodies provides the basis, if anything does, for knowledge of other persons. A similar distinction can be made in the realm of events—between bodily movements available to sight and hearing on the one hand, and mental events occurring inside people on the other. If we attached any serious theoretical status to this distinction, we should feel forced to ask upon which side of the division actions lie, and the visibility of actions would come to seem to be an issue of the sort that our objector suggested it was.

Someone might think not only that the traditional epistemological outlook prompts particular questions about what is strictly and literally visible, but also that the thesis that actions cause movements engenders such an outlook. It is sometimes said that there is a tendency to use the word 'behavior' ambiguously: bits of behavior may (i) be the colorless, unproblematically visible, "mere" bodily movements of the behaviorists; or they may (ii) be actions, things colored by their own significance.[22] Now what someone might think is that when movements are distinguished from actions, the distinction made runs along the lines of this ambiguity in 'behavior'. In that case, bodily movements would have to be credited with the special epistemological status that is assigned, from the traditional outlook, to colorless "mere" movements.

But here we need to use not one distinction, but two.[23] A distinction can always be made within the realm of events between those items there to which a particular predicate applies and those to which it does not; taking the predicate in question to be 'is an action', and granting the distinctness of the action and the movement of section II, we obtain a distinction between actions and movements. But this is different from any distinction between, so to speak, what is colorless and what is not—between different characterizations of events (or whatever), according as those characterizations do or do not presuppose a subject of mentality. This latter distinction will be required if the epistemology of other minds is to be conducted in the traditional way: we have to be able to separate what is psychologically uncontaminated from what is not; and such a separation would make a division in the realm of facts, and not in the realm of events. One cannot say of an event per se whether it is a psychologically neutral or a psychologically contaminated thing.

This last point may explain why it seemed impossible (in section IV) to tie questions about the strict and literal visibility of actions to anything of real epistemological interest. Concerned with epistemology, we might want to ask, say, whether someone can become acquainted with the psychological facts about others simply by keeping her eyes and ears open in their presence. But we should be no further forward with such a question if we were told only which events are seen. Suppose that we were told that actions are seen. Unless we could say that it was known *that* the things seen are actions, we should have made no advance in ensuring that vision gives us knowledge of "other minds."[24]

If one is guided by an epistemology that uses a division between what takes place strictly before an observer's eyes and what does not, and correlates that with a division between a kind of fact that is immediately accessible to an observer and a kind of fact that is not, then one will want a single line to be defined by both of the two distinctions I have made. But there is nothing in the thesis that actions cause movements which should make us expect to find such a line. And there is nothing there that demonstrates that bodily movements are the behaviorists' colorless items. Once both distinctions are in play, we can insist that bodily movements, even if they are not the same as actions, are not the colorless "mere" movements of the behaviorist: they may participate in all of the color of the actions that cause them.

The bodies that these movements are the movements of are, after all, the bodies of persons, and not "mere" bodies. Consider now how the relevant class of movements might be specified. A movement, one might say, is something that occurs in any normal case of an unparalyzed person who tries to do something that requires her to move her body. The psychological element in this specification is ineliminable. There need be no suggestion that what we pick out when we pick out bodily movements are events that could occur even if there were no "other minds."[25]

At this point, we can appreciate the proper source of the claim that the ordinary idea of seeing people do things is all that is needed for knowledge of actions. This claim need not spring from thinking that what we ordinarily say is all that ever matters; nor need it be the product of evasion. For there is no urgent question about how we get to know about one another that someone who makes this claim refuses to face up to. Rather the claim can derive from a reasoned rejection of the outlook from which putative questions about the strict and literal visibility of events are supposed to arise. Wittgenstein rejected the conception of a body required by the epistemological outlook discussed here.[26] We may reject any related conception of a movement of such a body.

VI

Nothing here has been intended to establish the thesis that actions cause movements; I have hoped only to displace one argument against that thesis.[27] I have tried to show that the metaphysical questions in the philosophy of action of section II can to a large extent be freed from epistemological questions that are posed as questions about the visibility of actions. And I have suggested that the two sorts of questions have wrongly been allowed to impinge upon one another: some people may have been deterred from adopting a particular view of actions for fear that that would require of them an epistemological outlook that they preferred not to take; again, some people may have allowed that same outlook to influence their view in the philosophy of action.[28]

This latter suggestion may seem mischievous. The epistemological outlook I have spoken of is not an attractive one. Has not philosophy learned to abandon it? How could it still influence thought?

Well, there is more prevalent than ever before in the philosophy of mind the idea that people's behavior can be given an exhaustive, colorless characterization (in the terms, say, in which a functionalist would wish to describe "outputs"), which combines with a characterization of the stimuli impinging upon them (of "inputs") to determine their psychology. This idea often appears to have the status of assumption. It is hard to see how it can seem so obviously correct unless some doctrine that appears evident from the traditional epistemological outlook makes it seem so. But whatever is in fact responsible for the idea about the determinants of people's psychology, the epistemological issues may be worth addressing. If the only escape from the epistemological outlook that I have considered, and that seems so unattractive, were to argue against the reality of the concept of bodily movement that that outlook requires, then the very possibility of colorless characterizations of behavior, the alleged determinants of psychology, would have to be cast into doubt. If so, exploration of the epistemological questions I have touched on could have far-reaching consequences in the philosophy of mind.

Notes

1. I am grateful to Michael Smith for discussion of the issues in section II and for comments on a draft of the present paper.

2. The use of 'physical' at the beginning of this sentence (and in the first paragraph of section II) is a stipulative one, which might be provisionally defined by this sentence itself.

3. This is a summary statement of Donald Davidson's thesis about actions, which is sometimes put by saying that actions are events that are intentional under some description. (See, e.g., his "Agency," reprinted in *Actions and Events* [Oxford, 1980]). Some of those who engage in the controversy I am introducing believe that we should recognize some "subintentional" items as actions, thereby recognizing more actions than Davidson's criterion defines; but they need not deny what is assumed here, that at least the items Davidson calls actions are actions.

My own statement relies upon a distinction between things that are done (which are not particulars: I can do the same thing as you) and actions (which are particulars: your doing something cannot be the same as my doing that thing).

4. I discover that the argument for this (and not only the more familiar analogous argument about perception) was given by H. P. Grice in his unpublished William James lectures (1967) and by D. M. Armstrong in "Acting and Trying," *Philosophical Papers, vol. 2* (Cambridge, 1973), 1-15. Brian O'Shaughnessy used the argument in "Trying (as the Mental "Pineal Gland")," *Journal of Philosophy* 71 (1974): 365-86; and I attempted to state a more general version in *Actions* (London, 1980), 33ff. O'Shaughnessy has since argued for a more general thesis still: he identifies actions with attempts even where the class of actions includes the subintentional (cf. n. 3); see *The Will,* chap. 11 (2 vol., Cambridge, 1980). (I refer to vol. 2 of *The Will* in notes below.)

5. Notice that 'and intentionally moves her body' is doing some actual work in this sentence. For one can accept that someone's action is her intentionally doing something that she does by moving her body without affirming that she intentionally moves her body. I am inclined to doubt that *move the body* is something that we intentionally do whenever we intentionally try to do something that requires a bodily movement. Because the claim about *trying* above is confined to what we intentionally do ('We try to do what we intentionally do'), I am not committed to thinking that whenever there is a ("physical") action, there is an event of trying to move the body—even if I confine myself to cases in which that is so.

6. The quotation is from Colin McGinn, *The Character of Mind* (Oxford, 1982), 90. McGinn there perspicuously sets out four different views.

7. For instance O'Shaughnessy (*The Will*), who accepts identities between actions and attempts, argues for them only by way of arguing against alternatives. Reviewing O'Shaughnessy, Frank Jackson dissents from the identities thesis, without contemplating arguments other than the negative ones that O'Shaughnessy uses (*Inquiry* 25 (1982): 255-70).

8. The generality of the schema may be doubted. (We do say such things as 'I'll arrive at the station on time by telephoning for a taxi', but we don't want to identify my arriving at the station with my telephoning.) But it need not be doubted that, whatever argument can be given for the account of action individuation, it will, with some regularity, yield statements of identity between actions and tryings.

9. This is by no means a novel thesis. Ryle must have accepted it (see *The Concept of Mind,* chap. 5, section 4). See also Davidson, "Agency."

It may be objected that we need to distinguish between attempts to move the body and attempts to bring about things beyond the body. That which is here called the attempt is someone's trying to wiggle her finger; and (it will be said) this can be distinct from her action, even if her action is to be identified with, say, her trying to get someone's attention. I think that there are difficulties about treating *trying to move the body* as a special case (cf. n. 16 below). But one's view of this matter is likely to depend upon whether one thinks that any moving of the body that is an action is an intentional moving of the body (cf. n. 5 above) and upon whether one accepts that we can have a uniform account of *trying* of the kind suggested below (penultimate paragraph of section II.)

10. This is evidently McGinn's motive when he writes, 'The composite conception of action . . . seems to meet our desideratum of displaying actions as inherently psychophysical more successfully than [three other conceptions]' (*Character of Mind*, 90).

Notice that someone might think that there was a point in insisting that *persons* are inherently psychophysical but be dissatisfied with a conception of a person (actually Descartes's) as composed out of something mental and something physical. It must then be possible to give serious content to a claim that something is psychophysical without introducing any notion such as composition to say how the psychological and the physical exist together, as it were.

11. Arguments are offered for an account of individuation of actions that regards as parts of actions things that on the present account are the consequences of actions. But these are not arguments for the specific claim that *movements* are parts of actions.

O'Shaughnessy (*The Will*) accepts the identity of the action with the attempt and takes the movement to be a part of the action; but he happily concedes that there is no straightforward specification of the action-minus-movement: he calls this a nonautonomous part, and he is not affected by the argument of the present paragraph. O'Shaughnessy's own argument for this view relies on the rejection of alternatives.

12. Another possible reason may be given, which bypasses any questions about the status of the attempt. Here I mean the consideration stated by McGinn when he says that a theory that identifies actions with movements 'fails to register the essential activity of actions' (*Character of Mind*, 88). It may be that this consideration gains some of its force from the idea that movements are "mere" movements—an idea that I challenge in section V. Still there does seem to be something right in the suggestion that there are certain predications that we can make of actions, but not of movements. For the kinds of predications that might be mentioned here, see O'Shaughnessy, *The Will*, 128. (It is true that O'Shaughnessy sets out these features in the course of preparing to argue for the conclusion that actions are *not* distinct from movements. But, given O'Shaughnessy's views, the nondistinctness in question cannot be identity; cf. n. 11.)

13. One may have a view of "deviant chains" that would lead one to qualify this.

14. This imports the idea that it is possible for someone to try to move her body and fail to do so. More controversial than that is the thesis that if someone succeeds in moving her body, then the very event that occurred and that was her trying to move her body could still have occurred even if she had not succeeded. (See Michael Smith, "Actions, Attempts and Internal Events," *Analysis* 43 (1983): 142-46.)

15. Acceptance of the thesis called more controversial in n. 14 may lead to a cleaner argument than that presented here against the idea that the action is both the attempt and the movement. It may also affect our view of the idea considered in the previous paragraph that the movement is a part of the action; and here it will make a difference whether one is with O'Shaughnessy in accepting the action/attempt identities, or with McGinn in denying them.

McGinn (*Character of Mind*, 89) argues as follows against the identity of action with attempt: "The trying could occur without the movement; but in those circumstances the action would not have occurred. In short, tryings are contingently successful, but actions are necessarily successful." Now the claim in the last four words is not: "Necessarily there is nothing to which 'action' applies unless there is a movement"; if this were the claim, it would be compatible with the idea that the trying/action might occur without the movement. The claim must be: "Any event that is an action could not have failed to be an action"; in this case the claim itself may be disputed, and the argument now also requires the thesis about trying that I have called "more controversial."

16. In the first two chapters of *Actions* I offered considerations different from any used or alluded to here in favor of the view that actions cause movements.

17. See, e.g., O'Shaughnessy, *The Will,* 130ff; and McGinn, who writes: "We can see someone's actions when we see him move his body; but on [this] theory [which identifies actions with attempts] all you see are the consequences of the agent's actions, never the actions themselves, since the tryings with which actions are identified are purely inner events invisible to the naked eye" (*Character of Mind,* 88-89).

In chap. 7 of *Actions,* I responded to the objection that my view had the absurd consequence that actions are invisible. But there I made the claim that "actions occur inside the body," misguidedly supposing that this was a vivid summary statement of my view. With that claim to one side, the defense against the objection can be conducted rather better. (At least this thought inspires my present effort.)

18. Philosophers single out the word 'action' to stand for events in a certain class (see the beginning of section I above, and n. 3). The word does not play that role in every use, and one does not preserve the sense of sentences if one switches between the philosopher's carefully delimited use and other uses. Here I think we have a case in point: I suggest that when we say that actions are visible, finding that obviously correct, we do not use 'action' in the delimited way. (This is not to say that it is false in any sense that actions are visible.)

I believe that the general point here is of use in defending against other objections to my view of actions that I do not take up here.

19. I take it that 'x saw a moving his finger' is to be assimilated to 'x saw a move his finger' (from which it differs in aspect), and not to 'x saw a's moving of his finger': in this last construction, but only here, the whole of what follows 'saw' is a noun-phrase in extensional position. I take it also that 'x saw a ϕ', unlike 'x saw that a ϕ-d', requires sight by x of a for its truth.

20. It seems as if McGinn thinks that the overtness of movements guarantees the overtness of attempt-plus-movements. For he thinks attempts are hidden (see the quotation in n. 17 above), but that attempt-plus-movements, which in his own view are actions, are visible. McGinn might use the principle that a thing is visible if it has a visible part. But this principle, though it may be correct for material objects, seems to have less to recommend it for events. (Suppose someone was worried that we could not see actions because he thought that they went on inside us. It is not obvious that he would be reassured if he was then told that only parts of them went on inside us—especially if he were told that the psychological part of an action is always on the inside.)

Similarly, O'Shaughnessy thinks that to allow that actions "encompass" movements is to ensure that actions are visible (*The Will,* 132). (Though he does not identify actions with attempt-plus-movements—cf. n. 11.)

21. 'At best less directly' is deliberately vague. The epistemological outlook that I describe here is associated with many different views about how we have knowledge of others and how much of it we have. (One's view of how and how much is not determined by the outlook because it depends upon how seriously one is able to take the predicament that the outlook creates, and on how one conceives knowledge of one's own mind, etc.)

22. See, e.g., Charles Taylor, *The Explanation of Behaviour* (London, 1964), chap. 3, n. 1, 55-56.

23. Until it is decided whether actions are distinct from bodily movements, it remains an open question whether a distinction between actions and movements is in fact (as I believe) a distinction between items within the realm of events.

One may make a distinction between two senses of 'movement': a movement may be a person's moving of her body (cf. "the action" of section II) or it may be a person's body's movement (cf. "the movement" of section II). This ambiguity in 'movement' can be acknowledged even by those who deny the distinctness of actions and movements, and who thus deny that the ambiguity corresponds to any distinction between items within the realm of events. This shows that we may have to detect two possible sources of ambiguity in 'behavior', even if we deny that one of them proves to correspond to the distinction "within the realm of events" just mentioned in the text.

24. Similarly one has made no advance in exposing the traitor if one only knows that one has seen the traitor. The point derives from the extensionality of the '*x* sees *a*' construction (cf. n. 19). (If our interest were in epistemology at its most general—do we see things in an external material world?—then we should have to concern ourselves with questions framed using the extensional construction. I assume that someone who raises questions about the visibility of actions doesn't [*pro hac vice*] have an interest in epistemology at its most general.)

25. This doesn't yet contradict someone who holds that there is, for any bodily movement, a colorless characterization of it. I confine myself here to arguing against those who think that we *must* start with colorless characterizations of movements if we distinguish these from actions.

26. *Philosophical Investigations* (Oxford, 1953). See John W. Cook, "Human Beings," in *Studies in the Philosophy of Wittgenstein,* edited by Peter Winch (London, 1969); and John McDowell, "Criteria, Defeasibility and Knowledge," *Proceedings of the British Academy* 68 (1982): 455-79. See also (without references to Wittgenstein) Douglas C. Long, *Philosophical Review* 73 (1964): 321-37.

27. Other arguments are given against the thesis (see, e.g., O'Shaughnessy, *The Will,* chap. 11). I should hope to use a consideration of the kind offered in section III above in reply (see n. 18).

28. I say *some* people. It is possible that someone should think that the argument of section III is inconclusive but not want to frame his response to that argument in the terms of the objector who speaks at the start of section IV. (O'Shaughnessy, for instance, may not be satisfied with section III—cf. n. 17; but it may be that he need not quarrel with what is said in section V.)

Kripke's Belief Puzzle

IGAL KVART

1. INTRODUCTION

In this article I offer a resolution of Kripke's belief puzzle.[1] The puzzle runs as follows, in Kripke's own words:

> Suppose Pierre is a normal French speaker who lives in France and speaks not a word of English or of any other language except French. Of course he has heard of that famous distant city, London (which he of course calls 'Londres') though he himself has never left France. On the basis of what he has heard of London, he is inclined to think that it is pretty. So he say, in French, "Londres est jolie."
> On the basis of his sincere French utterance, we will conclude:
>
> (4) Pierre believes that London is pretty.

> I am supposing that Pierre satisfies all criteria for being a normal French speaker, in particular, that he satisfies whatever criteria we usually use to judge that a Frenchman (correctly) uses 'est jolie' to attribute pulchritude and uses 'Londres'—standardly—as a name of London.
> Later, Pierre, through fortunate or unfortunate vicissitudes, moves to England, in fact to London itself, though to an unattractive part of the city with fairly uneducated inhabitants. He, like most of his neighbors, rarely even leaves this part of the city. None of his neighbors know any French, so he must learn English by 'direct method', without using any translation of English into French: by talking and mixing with the people he eventually begins to pick up English. In particular, everyone speaks of the city 'London', where they all live. Let us suppose for

the moment—though we will see below that this is not crucial—that the local population are so uneducated that they know few of the facts that Pierre heard about London in France. Pierre learns from them everything they know about London, but there is little overlap with what he heard before. He learns, of course—speaking English—to call the city he lives in 'London'. Pierre's surroundings are, as I said, unattractive, and he is unimpressed with most of the rest of what he happens to see. So he is inclined to assent to the English sentence:

(5) London is not pretty.

He has *no* inclination to assent to:

(6) London is pretty.

Of course he does not for a moment withdraw his assent from the French sentence, "Londres est jolie"; he merely takes it for granted that the ugly city in which he is now stuck is distinct from the enchanting city he heard about in France. But he has no inclination to change his mind for a moment about the city he still calls 'Londres'.

This, then, is the puzzle. If we consider Pierre's past background as a French speaker, his entire linguistic behavior, on the same basis as we would draw such a conclusion about many of his countrymen, supports the conclusion [(4) above] that he believes that London is pretty. On the other hand, after Pierre lived in London for some time, he did not differ from his neighbors—his French background aside—either in his knowledge of English or in his command of the relevant facts of local geography. His English vocabulary differs little from that of his neighbors. He, like them, rarely ventures from the dismal quarter of the city in which they all live. He, like them, knows that the city he lives in is called 'London' and knows a few other facts. Now Pierre's neighbors would surely be said to use 'London' as a name for London and to speak English. Since, as an English speaker, he does not differ at all from them, we should say the same of him. But then, on the basis of his sincere assent to (5), we should conclude:

(7) Pierre believes that London is not pretty.[2]

Of course, (4) and (7) seem to involve Pierre in a straightforward inconsistency. As Kripke puts it: "So we must say that Pierre has contradictory beliefs, that he believes that London is pretty *and* he believes that London is not pretty."[3] Yet, given the setup of the story, it seems clear that Pierre is *not* being inconsistent at all.

Let us call this form of the puzzle the *inconsistency version*. Kripke now presents the puzzle in an even stronger form:

Again, we may emphasize Pierre's *lack* of belief instead of his belief. Pierre, as I said, has no disposition to assent to (6). Let us concentrate on this, ignoring his disposition to assent to (5). In fact, if we wish we may change the case: Suppose Pierre's neighbors think that since they rarely venture outside their own ugly section, they have no right to any opinion as to the pulchritude of the whole city. Suppose Pierre shares their attitude. Then, judging by his failure to respond affirmatively to "London is pretty," we may judge, from Pierre's behavior as an *English* speaker, that he lacks the belief that London is pretty: never mind whether he disbelieves it, as before, or whether, as in the modified story, he insists that he has no firm opinion on the matter.

Now (using the *strengthened* disquotational principle), we can derive a contradiction, not merely in Pierre's judgments, but in our own. For on the basis of his behavior as an English speaker, we concluded that he does *not* believe that London is pretty (that is, that it is not the case that he believes that London is pretty). But on the basis of his behavior as a *French* speaker, we must conclude that he *does* believe that London is pretty. This is a contradiction.[4]

Let us call this version of the puzzle, in which we seem to be driven to a contradiction in describing a case that seems perfectly possible, the *contradiction version* of the puzzle.

To buttress the reasoning that lies behind his analysis of the case, Kripke provides the following plausible principles:

A. *The Disquotational Principle:* "If a normal English speaker, on reflection, sincerely assents to 'p', then he believes that p" (where " . . . 'p' is to be replaced inside and outside all quotation marks by an appropriate standard English sentence").[5]

B. *The Biconditional Form of the Disquotational Principle:* "A normal English speaker who is not reticent will be disposed to sincere assent to 'p' if and only if he believes that p" (where " . . . any appropriating English sentence may replace 'p' throughout").[6]

C. *The Principle of Translation:* "If a sentence of one language expresses a truth in that language, then any translation of it into any other language also expresses a truth (in that other language)."[7]

These three principles are indeed necessary for Kripke's reasoning. He needs the disquotational principle in order to move to (7) from Pierre's assent to (5), and also to move from Pierre's assent to 'Londres est jolie' to (8):

(8) Pierre crois que Londres est jolie,

and he needs his principle of translation to move from (8) to (4). Thus, in the inconsistency version of the puzzle, he needs the disquotational and the translation principles. In the contradiction version of the puzzle, however, Kripke needs the biconditional form of the disquotational principle in order to move from Pierre's nonassent to 'London is pretty' to the conclusion that Pierre doesn't believe that London is pretty. Thus, since by this principle, in our case, 'Pierre believes that p' implies 'Pierre would be disposed to sincere reflective assent to 'p' ', his not being disposed to sincere reflective assent to (6) would entail that he doesn't believe that London is pretty. This would contradict (4), which, again, resulted from (8) (via the principle of translation), which resulted (via the disquotational principle) from his assent to 'Londres est jolie'.

In this paper I shall treat Kripke's puzzle by drawing a sharp distinction between beliefs of a certain believer, which are constitutive of the believer's doxastic state, on the one hand, and belief sentences on the other; in other words, a distinction between 'p' being a belief of a cognizer r and the established, ordinary-language construction 'r believes that p'. I will treat beliefs as linguistic (symbolic) representations (at least where limited to cognizers with minimal logical, conceptual, and linguistic acumen)[8], and analyze what I shall henceforth call *belief sentences*—sentences of the form 'r believes that p' (read *de dicto*)—in terms of beliefs. It will be argued that such belief sentences do their reporting job *not* by displaying beliefs, but rather by describing them via the mechanism of *adequate paraphrasing;* whereas sentences to the effect that one is disposed to assent or not to assent do display one's beliefs. I will argue that the question of whether a believer is consistent lies squarely within the level of his or her belief. That is, the consistency of a believer r is a function of the logical relations between r's beliefs and of the structure of his representational system. It is not determined by the linguistically entrenched manner in which we report his beliefs, nor by the manner in which his beliefs hook up with the world (as by the reference relation). These contentions will allow us to propose a solution to both the consistency and the contradiction problems.

2. BELIEFS

In the discussion below, the notion of *'p' being a belief of r* (for a believer $r)$ will play a major role. My main working hypothesis involves taking beliefs as *linguistic representations.* At a given time $t,$ a cognizer can be said to be in a certain belief state, reflecting whatever beliefs he or she has at the time. Such belief states are classifiable via particular beliefs: if 'p' is a belief of our cognizer r (as I shall henceforth call our believer) at time $t,$ then r can be said to be in a 'p' belief state. (I remind the reader that I limit my discussion in this paper to cognizers with minimal logical, linguistic, and conceptual acumen.)[9]

Of course, having particular beliefs is a constituent of the causal order. The acquisition of beliefs can be caused by various stimuli,[10] and r's possession of certain beliefs can cause modes and dispositions of behavior, not the least of which would be his verbal dispositions to assert, or to assent to, various sentences, or to refrain from such assents. Beliefs, being linguistic representations (that is, sentences) are in one language or another: a cognizer r may have 'the king is bald' but not 'le roi est chauve' count as one of his beliefs.[11] This would be attested to by his disposition to assent to the first but not to the second in 'appropriate' circumstances (which would obtain, for instance, when he knows no French). If he assents to both in 'appropriate' circumstances, then they constitute two distinct beliefs of his. The perspective underlying the discussion here should be contrasted with the theory that takes beliefs to be propositions.[12] On the line taken here, a belief of r is a linguistic representation of his in a particular language, which need not (and normally would not) be context-independent: among one's beliefs there could be such as 'I am here' or 'the president is eating now'. A multilingual believer possesses beliefs in more than one language, and thus may possess various distinct beliefs in different languages he speaks that convey the same message.

I am thus operating within a framework in which beliefs are taken as linguistic representations, that is, sentences. That a cognizer r has a certain sentence as a belief of his is attested to primarily by his disposition to assent to that sentence or to assert it under 'appropriate' circumstances, whereas not possessing it as a belief is primarily attested to by his disposition not to assent to it in appropriate circumstances. Verbal dispositions to assent or not to assent to certain sentences are thus key indicators of such sentences being beliefs, and these two can be expected to be related via nomological connections (as I do not define beliefs as verbal dispositions or identify the two).

Beliefs belong, therefore, to the level of the internal representations of a believer; they fully reside, so to speak, *within* his or her belief world. To specify the beliefs of a cognizer is to characterize that belief world purely internally—that is, without making any essential use of, or having to assume the existence of, any particular object outside of the believer. Beliefs, being linguistic representations of a cognizer, can, of course, be characterized and classified in various ways. For example, certain causal relations that entities outside the cognizer's belief world bear to the cognizer's possession of particular beliefs can be called upon to characterize and classify those beliefs. Such characterizations are involved in analyzing belief sentences read *de re*,[13] but they can be ignored for my purposes in this essay.

In what follows I shall disregard most of the causal roles played by one's having certain beliefs, roles such as being an effect of various events, or being a cause of modes of behavior. Rather, I shall concentrate on the relation between having certain beliefs and the cognizer's dispositions to verbal behavior. A disposition to assent to 'p' by r at t under 'appropriate' circumstances will indicate that 'p' is a belief of r (at t); similarly, his disposition not to assent to 'p' in the appropriate circumstances will indicate that 'p' is not a belief of r.[14] Such 'appropriate' circumstances will involve, of course, r's sincerity,[15] consciousness, reflectiveness, and so on. Without attempting here to characterize these 'appropriate' circumstances under which a disposition to assent to 'p' indicates that 'p' is a belief of r, I shall call them belief-indicating circumstances (in short: BIC). Again, saying that r's being disposed to assent to 'p' in BIC indicates that 'p' is a belief of r is not intended as an analysis of the notion of belief. Rather, the relation between the two is taken as an empirical connection (or a bridge rule) associated with the notion of belief so conceived. The above remarks are thus to be taken as indicating sketchily the type of cognitive model I presuppose and work with here in assessing Kripke's claim that there is a puzzle about the belief construction 'r believes that p' in ordinary language. The notion of belief presupposed here can thus be taken as a theoretical notion in an appropriate model of a cognitive system.

Notice that taking beliefs as linguistic representations would suggest that the possession of different beliefs (differing, of course, as linguistic representations, i.e. as sentences, regardless of whether they differ in 'content') can play different causal roles in r's interaction with the world. If r, who knows no French, has 'today is Monday' as a belief of his (at a given time) and is now reliably informed that if 'aujourd'hui est lundi' is true then there are $100 in a barrel in the next street, he need not display the behavior of looking for that barrel in a way in which he would if he had 'aujourd'hui est lundi' as a belief of his (e.g., had he known French). Of course, having a verbal disposition to assent to 'aujourd'hui est lundi' is a primary behavioral indication of 'aujourd'hui est lundi' being a belief of r, regardless of whether 'today is Monday' is a belief of his.

In what follows we shall, on many occasions, need the notion of 'a disposition to assent to 'p' at BIC'. Instead of introducing a new symbol for that locution, I shall just use the phrase 'assent to 'p''. So, when I say 'r assents to 'p'' I shall assume that BIC prevail and that 'assent' is understood as 'disposition to assent'. (I shall call the believer under discussion r throughout, after Quine's famous Ralph, rather than use Kripke's 'Pierre' and 'Jones'.)

3. BELIEF SENTENCES

So far we have discussed beliefs, which pertain to the realm of facts concerning r's doxastic state, with no regard for how such facts are described in a constructionally entrenched way in ordinary language. At this point I wish to draw attention to the ordinary language construction 'r believes that p' in its *de dicto* reading. (Henceforth, unless otherwise stated, I shall confine myself to the *de dicto* reading of this sentence, even when I do not specifically say so). Surely, if '*p*' is an English sentence,[16] and *r* assents to '*p*' in the 'right' circumstances, thus indicating that '*p*' is a belief of his, then indeed *r* believes that *p*. To be on the safe side, we shall limit ourselves to cases where *r* understands the sentence '*p*' to which he assents and uses the linguistic items in '*p*' in a standard way (relative to the linguistic community to which he belongs, which uses the dialect to which '*p*' belongs).[17] Indeed, we shall conduct the discussion in the next few sections assuming this restriction, as does Kripke,[18] which is perfectly congruent with the puzzle under discussion.

Often, however, we claim that *r* believes that *p* on the basis of utterances of his to the effect that *p*, even though we have never heard him assert or assent to '*p*'. We *might* make such a claim to indicate that we would expect *r* to assent to '*p*'—that is, that '*p*' is indeed a belief of his. But if *r*'s assertions were expressed in another language, and *r* knows no English, such an expectation would no longer be defensible. It is clear, though, that this claim could still be made if *r*'s assertion '*q*' in another language is an *adequate paraphrase* of '*p*'. Thus, even though it is true that *r* believes that *p*, it need not be the case that '*p*' is a belief of *r*; but then there should be some other '*q*', which is a belief of *r*, which is an adequate paraphrase of '*p*'. If *r* assents to '*q*' in another language, it would be a matter of an *inductive* inference to conclude that '*p*', which is an adequate paraphrase of '*q*' in English, is a belief of *r*, given that he knows English. But it would be a matter of a valid *logical* inference to claim that *r* believes that *p*. This would hold as well when '*q*' and '*p*' belong to the same language, or to different dialects in the same language (e.g., when scientific jargon is involved: if *r* asserts 'John is blue', a psychiatrist may validy infer that *r* believes that John is depressed, regardless of whether *r* is familiar with the predicate 'is depressed'). Let us therefore introduce the predicate 'PB_r' as in 'PB_r'*p*'' as follows (the '*P*' in 'PB_r' is to serve as a reminder of 'paraphrase'):[19]

'PB_r'*p*'' is true iff for some '*q*' such that '*p*' is an adequate paraphrase of '*q*', '*q*' is a belief of *r*.

This, of course, is introduced for the purpose of claiming that (for an English sentence '*p*'):

*Analysis of '*r* believes that *p*'*: '*r* believes that *p*' is true iff PB_r '*p*'.

Of course, the idempotent paraphrase (of '*p*' by '*p*') is an adequate paraphrase; thus, if '*p*' is a belief of *r*, then *r* believes that *p*.[20] More generally, if 'α' is a sentence of *L*, and 'βr' is an adequate paraphrase of '*r* believes that' in *L*, so that '$\beta_r\alpha$' is a well-formed sentence of *L*, then:

'$\beta_r\alpha$' is true (in *L*) iff PB_r'α'.

The construction '*r* believes that *p*' therefore involves essentially a relation such as adequate paraphrase, which has the form ap ('α', 'β'), being read as 'α is an adequate paraphrase of β', where 'α' and 'β' are two linguistic items. (Of course, in full form it should involve the languages as well: it should have the form ap ('α', L_1, 'β', L_2), where 'α' is a phrase in L_1 and 'β' in L_2; for simplicity, however, we shall assume that phrases carry the languages they belong to 'on their sleeves', as is so often the case, and use the two-place form.) What we therefore get from the above analysis is the validity of the following inference pattern:

(I)
$$'q' \text{ is a belief of } r$$
$$ap('q', \, 'p')$$

r believes that p.

Adequate paraphrasing is a cornerstone of the indirect speech construction. It is often used within the boundaries of a given language (common to the believer and the speaker), but it figures critically in adequate translation. Now it will not be my business in this paper to analyze this adequate paraphrase relation, which lies at the heart of the belief construction 'r believes that p' (and, for that matter, of other constructions such as 'says that', 'denies that', and other propositional attitudes). The use I shall make of this notion of adequate paraphrasing for the purposes at hand will rely primarily on its intuitive force, and further elaborations will be made along the way as the need arises. My purpose here is to defend the ordinary-language belief construction against Kripke's charge that it is afflicted with paradox. For that purpose, a general and thorough analysis of the notion of adequate paraphrase will not be necessary. What I claim is that with it stands or falls the ordinary-language belief construction, which is free of the paradoxes imputed to it. The ordinary-language belief construction 'r believes that p' depends upon the notion of adequate paraphrase in a way that the notion of 'p' being a belief of r does not depend. My point will be that the sources of Kripke's puzzle can be brought to light, given this analysis of belief sentences that uses this notion of adequate paraphrase, in a way that does not make this notion paradoxical or even more suspect. It will become clear that the reasons for doubting the viability of the belief sentence 'r believes that p' that Kripke took to arise out of his puzzle do not in turn make the notion of adequate paraphrase suspect. Thus, the intuitive use of this notion (under the elaborations to be discussed below) can be maintained without providing a full-fledged analysis for it. Objections to this notion or requests for its analysis will thus have to be made *independently* of Kripke's puzzle. In attempting to free ourselves while working with the belief construction that is based on the notion of adequate paraphrase from the suspicion of paradox that Kripke has imputed to this construction, we need not worry (for *this* purpose) about possible inadequacies or unclarities in the notion of adequate paraphrase that are unrelated to the problem at hand, which is Kripke's puzzle.[21]

The implications of the foregoing analysis of belief sentences (which will henceforth be taken to be sentences of the form 'r believes that p') are in the main congruent with the spirit of various observations by Kripke. Thus, we get from this analysis that if r assents to 'p' in 'appropriate' circumstances, and therefore 'p' is a belief of r, then, if ap ('p', 'q'), r believes that q, where 'p' is, say, a French sentence (but 'q', of course, is English). Kripke's disquotational principle will lead him from r's assent to 'p' to 'r crois que p' and, via his translation principle, to 'r believes that q'.

It is important for the spirit of my general direction here that I should emphasize the distinction between, on one hand, what I take to be the (primarily doxastic) facts of the matter—r's having particular beliefs (as well as various features of those beliefs)—and, on the other hand, the level of the ordinary-language constructions that serve the communicative role of describing these facts. To say in our semitechnical jargon that 'p' is a belief of r is to *display* the belief in question; but to say that r believes that p is merely to *report* such a belief. This reporting construction has the force of an existential claim to the effect that there is a belief with such-and-such features (i.e., which is an adequate paraphrase of a given sentence; see the 'PB_r'p'' definition above), and thus it serves to report that r has a belief of a certain kind. The same holds for the *de re* reading of belief sentences, though this will not be discussed here.[22]

Linquistic constructions designed to serve a certain communicative role can play their role better or worse in comparison with potential alternatives; and communicative roles of ordinary-language constructions scarcely coincide with the roles of locutions that are to serve a particular scientific investigatory function.[23] It is therefore quite important, when elements relating to the doxastic level are discussed, to focus attention on the beliefs of the cognizer rather than on the linguistic construction that serves to report them in ordinary language and on the particular semantical features of that construction. Fit to fulfill its communicative role, a construction in ordinary language possesses semantical features that are adept in this role but need not be useful for specialized investigatory purposes. There is little doubt that the belief construction is quite useful for reporting through one formulation (in a certain language or dialect) beliefs formulated in another. This is made possible thanks to the adequate paraphrasing device. But since the belief construction doesn't *display* the beliefs in question but rather *describes* them in a certain way (or rather makes an existential claim under certain classificatory specifications), dealing with epistemological questions via the belief construction is comparable to watching a subject through a veil: it keeps us from a closer touch with the doxastic phenomena themselves. It would be a mistake then to attribute features that reside at the level of our doxastic phenomena to the level of the linguistic constructions that report those phenomena, and vice versa. Not keeping these two levels clearly separated is a mistake that can, and often does, easily lead us astray.

Thus, for instance, whether a cognizer is consistent or not is a question that lies wholly at the level of his or her beliefs. Reporting the beliefs of a cognizer via the belief construction amounts to presenting the cognizer's belief world from the perspective of the reporter's belief world; when the two differ—in particular, when the reporter's information is wider in certain ways than that of the cognizer—the resulting report can have awkward features. But we should be quite careful not to confuse that with inconsistency of the cognizer. Upon acquiring new information, the cognizer may become inconsistent (and may have to give up certain beliefs). Reporting the cognizer's beliefs from a framework equipped with such extra information by describing them rather than displaying them can thus be easily misleading regarding the actual doxastic state of the cognizer and can thus fail to reflect the specific features of the cognizer's doxastic state that determine whether the cognizer is consistent. These reflections will be seen to bear on the consistency subproblem of Kripke's puzzle[24] since, as I will claim, consistency is a purely internal feature of a cognizer's belief world. The belief construction 'r believes that p', however, instead of displaying a belief of r, only yields that there is a certain belief classified modulo the adequate paraphrase relation.

4. INFERENCES

In sections 2 and 3, we have presented the notion of belief and an analysis of belief sentences. Our discussion here, it will be recalled, has been limited to believers with minimal logical and linguistic acumen and to cases of stable dispositions to assent or not to assent to 'p'—that is, dispositions that are uniform under varying circumstances evoking assent or nonassent to 'p'.[25] We have also assumed that dispositions to assent or not to assent are taken in belief-indicating circumstances and that the cognizer under discussion uses terms in a standard way, that is, understanding correctly the items in the sentences under discussion to which he or she is disposed to assent or not to assent.[26] I shall now use our notion of belief, our analysis of belief sentences and the notion of one's disposition to assent or not to assent, to quickly go through some valid inferences that will connect them (and also some invalid ones) that will be useful in the sequel. The reader who wishes to move directly to the main thrust of our treatment of Kripke's puzzle may skim through this section and move directly to sections 5 and 6, where the puzzle is handled (returning later to the inferences here as the need arises, via the back-references in the following sections).

In section 3 we presented inference I, which we derived from the analysis of the belief sentence 'r believes that p' as 'PB_r'p''. Since, obviously, adequate paraphrase is a reflexive relation, we get as an immediate consequence:

(II)   'p' is a belief of r

r believes that p.

Under the limitations specified above (which we shall take to be operative throughout the following discussion unless specified otherwise), a disposition to assent to 'p' in belief-indicating circumstances (*BIC*) indicates that 'p' is a belief of r, and vice versa: 'p' being a belief of r would give rise to this disposition to assent to 'p' (in BIC). (Recall that we abbreviate 'r is disposed to assent to 'p' under BIC' by 'r assents to 'p' ' and 'r is disposed not to assent to 'p' under BIC' by 'r does not assent to 'p' '.) We thus have as valid:

(III)   r assents to 'p'

'p' is a belief of r.

and likewise:

(IV)   'p' is a belief of r

r assents to 'p'.

From (II) and (III) we get:

(V)   r assents to 'p'

r believes that p.

From (III) and (I) we get:

(VI)   r assents to 'p'
            ap ('p', 'q')

r believes that q.

Now for 'p' and '$-p$'[27] to be beliefs of r, in our present setup,[28] is for r to be inconsistent. For r to have neither 'p' nor '$-p$' as beliefs is for him to suspend judgment concerning 'p'. Thus, 'p' not being a belief of his is compatible with '$-p$' being a belief of his and is also compatible with '$-p$' not being a belief of his (even when he is consistent). Hence the inference:

(VII) × $-$('p' is a belief of r)

'$-p$' is a belief of r

is invalid (I shall use × on the side of the inference to indicate invalidity). Again, if '$-p$' is a belief of r, 'p' may not be a belief of his on pain of his being inconsistent; but since inconsistency of a believer is a prevalent phenomenon not to be disregarded, the inference:

(VIII) ×   '$-p$' is a belief of r

$-$('p' is a belief of r)

is invalid, even though:

(IX) r is consistent

'$-p$' is a belief of r

—

$-$('p' is a belief of r)

is valid. Thus, because of (VII) since 'p' not being a belief of r is compatible with '$-p$' not being a belief of r, the inference

(X) $\times$ $\dfrac{-(\text{‘}p\text{’ is a belief of } r)}{r \text{ believes that } -p}$

is also invalid. This is so since the conclusion will be true only if (by the analysis of 'r believes that p') there is a belief of r that is an adequate paraphrase of '$-p$'. But the premise, though *allowing* for '$-p$' to be a belief of r without an inconsistency on r's part, does not *require* that '$-p$' be a belief of r, much less that an adequate paraphrase of it be a belief of r. Therefore, (X) would be invalid even with the added premise that r is consistent; thus:

(XI) $-$('p' is a belief of r)

$\times$ $\dfrac{r \text{ is consistent}}{r \text{ believes that } -p.}$

The inference:

(XII) $\times$ $\dfrac{-(r \text{ assents to ‘}p\text{’})}{r \text{ believes that } p}$

is also invalid, since 'p' not being a belief of r is consistent, of course, with all adequate paraphrases of 'p' not being beliefs of r. (Notice that (VII) and (XII) would remain invalid even if we added to them a premise to the effect that r is consistent).

The construction 'r believes that p' can be true in case some 'q' (in some other language), which is an adequate paraphrase of 'p', is a belief of r, without 'p' being a belief of r. (The case in which r knows no English will be an obvious special case here; 'p' is in English, as we assume throughout when the construction 'r believes that p' is concerned, to ensure its being well formed.) It is therefore clear that the set:

$$\alpha' \quad \left\{ \begin{array}{l} \text{‘}q\text{’ is a belief of } r \\ ap\,(\text{‘}q\text{’}, \text{‘}p\text{’}) \\ -(\text{‘}p\text{’ is a belief of } r) \end{array} \right\}$$

is consistent, even when 'p' is an English sentence, in view of cases in which r knows no English. To become convinced that α can be consistent even when r knows English and uses the items involved in a standard way, we make use of the 'Londres' case in which:

$$\alpha' \quad \left\{ \begin{array}{l} \text{'Londres est jolie' is a belief' of } r \\ ap \text{ ('Londres est jolie', 'London is pretty')} \\ -(\text{'London is pretty' is a belief of } r) \end{array} \right\}$$

was a set of true sentences, thus consistent. That α is consistent when r knows no English, and yet is a consistent believer, is quite obvious. That α can be consistent when r knows English and is a consistent believer will depend on how we resolve the problem of r's consistency in the 'Londres' case. If we become convinced that r can be consistent in this case, then his consistency is compatible with α and his knowledge of English. In general, the consistency of α will not be affected if we add to it the extra member 'r is consistent'. To make this claim, in particular for cases where r knows English (and uses his terms in a standard way), we will have to await the resolution of the inconsistency version of the puzzle (section 5 below).

From the consistency of α [by(I)] it is clear that:

$$\left\{ \begin{array}{l} r \text{ believes that } p \\ -(\text{'}p\text{' is a belief of } r) \end{array} \right\}$$

is consistent. Hence the following inference is invalid:

$$\text{(XIII)} \quad \times \quad \frac{r \text{ believes that } p}{\text{'}p\text{' is a belief of } r.}$$

Consequently, obviously its converse:

$$\text{(XIV)} \quad \times \quad \frac{-(\text{'}p\text{' is a belief of } r)}{-(r \text{ believes that } p)}$$

is invalid too, and in view of (III), so is the inference:

$$\text{(XV)} \quad \times \quad \frac{-(r \text{ assents to '}p\text{')}}{-(r \text{ believes that } p).}$$

Its converse, therefore, is also invalid:

$$\text{(XVI)} \quad \times \quad \frac{r \text{ believes that } p}{r \text{ assents to '}p\text{'.}}$$

From the consistency of α we get the invalidity of:

$$\text{(XVII)} \quad \times \quad \frac{\begin{array}{l}\text{'}q\text{' is a belief of } r \\ ap \text{ ('}q\text{', '}p\text{')}\end{array}}{\text{'}p\text{' is a belief of } r}$$

as well as the invalidity of:

$$(\text{XVIII}) \quad \times \frac{\begin{array}{l} -(\text{`}p\text{' is a belief of } r) \\ ap\,(\text{`}q\text{'}, \text{`}p\text{'}) \end{array}}{-(\text{`}q\text{' is a belief of } r).}$$

Cases in which r knows no English ('p' being an English sentence) proved α to be consistent, even when the believer r is consistent, as we have seen above. Similarly, it can be easily seen that, more generally, cases in which 'q' and 'p' belong to different languages, one of which r doesn't know at all, would make α consistent for a consistent believer regardless of which of these languages (if any) is English. Such cases would therefore symmetrically show the set:

$$\left\{ \begin{array}{l} -(\text{`}q\text{' is a belief of } r) \\ ap\,(\text{`}q\text{'}, \text{`}p\text{'}) \\ \text{`}p\text{' is a belief of } r \end{array} \right\}$$

to be consistent too, when 'p' is an English sentence. Hence also:

$$\left\{ \begin{array}{l} -(\text{`}q\text{' is a belief of } r) \\ ap\,(\text{`}q\text{'}, \text{`}p\text{'}) \\ r \text{ believes that } p \end{array} \right\}$$

is consistent. Hence:

$$(\text{XIX}) \quad \times \frac{\begin{array}{l} -(\text{`}q\text{' is a belief of } r) \\ ap\,(\text{`}q\text{'}, \text{`}p\text{'}) \end{array}}{-(r \text{ believes that } p)}$$

is invalid as well. And similarly [from (XIX) and (III)], so is:

$$(\text{XX}) \quad \times \frac{\begin{array}{l} -(r \text{ assents to } p) \\ ap\,(\text{`}q\text{'}, \text{`}p\text{'}) \end{array}}{-(r \text{ believes that } q).}$$

Since α would remain consistent with the addition of 'r is consistent', inferences (XIII) through (XX) would remain invalid even with an added premise to the effect that r is consistent. Given the remark above [(before inference (III)], the claim that this will remain so in particular for cases in which r knows English (and uses his terms in a standard way) is conditional upon whether he can be consistent in a case such as the one described in the 'Londres' puzzle.

So far we have explored what we need for the resolution of Kripke's puzzle. But the situation will be clearer if we explore the viability of using a stronger premise in inference (XIV); that is, if we explore whether:

$$\frac{\text{'}-p\text{' is a belief of } r}{-(r \text{ believes that } p)}$$

is valid.

Kripke's case was one in which, as Kripke showed:

$$\beta \begin{cases} r \text{ assents to 'London is not pretty'} \\ ap \text{ ('Londres est jolie', 'London is pretty')} \\ r \text{ assents to 'Londre est jolie'} \end{cases}$$

are all true. Hence, the set

$$\lambda \begin{cases} r \text{ assents to '}-p\text{'} \\ ap \text{ ('}q\text{', '}p\text{')} \\ r \text{ assents to '}q\text{'} \end{cases}$$

is consistent. As Kripke correctly mentions, this also obtains with kind terms instead of proper names.

From (III) and the consistency of λ,

$$\mu \begin{cases} \text{'}-p\text{' is a belief of } r \\ ap \text{ ('}q\text{', '}p\text{')} \\ \text{'}q\text{' is a belief of } r \end{cases}$$

is also a consistent set. Hence, with (I), also

$$\rho \begin{cases} \text{'}-p\text{' is a belief of } r \\ r \text{ believes that } p \end{cases}$$

is consistent, and therefore similarly [using ρ with (IV)]

$$\begin{cases} r \text{ assents to '}-p\text{'} \\ r \text{ believes that } p \end{cases}$$

is consistent. Therefore (from ρ) the inference

$$\text{(XXI)} \times \frac{\text{'}-p\text{' is a belief of } r}{-(r \text{ believes that } p)}$$

is invalid, and so is (given [XXI] and [IV])

$$\text{(XXII)} \times \frac{r \text{ assents to '}-p\text{'}}{-(r \text{ believes that } p)}.$$

Notice that, as Kripke observes, it is intuitively clear in the situation described in his example that r may very well be consistent. Kripke, however, provides an argument for r being *in*consistent, which generates one aspect of the puzzle. Let us notice, then, that we would be in a position to rely on this intuition if we eliminate this suspicion of inconsistency; in this case, we would be able to add 'r is consistent' to β without endangering β's consistency and then add the assumption 'r is consistent' to all the inferences that follow, without changing their status as invalid.

From μ we thus conclude the invalidity of

(XXIII) $\times$ $\dfrac{\text{'}-p\text{' is a belief of } r \qquad ap\,(\text{'}p\text{', '}q\text{'})}{-(\text{'}q\text{' is a belief of } r).}$

From the consistency of ρ' we get the consistency of ρ' (by replacing in 'p' by '$-p'\rho$'):

$$\rho' \left\{ \begin{array}{l} \text{'}p\text{' is a belief of } r \\ r \text{ believes that } -p \end{array} \right\}$$

and thus the invalidity of

(XXIV) $\times$ $\dfrac{r \text{ believes that } -p}{-(\text{'}p\text{' is a belief of } r)}$

and hence also [with (IV)] the invalidity of:

(XXV) $\times$ $\dfrac{r \text{ believes that } -p}{-(r \text{ assents to '}p\text{'}).}$

Now from the consistency of ρ' we get the consistency of

$$\rho'' \left\{ \begin{array}{l} r \text{ believes that } p \\ r \text{ believes that } -p \end{array} \right\}$$

and hence the invalidity of

(XXVI) $\times$ $\dfrac{r \text{ believes that } -p}{-(r \text{ believes that } p).}$

Having established the invalidity of the inferences of the last group and the validity of the inferences of the first group, we can now proceed to analyze Kripke's puzzle.

Notice that if we dispose of the argument for r's inconsistency in the situation described in Kripke's puzzle, given our above remark [after inference (XXII)], inferences (XXI) through (XXVI) will remain invalid with an additional premise to the effect that r is consistent.

5. THE INCONSISTENCY PROBLEM

It will be recalled that, in the setup of Kripke's puzzle, the believer (Kripke's Pierre, whom I rename r) is a cognizer with minimal logical and linguistic acumen who understands the relevant phrases in French and English and uses them in a standard way.[29] This, however, does not protect him ipso facto from a charge of inconsistency. For convenience, we abbreviate the sentences 'London is pretty' and 'Londres est jolie' as '*Pln*' and '*Jlr*' respectively and their negation as '$-Pln$' and '$-Jlr$' respectively. (Thus, '*P*' and '*J*' abbreviate the predicates 'pretty' and 'jolie' respectively, and '*ln*' and '*lr*' the names 'London' and 'Londres' respectively.)

As we have seen,

(10) *r assents to 'Jlr'*

is true (taken as a disposition of *r* in the 'right' circumstances), as well as

(11) *r assents to '$-Pln$'*.

Consequently, under these conditions, given our discussion in the previous sections, we are entitled to infer both:

(12) '*Jlr*' is a belief of *r*

(13) '$-Pln$' is a belief of *r*

[cf. inference (III), section 4]. Given inference (II), we are entitled to infer from (13) that

(14) *r* believes that London is not pretty.

Similarly, under the above conditions, (12), together with (15):

(15) *ap('Jlr', 'Pln')*

yield the truth of [via inference (I)]:

(16) *r* believes that London is pretty.

We can safely conclude (16), because *r*'s use of the terms involved in his French belief in (12) is quite a standard use. Thus, if we consider *r* before the time of his arrival in London, he is, in our story, a normal French speaker in every relevant respect—in particular in his use of 'Londres' and 'jolie'. Surely his lack of knowledge of English does not in the least subject him to a charge of not using 'Londres' in a standard way; and the information he possesses with respect to 'Londres' is no different from (in particular, not richer than) that possessed by a great many French speakers. The fact that he has been unaware that 'Londres est la capitale d'Angleterre' does not detract from his standard use of the term 'Londres' but only leaves him short of some pertinent information concerning that city, which is not unlike information concerning its population, elevation, climate, and so forth.[30] Notice in particular that, given our story, by 'Londres' *r* indeed refers to the city London, and thereby a necessary condition for a standard use of a proper name is fulfilled here.[31] I shall not analyze this point,[32] but rather assume it to be obvious on intuitive grounds.[33]

But surely *r*'s learning another language—English—did not interfere with his knowledge of French, in particular with his standard use of the word 'Londres', since that use of his has not changed one bit: he still holds, after having learned English, the same French beliefs in which 'Londres' occurs that he held before (since he would not take himself to have learned anything concerning 'Londres' while in England, only concerning what he takes to be another city, called 'London'). Hence, since it is obvious that his use of 'Londres' (and, of course, of 'jolie') was standard before he came to England, it remained so thereafter, too. Thus, (14) and (16) help us vindicate Kripke's conclusion that, for 'p' taken as 'Pln', it is the case that

(17) r believes that p, and r believes that $-p$.

In section 3 I emphasized the need to separate the level of r's beliefs, on the one hand, from the reporting level of the construction 'r believes that p' on the other. We have seen that what such a reporting sentence conveys is that there is a belief of r that is an adequate paraphrase of 'p'.

Now the notion of the consistency of a believer r resides in whether his beliefs yield a contradiction. It resides in whether the use of logical tools alone can allow r to derive a contradiction from the beliefs he possesses, which is tantamount to whether he has contradictory beliefs. Thus, the subject matter of r's consistency lies at the level of r's beliefs[34] — in whether there is a set of beliefs of his such as ['p', '$-p$'], or, more generally, a set of beliefs of his ['p_1', . . . ,'p_n'] that is self-contradictory. Whether and to what extent this is reflected by conditions formulated at the reporting level must be carefully examined and not just taken for granted. Thus, whereas

(18) 'p' is a belief of r, and '$-p$' is a belief of r

will make r inconsistent by virtue of having contradictory beliefs,[35] it remains to be seen whether condition (17), which Kripke takes to make him inconsistent, indeed does so as well.

In so far as the 'Londres' case is concerned, it is clear that r's relevant beliefs involve

$$\alpha^* = \left\{ \text{'}Jlr\text{'}, \text{'}-Pln\text{'}, \text{'}ap\,(\text{'}J\text{'} \text{ (in } F), \text{'}P\text{'} \text{ (in } E\,))\text{'} \right\} \text{ [36]}$$

where the last item merely represents any one of various other possible beliefs to the same effect[37] [e.g.: 'J' (in F) is an adequate translation of 'P' (in E); or 'J' (in F) means 'P' (in E); or: 'J' (in F) and 'P' (in E) stand for the same thing; or even: whatever 'J' (in F) is true of, 'P' (in E) must be true of too; etc.]. Is this set of beliefs self-contradictory? Can a contradiction be derived from it? Of course not. If one wants to charge self-contradiction, one must include the belief 'ap('lr' (in F), 'ln' (in E))' (or some other belief to the same effect), and thus focus on the set of beliefs β^*:

$$\beta^* = \left\{ \begin{array}{l} \text{'}Jlr\text{'}, \text{'}-Pln\text{'}, \text{'}ap\,(\text{'}J\text{'} \text{ (in } F), \text{'}P\text{'} \text{ (in } E\,))\text{'}, \\ \text{'}ap(\text{'}lr\text{'} \text{ (in } F), \text{'}ln\text{'} \text{ (in } E\,))\text{'} \end{array} \right\}$$

But certainly no one could charge that α^*, which *does not* include the last item of β^*, is self-contradictory. To realize that, assume that r's use is nonstandard and that he takes 'Londres' to be a name of a cat, whereas 'London' for him is the name of the city. Surely α^* yields no contradiction here. But this interpretation is not possible for β^* because of its extra condition.

Thus, surely the set α^* is compatible with ' $-ap('lr'$ (in F), 'ln' (in E))'. Since '$ap('lr'$ (in F), 'ln' (in E))' is not a belief of r in our case (nor is any other sentence to the same effect), clearly α^* in itself is not self-contradictory. Above we have argued that r uses the items here in a normal way, and in this we are in agreement with Kripke. No logical acumen would enable r to derive a contradiction form the set α^*, which is not self-contradictory, given his normal use of the items there. We thus see that '$ap('lr'$ (in F), 'ln' (in E))' (or another sentence to the same effect) is a crucial item missing from r's beliefs, and that, as long as it is, a charge of self-contradiction is implausible and cannot be sustained. Thus, r is consistent in our case and sustains at the same time our assumption of standard use.

Yet, of course, as Kripke realized, (14) and (16) are true in our case, thus making true:

(17) r believes that p, and r believes that $-p$.

We therefore see that (17) *cannot* be a sufficient condition for r's being inconsistent. But how can that be? By our analysis of 'r believes that p', (17) would be true in case for some 's' and 'q', which are beliefs of r, $ap('s', 'p')$ and $ap('q', '-p')$ (when r uses the items in 'q' and 's' in a normal way). Thus, to check (17) vis-à-vis r's consistency, we must consider whether for r to have 'q' and 's' as beliefs, while $ap('q', '-s')$ (where r uses 'q' and '$-s$' normally) would render him inconsistent.

As before, the crucial question is whether $ap('q', '-s')$' (or another sentence to the same effect) is a belief of r. It must be for a charge of inconsistency to become serious. If it is not a belief of r, surely no logical acumen of r would help him derive a contradiction from his beliefs 'q' and 's'. If r doesn't realize, therefore, that $ap('q', '-s')$, he cannot be branded inconsistent. But can r fail to realize that $ap('q', '-s')$, while 'q' and 's' are beliefs of his, if his use of the linguistic items involved is standard? Here lies the catch: *normally,* he couldn't. Normally, a believer r with a normal understanding of the linguistic items he uses, whether in one language or more, would realize whether or not two items are adequate paraphrases of each other. In many cases, a failure to realize that would detract from the believer's normal use of these items. But not always. We have seen in our example that r can have a perfectly normal use of 'London' and 'Londres' despite his not realizing their being adequate paraphrases of each other. What can happen with 'Londres' and 'London' can happen with other proper names, and with kind terms, too.

Even though (to use an example of Putnam and Kripke) 'hêtres' and 'beech' are adequate paraphrases of each other (in French and English respectively), r might use them in a normal way and yet feel that they somehow differ from each other in a way he can't specify; he may feel that 'hêtres is a species that grows only on the continent, whereas beech grows only in North America. Such a mistake would not be grave enough to detract from his normal use of the terms involved. Kripke's example, once we have shown it to involve no paradox, can be taken to show how one can use two items in a standard way without realizing they are adequate paraphrases of each other.

We thus realize that (17) is *not* a sufficient condition for r being inconsistent since it does not entail that r has contradictory beliefs, even in cases with standard use of the items involved. We thus see that the characterization of the inconsistency of a believer r, belonging properly to the level of his beliefs, cannot be relegated to the reporting level. Thus, (17) will not suffice for determining inconsistency since it does not yield that 'p' and '$-p$' are beliefs of r, nor does it yield that 'q' and '$-q$' are beliefs of r, for any other 'q'. To conclude from (17) that r is inconsistent is thus a mistake, and this mistake underlies the seeming paradox of r's inconsistency in Kripke's puzzle.

Rather, inconsistency would occur (under the assumptions of the present discussion) in case

(18') 'q' is a belief of r and '$-q$' is a belief of r.

Of course, (18') → (17) via inference (I), when 'q' is a sentence in L such that $ap($'q' (in L), 'p' (in E)), and hence $ap($'$-q$' (in L), '$-p$' (in E)). But (17) may be true without (18') being true for *any* 'q'. [Of course, (17) → (18) [(18) involves 'p' as in (17) rather than a possibly different 'q' as in (18)'] since r need not know English (and 'p' is an English sentence).] As we saw above, (17) can be true in case r has two beliefs 'q' and 's' such that $ap($'q', 'p') and $ap($'s', '$-p$'), without '$ap($'q', '$-s$')' being a belief of r and without a violation of his normal use. In such a case, 'q' and '$-s$' need not, of course, be the same sentence, and they may well belong to different languages. Hence, (18') need not be true for *any* 'q' even when (17) is true. Thus, (17) does not *logically imply* that r is inconsistent; in our case, it is true *without* r being inconsistent. It is here that Kripke went wrong in the inconsistency problem, in assuming (17) to be a sufficient condition for r's being inconsistent. The separation of the level of r's belief world, that is, the level of his beliefs, from the reporting level of belief sentences in ordinary language—this separation being made possible by the conception of beliefs as linguistic representations—allows for the realization that consistency lies primarily at the level of beliefs and not at the reporting level of belief sentences. It also allows for the realization that condition (17), which resides at the reporting level of belief sentences, is *inadequate* as a sufficient condition for inconsistency. Indeed, one cannot, it seems, do better than (17) when only the reporting level is available. One must, therefore, move to define the notion of beliefs and to introduce (18) as a better sufficient condition for inconsistency. Not having the notion of beliefs presented here, Kripke was unable to clearly separate the two levels. Consequently, he uses 'r believes that . . . ' and 'that . . . is a belief of r' almost interchangeably in various places.[38] Kripke had therefore to remain at the reporting level, and the result is the misleading conception that (17) suffices for inconsistency.

And yet (17) is not wholly irrelevant to questions of inconsistency. Its seductiveness lies in the fact that *normally* r would indeed be inconsistent when (17) is true. This is so since the cases where (17) would fail to yield an inconsistency are cases in which two items that occur in r's beliefs, and that he uses standardly, are adequate paraphrases of each other without r realizing it. But this phenomenon, though possible, as we have seen, is relatively *uncommon*. Unless something like that happens, (17) does indeed yield an inconsistency. Since (17) yields an inconsistency in all cases but one rare sort, (17) therefore constitutes *good evidence* for inconsistency. Surely if r has two contradictory beliefs 'p' and '$-p$', (17) would hold. Thus, (17) is indeed a *consequence* of inconsistency of a certain kind (e.g., involving only two beliefs). Therefore, for practical purposes, (17) is a reliable *indicator* of inconsistency. But this is so by way of (17) providing the grounds for a good *ampliative* inference to the effect of r being inconsistent. Yet (17) fails to be a sufficient condition in that it does not *logically* entail that r is inconsistent. To determine inconsistency when (17) obtains, one must check whether we don't have a phenomenon of the type indicated, which would block an inconsistency despite (17).

Yet, surely there is a certain oddity in r's having the beliefs in α^*, even if this does not amount to an inconsistency. The believer r is in a doxastic state in which, were he to acquire and retain the belief ' 'lr' (in F) is 'ln' (in E)', or 'ap('lr' (in F), 'ln' (in E))', or something else to this effect, he would have to give up one of his beliefs in α^* (even though it directly contradicts none of them severally). One might say that having the beliefs in α^* would make r have *incongruent* beliefs. But to have incongruent beliefs is not to be inconsistent.[39]

I trust that we have now established that, in the situation in Kripke's puzzle, that r's use of his terms may well be normal and that r can hold his beliefs without being inconsistent since condition (18), the appropriate indication of inconsistency for such a case, is not satisfied. We can now go back to the last item left open in section 4. In discussing the set β there, describing the facts of the 'Londres' case, we left it open whether the addition of 'r is consistent' would leave β consistent. Now we are in a position to answer this question affirmatively. Our conditional conclusion in section 4 was that, if the answer to this question is affirmative, inferences (XXI) through (XXVI) would remain invalid with the additional premise '*r* is consistent'. We can now assert this conclusion unconditionally. Similarly, the consistency of α can now seem not to be affected if we add to it the extra premises '*r* is consistent' and '*r* knows English and uses his terms in a standard way'. Hence inferences (XII) through (XX) would remain invalid with these two extra premises as well.

Of course, since β in section 4 would now remain consistent after the addition of the sentence '*r* is consistent', so would λ there. It is therefore not surprising now that λ, with this added sentence, yields the consistency of [via (I) and (II)]:

$$\left\{ \begin{array}{l} r \text{ believes that } -p \\ r \text{ believes that } p \\ r \text{ is consistent} \end{array} \right\}$$

reflecting again the inadequacy of (17) as a sufficient condition for *r*'s inconsistency (not to mention the inadequacy of (17) as a necessary condition, which Kripke most likely never held it to be).

Let us illustrate how Kripke goes astray by not separating the reporting of beliefs via belief sentences on the one hand, and the beliefs themselves on the other, in his discussion of the inconsistency problem. Thus he says:

> Suppose that, in France, Pierre, instead of affirming "*Londres est jolie,*" had affirmed, more cautiously, "*si New York est jolie, Londres est jolie aussi,*" so that he believed that *if* New York is pretty, so is London. Later Pierre moves to London, learns English as before and says (in English) "London is not pretty." So he now believes, further, that London is *not* pretty. Now from the two premises, both of which appear to be among his beliefs (a) If New York is pretty, London is, and (b) London is not pretty, Pierre should be able to deduce by *modus tollens* that New York is not pretty. But no matter how great Pierre's logical acumen may be, *he cannot in fact make any such deduction, as long as he supposes that 'Londres' and 'London' may name two different cities.* . . . Yet, if we follow our normal practice of reporting the beliefs of French and English speakers, *Pierre has available to him (among his beliefs) both the premises of a modus tollens argument that New York is not pretty.*[40]

The apparent problem is that he should be able to draw the conclusion of a modus tollens argument whose premises he possesses among his beliefs, yet in fact he cannot. But this problem is generated by a failure to realize that the reporting belief construction does not *display* his beliefs. Thus, in light of our analysis, the italicized part of the last sentence in the quotation comes out as strictly false: his beliefs are 'Si New York est jolie, Londres est jolie aussi' and 'London is not pretty', and these are not premises of a modus tollens argument: (a) in the quotation is *not* a belief of Pierre. Since he has no premises of a modus tollens argument among his beliefs, he cannot be expected to draw any such conclusion. The mistake here lies again in examining, when exploring logical relations that the believer should realize, sentences in the scope of belief idioms in the belief-sentence construction rather than the beliefs themselves.

6. THE CONTRADICTION PROBLEM

We now come to the contradiction version of the puzzle. We still have as true:

> (10) r assents to '*Jlr*',

but, instead of (11), we have a suspension of judgment on r's part with respect to '*Pln*': r has no disposition to assent to or dissent from it; that is, we have the truth of both

> (19) $-(r$ assents to '*Pln*')
> (20) $-(r$ assents to '$-Pln$').

Under the assumed circumstances, (10) yields, as before [inference (III)]:

> (12) '*Jlr*' is a belief of r.

But (19) and (20) now yield [inference (IV)] both:

> (21) $-$('*Pln*' is a belief of r)
> (22) $-$('$-Pln$' is a belief of r).

Again, as above, in the assumed circumstances, (12), together with (15):

> (15) ap('*Jlr*', '*Pln*')

yield [via inference (I)]:

> (16) r believes that London is pretty.

Thus, (16) is reached via the analysis of 'r believes that p', according to which 'r believes that London is pretty' is true iff there is some 'q' in some language L, such that ap ('q' (in L), '*Pln*' (in E)), and 'q' is a belief of r. And indeed, (12) and (15) secure that '*Jlr*' in French is just such a requisite 'q'.

Can we infer the negation of (16) via (21)? Such an inference would be fallacious, given our analysis of 'r believes that p'. What is required in this analysis for the truth of 'r believes that p' is that, under the given circumstances of standard use, *some* adequate paraphrase of 'p' be a belief of r. If this requirement is fulfilled, the question of whether some adequate paraphrase of p is *not* a belief of r, or whether some adequate paraphrase of '$-p$' is a belief of r (as was the case in the inconsistency version), is immaterial to whether r believes that p according to this analysis, so long as it doesn't undermine the assumption of understanding and normal use under which the above requirement is to be fulfilled. But we have concluded in the previous section that having '*Jlr*' as a belief while having '−*Pln*' as a belief as well, in the circumstances of our case, does not reflect negatively on *r*'s standard use of the term involved. A fortiori, this is the case when *r* has '*Jlr*' with neither '*Pln*' nor '−*Pln*' as beliefs.

In particular, the move from (21) [or from (19)] to the negation of (16) will be an instance of inference (XIV) [or inference (XV)], which, we have seen in section 4, is invalid.

Let us buttress this point. The question is whether (19) or (21) implies the negation of (16), which is

(−16) *r* does not believe that London is pretty.

Now (−16) is true (via the analysis of belief sentences, section 3) provided there is *no* sentence '*q*' (in whatever language) such that $ap('q', 'Pln')$ and such that '*q*' is a belief of *r* (again, under our general assumption of normal use by *r* of the items in any pertinent belief of his in the language to which this belief belongs). But all that (19) or (21) provides us with is one sentence '*Pln*' that does *not* constitute a belief of *r*. Given, however, what it takes for (−16) to be true, the information that *some* sentence is not a belief of *r* tells us nothing about whether *r* believes that *p*, even if that sentence is an adequate paraphrase of '*p*', or even if that sentence is '*p*' itself. This is so since the fact that any given sentence, in particular '*p*' is not a belief of *r*, does not imply that there is no other sentence '*q*' such that $ap('q','p')$ and such that '*q*' *is* a belief of *r* (while satisfying the requirement of standard use by *r*). There may indeed be such a sentence '*q*' that would yet not endanger *r*'s consistency or standard use (in general, and in particular of '*p*', if *r* happens to understand '*p*'), as we have seen above, as long as *r* is not aware that $ap('q','p')$. Even if *r* understands '*p*' (e.g., if '*p*' is '*Pln*,' in our case) as well as '*q*', and both '*p*' and '*q*' are in the *same* language (e.g., English), *r* need not violate the standard use for '*p*' and '*q*' while failing to realize that $ap ('p', 'q')$, as Kripke's kind-terms example shows; a fortiori if '*p*' and '*q*' belong to *different* languages. So, if an English '*p*' is not a belief of *r*, *r*'s linguistic competence and consistency need not rule out even an *English* '*q*' as a belief of *r*, in case $ap ('q', 'p')$; a fortiori they need not rule out such a '*q*' in *another* language or dialect being a belief of his. Thus, (19) or (21) does not imply (−16).

We thus conclude that we have no contradiction here: (16) is true, and there is no valid argument that leads to its negation from the premises of our case.

But this is so provided, of course, we reject Kripke's biconditional form of the disquotational principle. According to this principle (quoted in section 1), under the appropriate circumstances *r* is disposed to assent to '*p*' iff *r* believes that *p*. What this principle adds to the disquotational principle is the validation of (in the appropriate circumstances, when 'p' is an English sentence):

$$\frac{r \text{ believes that } p}{r \text{ assents to '}p\text{'}}$$

that is, the validation of:

$$\frac{-(r \text{ assents to '}p\text{'})}{-(r \text{ believes that } p)}$$

which is inference (XV) in section 4, shown there to be invalid. And it is indeed this biconditional form of the disquotational principle that Kripke needs for his derivation of the contradiction version of the puzzle.[41] But if our analysis is correct, this principle is not valid. Hence Kripke's argument for the negation of (16) (which is based on this principle) and thus his argument for there being a contradiction are undermined. This principle, it will be recalled, is rendered false, given our analysis of belief sentences and the inferences based on this analysis (for an English sentence 'p', and under our usual assumptions), by cases in which some 'q', such that ap ('q', 'p') is a belief of r while 'p' is not a belief of r, where 'q' and 'p' are sentences whose items are used by r in a standard way. (That standard use can be retained in such a case has been observed before, in agreement with Kripke; we also showed that $r's$ consistency is not necessarily impaired in such a case.) According to our analysis, in such a case r will not assent to 'p' yet he will believe that p [from inference (I)], contrary to Kripke's principle.[42]

It is worth noting that, as Kripke's kind-terms example shows, the failure of this principle *does not* require knowledge of different languages or dialects on the part of the believer: r might not assent to 'furzes have shallow roots' while assenting to 'gorses have shallow roots', thus making true 'r believes that furzes have shallow roots' (owing to the truth of 'ap ('gorse', 'furze')'), without engaging in a nonstandard use of the terms involved (or in any inconsistency). Recall that the invalidity of (XV), hence of Kripke's biconditional form of the disquotational principle, was a consequence of our analysis of belief sentences in terms of beliefs. According to this analysis, 'r does not believe that p' is true in case of a variety of a certain kind of sentences is a belief of r, whereas nonassent to 'p' by r indicates only that a particular sentence, that is, 'p', is not a belief of r. Nonassent to 'p' leaves it open for *other* sentences to be beliefs of r and to give rise to the truth of 'r believes that p'.

So far we have examined the suspension of judgment case, and we have seen that one cannot derive a contradiction in this case on the basis of (10) and (19) [or (12) and (21); see the beginning of this section]. But when we discussed the inconsistency problem (cf. the beginning of section 5), we had a stronger premise than (19) [or (21)]: we had (11) [and thus (13)]. [Recall, (11) was: *r* assents to *'−Pln'*. (13) was: *'−Pln'* is a belief of *r*.] Are we likely to generate a contradiction with (11) and (10), or with (12) and (13)? As in the previous discussion, (10) [via (15)] yields (16). Can we also generate (−16), the negation of (16), in this stronger version?

Again, however, this is not the case. What we have here, and which we did not have in the suspension of judgment case, is the truth of (11) and thus of (13). But it is a mistake to conclude (−16) from (11): this is an instance of inference (XXII), which we have shown to be invalid (section 4). Similarly, it is a mistake to conclude (−16) from (13): this would be an instance of inference (XXI), which we have also shown to be invalid. Also, in this case we have (14) as true, which we did not in the suspension of judgment case. [Recall, (14) was: *r* believes that London is not pretty.] But it would be fallacious to infer (−16) from (14): this is an instance of inference (XXVI), shown there to be invalid too. And, furthermore, as indicated at the end of section 5, the invalidity of (XXI), (XXII), and (XXVI) would hold even for a consistent believer.

Let us make things a bit clearer: since (13) is equivalent to (11) (under our assumptions), and since (14) follows from (13), we can limit ourselves to showing that (13) does not imply (−16) even for a consistent believer. But now we are back to the case discussed above: (13) (i.e.: ''−*Pln'* is a belief of *r'*) does not exclude *r*'s having a belief *'q'*, such that *ap ('q', 'Pln')*, with *r* not being aware that this is the case (to protect his standard use and consistency). Is there such a belief of *r* in our case? Of course: *'Jlr'* can serve as the belief *'q'* that *r* can have together with *'−Pln'* without endangering his consistency and standard use, which will make (16) true, thus (−16) false.

Thus, it is the invalid inferences (XIV), (XV), (XXI), (XXII), and (XXVI) that reflect the mistakes in the arguments Kripke provides for (−16), and thus in the arguments he provides for the contradiction. Nevertheless, it is easy to see the temptation to follow these inferences. They become invalid, for a consistent believer, only when there are two items, α and β, which *r* uses in a standard way, such that *ap* (α, β), of which *r* is not aware. As we pointed out at the end of section 5, this is an unusual situation. Normally, when this is not the case, the above inferences would not fail us. Thus, normally, barring unusual cases of this sort, *r*'s nonassent to *'p'*, or his assent to *'−p'*, or his believing that not *p*, would indeed guide us safely to the conclusion that, being consistent, he does not believe that *p*. Thus, these are *good indicators* and provide *good evidence* for *r* not believing that *p*, which will fail us only in the unusual cases where *r* fails to be aware of the adequate paraphrase relation between two items he uses in a standard way. They would therefore provide for an adequate ampliative inference to *r* not believing that *p*, even though they do not logically entail it. Such an inference fails us only in fairly recondite cases; but the case under discussion is just such a case.

We thus conclude that we resolved Kripke's two versions of the puzzle in his *own* terminology. We have pushed the notion of the consistency of a believer back to the level of beliefs and have concluded that the level of belief sentences does not allow for a formulation of sufficient conditions for inconsistency; in particular (17) was not a sufficient condition for inconsistency. Thus, concerning the consistency problem, we have seen that when there are two sentences 'p' and 'q' that are adequate paraphrases of each other, even though r is not aware of it, with his standard use intact,

'p' is a belief of r and '$-q$' is a belief of r

may be true, thus yielding:

'$-q$' is a belief of r and r believes that p,

as well as:

r believes that p and r believes that $-p$,

which is *not* sufficient for inconsistency, thus not yielding:

'p' is a belief of r and '$-p$' is a belief of r,

which *would* reflect an inconsistency. In the contradiction version we have confirmed (16), as Kripke does, but rejected its negation; and we have rejected the argument Kripke presented for its negation by rejecting Kripke's biconditional form of the disquotational principle, on the basis of our analysis of belief sentences in terms of beliefs (acknowledging that Kripke's arguments based on this principle were valid, and without rejecting his other two principles of disquotation and translation).

Kripke issues the following warning:

> It is no solution in itself to observe that some *other* terminology, which evades the question whether Pierre believes that London is pretty, may be sufficient to state all the relevant facts . . .
>
> But none of this answers the original question. Does Pierre, or does he not, believe that London is pretty? I know no answer to *this* question that seems satisfactory. It is no answer to protest that, in some *other* terminology, one can state 'all the relevant facts'.[43]

I believe that my account heeds Kripke's warning and provides an answer to his puzzle as he presents it in his own terminology.

Facing what seems to him to be an insurmountable difficulty ("Since our backs, however, are against the wall. . . ."),[44] Kripke considers a radical suggestion to this effect: "decree that no sentence containing a name can be translated except by a sentence containing the phonetically identical name."[45] But he finds this suggestion ". . . both contrary to our normal practice of translation and very implausible on its face."[46] He therefore asks: "What is it about sentences containing names that makes them—a substantial class—

intrinsically untranslatable, express beliefs that cannot be reported in any other language?"[47] Our handling of the 'Londres' case finds no fault in translating proper names from our language to another in the standard way: it finds no fault in Kripke's principle of translation. Furthermore, it surely does not endorse the conclusion that beliefs that include proper names can't be reported in other languages. They certainly can—and the mechanism for that is indeed supplied via the '*r* believes that *p*' construction, based on the notion of adequate paraphrase, which allows 'Londres' and 'London' to be adequate paraphrases of each other. According to my analysis, '*r* believes that London is pretty' is indeed a correct reporting of *r*'s having the belief 'Londres est jolie'. Therefore, such radical moves as disallowing standard translation of proper names are indeed avoided in my analysis.

Kripke delineates four possibilities for resolving the puzzle. The one closest to our approach is his "(b) that we do not respect his English utterance (or lack of utterance)."[48] Of course, this formulation is indicative of Kripke's failure to distinguish between beliefs and belief sentences. For him, either we apply the biconditional form of the disquotational principle to '*r* does not assent to '*Pln*' ' or else we don't consider this nonassent as reflecting *r*'s doxastic state, in which case we 'don't respect it'. According to the approach we have taken, we very much respect this nonassent, and we do not disregard it at all: we take it as fully reliable in indicating that '*Pln*' is *not* a belief of *r*. We part ways with Kripke in that we do not have to choose between concluding that *r* does not believe that London is pretty and disregarding this nonassent. It is simply that in the case in question this nonassent, though reflecting the lack of the corresponding belief, *does not* entail that *r* does not believe that London is pretty. The implausibility of disregarding, or not respecting, this nonassent is thus avoided, without affecting the viability of rejecting the conclusion that *r* does not believe that London is pretty.

However, by using the reporting construction '*r* believes that *p*' we seem to be giving an incomplete description of the situation involved in the contradiction version. The belief sentence '*r* believes that *p*' is true in case some adequate paraphrase of '*p*' is a belief of *r*, and its negation is true in case no such adequate paraphrase is a belief of *r*. But in cases such as the ones brought to light by the contradiction version, *r suspends judgment* with respect to '*Pln*' (in addition to assenting to '*Jlr*'), althouth he understands it in a standard way. We lack a way of reporting this because the issue of whether *r* believes that London is pretty is being preempted by *r* having *another* belief (which is an adequate paraphrase of '*Pln*'). It seems that our only way of reporting a situation in which *r* suspends judgment regarding '*Pln*' in the indirect mode is to say that *r* does not believe that London is pretty. But this would be false in case there is an adequate paraphrase of '*Pln*' that is a belief of *r*, as in our case. But even when there is no such paraphrase, saying that *r* does not believe that London is pretty would not report the fact that r here suspends judgment regarding '*Pln*' with sufficient discriminating adequacy, since saying so would equally apply to a case in which r has '$-Pln$' as a belief, which he indeed does *not* have in our case.

In reporting the case in the inconsistency version of the puzzle, we were able to take into account r's assent to '$-Pln$' by resorting to (17). But no such comparable reporting mode is available here. Nor would we be helped by correctly saying that r does not believe that London is not pretty. Even though by saying this we would be excluding a situation of the type in the inconsistency version, we would still fail to report suspension of judgment (as contrasted with a case in which an adequate paraphrase of '*Pln*' is a belief of r, in a language in which he understands it correctly). To say that r does not believe that London is pretty and does not believe that London is not pretty would be true only in case of suspension of judgment in all the languages r understands, and it will not be true in the situation envisaged in the contradiction version, in which there is a suspension of judgment in *one* language but not in another. All this is not to say that we should reconsider our analysis of belief sentences: they have, I believe, been analyzed here correctly. It is just that the belief-sentence construction is not versatile enough to allow for a sufficiently full description of certain situations.

It therefore seems warranted to introduce *another* propositional attitude—r suspends-judgment that p.[49] Now we do *not* need a new construction to say that r suspends judgment *with respect to (the sentence)* 'p'—that is, that neither '*p*' nor '$-p$' is a belief of r; but we may want a *reporting* construction, not a *displaying* construction.[50] We can thus define a reporting suspension-of-judment construction as follows:

r suspends-judgment that p iff for some 'q', such
that ap ('q', 'p'), neither 'q' nor '$-q$' are beliefs
of r, though r uses the items in 'q' in a normal way
in the language to which 'q' belongs.[51]

(Of course, this construction appears here in a *de dicto* form.)

This will allow us to describe the situation under discussion in the following way. In the contradiction version of the puzzle, when r suspends judgment with respect to '*Pln*', we shall be able to say:

(23) r believes that London is pretty and r suspends-judgment
that London is pretty.

Of course (23) is not at all contradictory, even though:

(24)   '*Pln*' is a belief of r and r suspends-judgment
with respect to '*Pln*'

is a contradiction. Thus, (23) is true in a case of *two* adequate paraphrases, 'p' and 'q', of 'London is pretty' (such that r is not aware that ap ('p', 'q'), to preserve his consistency and standard use), where 'p' is a belief of r, but neither 'q' nor '$-q$' are beliefs of r (though r uses the items in 'q' as well as in 'p' in a standard way in the languages to which they belong). Nor, of course, does (23) imply that r is inconsistent: (17) does not, and so, a fortiori nor does (23).

Thus prior to the introduction of this new construction, it could be argued against us that in the situation that gives rise to the contradiction version (suspension of judgment regarding 'Pln' and assent to 'Jlr') all we could do to describe the situation on the reporting level is to say that r believes that London is pretty, thereby 'respecting' r's assent to 'Jlr', but ignoring his nonassent to 'Pln'. But this fact does not tell against our analysis of belief-sentences: it simply calls for the introduction of a new construction that will enable us to take account of the situation on the reporting level. The suspend-judgment propositional attitude is such a new construction. It allows us now to describe r's suspension of judgment regarding 'Pln' together with his assent to 'Jlr' by (23).

It should be noticed that the move made here in no way ignores Kripke's request that we answer the question he posed in the terminology in which he posed it. We have done so. We have fully answered the question of whether r believes that London is pretty in the case described and have answered it affirmatively, claiming that our answer is anchored in the nature of the belief construction, as reflected in our analysis of that construction. We have only added *another* construction in a way that is independent of our treatment of Kripke's puzzle. This addition is not *required* for the resolution of the puzzle. The use of this added terminology is *not* at the expense of providing an answer for the puzzle in Kripke's terms. The suspend-judgment construction is merely a convenient and useful construction to have in *addition* to the belief construction in order to report such a situation more accurately.

Kripke summarizes the puzzle as follows: " . . . the present puzzle presents us with . . . a challenge to formulate an acceptable set of principles that does not lead to paradox, is intuitively sound, and supports the inferences we usually make."[52] I have attempted in this paper to meet this challenge. At the core of our proposal lies the distinction between beliefs, conceived as symbolic (linguistic) representations, and belief sentences, which are analyzed in terms of beliefs and which *describe* beliefs rather than *display* them. It is primarily the level of beliefs that is attached to verbal dispositions, and it is primarily at that level that the notion of the consistency of the believer belongs.[53]

7. ANALOGY WITH THE
HESPERUS-PHOSPHORUS CASE

It would be instructive to notice the analogy between Kripke's puzzle and the Hesperus-Phosphorus case (taken as a form of Quine's Ortcutt puzzle),[54] and the way they can both be handled. The Hesperus-Phosphorus puzzle runs as follows:

> A believer r was accustomed to see a certain celestial body in the mornings at a certain place in the sky, which he came to know as Phosphorus, and believe it to be large, bright, and so forth. But he suspended judgment as to the question of whether it was a star (rather than a planet); though he considered the question, he did not believe it to be a star, nor did he believe it not to be a star.
>
> On other occasions he became aware of a certain celestial body, which he came to know as Hesperus, and which appeared regularly in the evenings in the western sky. He came to believe it to be small, dim, and so forth, and in particular came to believe it to be a star. Unbeknownst to r, Hesperus and Phosphorus were the same planet (Venus).
>
> But now r is in a strange situtation vis-à-vis Venus. It seems that, not having changed his beliefs concerning Phosphorus, which resulted from his experiences in the mornings, he still does not believe it to be a star; yet, via his acquaintance in the evening hours with what he takes to be a small and dim celestial body, he does believe it to be a star. This seems to be a straightforward contradiction.

The handling of this case relies primarily on the exportation inference. The construction 'r believes 'F' of a'[55] indicates a belief relation between the cognizer r, the predicative expression 'F', and the object a, a relation that would make 'r believes of a that it is F' true.[56] We shall symbolize this construction as '$B_r{}^r$ 'F'a' (the superscript 'r' indicates '$de\ re$').

The primary working assumption for this case is that a valid exportation inference connects ' 'Fa' is a belief of r' with the $de\ re$ '$B_r{}^r$'F'a'. The connecting premise relies on what I have proposed to call the R-$function$ R_r ('a', 'Fa'),[57] a function whose arguments are the singular term 'a' and the belief 'Fa' in which it occurs (for the believer r), and whose value is the object that is to be the $referent$ of the singular term 'a' in this belief (for r). ('Referent' here is meant in the sense of speaker-reference.) For instance, consider the famous case in which r stands at a party, believing wrongly that the man in the corner is drinking a martini—in fact he drinks water—and asserts: The man drinking a martini is tall. His referent here by the phrase 'The man drinking a martini' is the man in the corner, not the man who in fact drinks a martini (assuming there is one such man at the party). Thus, in this example:

R_r ('the man drinking a martini', 'tall (the man drinking a martini)') = the man in the corner.

Now valid exportation has the following form:

A.   'Fa' is a belief of r
R_r ('a', 'Fa') $= a$
_____

B_r^r'F'a.

More generally, it has the form:

B.   'Fa' is a belief of r
R_r ('a', 'Fa')$=b$
_____

B_r^r'F'b

for cases in which the referent for 'a' in r's belief 'Fa' is not (as it need not be) the object a (if there is one).[58]

The problem thus stands as follows: r's suspension of judgment as to whether Phosphorus is a star yields:

(25) $-$('Sp' is a belief of r)

(p * Phosphorus, S * star). Given that in various beliefs of r's his referent by 'Phosphorus' is Phosphorus, as is clear from the description of the case, it seems that this nonbelief of his is also *of* Phosphorus, and that we should thus be in a position to infer:

(26) $-B_r^r$ 'S'p.

However, his assent to 'Hesperus is a star' yields (h = Hesperus):

(27)   'Sh' is a belief of r,

for which it is the case that

(28) R_r ('h', 'Sh') $= h$.

(27) and (28) together yield, via exportation:

(29) B_r^r'S'h.

But since $h= p$ (= Venus), (26) and (29) yield a contradiction (the position of 'a' in 'B_r^r'F'a' being referential).

The catch in this puzzle is that the exportation inference B allows 'B_r^r 'F'b' to be made true by *various* beliefs (of r) of the form 'Fa', which fulfill that 'R_r ('a', 'Fa') $= b$', and not necessarily by 'Fb' being a belief (of r). Thus the falsehood of the double-condition ' 'Fa' is a belief of r and R_r ('a', 'Fa') $= b$', for a given singular term 'a', is *not* sufficient to establish the falsehood of 'B_r^r'F'b', since the latter could be made true by *another* double-condition ' 'Fc' is a belief of r and R_r ('c', 'Fc') $= b$'. In our case, such a double-condition is false because ' '*Sp*' is a belief of *r*' is false. But it is a mistake to infer from that alone that 'B_r^{r}'*S*'*p*' is false too, which is the transition that leads from (25) to (26), a transition that is therefore unwarranted. Indeed, 'B_r^{r}'*S*'*p*' is true in our case owing to (27) and (28).

The analogy to Kripke's puzzle is quite obvious: just as much as the *de re* sentence '*r* believes '*F*' of *a*' (i.e., 'B_r^{r}'*F*'*a*') can be made true via '*Fb*' being a belief of *r* plus the auxiliary condition 'R_r ('*b*', '*Fb*') = *a*', in the case of Kripke's puzzle the *de dicto* reading of '*r* believes that *a* is *F*' can be made true by '*Gb*' being a belief of *r* plus the auxiliary condition that *ap*('*Gb*', '*Fa*'). *Normally,* when the referent of *r* by '*a*' is *a*, then indeed, if ' '*Fa*' is a belief of *r*' is false, so would be '*r* believes '*F*' of *a*'. Analogously, *normally* when *r*'s use of the terms involved is standard and ' '*Fa*' is a belief of *r*' is false, so would be '*r* believes that *a* is *F*'. But not always. And just as much as '−B_r^{r}'*F*'*a*' does not logically follow from the falsehood of ' '*Fa*' is a belief of *r*', even when the referent of '*a*' by *r* is *a* (although the falsehood of the latter constitutes good *evidence* for '−B_r^{r}'*Fa*'), so doesn't '−(*r* believes that *Fa*)' logically follow from the falsehood of ' '*Fa*' is a belief of *r*' (with standard use), although making such an inference would lead one astray only in relatively recondite cases. In both cases, the epistemic facts belong primarily to the level of *r*'s beliefs. In both cases, we possess linguistic constructions for describing beliefs without displaying them: in one case by specifying the predicate involved and the object that constitutes the referent in question, via the construction '*r* believes '*F*' of *a*',[59] and in the other case by describing the belief by adequate paraphrases, via the entrenched construction '*r* believes that *a* is *F*' (read *de dicto).* But by so describing beliefs, or by so asserting that there are such-and-such beliefs, one does not necessarily specify a *unique* belief, but rather asserts that there are beliefs of a *certain sort.* And, therefore, in both cases, the failure of a given candidate to be a belief of the sort specified does not imply that there is no *other* belief of that sort. Ignoring this point underlies the fallacious reasonings that lead to the falsehood of 'B_r^{r}'*F*'*a*' and of '*r* believes that *Fa*' (read *de dicto)* on the basis of the failure of a *particular* belief candidate to yield them respectively via exportation or via the belief inferences [inferences (I) and (II)]. [The latter fallacy is exemplified in (XIV) and (XIX), section 4.] Thus, in the Hesperus-Phosphorus case, '*r* believes 'Star' of Phosphorus' was fallaciously judged false on the basis of the falsehood of ' '*Sp*' is a belief of *r*' (even though the referent of *r* by '*p*' was indeed Phosphorus); whereas in the 'Londres' case, '*r* believes that London is pretty' (read *de dicto)* was fallaciously judged false on the basis of the falsehood of ' '*Pln*' is a belief of *r*'. The similarity between the fallacies in the two cases is thus obvious, though one involved a relation between the nonpossession by *r* of a certain belief and a *de re* construction, and the other a relation between the nonpossession of a certain belief and a *de dicto* construction, thus involving distinct sorts of inferences. We have just seen that in both cases the fallacious nature of the inferences involved lies in ignoring that, given the falsehood of ' '*Fa*' is a belief of *r*', there might still be another belief of *r* '*Fb*', such that '*Fb*' is an adequate paraphrase of '*Fa*' (in the *de dicto* case), or such that R_r ('*b*', '*Fb*') = *a* (in the *de re* case). A situation of this sort requires that *r* possess two singular terms, '*a*' and '*b*', such that *ap*('*a*', '*b*'), although *r* is not aware of it, in the one case; or that the referents for both '*a*' and '*b*' by '*r*' be the same, though *r* is not aware of it, in the other. It is fairly easy to realize that the latter (the *de re*) sort of case is perfectly possible for a consistent believer whose use of the linguistic items involved is standard; it takes some more elaboration to establish the same point in the first (the *de dicto*) case.

In section 4 we have pointed out a certain incompleteness in describing the situation typical to the contradiction version by merely using the *de dicto* reporting construction and sanctioning '*r* believes that *Pln*'. A similar dissatisfaction can be expressed concerning the Hesperus-Phosphorus case against the use of the *de re* reporting construction '*r* believes '*F*' of *a*'. Having told the whole story as in the beginning of this section, all we seem to be able to do by way of describing the situation in the *de re* mode is to say that *r* believes 'Star' of Venus, without, on *this* level, reflecting the fact that *r* suspends judgment with respect to 'Hesperus is a star', even though *r* refers to Venus via '*h*' (in some belief of his). Let us abbreviate the latter (that R_r ('*Gh*', '*h*') = Venus, for some '*G*'), as R(r, 'h', v), which basically means that 'h' serves as a vehicle of *r* for referring to *v* (*v* = Venus). To remedy this aspect of the situation presented in section 6, we have introduced a *de dicto* reporting construction '*r* suspends-judgment that *p*'. We can similarly help things here if we introduce the *de re* reading of this suspension-of-judgment construction, as follows:

'*r* suspends '*F*' of *a*' is true iff for some singular term '*b*' neither '*Fb*' nor '−*Fb*' is a belief of *r*, yet R(r, 'b', a).[60]

This construction is of course *de re* (with '*a*' occurring in a referential position). It conveys that *r* suspends judgment as to whether '*F*' is true of *a*. Having familiarized ourselves with this construction, we shall now be able to accept that:

(30) *r* believes 'Star' of Hesperus, and *r* suspends 'Star' of Hesperus

as correctly reporting the situation under discussion, given our story in its entirety. So (30) will be true in case, for some singular term '*b*', '*Sb*' is a belief of *r* such that R(r, 'b', h), while for *another* singular term '*c*', neither '*Sc*' nor '−*Sc*' is a belief of *r*, although R(r, 'c', h). (The logical acumen of *r* could still be faultless as long as he does not take '*c*' and '*b*' to be coreferential.)

The above charge, that '*r* believes 'Star' of Hesperus' does not fully describe the situation at hand, is thus justified. Before the introduction of this new construction, it could be argued against us[61] that we cannot distinguish on the reporting *de re* level between a case such as the Hesperus-Phosphorus case described in the beginning of this section and a case in which *r* indeed satisfied the second part of our story concerning 'Hesperus' but not the first part concerning 'Phosphorus'; that is, a case in which *r* would have 'Hesperus is a star' as a belief, thereby referring to Venus, without ever having heard the name 'Phosphorus' and without having any singular term '*b*' by which he refers to Venus without having the belief '*b* is Hesperus'. Just to say '*r* believes 'Star' of Hesperus' would equally apply to both cases. Of course, even in the case just introduced, *r* would suspend judgment with respect to 'Phosphorus is a Star' (he has never heard, in this case, the word 'Phosphorus'); but, on the reporting *de re* level, without the introduction of our new construction, we would have no way of distinguishing the two cases, which are worth being distinguished.

But the construction '*r* suspends '*F*' of *a*' will now allow us to do just that, in a *de re* construction. (30) will be true in the Hesperus-Phosphorus case as described above, but it will *not* be true in the modified version alluded to in the previous paragraph, since in this case '*R(r, 'p', h)*' is false, while being a necessary condition for the truth of '*r* suspends 'Star' of Hesperus' to be made true on the basis of both '*Sp*' and '$-Sp$' not being beliefs of *r*.

Notes

1. I wish to thank Gilead Bar-Elli, Yael Cohen, Gideon Makin, and David Siegel for stimulating discussions of earlier drafts of this paper.

2. S. A. Kripke, "A Puzzle about Belief", 254-56, in *Meaning and Use,* edited by A. Margalit (Dordrecht, 1979).

3. Ibid., 257.

4. Ibid., 258.

5. Ibid., 248-49.

6. Ibid., 249.

7. Ibid., 250.

8. In the course of this essay we shall not need to, nor shall we, consider believers who do not possess these faculties.

9. Thus, I excuse myself from discussing the notion of belief for prelinguistic children, animals, and so forth, even though I would hold that in every case a belief is a symbolic (if not linguistic) representation. Since our discussion here will be limited to beliefs the possession of which is indicated by verbal dispositions, I can safely ignore in the present discussion cases of beliefs that might be taken to constitute symbolic, but not necessarily linguistic, representations. For more along similar lines, see D. M. Armstrong, *Belief, Truth and Knowledge* (Cambridge, 1973), chap. 3; G. Harman, *Thought* (Princeton, N.J., 1973), chap. 4, sec. 2; and H. Field, "Mental Representation," *Erkenntnis* 13 (1978): 1-61; J. Perry, "Belief and Acceptance," *Midwest Studies in Philosophy* 5 (Minneapolis, 1980); and my forthcoming "Beliefs and Believing."

10. With or without attendant mental states; cf. N. Block, "Troubles with Functionalism," in *Perceptions and Cognition: Its Use in the Foundation of Psychology,* edited by C. W. Savage (Minneapolis, 1978), 261-325.

11. At time *t*, of course. I shall omit obvious time relativizations in the sequel. For further discussion concerning this notion of belief and the role it plays in exportation, cf. my "Quine and Modalities *de re:* A Way Out?" *Journal of Philosophy* 79 (1982): 295-328.

12. This contrast is dealt with a great length in part II of this essay (unpublished).

13. According to my conception, beliefs *de re* (to be distinguished from belief *sentences* read *de re)* form a subclass of the class of beliefs whose special feature is the existence of reference to a certain object by a singular term in the belief, which invokes a dependence on facts outside the purely internal realm of *r*'s belief world; cf. my (unpublished) book manuscript *Reference and Knowledge;* but this conception does not play any role in the present essay.

14. Through the first part of this essay I shall confine myself to cases where dispositions to assent or dispositions not to assent to a given sentence are *uniform,* that is, independent of the context of questioning (as long as it is an 'appropriate' context of questioning), which will assure us that a disposition not to assent to '*p*' in one context of questioning implies that there is no 'appropriate' context of questioning in which a disposition to assent would be forthcoming (at the same time, of course), and thus that '*p*' is not a belief of *r*. Such a lack of dependence on the context of questioning characterizes the 'Londres' case. Because of limitations of space, I do not discuss in this paper what happens when this uniformity breaks down; I do so in part II of this essay (unpublished).

15. Sincerity need not lead us circularly back to the notion of belief (as R. Chisholm held: cf. his "Sentences about Believing," in *Intentionality, Minds and Language,* edited by A. Marras [Urbana, Ill., 1972]) if it is taken, for instance, to be a desire to tell the truth.

16. In the construction '*r* believes that *p*' I shall always assume that '*p*' is a well-formed English sentence; otherwise, the construction is not a well-formed sentence.

17. This restriction is dealt with in a greater detail in part II of this essay.

18. "Puzzle about Belief," 249.

19. I allow myself a liberal use of single quotes when corner-quotes or the like are called for, trusting that this will generate no confusion.

20. Again, when '*p*' is an English sentence, which I will normally not repeat henceforth. Issues related to this analysis will be further discussed below in this section and in part II of this essay. Let me also repeat that the 'PB_r'*p*' ' definition is offered under the proviso, which we have adopted for this part of the essay, that *r* uses the items in the sentence '*q*', which is a belief of his, in a standard way.

21. Notice though that it seems that adequate translation often connects two items that are somewhat less than synonymous. Thus, it seems that adequate paraphrase is somewhat looser than the notion of synonymy. For that matter, the notion of adequate paraphrase might also be less susceptible to some of the criticisms launched against the notion of synonymy. Cf. D. Davidson's use of the notion of 'samesayers', reflecting on akin perspectives (in some respects) in his "On Saying That," in D. Davidson and J. Hintikka, *Words and Objections* (Dordrecht, 1969).

22. As mentioned before in my review, all there is, in so far as beliefs are concerned, are beliefs conceived as linguistic (or symbolic) representations (that is, *de dicto* beliefs); beliefs *de re* are a subclass of these, which maintain certain causal and justificatory relations. The *de re* construction of the form '*r* believes of *a* that it is *F*' has the force of asserting the existence of a belief of *r* of a certain sort, classified via the object that is the referent of the singular term in that belief and the class of descriptive phrases that are adequate paraphrases of '*F*'.

According to the conception I develop in my *Reference and Knowledge,* for each believer there is a special class of definite descriptions, called *strict anchors,* through which the reference relation is secured. Beliefs that include these terms will thereby be *de re,* and so will other beliefs involving other singular terms that are coclusteral with a strict anchor and maintain certain parasitic connections to a belief that includes a strict anchor. Roughly speaking, to be a strict anchor, a definite description $\iota x H x$ must satisfy the condition that the believer (latently) knows (*de dicto*) that $\iota x H x$ being *H* is a cause of his having some belief involving '*ixHx*'. This condition thus confers both causal and justificational components on the reference relation. The inference relation is thus not a purely causal, or naturalistic, relation, nor does it involve any intentional element whatsoever. That the reference relation involves a justificational component provides a basis for arguing that knowledge must also involve justification (and similarly for the rest of the propositional attitudes). See also my forthcoming "A Theory of Speaker Reference."

23. For more on this subject in the context of another type of construction—the counterfactual construction—cf. my book *A Theory of Counterfactuals* (Hackett, Ind., 1985), chap. 2, sec. 7, 2, and sec. 8, 1 and 3; chap. 7, sec. 5; chap. 9, sec. 5, 2.

24. See below, section 5.

25. I go beyond this limitation in part II of this essay.

26. This limitation too is discussed further in part II of this essay.

27. The term '$-p$' is a place-holder for an English sentence that is the negation of the English sentence 'p'.

28. In particular, the limitation of the uniformity of verbal dispositions.

29. We shall further defend the feasibility of taking this feature as a part of the setup of the example below in this section.

30. In a context in which political matters are quite insignificant, one may use 'Londres' in a perfectly standard way, without realizing it names a capital, for example, when one has no opinion what the capital is. The point is not crucial for our example, however, since the puzzle can be generated with respect to other cities that are not capitals, and therefore there is no need to dwell on it here. Also, one may assume, r is aware that 'Londres' names a capital but is not aware that 'London' does. Since he know 'London' to be the name of the city he lives in, this will clearly not reflect on his normal use of 'London', but only on his ignorance.

31. This point is discussed in greater length in part II of this essay.

32. In this case, r would acquire his reference to London via 'Londres' through the sources form whom he acquired his beliefs concerning 'Londres'; cf. also my (unpublished) manuscript *Reference and Knowledge*.

33. As Kripke seems to do, thus: "Of course, he has learned of that famous distant city, London (which he of course calls 'Londres') . . . " ("Puzzle about Beliefs," 242). Notice here the *de re* use by Kripke, who has previously stated that he excluded *de re* statements from his concerns in this paper. Kripke must have realized that r's referring by 'Londres' to London is a necessary condition for his standard use of 'Londres', and it was for that reason that he seems to have felt that he needs the *de re* mode here.

34. The key issue, of course, is what his beliefs really are. I continue here on the basis of the sketchy account developed in section 2. The consequences for the propositional theory of belief are discussed in part II of this essay.

35. Under the assumptions we hold in this part of the essay, i.e., of uniformity of response and standard understanding.

36. 'French' and 'English' are abbreviated as 'F' and 'E' respectively.

37. Of course, it is unrealistic to expect any *arbitrary believer* to have the notion 'adequate paraphrase' in his or her vocabulary.

38. Cf., for instance: "According to such a supposition a belief that Hesperus is a planet is a belief that a certain heavenly body, rigidly picked out as seen in the evening . . . " ("Puzzle about Belief," 280); or " . . . that he lacks the belief that London is pretty" (ibid., 258). Or: "We may give a rough statement of his beliefs. He believes that . . . " (ibid., 259). Of course, failing to separate the two levels is indicative of the propositional theory of belief, which lurks behind Kripke's formulations. Cf. also part II of this essay.

39. The notion of incongruent beliefs is discussed further in part II of this essay.

40. "Puzzle about Belief," 257-58.

41. Ibid., 258; cf. also section 1 above.

42. Of course, if r knows no English, the invalidity of the principle will be glaring, but Kripke limits himself to an English speaker.

43. "Puzzle about Belief," 259.

44. Ibid., 263.

45. Ibid., 263.

46. Ibid., 264.

47. Ibid., 264.

48. Ibid., 258.

49. Some philosophers have taken the view that to provide such a full account we must go beyond the level of propositional attitudes and use construction that display the beliefs involved by explicitly bringing in a relativization to a mode of presentation (cf. D. Kaplan, "Quantifying In," in *Words and Objections,* edited by D. Davidson and J. Hintikka (Dordrecht, 1969), 206-42; and S. Schiffer, "Naming and Knowing," in *Contemporary Perspectives in the Philosophy of Language,* edited by P. A. French et al. [Minneapolis, 1977]). If this is taken as a motivation for a different analysis of belief sentences, it is I believe, too radical a proposal; it breaks the inherent character of propositional attitude constructions, the fundamental function of which is to enable reporting without displaying the beliefs involved. The proposal I make below should, I believe, allow for the descriptive incompleteness noted in the text to be remedied *within* the sphere of standardly structured propositional attitude idioms. That such a propositional attitude as the one proposed here is not to be found in natural language is all but puzzling: the kind of situations it helps describe more fully is rather rare, and it does not therefore justify a separate entrenched construction.

50. Note that my coined phrase '*r* suspends-judgment that *p*' is designed to be akin in form to other propositional attitude constructions.

51. We will operate, of course, under our general assumption in these sections of uniformity of verbal dispositions. If this assumption is withheld, the above definition should be modified. What happens when this assumption is withheld is more fully discussed in part II of this essay.

52. "Puzzle about Belief." 259.

53. In this paper I have not addressed myself to the Paderewski case, which involves a violation of the uniformity assumptions. I do claim, however, that it can be treated along lines similar to the treatment above. I deal with this and other related issues in part II of this essay.

54. Cf. W. V. Quine, "Quantifiers and Propositional Attitudes," in his *The Ways of Paradox and Other Essays* (New York, 1966), 183-94.

55. Cf. Quine's use of this construction in his "Intensions Revisited", in *Contemporary Perspectives in the Philosophy of Language,* edited by P. A. French (Minneapolis, 1979), 268-74.

56. But not vice versa. I take the construction '*r* believes of *a* that it is F' to be true just in case, for some singular term '*b*' and for some predicative expression '*G*' such that ap ('*F*', '*G*'), '*Gb*' is a belief of *r*, and *r* refers (by '*b*', in his belief '*Gb*') to *a*. Accordingly, *r* believes '*F*' of *a* iff for some singular term '*b*', '*Fb*' is a belief of *r*, and he refers (in it) by '*b*' to *a*. Thus, *r* may believe of *a* that it is F without knowing English (in particular, without commanding the expression '*F*'); but for him to believe '*F*' of *a*, '*F*' must belong to his vocabulary.

57. Cf. my "Quine and Modalities *de re.*" I used there the notation 'IR_r ('*a*', '*Fa*')', where the '*IR*' indicated intended reference. But since the reference relation, as I see it (and as I attempt to analyze it in *Reference and Knowledge)* is emphatically *non*intentional, the notation '*R*('*a*', '*Fa*')' seems preferable in preventing confusions and misunderstandings.

58. For further details, see my "Quine and Modalities *de re.*" Obviously, the problem of analyzing the reference of singular terms resides primarily in the analysis of the R-function. Exportation, classically conceived (by Quine), was to connect the *de dicto* readings and the *de re* readings of, e.g., belief sentences. In the exportation inferences A and B, ' '*Fa*' is a belief of *r*' was used instead of the *de dicto* reading of '*r* believes that *p*'. But the analysis of belief sentences in section 2 of this article allows for the extension of inferences A and B to the case in which a belief sentence (read *de dicto*) occurs as the first premise. Similar obvious linkages connect the construction '*r* believes '*F*' of *a*' and the *de re* belief sentence '*r* believes of *a* that it is F'. Because of scope limitations, however, I shall not develop this point further here. Cf. "Quine and Modalities *de re,*" n. 24. Cf. also my "The Hesperus-Phosphorus Case," *Theoria* 62 (1984).

59. And more generally in the *de re* construction *r* believes of *a* that it is *F'*, for which we need not specify the predicate in a belief that makes this construction true, but only an adequate paraphrase of it.

60. The coining of '*r* suspends '*F*' of *a*' may sound somewhat awkward as a semi-English construction—even more so, perhaps, than '*r* believes '*F*' of *a*'; but no better candidate occurs to me.

61. This point was made by S. Schiffer in private communication. Cf. also his article "Naming and Knowing."

Is It Possible to Have Contradictory Beliefs?

RICHARD FOLEY

I

What is it to have a belief? It is notoriously difficult to answer this question. But, of course, it is not significantly easier to say what a thought is, or what a desire is, or what a fear is. All such questions are difficult to answer, and they are difficult precisely because providing a fully adequate answer to any one of them inevitably would involve an answer to some of the most fundamental questions in the philosphy of mind. Indeed, a fully adequate answer to any one of these questions inevitably would involve nothing less than a defense of some general conception of the mental.

I do not propose to try to give a fully adequate answer to the question, What is a belief? Rather, I propose to do something more modest: to defend a few simple rules concerning what it is possible and what it is not possible for a person to believe. These rules can be regarded as constituting a first step towards a logic of believing.

I realize that to some this will seem to be just the reverse of the proper procedure. They will recommend that questions concerning what it is possible for a person to believe be answered in light of some general theory of belief. An adequate logic of believing, they will recommend, is to be derived from an adequate theory of belief.

I do not have any a priori objection to such a recommendation. Indeed, it is hard to see what objections there could be to such a recommendation if we knew of some fully adequate theory of belief. And even in the absence of such a theory, we may have reasopns to think that certain questions concerning the logic of believing cannot be answered convincingly in advance of such a general theory. But, on the other hand, there is no reason to think that all questions concerning the logic of believing are like this. More to the point, in the absence of any fully adequate theory of belief, there is no reason to think that conclusions—even provisional ones—concerning what it is possible or impossible to believe cannot sometimes be of help in judging the plausibility of various proposed, general theories of belief.

In any event, I will try to defend some conclusions of this sort.

II

Consider a pair of questions. Is it possible to believe a proposition p and to believe also its negation not p. And is it possible to believe the proposition that p and not p? The difference between these two questions can be represented in the following way, where "Bsp" stands for "S believes that p is true":

1. $\sim\lozenge(\mathrm{B}sp\ \&\ \mathrm{B}s\ \mathrm{not}\ p)$.

2. $\sim\lozenge(\mathrm{B}s(p\ \&\ \mathrm{not}\ p))$.

Principle 1 says that it is impossible to have contradictory beliefs; 2 says that it is impossible to believe a contradiction.

Notice that neither of these principles says that it is impossible to have inconsistent beliefs. A set of beliefs is inconsistent just if it is impossible for the set of propositions that are believed all to be true. So, for example, S's beliefs are inconsistent if S both believes p and believes q and if p implies not q, where one proposition implies another just if necessarily the second is true if the first is true. It is possible for a person to have beliefs of this sort because it is possible for a person to believe p but not to realize that p implies not q. For instance, let p be the proposition that triangle T is equilateral and q be the proposition that T has one angle that is forty-five degreees; and suppose that S both believes p and believes q because he does not realize that all equilateral triangeles are equiangular. Here S has inconsistent beliefs, but he need not have contradictory beliefs because he need not, for example, believe q and believe not q.[1]

Indeed, whenever a person believes a necessarily false proposition he will have inconsistent beliefs. Suppose, for example, that as a result of faulty computations a person comes to believe that $43 \times 33 = 1,319$. This proposition is necessarily false. But then, it is impossible for all of the members of a set of propositions to be true if the set contains this proposition. So, a person who believes such a proposition will have inconsistent beliefs. But again, the fact that one's beliefs are inconsistent in this way in no way implies that one both believes a proposition and believes its negation. It in no way implies, that is, that one has contradictory beliefs.

Moreover, it is even possible for a person to have inconsistent beliefs and for him to realize that his beliefs are inconsistent and yet not have contradictory beliefs.[2] Indeed, this probably is not even very unusual. Suppose a person S is properly humble about his ability to believe only truths. Suppose, in particular, that he believes of a set of propositions he believes that at least one, he knows not which, is false. If S has such a belief, it is impossible for all of his beliefs to be true. So, his beliefs are inconsistent. And S might very well recognize this, without having contradictory beliefs. For example, suppose S believes each proposition in the following set, $(p^1, p^2, p^3 \ldots p^n)$. If S also believes that at least one of these propositions is false, he believes that not $(p^1 \& p^2 \& p^3 \ldots \& p^n)$. On the other hand, from the fact that he believes each proposition in the set $(p^1, p^2, p^3 \ldots p^n)$, it does not follow that he believes the conjunction $(p^1 \& p^2 \& p^3 \ldots \& p^n)$. And thus, it does not follow that he has contradictory beliefs.

This does not follow because a conjunctive rule does not apply to beliefs. There *is* a simplification rule that applies to beliefs. Necessarily, whenever someone believes a conjunction, that person believes each conjunct. More formally, the following is true:

3. $\Box$(If Bs $(p \& q)$ then Bsp & Bsq).

But the converse does not hold. It is possible for a person to believe two propositions without believing their conjunction. More formally,

4. $\Diamond$(Bsp & Bsq & not Bs $(p \& q)$).[3]

This latter principle, at least at first glance, may not seem as obviously true as the former, but a little reflection indicates that it is indeed true. To believe a proposition one must be capable of conceiving it;. But if a conjunctive rule applied to beliefs, such that Bs$(p \& q)$ whenever Bsp and Bsq, and if, as is plausible to assume, people can have a very large number of beliefs, then they must be capable of conceiving very complex propositions. If, for instance, S believes the propositions $p^1, p^2, p^3 \ldots p^n$, where $n = 1,000$, then given such a conjunctive rule S must believe and hence be capable of conceiving the conjunctive proposition $(p^1 \& p^2 \& p^3 \ldots \& p^{1000})$. And if n is greater than 1,000—if n, for example, is infinitely large (and it is not completely implausible to suppose a person might have an infinite number of beliefs)—then S must be capable of understanding even more complex, perhaps even infinitely complex, propositions. But for the lack of time, if nothing else, humans are not capable of conceiving propositions of this complexity. And so, a conjunctive rules does not apply to beliefs, and principle 4 is true.

Given that a simplification rule does apply to beliefs and that a conjunctive rule does not, it follows that principle 1 makes a stronger claim than does principle 2. In particular, given the truth of principle 3 (the simplification rule), it follows that if principle 1 is true—if it really is impossible to have contradictory beliefs—then 2 also must be true. It must, that is, be impossible to believe a contradiction. To see this, assume for purposes of a *reductio* that it is possible for S to believe a contradiction. It then would follow by virtue of 3 that it also must be possible for S to have contradictory beliefs. But this is what principle 1 denies.

On the other hand, it is not obvious that if 2 is true, then principle 1 must also be true. If a conjunctive rule applied to beliefs, then the truth of 1 would follow from the truth of 2. For given such a conjunctive rule, if S had contradictory beliefs, he would of necessity also believe a contradiction. But precisely what principle 4 denies is that such a rule is applicable to beliefs.

Thus, 1 is a stronger claim than is 2. If 1 is true, then so too is 2, but it is not obvious that the truth of 1 follows from 2.

So, is 1, and hence 2, true? Is it really impossible to have contradictory beliefs? The answer, I think, is "yes"; but there are, it must be admitted, cases where it might appear, at least at first glance, as if a person does have contradictory beliefs. But in all of these cases, the first appearance is misleading.

Some of these are cases of the sort already mentioned, where a person has inconsistent but not genuinely contradictory beliefs. But there are a number of other sort of cases as well. For example, a person who believes p may nonetheless act as if she believes not p, and in this way it may appear as if she has contradictory belief. Thus, a person who believes that walking under ladders need not bring bad luck may nonetheless act as if she believes it does. She may avoid walking under ladders, perhaps out of habit or out of fear that the ladder will slip down on top of her. But, of course, such a person need not have genuinely contradictory beliefs.

A special case of a person believing p even though she acts as if she believes not p occurs when a person for the sake of argument accepts a proposition that she believes to be false. In such cases, the person voluntarily commits herself to the truth of a proposition, as least for the duration of the argument, even though she believes that the negation of the proposition is true. Here again it might appear to someone as if the person has contradictory beliefs, although in fact she does not.

In addition, if a person changes her mind about some proposition, it may very well appear is if she has contradictory beliefs. But in such cases the person merely believes at a time t some proposition whose negation she believed at some former time t *, and hence the person at no time need have genuinely contradictory beliefs. (For the sake of simplicity, I have not explicitly inserted a temporal qualifier in principle 1; but it should be understood to contain an implicit one, so that it asserts only the impossibility of S at a time t believing p and at the same time believing not p).

Similar points hold for repressed, unconscious beliefs. If one thinks there are such beliefs, one might think it is possible to have beliefs of this sort that are contradictory; or at the very least that it is possible to have "mixed contradictory beliefs," such that a person in the ordinary, nonrepressed sense believes p while in a repressed sense that same person believes not p. I do not want to claim that there are not contradictory beliefs of this sort. All I want to claim is that a person cannot in an ordinary, conscious, nonrepressed sense believe p and also in an ordinary, conscious, nonrepressed sense believe not p.

By "ordinary, conscious, nonrepressed belief," I mean to include not just occurrent beliefs but also nonoccurrent beliefs. In the nonoccurrent sense of belief, a person at a time t need not be explicitly considering a proposition p to believe p at that time. A person, for example, in this sense can believe that he is alive even at those times when he is not explicitly considering the proposition.

It is none too easy, however, to say what a nonoccurrent belief is; moreover, this is none too easy even if we presuppose the notion of an occurrent belief and try to understand nonoccurrent belief in terms of it. It may be tempting to think that S nonoccurrently believes p just if he is able to consider p and if he were to consider p, he would occurrently believe p. But, this won't do. Let p be the proposition that S is considering some proposition. According to the above suggestion then, it presumably will be the case that S at most times of his life believes this proposition p—even at those times when his mind is blank and he is not considering any proposition at all. For at those times, it presumably will be true that if he *were* to consider the proposition p, where p is the proposition that he is considering some proposition, he would occurrently believe p. What this example makes clear is that the above suggestion fails to distinguish between cases where S nonoccurrently believes p and cases where he lacks this belief but is nonetheless disposed upon considering p to *acquire* the belief p. The suggestion, in other words, fails to recognize that what a person believes might be altered by what propositions he considers. This applies not just to "trick" situations, as where a person is considering the proposition that he is considering a proposition, but also to ordinary situations where a person upon considering a proposition notices something that had not occurred to him previously and thereby comes to believe what he formerly did not believe.[4]

Of course, this does not show that there might not be some way or another of patching up this general approach to nonoccurrent beliefs, which presumes that nonoccurrent beliefs are to be understood in terms of what a person would believe occurrently under certain conditions. But perhaps this assumption should be questioned. After all, the notion of an occurrent belief probably is no more and no less difficult to understand than the notion of a nonoccurrent belief. Moreover, if we had a good idea of what a belief *simpliciter* is, we would also have a good idea of how to distinguish occurrent beliefs from nonoccurrent beliefs. We then could say that S occurrently believes p just if he believes p and is consciously considering p, and S

nonoccurrently believes p just if he believes p and is not consciously considering p.

What I am suggesting, in other words, is that perhaps the most promising approach to developing a general theory of belief is not one that first tries to say that an occurrent belief is and then tries to explicate nonoccurrent belief in terms of a disposition to have an occurrent belief. Rather, it is one that tries to say what a belief *simpliciter* is. If one succeeds, there then will be no problem in distinguishing occurrent from nonoccurrent beliefs. Likewise, there will be no problem distinguishing cases where a person's considering p results in his *acquiring* a belief p from cases where a person's considering p merely results in his occurrently believing what he previously nonoccurrently believed. All we need say is that in the latter kind of case, before explicitly considering p the person already nonoccurrently believed p, but that in the former kind of case this is not so.

In any event, the primary concern here is with principle 1. What principle 1 is to be understood as asserting is that it is impossible for S in a conscious, nonrepressed sense to believe p, either occurrently or nonoccurrently, and also in a conscious, nonrepressed sense to believe not p, either occurrently or nonoccurrently. What I am claiming is that this principle will be true on any plausible account of belief and on any plausible account of the difference between occurrent and nonoccurrent beliefs.

I will say more about why I think this later, but first it is necessary to say something about *de re* beliefs. I have been presupposing up until now that to have contradictory beliefs is just to believe contradictory *propositions*. Principle 1, for example, is expressed in terms of the impossibility of believing such propositions. Strictly, therefore, *de re* beliefs are as irrelevant to an assessment of principle 1 as are unconscious, repressed beliefs. Nevertheless, it is of interest to inquire whether (or in what sense) it is possible to have contradictory *de re* beliefs, if for no other reason than that many cases where it might appear as if a person has beliefs that violate principle 1 may actually be cases where a person has contradictory *de re* beliefs.

Let us begin simply by assuming (later the assumption will be examined) that it is possible for a person to have a number of *de re* beliefs about an object without realizing that her beliefs in fact are about one and the same object. Assume, in other words, that it is possible for a person to have *de re* beliefs about objects that are in this way *epistemically remote* from her. There then would seem to be a sense in which it is possible to have contradictory *de re* beliefs. It would seem possible, that is, for a person to believe *of* an object that it has a property and also to believe *of* the same object that it lacks that property.

To get clearer on how this might be so, consider various accounts of *de re* belief. Such accounts can be divided, very crudely, into two classes: those accounts that make it relatively difficult to believe *de re* of an object that it has some characteristic, because they require believers to have a special, intimate relation of some sort with objects about which they have *de re* beliefs; and those accounts that do not require there to be such a relation and that thus make it relatively easy to have *de re* beliefs. As an example, suppose that *S* lives in Hollywood and is interested in the sleeping habits of film stars. He knows that some film stars rise very early in the morning and he knows also that some film stars don't go to sleep until very late at night. In addition, he knows the relatively uninteresting proposition that the film star who regularly rises first in the morning is a film star. If we call the film star who regularly rises first "the morning star," then what *S* knows here is that the morning star is a star. He also knows the equally uninteresting proposition that the film star who regularly goes to bed the latest at night is a film star. That is, he knows that the evening star is a star. Moreover, *S* knows some film stars personally. For instance, he has met *T*, who is one of the most famous film stars. On the other hand, he has never met *R*, who also is a film star, and in addition has not seen any of her films and has not seen a photograph of her.

Now, some accounts of *de re* beliefs allow *S* to have *de re* beliefs about *R* as well as about *T*. In particular, if we suppose that *R* is the evening star, some accounts of *de re* belief allow us to conclude that since *S* believes *de dicto* that the evening star is the evening star and since *R* in fact is the evening star, he also believes *de re* of *R* that she is the evening star.[5] But if *S* can have *de re* beliefs about such epistemically remote objects, it is not hard to see how he might have contradictory *de re* beliefs. Suppose, for example, that *S* regards it as unlikely that the film star who regularly goes to sleep the latest at night should also be the film star who regularly rises the earliest in the morning and that he thus comes to believe that the morning star is not the evening star. But suppose he is wrong and that *R* in fact is both the morning and the evening star. An account of the above sort then allows us to conclude not only that *S* believes *de dicto* that the morning star is not the evening star but also that he believes *de re* of the morning star that she is not the evening star. But since the morning star and the evening star are one and the same star and since we have already granted that *S* believes *de re* of the evening star that she is the evening star, *S* believes *de re* of one and the same star that she is the evening star and that she is not the evening star. In other words, *S* has contradictory *de re* beliefs.

Other accounts make it somewhat harder to have a *de re* belief about an object. Some accounts imply, for instance, that although *S* cannot have a *de re* belief about *R*, because he has never met nor seen her, he can have *de re* beliefs about *T* because he is on more intimate terms with *T* than with *R*—he has seen her, talked to her, etc.[6] Nevertheless, even these more restrictive accounts typically allow the possibility of contradictory *de re* beliefs since they typically allow the possibility that *S* might have a number of *de re* beliefs about an object and yet not realize they are beliefs about one and the same object. Suppose, for example, that when *S* is up early in the morning he almost invariably sees *T,* who has dark hair and a dark complexion, and that as a result he comes to believe that *T* is the morning star. Because *S* regularly sees and perhaps even talks to *T,* let us suppose that he has the requisite "closeness"—however this is explicated—to believe *de re* of *T* that she is the morning star. But, suppose in addition that when *S* is up very late at night he invariably sees and talks to someone with very light hair and a very light complexion. Since this person is glamorous looking and often talks of "taking a meeting," *S* takes her to be a film star and comes to believe that she must be the evening star. Suppose he is right about this; the person he sees is in fact the evening star. Now, suppose *S* also thinks that the evening star is not the star who regularly rises the earliest in the morning. He thinks, in other words, that the evening star is not the morning star. Because *S*'s acquaintance with the evening star is as intimate as is his acquaintance with the morning star, let us suppose that he believes *de re* of the evening star that she is not the morning star. But, finally, suppose that contrary to what *S* thinks, the morning star *is* the evening star. When out at night, *T* wears makeup and a wig that prevents her from being recognized. In such a case, *S* believes *de re* of the morning star that she is the morning star and believes *de re* of the evening star that she is not the morning star. But since the morning star and the evening star are one and the same star *S* believes *de re* of one and the same star (viz., *T*) that she is the morning star and that she is not the morning star.

The lesson here, then, is that even accounts of *de re* belief that are relatively restrictive, in that they require a person to have a particularly intimate relation with an object in order to have a *de re* belief about it (to see it, to touch it, or in some other way to interact causally with it) tend to allow the possibility of contradictory *de re* beliefs. Ordinarily, the relation such accounts require won't be sufficiently intimate to prevent the possibility that the objects about which a person has *de re* beliefs are epistemically remote from him. Thus, for example, even if it is claimed that a person can have *de re* beliefs only about objects he has perceived, this won't prevent the possibility of his having two *de re* beliefs about an object even though he doesn't realize they are about the same object. And insofar as this is possible, it will be possible to have contradictory *de re* beliefs.

But, shouldn't this make us suspicious of such accounts of *de re* belief? In other words, shouldn't we be suspicious of any account that makes it so *easy* to have contradictory *de re* beliefs? After all, even on the relatively restrictive accounts of *de re* belief, which require a believer to have a relatively intimate relation with the objects about which he has *de re* beliefs—which require that the believer perceive objects about which he has *de re* beliefs—it very likely will be plausible to think that most of us most of the time have at least some contradictory *de re* beliefs.

The answer to these questions, I think, is a qualified "yes." It shouldn't be this easy to have contradictory *de re* beliefs. However, the "yes" needs to be qualified because perhaps *de re* beliefs—or at least some *de re* beliefs, including those that appear to be contradictory—are reducible to *de dicto* beliefs. That is, perhaps some *de re* beliefs—as in the *de re* belief of object O that it has characteristic X—can be reduced to belief in a proposition, such as the proposition that the so-and-so has X. If so, then perhaps in cases where it appears as if S has contradictory *de re* beliefs the appearance of a genuine (or irreducible) contradiction can be explained away in terms of the person believing noncontradictory propositions.

In suggesting that some (or perhaps even all) *de re* beliefs might be reducible to *de dicto* beliefs, I mean something relatively loose. I do not mean, for example, that when a person S believes *de re* of an object O that it has characteristic X, his having this belief is *just* a matter of his believing a proposition of the form, the so-and-so has X. At a bare minimum, there has to be an object of the sort implied by the proposition. *De re* beliefs, in Quine's words, are "relational" and not merely "notional."[7] To have a *de re* belief, there has to be something that stands in the appropriate relation with the believer. So, to say that a *de re* belief is reducible to a *de dicto* belief is not to say that the former is identical with some instance of the latter. Rather, it is to say that to have this *de re* belief is to have a *de dicto* belief *and* to have certain other nonbelief conditions satisfied: for example, the condition that there in fact be an object of the sort the proposition implies, that the believer stand in an appropriately close causal relation with this object. It is to say, in other words, that the person S has the *de re* belief in virtue (at least in part) of his having an appropriate *de dicto* belief. Correspondingly, to say that a *de re* belief is *not* reducible to a *de dicto* belief is to say that there is no *de dicto* belief in virtue of which he has the *de re* belief. More specifically, it is to say that it is possible for S to have had this *de re* belief about object O that it has characteristic X even if he were to believe no proposition entailing that the so-and-so has X, where the so-and-so is object O.[8] If this were *not* possible, there would be reason to suspect that S has the *de re* belief about O in virtue (at least in part) of believing a proposition of the above sort.[9]

On the other hand, to claim that a person S has a *de re* belief by virtue of believing an appropriate proposition is not to claim that there is some mechanical way of identifying the believed proposition. There need be no rule to identify the *de dicto* belief in virtue of which a person believes *de re* of O that it has X—other than perhaps the very general rule that he must *de dicto* believe *some* proposition of the form the so-and-so has X, where the so-and-so in fact is O. So, for example, if S believes *de re* of T, that she is the morning star, perhaps the believed proposition in virtue of which S has this *de re* belief is the proposition that the person whom he regularly sees and to whom he speaks whenever he is up early in the morning is the morning star; or perhaps it is the proposition that the person with the low voice, dark complexion, and purple sunglasses who lives on the 1600 block of Rose Avenue is the morning star; or perhaps it is some other proposition. And if *S* also believes *de re* of *T* that she is not the morning star, perhaps the believed proposition in virtue of which he has this *de re* belief is the proposition that the person whom he sees and to whom he speaks whenever he is up late at night is not the morning star; or perhaps it is the proposition that the person with the high voice, the light complexion, and the rose sunglasses who lives on the 1700 block of Rose Avenue is not the morning star; or perhaps it is some other proposition.

The most important point here, however, is that insofar as *S* when he believes *de re* of *T* both that she is the morning star and that she is not the morning star has such beliefs by virtue of believing propositions of the above sort, *S* need not have genuinely contradictory beliefs. Alternatively, he need not have *contradictory beliefs that are irreducibly contradictory*. For, we can say if we so wish that *S* here *does* have contradictory *de re* beliefs because he believes *de re* of an object both that it has a property and that it lacks that same property. We can say this as long as we remember that this need not imply that *S* believes contradictory propositions. All it implies is that *S* believes two noncontradictory propositions (e.g., that the woman he sees regularly in the morning is the morning star and that the woman he sees regularly in the evening is not the morning star) that together with a third true proposition that he doesn't believe (e.g., that the woman he sees in the morning is the same woman he sees in the evening) implies that something both has and lacks a property.

Of course, this way of dealing with cases of contradictory *de re* beliefs depends on the *de re* beliefs in question being reducible to *de dicto* beliefs. But suppose this is denied. Suppose it is claimed that although perhaps one kind of *de re* belief is had in virtue of having *de dicto* beliefs, there is another sense of *de re* belief that is not so reducible. Suppose it also is claimed that these irreducible *de re* beliefs, like the reducible ones, might very well be contradictory. What then? Is it plausible to accept such claims? Is it plausible, for one, to think that there are *irreducible de re* beliefs, such that a person believes of an object *O* that it has characteristic *X* but such that he need not in order to have this belief believe any proposition of the form the so-and-so has *X*, where the so-and-so in fact is *O?* If this is plausible, is it also plausible to think that a person might have beliefs of this sort that are contradictory, such that he might have an irreducible *de re* belief of *O* that it has *X* and also an irreducible *de re* belief of *O* that it does not have *X?*

I think that perhaps it is plausible to say that there are irreducible *de re* beliefs. But at the same time, there is a significant restriction upon having such irreducible beliefs, which makes less plausible the idea that there can be *de re* beliefs that are both irreducible and contradictory. The restriction is that it is possible for a person to have irreducible *de re* beliefs only about objects that are not epistemically remote from him. So, insofar as a person *S* has two or more *de re* beliefs about one and the same object and insofar as neither are reducible to *de dicto* beliefs, *S* must realize that the beliefs are about one and the same object. Expressed in yet other words, the idea here is that whatever precisely it is to have irreducible *de re* beliefs about an object, it must turn out that the object about which one has such beliefs is not epistemically remote from the believer.

To see why it is plausible to think that this is so, recall that for *S* to have an irreducible *de re* belief about an object *O* that it has a characteristic *X* he must not have this belief in virtue of believing some proposition. In particular, it must be possible for him to have this belief without believing a proposition that entails that the so-and-so has *X*, where *O* is the so-and-so. Otherwise, it would be plausible to think that the *de re* belief is reducible. But in effect this means that if *S* is to have an irreducible *de re* belief of *O* that it has *X*, he must believe this of *O* in a way that does not require him to have any mediating characterization of *O*, in virtue of which he ascribes *X* to *O*. In this sense, he must be able to ascribe *X* to *O* directly. But insofar as the attribution of *X* to *O* is direct and insofar as an attribution of another characteristic *Y* to *O* is likewise direct, it is hard to see how *S* could fail to realize that it is one and the same object that has both *X* and *Y*. It is hard to see, that is, how the object could be epistemically remote from *S*. For, suppose that it were remote. Then, *S* simultaneously must be "close enough" to *O* to permit direct ascriptions of properties to it, without the help of some mediating characterization of the object; and yet also be "far enough away" from it not to realize that two such direct ascriptions are ascriptions to one and the same object. How could this be?

I want to suggest that it cannot be. In other words, I want to suggest that insofar as a person *S directly* ascribes a number of properties to an object *O* —insofar as *S* has a number of irreducible *de re* beliefs about an object *O* —the object of those ascriptions (or beliefs) must be transparent. At a minimum, this means that *necessarily insofar as* S *directly ascribes to an object the property* X *and also directly ascribes to an object the property* Y *and insofar as he takes both ascriptions to be correct and insofar finally as it is to the same object* O *that he ascribes these properties, then he believes that something has both* X *and* Y. This formulation recognizes the possibility that *S* might not be confident that both of his direct ascriptions are correct. For example, he might regard the ascription of property *X* as being somewhat risky and also regard the ascription of property *Y* as being somewhat risky. As a result, he might not think that both ascriptions (i.e., their conjunction) are likely to be correct. But necessarily, *if* he does think that both are correct and if in addition both are ascriptions of a property to the object *O*, then he believes something has both *X* and *Y*.

This is one mark of an ascription of a property to an object being direct. It is, in other words, one mark of irreducible *de re* beliefs.

Notice that an analogous rule does not apply to indirect ascriptions of a property—in other words, to reducible *de re* beliefs. A person might indirectly ascribe a property X to object O, by virtue, say, of believing a proposition that entails that the so-and-so has X, where the so-and-so is O, and in addition indirectly ascribe a property Y to O, by virtue, say, of believing a proposition that entails that the such-and-such has Y, where the such-and-such is Y, and yet not believe that there is something that has both X and Y, even though he thinks both of his ascriptions are correct. For example, in the morning star-evening star case, S indirectly ascribes to an object the property of being the morning star and also indirectly ascribes to an object the property of being the evening star. In addition, he may well think that both ascriptions are correct. Moreover, each ascription is an ascription to the same object—to the person T. Yet, S in that case does not believe that some person is both the morning star and the evening star.

Assuming, then, that the objects of irreducible *de re* beliefs must in this way be transparent, about what kinds of objects is it plausible to think that a person can have irreducible *de re* beliefs? That is, to what kinds of objects can a person directly attribute properties? One good candidate, of course, is oneself. So-called *de se"* beliefs are irreducible *de re* beliefs about oneself.[10] Thus, for example, when a person S believes of himself that he is thinking of Paris and also believes of himself that he wants to be wealthy, it is not altogether implausible to think he might be ascribing these properties to himself directly, without needing any mediating characterization of himself (as the person with such-and-such characteristics). And if he is directly ascribing to himself such properties, and if he takes both ascriptions to be correct, it likewise is not implausible to think that necessarily as a result he believes (either occurrently or nonoccurrently) that something has both properties—that something is both thinking of Paris and wanting to be wealthy.

On the other hand, even if it is granted that a person S can have irreducible *de re* beliefs about himself, this need not preclude his at the same time having reducible *de re* beliefs about himself. Suppose S sees a reflection of himself in a mirror, and suppose not realizing that it is he himself whom he is seeing he comes to believe that the man in the mirror is well-to-do. In virtue of having this *de dicto* belief (and perhaps also in virtue of his standing in an appropriately close relation to the man whose image is in the mirror), he might have (at least on many accounts) a reducible *de re* belief about himself.

But given that this is so, a person might be epistemically remote from himself. He might, that is, have another reducible *de re* belief about himself and not realize they are about one and the same thing. Imagine, for example, that unbeknownst to him the back of his jacket is tattered and that he sees a reflection of himself in a second mirror. Once again not realizing that it is he himself whom he is seeing and not even realizing that the man he sees in this second mirror is the same man he sees in the first mirror, he comes to believe of this man—himself—that he is not well-to-do.

If all this is so, then it follows that a person *S* might be simultaneously both epistemically remote from himself and not epistemically remote from himself.

What this shows, in turn, is that the notion of epistemic remoteness must be made more precise. This can be done by relativizing the notion to a particular set of beliefs. Thus, insofar as *S* directly ascribes characteristics to himself, without the need of mediating descriptions, he has irreducible *de re* beliefs about himself. And relative to such beliefs, he cannot be epistemically remote from himself. The nature of this kind of believing precludes such remoteness. But with respect to other ways of believing, he can be remote from himself. Insofar as he ascribes properties to himself indirectly, by virtue of mediating characterizations (the man whom he sees in the first mirror, and so on), he has reducible *de re* beliefs about himself. And relative to these beliefs (or relative to a mixture of his reducible and irreducible *de re* about himself), he might be epistemically remote from himself.

So, the fact that with respect to some of his *de re* beliefs a person is epistemically remote from an object does not preclude him from having other *de re* beliefs about that object that are irreducible. This holds for other objects as well as for himself. Thus, from the fact that a person is epistemically remote from an object other than himself (with respect to some of his *de re* beliefs), it doesn't follow that he cannot also have irreducible *de re* beliefs about that object. Of course, it doesn't follow that he *can* have irreducible *de re* beliefs about that object either. What, then, are we to say about this possibility? Might not a person have irreducible *de re* beliefs about objects other than himself? In other words, might not it be possible for there to be irreducible *de re* beliefs that are not *de se* beliefs? For example, might not a person with good eyesight and in good light believe of an object in front of him that it is red and also believe of it that it is round and believe these things not in virtue of some mediating characterization of the object? Might not he directly ascribe these properties to the object?

No doubt it is tempting to answer "yes" to these questions. But, the problem with such an answer is that it is at least as tempting to think that whenever a person has a *de re* belief about an object other than oneself, there is readily available to the person *S* a characterization of the object that is a good candidate for being a *mediating* characterization—a characterization in virtue of which he ascribes a property to the object. Thus, in precisely those cases where it might seem most plausible to think that *S* directly ascribes a property to an object *O* other than himself that it is, say, red—cases where *S* is in good light and has good eyesight, etc., and is looking at *O*—it is also plausible to think that there is available to S a characterization of the object—such as, "the ball I see in front of me"; or, if there are many balls in front of him, perhaps the characterization "of the three balls I see in front of me the one in the middle"; or the characterization "the ball I see in front of me and upon which I am now focusing attention." Accordingly, it is not unnatural to think that perhaps it is in virtue of S having a belief *de dicto* that the object to which such a characterization applies is red that he has the belief *de re* of O that it is red. On the other hand, those cases where it is most plausible to think that S has an irreducible *de re* belief about himself that he has some property, there often seems to be no such readily available characterization. That is, there is no readily available characterization that it is natural to think might be a mediating characterization in virtue of which he ascribes the property to himself. Hence it is natural to think that perhaps in the latter sort of case, but not in the former sort of case, S's *de re* belief sometimes really is irreducible.[11]

This, of course, is controversial. If, for example, each person has a haecceity *and* is acquainted with it, then in plausible cases of self-ascription there *will* be available to the person a characterization of himself in virtue of which he might make the self-ascription (just as in plausible cases of other-ascription there ordinarily seems to be such a characterization). But even so, on *either* view—the haecceity view, which suggests that *de re* beliefs about oneself might be reducible to *de dicto* beliefs (about "first-person propositions" involving the person's haecceity) and the direct ascription view—there is likely to be readily available characterizations in virtue of which it is not implausible to think the person S ascribes properties to things other than himself. On the haecceity view, the characterization will be "built in" to a first-person proposition, so that S might believe of O that it has X by virtue of believing the proposition expressed by the sentence "the object I see has X," where "I" expresses S-ness (the haecceity of S) and where the object that the person with S-ness sees is O. On the direct ascription view, by contrast, the characterization will be "built in" to a property that S self-ascribes, so that it might be by virtue of his having an irreducible *de re* belief about himself that he sees an object with X, where O is the object he sees, that he believes of O that it has X. Thus, on either view (the haecceity view or the *de se* belief view), one has a way of claiming that most, or even all, *de re* beliefs about objects other than oneself are reducible. Given the haecceity view, they will be reducible to *de dicto* beliefs in first-person propositions. Given the *de re* view, they will be reducible to irreducible *de se* beliefs about oneself.[12]

For this reason, it is best to broaden the notion of what makes *de re* beliefs reducible so that such beliefs can be reducible even if they are not reducible to *de dicto* beliefs. In particular, let us say that a *de re* belief is reducible if the person has this belief either by virtue of having a *de dicto* belief or by virtue of having an irreducible *de re* belief.

What does all this suggest about the original problem, having to do with contradictory *de re* beliefs? It suggests that although it may well be possible to have contradictory *de re* beliefs—to believe of O that it has X and to believe of O that it does not have X—the kind of case where it is most plausible to think that a person has such beliefs (e.g., the morning star-evening star kind of case) is a case where the object about which the person has these beliefs is epistemically remote from the person with respect to those beliefs. It is a kind of case where the person does not realize that his beliefs are about one and the same object. But cases involving *de re* beliefs about epistemically remote objects are cases where it is plausible to think that the person has these beliefs in virtue of having other beliefs, say in virtue of having appropriate *de dicto* beliefs or appropriate *de se* beliefs. It is a kind of case, in other words, where it is plausible to think that the *de re* beliefs are reducible to other sorts of beliefs and where there is no particular reason to think that these other beliefs need be contradictory. Expressed in yet another way, it is a kind of case where there is no reason to think the beliefs are irreducibly contradictory.

The conclusion that in such cases the person's beliefs are not irreducibly contradictory, besides being intuitively plausible, has a welcome epistemological consequence as well. Namely, we need not say that a person's *de re* beliefs can be both irreducibly contradictory *and* epistemically rational.

To appreciate this, reconsider the morning star-evening star case. It is easy enough to describe that case, in which S believes of T both that she is the morning star and that she is not the morning star, in such a way that S is guilty of no epistemic blunders. At the very least, it is easy to describe the case so that he makes no epistemic blunders with respect either to his *de dicto* beliefs or, if there be such, to his *de se* beliefs. To be sure, he believes false propositions or ascribes properties to himself that he does not have, but the case can be described so that given his evidence it is rational for him to do so. It can be described, for example, so that it is rational for him to believe both the proposition that the woman he sees in the morning is the morning star and the proposition that the woman he sees in the evening is not the morning star. Or, assuming that there are *de se* beliefs, it can be described so that it is rational for him to ascribe to himself the property of seeing someone in the morning who is the morning star and also rational for him to ascribe to himself the property of seeing someone in the evening who is not the morning star. Indeed, it is difficult to see what there *could* be about the nature of such cases such that *necessarily* in cases of this sort at least some of S's beliefs had to be irrational. But if so, it is possible for S to have contradictory *de re* beliefs that are rational.

As long as these *de re* beliefs are reducible to *de dicto* beliefs or to *de se* beliefs, the fact that there are such contradictory but epistemically rational *de re* beliefs need be neither surprising nor alarming. After all, although we may very well *say* that *S* believes of the same person that she is the morning star and that she is not morning star, by this we only mean that *S* has such beliefs either by virtue of believing two noncontradictory propositions or by virtue of ascribing to himself two noncontradictory properties (two properties that are not the "negations" of one another, unlike, e.g., the property of being red and the property of not being red). What he believes, for example, may be the proposition that the woman he sees regularly in the morning is the morning star and the proposition that the woman he sees regularly in the evening is not the morning star. And even if there is a third proposition that is not believed by *S* and whose truth implies that one of these two propositions must be false (e.g., the proposition that the woman *S* sees in the morning is the same woman that he sees in the evening), it is not at all surprising that *S* could rationally believe the first two propositions to be true. For, it is not at all surprising that *S* could rationally believe a proposition that in fact is false. Similarly, it is not at all surprising that *S* might rationally ascribe to himself a property he does not have—the property of seeing someone in the evening who is not the morning star.

On the other hand, if *S*'s *de re* beliefs are not reducible, we cannot in one of these ways account for the rationality of both of *S*'s *de re* beliefs. On the contrary, we will be forced to say of *S*'s contradictory *de re* beliefs that both are epistemically rational despite the fact that their rationality is *not* just either a matter of his rationally believing two noncontradictory propositions or a matter of his rationally ascribing two noncontradictory properties to himself. We will be forced to admit, in other words, that *S*'s *de re* beliefs are in this sense *both irreducibly contradictory and epistemically rational*.

Such a conclusion is unacceptable. One prerequisite of an adequate theory of belief is that in conjunction with a plausible theory of epistemic rationality it preclude the possibility of a person having beliefs that are both genuinely (i.e. irreducibly) contradictory and epistemically rational. A theory of belief and a theory of epistemically rational belief ought to combine to make this impossible. But an account of *de re* belief that allows for irreducible *de re* beliefs about objects epistemically remote with respect to those beliefs will not satisfy this requirement. Evening star-morning star kind of cases can be described in such a way that on any plausible account of epistemically rational belief, whether it be a coherentist-inspired account or a foundationalist-inspired account or some other account, *S* is perfectly rational. But given that this is so and given the above restriction on a theory of belief, it follows that *S* in that case cannot have contradictory and irreducible *de re* beliefs about the person *T* (who is both the morning star and the evening star) and that any account that implies that he does is unacceptable.

So anyone who says that *de re* beliefs about objects epistemically remote with respect to those beliefs provide good examples of contradictory beliefs faces a dilemma. If the purported contradictory beliefs are reducible to *de dicto* beliefs, the example is not one of beliefs that are genuinely, or irreducibly, contradictory. On the other hand, if the purported contradictory beliefs are not so reducible, either there are no such beliefs or it is relatively easy to have contradictory beliefs both of which are epistemically rational. But since the latter disjunct is unacceptable, it must be that there are no such beliefs.

III

If situations in which a person has *de re* beliefs cannot be used to generate convincing examples of genuinely (i.e., irreducibly) contradictory beliefs, what other kind of situation might do so? What about situations in which a person has what might be called "linguistic beliefs"—that is, beliefs that a linguistic item, say, a sentence, is true?

It obviously is possible for a person S to believe that a sentence P is true (as least as uttered by a person in a certain situation at a certain time) and that a sentence Q is true, where P and Q express contradictory propositions. One situation in which this can happen occurs when S does not know the language in which sentence P and sentence Q are expressed but nonetheless believes each to be true, perhaps because a friend whom he thinks does know the language says that this is so. If S in such a situation believes each of these sentences to be true, must he have contradictory beliefs?

Hardly. Although sentences P and Q express contradictory propositions, it is not those propositions that S believes. By hypothesis, he doesn't know what propositions are expressed by P and Q. What he *does* believe are the following two propositions: (1) that sentence P is true and (2) that sentence Q is true. Of course, even if sentence P and sentence Q express contradictory propositions, propositions (1) and (2) are not contradictory. It is not impossible for both to be true. If, for example, P had expressed a different proposition from the one it in fact expresses, both might be true.

On the other hand, in such a case there may well be a sense—albeit, not a very interesting sense—in which S does believe the contradictory propositions expressed by P and Q. Namely, he might believe *de re* of the proposition p expressed by P that it is true and believe *de re* of the proposition q expressed by Q that it is true. Since S believes that the proposition expressed by P is true and since the proposition expressed by P in fact is p, at least on relatively unrestrictive accounts of *de re* belief he believes *de re* of p that it is true. Similarly, since he believes that the proposition expressed by Q is true and since the proposition expressed by Q in fact is q, he believes *de re* of q that it is true. Thus, he in this way believes p to be true and believes q to be true, although p and q are contradictories.[13]

However, this kind of case is no more convincing as an example of genuinely (irreducibly) contradictory beliefs than other, more standard cases of apparently contradictory *de re* beliefs—e.g., the evening star-morning star case. What makes this case initially a bit more confusing is that the object of the *de re* beliefs here are propositions. So, the beliefs in one sense *are* propositional, but the sense is a derived one. *S* has beliefs *about* these propositions by virtue of believing *that other* propositions are true—by believing the proposition that sentence *P* is true and by believing the proposition that sentence *Q* is true. These other propositions, in turn, are not contradictory.

There are, however, more difficult cases—cases involving people who are familiar with the language. Consider two kinds of cases. In the first, suppose *S* who knows English believes that the following sentence is true: "The flipping of the switch caused the light to go on." Call this sentence "*A*". Now, suppose that a second sentence, call it "*A**", expresses the same proposition as does sentence *A:* "The flipping of the switch stands in relation *R* to the light going on," where *R* is a successful analysis in ordinary English of what is involved in the causal relation. Might not *S,* who by hypothesis is a competent speaker of English, believe that sentence *A* is true and that sentence *A** is false, even though *A* and *A** express one and the same proposition?[14]

Consider a second case. Call the following sentence "*B*": "It either is raining or it is snowing." Let sentence *B** be: "It is not the case that it is both not raining and not snowing." Sentences *B* and *B** express the same proposition. But again, isn't it possible even for a competent speaker of English to believe that *B* is true and to believe also that *B** is false?

In both of the above cases, two relatively ordinary sentences in English express the same proposition, and yet an ordinary speaker of English might very well believe the one sentence to be true and the other to be false. In an analogous way, it is possible to generate examples of two relatively ordinary English sentences that express contradictory propositions and that are such that an ordinary speaker of English might believe both to be true. For example, let sentence *A*** be: "It is not the case that the flipping of the switch stands in relation *R* to the light going on." Sentences *A* and *A*** express contradictory propositions and yet it seems that an ordinary speaker *S* might believe both to be true. Similarly, let *B*** be: "It is not the case that it is not the case that it both is not snowing and not raining." *B*** and *B* expressed contradictory propositions and yet, once again, *S* might believe both to be true.

What is to be made of these cases? Do they provide convincing examples of contradictory beliefs? The answer, once more, is "no."

The problem with using these kinds of linguistic examples to try to illustrate how it might be possible to have genuinely contradictory beliefs is that insofar as it is plausible to think that a person *S* believes one sentence to be true and a second sentence to be false, where both express the same proposition—or insofar as it is plausible to think that S believes that two sentences are true, where one expresses the contradictory of the other—it also is plausible to think that S does not understand exactly what proposition is being expressed by one or both of the two sentences. But insofar as he does not understand the exact proposition being expressed by one or both of the sentences, then from the fact that he assents to both sentences—believes both sentences to be true—it does not follow that he believes the proposition expressed by each sentence. If a person assents to a sentence and if he understands exactly what proposition the sentence expresses, then perhaps it does follow that he believes that proposition. But precisely what is in question here, where the sentences to which S assents express contradictory propositions, is whether S does understand exactly what proposition each sentence expresses. This question cannot be answered simply by pointing out that the above sentences are English sentences and that S by hypothesis is a competent speaker of English. For, whatever linguistic competence is—and no doubt it is difficult to say exactly what it is—it is not a matter of knowing the exact proposition expressed by every sentence in the language in question, and it is not even a matter of knowing the exact proposition expressed by every sentence in the language to which one assents. So, from the fact that a person is a competent speaker of English and from the fact that he assents to an English sentence that expresses a proposition $p,$ it does not follow that he believes $p.$[15] *A fortiori,* from the fact that a person is a competent speaker of English and that he assents to two English sentences that express contradictory propositions, it does not follow that he believes contradictory propositions. Indeed, the very fact that these sentences express contradictory propositions and that the person nonetheless assents to them suggest that he does not understand exactly what proposition at least one of the sentences expresses.

To see this, consider what kind of linguistic beliefs are *least* likely to provide initially plausible examples of contradictory beliefs. The least likely candidates are those that involve sentences in the believer's own language that express relatively simple propositions. For example, let sentence C be: "A square is a kind of rectangle." Let C^* be: "A square is not a kind of rectangle." Here it is hard to convince oneself that a competent speaker of English could believe that both of these sentences are true. In turn, this is so hard to convince oneself of because it is so hard to convince oneself that a competent speaker of English does not understand precisely what propositions are expressed by the two sentences.

On the other hand, the more complex the propositions are that are expressed by a pair of sentences that express contradictory propositions, the easier it is to convince oneself that a competent speaker could believe both sentences to be true. For example, let sentence D be: "No number that is represented by numerals whose sum is 9 is a prime number; moreover, 9, 18,

27, 36, 45, 54, 63, 72, 81, 90, 108, and 207 are all examples of such nonprime numbers." Let D^* be: "All of the numbers in the following set are prime numbers: 3, 5, 7, 11, 37, 41, 43, 47, 61, 72, 73, 79, 83, 87, and 89." It is not too hard to convince oneself that an ordinary speaker of English, even one who knows mathematics well, could believe both of these sentences to be true. But the propositions expressed by these two sentences entail contradictory propositions. They entail the contradictory propositions that 72 is not a prime number and that 72 is a prime number.[16]

The complexity of the propositions expressed by D and D^* thus make it relatively easy to imagine that a competent speaker S could believe both sentences to be true. However, this very same complexity makes it all the more plausible to think that when S believes both sentences to be true, he does not really understand the precise proposition expressed by each. But if S does not really understand precisely what propositions D and D^* express, the fact that he believes both sentences to be true need not indicate that he has genuinely contradictory beliefs. Suppose, for example, that although he understands precisely what proposition is expressed by D, he does not quite grasp, perhaps because of carelessness, the proposition expressed by D^*. It then does not follow that he believes this proposition, although he may very well believe the proposition that sentence D^* is true. Thus, even though D^* expresses a proposition that entails the contradictory of a proposition entailed by the proposition expressed by D, it does not follow that S has contradictory beliefs. Call the proposition expressed by D "the D-proposition." Then, S believes the D-proposition as well as the proposition that sentence D^* is true. But these two propositions are not contradictories, and neither do they entail propositions that are contradictories. For, it is possible for both to be true. This is possible because it is possible for the sentence D^* not to express the proposition it in fact expresses.

But is the case here, and the other cases mentioned, really this simple? Isn't it at least somewhat tempting to think that if a competent speaker of English believes a relatively ordinary English sentence to be true, then there must be *some* sense in which he believes the proposition expressed by the sentence to be true, regardless of whether he understands precisely what proposition this is? After all, many of the words and phrases that an ordinary speaker of English uses regularly are words and phrases that he cannot precisely define. Yet, such a speaker uses such words and phrases perfectly well. He can make himself understood. Are we then to say, despite his obvious success in communicating, that he does not really believe, much less know, what he is saying or hearing or reading, since he cannot provide exact analyses of the words and phrases in the sentences he is saying, hearing, or reading?

No. For one, nothing I have said precludes S believing *de re* of the precise propositions expressed by the sentences he utters, or hears, or reads, that they are true, even if he cannot provide correct analyses of all the words and phrases contained in them. Even if we restrict ourselves to *de dicto* beliefs, all that follows from what I have said is that for sentences containing words and phrases for which S cannot provide adequate analyses, S does not know the *precise* propositions such sentences are expressing. But this is not to say that he is in the position of one who is ignorant of the language and who as a result has little or no idea what propositions are being expressed by the sentences. No doubt he does know roughly what propositions are being expressed, and in most situations this is more than enough for successful communication. It is enough, for example, to allow him to reach agreement with other competent speakers of English concerning the truth of many of the sentences he asserts, reads, hears, and so forth. For those sentences on whose truth values he cannot reach agreement with others, it usually is enough to allow him to reach agreement with others on what it is they disagree. That is, it is enough to allow them to reach agreement concerning what it is that makes one of them think the sentence is false and the other think that it is true. The only point I am insisting upon here is that if a competent speaker assents to two sentences that express contradictory propositions and that in addition are such that S is not aware of precisely what propositions they express, he need not have genuinely contradictory beliefs as a result of believing both sentences to be true. In other words, he need not believe that a proposition is true and that the very same proposition also is false.

This general point can be expressed in a slightly different way as well. If we let E and E^* be any two sentences that express the same, relatively complicated proposition, the crucial question to be asked is this: Does some person S believe sentence E to be true and sentence E^* to be false and in addition realize they express one and the same proposition? I am claiming that it is not possible to describe a situation in which it is plausible to answer "yes" to this question. On the other hand, in situations where the answer is "no," S need not believe genuinely contradictory propositions. In such situations, S either does not believe one sentence to be true and the other to be false or he does not understand precisely what proposition at least one of the sentences expresses. Otherwise, he would realize that the two sentences express the same proposition.

Of course, one might try to retreat once again to the claim that even if S does not understand precisely what proposition at least one of the sentences expresses, he nonetheless can believe *de re* of the proposition expressed by E (as well the one expressed by E^*, since they are the same) both that it is true and that it is false. But if one does claim this, one is claiming yet again that it is possible to have contradictory *de re* beliefs about an object that is epistemically remote with respect to those beliefs—in this case, the epistemically remote object is the proposition expressed by E and E^*. This claim, however, can be treated in just the way that other claims concerning *de re* beliefs about an object epistemically remote with respect to those beliefs are treated: either there are no such beliefs or at least one of the beliefs can be reduced to a *de dicto* belief (or perhaps a *de se* belief), in which case the person need not have genuinely contradictory beliefs. For example, the *de dicto* belief here may be the belief that sentence E^* is false.

Therefore, any linguistic attempt to provide a convincing example of contradictory beliefs faces a dilemma. Either the sentences purportedly providing the example express relatively simple propositions or they do not. Insofar as they do, it will be implausible to think that a person is both a competent speaker of the language and that he believes both to be true. Insofar as the sentences express propositions that are relatively complex, it will be implausible to think that a person is a competent speaker of the language, believes both to be true, *and* genuinely understands the exact propositions expressed by both sentences. He may know roughly what propositions are being expressed, but this is not enough to indicate that he has genuinely contradictory beliefs. Neither is it plausible to say that he has genuinely contradictory *de re* beliefs about the proposition expressed by one of the sentences. There are no irreducible *de re* beliefs about an object epistemically remote with respect to those beliefs; and if the *de re* beliefs can be reduced to *de dicto* beliefs, the beliefs need not be genuinely contradictory.

I am claiming that *any* linguistic attempt to provide a convincing example of contradictory beliefs can be handled in one of these ways. Suppose, for instance, one tries to use a "purely referential" account of proper names and corresponding account of "singular propositions" to generate such an example. Suppose, in particular, that S believes the following sentences (1) and (2) to be true and the following sentence (3) to be false: (1) Smith is a spy; (2) Jones is not a spy; (3) Smith is not a spy. Further suppose that the proper names in these sentences are not thought to be disguised definite descriptions but rather are thought to be purely, or directly, referential.[17] Finally, suppose that the name "Smith" and that the name "Jones," unbeknownst to S, refer to one and the same person. Each of these sentences, then, might be thought to express a singular proposition. For example, the proposition expressed by sentence (1), given this view of proper names, might be regarded as an ordered triple consisting of a person S (who is called "Smith" and who also is called "Jones"), a time t, and the property of being a spy. The proposition expressed by sentences (2) and (3), by contrast, might be regarded as the ordered triple consisting of person S, time t, and the property of not being a spy. Accordingly, sentences (1) and (2) express contradictory singular propositions and sentences (2) and (3) the same singular proposition. But then, given this understanding of the propositions expressed by the three sentences, might not S by believing (1) and (2) to be true and (3) to be false have genuinely contradictory beliefs? Might not he believe contradictory singular propositions?

No, and for the same reasons given above. By hypothesis, S believes (1) and (2) to be true and (3) to be false without realizing that the names in the three sentences pick out the same person. Thus, insofar as the person named "Smith" (as well as "Jones") is a constituent in the propositions expressed by these three sentences, S does not understand precisely what propositions are expressed by each of the sentences. Were he to realize that "Smith" and "Jones" pick out the same person (and were he to know who this person is), he presumably would understand exactly what proposition each of the sentences express and hence would realize, for example, that (2) and (3) express the same proposition. But by hypothesis he doesn't realize that "Smith" and "Jones" pick out the same person, and accordingly he need not understand, nor believe, the exact proposition expressed by, for example, (1) and (2). He need not, in other words, believe contradictory, singular propositions.[18]

Here again, to say that S does not understand exactly which singular proposition is being expressed by each one of these sentences is not to say that S might not have a fairly good "feel" for the singular propositions being expressed. Moreover, he might well believe *de re* of the proposition expressed by (1) that it is true and also believe *de re* of the proposition expressed by (2) that it is true, even though these propositions are contradictory. Likewise, he might well believe *de re* of Smith herself (and hence of Jones) that she is a spy and also believe *de re* of her that she is not a spy. He might believe this, for instance, by virtue of believing *that* the person who is picked out by his use of the name "Smith" (i.e., given the direct reference view, the person who stands in the appropriate causal relation to his use of the name "Smith") is a spy and by virtue of believing *that* the person who is picked out by his use of the name "Jones" (i.e., the person who stands in the appropriate causal relation to his use of the name "Jones") is not a spy.[19] But insofar as S does have such *de re* beliefs either about the propositions expressed by (1) and (2) or about Smith (and Jones), the beliefs—like other *de re* beliefs about remote objects—need not be genuinely (i.e., irreducibly) contradictory.

So, the claim that proper names are directly referential and the accompanying claim that sentences containing proper names as their subjects express singular propositions, even if acceptable, are of no help in generating examples of genuinely contradictory beliefs. Accordingly, we are left still with no convincing examples of contradictory beliefs.

However, I suppose it might be charged that given my approach the failure to find convincing examples is hardly surprising. After all, don't all the responses I have made to purported linguistic examples of contradictory beliefs in effect simply assume that it is impossible to have contradictory beliefs? In particular, hasn't my strategy in effect been simply to claim that with respect to any pair of sentences that express contradictory propositions, a person *S must* either not understand exactly what proposition is being expressed by at least one of the sentences or not really believe one of the sentences to be true? But, it might be claimed, if we don't initially assume that it is impossible to have contradictory beliefs, is there any reason to think one of these disjuncts must be true? And if not, doesn't my discussion beg the question?

I think not. The above discussions, of both linguistic and nonlinguistic examples, present a challenge. The challenge is to describe a convincing example of a person with contradictory beliefs. That is, the challenge is to describe an example that cannot be explained away, and explained away relatively easily, in one of the ways I have suggested. In particular, I have suggested that *any* purported example of a person having contradictory beliefs plausibly can be understood as a case where either (1) the person has inconsistent but not contradictory beliefs; or (2) the person believes *p* although his behavior may make it seem as if he also believes not *p* ; or (3) the person now believes *p* although at a earlier time, perhaps only a slightly earlier time, he believed not *p;* or (4) the person believes *p* although in some other sense, perhaps an unconscious, repressed sense, he believes not *p;* or (5) the person has contradictory *de re* beliefs about an object that is epistemically remote with respect to these beliefs, where such *de re* beliefs are reducible to noncontradictory *de dicto* or *de se* beliefs; or (6) the person believes two sentences to be true, where the sentences express contradictory propositions but where in addition the person does not understand precisely what proposition at least one of the sentences expressed.

There is a simple way to respond to this challenge. Describe some situation in which it initially appears as if the person may have genuinely contradictory beliefs but in which this initial appearance cannot be explained away plausibly in any of the ways (1)–(6). My claim is that this cannot be done.

IV

For convenience let us ignore the complications posed by *de re* beliefs, *de se* beliefs, and linguistic beliefs. Simply assume that the phrase *"S* believes *p"* refers to cases where *S* fully understands a proposition *p* and believes the proposition to be true. With this restriction in mind, consider whether it is possible for a person to believe *p* and to believe also the proposition that he falsely believes *p*. Is it impossible for a person to have both these beliefs? In other words, is the following principle true?

5. $\sim \Diamond (\mathrm{B}sp \ \& \ \mathrm{B}s(\mathrm{B}sp \ \& \ \mathrm{not} \ p))$.

I think that it is. Indeed, the truth of 5 can be deduced from the principles already defended. For purposes of a *reductio,* assume that 5 is false. Assume, in other words, that it is possible for (a) to be true.

(a) Bsp & Bs(Bsp & not p)

From (a) follows (b) and (c):

(b) Bsp

(c) Bs(Bsp and not p).

Using principle 3, the following can be deduced from (c):

(d) Bs not p.

But given principle 1, it is impossible for both (b) and (d) to be true. That is, it is impossible to have contradictory beliefs. So, contrary to what was initially assumed, (a) must not be possible and hence 5 must be true. It is impossible for a person to believe p and at the same time to believe that he falsely believes p.

A corollary of principle 5 is that it is impossible for a person to believe truly that he believes p falsely. If "B*sp" is used to imply that S believes p and p is true, then this corollary of 5 can be expressed as follows:

6. $\sim\diamond(B^*s(Bsp \text{ \& not } p))$[20]

The truth of 6 is at least somewhat surprising. After all, it obviously is possible for a person S to believe p falsely. It is thus tempting to think that it should be equally possible for him to be in the state of believing p falsely and at the same time believe that he is in that state. Others can believe that S in such a state. Why, it is tempting to ask, couldn't S also believe that he is in this state?

There is a quick answer to this question. Namely, someone other than S can believe that S falsely believes p without having contradictory beliefs; but if S were to believe this, he would have to have contradictory beliefs, and this is impossible.

Moreover, the truth of 6 becomes less surprising when one realizes that there are other true propositions dealing with the psychological states of a person S that others can believe but that S himself cannot believe. For example, others can believe the true proposition that S has forgotten that the name of his best friend is "Harry," but S cannot believe this true proposition. He cannot, that is, believe the true proposition that he himself has forgotten that his best friend's name is "Harry."[21]

Similarly, it is not particularly surprising that it should be impossible for S to believe truly that he believes p falsely, even though it is possible for him to believe p falsely.

Moreover, it is this impossibility that provides a solution for Moore's paradox. G. E. Moore worried that although a sentence of the form "S believes p but p is false" can be true, it is at the very least extremely odd for S himself to assert the sentence. But if the sentence can be true, why is it so odd for S to assert it?

The answer is provided by 6. The oddness is caused by the fact that it is impossible for both what the sentence asserts to be true and for S to believe it to be true.

Of course, it is not at all odd for S to assert what in fact he does not believe or what in fact is not true. This happens whenever S either sincerely asserts something false or tries to deceive his listeners about what he believes. But when it is impossible for S to believe a proposition and for the proposition to be true, there *is* something odd about S asserting a sentence expressing that proposition. Asserting a sentence normally has two closely related functions. One is to make a claim about the world and the second is to report what the speaker believes about the world. But if S asserts a sentence of the form "Bsp and not p," the listener can deduce that one of these functions is thwarted. Either it is not the case that (Bsp and not p) or S does not believe this to be the case. In this way, S asserting a sentence of the form "Bsp and not p" tends to be self-defeating. It tends to be self-defeating in just the same way that a person's asserting "I have forgotten that 'Harry' is the name of my best friend" tends to be self-defeating.

CONCLUSION

A belief is a mental state that, to put the point metaphorically, "aims at truth."[22] More than anything else it is this quality of belief that accounts for the truth of the principles I have been defending. And it is the fact that other kinds of mental states lack this quality that account for why some of the principles I have been defending do not have analogues for other kinds of mental states. It is possible, for example, to think about a proposition p without regarding it as true. It likewise is possible to desire p or to be afraid that p without regarding p as true. Accordingly, it is possible to think about two contradictory propositions, p and not p, and to desire each, and to be afraid that each is true.[23] But to believe each, it is necessary to regard the world as being such that each in fact is true. It is this distinctive mark of belief that makes it impossible to have contradictory beliefs, even though it is impossible to have contradictory thoughts, desires, and fears.[24]

For convenience, I summarize the principles I have defended:

1. $\sim\Diamond$(Bsp & Bs not p).
2. $\sim\Diamond$(Bs(p & not p)).
3. $\Box$(If Bs(p & q) then Bsp & Bsq).
4. $\Diamond$(Bsp & Bsq & not Bs(p & q)).
5. $\sim\Diamond$(Bsp & Bs(Bsp & not p)).
6. $\sim\Diamond$(B*s (Bsp & not p)).

Notes

1. Cf. John Williams, "Believing the Self-Contradictory," *American Philosophical Quarterly* 19 (1982): 279-85, who used "self-contradictory" in much the same way as I use "inconsistent." As a result, he has little trouble finding examples of "self-contradictory" beliefs.

2. Cf. Wilfred Hodges, *Logic* (New York, 1977), 15.

3. An analogous principle is true for epistemic rationality. That is, it can be epistemically rational for S to believe p and epistemically rational for S to believe q without it being epistemically rational to believe (p & q). See Richard Foley, "Justified Inconsistent Beliefs," *American Philosophical Quarterly* 16 (1979): 247-57.

4. See Robert Audi, "Believing and Affirming," *Mind* 91 (1982): 115-20, for further discussion of this distinction.

5. Roderick M. Chisholm, *The First Person* (Minneapolis, 1981, esp. 107-81; Ernest Sosa, "Propositional Attitudes *De Dicto* and *De Re*," *Journal of Philosophy* 67 (1970): 883-96.

6. Chisholm provides an example of this sort of account as well. Chisholm's view is that the notion of *de re* belief is ambiguous. Very roughly, he thinks that S in a broad sense believes *de re* of O that it has X if S believes that the so-and-so has X, where the so-and-so in fact is O. But in the narrow sense, S believes *de re* of O that it has X only if S in addition can "identify" O as the thing that has X, where "identify" is a epistemic notion. For further details, see *The First Person*, especially 108-20. Also see David Lewis, "Attitudes *De Dicto* and *De Re*," *Philosophical Review* 87 (1979): 513-42, who says that S can have a *de re* belief about O only if he knows of a description of O that either captures the essence of O or captures an acquaintance relation he bears to O (i.e., "an extensive causal relation between S's states and O's states"). Similarly, David Kaplan, "Quantifying In," *Synthese* 19 (1968): 178-216, requires S to have a causal rapport with O in order to have *de re* beliefs about O.

7. W. V. O. Quine, "Quantifiers and Propositional Attitudes," *Journal of Philosophy* 53 (1956); reprinted in Quine, *The Ways of Paradox* (New York, 1966).

8. As I employ the notion, entailment is to be distinguished from a broader notion of implication. Specifically a proposition p entails a proposition q just if p implies q and necessarily whoever believes p also believes q and believes it with as much confidence as p and whoever thinks (i.e., entertains) p also thinks q. Compare with Chisholm's distinction between entailment and implication in *The First Person*, 7.

9. For simplicity I assume here that S's *de re* belief about O that it has X, if reducible at all, is reducible to a *de dicto* belief in a proposition that *uniquely picks out* object O; e.g., the proposition that the so-and-so has X, where the so-and-so is O. But, it is at least possible to hold (although in my opinion not very plausible) that S might believe *de re* of O that it has X by virtue of believing a proposition (or perhaps by believing many such propositions) that implies, for example, that a such-and-such has X, where O is in fact a such-and-such but not the only one and where this fact in conjunction with, say, social or contextual features turn this *de dicto* belief into a belief *de re* about O (rather than about one of the other objects with characteristic such-and-such). With respect to the claims I make about contradictory beliefs, either of these views about how *de re* belief might be reducible to *de dicto* belief will do. On either view, there will be no reason to think that the believed propositions in virtue of which S has contradictory *de re* beliefs will themselves be contradictory.

10. See David Lewis, "Attitudes *De Dicto* and *De Se*." Also, see Chisholm, *The First Person;* John Perry, "Frege on Demonstratives," *Philosophical Review* 86 (1977): 474-97; and Hector-Neri Castaneda, " 'He': A Study in the Logic of Self-Consciousness," *Ratio* 8 (1966): 130-52).

11. However, *if* the mediating characterization in virtue of which S has a *de re* belief about an object O need not uniquely pick out O (see n. 9), it is easier to avoid a commitment to *de se* beliefs.

12. See Lewis, "Attitudes De Dicto, " and Chisholm, *The First Person.*

13. On more restrictive accounts of *de re* belief it might be thought that it is not so easy to have *de re* beliefs about propositions. It might be thought not so easy if, for example, a close causal relationship with an object is a prerequisite of having a *de re* belief about that object (see n. 6). But this depends on one's view of propositions. For example, on Chisholm's view of propositions, which makes a proposition a kind of state of affairs, a person might very well stand in causal interrelations with true propositions (see *The First Person*). Similarly, it is hard to see why one couldn't stand in a close causal relationship with so-called "singular propositions."

14. For the purpose here of trying to find a convincing example of genuinely contradictory beliefs, I assume that if *R* is a successful analysis of a term or phrase *T,* then substituting *R* for *T* in a sentence will not alter the proposition expressed by the sentence. For an attack on this assumption, see Diana Ackerman, "Proper Names, Propositional Attitudes, and Non-descriptive Connotations," *Philosophical Studies* 35 (1979): 55-69.

15. The principle that if a competent speaker of a language *L* assents to a sentence in *L* that expresses the proposition *p* then he believes *p* sometimes is called the "disquotation principle." For another, differently motivated criticism of the disquotation principle, see Ruth Barcan Marcus, "Rationality and Believing the Impossible," *Journal of Philosophy* 80 (1983): 321-38. Also see Saul Kripke, "A Puzzle about Belief," in *Meaning and Use,* edited by A. Margalit (Dordrecht, 1979).

16. Recall that I am distinguishing entailment from a broader notion of implication. See n. 8.

17. See, e.g., David Kaplan, "Quantifying In"; Saul Kripke, "Naming and Necessity," in *Semantics of Natural Language,* edited by D. Davidson and E. Harman (Dordrecht, 1972); Keith Donnellan, "Reference and Definite Descriptions," *Philosophical Review* 75 (1966): 281-304.

18. Similarly, suppose Pierre who is a competent speaker of both French and English believes the French sentence "Londres est jolie" to be true and the English sentence "London is pretty" to be false (see Kripke, "A Puzzle about Belief."). Might Pierre in such a case understand precisely what proposition is expressed by the French sentence? Perhaps. Might he understand precisely what proposition is expressed by the English sentence? Again, the answer is perhaps. What is impossible, I am suggesting, is for (1) the French sentence and the English sentence to express exactly the same proposition, (2) Pierre to understand precisely what proposition each sentence expresses, and (3) Pierre to believe one sentence to be true and the other to be false. (To say that this is impossible is not, however, to solve Kripke's puzzle about belief. As Kripke emphasizes, his puzzle is one that concerns belief ascription. In particular, his puzzle concerns the question of under what conditions a competent speaker by believing a sentence to be true (e.g., "London is not pretty") can be said to believe the proposition expressed by that sentence (e.g., that London is not pretty). One of Kripke's theses is that on any view of proper names—say, a direct reference view or a Fregean view—it is hard to answer this question. I have not been trying to answer this question. Rather, I am doing something more modest—claiming that *if* Pierre by believing true the above English sentence believes the proposition expressed by that sentence, then it is *not* the case that by believing the French sentence "Londres est jolie" he believes the negation of this proposition. On the other hand, if this claim is accepted, it does put a constraint on what would be a plausible answer to Kripke's puzzle.)

19. See Ackerman, "Proper Names," who argues that the analysis of a proper name "*N*" is: "(the entity who stands in relation *R* to '*N*') in alpha," where "*R*" picks out an appropriate causal relation and "alpha" rigidly designates the actual world. However, Ackerman rejects the view that an analysandum and its analysans need be synonymous. Accordingly, she also rejects the view that the sentence "*N* is a spy" and the sentence "(the person who stands in relation *R* to '*N*') in alpha is a spy" need express the same proposition.

20. The proof is as follows. Assume 6 is false. That is, assume, it is possible for (1) to be true: (1) B*s (Bs*p* & not *p*). From (1), it follows that (2) Bs*p* & Bs (Bs*p* & not *p*). But given 5, (2) is impossible. So, (1) must be impossible. In other words, 6 must be true.

21. For convenience I assume here that when S believes that he himself has characteristic X he believes a first-person proposition. But an analogous point can be made if it is assumed instead that when S believes he himself to have X, he has a *de se* belief—that he directly ascribes X to himself. Namely, given this assumption, the point becomes: If X is the property of having forgotten that the name of his best friend is "Harry," others might correctly ascribe this property to S but S cannot correctly ascribe it (as least directly) to himself.

22. This phrase is Bernard Williams's. See "Deciding to Believe," in *Problems of the Self* (Cambridge, 1973).

23. There may, however, be some kinds of desire (as well as other intentional attitudes) that it is not possible to have towards contradictory propositions. Suppose we say that S basically desires proposition p to be true just if he has a positive psychological feeling towards it being true; and let us say that S, all things considered, desires proposition p to be true just if the positive psychological feelings he has towards the nomological prerequisites and consequences of p being true outweigh the negative psychological feelings (i.e., the basic aversions) he has toward these prerequisites and consequences. *If* there are these two senses of desire, it may be possible to have contradictory basic desires (to have a positive psychological feeling both towards a proposition being true and towards its negation being true) even though it is impossible to have contradictory desires, all things considered. Analogous remarks may apply to, for example, wishing and fearing.

24. *Some* of the above principles have analogues for *some* mental states. For example, the simplification rule, principle 3, has an analogue for thinking but not for desiring. It is not possible to think a conjunctive proposition without thinking each conjunct, but it is possible to desire a conjunctive proposition without desiring each conjunct separately.

What Is a Belief State?

CURTIS BROWN

What we believe depends on more than the purely intrinsic facts about us: facts about our environment or context also help determine the contents of our beliefs.[1] This observation has led several writers to hope that beliefs can be divided, as it were, into two components: a "core" that depends only on the individual's intrinsic properties; and a periphery that depends on the individual's context, including his or her history, environment, and linguistic community. Thus Jaegwon Kim suggests that "within each noninternal psychological state that enters into the explanation of some action or behavior we can locate an 'internal core state' which can assume the causal-explanatory role of the noninternal state."[2] In the same vein, Stephen Stich writes that "nonautonomous" states, like belief, are best viewed as "conceptually complex hybrids" made up of an autonomous component together with historical and contextual features.[3] John Perry, whose term I have adopted, distinguishes between belief states, which are determined by an individual's intrinsic properties, and objects of belief, which are not.[4] And Daniel Dennett makes use of the same notion when he asks:[5]

> What, then, is the *organismic contribution* to the fixation of propositional attitudes? How shall we characterize what we get when we subtract facts about context or embedding from the determining whole? This remainder, however we ought to characterize it, is the proper domain of psychology, 'pure' psychology, or in Putnam's phrase, 'psychology in the narrow sense'.

I propose to explore the notion of a belief state. In section I, I will propose an account of the idea of a belief state that is neutral with respect to such questions as how belief states are best characterized and whether they play a central role in psychology or epistemology. In section II, I use this account to describe some recent positions in the philosophy of psychology as sharing the *notion* of a belief state but disagreeing about the *nature* of belief states. The remaining sections develop my own preferred account of how best to characterize belief states. The account I favor takes belief states to be relations between people and semantic or intensional objects. Section III explains why propositions will not do for this purpose: depending on how we specify the relevant propositions, there will either be too many to characterize belief states completely or too few to characterize them essentially. Following David Lewis and Roderick Chisholm, I suggest that belief states are best characterized by properties. Finally, section IV sketches an account of how the properties that characterize one's belief state are determined by one's intrinsic properties. The account of belief states defended in sections III and IV is an important part of a larger account of belief proper—an account that, however, can only be hinted at here.

I

I shall assume without defense that the objects of belief are propositions, and in particular that if a sentence of the form 'Joe believes that S' is true, then the proposition expressed by S is an object of Joe's belief. I believe that this view is correct,[6] but it is certainly a minority view. Those who reject it may want to regard it here as merely a simplifying assumption; it should be possible to adapt my account of the notion of a belief state to any view according to which beliefs have objects (whether propositions or something else) that are determined (in some not necessarily straightforward way) by the 'that'-clauses of true ascriptions of belief.

Dennett's helpful term 'organismic contribution to belief' suggests two conditions that must be met for something to be a belief state. First, a belief state is an *organismic* contribution to belief: it is the organism's contribution to belief, not the environment's. We might put this by saying that one's belief state depends only on one's *intrinsic* properties. An "intrinsic property" of an organism is one that involves only facts solely about the organism. Facts about the organism's environment are wholly irrelevant to its intrinsic properties. Seeing an apple does not depend only on intrinsic properties of an organism, since whether one sees an apple depends not only on facts solely about one's body, but also on whether one's environment includes an apple. For precisely the same reason, believing a singular proposition about something in one's environment does not depend only on one's intrinsic properties. Further, the belief state of an organism at a time should involve only properties of the organism *at that time*. Thus we have *condition 1:* the belief state of an organism at a time should supervene on the intrinsic properties of the organism at that time.

Second, a belief state is an organismic *contribution to belief.* One believes the things one does because of the total state one is in. But not every facet of one's total state contributes to determining what one believes. One's belief state does not depend on facts about one, such as whether one's body has an odd or even number of water molecules, which make no contribution to what one believes. The notion of a belief state must be such as to allow that if all the intrinsic facts about me were exactly as they are except that my left big toe contained one less water molecule, I would be in the same belief state I am in fact in. Thus we have *condition 2:* a belief state must be a state of the organism that depends only on those facts about the organism that are relevant to what it believes.

Both of these requirements rule that certain facts are irrelevant to what belief state one is in. They give information about the conditions under which one is in a particular belief state.

Suppose that I am at the moment in a particular belief state. Under what circumstances would I be in this belief state? We know already of one set of circumstances in which I am in it: the actual one. But there are more. Some conditions met by my present circumstances do not need to be met for me to be in the same belief state. If we rule that certain facts about my present situation are irrelevant to what belief state I am in, we thereby increase the number of circumstances in which I would be in it.

Some such facts are ruled out by the first condition. Only facts solely about me are relevant to what belief state I am in. No matter how the facts about my environment alter, as long as the intrinsic facts about me remain the same, my belief state remains the same. According to the first condition, then, I would be in the same belief state in all those circumstances in which, however different my environment might be, the intrinsic facts about me remain the same.

The second condition relaxes the conditions on my being in the same belief state still further. Not all the intrinsic facts about me are relevant: just those facts a difference in which would involve a difference in what I believe. Thus the circumstances in which I would be in the same belief state include not only those in which my environment differs but also those in which the intrinsic facts about me differ in ways that do not affect what I believe.

Let us now try to make this intuitive picture a little more precise. I will employ some quasi-technical abbreviations that are admittedly no more precise than the English expressions they abbreviate. Nevertheless, they are helpful because the complexity of the account, despite the simplicity of its basic idea, makes it difficult to state unambiguously in ordinary English.

I begin by dividing the world up in a mildly unusual way. The facts that determine what an individual believes divide into facts solely about the individual and facts about the individual's environment or situation. So we need two theoretical notions. First, we need the notion of the *total intrinsic state,* or simply "total state" for short, of a person, at a time, in a world. Let

'TS' be a variable over total intrinsic states, and let 'TS(x,t,w)' denote the TS of person x, at time t, in world w. For vividness only, I will think of a total state as a concrete, momentary, physical entity. (We could almost think of a total state as a time-world slice of an individual. But not quite: the facts about a total state do not include facts about whose state it is. TS(me, now, the actual world) is the very same total state as TS(Twin Curtis, now, the actual world), although our current time-world slices are different.)

Our second notion is that of a *situation*. The situation of x, at t, in w— S(x,t,w)—is the sum of the intrinsic facts about x's environment up to t, including the environment's and x's own past history. S(x,t,w) includes all the intrinsic facts about w, up to and including time t, *except* those that constitute TS(x,t,w). Again for vividness, I will think of a situation as a concrete physical entity. If possible worlds are thought of as concrete, we can get the situation of x at t in w by taking w, cutting off everything after t, and then cutting out the stage of x at t.

A TS and an S together determine a set of propositions P. Let P(TS,S) be the set of those propositions P such that, for all x, necessarily, if x is in TS and x's situation is S, then x believes P. If we ignore complications introduced because situations contain facts about a world only up to a certain time, and we think of situations and total states as concrete building blocks, then we can visualize P(TS,S) as follows: TS and S fit together to form a world, and P is the set of propositions believed in that world by the person of whom TS is a slice (at the time of the gap into which TS was inserted).

Recall Putnam's Twin Earth example.[7] I believe that water is wet; but were I on Putnam's Twin Earth in the very same TS I am in fact in, I would believe instead that XYZ is wet. The very same TS, embedded in different contexts, warrants different belief ascriptions. We might diagram this situation as shown in the accompanying figure (letting 'ts_1' name a particular total state, the one I am in now). Here, s_1 is a particular situation—my actual situation, let us say. Then p_1 is the set of propositions that my actual total intrinsic state, ts_1, determines in s_1; that is, $p_1 = P(tis_1, s_1)$. Assuming, as seems plausible, that my total state together with all the facts about my environment, including my own past history, determines all the things I believe,[8] p_1 will be the set of all the things I actually believe. Thus p_1 includes the proposition that water is wet, but not the proposition that XYZ is wet.

Now s_2 is another situation—perhaps the situation of my Twin Earth counterpart. p_2 is then the set of propositions determined by my actual total state, ts_1, together with that situation. p_2 will be the set of propositions

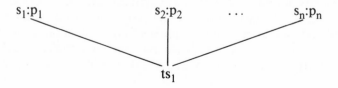

believed by my Twin Earth counterpart—including the proposition that XYZ is wet, but not the proposition that water is wet.

The list of situations is then extended to include all the situations, actual and possible, into which ts_1 could be fitted. (The list will include, for example, a counterfactual situation in which I myself grow up on a planet where XYZ fills the lakes. The set of propositions determined by ts_1 and *that* situation will be like p_2 and unlike p_1 in containing the proposition that water is wet; but it will be like p_1 and unlike p_2 in containing the proposition that I, CB, am named 'Curtis'. Instead, p_2 contains the proposition that Twin Curtis is named 'Curtis'.)

Now, condition 1 says that I am in the same belief state, no matter what situation I am in, provided that I am in ts_1. But according to condition 2, there are also other total states that I (or others) could be in and be in the same belief state: namely, all those total states that make no difference to my beliefs. A total state would make a difference to my beliefs if there were *some* situation in which it led to different propositions believed. So those total states that make no difference to what I believe are those for which there is no situation in which they produce different propositions believed than ts_1: namely, all those TS such that $P(TS,s_1) = p_1$, $P(TS,s_2) = p_2, \ldots , P(TS,s_n) = p_n$.

The belief state I am actually in, then, is the state anyone would be in if and only if they were in one of the total intrinsic states just described. For at least some, and perhaps all, purposes we could simply identify this state with the corresponding set of total intrinsic states, just as for at least some and perhaps all purposes we can identify the property of being wooden with the set of all actual and possible wooden things. We can then generalize our account as follows: the belief state of individual x, at time t, and in world w —$BS(x,t,w)$—is the set of all those TS such that: for all S, if $P(TS(x,t,w),S) = Q$, then $P(TS,S) = Q$. In something closer to English, x's belief state (at time t and in world w) is the set of total states that determine, with respect to any situation, the same propositions x's total state (at t and in w) determines with respect to that situation.

My belief state, then, is determined as follows. First, consider the total state I am actually in. Next, consider what beliefs that TS would give me (or others) in all situations of interest. Finally, consider the set of all the TS's that would produce exactly the same beliefs as my actual TS, no matter what the situation. This set of TS's is my belief state.

So my current belief state is the set of all those total states that would produce, in my actual situation, the belief that water is wet (but not the belief that XYZ is wet), together with all the other beliefs I have in the actual situation, *and* would produce, in the Twin-Earth situation, the belief that XYZ is wet (but not that water is wet), together with all the other beliefs of my Twin-Earth counterpart.

It may be helpful to compare my belief state with my weight state. Consider first the TS I am actually in. Next, consider what weights that TS would produce in all situations of interest (on the Earth, on the Moon, if the Earth were twice as big, etc.). Finally, consider the set of TS's that would produce the same weights as my actual TS, no matter what the situation. Some of these will specify shortness and fatness, some tallness and slenderness; some will specify that their possessor be made of flesh, some that it be made of stone. The set of all of them is my weight state. Or, perhaps more clearly, what they all share and nothing else does is my weight state.

As it happens, weight states are very interesting and important for physics, for a particular weight state is just the property of having a particular mass. Belief states *may* turn out to be as important for psychology as weight states are for physics. But nothing said so far guarantees that they will be. There may be nothing of interest shared by all and only the total states that make up one's belief state. Belief states as here defined would still *exist,* but would be of no systematic importance—like the scattered object consisting of my left thumb and a certain beetle in Africa, or like the property of being a Virgo.

II

We have reached an account of what it could mean to talk about "belief states" or about the "organismic contribution to belief." A good deal of recent discussion can be understood as addressed, more or less explicitly, to the question how best to *characterize* belief states so understood, or what the *nature* of belief states is. We have thought of one's belief state as a set of total intrinsic states: those states, roughly, in which one would believe the same things as in one's actual state, no matter what the circumstances. The question of what the nature of a belief state is might then be understood as the question of what, if anything, these total intrinsic states have in common *besides* the fact that one believes the same things in each of them. If they do share something interesting, then it will seem plausible that it is in virtue of that something that a person in a given belief state believes the things she or he does.

An analogy may help make this clear. We can pick out a certain collection of physical states of material objects as those states that produce in us the sensation of red; and we might then call the whole collection the "state of being red." If all the states in the collection (and no others) share some interesting feature, then it will seem reasonable to say that it is because of that feature that objects appear red to us, and redness will seem to be an intrinsic property of objects. If the states do not share such a feature, then it will seem that the "state of being red" is a gerrymandered state hardly deserving the name at all; redness will seem to be irreducibly a relational property, a property an object has just in case it affects people in a certain way.

Similarly, if the physical states comprised by a given belief state (and no others) share some interesting feature, then it will seem natural to say that it is in virtue of possessing that feature that one believes the things one does, and belief will seem to be an intrinsic property of individuals. If they do not, then "belief states" will seem hardly to be states at all, and belief will seem to be irreducibly relational.

If there is an intrinsic property of redness, then it will be reasonable to say that if things had been different—if people had been constructed differently—redness might have looked blue; if not, there will seem to be a necessary connection between being red and looking red. Similarly, it will seem natural to say that one's belief that P might not have been a belief that P just in case there is an intrinsic property of individuals in virtue of which they believe the things they do.

Recent views about the nature of belief states divide into three groups. First, it may be that they simply have no nature: the various total states that constitute a belief state may share nothing but some long, disjunctive physical property. The "organismic contribution" to belief may simply not be interesting by itself, just as the object's contribution to redness may not be interesting by itself. This seems to be the view of Gareth Evans[9] and of some Wittgensteinian writers;[10] it also seems to be the view of those who think that cognitive psychology needs to devise its own theoretical terms and that these will have no interesting connection with the folk psychological notion of belief. This view is held by Paul and Patricia Churchland[11] and is entertained seriously by Stich.[12] Second, it may be that what the states that constitute the belief state share is somehow specifiable formally or syntactically, as a relation between the believer and a sentence in a "language of thought." This seems to be the view of Jerry Fodor and Hartry Field,[13] and is entertained by Stich, who calls it the "modified Panglossian prospect."[14] Finally, it may be that belief states are best characterized as relations to semantically defined objects such as propositions or properties. This sort of view is at least suggested by work of Robert Stalnaker and David Lewis,[15] and it is a view of this sort that I propose to explore.

The most obvious candidates for semantic objects that characterize our belief states are the propositions we believe. But these propositions clearly do not characterize our belief states essentially. That is the moral of examples like Putnam's: since I could be in the same belief state but believe different propositions, the propositions I in fact believe are not essential to my belief state. This is one reason why many have found the view that belief states are best characterized by semantic objects implausible.

But it would be fainthearted to abandon the idea of a semantic characterization for this reason. Granted, the same belief state yields different propositions believed in different situations. It may nevertheless be that there are *some* propositions that a given belief state determines in *every* situation, and it may be that these provide the characterization we seek.

The leading idea of the account of belief I favor is that of an *immediate object of belief*. Among the things I believe, some are believed indirectly or mediately. The belief that water is wet, the belief that I am married to Karen, the belief that Aristotle wrote the Nicomachean Ethics—all these I believe indirectly, since I could be in the same belief state and yet not believe them. Had I grown up on Twin Earth calling XYZ 'water' I would now believe that XYZ is wet, not that water is. Some of my beliefs, then, differ between the actual situation and the counterfactual one. But surely others of my beliefs hold constant across them, and surely it is in virtue of some of these more constant beliefs—such as the belief that the odorless substance that fills the lakes and is called 'water' is wet—that I believe in the one situation that water is wet, and in the other that XYZ is wet. I suggest that there are some propositions that I believe in every situation in which I am in the same belief state; and that it is in virtue of believing these, together with the varying facts of the situations I could find myself in, that I believe in those situations the rest of the propositions I believe in them. These constant propositions are the immediate objects of belief.

We can define the notion of an immediate object of belief as follows. A proposition P is a (partial) immediate object of (say) Joe's belief just in case, for any possible situation S, if Joe is in the same belief state in S he is actually in, then Joe believes P in S. One's *total* immediate object of belief is then simply the collection of all one's partial immediate objects of belief.

Suppose we want to find an illuminating and helpful way to characterize belief states by means of semantic objects. What is it exactly that we want? I suggest that it is a means of determining, given only intrinsic facts about an individual, a set of semantic objects such that: (1) anyone in the same belief state will determine the same objects—that is, the objects characterize the belief state *essentially*; (2) no one in a different belief state determines exactly the same objects—that is, the objects characterize the belief state *completely*; and (3) the facts about these special objects, together with the facts about one's environment, determine the facts about what one believes in that environment.

My initial hope was that the semantic objects that would meet these conditions would be propositions—in particular, the immediate objects of belief. But it appears that no set of propositions can satisfy both (1) and (2). So the account I will offer is slightly more complex.

This account involves two related notions. The first is the notion of an immediate object of belief. The second, adapted from David Lewis and Roderick Chisholm,[16] is the notion of the property (immediately) self-ascribed by an individual. The total property self-ascribed by an individual is what essentially and completely characterizes the individual's belief state. One's total immediate object of belief characterizes *one's being* in a particular belief state rather than the belief state itself; and it determines, in conjunction with contextual features, the rest of one's beliefs. But the two are intimately connected: from one's total immediate object of belief it is possible to recover one's total self-ascribed property; and one's total self-ascribed property, together with who (and when) one is, determines one's total immediate object of belief.

In the remainder of this paper I will do two things. In section III I will explain why it seems impossible to find a set of propositions that characterizes one's belief state both essentially and completely. Reflection on this difficulty will lead to the notion of a self-ascribed property as what best characterizes one's belief state. In section IV, I will sketch an account of how one's intrinsic properties determine one's total self-ascribed property.

III

One's total immediate object of belief, as I have defined it, does not characterize one's belief state essentially. I believe that I am named 'Curtis'. Very likely I would believe this in any situation in which I were in the same belief state I am actually in, so the proposition that I am named 'Curtis' is an immediate object of my belief. Nevertheless, although *I* cannot be in this belief state without believing that I am named 'Curtis', someone else can be. My Twin Earth counterpart is in exactly the same belief state I am in, but does not believe that I am named 'Curtis'—indeed, he has no beliefs about me at all. So although *my being in* this belief state is essentially characterized by the proposition that I am named 'Curtis', the belief state itself is not. Of course, if any partial immediate object does not characterize my belief state essentially, neither does my total immediate object of belief.

The definition of 'immediate object of belief' could be modified so as to avoid this result. We could say that an immediate object of my belief is a proposition which anyone in my belief state would believe in any situation. But given this definition, my total immediate object of belief does not characterize my belief state completely.

For consider: Twin Curtis and I are in the same belief state. I believe that I am named 'Curtis', but not that Twin Curtis is; Twin Curtis believes that *he* is named 'Curtis' but not that I am. There must be something about the belief state we share in virtue of which we believe these different propositions. If our belief state can be completely characterized by means of immediate objects of belief, then there must be some immediate object of belief that we share and in virtue of which we indirectly believe these different propositions. But it seems that there is no such proposition.

The needed proposition cannot be the proposition that the sentence "I am named 'Curtis' " is true: I know that the sentence is true or false only relative to context. Do I believe that the proposition the sentence expresses *in the present context* is true? Let us pass over for the moment problems about direct belief of singular propositions about the present time. There are many different present contexts—for instance, one for me and a different one for Twin Curtis. So perhaps what I really believe is that the sentence "I am named 'Curtis' " is true in the context I am now in. But then our semantic ascent has accomplished nothing. This cannot be the proposition both Twin Curtis and I believe in virtue of which each of us believes that he is named 'Curtis': Twin Curtis does not believe that he is named 'Curtis' in virtue of believing that the sentence "I am named 'Curtis' is true in the context *I* am now in.

We were evidently wrong to think that the immediate belief we seek is metalinguistic. It might be thought instead that Twin Curtis and I each believe that the unique person who satisfies a certain description is named 'Curtis'. But surely we don't, for we acknowledge that any description we immediately believe we satisfy may be satisfied by someone else as well. Nor does each of us believe that he is named 'Curtis' in virtue of believing that all people who satisfy some description are named 'Curtis', for any description I immediately believe I satisfy could be satisfied by someone who is not really named 'Curtis', and I am aware of this.

If we now take the subjects of attitudes to be person stages rather than people proper, we may construct similar examples involving different stages of the same person rather than different people. I will present an example showing that if we do not allow singular propositions about oneself (where 'oneself' may refer to a temporal stage of a person), we cannot find propositions in virtue of immediately believing which we believe indirectly some singular propositions about the present time.

Consider first an example that might be thought not to work. In situation 1, Andrea believes, at t_1, that it is then raining. In (counterfactual) situation 2, Andrea is in exactly the same belief state as in situation 1, but she believes at t_2, a different time than t_1, that it is *then* raining. In situation 1, Andrea does not immediately believe the proposition that it is raining at t_1, since she is in the same belief state in situation 2 but does not believe that proposition. If we are to characterize her belief state, we need something that stays constant across situations 1 and 2.

Let S be the sentence 'It is now raining', P_1 be the proposition that it is raining at t_1, and P_2 be the proposition that it is raining at t_2. If Andrea's belief state can be characterized in terms of propositions, then there must be a proposition Q that she believes in both situations and in virtue of which she believes P_1 in S_1 and P_2 in S_2.

In most such examples, it is plausible that there is an immediate object of belief Q in virtue of which Andrea believes the things she does. We typically identify the present time, I suggest, as the time at which we have a total experience of a certain character. Let F characterize Andrea's total experience. Then she believes in both S_1 and S_2 that it is raining at the time at which she has F. But the time at which she has F is different in S_1 than in S_2, so in virtue of this immediate belief she has different mediate beliefs in the two situations.

But even if this strategy works for the present example, it will not always work. For consider the following case. Sarah is the subject of a psychological experiment. The experimenters have discovered that by means of a particularly effective hypnotic technique they can get people to relive experiences they have had in the past so exactly that there is no difference at all between the original experience and its later counterpart. They explain this carefully to Sarah. They tell her that on a cold day in January they will take her into their laboratory, hook her up to a variety of devices, and then do nothing but monitor her. On a hot day the following July they will take her into the same laboratory, hook her up to the same devices, and then recreate exactly the same experience she had the previous January. In January, brought into the room and hooked up, she thinks: this is the first time that I have had just this experience, but I will have it again next July. The following summer, hooked up again, she thinks: this is the first time that I have had just this experience, but I will have it again next July. Thus if the character of her experience is F, then at each time she knows that there are two times at which she has F, but also thinks each time that she has never had F before.

Suppose that at both times Sarah accepts the sentence "It is now cold outside." There seems to be no immediate propositional belief on the basis of which she accepts this sentence. She does not believe that it is cold outside at *the* time at which she has F, since she believes that there are two such times. Nor does she believe that it is cold outside at *all* times at which she has F, since she believes that she has F once when it is hot. She does believe that it is cold outside at the *first* time at which she has F. Does this give her reason to accept "It is now cold outside"? Not unless she also has reason to accept "It is now the first time at which I have F." But if she identifies the current moment as the first time at which she has F, then it seems that the only propositional basis for accepting the latter sentence would be the proposition that the first time at which she has F is the first time at which she has F, and this is no help at all. It seems that there simply is no propositional belief on the basis of which she accepts the sentence "It is now cold outside"; thus, on the revised definition of 'immediate object of belief' we have been considering, there are not enough immediate objects of Sarah's belief to characterize her belief states completely.

Let us revert to the official definition of an immediate object of belief, and let us take the relevant subjects of belief to be temporal stages of Sarah rather than Sarah as a whole. Then we can suggest that in January, the January-stage of Sarah immediately believes that she (it?) exists at a time at which it is cold. In July, the July-stage of Sarah believes that *it* exists at a time at which it is cold. We now have enough immediate beliefs to fully characterize Sarah's belief state. But too much information, rather than too little, is now captured in the immediate objects of one's belief, so that Sarah's immediate objects of belief do not characterize her belief state essentially. The two Sarah-stages are in exactly the same belief state but do not have the same immediate objects of belief.[17]

Thus it seems that no matter what set of propositions we term one's "immediate object of belief," it will either fail to characterize one's belief state essentially or it will fail to characterize it completely. Is there anything that does both? The account offered by David Lewis and Roderick Chisholm offers hope. I will discuss Lewis's version of this account.

On Lewis's view, belief states are characterized not by the propositions we immediately believe but by the properties we or our temporal stages "self-ascribe." In both winter and summer, temporal stages of Sarah self-ascribe the property of existing at a time at which it is cold outside. The property may be thought of as a set of "centered worlds,"[18] in this case worlds centered on a person-stage that exists at a time at which it is cold outside.

When one self-ascribes a property, one thereby believes that one is the center of one of the centered worlds in the set that constitutes the property. Thus one believes the proposition that one has the property in question. This proposition is an immediate object of one's belief, in my sense, since one believes it in any situation in which one is in the same belief state. Again, it is a proposition that one believes but does not believe in virtue of believing anything else. We have seen that such propositions do not characterize belief states essentially, since someone else could be in the same belief state without believing the same propositions. If Lewis is correct, however, anyone in the same belief state will (immediately) self-ascribe the same properties.

The transition from the account I have given of the immediate objects of belief to the properties that characterize belief states is quite smooth and natural, given the account of belief states in section I. On my account, the immediate objects of one's belief are those propositions that one believes in any situation in which one is in the same belief state. Call this the "official definition." It is instructive to consider the relation between the official definition and an alternative that bears some resemblance to what Lewis and Robert Stalnaker mean by the term 'object of belief'. On this second formulation, the total immediate object of someone's belief is the proposition true at all and only those worlds in which one is in the same belief state one is actually in and all one's beliefs are true. Call this formulation the "alternative definition."

The alternative definition sorts most propositions into the immediate/ mediate categories in the same way the official definition does. Consider first a proposition that Ralph believes but that is not an immediate object of his belief: the proposition that water fills the lakes. It is not an immediate object of Ralph's belief on the official definition, since Ralph does *not* believe it in every situation in which he is in the same belief state: there are Twin-Earth-type situations in which Ralph is in the same belief state but believes rather that XYZ fills the lakes. Also it is not an immediate object of Ralph's belief on the alternative definition, for there are worlds in which Ralph is in the same belief state he is actually in, and all his beliefs are true, but XYZ rather than water fills the lakes.

Consider next a proposition that *is* an immediate object of Ralph's belief. Let us suppose that the proposition that 'Ralph has arthritis in his thigh' is true is such a proposition. If so, it satisfies the official definition — it is a proposition that Ralph believes in any situation in which he is in the same belief state. But then it also satisfies the alternative definition: if Ralph believes it in every world in which he is in the same belief state, then it must be true in every world in which he is in the same belief state and all his beliefs are true.

The strange case of Sarah shows that the official definition does not provide enough immediate objects of belief to say what it is about Sarah's belief state that remains the same at the two times at which she has the same experience. But Sarah's case also poses an instructive difficulty for the alternative definition: it gives us no clear advice on how to classify certain worlds. Consider the world at which Sarah has the same experience at two different times. And suppose that in the actual world the experiment failed, so that in fact Sarah had the experience in question only once. Is the world in which she had it twice a world in which she is in the same belief state and all her beliefs are true? It depends on which of the occasions when she was in the same belief state we consider. In January she was in the relevant belief state, and all her beliefs (let us suppose) were true; whereas in July she was in exactly the same belief state, but at least one of her beliefs — the belief that it was cold outside — was false. Yet both of these situations are located in the same possible world.[19]

Earlier I compared situations with possible worlds having holes in them. Take the possible world we have just been considering: cut out the relevant stage of Sarah in January and you get the first situation; cut out the relevant stage of Sarah in July and you get the second situation. Plug a Sarah-stage in the relevant belief state into situation 1, and you get a Sarah-stage all of whose beliefs are true; plug the same Sarah-stage into situation 2, and you get a Sarah-stage one of whose beliefs is false.

Situations are similar to the "centered worlds" introduced by Quine and discussed by Lewis. Just as there are many centered worlds for each possible world, so there are many situations for each possible world.

The natural move here seems to be to take as basic not possible worlds but situations. What characterizes one's belief state is not the set of possible worlds that constitutes one's total immediate object of belief, but rather the set of situations in which all the beliefs of anyone in the same belief state one is actually in are true. When we first began considering belief states, we found that the notions we needed were that of a state of a person and that of a situation, which might be regarded as a state of the person's environment. These now seem again to be the notions we need to characterize belief states: possible worlds have just gotten in the way.

The picture that emerges from this discussion is one of belief as a three-tiered rather than a two-tiered phenomenon. Instead of having two levels only, those of mediate and immediate belief, we have three: mediate belief, immediate belief, and self-ascription. We believe the things we believe mediately in virtue of believing other things immediately; and some of the things we believe immediately, we believe in virtue of self-ascribing properties.

This can be illustrated as follows. I believe that I am in San Antonio. This is a belief in a singular proposition about San Antonio, and so not an immediate belief. I believe it in virtue of certain further beliefs: for instance, the belief that I am in a town called 'San Antonio'. This latter proposition may be an immediate object of my belief, one I believe but not in virtue of believing anything else. Still this proposition does not characterize my belief state essentially, since others in the same belief state need not believe the proposition that I am in a town called 'San Antonio'. What characterizes my belief state essentially is not the proposition I believe immediately but rather my self-ascription of the property of living in a town called 'San Antonio'.

There is an easy way to derive one's total self-ascribed property from one's total immediate object of belief. For any person-stage x, we can express x's total immediate object of belief by means of a sentence of the form 'x is F'. We can see this as follows. Some of x's immediate objects of belief will be propositions that x has a certain property; some will be propositions that something is the case at a time t; and all will be propositions of some sort or other. So all ascriptions of immediate belief will have one or another of the following forms:

x immediately believes that x is F
x immediately believes that Q at t
x immediately believes that P.

The first is already in the desired form. For the second, let F be 'exists at a time at which Q'. All remaining cases have the third form; for them let F be 'is such that P' or 'exists in a world in which P'.

Now, if x's total immediate object of belief is the proposition that x is F, then, I suggest, x's belief state is essentially and completely characterized by the property F, the total property self-ascribed by x. Conversely, if x's belief state is essentially and completely characterized by F, then x's total immediate object of belief is the proposition that x is F.

IV

We now have a sketch of an account of belief that takes the notion of an immediately self-ascribed property as basic. But this fundamental notion has been left somewhat obscure. In particular, we need an account of the relation between the intrinsic properties that ground one's belief state and the property that characterizes it. How do the intrinsic facts about me determine the relevant property?

Let us begin by pretending that we are trying to find how one's intrinsic properties determine a set of propositions (the immediate objects of one's belief) rather than of properties. We will be led back to properties soon enough; but it is simpler to begin by considering propositions, and the eventual modification will be minor.

The account we now seek would tell us how to get from information about someone's belief state to information about what propositions are immediate objects of that person's belief. Belief states are in this respect analogous to sentences. Sentences express (in context) propositions, and a semantics of sentences tells us how to get from information about sentences to information about the propositions they express. (A compositional semantics will tell us, for instance, that 'P & Q' is true in any possible world just in case P is true in that world and Q is true in that world.) So it may be appropriate to call the account we seek a "semantics of belief states."

This analogy suggests that consideration of semantics proper may help us to find the sort of account we need of the immediate objects of belief. It is helpful to begin by considering an oversimple picture of the semantics of sentences. This picture is sometimes associated with the term 'procedural semantics'.[20]

The picture begins from the idea that the meaning of a sentence is the proposition it expresses and that propositions are functions from possible worlds to truth values. Sentences mean what people mean by them. So it may seem natural to suppose that what a sentence means (for a person) is a function from worlds to truth values, a function that the person somehow determines. One way to determine such a function would be to be disposed, upon inspection of any world, to pronounce the verdict 'true' or 'false'. Consider for instance the sentence 'The earth is round'. On the simple picture, one understands 'The earth is round' to express the proposition that the earth is round just in case, if asked "Is 'The earth is round' true?" and shown enough of any possible world, one would answer "yes" if the earth were round in that world and "no" otherwise.

Many problems with such a view are immediately apparent. For instance, one can't actually investigate any world but one's own, and the facts about what investigations one pursues are among the facts about that world. But perhaps the picture being considered could be captured along these lines: in any possible world in which all the facts about one relevant to one's understanding of 'The earth is round' are the same as they actually are, and in which one pursues the relevant investigations far enough, one assents to 'The earth is round' if the earth is round in that world and dissents from it otherwise. If this approach will not work, then let us simply indulge in the helpful fiction of the Verne-o-scope, a sort of telescope by means of which we can examine as carefully as we like possible worlds other than our own.[21]

More serious difficulties with the simple picture remain. One such difficulty is that we can intend to mean by our expressions propositions that we don't, and know we don't, internalize. Hilary Putnam intends to use the sentence 'There are elms in North America' in such a way that he could not, and knows he could not, reliably say in all situations whether it was true or not. Most of us have similar intentions with regard to sentences containing natural kind terms, indexicals, demonstratives, and proper names. We understand any such sentence to mean some proposition in particular, but *which* proposition we understand it to mean is not determined by facts solely about us.

There is a second difficulty, related to but distinct from the first: the simple picture assumes that a verificationist theory of meaning is correct—that truth conditions for even theoretical sentences depend only on observable facts. This seems plainly false. Suppose that I am an expert on elms. I know not only the way they appear but also the genetic structure that distinguishes them from other trees. I suppose there might be trees that look just like elms but were not. But: show me through the Verne-o-scope a world in which there are in North America trees that look just like elms, but in which people never evolve and so in which there are no microscopes or other technological aids that enhance our observational skills. I may well not know whether 'There are elms in North America' is true or not. Surely this does not show I do not know what proposition the sentence expresses. If I were given enough information about the world in question, I would know whether the sentence was true. It's just that "enough" information is more than I can glean by unaided observation. But if we try to avoid presupposing verificationism by allowing more information about the world than observation can provide, how are we to specify *how much* more? If it seems too restrictive to limit the information to the observational, it also seems too generous to admit the information that there are elms in North America,[22] and it is not clear how to steer a middle course.

Now let us return to the immediate objects of belief. A simple proposal similar to the simple semantic picture just considered is this: one's total immediate object of belief is a function from worlds to truth values, determined in the following way. The worlds that are assigned the value T are those that, upon examination, the subject would agree could for all he knew be actual. (Notice that not all the worlds the subject would agree could for all he knew be actual will be worlds that really are compatible with all his beliefs. I believe that the lakes on earth are full of water. But show me a world where they are full of XYZ, and I will wrongly claim that it could for all I know be actual. I know more things than I realize.)

Look again at the two criticisms I made of the simple semantic picture. First, we can use sentences to mean propositions we haven't internalized, even ones we couldn't internalize, since we intend social and historical facts to play a role in determining what we mean. The same is true of belief: we believe propositions we haven't, or couldn't, internalize, and for something like the same reasons. But nothing of the sort *could* be true of immediate or direct belief. It is no shortcoming of a procedure for determining the *immediate* objects of belief that it finds no place for social or historical factors.

Second, the simple semantic picture is verificationist, whereas any adequate semantic theory must not be. But perhaps verificationism is not a fault in a semantics of belief states.

The trouble with verificationism is that many sentences have truth conditions that we do not, even could not, have immediate access to. But to be related to a proposition in such a way that one does not have immediate access to its truth conditions is to be related to it in virtue of features of one that might, had matters been different, have related one to a different proposition. Being related to P as things are, and being related to Q as things might have been, are indistinguishable from the point of view of the subject. But a proposition that is an immediate object of one's belief is a proposition one is related to in a way that could not relate one to any other proposition.

Verificationism as a theory of meaning for a public language assumes that there has to be too strong a connection between what a sentence or term means and what is understood by someone who is able to use it correctly. Putnam and others have provided a strong corrective to this view of language. (I do not mean to imply that theirs has been the only important criticism of verificationism.) But the price is to concede that in a sense we don't know the public meaning of most of the terms we use capably enough. We can't immediately believe anything we don't completely understand, so the maneuver that saves us from verificationism with respect to the public language will not save us from verificationism with respect to belief states.

The account we have been considering, according to which the immediate objects of one's belief are determined by which worlds one would agree could be actual, seems able to meet the objections we have so far considered. But a more serious one remains: the account requires us not only to have beliefs but to be aware of what they are. Dogs have beliefs, but could hardly assent or dissent when presented with alternative possibilities and asked whether they might be actual. Perhaps some of our beliefs are like all of a dog's are in this respect. We need a notion of various possible worlds being compatible with a subject's belief state that does not require the subject to have views about whether they are or are not so compatible. We need a way to determine what a subject's immediate objects of belief are without supposing that the subject can tell us.

Such a procedure for determining what the immediate objects of someone's (say, Art's) belief are, given only nonintentional facts about Art, would be a method of what has been called "radical interpretation." Much of the literature on radical interpretation urges us to adopt one or another "principle of charity": assume that Art's beliefs are mostly *true,* or that his terms mostly refer, or that words mean the same when he uses them as when we do.[23] If we want to find the immediate objects of Art's belief, however, we will be careful *not* to apply any such principle. For each of these principles will yield different results in different possible situations in which Art himself remains exactly the same. Take, for instance, the principle that we should interpret Art in such a way that as many of his beliefs as possible come out true. Surely the facts could be different than they in fact are, even radically different, in a situation in which Art was nevertheless exactly the same; and in such a situation the principle would lead us to attribute very different beliefs to Art than we would in the actual situation. Since Art's immediate beliefs remain the same in any situation in which Art's intrinsic properties are the same, this principle of charity will not lead us to make the correct attributions of immediate belief to Art.

We need instead specific instances of the following two general principles: that we should attribute those direct beliefs that Art would most likely have been led by his experience to acquire; and that we should attribute those direct beliefs that would best explain Art's actions.[24] Even these principles will lead to the desired results only if they employ descriptions of experience and action that are not themselves situation dependent: we shall need to have at hand individualistic accounts of perception and action.

Suppose that there are such principles: principles that will take us from complete descriptions of Art's perceptual input and behavioral output to a correct account of his total set of direct beliefs. Then these principles together with descriptions of Art's perceptions and actions provide something like a functional account of Art's total set of immediate objects of belief. Once we have this general characterization, we can provide a derivative object-by-object account of Art's immediate beliefs: P is a partial immediate object of Art's belief if and only if there is a Q such that Q is Art's total immediate object of belief, and Q implies P.

At its simplest, the account I am suggesting may be put, following Dennett,[25] like this. The set of worlds at which one's total immediate object of belief is true contains those worlds in which one would be most at home or to which one is best adapted: those in which one's behavior would make the most sense and one's expectations be least thwarted. Which worlds these are is determined solely by the intrinsic facts about one, so the appropriate set will not differ with differences in one's environment alone. And this account should make it seem plausible that there are immediate objects of belief, since it should be clear that there will be worlds to which one is especially well adapted.

But now we are in a position to see the need for a modification we have been expecting from the start. Is there really a set of *worlds* to which Art is best adapted? I am reasonably well adapted to the world *I* am currently in—provided that I am located toward the end of the twentieth century. Were I in precisely the same intrinsic state, but located in the twelfth century, however, I would be disastrously ill adapted. Again, if I were in my present intrinsic state but located on Venus, I would be ill adapted. What I am well or ill adapted to, then, are *situations* rather than worlds. To characterize my belief state, we need to consider the set of situations to which I am best adapted.

As noted earlier, a set of situations, like a set of centered worlds, corresponds not to a proposition but to a property: the property one has if and only if one is *in* one of those situations. One's total self-ascribed property is, then, the property of being in one of the situations to which one is in fact best adapted. For any person x, if x is in the belief state characterized by property F, then x's total immediate object of belief is the proposition that x is F.

We have now seen how one's intrinsic properties determine one's total self-ascribed property and how one's total self-ascribed property, together with who (and when) one is, determines one's total immediate object of belief. Thus, to complement the neutral answer to my title question given in section I, we have a sketch of a more substantive answer. To do more would be to go beyond the bounds of the present paper.

But I see this account of belief states as forming part of a larger account of belief proper. Our ordinary or mediate beliefs are propositions we believe in virtue of our immediate beliefs, together with facts about our environment. If the dependence of mediate on immediate belief is systematic, it should be possible to find the principles that govern it; it should be possible, that is, to give an account of belief in general in terms of immediate belief and contextual factors. Such an account would resemble Alvin Goldman's account of action in general in terms of basic actions and "level generation."[26] I believe that such an account *is* possible, but this is not the place to provide it.[27]

Notes

1. Many examples have been used by recent writers to illustrate this point. Such examples all involve cases in which, although all of the relevant intrinsic properties of individuals x and y are the same, x nevertheless has different beliefs than y. One of the most familiar of these examples, provided by Hilary Putnam (see "The Meaning of 'Meaning'," in *Mind, Language and Reality: Philosophical Papers,* vol. 2 (Cambridge, 1974), esp. 223-27), invites us to imagine that I have an exact duplicate on Twin Earth, a distant planet exactly like Earth except that the colorless, odorless liquid that falls from the sky, fills the lakes, and is called 'water' by the inhabitants is not H_2O but XYZ. Despite sharing all our relevant intrinsic characteristics, my counterpart and I do not share all our beliefs: whereas I believe that water is wet, he does not, believing instead that XYZ is wet.

In Putnam's example, the two individuals considered—myself and my counterpart—are both actual and are exactly alike. Other examples involve individuals who are both actual and who are *not* exactly alike, but who are presumed to be similar in all relevant respects. (See, e.g., John Perry, "The Essential Indexical," *Nous* 13 (1980): 3-21; Robert Stalnaker, "Indexical Belief," *Synthese* 49 (1981): 129-51; and Stephen P. Stich, *From Folk Psychology to Cognitive Science: The Case against Belief* (Cambridge, Mass., 1983), 63-64). These examples are very useful and illuminating. One could object, though, against Putnam that he requires us to imagine something desperately unlikely (that two actual people could be exactly alike), and against Perry and Stich that differences supposed to be irrelevant might turn out not to be. Both these difficulties are avoided in examples employed by Tyler Burge, which involve the same person in exactly the same state in different situations, at least one of them counterfactual. Having noted that such examples are available, I will continue to use Putnam's for illustration.

That I believe that *water* is wet, and not that XYZ is wet, results in part, Putnam's example suggests, from the actual chemical structure of the salient liquid portion of my environment and not simply from such intrinsic facts about me as how my rods and cones are being stimulated, what words are running through my mind, and how I am disposed to move my body. Other examples in the literature make a similar point about other beliefs—for example, the belief that I have arthritis in my thigh, and the belief that chicory is bitter.

2. Jaegwon Kim, "Psychophysical Supervenience," *Philosophical Studies* 41 (1982): 51-70, at 65.

3. Stich, *From Folk Psychology,* 168-70.

4. See Perry, "The Essential Indexical," as well as "Belief and Acceptance," *Midwest Studies in Philosophy* 5 (1980): 533-42; "A Problem about Continued Belief," *Pacific Philosophical Quarterly* 61 (1980): 317-32.

5. Daniel Dennett, "Beyond Belief," in *Thought and Object,* edited by Andrew Woodfield (Oxford, 1982), 19. A similar notion is employed in Jerry Fodor, "Methodological Solipsism Considered as a Research Strategy in Cognitive Psychology," in *Representations* (Cambridge, Mass., 1981).

6. See, for example, Tom McKay, "On Proper Names in Belief Ascriptions," *Philosophical Studies* 39 (1981): 287-303; Takashi Yagisawa, "The Pseudo-Mates Argument," *Philosophical Review* 93 (1984): 407-18; and chapter 3 of my *Beliefs and Their Objects* (Ph.D. dissertation, Princeton University, 1982).

7. The example is summarized in note 1.

8. Since situations include facts about a world only up to a certain time, this involves the assumption that future things and events do not affect the *content* of one's beliefs, though they may affect their truth or falsity. David Kaplan once introduced the name 'Newman 1' as a rigid designator of the first child actually to be born in the twenty-first century. ("Quantifying In," in *Words and Objections: Essays on the Work of W. V. Quine,* edited by D. Davidson and J. Hintikka (Dordrecht, 1969), 206-42, at 228-29.) Did he then believe singular propositions about Newman 1? Not if the account sketched here is correct. The facts about Kaplan's situation and

his total state were compatible with Newman 1's being either Sally or Joe, so if anything determined that Kaplan believed singular propositions about one rather than the other, it was something other than the facts about his situation and total state. But on the present account, there is nothing else that determines the contents of our beliefs.

This conforms to Kaplan's view in "Quantifying In," though he seems to disagree in his later "Dthat," in *Contemporary Perspectives in the Philosophy of Language,* edited by Peter A. French, et al. (Minneapolis, Minn., 1979), 383-400, at 397. The account also meshes with Keith Donnellan's treatment of Kaplan's example in "The Contingent *a Priori* and Rigid Designators," in ibid., 45-60, at 53-58.

9. See his response to Jerry Fodor's "Methodological Solipsism," in *Behavioral and Brain Sciences* 3 (1980): 79-80.

10. See, e.g., Bruce Goldberg, "The Correspondence Hypothesis," *Philosophical Review* 77 (1968): 438-54.

11. See esp. Paul M. Churchland, "Eliminative Materialism and Propositional Attitudes," *Journal of Philosophy* 78 (1981): 67-90.

12. Stich, *From Folk Psychology,* chap. 10 and 11.

13. Fodor, *Representations;* Hartry Field, "Mental Representation," *Erkenntnis* 13 (1978): 9-61; reprinted in *Readings in the Philosophy of Psychology,* edited by Ned Block, vol. 2 (Cambridge, Mass., 1981), 78-114.

14. Stich, *From Folk Psychology,* chap. 11.

15. Robert Stalnaker, "Propositions," in *Issues in the Philosophy of Language,* edited by Alfred F. MacKay and Daniel D. Merritt (New Haven, Conn., 1976), 76-91, and "Indexical Belief"; David Lewis, "Attitudes *De Dicto* and *De Se,"* *Philosophical Review* 87 (1979): 513-43. Neither Stalnaker nor Lewis employs the notion of a belief state, and Stalnaker at least regards the notion with suspicion (private communication).

16. David Lewis, "Attitudes *De Dicto* and *De Se";* Roderick Chisholm, *The First Person* (Minneapolis, Minn., 1981).

17. Interestingly, Robert Stalnaker ("Indexical Belief," 143) considers an example similar to the present one and takes something similar to the line of the previous paragraph. (Instead of allowing Sarah-stages to have singular propositions about *themselves* as immediate objects of their belief, Stalnaker would allow Sarah to have singular propositions about particular thought tokens as something like immediate objects of belief.) But it is not clear whether he realizes that the price of adopting this line is acknowledging that immediate objects of belief do not characterize belief states essentially. I should note here that Stalnaker does not use the notion of an immediate object of belief, and my attempts to cast his views in my terminology may well be misleading.

18. Lewis takes the notion of a centered world from W. V. Quine, "Propositional Objects," in Quine, *Ontological Relativity* (New York, 1969).

19. Compare a passage from Quine's "Propositional Objects." Quine is considering a cat that wants to escape from a dog onto a roof: "One of those possible worlds will have a cat like him on a roof like his, and another cat like him in the dog's jaws; does it belong to both the desired state of affairs and the feared one?" (quoted by Lewis, "Attitudes *De Dicto* and *De Se,"* 531). Stalnaker avoids this sort of example by postulating distinct but indiscernible possible worlds ("Indexical Belief," 143-45).

20. I do not mean to imply that the oversimple picture is all there is to procedural semantics. Some lively discussion and criticism of procedural semantics may be found in Fodor, "Tom Swift and His Procedural Grandmother," 204-24 of *Representations.*

21. The Verne-o-scope was invented by David Kaplan. See his "Transworld Heir Lines," in *The Possible and the Actual,* edited by Michael J. Loux (Ithaca, N.Y., 1979), 88-109, at 93.

22. What I have in mind is that my observations through the 'scope are supplemented by something like a written list of information about the world in question. The list is too generous if it includes the sentence 'There are elms in North America', since being able to tell that a

sentence S is true in a world on the basis of a list that includes S itself hardly guarantees that one understands S. The information that there are elms in North America would be admissible if it were not conveyed by the *sentence* 'there are elms in North America'. But how else can it be conveyed?

23. See, among other writings of Donald Davidson, his "Radical Interpretation," *Dialectica* 27 (1973): 313-28; see also Hilary Putnam's discussion of the "Principle of Benefit of Doubt" in "Language and Reality," 272-90 of *Mind, Language and Reality,* esp. 274-77.

24. Such principles are offered, along with others, in David Lewis, "Radical Interpretation," *Synthese* 27 (1974): 331-44. There is an extremely interesting discussion of the sort of radical interpretation I have in mind in Daniel C. Dennett, "Beyond Belief," sec. 4.

25. See "Beyond Belief," sec. 4, 40-44.

26. Alvin Goldman, *A Theory of Human Action* (Princeton, N.J., 1970).

27. I offer the beginnings of such an account in *Beliefs and Their Objects,* chap. 4.

Seeing Surfaces

AVRUM STROLL

I

In this paper I wish to raise some questions about the seeing of surfaces: what conditions must be satisfied before one can be said to be seeing the surface of something, and what it is that one is seeing in such a case. The main focus of the paper will be on the questions: "Can one see X without seeing its surface?" and "Can one see the surface of X without seeing X?" These are questions to which I will try to provide some cogent answers. They are, of course, closely connected with a celebrated epistemological tradition whose main proponents—Moore, Price, Broad, Prichard, Russell—were concerned about the relationship between what one perceives "directly" and the constituents that formed the "external world." By "directly," they meant that there was an X in one's visual field whose presence was obvious and required no inference or judgment as to its existence. It was just there. They were thus working with a distinction between mediate and immediate perception that they inherited from the Cartesian tradition and that they never really called into question. Nearly all of them agreed that what we directly perceive are "sense-data," but they differed markedly in the inferences they derived from this supposition.

Moore, in particular, is of special importance for anyone who wishes to study the role that surfaces play in this story. As a realist, he held that in what he called the "veridical perception" of an opaque "physical or material" object, say a box, it was a necessary condition for seeing the object that one see (or sense) a sense-datum; and he explored at length the question whether the datum in such cases could be identical with the surface of the perceived object. Had he been able to show that it was, it would have been an optimal result; for it would have entailed that one was seeing a physical object (or more exactly, some part of its surface) directly. This, in turn, would have meant that some of the knowledge we have of the external world arises from the direct perception of some of its constituents. It is, of course, well known that in his last paper—"Visual Sense-Data," 1957—he arrived at the decisive judgment that no sense-datum could be identical with part of the surface of a physical object, and accordingly that the most simple form of Realism, so-called "Naive Realism," could not provide a correct analysis of how perception gives rise to such knowledge.

I mention this earlier tradition because it forms a background that must be kept in mind if the present discussion is to be put into proper perspective. What I have to say in this paper will bear upon the main questions that these sense-data theorists addressed, but with some important differences. The conceptual model they were working with contained three notions that were problematical: *seeing, sense-datum,* and *physical* (or *material) object.* There was an enormous literature on the first two of these concepts, and a considerable discussion of the third. But to my knowledge, nobody in this tradition tried to analyze what surfaces were, and what their relationship to "physical or material" objects might be.[1] In what follows, I will not be discussing the concepts of "sense-data" or "physical objects" at all, as they used these terms. The paper is altogether about seeing and surfaces, or, more precisely, about the conditions that must be satisfied before one can be said to be seeing a surface or part of one.

In dealing with these matters, I want to explain how my approach to the nature of seeing differs from theirs, and then I want to draw some preliminary distinctions that will provide a bridge to the more substantive issues that follow.

First, then, about "see." It became part of the received opinion that "see" was ambiguous: that it was, or could be, used in three distinct senses. In each of these, a contrast was drawn between seeing all of something or only part of it. One could be said to be seeing a whole opaque object—for example, a wooden block—if all visual conditions were normal, nothing covered or partially covered the block, or if nothing were interposed between the observer and the block that would interfere with or obscure one's view of it. In this "ordinary" use, one would not be seeing all of the block if, for example, something opaque were superimposed upon part of it. But there was a second sense of "see" in which it was agreed that one could not be seeing all of the block even when the conditions for seeing all of it, in the preceding sense, were satisfied. This would be a case where, from a given perspective and at a given moment, there would be a part of the block that one couldn't see. One couldn't see, for example, from a particular angle and at a precise moment, whether the backside of the block was scratched or whether it was a different color; and one couldn't from any perspective or at any time see its interior if the block were left whole. Moore and others said that, in such cases, *maximally* what one could be seeing was that part of the surface of the block that faced the observer.

But beyond this, they distinguished a third sense of "see." In so doing, they again drew a contrast between seeing all or less than all of something. In this case, the something was a sense-datum, and the distinction between seeing all of it or less than all of it was identified with the distinction between apprehending all or only some of its properties. Moore went to infinite pains to explain what he meant by a sense-datum. In some of his articles, he explicitly defined the term as denoting that which one directly sees in any act of perception. But more typically, he tried to illustrate what sense-data were by providing examples of them: afterimages, and so forth. He did not intend to imply with the use of such examples that sense-data were always and only the products of illusory perception—quite the contrary. It was rather that by using such examples he could perspicuously bring out that sense-data were the sorts of things one sees directly. By "directly," as I have indicated, he meant that there was an X in one's visual field whose presence did not need to be confirmed or established by any process of inference. But granting the existence of X, it still remained an open question whether X could be part of a material object or not.

All these theorists agreed that sense-data were the sorts of things seen directly and that an afterimage was an example of a sense-datum. But they differed over the question of whether, in general, in seeing a sense-datum one was apprehending all of its properties. Moore in particular had reservations about equating "A is directly seeing X" with "A is directly apprehending all of X's properties." He noted that if one looked at a surface with a magnifying glass, one might see scratches and blemishes not visible to the naked eye. But if a sense-datum could be identical with part of the surface of the material object, then it could have properties it did not appear to have.

But most sense-data theorists disagreed with Moore. They thought that the basic distinction between a sense-datum and a material object was that the latter could have properties it did not appear to have whereas the former could not. Thus, an opaque wooden block could have properties on its backside or interior that at a given moment or from a given perspective it did not appear to have. But a sense-datum couldn't; it had to be just what it appeared to be; otherwise one was subtly converting it into a "thin" kind of material object. Moore left the question open; as a realist, his main question was whether what one saw directly, in this third sense of "see," could be identical with what one saw in the second sense of "see"—in other words, whether the sense-datum being directly perceived could be identical with part of the surface one saw in perceiving an opaque object. And, of course, had he decided that it could have been, there is no reason why that part of the surface of the object could not have properties it did not appear to have.

The vast bulk of the literature in this tradition was thus concerned with whether "see" was ambiguous in these three ways, and what implications this had for the relationship between sense-data and external objects; and because this is so, I wish to explain why I shall not be adding to their discussion now. To come to the main point immediately, I will begin by saying that it strikes me as extremely dubious that there is any ambiguity between the first and second supposed senses of "see." There is simply no reason to believe that if I can see only part of an object, rather than all of it, I am using "see" differently in describing the two situations. If my car is parked behind a fence and I can only see the rear part of it, and say so, or if it is parked in the open and I can see all of it, and say so, there is no reason to believe that I am using "see" differently in these cases. To think so is simply to conflate the meaning of the term "see" with the range of items to which it can be correctly applied, and this would clearly be fallacious.

On the other hand, it is possible that "see" as used in speaking about afterimages does differ in meaning from its use in the supposed first two "senses." Moore meant by an afterimage the faint glow that is apprehended when, after staring fixedly at a light bulb for a moment or two, one closes one's eyes and then "sees" a white patch that has roughly the same shape as the bulb. The important point here is that even though one's eyes are shut, one does speak about "seeing" the object in such cases. There does then seem to be a different sense of "see" involved from that which is used when we speak about seeing the bulb itself. Moore thought this example was a case par excellence of seeing directly.

But one has to be careful not to extend this particular example beyond its proper range and argue that whenever we say we see anything that in Moore's sense is not a material object—for example, hallucinations or "negative after-images"[2]—that we can be said to be using "see" in this third sense. For in some of these cases—for example, with respect to negative after-images—we have our eyes open and see the image only when they are open. To be sure, there is no "physical object" actually located where the negative afterimage appears to be located; but there is no reason to believe that in saying we "see" it we are using "see" differently from the way we use it when we are said to be seeing tables or chairs, upon which the negative afterimage appears to be superimposed.

But whether "see" is ambiguous between this sense and that, or those in which we "see" tables or parts of tables, is not relevant to my purposes here. I do not think that the seeing of surfaces is like the seeing of an afterimage. It is something we normally do with our eyes open, and we can often touch the surface we see: feel it to see if it is rough or smooth, polished or unpolished, and so on. In these respects, seeing surfaces is not substantially different from seeing the tables and chairs that have such surfaces. My basic point is that if one wishes to discuss what it is one sees when one is seeing a table, one wouldn't have to distinguish between different senses of "see"; and *mutatis mutandis* for surfaces. I do not wish to deny, of course, that "see" is ambiguous; in fact, I think it is. When we say we "see" the point of a joke, or the hidden meaning in a remark, we are using the word in a different sense from that which is employed in saying that we see a table or its surface. I am even willing to say, though with some hesitation, that the latter use of "see" captures its literal meaning whereas the former does not. There may well be interesting and important problems connected with such ambiguities; but these we can also set aside for the inquiry to be pursued here. In what follows, therefore, I will be using "see" in what the tradition would have called its "ordinary sense"—whatever that "sense" is in which one talks about seeing tables and chairs, or parts of them.

II

I turn now to the first of our two questions: "Can one see X without seeing its surface?"

1.

It is important to realize in the study of surfaces that not every opaque physical object has a surface. Moore, on the contrary, assumed that every such object had a surface; indeed, he assumed that it has exactly one surface, and then argued that it was a necessary condition of seeing the object that one see at least part of its surface. In a previous paper,[3] I developed a series of arguments to show that it is not true that every opaque object, in Moore's use of the term, has a surface, and accordingly that we can see such objects without seeing their surfaces. I will not rehearse those arguments here; I merely restate some of their conclusions. Mountains and clocks have faces but not surfaces; water lying flat in a lake has a surface, but water gushing out of a hydrant does not. Such things as tall grass seen from close up, clouds, and Afro wigs do not have surfaces. Persons and animals do not; but a person's skin has a surface, and statues of persons and animals, if made from the right sort of material, do.

A decisive counterargument to the claim that it is a necessary condition of seeing X that one see its surface is the following. On a clear night, a person standing on the earth can see the surface of the moon without using any special optical equipment. The person can see ridges, shapes, rays, and so forth. On a clear night, a person standing on the earth can see Jupiter, which is an opaque object. But nobody has ever seen the surface of Jupiter; indeed, it is not even clear that Jupiter has a surface. Since on this sort of occasion one can see Jupiter without seeing its surface, it cannot be a necessary condition for seeing an opaque object that one see its surface.

In this connection it is possible to make the further observation that even when X has some surfaces, there may be nothing called "the surface of X" or "X's surface." A die has six surfaces because it is a cube. Suppose that from a given observational standpoint we can see only three of them. In such a case, we would not be said to be seeing part of *the surface* of the die. We could be said to be seeing three of its surfaces, or some of its surfaces. But we could not be said to be seeing part of *its surface*. It seems to be the case that there are contexts in which there is nothing that can be described as *the surface* of the die. In other words, from the fact that a die has a number of surfaces, it does not in general follow that there is something that is *its surface* or *the surface* of the die. And this inference seems in general to hold of opaque objects: there may be things that have surfaces, but nothing that in certain circumstances can be called "the surface" of the object. Compare and contrast a die with a solid-steel ball bearing, for instance. In seeing the ball bearing from a certain perspective, we may not be able to see all of its surface; but the locution "all of its surface" applies to the ball bearing. This is probably because its surface is continuous, whereas the surface of a die is not. We can, in speaking about the ball bearing, also say that we are seeing some or part of its surface. But the point is that such phrases do not in general apply to all "physical" objects. Moore's view that a necessary condition for seeing any opaque object is that we see parts of its surface is simply false; there is nothing, in certain cases, where we see such an object that qualifies as part of its surface.

2.

There is a second point to be made in connection with the preceding. Moore's language strongly implies (and most commentators have taken him to mean this) that we *never directly see more than part* of the surface of an opaque 'physical' object. In "Some Judgments of Perception," Moore contrasts the seeing of a soap bubble, which is transparent, with the seeing of an opaque object. He implies that we can *directly* see *all* of the soap bubble, but only part of the opaque object; namely, that part of its surface that is facing us. In "A Defense of Common Sense," he writes:

> I think it certain, therefore, that the analysis of the proposition 'This is a human hand' is, roughly at least, of the form 'There is a thing, and only one thing, of which it is true both that it is a human hand and that *this surface* is a part of its surface'. In other words, to put my view in terms of the phrase 'theory of representative perception,' I hold it to be quite certain that I do not *directly* perceive *my hand;* and that when I am said (as I may be correctly said) to 'perceive' it, that I 'perceive' it means that I perceive (in a different and more fundamental sense) something which is (in a suitable sense) *representative* of it, namely, a certain part of its surface. (P. 55)

Moore is emphasizing the distinction between seeing and seeing directly, and the distinction between seeing all of something or only part of it. What is interesting for our purposes is his claim that the part of an opaque object that one can see is its surface. But still more interesting is the strongly implied claim that one can see *only* part of the surface. Or, to put the point differently, that maximally what one can see *directly* is only part of the surface of the object. Moore, to be fair, never *states* that one cannot see or directly see the whole *surface* of an opaque object; but he strongly implies that this is so. But if this is his intention then he is clearly, and, for our study here, importantly wrong. It is obviously possible to see all the surface of an opaque object even in Moore's sense of "directly."

Two brief examples will suffice to make the point. Suppose that, like J. H. Speke, someone is standing on the southern shore of Victoria Nyanza, a lake that is about two hundred miles long. It is obvious that from ground level one cannot see the whole of its surface. But suppose the question arises whether the whole surface or only a part of the surface of a neighbor's pond is covered with algae. If the pond is small enough, the question can be answered. One can see the whole surface, and one can see—if that turns out to be the case—that part of it that is covered by algae.

Suppose one wishes to have the surface of a Cheval mirror refinished. Like all mirrors, a Cheval mirror is an opaque physical object, as Moore uses these terms. One can't see right through it; indeed, if one could it wouldn't function as a mirror. Again, the question might arise (because of the cost) whether the whole surface should be refinished or only part of it. After carefully scrutinizing its surface, noting where it is pitted or chipped, an expert might inform one that he has examined it and only part of it needs to be refinished. One would understand him to mean that he has looked at the whole surface. But one doesn't have to be an expert to see the whole surface; if the mirror is small enough, anybody can take in all of it at a glance.

I have cited these *two* cases (Lake Victoria and the Cheval Mirror) not merely to bring out that Moore's suggestion that we can see only (maximally) part of the surface of an opaque object is wrong, but because the two cases are instructively different from one another. In the case of seeing Victoria Nyanza, it is *impossible,* given the stated conditions, to see all of its surface. But it is possible to see part of its surface from ground level. In the case of the Cheval mirror, it is possible both to see all of its surface and to see part of it—for example, those places where it is pitted or chipped. But now we come to an interesting contrast. In the case of Victoria Nyanza, one can sensibly say that it is possible, standing at ground level on the southern shore, to see only (or maximally) part of its surface. Here the concept of seeing *only* part of the surface of X plays more than a spear-carrying role. But could we under the circumstances described say that the expert could see only part of the surface of the Cheval mirror? The answer seems to be "no." *In the circumstances described,* there is no way that he can be seeing only part of the surface of the mirror. As he approaches the mirror to examine it, he takes in at a glance the whole surface. Is there some "natural" way that he could take in only part of it as he approaches it? The answer is clearly "no." Of course, we can describe circumstances in which he could maximally see only part of its surface; for example, if part of the surface had been painted over. Then as he examined the mirror he would be seeing only part of its surface. Or if the mirror were embedded in a wall and part of its surface was covered by the wood holding it in place, he could be said to be only seeing part of its surface.

What is basically wrong with Moore's approach is that he has generalized from a few cases—the usual epistemologist's collection of tables, chairs, inkwells—thinking that what it is true to say of them is true to say of all opaque objects. But this is simply wrong. Opaque objects fall into a variety of classes. As we have just seen, some of them (a solid-steel ball bearing) have exactly one surface, and from a given point it may be possible to see maximally only part of it; some of them do not have surfaces, so it may not be possible even to see part of their surfaces; some of them may be described as having one surface or as having more than one surface (for example, if I ask you to paint the surface of this table you will probably paint its top; but if I ask you to measure its surface you will probably measure its top, undersides, and legs). In response to these criticisms, one may say, defending the tradition, that with respect to the objects he was talking about Moore was right; we can't see all of the surface of a solid wooden block, for example, but only and maximally that part of it that faces us. But even here Moore's generalizations go wrong. As I have indicated, if seeing is like painting, then to see the surface of a table is to see its top, and this is something all of which we see in normal circumstances.

As we shall find in what follows, there are some interesting questions connected with the conditions that must be satisfied before we can be said to be seeing only part of the surface of something; the distinctions we have drawn above will be presupposed in that inquiry.

III

The preceding discussion shows that we can see an object without seeing its surface or part of its surface. But an issue that is more difficult to adjudicate is the question of whether we can see the surface of something without seeing that thing. To come to grips with this issue, we must draw yet another distinction. We shall ultimately want to ask whether seeing is like scratching or polishing. For some objects—for example, the solid-steel ball bearing we spoke about earlier—there is no way of scratching the surface without scratching the object; conversely (assuming the object is intact) there is no way of scratching the object without scratching its surface. Our previous discussion has shown that for some objects it is possible to see the object without seeing its surface (say, Jupiter); and for those objects, seeing and scratching clearly will not have the same logic. But for those objects, can we also show that we can see their surfaces per se, see them without seeing the object at all? The question is a difficult one; the answer in part will turn on what is meant by a surface. For this reason, it is necessary to make the following distinction.

It is important in investigating the subject of surfaces to notice that the word "surface" is used in everyday speech in two different, and possibly even incompatible, ways. Whether the term is a genuine homonym or not is a question I have previously discussed in this journal,[4] and therefore I will not repeat the arguments pro and con here. But independently of how this question is resolved, one can safely say the following. Sometimes when we speak of a surface we are speaking of something that can be the bearer of certain kinds of 'physical' properties or be subject to certain sorts of 'physical' operations. For example, the surface of a mirror can be pitted, rough or smooth, damp or dry; and it can be polished, dusted, or refinished. Sometimes when we speak of a surface we are speaking of something that cannot be the bearer of such properties or be subject to such operations. Roughly speaking, this second way of talking about surfaces strongly suggests that they are conceived of as boundaries or as limits. Like the equator that divides the northern and southern hemispheres of the globe, a surface under this conception cannot be scratched, cannot be washed or waxed, and of course cannot be seen. Just as the equator reflects no light, so a surface—thought of as a boundary or limit—reflects no light. In such a case, there is nothing to be seen.

When surfaces are spoken about in the former sense, I call them "Somorjai surfaces,"[5] naming them after a distinguished contemporary scientist who is one of the leading investigators of the chemical properties of surfaces. When they are thought of as limits or boundaries, I call them "Leonardo surfaces," after Leonardo da Vinci, who provides an argument in his notebooks whose conclusion is that surfaces are not things or parts of things, but are what we today would call "interfaces."[6]

The differences between the two conceptions can be illustrated by some simple examples. Let's assume that city officials decide to resurface a road. They may decide to go about this in several ways, the least expensive of which would be to pour a layer of macadam over the old surface. After they have finished doing so, there may be some complaints to the effect that the new surface is rough, or wavy, or has a washboard quality to it. So they may decide to "shave" it down, smoothing it out, removing the dips, peaks, or ridges that gave it an unacceptable finish. As so described, the surface is something that has such properties as being rough or smooth, as being susceptible to shaving down, sanding, polishing, and so forth. We are here talking about a Somorjai surface.

But now let's assume that after the city has shaved down the surface, there is still a bulge in it at a certain point. An investigation reveals that this is caused by a rock in the macadam. Where shall we say the rock is? Of course, it's quite correct to say it's in the macadam; somehow the rock got picked up in the macadam, and was deposited with it when they laid the surface. Since the macadam *is* the surface, can we say the rock is *in* the surface? Shall we say it is three inches deep *in* the surface? Both of these ways of describing where the rock is sound a little strange. One wishes to say that the rock is in the macadam all right, but not that it is "in" the surface; instead, that it's three inches *below* the surface, and that is what is causing the bulge. In these latter ways of speaking, a different use of "surface" is coming into play: the Leonardo conception. Now the surface is an outer boundary; on that conception it makes sense to say that the rock is below the surface rather than in it, or that it is three inches below the surface, and so forth. What has happened here is that we seem to be using "surface" in two different ways—first as something that can bulge, that can be rough or pitted, and then as a kind of limit or boundary that cannot be pitted or rough: indeed, as something that cannot have any physical properties at all.[7]

The distinction is an interesting and important one, and it can be investigated and described in greater length than I have done here. But for our present purposes, what we have said should suffice. The important point is that if we wish to describe what is seen when one is said to be seeing a surface, or if we wish to describe the conditions that must be satisfied before one can be said to be seeing a surface, it is clear that we must be talking about a Somorjai rather than a Leonardo surface. We have to be talking about something that in principle can be scratched, waxed, polished, or can be rough, pitted, damp, and so forth. We cannot see the equator and we cannot see a Leonardo interface.

IV

If it is agreed that we can see an object without seeing its surface, let us then turn to the more difficult issue of whether we can see the surface of an object without seeing the object. Why should this question be more difficult? The answer, at least in part, is that surface talk (about Somorjai surfaces) seems expendable, whereas object talk is not. For certain kinds of objects, there seems to be no difference between saying (for example) that an object like a ball bearing is dirty or that its surface is dirty, or that one has polished it until it shines or that one has polished its surface until it shines, or that it reflects light or that its surface does. This sort of example makes it seem that surface-talk in principle is otiose; of course, if that were so then the word "surface" would play no significant role in everyday discourse. But since most words do play some special role in ordinary speech, we shall have to assume that it does; if so, there must be some substantive difference between talk about surfaces and talk about the objects that have such surfaces.[8]

The problem can be posed in yet a different way. If one is talking about Somorjai surfaces, it seems plausible to believe that surfaces are always parts of objects. To scratch the surface of a mirror is to scratch the mirror. The issue is: Can we distinguish or separate—at least in talk—part of an object from the rest of it? In particular, if surfaces are parts of objects, can we somehow treat them independently of any discussion of the object per se? The presumption would have to be "yes" for the general case and, accordingly, "yes" for the particular case of surfaces. To illustrate what is at issue here, one might take, as an example, talk about the leg of a table.

A leg is normally considered to be part of a table and, indeed, "a part of it," especially if it is detachable. We can describe it as cylindrical or round, or as a foot long, or as made of steel, whereas none of these terms might apply to the table itself. We can remove a detachable wooden leg, sand it down, change its shape, and so forth, without doing any of these things to the table itself. Of course, if we repair a damaged leg we might also be said to be repairing the table, so that with respect to this predicate, and on this occasion, doing the one would be doing the other. But more importantly, if we take the leg to a repair shop one can be said to be examining or looking at it without examining or looking at the table. There is thus a clear sense in which one could be said to be seeing the leg without seeing the table. The question is: "Is there such a relatively clear sense in which we can be said to be seeing the Somorjai surface of an object without seeing the object?"

The analogy between surfaces and legs, with respect to being parts of objects, thus seems to be a persuasive one. Both surfaces and legs clearly seem to be parts of the objects that have them. In some cases, not only legs but surfaces can be removed. If, for instance, one removes the paint from a table, it may be because the surface is scratched or rough or chipped; in such a case, it might be said that we have removed the old surface and replaced it with another. But the analogy is also misleading. The pile of old chips on the floor is no longer a surface in the way that the damaged leg is still a leg, even when it has been removed from the table. It's a little like saying that the peel of an apple is its surface and that when we peel the apple we are peeling its surface, so that what we throw into a garbage pail is the old surface. At some point we stop calling the peel "the surface" of the apple, possibly because this would seem to entail the counterintuitive result that a roughly round, more or less intact object can have two different surfaces and have them in two different places at the same time. Moreover, there is a second respect in which the analogy is misleading. In general, one can't remove the surface of an object in the way that one can remove old paint. Some table legs may be difficult to remove, but in principle all can be. But the difficulty of removing some surfaces is logical. There is in principle no way of removing the surface of a solid-steel ball bearing. One can "resurface" the object by grinding down or sanding the surface it has. But one can't take away its old surface in the way that one can take away old paint. One can do this with paint because paint is a mantle or a cover; it is made of different material from the underlying wood of the table. The surface of a solid-steel ball bearing is not a mantle; its surface is not made of a different stuff, and because that is so, it cannot be removed or chipped off in the same way that paint can be. Its relationship to the object that has it is thus different from the mantle relationship of paint to a painted wood object. The difficulty being described is more like that of trying to remove the surface of a lake; what would it be like to try, and what would it be like to succeed?

Still, despite these objections, there is also something right about the analogy. What is right about it is that, like a leg, a surface can have properties[9] and be subject to operations that the object does not have and is not subject to. As I have indicated, we can remove the surface of a table without removing the table, or remove the old surface of a road without removing the road. It is, to be sure, easier to find such examples when one is dealing with surfaces that are mantles; but similar results can be obtained even when one is not. An X-ray might reveal a cavity just beneath the surface of a tooth, but of course not beneath the tooth; and a machinist might have just penetrated beneath the surface of a solid-steel ball bearing with a fine drill to remove a foreign particle, without having just penetrated beneath the ball bearing itself for this purpose. The interesting question here, however, is whether seeing is like "penetrating beneath" or "removing." Can one be said to be seeing the surface without seeing the object that has it?

V

In dealing with that question, we encounter two broadly different kinds of cases. In some instances, it may appear plausible to say that we see *only* the surface of only part of the surface because of an inability to discriminate any details within the surface or within the object. In the other, we may say we see *only* the surface because the level of detail is so great that we cannot be said to be seeing the object at all. In this section I will be dealing with cases falling into the first of these categories, and in the next section with cases falling into the second.

It will be helpful in initiating this discussion to distinguish between the concepts of *magnification* and *resolution*.[10] In science the distinction is a familiar and important one, but it is often put in a way that can be misleading. For a scientist, "magnification" refers to the enlargement of an *image* of something, whereas "resolution" refers to the fineness of detail with which a certain X is seen, where X may either be an image of something or that something itself. The reason for the ambiguity is fairly easy to diagnose.

Scientists use various sorts of instruments, microscopes, telescopes, X-ray machines to look at various features of the world. If one takes an X-ray of somebody's arm, one does not magnify the arm in looking at the X-ray, but rather the image that appears on the X-ray film. There are ways of using instruments so that we can speak about having greater resolution for the image we see—say, in a photograph of a planet taken through a telescope. But sometimes we wish to say that it is finer detail in the object that one is seeing, rather than finer detail in the image. The point is relevant to seeing surfaces. In using the naked eye to see the surface of something, we are not normally seeing images—this would be to adopt something like the Cartesian assumption mentioned earlier. We are seeing the object directly. And if we look at the surface of a table with a magnifying glass, we are still not seeing an image but rather the surface. Scientists, of course, tend to think of the human eye as an instrument, and accordingly may talk as if what a human being sees in using the eye is an image, or something analogous to what one would be looking at when one looks at a photograph of someone. But the analogy is misleading if it disposes one to talk as if in seeing with the naked eye one is apprehending images. In that sense, the eye is not an instrument.

Since in what follows we shall be talking about what we see with instruments and with the naked eye, let us characterize the concepts of magnification and resolution in a way that will be relatively neutral with respect to whether we are speaking about images of objects or the objects themselves. By "magnification," we shall then mean the enlargement of a certain X that is in our visual field; by "resolution," the effect of a process that allows us to ascertain finer detail in X. Therefore, in talking about these notions in connection with surfaces, we can be understood to be speaking either about images or about the objects themselves, depending on the context.

As I mentioned, the distinction between magnification and resolution is important in science. For such instruments as microscopes or telescopes, their capacity for resolution is characterized quantitatively by measuring the minimal distance between two objects that that instrument can still discriminate as two separate objects.

Suppose one is photographing Jupiter on a clear, dark night. Near Jupiter there is a spot of light. Is it a satellite of Jupiter; is it two satellites? One can't answer the question merely by blowing up the photograph. When one has done this what one has is a larger single blob of light. Enlargement of the photograph does not give one sufficient detail to determine whether one is looking at one or two objects. However, if one uses a telescope that both magnifies and resolves the object, sufficient resolution may be achieved to distinguish the two objects (if there are such) even at a great distance, though even this ability would be lost if it turns out that the blob of light is not a planet but a star.

Similarly, the standard optical microscope has the capacity for resolution of tiny objects. This capacity is equal to one-half the wave length of the light used to illuminate the object. For reasons that the physicists can easily give us, no two objects or parts of an object closer together than that distance can be perceived as separate entities. In actuality, this value for a good optical microscope is approximately 0.25 micrometers (microns); by comparison, a red blood cell is 8 microns in diameter. This is why we can't see most viruses with the standard optical microscope: theoretically, we could magnify the image an infinite number of times by stacking microscopes on top of microscopes, but the *clarity* of the image would not be improved. Instead, scientists use the electron microscope because electrons have a very short wave length that can be calculated by non-Newtonian physics. This vastly improves resolution and allows viruses and even molecules to be seen with considerable detail.

The distinction between magnification and resolution is important with respect to the question of whether we are seeing *only* the surface of X. The connection can be established as follows. Suppose you have a leather bag with some objects in it. With the naked eye you can see the surface of the bag; you can see rough spots, some abrasions, and some differences in color. If you examine the bag with a magnifying glass, you can see scratches and marks not visible to the naked eye. In such a case, as Moore noted, we are still inclined to say that you are seeing the surface of the bag. The magnifying glass gives one greater resolution than the eye. But if you run the bag through an X-ray machine at the security gate of an airport, you can see through the bag—you can see some of its contents, especially if they are metal. But with an X-ray machine you do not see the surface of the bag: its degree of resolution is so great that it renders the surface transparent.[11] The question is: where does the surface of the bag stop? Clearly, some degrees of resolution reveal more than the surface. But how much resolution gives us only the surface? If we gradually lessen the resolving power of whatever instrument we are using, it is plausible to suggest that if we reach a point of zero resolution, then the only thing we could be seeing would be the surface of the object we are looking at. If this were a correct analysis, then we should look for some cases where the resolving power of the naked eye is either zero or virtually zero; and those might be cases where we could be said to be seeing only the surface or X, but not X itself. In the limiting case we would be apprehending only the surface, and without any detail.

The following might be a case like that. Suppose we are flying over Victoria Nyanza. From a low altitude we can see, with the naked eye, the surface of the lake. We can see that it is dotted with boats, that it is rough, that there is foam on it. We, of course, can also be said to be seeing the lake itself. As our plane flies higher and higher there will come a point when all resolution of surface features will disappear. We can no longer see whether there are boats on the surface or whether it is rough or smooth. What now exists in our visual field is a bright, bluish-looking, approximately elliptical dot, set against a background of hills and rolling terrain. Shall we say that we are seeing the lake, but not its surface, since we cannot discriminate any features of the surface; or shall we say we are seeing *only* the surface since we cannot discriminate any features of the lake; or shall we say we are seeing both? (Is the photograph we have taken of the stellar object near Jupiter a photograph of the object, its surface, both, or neither?)

As the plane flies still higher, there will come a point when we have lost all powers of magnification and of resolution. There will no longer even be a bright spot in our visual field. In this circumstance, it would clearly be correct to say that we can no longer see the lake or its surface. But the question we wish to come to grips with is whether, shortly before this happens, the bright spot we are seeing is the surface of the lake or not? And if so, is it *only* the surface we are seeing, but not the lake? Will this case, where all resolution has vanished, count as a case of seeing only a surface but not the object that has it?

In trying to answer these questions, I should like to emphasize that the questions themselves are much less clear than the question of whether I can see the leg of a table without seeing the table. The answer to that question was relatively free of context. But in this situation, contextual factors play complicating and perhaps even determinative roles. That is, the kind of answer one gives will not depend so much on *what* one is seeing—it is agreed that there is a dotlike object in one's visual field—but on what kind of response would be appropriate to the question asked. If the question is: "From this altitude, how many lakes can you see?" I might respond by saying, "Three"—from here I can see not only Victoria Nyanza but also Lake Kiwu and Lake Albert Edward; but I can't see Lake Tanganyika. The question thus does not require an answer mentioning surfaces. How, then, shall we couch the question so as to refer only to surfaces but not to the lake? Here it seems to me that the question would call for an answer that would discriminate surface features of the lake. One might ask: "How much of the surface is still covered with oil?" or "Is the surface still as rough as it was at nine o'clock?" and so on. If a person responded to these questions by saying, "We're up so high I can't see the surface any more," we could infer that in this case the person was seeing the lake but not the surface. But of course this doesn't help us answer the question of under what conditions one would be seeing *only* the surface and not the lake? Still, we have what seems to be a significant negative result; namely, that where all resolution has been lost so that no "surface features" are discernible, one cannot be said to be seeing the surface *at all*, let alone *only* the surface. In such a case, the disposition is to say that one is seeing the object rather than the surface or some part of it.

This case is thus a variant of the case of seeing Jupiter—in other words, a case where we can say that we are seeing an object without seeing its surface. But in terms of the tradition, even this result is significant; recasting the views of Moore, Broad, Price, Russell inter alia in our teminology here, we can say that what they insisted upon is that when all resolution is lost, one is seeing maximally a surface (one at best is seeing *only* part of the surface of an opaque object). They held that in cases of the veridical perception of an opaque physical object, one was seeing its "outermost aspect"; and this was maximally part of its surface. On their view, the dot that appeared on our photograph of the night sky around Jupiter was at least and also at most part of the surface of a certain object.[12] But if the preceding argument is cogent, they could not be correct in this contention: at the distance from which the photograph was taken it would be impossible, without some degree of resolution, to see the surface or any part of it at all.

What these findings show, I think, is that we must be able to discern some detail in the surface of an object before we can be said to be seeing the surface. Returning to our problem, then, we may ask whether we can find a case involving a minimal degree of resolution that allows us to say we are seeing the surface, or some part of the surface, of X, but not seeing X? Clearly, it is not easy to do so. I have two suggestions in this connection.

Take the case of a very transparent lake on a day with no winds, when viewed from above. Under those circumstances, one may see the lake bottom without being aware of the existence of the surface at all. But even under those circumstances, when viewed from a glancing incidence the surface would be apparent. Let us turn this situation around. Suppose one is lying supine at the bottom of the lake under the same conditions and looking directly at the sky. It is possible that one might not see the water at all, but might see the interface between water and air. In such a case, one might be seeing the surface without seeing the object that has it. But the case is certainly not clear-cut.

A second possibility is the following. Suppose one is led blindfolded to the wall of a room, and suppose that the wall is a homogeneous color, say beige. If one's face were pressed against the wall or were very close to it, and the blindfold were removed, one might have in one's visual field at that moment only a beige expanse. Let us assume that the conditions are such that one does not know that it is a wall she is looking at. Then, of course, she would not know that what she is seeing is the surface of a wall. The question here is whether we can say under those conditions that she is seeing a surface without seeing the object that has it?

The case is again not clear-cut, in the sense in which it was clear-cut that one could see the leg of a table without seeing the table. One is disposed to say that the person is seeing the outer aspect of something, so that she is seeing a surface even if she doesn't know that it is one. But then is she also seeing the wall, even if she doesn't know that what she is seeing is a wall?

The issue is complicated by *de re* and *de dicto* problems. In the *de re* sense, one is inclined to say that she is seeing a surface, since in fact what she is seeing is the surface of a wall. But if that is so, then in the *de re* sense she is also seeing a wall. So this can't be a case of seeing only a surface. Can she see the surface in the *de dicto* sense without seeing the wall? The *de dicto* distinction introduces epistemological considerations. She will know that what she is seeing is a surface without knowing what it is the surface of. So on this reading, we can only conclude that *she knows* she is seeing the surface of X without knowing what X is. But this does not give us the result we need: namely, that she is only seeing the surface of X but not seeing X.

VI

The preceding cases were instances where the amount of data in one's visual field was so minimal that it seemed initially plausible to say that the degree of resolution involved was zero or virtually zero, and accordingly that one was seeing only the surface of X but not X itself. Let us look at a different sort of case. Here the amount of detail and information given to a person fills his visual field; and since presumably all of it will be information about a surface, would that count as a case of seeing the surface of X without seeing X?

In this case, it is also important to eliminate or minimize epistemological considerations in trying to arrive at a decision. That is, the question of whether A is seeing only the surface of X must be sharply distinguished from the question of whether A knows what X is—whether he can identify the object whose surface he is apprehending.

In my previous paper in this journal,[13] I reproduced a drawing of a surface at the atomic scale. In the article in *Science* that contains this sketch,

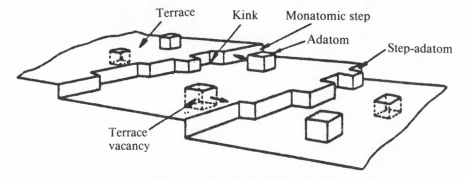

Figure 1. Schematic representation of the heterogeneous surface on the atomic scale. Terrace, step, and kink atoms as well as point defects (adatoms and vacancies) have been identified by experiments. From G. A. Somorjai, "Surface Science," *Science*, vol. 201, No. 4355 (11 Aug. 1978, pp. 489-97). Reproduced with permission of author and publisher. Copyright 1978 by the American Association for the Advancement of Science.

Dr. Somorjai does not tell us what object the surface belongs to. Suppose that it is the surface of a solid-steel ball bearing, and also suppose that it is an exact representation of what one would see if one were looking at the ball bearing through an electron microscope. Let us also assume that what we see through the electron microscope entirely fills our visual field, so that there are no other features that creep in from the sides or top or bottom. In this situation, then, what are we seeing? Is it only the surface of *X,* but not *X*? The case for saying so would go as follows. It is agreed that Somorjai surfaces are parts of objects, so what we are seeing is part of some object. What we are seeing is part of the surface of that object. Most importantly, it is the only thing we are seeing. It therefore seems to follow that we are seeing only the surface of *X.* Does it also follow that we are not seeing *X*? The argument in favor of saying so would continue as follows. To say we see *X,* in this case a ball bearing, we would have to say that we see some of the features normally associated with an object of that kind: being circular, being made of steel, being of a silver color, reflecting light, and so forth. To say we are seeing part of *X* would mean that we would be seeing some of the group of features normally associated with seeing objects of that sort, but not all of them from that standpoint and at that time. But what we are seeing in fact exhibits none of the features we normally associate with ball bearings; they do not normally exhibit such 'surface' features as terraces, kinks, monatomic steps, adatoms, and so forth. But these are just the features that what we are seeing exhibits. It follows that we are not seeing *X.* By hypothesis, what we are seeing is part of the surface of *X*; therefore, we are seeing part of the surface of *X,* but not seeing *X.* Therefore we have a case of seeing part of the surface of something without seeing that thing.

Whether this argument is cogent is not something I wish to discuss here. It is clear that it is pretty slippery, and surely not as clear-cut as the case of seeing a leg without seeing the table of which it is a part. I think it is persuasive but not wholly convincing. But suppose it were sound, then what would it prove? Would it prove that the epistemological tradition was, after all, correct? This is what I am concerned to deny.

VII

In the realist epistemological tradition of the twentieth century, and in some of the most recent and important psychological studies of perception,[14] it was believed and sometimes even argued that we do, sometimes, perceive the 'external world' directly. This claim was interpreted to mean that we don't literally see all of an object from a given perspective and at a given moment, but at most a certain part of it. This latter claim was taken to mean that we see a certain part of its surface. This idea we formulated earlier as the thesis that it was a necessary condition of seeing an object that we see at least part of its surface. We have shown that this thesis is wrong—the Jupiter example being a decisive counter case to it.

But along with the preceding important thesis, there was another of almost equal weight. It was held by Moore (among others) that *at most,* in cases of veridical perception, one could be seeing *only* part of the surface of any opaque object. We have shown, with our Victoria Nyanza and Cheval mirror examples, that this view is also wrong.

We have also tried to show that this entire tradition and its current psychological counterparts have been unaware of how difficult it is to see the surface of something under certain conditions and how really difficult it is to see *only* the surface of something under certain conditions. It is even more difficult to see *only* part of the surface of something under those conditions, if one means by "only" that one is not seeing the object as well. We conclude from this investigation that even if Moore were correct that sometimes we can see *only* the surface, or part of the surface of *X,* this principle could not be foundational for a whole theory of perception.

Notes

1. The notion of a material object is crucial in Price's account of perception. His definition partly analyzes this concept via the notion of a surface, but the latter concept is left unexplored. His definition is: "By 'material thing' is meant something which is a single three-dimensional whole, having one closed surface, one shape, one size, and one position in relation to other material things." *Perception* (Westport, Conn., 1973), 35.

2. For an account of Moore's use of 'after-image', 'negative after-image', 'to be met with in space', and related notions, see his "Proof of an External World," *Philosophical Papers* (Winchester, Mass., 1959), 130-35. His discussion is too subtle to be summarized here. For a critical appraisal of this paper, and especially of Moore's use of these notions, see my "Moore's Proof of an External World," *Dialectica* 33 (1979): 379-97.

3. "Talk about Talk about Surfaces" (coauthored with Robert Foelber), *Dialectica* 31 (1977): 1-21.

4. See "Two Conceptions of Surfaces," *Midwest Studies in Philosophy* 4 (1979): 277-91.

5. Ibid, 277ff.

6. Ibid, 266ff.

7. These remarks would have to be qualified. In "Two Conceptions of Surfaces," I pointed out that one could speak of a Leonardo surface as having a bulge. Therefore even Leonardo surfaces have properties, but these are not 'physical' properties. We cannot shave down the bulge in a Leonardo surface, but we can give a topological representation of it.

8. When tennis players speak about fast and slow surfaces they are not speaking about fast and slow courts.

9. The property, *being a part of,* applies to Somorjai surfaces, but not to the objects that have such surfaces. In general, this is not a physical property, as I am using the term, though there are doubtless some cases where we might wish to say the contrary.

10. I am greatly indebted to Robert Buccini with respect to this discussion, even though he disagrees with me in holding that one need not be able to distinguish features of a surface to be said truly to be seeing it.

11. Moore explicitly denied ("A Defense of Common Sense,") *Philosophical Papers* (Winchester, Mass., 1959), 55, that, if you could see so deeply into the hand as to see its bones, you would then be seeing its surface or part of its surface.

12. In effect they wished to identify what was "directly seen," the sense-datum, with the object apprehended when there is zero visual resolution. Unless there is some resolution, we cannot be said to be seeing the surface at all. But how much resolution is a matter of degree: it thus appears that what is directly seen can have properties it does not appear to have.

13. "Two Conceptions of Surfaces," 283.

14. I am here thinking primarily of the recent work of the distinguished psychologist, J. J. Gibson. In his monumental study *The Ecological Approach to Visual Perception* (New York, 1979), Gibson argues that surfaces play a key role in the perception of the environment. They provide the edges, corners, boundaries, and perceptual invariants that allow us to apprehend the sizes and relative positions of objects as we move through an environment while scanning it. In holding that every object has a surface, that it is a surface, that it is a condition of seeing the object that we see its surface, Gibson espouses many of the same theses as Moore. But he would categorically deny that in normal perception—what he calls cases of "ambulatory vision"—we typically apprehend images or any of their analogues, such as sense-data, *directly*. Instead, he argues that we apprehend surfaces and (in so doing) the objects that have them *directly*. There is thus a direct visual "uptake" of depth, roundness, relative position, etc. His views are too complicated to be described here, but their resemblance to those of Moore is striking.

The Historicity of Psychological Attitudes: Love Is Not Love Which Alters Not When It Alteration Finds

AMELIE OKSENBERG RORTY

There is a set of psychological attitudes—love, joy, perhaps some sorts of desire—that are individuated by the character of the subject, the character of the object, and the relation between them. Of course, such attitudes can typically be identified without reference to their objects: Mr. Knightly, Raskolnikov, Swann, Humbert Humbert all love, though Emma, Sonia, Odette, and Lolita are quite different sorts of women. Still, the details of their loves—the dispositions and thoughts that are active in their loving—are radically different in these cases, so much so that each, looking at the others, might wonder whether they really love. When such psychological attitudes are directed to other people, those concerned characteristically want the attitude to be directed to *them,* rather than to this or that trait. "Do you love me for myself alone, or for my yellow hair?" asks one of Yeats's beautiful ladies, and Yeats has a sage reply, truthfully and sadly: "Only God, my dear, could love you for yourself alone, and not for your yellow hair." This concern about the proper object of the attitude is a way of expressing a concern about its constancy or endurance.

The individuation of such psychological attitudes might be thought a consequence of a general metaphysical fact, that relations are individuated by their subjects and objects. But these relational psychological attitudes are not states identified by the functional relation between the subject and some object: a person, a state of affairs, a propositional content. Although for some purposes it may be convenient to treat such attitudes as states, they arise from, and are shaped by, dynamic interactions between a subject and an object. (As slides of frozen cells stand to a living, working organism, so do psychological attitudes construed as *states* stand to phenomena of dynamic interaction.) It is this feature of such attitudes—what we might call their *historicity*—that generates a concern about their constancy and that can, as

I hope to show, also assuage that concern. (In calling psychological attitudes *activities,* and focusing on interactive attitudes, I do not intend to classify them with voluntary or responsible actions. Interactive attitudes are not necessarily caused by intentions or under voluntary control, even though they are certainly intentional, and sometimes voluntary.) These psychological attitudes are identified by the detail of the narrative of the interactions between the subject and the object, interactions that also individuate the persons involved. Not only are such relational psychological attitudes individuated by their objects, but also the trajectory of the subject's life—the subject's further individuation—is affected by this relational attitude, this activity.

For the moment, I want to set aside the question of whether this characterization defines only a very small class. Because I do not believe passions or emotions form a "natural class," as distinct from (say) desires or motives, or some sorts of beliefs and judgments, I shall not even try to determine whether those conditions we now roughly classify as *passions* or *emotions* are historical, dynamic, and interactive, and whether their rationality is thereby endangered. I want rather to trace one such interactive attitude through some of its ramifications, to give a sketch of its historicity, showing that far from threatening rationality, it is just this interactivity that shores, though it cannot possibly assure, the sane emendation and corrigibility we want when we try to account for the rationality of such attitudes. I shall take love, rather than joy, desire, indignation, or fear, as an example. We seem to know more about loving than we do about many other psychological attitudes, not because we are more adept at loving than we are at being joyful or indignant, but because, wanting to be loved, we have given thought to what we want, in wanting to be loved. The characteristics that such an examination uncovers are, as I hope to show, historically specific: they arise in particular social, political, and intellectual contexts. The conditions and criteria set on the identification of love reveal the preoccupations of the era.

Although I shall sketch the place of contemporary conceptions of the conditions of love in its historical context, I want for the moment to set aside the question of whether the contemporary forms provide the central and definitory example of love (if there can be such a thing). Though romantic and erotic love are primary examples, they are by no means the only, or even the clearest examples of this sort of attitude. The kind of love I have in mind is the love of friendship, and sometimes (though in our culture, rarely) the love of parents and children. The account I sketch does not assume that such friendship-love is symmetrically reciprocated or even that it is reciprocated at all. Nor does it assume that there is a strict economy of love, such that its expansion to others automatically constitutes a diminution or loss elsewhere. Nevertheless, although such love is by no means exclusive, it cannot include more people than the lover is able to attend closely. If there is an economy involved, it is the economy of focused, interactively forming attention, one that not only wishes but acts to promote the thriving of the friend.

I want to examine some characteristics of dynamic, interactive, historical psychological attitudes: (1) Their proper objects are a person, rather than this or that characteristic of a person.[1] (2) Such attitudes are permeable; that is, the lover is affected, changed not only by loving but by the details of the character of the person loved. (3) Because such attitudes affect the person, they affect the person's actions. Although some lovers do not act on behalf of the welfare of those whom they love, their not doing so raises a doubt about whether they do truly love. (Parallel: although someone who desires to learn does not necessarily forthwith set about learning, still, not doing so raises a doubt about the desire). (4) These attitudes are identified by a characteristic narrative history. Although there are pangs of love, stabs of fear, twinges of longing, and thrills of joy, these are identifiable as the feeling of love, fear, longing, or joy only within the complex narrative of the living attitude. These psychological attitudes often feature a particular feeling tone that so magnetizes our attention that we tend to confuse it with the dynamic attitude as a whole.[2] But it is the whole history, and not only the focused and highlighted affective aspect, that constitutes the attitude. In the case of love, there is a presumption of some nonaccidental continuity, assured either by the constancy of a particular relation between the lover and the friend or by the character of their interaction.

Let's begin by distinguishing different ways that the continuity of love can be assured, distinguishing its enduring constancy from its interactive historical continuity. When love is constant and enduring, it persists despite changes in the friend's traits, even changes in those traits that first awoke the love and that were its central focus. This kind of constancy is assured only at a very general level: it is directed to the same person, extensionally identified, and the attachment remains at roughly the same level of devotion.[3] If Louis's love for Ella when he is 20 is radically different from his attitude at 60, has his love been constant? Presumably, constancy can be preserved by defining the object and the functional roles of his attitude in a sufficiently general manner. But such generality is unlikely to reassure those who wonder if they still love, when little they desire or do has remained the same.

When Louis and Ella are concerned about the continuity of their loves, they are not only interested in constancy, though perhaps some of their concerns could be rephrased in that way. What might concern Ella is whether *she* influences or affects the character of Louis's love and whether his delight in her ramifies to affect other things about him. When Ella does not want Louis to love her as Don Juan might have loved Elvira, her concern for his fidelity might be a way of expressing her concern for whether his delight focuses on her rather than on his dazzling gifts as a lover. She wants his speeches, his charming attentions and deftly winning ways to be not only directed *at* and *to* her, but to take their tenor and form from his delighted recognition of what is central to her. It is not enough that he gets the color of her eyes right, when he gets to that part of the serenade describing their enchantment. Nor is Ella's worry laid to rest by being assured of his fidelity, assured that Louis is no Don Juan, ranging over variables for his joys as a connoisseur of the subtle and interesting differences between women and their ever so wonderful effects on him. For whatever good such assurance might do her, Ella could be convinced that if she were to die, or if they were to have an irreconcilable falling out, Louis would feel lost, mourn, and only gradually be healed enough to love someone else. But both she and her successor Gloria might be aggrieved that Louis always brings the same love, a love that is contained within *his* biography, to be given as a gift. Presumably Gloria does not want to inherit Louis's love for Ella: she wants Louis to love her in a wholly different way, defined by the two of them. This is a complex and compounded hope: that Louis's love will be formed by his perceiving—his accurately perceiving—the gradual changes in her, and in his responses being appropriately formed by those changes. If Ella and Gloria love *Louis,* they want the changes they effect in him to be consonant and suitable to him as well as to them, conducing to his flourishing as well as theirs. It is because they want their love to conduce to his flourishing that it is important that they see him accurately and that their interactive responses to him be appropriate.

There is a kind of love—and for some it may be the only kind that qualifies as true love—that is historical precisely because it does not (oh so wonderfully) rigidly designate its object. The details of such love change with every change in the lover and the friend. Such a love might be called *dynamically permeable.* It is *permeable* in that the lover is changed by loving and changed by truthful perception of the friend. Permeability rejects being obtuse to change as an easy way of assuring constancy. It is dynamic in that every change generates new changes, both in the lover and in interactions with the friend. Having been transformed by loving, the lover perceives the friend in a new way and loves in a new way. Dynamism rejects the regionalization of love as an easy way of assuring constancy: the changes produced by such love tend to ramify through a person's character, without being limited to the areas that first directly were the focus of the lover's attention.

To see how this works out, let's gossip a bit about Ella, Louis, and Gloria. Louis's love for Ella began with his enchantment at her crisp way of playing Scarlatti, the unsentimental lyricism of her interpretation of Schubert, her appreciation of Orwell's journalism. After a while, he found that he was enchanted by traits he'd never noticed or admired in anyone else: the sequence of her moods, the particular way she had of sitting still, head bent when she listened to music. He came to love those traits in her, or her in those traits—he could hardly tell which. He came to appreciate such traits in others because her having them had delighted him. And he changed too, not necessarily in imitation of her, but because of her. An acute observer could discern changes in Louis that had their origins and explanation in his love of Ella, changes that were deeper than those that arose from his desire to please her. Some of these changes might conflict with, and threaten, other long-standing traits. If Louis's interest in Ella brings an interest in medieval music, it brings him into new company as well. The ramified consequences of his new interests are likely to interfere with his Friday night jam sessions with his old friends in the hard rock group. Either his responses to Ella ramify, and he acquires a new taste in companions, or he attempts to regionalize the changes that Ella effects on him. Both alternatives have significant consequences on them, and on him. If his dynamic interactions do not ramify, there will be conflicts between his pre-Ella and his post-Ella self. But if they do ramify, his psychological continuity is loosened by his being formed and reformed by each new friendship. (Of course, such problems are often solved by Louis and Ella sharing important parts of their lives, partners in common enterprises. Sharing their lives and activities assures their both being formed by a common world as well as by each other.) If Louis and Ella are wise, they are careful to avoid the extremes of both regionalization and ramification. Fortunately, this is not wholly a matter of insight and foresight: a person's previous traits resist transformation. If Louis *interacts* with Ella, he cannot become a person formed by and designed to suit her fantasies.

We shall return to the difficulties of regionalization and ramification, the difficulties of abstract constancy and hypersensitivity. For the moment, let us suppose that in this idyllic fairy tale, Louis came to realize that he would continue to love Ella even if she were to lose those traits that first drew him to her and that were still the focus of his joy in her. Even if someone else played Scarlatti more brilliantly, Schubert more discerningly, and had even more trenchant views on the relation between Orwell and Brecht, he would not transfer his love. This does not mean that he would see or love her *de re,* whatever that might mean. Nor does it mean that the character of his devotion would remain unchanged by whatever changes might occur in her. He'd be lunatic to love her at 60 in just exactly the same way as he had at 20; and he'd be cruel to love her way of playing Scarlatti if her hands had been mangled in an accident. Nor can his love be analyzed by a set of counterfactuals.[4] If she became Rampal's accompanist, he would . . . . If her mother moved next door, he would . . . . If she became paralyzed, he would . . . . If she declared herself impassioned of a punk-rock-shlock electronic guitar player, he would . . . . If Glorious Gloria, the Paragon of his Dreams, invited him to join her in a trip to Acapulco, he would . . . . If this kind of love could be analyzed in a set of counterfactuals, that set would have to be indefinitely large. For there are an indefinite number of changes that will occur and that will affect Louis if he loves Ella.

This explains why even a true historical love might end in dissolution and separation. That it did end would not prove that it had not existed, or that either its permeability or its dynamism were defective. On the contrary, it might be just these that establish—if it is at all sensible to speak of demonstration in this area—that it was indeed Ella that Louis loved, and that he did indeed love rather than swoon. But we have come to a strange outcome. The internal momentum of their interaction—for instance, the consequences of its ramification or its regionalization—might lead to its dissolution. And this might comfort them both: if they parted, it was because they had truly affected one another, and not because Louis's love had accidentally lost its rigidity or acquired a new direction, however slowly or grievously. In such cases, what marks theirs as a historical love that could not endure (though it might have remained constant over appropriate counterfactuals) is not that it was a love *de re* that got transferred to another *rem,* or that their resistance to transference or substitution was expressed by a suitable period of mourning. What marked it as historical was that they had both been permanently transformed by having loved just *that* person. In short, such love is not only individuated by its objects; more significantly, the lovers are individuated by their love. Louis's subsequent history, his new loves, joys, indignations, the details of his continuing individuation—even his love of Gloria—are affected by his loving interaction with Ella. Both the continuity of their love, and its eventual rupture, arose from their interaction.

That dynamic permeability can lead to dissolution should not impel lovers to assure the continuity of their love by preferring constancy assured by rigid nonpermeability. If historical love runs the danger of phasing itself out, constant, rigid, nonpermeable love also has its dangers. If Louis's love is fixed only by his own character, its active expression may not respond to Ella's needs, even though he may be, in an abstract way, supportive. When Ella worries about the constancy of Louis' love, she may be expressing her sense of her vulnerability in the world, the ways that she has come to need and to depend on him for her thriving.[5] Besides expressing a fear of being harmed, a desire for constancy can itself sometimes be harmful: Ella's fears about Louis's constancy might betray a self-fulfilling sense of dependency. She may have come to be so dependent on the responsive sensitivity of Louis's attunement to her, as a supporting force in her thriving, that she has diminished herself, perhaps even muted the very things that Louis originally admired in her. And Louis, initially charmed by Ella's need of him, may for his part have colluded in her dependency. On the one hand, constancy assured by dynamic permeability does not always automatically work to the benefit of lovers: insight and foresight (of a sort that is, unfortunately, acquired only through experience, and even then, only rarely) is required to direct and to prune the modifications that dynamic permeability fosters. Without the tempering of sound good sense, dynamic permeability might simply produce a severe case of *folie a deux*. If Ella knows herself to be affected by the ways Louis perceives her, if her sense of herself—and, so, in a way, the self she becomes—is in part constituted by the way Louis sees her, she wants more than that Louis's love be historical and dynamically permeable. On the other hand, if she hopes to assure continuity by constant rigidity, she may find Louis's love to be a conserving, conservative prison, binding her to continue as the person Louis originally loved or chooses to see in her. Both those who want the sort of sensitivity assured by dynamic permeability and those who want the sort of security assured by a rather more rigid constancy want their friends to be wise, wiser than either a rock or a sensitive chameleon with a skin of litmus paper can be.[6]

It might be useful to ask *why* we want all this from our loves. There are two reasons, both obvious, both also sobering. Those who are concerned about the constancy and historicity of love are not necessarily self-important or self-obsessed; they suffer the diseases of the time. It is after all rather remarkable that an attitude and an activity that begins in delight, that carries a desire to share the activities of life, and that brings an active wish for well-being should so quickly move to a concern about continuity. The first reason that contemporary love focuses on constancy is that we sense ourselves fragile, vulnerable in the world. In being aware of our vulnerability, we recognize that among the harms that can befall us are those that endanger or erode just those traits for which we are loved. Because those who delight in us seem to vanquish our sense of vulnerability, we think of them as among our strongest protections in the world. And because lovers characteristically want the flourishing of their friends, they often are actively and objectively central to their thriving. Because the continuity of protective devotion is not automatically assured by the permanent individuating effects of interaction, we want to be loved "for ourselves alone" rather for our most lovable traits, traits we realize we may lose. Not surprisingly, the idea of individuality and the sense of vulnerability are closely associated. Those who concentrate on the sense of invulnerability that loving delight can sometimes bring, and on the objective protections that devoted lovers often assure, might want constancy and think of nonpermeable rigidity instead of historicity as the best way to achieve it. (The pathological form of this attitude is an attempt to control and to bind the friend.)

The second reason we want continuity is that we are aware of being constituted by the perceptions of others, particularly by the perceptions of those who love or hate us, rejoice in us, fear or admire us. We come to think of ourselves, as we perceive they see us. For that reason, it is important to us that our enemies and lovers—the objects of psychological attitudes— perceive us aright, sensitive to the changes in us. Because we crystallize around what they focus, it is important that they continue to love or hate us for what we are—for what conduces to our thriving—rather than for what we were or what they need us to be. (The pathological form of this attitude is failure of integrity, the readiness to abandon parts of oneself.)[7]

This baroque description of the desire for constancy or continuity of historical psychological attitudes might be thought well replaced by a rather more streamlined Bauhaus approach, a functionalist account of psychological attitudes. They are, we might say, identified by their causal roles, by their etiologies and their effects: that is all that is needed to make sense of the different effects of a preference for rigid constancy or for dynamic permeability. But if we favor Bauhaus functionalism about psychological attitudes we must accept functionalism everywhere. Not only Louis's love but also his beliefs, his perceptions, hopes, and desires are identified by their functional roles. But the functionalist account will not itself explain *why* Louis's attitudes play their various typical functional roles. There is, in a way, nothing wrong with functionalism except that it is radically incomplete: it cannot by itself explain why psychological attitudes have their typical—and typically interactive and clustering—roles. (Bauhaus architecture reveals a great deal about how architects solve heating problems; but it does not thereby provide a clear understanding of the needs or even the constitutions of the people who live or work in those buildings.)

Reflecting on *why* our contemporaries seem to want love to take these forms—why they want their loves to be appropriately interactive and to be enduring—suggests yet another, quite different way that such psychological attitudes are historical. Because the roles that loving friendship play in a person's life vary historically, conceptions of their proper causes and objects and of the behavior that is appropriate to them also change historically. The standard narratives of such attitudes (the usual tales of their dynamic permeability) vary culturally. The story of a dynamic permeable love that I sketched tends to appear quite late and regionally: it arises after Romanticism, after the Industrial Revolution, in a context in which the sense of vulnerability takes quite specific forms. Vulnerable we are, and vulnerable we have always been. But the particular conditions that constitute our sense of our vulnerability varies historically. It takes a particular conception of the course of the life of an isolated individual as some thing fashioned by that person alone to produce the sense of vulnerability that might seem to make a particular form of love—which after all begins in attentive rejoicing—a protection and a mode of development.

The functional identification of psychological attitudes characterizes their typical causes and effects: to understand *why* such attitudes as love, indignation, and respect have just those characteristic etiologies and consequences, we need to understand the conceptions of individuality, needs, and vulnerabilities that constitute a typical life. (It is not always *needs* and *concerns* that identify the functional roles of psychological attitudes. But because needs and concerns seem to be the primary focus of current theoretical and practical preoccupations, I'll concentrate on them, without being committed to the general view that the functions of psychological attitudes are always defined by needs.) The vicissitudes from which we need protection vary historically: they vary with the sorts of dangers and fortunes that typically arise, with a person's class and condition, with conceptions of individuality.[8] As our conceptions of individuality change, our vulnerabilities change; as our vulnerabilities change, our needs change; as our needs change, our activities take distinctively different forms; as our activities take characteristically different forms, so do our psychological attitudes.

A short and absurdly superficial sketch of the history of changes in the conception of love may help to make this more plausible. Platonic *eros* is a cosmological as well as a psychological force: it has one proper cause and one proper object—the Beautiful Good—that draws us to it. Acting within us as well as on us, it provides the energy and direction of all we do. Although *eros* has nothing to do with individuality or vulnerability—and indeed is meant to transcend particular individuals—it is the principle that assures our real well-being. Aristotle's account of *philia* as a relation among the virtuous, sharing the activities of life together, each actively wishing the other well and seeing his own virtues mirrored in his friend, is hardly recognizable as the ancestor of our notion of loving friendship. The role of loving friendship in that world was radically different from its role for us. Perhaps because family rather than friends provided the primary protections against vulnerability, the philosophical problems concerning *philia* were, for the Greeks, questions about whether friends are primarily like-minded or complementary and whether it is better (more beneficial) to love than to receive love. Christian preoccupations with *eros, philia, caritas,* and *agape* reflect still different conceptions of individuality. When it is God rather than kin who determines and secures the shape of a life, the primary questions about the fidelity of love are whether it conforms to divine intention, whether it is modeled after Christ's love. Renaissance *amor* brings yet other transformation: it is the descendant of Platonic *eros,* the active energy that moves a person to the realization of excellence. The love of Glory, of the City, of a Lady or Muse are simultaneously passions and the very springs of action. Because the object draws the person towards it, *amor* is classified as a passion, a passive condition. Yet the lover's nature is perfected and fulfilled by *amor* and by the active desires that it engenders. The central question becomes: what is the relation between this one primary motivational force and the many various desires that follow from it and that are its expression? Hobbes transforms *eros* and *amor* into particular desires: the desire for the realization of the Good becomes a desire for the objects and actions that promote self-preservation and self-interest. Following Hobbes, but echoing a secularized version of Platonic Christianity, Rousseau makes an individual's self-love the source of all that person's desires. But self-love has a proper and a corrupt form. *Amour de soi* is an unselfconscious, noncomparative sense of one's own well-being in healthful activity; by contrast, *amour propre* is comparative and depends on a perception of the estimation of others. (Rousseau would regard the story of Louis and Ella as a story of the fallen condition, generated by *amour propre* rather than healthful *amour de soi.)* Against this historical background, Freud's account of libidinal *eros* as the basic energetic principle, whose social formation and direction provide the vicissitudes of an individual's psychological history, no longer seems startling.

Now what does all this mean about the *rationality* of such psychological attitudes?[9] Those who would like to make emotional and psychological attitudes respectable as appropriate sources of action want to assure that their corrigibility and redirection take the same form as the corrigibility of beliefs. To rescue such attitudes from the Seething Cauldron of the Irrational, they attempt to show that psychological attitudes can be rationally reconstructed on the model of the structure of propositional or intellectual attitudes. But this philosophical reconstruction cannot—nor was it ever intended to—assure that the corrigibility of the propositional content of a psychological attitude is sufficient to secure its psychological appropriateness. Presumably we want psychological attitudes to be corrigible because we want them to serve us well, to conduce to our thriving. Certainly psychological attitudes that can be propositionalized are at least in principle corrigible insofar as the truth value of their intentional content can be determined. But although the corrigibility or emendation of the beliefs and perceptions associated with psychological attitudes conduces to their appropriateness, an account of the ability of such attitudes to be propositionalized need not provide the most perspicuous account of either their appropriateness or their functional roles in thriving.

It might be helpful to take an indirect approach to the analysis of the connection between the ability of psychological attitudes to be rationalized and their being well formed to conduce to thriving. In principle at any rate, propositional attitudes differ from psychological attitudes in being affected only by changes in a person's relation to evidence and other epistemically relevant factors. They are not (or should not be) affected by changes in one's character—by whether, for example, one is depressed or elated, angry or affectionate. But some intellectual or propositional attitudes may be historical in the same way that love and hate, fear and admiration can be.

Classes of psychological and propositional attitudes cannot be so sharply and neatly distinguished from one another. The distinction between dynamically permeable activities and epistemically oriented activities does not serve to distinguish between psychological and propositional attitudes just like that, *überhaupt*. There are some people who love constantly and rigidly, nonhistorically. The functional character of their love is assimilable to that of propositional attitudes that are not dynamically permeable to the objects or contents of their attitudes. The psychological attitudes of such people might be said to be intellectualized. But there are others who believe, doubt, and think in a dynamically permeable way. It would be true of them that their cognitive propositional attitudes are psychologized: their thinking, doubting, believing is affected by their character traits, by their irascibility, melancholy, cheerfulness. Their propositional attitudes are dynamically responsive to nonepistemic features of the contents of their propositional attitudes. Psychological associations (puns, visual associations, memories) connected with the cognitive or propositional content of their attitudes affect their propositional attitudes. They do not stand in the same epistemistic relation to someone they dislike as they stand to those whom they like: they cannot hear what that person says in the same way that they would hear just those words from someone they like. They cannot think about what they fear with the same epistemically sensitive attitude as they take to what does not frighten them. It is more difficult for them to evaluate a core belief about what they fear than it is for them to determine the truth of a belief about what brings them pride, and both are more difficult for them to evaluate than a belief about what does not directly affect them. Not only the system of beliefs, but *they* are changed by their doubts, distrusts, loves. For such people, thinking is, as one might say, psychological, affected by moods, by likes and dislikes.

Still, one might object that this sort of Proustian differentiation of types of believers and lovers does not affect the basic point, that at least *knowledge* is not psychologically dynamically permeable. If our propositional attitude is formed by associations rather than by our epistemic relation to its propositional content, then our propositional attitude does not qualify as *knowledge*. And if our beliefs about our acquaintances is affected by our likes and dislikes, then those beliefs are not rational, however true or appropriate they may otherwise be. Still, even if the conditions for knowledge guarantee its immunity to epistemically irrelevant psychological attitudes, the beneficial functioning of such attitudes is not thereby necessarily best assured by their rational corrigibility. Though a propositional attitude becomes epistemically suspect when it is formed by a person's psychological condition (fears, elation, or melancholy), propositionalizing or intellectualizing psychological attitudes need not be the best way to assure sanity and soundness.

What is it then that we want, when we want psychological attitudes to be rational? There is often no one whose inferences are more logical, more formally impeccable, and often there is no one more truthful, than the local lunatic. It is because his impeccable and exemplary truth-preserving inferences do not serve him in the right way that the local lunatic is in trouble. No particular additional truth or inference can help him. His problem is that his rationality cannot guide or form what he does because it is not appropriately rooted in his character. Because we want to avoid the lunatic's troubles, we want more than that our attitudes be corrigible by considerations of truth and validity. We also want them to be appropriately formed to serve our thriving.

The direction we take in assuring the correctness and appropriateness of psychological attitudes may vary, as we focus primarily on their correction or on their formation. If we concentrate on avoiding the harms of malformation, we emphasize rational corrigibility. We are then likely to favor propositionalizing the contents of our psychological attitudes. On the assumption that we at least attempt to free ourselves of attitudes clustered around false beliefs, we attempt to secure the appropriateness of psychological attitudes by assimilating them as closely as we can to propositional attitudes oriented to truth. If, however, we concentrate on developing and forming appropriate psychological attitudes, we emphasize their historicity, attempting to discover the conditions under which dynamic permeability conduces to flourishing.

Rather than assimilating appropriateness and thriving to rationality, construed as preserving truth through inferential sequences, we might construe rationality as itself partially constituted by what serves us well. If the difference between the lunatic and the wise person is a difference in their rationality, then rationality has acquired a substantive as well as a formal condition. If rationality is understood to serve thriving, the rationality of a person of practical wisdom is as much a function of her character—her having appropriate habits arising from well-formed perceptions and desires—as it is from her drawing the right inferences from the right premises. It is what the wise person knows, and the role that knowledge plays in the fine attunement of action, as well as the logically impeccable character of reasoning, that makes the person rational. It is by doing the right thing at the right time in the right way that rationality serves the wise person; it is this that keeps her truth-telling and valid inferences from being inconsequential, inappropriate, blind, stubborn, or silly.

How does any of this help Louis and Ella determine what they require from their psychological attitudes, if those attitudes are to conduce to their thriving? Certainly, if their interactions are to be beneficial, they had better perceive one another accurately. To avoid their responses being formed by mere perceptions of the moment, to avoid the *folie a deux* problem, it is also important that their attunement be appropriate. But how is that to be determined? As we saw, what conduces to the continuity of their love might serve neither of them well, and what conduces to Louis's developing and thriving need not serve the interactive harmony between him and Ella. Although the historicity of their attitudes—their attunement—initially seemed to promise the appropriateness of their responses, there can be difficulties in that promise being fulfilled. The beneficial functions of psychological attitudes seem no more assured by their historicity than by their ability to be rationalized.

Standardly, but not necessarily, rationality, appropriateness, and thriving are interwoven. It is the dream of rational social politics that in the long run these converge even if they cannot coincide. Of course these three conditions can vary independently: the lunatic shows that rationality does not assure appropriateness; the dangers of *folie a deux* show that adaptability and attunement do not assure thriving. Still, such counterexamples do not undermine the presumptive interconnections: rationality (as defined by truthfulness supported by validity) is a central guide to appropriateness, and appropriateness a central guide to flourishing. That the separation of rationality from appropriateness produces the lunatic, and the separation of appropriateness from thriving produces the unhappiness of those who suffer *folie a deux,* proves the point.

Still, how have we spoken to Louis and Ella? It would be a mistake to think we've left them in a sound as well as a safe place. Even if they are assured of the connection between rationality, appropriateness, and thriving, they have yet to discover just what these require of them in particular situations. How dynamically permeable should Louis be without endangering his integrity or joining Ella in a case of *folie a deux?* How ramified or regionalized should his responses be? What *does* rationality require? What *would* constitute thriving? How are the thriving of Louis, Ella, Louis-and-Ella to be appropriately weighted when they seem to go in different directions?

We've left them just where they were: in the continuous, delicate, and delicious balancing acts of their lives. But that is just exactly where we should leave them. It is only the details of their particular situation that can determine what would be rational, what would be appropriate, what would constitute (whose?) thriving. No general philosophical conclusion about the presumptive connections between rationality, appropriateness, and thriving can possibly help them determine just what corrections rationality recommends or requires as appropriate to their condition. It can't even help them determine whether their sensitivities are sound or pathological, insufficient or excessive, let alone whether they should ramify or regionalize their responses to one another, to balance integrity with continuity in such a way as to conduce to thriving. The confluence of rationality, appropriateness, and thriving cannot help them to determine the directions in which rationality or appropriateness or even thriving—taken singly or coordinately—lie. And that is as it should be. Our task cannot be to resolve but only to understand the quandaries of Louis and Ella. Since their condition and its problems are historical, that is, particular, their solutions must be particular.

Notes

1. An earlier, shorter version of this paper was presented as a commentary to Robert Kraut's "Love *De Re*" (chap. 18 of this volume) at a meeting of the Eastern Division of the American Philosophical Association. In that paper, Kraut examined an account of love as a *de*

re, rather than a *de dicto* attitude; he also analyzed it on the model of naming, as a rigidly designating relation. In a later paper, he proposed an account of love as defined by a series of specific counterfactuals: if the beloved were to die, the lover would grieve . . . etc.

2. This "feeling" or "affective" tone of psychological attitudes is, as Stocker has argued, a central feature of their motivating force. Often the effects of psychological attitudes are a consequence of what it feels like to have them.

3. The analysis of the constancy of love rests on an account of the criteria for personal identity, as well as the criterion for the identity of psychological attitudes whose functional roles change over time.

4. Cf. Robert Kraut, "Love *De Re.*"

5. Cf. L. Tov-Ruach, "Jealousy, Attention and Loss," *Explaining Emotions,* edited by A. O. Rorty (Berkeley, Calif., 1980).

6. But friends who are not equally wise also have special problems. Perhaps this is why Aristotle thought true friendship could only exist among *phronimoi.*

7. Not all lovers want all this Proustian-Jamesian sensibility from their loves. If Ella is strongly autonomous, so that the details of Louis's love for her do not affect the person she becomes, if his perceptions of her do not further individuate her, she may not care whether Louis's love is historical: appropriate, not-too-rigid constancy may be all she wants, and indeed all she prefers. Ella might be the sort of person who finds an acutely historical love too demanding and time-consuming, preventing her from getting on with other things to which she wants to attend. It is just this sort of difference about preferences for historicity or for mere decent, not-too-rigid general constancy that leads lovers to be baffled by one another's disappointments in what seems to each of them a perfectly adequate fidelity.

A set of observations of prudence seems to follow from this analysis. (1) A friendship between a person who hopes that the constancy of love comes from its historicity and one for whom constancy is a matter of rigidity is likely to lead to deep misunderstanding. But such friends might reach an agreement about asymmetry: one of the friends might want to receive, but be disinclined to give, historical sensitivity; the other might have the appropriate corresponding desire, to give a historical sensitivity but be reassured by a rigid constancy rather than a dynamic permeability. Such a love might be very stable, even though there was considerable asymmetry of understanding between the pair. (2) Although a friendship between two constant, nonhistorical lovers is not likely to lead to misunderstanding, it is also likely not to assure very deep understanding. But both people might prefer to get on with other things in their lives. (3) A friendship between two strongly historical types might phase itself out. It is a difficult empirical question, one which we are not now in any position to answer, whether such differences—differences between a desire for dynamic permeability and a desire for rigidity—are associated with gender or with socioeconomic dependency.

8. See my "Literary Post-script: Characters, Persons, Selves, Individuals," *The Identities of Persons,* edited by A. O. Rorty (Berkeley, Calif., 1976).

9. The early version of this paper was expanded and presented to a colloquium on the emotions sponsored by La Maison des Sciences de l'Homme, 23-25, March 1984. Because organizers of that conference asked participants to address issues concerning the rationality of the emotions, I argued that evaluating psychological attitudes for their rationality is not a particularly perspicuous way of evaluating their appropriateness, their utility, or their soundness. Cf. "Varieties of Rationality, Varieties of Emotions" *Social Science Information,* 1985.

Love *De Re*

ROBERT KRAUT

A quite prevalent account of human emotion—the *cognitive evaluative theory*—treats occurrent emotional episodes as composites, one element of which is a set of physiological changes, the other of which is a set of judgments or evaluations that cause the changes. The intentionality of felt emotion—the "aboutness" of the emotion—derives from the intentionality of the judgments or evaluations that give rise to the physiological changes. Thus, my feelings are "conceptually directed" toward a certain object if they are caused by judgments or evaluations about that object.

On might, for various reasons, have misgivings about such a theory; I thus want to explore alternative approaches to the intentionality of emotion. Against the backdrop of a functionalist account of experiential states, I pursue an analogy between emotion and perceptual experience and examine one possible way of "getting the conceptual content into the feelings themselves"; a consequence of the approach is that ascriptions of emotional content involve a covert counterfactual element. Part II further attempts to understand distinctions of affective intentional focus, and it examines Robert Nozick's claim that "love is historical, attaching to persons . . . and not to characteristics." Some clarification is achieved by exploring analogies between the referential behavior of linguistic items and the content of emotions. My substantive suggestion for construing the "historicity" of certain emotions in terms of counterfactuals about replaceability is briefly outlined in part III.

I

Data: Sandra and Walter have been living together for some time. He tells her that he loves her. He surely exhibits the kind of behavior

> toward her that we are inclined, given other details of Walter's global psychology, to call love behavior.
> Sandra is upset. One evening she tells him: "It isn't really *me* you love."
> Walter is confused. "But you're the only one I share my joys and sorrows with, the one I most enjoy talking to, etc. And you're the only one I sleep with."
> Sandra says: "I know I'm on the receiving end of your love behavior. But that's not enough. I want to be on the receiving end of your love. And I'm not."

For the present, we need not discuss the kind of evidence that leads Sandra to make such remarks. What is essential is that she does not feel that Walter's emotional state—the state of love—is really directed toward *her*. Well, what *would* have to obtain, for her to really be the individual toward whom his attitude is directed?

This is a problem in the theory of intentionality—the theory, that is, of the directedness, aboutness, or "of-ness" of psychological states. The issue here is *not* that of distinguishing emotions from perceptions or judgments or from whatever else befalls the mental lives of persons. In general, emotions have the feature of intentionality: I am angry about something, I have an aversion to someone, I fear something, etc. There are, of course, prima facie examples of object-less emotions—nameless dreads, free-floating anxieties, general annoyance aimed at nothing in particular—but for the present we may ignore these.

Emotions are not, of course, the only kind of mental phenomena that have the feature of intentionality. Cognitive states—belief and knowledge, for example—have this feature, as do desires and perceptual states. Thus, I perceive *something,* and my perceptual state is directed toward an object— whether we construe such an object as a sense-datum or a physical entity that stands in an appropriate causal relation to the state in question. I will be suggesting here that the intentionality of emotion can be understood on the model of the intentionality of perception. And this latter phenomenon is not to be understood in terms of the intentionality of judgment or belief. One orthodoxy has it that intentionality—and opacity, its linguistic correlate—is always to be understood in terms of propositional content, the linguistic correlate of which is sentential embedding.

But this is only one orthodoxy; others reject it, arguing that not all opacity results from sentence embedding.[1] The dispute is obviously relevant to the theory of perception and the theory of emotion. For, on the one side, there are those who think that the possibility of reducing direct-object intensional constructions ("Macbeth sees a dagger," "Jones is terrified of lions," etc.) to sentential complement constructions ("Macbeth sees that a dagger is before him," "Jones is terrified that lions will rip him to pieces," etc.) is necessary if we are to adequately explain the intentionality of the notions involved (perception, terror, etc.). Thus, on such a view, perceptual awareness and terror have a judgmental component.[2]

That's one view. Another is that perceptual awareness is basically nonpropositional, and involves a nonsentential mode of representation. In traditional terms, we may claim that perception involves singular representations that have not yet entered into a predicational structure. In more modern terms, we may claim that it involves analogue, as opposed to digital, informational coding.

Such considerations are critical in connection with the analysis of emotion. Several writers (for example, Robert Solomon and Robert Gordon) have been inclined to regard emotions as somehow propositional or judgmental in character.[3] Thus, affective states are viewed as driven by, or reducible to, or somehow essentially related to cognitive states. In a recent discussion of fear, for example, Gordon claims that the fundamental linguistic construction is "Jones fears *that* P"—that is, a sentential complement construction (see n. 3). According to his account, direct object constructions like "Jones fears dark places" are generated from *fears that* constructions by the application of some sentential transformation (the character of which he never discloses). But why this urge to *propositionalize* the emotions? Why the tendency to taint affect with cognition?

Various familiar lines of argument, some more plausible than others, tend to foster such cognitivist accounts:

Emotions are subject to rational appraisal. Emotional reactions may be deemed reasonable or unreasonable, justified or unjustified, warranted or unwarranted, depending upon circumstances. The cognitivist often cannot see how "pure feelings" could be susceptible to criticism or justification. (George Pitcher, for example, claims that any view according to which emotions are feelings "does not allow the notions of reasonableness and justifiability to gain any foothold in the concept of an emotion."[4] So he remedies the difficulty by postulating a propositional component (a belief or judgment) as part of the emotion; if that component is epistemically unwarranted, then any emotional state "based upon" it is thereby unwarranted. Thus, the justificational status of an emotional state derives from the justificational status of beliefs or judgments.

A second pull toward cognitivism derives from an inability to understand how anything other than beliefs or judgments could have intentional content; thus the intentionality of emotion is analyzed in terms of the intentionality of underlying cognitive states. The cognitivist often cannot see how to get content into emotion without exploiting putative judgments in which the emotion is grounded.

Yet a third pull has already been discussed: verbs of emotion induce

opacity. Any linguist convinced that the source of all intensionality is sentential embedding will postulate implicit propositional complementation. This
in turn motivates the view that emotion verbs characterize states which are,
in part, cognitive. The intensionality of fear attributions, for example, is thus
explained in terms of the intensionality of belief ascriptions.

Additional arguments lead in similar directions; some turn on the
differentiation or individuation of distinct emotions that are phenomenologically indistinguishable (e.g., anger and indignation); others involve general
qualms about feelings and how we could learn to properly characterize them.
The usual upshot of such considerations is admirably stated by Robert
Gordon: "the intentionality of emotion sentences is derivative from the
intentionality of sentences that ascribe beliefs and wishes."[5] This is, I think,
false. It is, moreover, importantly false.

Suppose that Karl is now experiencing the kinds of feelings and physiological upsets characteristic of occurrent anger. Perhaps the feelings are not
identical with anger; perhaps they are not even a necessary component of
anger. It's commonly granted that the sensation of physiological change does
not provide adequate basis for the differentiation of distinct emotions.[6] For
example, jealousy may be argued to be phenomenologically indistinguishable from envy, annoyance from indignation, sadness from depression, affection from lust, and so on. Something must be added to make the more
fine-grained discriminations. The Schachter-Singer experiments suggest that
various details of the subjects' cognitive states play just this role.[7] Thus,
Karl's cognitions of the context around him play an essential role, not only
in his identification of his emotional state but in the very constitution of it.
And thus the intentionality problem is solved: Karl's feeling constitutes
anger toward *Jones,* on this occasion, if the feeling was caused by, say, the
judgment that Jones has just deliberately done him damage. This judgment,
and other like it, induced physiological changes in Karl, thus conferring upon
the corresponding feelings an intentional directedness toward Jones.

This kind of account might be plausible in connection with certain
emotions. But it seems inapplicable to the problem with which we began.
Sandra, you'll recall, was afraid that Walter didn't really love *her.* She wants
his emotion to be conceptually directed toward her. What precisely does this
amount to? Given the cognitivist account recently considered, it amounts to
this: Walter has certain feelings caused by the appropriate sorts of judgments
and evaluations directed toward Sandra. But this is implausible; it is hard
to find any corresponding judgments that would serve the purpose here.
Granted, Walter might judge Sandra to be the most marvelous person in the
world, and these judgments might evoke feelings. But it seems to work
precisely the other way around. The amorous feelings often come first; the
favorable judgments and evaluations are already "guided" by—that is, are
a consequence of—the emotional responses. Thus we cannot explain the

intentionality of the emotion in terms of the intentionality of the judgments that caused it, since no judgments caused it.

Perhaps the *object* of Walter's affection is not really at issue here. Sandra's qualms might not involve matters of intentionality at all. He loves her alright, but he has certain *reasons* for loving her, and Sandra is not especially pleased with those reasons. *What* (or *whom*) the emotion is directed toward is one thing; *why* the emotion is present is quite another. Sandra's self-concept turns on her sense of humor, her cleverness, her emotional insight into herself and those around her; but these features seem to play a minimal role in drawing Walter to her. It's thus clear why she's upset: she wants to be loved for the right reasons, reasons that involve the features she values in herself. Walter, however, loves her only because of her superb piano playing skills—and this, according to Sandra, is a silly and depersonalizing reason.

I don't think this diagnosis in terms of reasons is adequate. It is hardly clear that emotions like love are based upon reasons; they might be, but they needn't be. Just as some beliefs are noninferential—that is, not derived from or based upon other beliefs—some emotional states are the result of various causal factors none of which deserve to be called *reasons*. Consider: Karl might hate George for a reason (he believes that George is a Modal Logician, that Modal Logic was conceived in sin, and thus that such people are despicable). But he might hate him simply because of the way the chemistry works—he's met him several times, was made extremely uncomfortable by him, and now wishes he were dead. This hatred is not based upon *reasons,* though it's surely causally explicable in terms of the character types involved. Reasons for an emotional state are one thing; causes quite another.

So Walter's love for Sandra, though causally explicable in terms of the subtle factors that determine human attraction, might not be based upon reasons; in that case, the intentionality problem is still with us. But now suppose that Walter's love *is* based upon reasons. I think the intentionality problem is still with us (though now we would have its solution); for in this case, and in many cases, *the reasons for an emotion partially define or determine its intentional object.*

This latter claim is implausible; surely the reasons for an emotion are one thing and the content or object of the emotion are quite another. Emotions with the same intentional focus can surely be based upon quite different reasons. For example, Walter's reason for loving Sandra is that she has remarkable musical ability, whereas Karl's reason for loving Sandra is that she is a superb conversationalist. Aren't their attitudes nonetheless directed toward the same object? After all, they both want to marry Sandra.

On some coarse-grained level of description, this is obviously right. But strictly speaking, Walter's attitude is directed toward Sandra's musicianship; Karl's attitude is directed toward her conversational skill. These are distinct objects indeed. We could use various idioms, depending on our semantical and metaphysical preferences, for capturing the difference: thus, Walter loves *Sandra qua musician* whereas Karl loves *Sandra qua conversationalist*. The sense in which their attitudes are directed "toward the same object" is a loose and popular sense. A more rigorous, fine-grained characterization of the intentional object of the love discloses a genuine disparity of content, generated by the disparity in reasons. The reasons for the love *constitute* the intentional focus of the love. If this is right, then our problem is solved: what Sandra wants is to be festooned with the appropriate *qua* clauses so far as Walter's love is concerned; this will, in turn, be guaranteed by her being loved for the right reasons. The wrong reasons generate the wrong *qua* clauses, which generate the wrong object. Simple—at least if Walter's love is based upon reasons. But it probably isn't; thus we still have work to do.

Perceptual states, though intentionally directed, are not based upon reasons. Perhaps we can learn something about emotion by reflecting upon perception. What gives a perceptual state—or, more broadly, an experiential state—its content? One familiar though controversial answer is couched in terms of *causal role*. Thus, experiential states are functionally definable in terms of their syndromes of typical occasions, typical manifestations, and typical relations to other states. Challenges to such an approach are common—witness the concerns with absent qualia, inverted qualia, structural isomorphs who react deviantly, and general qualms about whether functional specification underdetermines qualitative (experiential) character. I ignore such problems here because I think they are tractable; at any rate, let us suppose they are.

Suppose that, as the story goes,

(1) Macbeth sees a dagger.

Note that the truth of (1) is perfectly compatible with there not actually having been a dagger in Macbeth's physical vicinity. Macbeth might be sitting in a dark, empty room. The perceptual verb, when embedded in a direct object or nominal complement construction, is drained of its "success" entailments. (It is perfectly natural, for example, to describe someone as seeing pink rats, despite our knowledge [and even *his*] that no such items actually exist in his vicinity.) Moreover, (1) supports such inferences as

(2) Macbeth sees something.

and allows for pronominalizations like

(3) Macbeth sees a dagger, and it's green.

[A quick methodological observation: certain cautious philosophers, motivated by some theory or other, might reject (1)-(3) as being literally false, though warranted according to some vulgar conversational conventions.

This is a bad strategy, which widens the gap between semantical theorists and more traditionally oriented philosophers. Instead of denying the literal truth of (1)-(3), we ought rather to find a plausible account of the logical form and the semantics of such sentences that explains the logical consequence relations among them and that, moreover, coheres with our philosophical intuitions. Such an account is indeed available.[8]]

At any rate, the kind of causal role account of experiential content we are exploring dictates truth conditions for (1) of the form

(1S)   Macbeth is in that state that is typically caused by retinal irradiation induced by a dagger under normal conditions and that typically induces dagger reports, beliefs that a dagger is present, and any other behavior appropriate (given Macbeth's global psychology) to the presence of daggers.

The distinction, then, between the content of an "of a dagger" perceptual state and an "of a bear" perceptual state would be grounded in distinctions among the typical inputs and typical outputs associated with each. Thus the distinctions among actual phenomenal content are to be specified in terms of counterfactuals. This is not bizarre; the distinction between, for example, being a Pawn and being a Bishop, though genuine, consists of distinctions between ways the pieces could appropriately be moved, given various counterfactual conditions. The fact that phenomenal properties are thus construed as functional properties in no way subverts their reality.

When Karl sees a bush as a bear, he's occupying an experiential state typically associated with bear irradiations (insert here a more detailed functional specification of the state). Any self-respecting bush that had induced such a state in Karl probably wouldn't feel very good about the way it's being perceived. In some vital and important sense (the sense that involves intentional content), Karl really isn't seeing the bush at all; he's seeing a bear.

We want to take this analysis of perceptual content and apply it to the emotions. Why? Because we're looking for an alternative to a cognitivist account of the intentionality of emotion, and reflection upon this account of perceptual content seems to provide just such an alternative. The point is *not* that emotions are perceptions: there are, after all, no specific organs of emotion as there are organs of perception. Emotions tend to be caused by beliefs, judgments, and evaluations in a way that perceptions are not. Perception provides information about the external world, whereas emotion, at best, provides information about our attitudes toward the world.[9]

But, for all that, there's an obvious and tempting analogy: Karl's perceptual episode has a physical object (the bush) and an intentional object (a bear); similarly, Sandra seems to be the physical object of Walter's affection, but (if her suspicions are correct) not the intentional object of his affection. It's the latter that she wants. The difference between phenomenal bush-content and bear-content is explicated nonpropositionally, and that's just the kind of account we wanted in distinguishing Sandra-affection from some of its alternatives (e.g., "excellent-musician" affection).

It's clear that disanalogies are also present. The bush simply isn't a bear; Karl's perception thus involves a mistake and thus a disruption in the normal causal connections. However, the emotional case involves no such identificatory error, only a failure to conceptualize a situation with sufficient richness—for Sandra is, among other things, a fine musician.

I think the similarities here are more important than the differences. We want to view the intentional content as exemplified by the very feelings themselves; perhaps we can get the content into the feelings in the same way that we get it into the perceptual states, *via* the mechanisms of causal role. This suggests the following kind of analysis:

(4)   Walter loves Sandra.

is true if and only if

(5)   Walter is disposed to occupy occurrent states of affection that are such that (among other things) their typical causes involve Sandra and only Sandra.

(N.B. It was not part of our project to specify the earmarks of an affection state; our task was to pack the intentional content into such a state.)

What's making Sandra nervous is her belief that something like the following comes closer to the truth:

(6)   Walter is disposed to occupy occurrent states of affection that are such that (among other things) their typical causes involve the presence of (not only Sandra but) women with noteworthy musical skill.

Thus the functional states imputed in (5) are vastly different from those imputed in (6). It's as if, although Sandra does indeed trigger off amorous feelings in Walter, she plays no essential role in the triggering process—persons other than she might have put Walter into precisely the same state. Thus the state is not "of" her—for the state's syndrome of typical causes is defined over a fairly wide class of persons.

If this is right, then it's clear why a certain class of counterfactuals matters to Sandra. Having gotten to know Walter fairly well, she's isolated certain characteristic love behavior; and she suspects that such behavior would likely be manifest toward Ruth or toward Carol, were he to become familiar with them. She feels indiscernible from these other people *modulo* the behavior associated with Walter's love.

Why should these counterfactuals matter? Why should they vindicate Sandra's skepticism? After all, Walter persists in reminding her that behaviorism is false.

They matter because the emotional state, as well as its intentional focus, is now being functionally defined in terms of typical inputs and typical outputs. Thus these counterfactuals are essential to the very specification of the object of Walter's affection.

This kind of approach, if workable, generates various familiar perplexities. For example, in wanting (5) to be true, what exactly does Sandra want? She wants to be discernible from her competitors in an important way. But who are her competitors? Suppose that, like most of us, Sandra has a doppelgänger on Twin Earth; and suppose that Walter would react to this doppelgänger precisely as he responds to Sandra. Would this undermine the claim that he *really* loves Sandra? Maybe not; perhaps ascriptions of love must be relativized to a specification of "relevant alternatives." And perhaps we must discuss the distinction, if any, between *de re* and *de dicto* emotions. For such a distinction seems somehow related to Sandra's misgivings.

II

"That dame ain't in love with you . . .
she's in love with the championship."
Jimmy Durante to Joe Palooka,
World Heavyweight Boxing Champion

It is one thing to love a particular person and quite another to love some property or properties that s/he happens to possess. Similarly, it is one thing to love a particular person and quite another to love some role or office (e.g., Heavyweight Champion of the World) that the person happens to fill.

However we ultimately analyze this intuitive distinction, it is a distinction that seems to matter. One feels, upon viewing the movie from which the opening line is lifted, that Palooka is indeed being a fool—for it is not him but rather the office that he fills toward which Nina's love is directed. Similarly, it matters to Sandra that her lover's affection be genuinely directed toward *her* and not simply toward her musical skills, or toward her emotional sensitivity, or toward any other properties that she happens to possess.

The distinction is puzzling both philosophically and psychologically; for love of general characteristics often manifests itself as prima facie directed toward the individuals who instantiate the characteristics. How are we to determine, then, the real intentional focus of the love? Epistemic problems aside, how are we ultimately to analyze these distinctions of intentional focus?

We already have a tentative account before us; in what follows, we further explore the relation between love for a person and love for general characteristics. In the course of the discussion, light will be shed on the ontology of personal identity—for, though our felt distinction invites the postulation of "bare particulars" by the unwary ontologist ("She wants to be loved for herself alone, and not for any of her characteristics . . . "), it emerges that such postulation is either unnecessary or metaphysically unobjectionable.

Consider a relevant question that Robert Nozick poses about the nature of love:

> love is an interesting instance of another relationship that is historical, in that (like justice) it depends upon what actually occurred. An adult may come to love another because of the other's characteristics; but it is the other person, and not the characteristics, that is loved. The love is not transferable to someone else with the same characteristics, even to one who "scores" higher for those characteristics. And the love endures through changes of the characteristics that gave rise to it. One loves the particular person one actually encountered. Why love is historical, attaching to persons in this way and not to characteristics, is an interesting and puzzling question.[10]

Note first that Nozick's own phrasing is misleading, for surely one *can* love characteristics or repeatable properties that particular persons possess. Thus we are led back to the initial distinction: some loves are directed toward particular persons, others are directed toward general characteristics. Why does the love that attaches to *persons* have this historical, nontransferable character? And does it always?

Everything depends, of course, upon our definition of "historical" (or "nontransferable"). We might call a relation R *historical* if and only if

(D1) $R\,(t,o) \rightarrow [(o')(P)[o \neq o' \;\&\; (Po \longleftrightarrow Po')] \rightarrow -R\,(t,o')]$.

That is, if t stands in relation R to o, then t does not stand in relation R to any object o' distinct from o and qualitatively indiscernible from it. However, another formulation suggests itself:

(D2) $-[R\,(t,o) \rightarrow [(o')(P)(o \neq o') \;\&\; (Po \longleftrightarrow Po')) \rightarrow R\,(t,o')]]$.

That is, t standing in relation R to o does not in itself guarantee that t is R related to any o' indiscernible from o; the relation R doesn't automatically transfer from o to any other o', however similar to o it might be.

Which of these formulations, if either, best captures Nozick's intuitions about the historical or nontransferable character of love? (D1) is surely too strong. It rules out the possibility of Karl's loving each of two identical twins (not a case of total indiscernibility but close enough—let the above predicate variables range only over enough properties to capture Nozick's notion of "someone else with the same characteristics"). Such multiply directed loves are ruled out if (D1) captures the relevant notion of historicity.

Yet for all its implausibility, (D1) has a tempting consequence. Suppose that Karl claims to love two women and that these women "have the same characteristics." If love is historical in the sense of (D1), then Karl doesn't really love either of them. What he loves, rather, is some properties that both women possess. This might explain why one of the women feels insecure, for she is convinced that Karl's love is only prima facie directed toward her.

Whatever we ultimately say about historical relations, things are perhaps getting unnecessarily complex. Love, like other attitudes, surely comes in both *de re* and *de dicto* varieties; and it is this very distinction that bears upon our cited cases. Moreover, Nozick's claim that love is historical is no more puzzling than the claim that love is a basically *de re* attitude, an emotional relation that puts a person directly en rapport with another person.

This kind of gambit provides no answer to Nozick's question. It simply introduces technical vocabulary that, depending upon our views about reference, personal identity, the essence/accident distinction, and so on, might correspond to very different diagnoses of the situation. Besides, though perhaps some sense can be made of the *de re/de dicto* distinction in connection with belief and other propositional attitudes, it is not yet clear how we might extend the distinction to *emotional* attitudes like love—attitudes that seem to be nonpropositional in character.

The classical cognitivist strategy, which we earlier discussed and dismissed, might claim that *de re* loves are those that rest upon a foundation of *de re* beliefs. In contrast, generalized loves (loves for characteristics) are those that rest upon a foundation of *de dicto* beliefs. But our present strategy has been to seek an alternative account. Love is a feeling. It is directed toward the world—however "general" its intentional focus might be—in a way that does not seem to involve the mediation of judgment or belief. Someone's love for a specific person is not "based upon" the belief that the person has superb qualities; if anything, it is the other way around.

There's nothing novel about this sentiment; the challenge is to find an adequate implementation of it. In 1907 the psychologist W. Wundt expressed a similar commitment to the "primacy of affect":

> When any physical process rises above the threshold of consciousness, it is the affective elements which as soon as they are strong enough, first become noticeable. They begin to force themselves energetically into the fixation point of consciousness before anything is perceived of the ideational elements. They are sometimes states of pleasurable or unpleasurable character, sometimes they are predominantly states of strained expectation.... Often there is vividly present ... the special affective tone of the forgotten idea, although the idea itself still remains in the background of consciousness.... In a similar manner, ... the clear apperception of ideas in acts of cognition and recognition is always preceded by feelings.[11]

The traditional model of affect construes it as driven by cognitive representations; with Wundt, I reject this model. Richard Rorty speaks of the "Platonic urge" to say that every emotion "should be based on the recognition of an objective quality in the recipient"; with Rorty, I resist this urge.[12] So we resist the attempt to explain the intentionality of love, and to ground any distinctions concerning its focus, in terms of putative cognitive foundations upon which the love rests. The sole purpose of this discussion is to explore alternative strategies.

There is a suggestive analogy between the behavior of linguistic items and the behavior of human emotions. The kind of "historical tie" of which Nozick speaks is precisely the kind of tie that holds between a proper name and its semantic referent (at least, according to several popular accounts of proper names). Once a name n comes to denote object o (and this might come about by virtue of o's having certain general characteristics), the name comes to be hooked up with o in a way that does *not* warrant the applicability ("transferability") of n to some distinct though relevantly similar object o'. This is what rigid designation is all about. So we might say: a proper name is committed to its bearer, in much the way that a lover is historically committed to the object of his love.

The analogy between the name relation and the love relation goes further. Suppose that a lexical item t is candidly and spontaneously volunteered in response to a portion of the passing show in which object X is especially salient. A first tentative hypothesis is that t names X. But this hypothesis is obviously premature and radically underdetermined by the data. An alternative hypothesis is this: t is a general term, applicable to any items that instantiate property P—a property that, under the circumstances, X possesses. How are we to decide among these hypotheses? Here's one way: if the speaker proceeds to apply t to some numerically distinct item Y, also possessed of P, the general-term hypothesis suggests itself. The expression t, though *applicable* to X, does not *name* X. Rather, t is a general term that applies in the presence of certain general characteristics that both X and Y possess, by virtue of which they fall into its extension. A necessary condition for t's being a name of X is that it be inapplicable to any entity distinct from X.

But this isn't quite right either. There are, after all, ambiguous names— lexical items that, though not general terms, are applicable to more than one entity. Thus we have several semantical hypotheses on our hands: 1) t names X and nothing else (in which case we need an alternative explanation of t's apparently having been applied to Y); 2) t is not a name at all but a general term applicable to any entity with certain general characteristics; or 3) t is an ambiguous name referring both to X and to Y (and, perhaps, to other objects as well).

Consider now the emotional analogue to this semantical puzzle. Karl claims to love two women. He displays "love behavior" (determined on the basis of his global psychology) in the presence of each of them. Well, maybe he does love each of them. Or perhaps he doesn't love either of them but rather loves some property that both women possess. Corresponding to the semantical question about the "referential focus" of the expression *t,* we have the emotional question about the focus of Karl's love.

The distinction between (2) and (3) can't be resolved without additional data; we need information about the way the expression entered the language or about the kinds of stories a speaker tells in providing reasons and justifications for his application of the expression. Let us pose, then, a semantical correlate of Nozick's question: Why is the relation between a proper name and its bearer historical, attaching to individuals and not to properties? The answer, I think, is straightforward: Because that's what it *is* for an expression to be a name, rather than a general term. "Nonhistoricity" is an earmark of general terms rather than of proper names.

I am suggesting that attitudinal (and emotional) relations are isomorphic to semantical relations. This puts us in a position to answer Nozick's question: An attitude *is* one of love toward a particular person, rather than toward general characteristics, by virtue of its historical character. The nontransferability, or historical nature, of love is a defining condition of its being directed toward a unique individual. Thus construed, a nonhistorical love is one that is directed toward general characteristics instantiated by a person rather than a love directed toward the particular. This does not, however, entail that genuinely "person-directed" loves endure through *all* changes of characteristics. Historicity may only require endurance through *certain* changes in *certain relevant* respects. Thus historicity would emerge as a pragmatically sensitive notion; questions about whether one's love was historical, and thus about the object of one's emotional attitude, would be vacuous pending contextual directives about relevant characteristics and permissible variations. Historicity does not entail permanence; analogously, proper names are not eternally bound up with their referents. Every proper name can lose its use. Every love has it limits.

Conversely: Can we say that *if* a love is historical, then it is person directed (rather than "general-characteristic directed")? Here is a possible counterexample to such a claim: Consider Mrs. Smith's parental love for her only child Lisa. Lisa finds her mother's "love" useless and unreassuring, and once observed, "*Love* me? She doesn't really love *me;* how can she love me if she doesn't even know who I am?" How indeed; Lisa feels that, in some important sense, she is *not* the object of her mother's love at all since Mrs. Smith is totally ignorant of her daughter's personality. Yet Mrs. Smith loves her daughter in a "nontransferable" way. So, if Lisa is right, then we have a case of a love that, though historical, is nonetheless not really directed toward a particular person. It is, rather, directed toward the office that Lisa fills.

Lisa's complaint is that her mother does not know her—at least, not sufficiently. From this she infers that her mother does not love her. What could possibly warrant such an inference? Clearly, we need a premise that relates love of x to knowledge of x. Is there any such plausible premise to be had? Is Lisa's complaint at all legitimate? And what's a mother to do?

On Lisa's behalf, we might offer the following: Lisa plays a certain role in her mother's life—she is her mother's only child. *Being Mrs. Smith's only child* is, we might say, an office that Lisa holds, and Lisa is the unique holder of that office. Needless to say, no one else is going to "score higher for those characteristics"—mother's love is not likely to be transferred to someone else. Yet Lisa feels that the identity of the office *holder* is irrelevant to her mother's love. Mother's attitude seems directed, rather, toward the office itself. The distinction between offices and officeholders is as straightforward as the distinction between definite descriptions and the items that satisfy them. Lisa accuses her mother of Office Love. If she knew some modal logic (but not too much), she might accuse her mother of *de dicto* love. Yet her mother's love for her is historical.

Intuitions differ here, but I suspect that Lisa's complaint is not legitimate. For, whether or not Mrs. Smith's love for her daughter involves character traits that Lisa values in herself, the fact is that, by any plausible criterion for *knowing who* someone is, Mrs. Smith knows who Lisa is. She has the ability to identify and reidentify Lisa, both through time and through nonbizarre counterfactual situations, and she is familiar with an acceptably large portion of Lisa's *curriculum vitae*. Of course, she might not know everything there is to know about Lisa or even everything that matters to Lisa herself. But this is as it should be. Having an emotional attitude toward a person does not demand omniscience with respect to that person.

So we do not have a love that is both historical and not person-directed. Lisa's accusations against her mother rest on an implausibly strong criterion for *knowing who*. It is, of course, true (here we agree with Lisa) that having attitudes toward an object x demands some recognitional and individuative skills with respect to x. But Lisa's mother satisfies this condition with respect to Lisa; contra Lisa, one can know who (or what) x is without knowing all there is to know about x.

An additional subtlety should be noted: exactly how much does Lisa's mother have to know about Lisa to qualify as *knowing who* Lisa is, thus satisfying a necessary condition for having attitudes directed toward her? The standards or criteria for *knowing who* are variable and dependent upon context; there is no such phenomenon as *knowing who simpliciter*. One knows who someone is if one knows enough of the right kind of things about the person. Lisa and her mother seem not to agree about which things are important. Upshot: Lisa and her mother ought to get together and agree upon criteria for knowing who someone is (or, equivalently, upon which of Lisa's characteristics are "really important"), and thus upon criteria for an emotional attitude's being genuinely directed toward *her*.

Certain properties are essential to Lisa. We may argue about which properties have this status, but it is ultimately not a factual matter; it is a matter to be settled by the social practices within the community in which "Lisa reidentification" is of some import. It is usually agreed that Lisa's history and origin are essential to her. If so, a name that uniquely refers to Lisa is not properly applicable to any possible object with a history and origin different from Lisa's. And, analogously, a love that is genuinely directed toward Lisa does not get directed toward any object with a history and origin different from hers. It is that that confers upon love the property of being directed toward Lisa. And it is that that makes love, at least love of individual persons, historical.

III

Neither of our earlier formulations adequately captures the interesting and relevant notion of historicity. The important concept is *not* that of multiplicity, as is suggested by (D1); we certainly ought to allow, for example, that a parent has historical love for each of his identical triplets—he loves each of the children individually, *not* their characteristics. The important concept is, rather, that of *irreplaceability* or *nonsubstitutivity;* to capture this notion, we need somewhat richer resources.

Suppose that Walter prima facie loves Sandra and lives with her for three years. After that time, Gloria moves in next door, strikes Walter's fancy, and claims his heart. Has he now "transferred" his love from Sandra to Gloria? Or, rather, has the one love dissipated and another love taken its place? Perhaps his love for Sandra is not historical since it has not "endured through all changes of the characteristics that gave rise to it." But it has endured through some rather drastic and important changes. So did he really love Sandra? Can he have loved her *without* his love having been historical?

One wants to know whether Gloria came to play precisely the same role in Walter's life that Sandra had played, or, since the individuation of roles is always a matter of degree and interest relativity, just how similar the roles were. The real force of Durante's opening claim ("That dame ain't in love with you . . . she's in love with the championship") is that Palooka himself is expendable or replaceable in Nina's life. Any heavyweight champ would come to play just about the same role in her life. Perhaps Durante's suspicions are correct—one champ is as good as another insofar as she is concerned. But why should Palooka's replaceability undermine the claim that Nina genuinely loves *him*? Probably because the concept of her genuinely loving *him* is intimately related to the concept of his being replaceable.

Did Walter really love Sandra? He loved her if and only if she was not replaceable. But not replaceable by *whom*? And what are the earmarks of replaceability?

As with the phenomenon of *knowing who* (and for precisely the same reason) there is no such phenomenon as his "really having loved her" *simpliciter*. The notion of object directedness of an attitude is relativized to several parameters the values of which are contributed by the context of discourse. Perhaps we can say something about these parameters.

Consider a simple case. Linus appears to love his security blanket—the particular one he always clutches. Nothing about the notion of historicity, as construed so far, obliges us to limit it to love of persons. So we ask: Is his love for the blanket historical? Or is his attitude toward it rather like Nina's attitude toward Palooka—a generalized or nonhistorical love? First ask whether the blanket is replaceable. Take it away and watch the results. Linus mourns and laments and accepts no substitutes—in fact, he is repulsed by any available successor blanket. It looks as though the particular blanket we removed was indeed irreplaceable, was itself the object of his love. But time heals all wounds and complicates the situation: after two days he calms down; after three days he is more receptive to alternatives; after four days he is bonded to a new blanket. It now looks as though the first blanket was *not* irreplaceable after all.

The notion of a historical attitude is characterized in terms of a kind of *bonding*, whether to an inanimate object or to a person. Bonding is, in turn, a matter of replaceability; and this latter notion involves counterfactuals about substitutes—about whether a certain item *could* take the place of the original. This modality involves at least two parameters:

First, what is the relevant substitution class? Does it matter, for example, that Sandra$_2$ (a clone) could replace Sandra in Walter's life? The fact that one is substitutable for the other vis-à-vis his love behavior might not undermine the claim that he really loves her. It depends upon whether clones loom as relevant alternatives in such discussions; perhaps this involves the likelihood of Walter's vacationing on Twin Earth. Second, the case of Linus and his blanket underscores the fact that we need explicit criteria for replaceability (substitutivity). How long must Walter lament for his lost Sandra to qualify as not willing to substitute another for her? Three days? Three years? A lifetime? Must Walter turn suicidal to qualify as having really loved her? These criteria, like the earlier ones, are likely to shift with the context of discussion.

There is thus an intimate tie between historicity, construed in terms of counterfactuals about replaceability, and the intentional focus of emotional attitudes. We can now provide a diagnosis of the opening situation. Suppose that Sandra and Walter share the view that irreplaceability demands four years of celibacy. Suppose also that the following is true: If Sandra were to disappear, within two years Gloria would play the role in Walter's life that

Sandra plays now. Given the truth of this counterfactual, Sandra's suspicions about the nonhistoricity of Walter's love are vindicated (at least, relative to the context of her and Walter). It isn't really Sandra whom Walter loves.

POSTSCRIPT (1985)

This paper was conceived after I had canvassed much of the available literature on the emotions. It was a reaction to what I found to be an excessive cognitivist tendency in the theory of emotion. The final straw was Robert Solomon's work in which emotions are construed as judgments. This seemed misguided and based upon confusions concerning intentionality generally, and concerning the relation between doxastic and affective processing. Around that time I discovered an article by the psychologist Robert Zajonc, who claims to have provided evidence for the "primacy of affect"—for the view, that is, that certain "gut" reactions, though intentionally directed, may precede the formation of belief.[13] If Zajonc is right, it may emerge that affect does not require cognitive processing; the *judgment* that one is in danger, for example, instead of causing the fear or somehow constituting it, may itself be the causal outcome of the fear.

There are two factors that I underestimated at the time. One is the possibility of accounting for these affective states in terms of desires and volitions, and accounting for the intentionality of certain affective states in terms of the intentionality of the desires to which they give rise (rather than the intentionality of any putative judgments that give rise to them). We would still need an account of the intentionality of desire, but it might be easier. The other factor is that there are importantly different *kinds* of judgment from which one might try to separate affective states. Love may not mobilize the judgment or evaluation that a person has "excellent qualities," but it certainly mobilizes more rudimentary identificatory or recognitional judgments—for example, the judgment that one is in the presence of Sandra, or in the presence of a superbly sensitive person, or in the presence of a fine pianist. Sandra might have wanted some of these judgments, as opposed to others, to be the proximate cause of Walter's amorous feelings.

One may, perhaps, *be* in love without having any specific feelings associated with it. The state of being in love may be constituted by the possession of certain desires, or by certain kinds of commitments, or by dispositions to form certain thoughts rather than others. But reductionist attempts to construe emotion in terms of judgment, evaluation, and/or desire often ignore the intuition that some emotional episodes characteristically have feelings associated with them. There is (at least for some people) something that it feels like to be in love, something that no adequate taxonomy of mental phenomena can ignore. This paper was spawned by the feeling that cognitivist theories of emotion had gone too far—especially given the arguments on which they often rest. Like any reactive paper, the present discussion may go too far in the other direction.[14]

Notes

1. See, for example, Barbara H. Partee's discussion of the options in her "Opacity and Scope," *Semantics and Philosophy,* edited by M. Munitz and P. Unger (New York, 1974), 81-102.

2. See Jaakko Hintikka, "On the Logic of Perception," *Models for Modalities* (Dordrecht, 1969), 151-83; "Knowledge by Acquaintance—Individuation by Acquaintance," *Bertrand Russell,* edited by D. F. Pears (New York, 1972), 52-79; and *Intentions of Intentionality and Other New Models for Modalities* (Dordrecht, 1975). See also Romane Clark, "Old Foundations for a Logic of Perception," *Synthese* 33 (1976): 75-99.

3. Robert Solomon, "Emotions and Choice," *Explaining Emotions,* edited by Amelie Oksenberg Rorty (Berkeley, 1980), 251-82; Robert Gordon, "Fear," *Philosophical Review* 89 (1980): 560-78.

4. George Pitcher, "Emotion," *Mind* 74 (1965): 330.

5. Robert Gordon, "The Aboutness of Emotion," *American Philosophical Quarterly* 11, 1 (1974): 36.

6. See, for example, Errol Bedford, "Emotions," *Essays in Philosophical Psychology,* edited by Donald Gustafson (New York, 1964), 77-98; Daniel Farrell, "Jealousy," *Philosophical Review* 89 (1980): 527-59.

7. S. Schachter and J. Singer, "Cognitive, Social, and Physiological Determinants of Emotional States," *Psychological Review* 69 (1962): 379-99.

8. See my "Sensory States and Sensory Objects," *Nous* 16 (1982): 277-93.

9. For an excellent discussion of these and other differences, see Anthony Kenny's *Action, Emotion, and Will* (London, 1976), esp. chap. 3.

10. Robert Nozick, *Anarchy, State, and Utopia* (New York, 1974), 167-68.

11. W. Wundt, *Outlines of Psychology* (Leipzig, 1907), 243-44.

12. Richard Rorty, *Philosophy and the Mirror of Nature* (Princeton, 1979), 191.

13. R. B. Zajonc, "Feeling and Thinking: Preferences Need No Inferences," *American Psychologist* 35 (1980): 151-75.

14. Portions of earlier versions of this paper were presented at the University of Cincinnati, APA Western Division Meetings (April 1982), APA Eastern Division Meetings (December 1982), and at the Chapel Hill Philosophy Colloquium (October 1982). I am grateful to all those who provided comments and participated in discussion. I would especially like to thank Wallace Anderson, Keith Gunderson, John Haugeland, William Lycan, William Lyons, Gerald Massey, Amelie Oksenberg Rorty, David Sanford, and Robin Vachon-Kraut for providing extensive and valuable criticisms of earlier drafts.

MIDWEST STUDIES IN PHILOSOPHY, X (1986)

The Indeterminism of Human Actions

RICHARD SWINBURNE

This paper aims to show that it is unlikely that prior physical states, such as brain states, totally determine which public intentional actions agents perform—given two crucial assumptions.[1] The first assumption is that of the causal efficacy of purposes: that, for given beliefs, an agent's purposes bring about his or her bodily movements. The second assumption is that of event dualism: that an agent's purposes and beliefs are distinct events (or states) from any physical events (or states) occurring to the agent, including brain events. These assumptions are, or course, the subject of acute philosophical controversy. Although I find them highly plausible, my concern is not so much to argue in their favor but to show what follows from them—that there is probably an element of indeterminism in human agency.

I

I begin by defining my subject matter in largely familiar and uncontroversial terms. An intentional action is something that an agent does, meaning to do it. There are basic actions and mediated actions. A mediated action is one that an agent does by doing some other action or actions: I open the door by grasping the handle and pulling it toward me; I insult you by saying, "You are a fool." A basic action is one that the agent just does, and not by doing some other action—apart from actions of trying, endeavoring, intending to do some action, which I shall call prebasic actions.[2] Basic actions, in contrast both to prebasic actions and to many mediated actions, consist in bringing about some state of affairs that could in all its intrinsic detail have been brought about by a cause other than an intentional agent. This state of affairs is called the result of the action. I open the door by turning the handle and pulling it toward me; I pull it toward me by grasping it with both hands and pulling my hand toward me. But I do not pull my hand toward me by doing any other intentional action (other, maybe, than trying or intending to pull it). So pulling my hand toward me is a basic action. This consists in my bringing about the motion of my hand toward me. Such motion could have been caused by someone else moving my hand or by a nervous discharge over which I had no control. Prebasic actions do not consist in my bringing about any independently describable result, nor do many mediated actions.

My insulting you cannot be so analyzed. It is my bringing it about that you are insulted by me—which is not a state that could have been brought about by a cause other than an intentional agent. But the basic action that I perform thereby to insult you is so analyzable. I insult you by saying, "You are a fool." I say "You are a fool" by bringing about such motions of my lips and larynx that the words "You are a fool" come out of my mouth. These motions of lips and larynx could have had other causes. An intentional action is a public intentional action if the basic action by which it is performed has as its result a publicly observable state of affairs. The basic actions by which humans perform public intentional actions consist in their bringing about movements of parts of their body (with possible exceptions of those who can bend spoons at a distance, without bending them by a means of limb movement!). The bodily movement that is the result of the basic action must be describable under some description as a movement that the agent means to bring about, but the description may be only as the movement that has such-and-such effects. I bring about those movements of lips and larynx that cause the noises "You are a fool" to come out of my mouth. The movements thus described in terms of what they cause may also be described in more intrinsic terms of the rate of change of shape of lips and larynx. I do not know which of such descriptions apply to them. Yet I intentionally bring about the movements because I intentionally bring them about under some description.

Which intentional action an agent performs does not depend solely on factors accessible in consciousness to the agent. Whether what the agent means to do will be achieved depends first in the case of mediated actions, on whether the circumstances in which the basic action is done and the effects brought about by the basic action are as the agent believes that they will be. By saying "You are a fool," I mean to insult you; but whether I do or not depends on whether you are there to be insulted. By grasping the handle and pulling it toward me, I mean to open the door; but whether I do or not depends on the effects of my pull, and that depends on whether the door is unlocked and the handle securely attached. Second, whether one does what one means to do depends on whether one performs the basic action that one means to perform—and that depends on whether one's limbs are free from constraint and whether brain, nerves, and muscles are functioning properly. I only move my hand when I mean to move it if it is not tied down, the muscles are in good order, and the hand is connected to my body by the normal nerve connections; and, no doubt, if certain neurons in my brain are functioning normally and connected to other neurons in the right way.

Yet when a person tries and fails to do an intentional action, basic or mediated, that person still does something intentionally. This intentional action that the agent performs when succeeding in performing any intentional action, or trying to perform one but failing, I shall call "purposing." The difference between success and failure lies in what happens subsequently to the purposing in the agent's body and in the world beyond it—over which the agent can have no control except by purposing. All prebasic actions are actions of "purposing." The more usual words by which we describe them pick out in a rather vague way overlapping subclasses of such actions; a prebasic action is an action of trying if effort or failure is involved, or seeking or endeavoring if it takes a little time. What I have called "purposing" has been called "volition" by some philosophers of the past and "desire" by many philosophers of the present. Both these words seem to me misleading: "desire" suggests something involuntary, not subject to the agent's control; and "volition" suggests something solemn and deliberate.[3]

So, on this account, my intentionally moving my hand—me intentionally bringing about the motion of my hand—consists in my purposing to move my hand followed by the motion of my hand. My trying but failing to move my hand consists in my purposing to move my hand occurring without any such consequence. When one acts intentionally in the normal full-blooded sense, one is conscious of what one is purposing to do—for one would not otherwise mean to do the action in a full-blooded sense.

Every action involves a purposing, but when an agent performs one action in order thereby to perform another (e.g., a basic action, in order thereby to perform a mediated action), there is involved also a belief that circumstances and causal relations are such that performing the first action intentionally will have the consequence of performing the second. I can only pull the handle toward me in order thereby to open the door if I believe that pulling the handle will have the consequence that I open the door. I can only insult you by saying "You are a fool" if I believe that those words have a certain meaning in English, you are present and understand English, and the conventions of society are such that telling someone that sort of thing (unless there are special circumstances) constitutes an insult.

II

The about account of intentional action should be fairly uncontroversial. Controversy begins to enter in with the assumptions by which I fill it out. In this section, I lay out these assumptions and show what is involved in them; I also give a brief argument for the first assumption, which is today the subject of less philosophical controversy than the second.

The first assumption is that the purposing involved in intentional action is, in the context of the agent's belief, not merely an accompaniment of the results of the action but a cause of them. When an agent performs a basic action for its own sake (say, tapping the fingers), a cause of the result of the action (the movement of the fingers) is a purposing to perform the action. When an agent performs a mediated action by performing a basic action, a cause of the result of the basic action is a purposing to perform the mediated action in the context of a belief that performing the basic action would achieve that.[4] If I twist the wrist of my hand holding the handle in order to open the latch, a cause of the twisting of my wrist is, in the context of my belief that the twisting of my wrist while holding the handle will effect the opening of the latch, my purposing to open the latch.

Clearly, I would not on this occasion have twisted my wrist unless I had sought (purposed) to open the latch and believed that twisting my wrist would achieve this. But what is at stake is whether the purposing and belief are further effects of whatever causes the twisting of the wrist (as the fall of the mercury level in the barometer is an effect of the rise of air pressure that causes the bad weather), or whether they themselves cause the twisting of the wrist.

Epiphenomenalists deny that purposings and beliefs are ever causally efficacious. They claim that they are mere epiphenomena that accompany the bodily movements that are the results of the basic actions without ever bringing them about. They hold that both the purposings and beliefs and also the bodily movements have a common cause in some brain event, which produces the illusion that the former causes the latter. The trouble with epiphenomenalism is, however, that no agent can think in this way and yet purpose to do anything. For the purpose is to try, minus any implication of effort or failure. And to try and so purpose to bring about something is just to do intentionally whatever, in the agent's belief, makes it causally more likely that that thing will occur. Yet since epiphenomenalists do not hold that purposing is causally efficacious, they cannot purpose; for no purposing of theirs would be doing anything that in their belief made anything causally more likely to occur. If I am an epiphenomenalist, I consider that trying to move my arm will not make my arm any more likely to move. But trying is not saying "Let it move"; it is just doing intentionally what in my view will make it more likely to move. But since, in my view, no such thing will make any difference, I cannot do it. We cannot be epiphenomenalists and also act in the world. I conclude that epiphenomenalism is not a live option and that we must revert to the normal view that purposings are causally efficacious parts of actions. That is certainly the way it seems to an agent when he or she tries very hard to move some damaged limb and finally succeeds.

My second assumption is the assumption of event dualism: that purposings and beliefs are not brain events or states, but mental events distinct from any brain events. I do not wish to deny (at any rate, in this context) that purposings and beliefs are events or states of a person that we may suppose to be the same thing (or substance) as that person's body. But the occurrence in the body of this or that nervous discharge is a different event from the person purposing to bring about some effect. A history of the world that told only of the former would have told only half the story. Purposings and beliefs are not contingently identical with brain events of certain types, nor are they to be defined functionally—for example, as whatever is causally likely to have such and such effects. For there will be some brain event that is causally likely to have those effects without being the event of the agent doing intentionally what the agent believes is causally likely to have those effects. Also, one may, when one's brain has been damaged in ways of which one is unaware, purpose to bring about some event; because of the brain damage, however, the purposing does not make that event in the least causally likely to occur. However, I do not argue further for the assumption, although it seems to me highly plausible. I merely state it and, in due course, draw the consequences.

I do, however, need to draw out just a little more fully what is involved in the assumption. Which bodily movements an agent will bring about intentionally depends not only on the agent's purposings and beliefs, but also on the agent's capacities. By an agent's capacities I mean the agent's abilities to perform basic actions: an agent has a capacity to bring about some bodily movement M if and only if, when the agent purposes to bring about M, M occurs. Talk about an agent's capacities is not therefore talk about the occurrence of mental events of a certain kind, but talk about the causal efficacy of mental events of a different kind—purposes. Most humans, of course, have very similar capacities to each other, though some can produce at will movements that most of us cannot bring about at will (say, ear wagglings), and some of us lose normal capacities. But when we meet Martians, it will not be at all obvious which of their movements are under their voluntary control and which are not.

An agent's purposings, beliefs, and capacities are not necessarily what the best-justified inference from that person's public behavior would lead us to suppose. We infer from an agent's public behavior a pattern of belief, purpose, and capacity that leads us to expect that behavior. We say that if the agent had these purposes and those beliefs and if the production of those bodily movements was within the agent's capacity, they would occur. We attribute purposes, beliefs, and capacities to others in accordance with the principles of simplicity and charity to which writers have drawn our attention (though they have not always brought out the relevance of hypotheses about capacity).[5] We attribute to others purposes and beliefs (or, at any rate, ways of acquiring beliefs) and capacities similar to our own. We suppose that others have from time to time the purpose of eating bread, not the purpose of eating inkwells; that they believe it hurts when you put your hand in the fire (or, at any rate, come to believe this after putting their hand in the fire once); and that they can open their hands but not stop their heart from beating at will. We also seek to attribute to agents constant purposes and capacities, and beliefs that change in response to sensory stimuli in regular ways. In this, the principle of simplicity is at work, as it is also in supposing others to be similar to ourselves—not to differ in inexplicable ways. We seek the simplest account of the purposes, beliefs, and capacities of others that will enable us to explain the movements that occur in and of their bodies. However, there are different schemes of purpose, belief, and capacity by which a set of movements may be explained. If we suppose capacities to be known, and so it is to be known which movements are the results of basic actions, still there are different systems of purpose and belief that will explain the performance of those basic actions. I sign my name, that is, bring it about that my hand and fingers move in such a way as to bring about an inscription of my name. The signature is on a check for £100 addressed to you. When asked why I thus gave you £100, I say, "I owe you £100." Much of my behavior can be explained by supposing that normally I repay debts that I believe I have and tell what I believe to be the truth. However, I do not owe you £100, nor did anything happen to me that, by the principles for acquiring beliefs that are reasonably attributed to me on the basis of my other behavior, would cause me to believe that I did. An alternative explanation of my action is that I did not realize I was signing on the bottom of a check; I was just doodling absentmindedly, trying out my new pen. Having discovered what happened, I was too ashamed to admit my absentmindedness and so told a lie about my beliefs. The alternative hypotheses that purport to explain my first basic action, my bringing about my signature—my belief that I owed you £100 and my purposing to repay it; and my purposing to produce the signature for its own sake—are combined with other hypotheses to explain the second basic action—my bringing about movements of my larynx and lips so that the words "I owe you £100" come out of my mouth. The first hypothesis is combined with a hypothesis of a purpose of mine to tell the truth about my beliefs and a belief that those words mean that I owe you £100; the second hypothesis is combined with a hypothesis of a purpose to ensure that others believe that I am not absentminded, a belief that those words mean that I owe you £100, and a belief that others will believe that I believe what I say. The two rival hypotheses have roughly equal complexity, each of them having to attribute to me one purposing or method of acquiring belief that fits badly with hypotheses able to explain other of my behavior. Subsequent behavior of mine might (on the assumption that my purposes and methods of acquiring belief remain constant) be better explicable by one hypothesis rather than another. But they might not be; and, anyway, my purposes and methods of acquiring belief may change. Compatible with any observed set of actual bodily movements, we can construct an endless number of hypotheses of the purposings and beliefs that bring them about. Some such hypotheses will be simpler than others and some vastly simpler than others, and that will be evidence of their truth.

But what my second assumption is claiming is that in such cases there is a true hypothesis—there is a truth about what my purposings and beliefs are—and that the true hypothesis is not necessarily the hypothesis rendered most probable by being the simplest account of my public behavior. For an agent knows what that agent is up to or is trying to achieve better than does any outsider making an inference from public behavior. The agent could know all that the outsider knows and yet know something further and different—what he or she is really trying to achieve. What in many cases (though not always) "stares us" more evidently "in the face" than any facts of our public behavior is the goal of our activity. I am not claiming that an agent's knowledge of his or her purposes is infallible (psychoanalysis could help the agent see that he or she has made a mistake): only that the agent is better positioned to know about them than any outsider. In my example, I would normally know very well whether I was trying to repay a debt or whether I was just doodling.

The last few paragraphs sought to bring out what was involved in the second assumption—that purposings and beliefs are not mere logical constructs, but events or states separate from each other and from brain events known best to the subject but inferred with justification by others. The first assumption stated that purposings and beliefs are causally efficacious in the production of bodily movements.

III

It follows from these two assumptions that if physical states—and the only plausible candidates for such physical states are brain states—bring about agents' public intentional actions, they do so in the following way. Brain states bring about an agent's beliefs and purposings. The beliefs and purposings together bring about other brain states that in turn bring about bodily movements. If the purposing includes a purposing to bring about the bodily movement that in fact occurs, then we have the basic intentional action of bringing about that bodily movement and also further mediated actions, dependent on which beliefs and purposes produce the basic action, the effects of the bodily movement, and the circumstances in which it is done. Insofar as the brain event caused by a belief-purpose state that includes a purpose to bring about a bodily movement M itself causes M—to that extent, the agent has the capacity to bring about M. We may reasonably suppose that the process whereby brain events cause bodily movements is as deterministic as most physical processes; and we may suppose that if indeterminism affects the production of intentional actions, it does so by affecting the other processes.

Thus, the issue of whether human intentional actions are predetermined by brain states turns on the issue of whether the laws of the form ($B \rightarrow K$), ($B \rightarrow P$), and (($K + P$) $\rightarrow B$), where B ranges over human brain states, K over human belief states, and P over human purposings, are deterministic. Such laws will follow from more general psychophysical laws that apply to all conscious organisms; they will be the special cases of such laws that apply where the brain states (and so mental states) are those of humans. I consider in this section what the scientific evidence of kinds normally considered suggests about whether the brain-mind and mind-brain laws for humans are deterministic or indeterministic. This evidence is of three kinds. First, there is general evidence of what natural laws in general are like, which may suggest something about how far psychophysical laws are deterministic. Second, a detailed psychophysiological study of the particular processes in humans might enable us to postulate justified laws of those processes in humans. Third, a study of the evolutionary processes by which humans come to have a particular brain and a range of possible brain states as causes and effects of their mental states may suggest that evolution is likely to select brains whose states are correlated with mental states either in deterministic or in indeterministic ways.

First, then, what can we conclude from the study of other natural laws (and that means purely physical laws) about the likelihood of general psychophysical laws being deterministic? It has been evident since Descartes that the three processes—the production by brain states of purposings, the production by brain states of beliefs, and the production of brain states (which in turn produce bodily movements) by purposings and beliefs—are totally different from any physical process, whether a process of a kind hypothesized by Descartes or of kinds hypothesized by Einstein or Heisenberg. For beliefs and purposings possess built-in intentionality, built-in meaning, something totally lacking to physical processes. Indeed, the fact that the dualist is forced to postulate an interaction totally different in character from any physical interaction has seemed to the physicalist to constitute a sound objection to dualism. However, in making my second assumption, I am assuming that this objection does not have much force.

The fact that these processes are so totally different from any physical process has the consequence that even if all physical processes were totally deterministic, there would be little reason for supposing that the body-mind and mind-body processes were similarly deterministic. However, quantum mechanics suggest that physical processes are not deterministic on the subatomic scale. Certainly, quantum mechanics also suggests what we know anyway—that most large-scale physical processes are virtually deterministic, wherein causes bring about effects with very high degrees of physical probability but not with necessity. The very high degrees of probability are normally so high that an improbable macroscopic physical process of a given kind occurs only once in several millenia. Most macroscopic physical systems are such that variations of subatomic variables from their most probable values normally average out. There are, however, macroscopic physical systems in which small-scale variations from most probable values normally produce large-scale effects. (We can make a machine that displays a sequence of digits, the sequence being determined by a small-scale quantum process. We could even make an atomic bomb, such that whether and when it exploded was determined by whether some radioactive atom decayed within a certain period.) Even on the macroscopic level, therefore, not all physical processes are virtually deterministic.

Given that background, analogy offers little guidance about what to expect about the extent to which mind-body and body-mind processes are deterministic. We would need to reach a justified view on what is the natural analogue in the mental world of those differences in the physical world that are of quantum significance. Is the difference between purposing to go to London and purposing to go to Moscow like a difference in length of 10 cm or like a difference in length of 10_{-13} cm? Analogy suggests no answer, and that is why any conclusion that we might reach about the level on which the physical world is indeterministic will suggest very little about the amount of indeterminism outside that world.

Perhaps, however, a detailed study of the three psychophysical processes in question will suggest an answer as to whether the processes operative in humans are deterministic. A start would be to consider how far uniform correlations exist between kinds of brain states and resultant beliefs, kinds of beliefs-and-purposes and resultant brain states, and kinds of brain states and resultant purposes. In the way of establishing such correlations, there is the very considerable difficulty that the subject is better positioned than outsiders to know about his or her mental events, including purposes and beliefs; even if the subject seeks to be honest, the subject may not mean by the words by means of which he or she describes them the same as others mean. There will, therefore, always be some doubt about the extent to which various correlations have been established. But let us ignore this difficulty and suppose that we can trust absolutely speakers' descriptions of their purposes and beliefs. Given that, there is evidence of much uniform correlation between kinds of brain state and kinds of subsequent belief. Since our beliefs about the state of the world around us often have a high degree of correlation with the states of the world around us, and the latter operates on our sense organs to cause the brain states connected with our beliefs, that shows that there must often be a high degree of correlation between kinds of brain state and kinds of subsequent belief. Similarly, there is evidence of much uniform correlation between kinds of purpose to effect some goal together with beliefs about which bodily movement will effect that goal and kinds of resulting bodily movement (when the beliefs about the necessary bodily movements are of a certain kind—say, to move a whole finger rather than a fingernail). That shows that there must often be uniform correlations between beliefs and purposes and the brain states that cause the bodily movements. But, of course, these correlations do not always hold: sometimes people acquire false beliefs or cannot move the limbs they require. There is also little evidence of uniform correlations between kinds of brain state and kinds of subsequent purpose. People may habitually do certain things in certain circumstances; but when people have to make choices, there is little certainty about how they will choose—either because different people in similar circumstances have different brain states or because the correlations between brain states and purposes are far from uniform, or both.

In all these cases, however, there is a very substantial difficulty in supposing that any uniform correlations show the operation of deterministic laws. To have a theory of the body-mind and mind-body connections, we need more than a list of well-authenticated correlations between events of one kind and events of the other. We need a theory with a few simple laws by which we explain why there is this correlation rather than that: why this brain state is correlated with this belief and that brain state with that belief; or (to take an example of a different brain-mind connection, that between brain states and sensations) why the brain events caused by tasting sugar give rise to a sweet taste and those caused by tasting salt give rise to a salty taste, and so on. The theory would find intrinsic features of brain events of different kinds that made natural a connection with mental events of different kinds. But how can brain events vary except in electrochemical properties, and how can one set of such properties have any more natural connection with one kind of sensation or belief than another? Yet in the absence of such a theory, we would not know why the correlations hold that do hold; thus, we would have some reasonable doubt whether they would continue to hold when circumstances change—for example, when the brain environment was slightly different (as in different people).[6] We may attempt to bypass the mental and establish correlations between the brain processes prior to purposings and the brain processes that initiate bodily movements or (for agents of normal capacity) the bodily movements themselves. However, any such regularities would be brought about by the operation of purposings and beliefs. If we were ignorant of these causal processes that brought about the observable physical correlations, we could have no well-justified theory of why the correlations that occur do occur, and in the absence of such a theory, we would have no strong reason for supposing that the observed correlations would hold in different environments (as for different kinds of people).

Even if deterministic laws do govern the body-mind and mind-body relations, these difficulties thus stand in the way of having good evidence that they do. In fact, as we have seen, we have no evidence of unvarying correlations even for the connection between brain states and beliefs. If we did have good evidence that the $(B \rightarrow K)$ and $((K + P) \rightarrow B)$ connections were deterministic, that would provide some weak evidence by analogy that the $(B \rightarrow P)$ connection was also deterministic. But the analogies are weak: purposings are active states, things that agents do; whereas beliefs are passive states, things that happen to them. One might well expect beliefs and not purposings to be caused; the efficacy of the mental $((K + P) \rightarrow B)$ is, because it involves active intentional choice, very different from the efficacy of the physical.

Our third kind of evidence comes from the fact that humans, like other animals, have evolved by natural selection. Organisms that are ill adapted for survival would have been eliminated. To survive, an organism with beliefs and purposes needs largely true beliefs about its environment and largely efficacious purposes. A species of animals whose beliefs about the presence of food, predators, and mates were largely false would not survive for long; the same goes for a species whose attempts to avoid predators and secure food and mates were always frustrated by their purposes to move one limb causing instead the movement of a different limb. To have such largely true beliefs, animals need to have brains "wired in" to their bodies in the right way and also largely deterministic connections between brain states and beliefs. For example, the presence of a predator must often cause a brain state that causes the belief that the predator is present. The former depends on the "wiring" (that the requisite brain state be caused in a sense organ, when and only when the predator is present); the latter depends on the operation of largely deterministic laws. If mutations produce animals whose brains are wired in in the wrong way, they will be eliminated. Similarly, if mutations produce brain states that cause certain beliefs only probabilistically, not with any high degree of necessity, they too will be eliminated. A mutation cannot cause a given brain state to have an effect other than its normal one. That depends on the general psychophysical laws; however, it may be that a given belief (K_1) can be produced either by B_1 or B_2, but the $B_1 \rightarrow K_1$ connection is invariable whereas the $B_2 \rightarrow K_1$ connection only operates with a moderate degree of physical probability. Natural selection will favor animals that have brain states connected deterministically rather than only probabilistically to a given belief; only in such animals can beliefs be fully sensitive to how things are. A similar argument shows that evolution favors animals in whom there are deterministic belief-and-purpose/brain state connections; only such animals can achieve their purposes. If there are alternative sets of $(B \rightarrow K)$ and $((K + P) \rightarrow B)$ laws, then evolution will favor the evolution of animals with brains having brain states governed by the more deterministic laws. Evolution gives no indication as to the particular forms these deterministic laws must take; it merely insists that whatever the brain correlates are, they must be "wired in" in the right way.

What of the $(B \to P)$ laws? There are certain restrictions upon them needed if organisms are to survive. Organisms need to have the purpose of escaping predators (ever present, so that when a belief arises that there is a predator present, it leads to action) and the purposes of eating, drinking, and mating (from time to time). (Perhaps also the purpose of lying down where it is convenient to sleep.) Or rather, what is necessary if a species is to survive is that, in general, organisms of that species shall have such purposes; the laws that produce such purposes must give quite a high probability to their occurrence. This would be the case if brain states gave rise to the desires to eat or drink when eating or drinking were good for survival; but the organisms might choose sometimes for some good reason to resist such desires. The species will still survive so long as most members yield to such desires after a time and if they yield immediately to the desire to escape a predator believed to be present. But, that said, there are many ways of escaping predators, of eating and drinking, and there are many other things to do between morning and night. There would seem to be no evolutionary advantage for the organism to be determined in these respects. On the contrary, there would be an evolutionary advantage in the laws being indeterministic. Purposes that are not determined cannot be predicted, however sophisticated the predictor; and if the details of an organism's behavior are not predictable, that organism will be able to escape predators and those who seek to control that organism. If for a given purpose there were two brain states, one that produced the purpose deterministically and one that produced it only with a moderate degree of physical probability, then there would be an evolutionary advantage for an organism that had a brain state of the latter type only.

The fact that there are evolutionary pressures favoring the selection of animals with brain states connected deterministically or indeterministically, as the case may be, with mental states of certain kinds, is some small evidence for supposing that those animals that have survived do have brain states of those kinds: that in humans the $(B \to K)$ and $((K + P) \to B)$ laws are as deterministic as such connections are allowed to be by the general psychophysical laws, whereas the $(B \to P)$ laws are (within the limits mentioned above) indeterministic. At least, it is such evidence if this conclusion is compatible with the other information that we have about the current laws and about the kinds of mutations available to organisms. It is indeed so compatible. The fact that quite a bit of human behavior is currently unpredictable is compatible with, and indeed would be explained by, the $(B \to P)$ laws being indeterministic. Although we do not know that mutations can give rise to alternative deterministic and indeterministic routes of production of a given purposing, we do know both that in the physical world there can be alternative routes of production of some given physical state (and mutations often give rise to different mechanisms for producing some bodily state or capacity) and also that some effects that can be produced with virtual determinism can also on other occasions be the result of nondeterministic processes.

Having set out the normal scientific evidence, I suggest that it points neither toward nor against the thesis that human intentional actions are predetermined by brain states, although it indicates that if they are not it is because the (B $\rightarrow$ P) laws are indeterministic.

IV

Finally, I wish to draw attention to a crucial human phenomenon that (I shall suggest) tips the balance of evidence in favor of the (B $\rightarrow$ P) laws being indeterministic—the phenomenon of human countersuggestibility. Among the purposes that humans acquire are the purposes of testing knowledge claims and thereby showing them false or making them more secure. Among the knowledge claims that any agent who seeks a well-justified understanding of the world will seek to test is the claim of any theory about the springs of human behavior, and especially the agent's own behavior; above all, whenever the theory is well supported and taken seriously in the scientific community. Such agents need not be fanatical antideterminists, but simply seekers after truth on important matters—in other words, scientifically minded persons. I call such agents countersuggestible, but I suggest that most of us are in this sense countersuggestible. Countersuggestibility in this sense is clearly open only, among animals, to humans; and so the conclusion that I wish to derive from it has no application to animals other than humans.

If, despite the difficulties outlined in the last section, there were a true deterministic theory of the correlations between brain states before the formulation of purposes and beliefs and subsequent bodily movements, it would have to apply to agents who, if they knew of the theory, knew it to be well supported, and knew its prediction about their own behavior, would sometimes put it to the test if they could do so easily. A countersuggestible agent, informed of the prediction of such a theory that he or she would do some simple basic action, would sometimes clearly try to do the opposite and would succeed because not doing such a basic action lies easily within his or her power. It follows that if there is a true deterministic theory of human behavior, scientists could not get countersuggestible subjects to know the predictions of that theory about that subject's immediate future basic actions.

The suggestion (often only implicit) in much writing is that the latter will always be the case with any theory of human behavior. The point is often made that if a scientist examines your brain state at t_1, predicts on the basis thereof what you will do at t_4, and then tells you the prediction at t_2, this will alter your brain state in such a way that the prediction no longer follows from the scientist's theory. But what is at stake is whether the scientist can get you to know what the theory predicts about your behavior when your brain state is that resulting from your having been given the prediction. I know of no discussion in the literature of whether this can be done. I wish to show that whether it can be done depends on the laws in accord with which beliefs are caused by brain states—depends on what are the $(B \rightarrow K)$ laws—and that for almost all logically possible such laws, this information can be transmitted. Only for $(B \rightarrow K)$ laws of a very narrow (and complex) kind can this not be done; in consequence, there are good inductive reasons for supposing that the true laws are not of that narrow kind.

A deterministic theory of the brain T that bypassed purposes and beliefs would show how brain states were altered by input and were followed (after the formulation of purposings and beliefs, which it ignores) by bodily movements. The theory would show how different brain states $(B_1 \ldots B_n)$ plus different input to the brain $(I_1 \ldots I_m)$ leads to different bodily movements $(M_1 \ldots M_x)$. Let us hold constant all nonsensory input to the brain— for example, keep the blood flowing at a constant rate with its chemical composition constant—or, if this is not possible, allow it to vary in a predictable way of which we can take account. Let us represent the different sensory input by $S_1 \ldots S_m$. The S's represent not the sensations themselves ('a red flash') but the input along the sensory nerves that gives rise to sensations and also (or thereby), if the sensation is recognized as a means of transmitting information, to beliefs. Then the laws of the theory will have the form:

$$B(t_1) + S(t_2 - t_3) \rightarrow M(t_4),$$

showing for different B and S the different resulting M. Here, t_1 represents an instant of time before the formation of the relevant purpose, $t_2 - t_3$ represents the period during which sensory input is sent to the brain, and t represents the instant at which the bodily movement is complete. I stress that this theory is concerned with relations between physical variables only. If determinism governs bodily movements, then laws of such a theory can be provided for any choice of intervals t_1 - t_2, t_2 - t_3, and t_3 - t_4.

Suppose a scientist has discovered a theory T of the above type and regards it as well confirmed. Take a simple basic action having as its result a simple bodily movement M_a, which is such that its occurrence is under the voluntary control of normal subjects—for example, the movement of a subject's left arm so that it touches a switch at a certain time t_4. Equipped with various measuring instruments, the scientist now examines the brains of many subjects, normal in the above sense, at t_1 and determines of which of two kinds is each subject's brain state: $B(1)$, which is such that if the digit 1 is flashed on the screen in front of the subject, causing S_1 to be propagated along the optic nerve during the period t_2 - t_3, T predicts that the subject's brain state will cause M_a at t_4; or B(0), which is such that if the digit 1 is flashed on the screen in front of the subject, causing S_1 to be propagated along the optic nerve during t_2 - t_3, T predicts that the subject's brain state will cause a bodily state that does not include M_a—call it $\overline{M}_a$. Each subject is told beforehand that if the subject is found in a brain state of kind $B(1)$, the signal S_1 will be transmitted to that subject to convey that information; if the subject is found in a state of kind B(0), no signal will be transmitted. Call this method of transmitting information the use of code W. Many subjects are examined; such as are found to be in a state of kind $B(1)$ are sent signal S_1. They will then know that T predicts of them that they will bring about M_a. Being countersuggestible, some of them show the theory to be false by not doing so, by bringing about $\overline{M}_a$.

Suppose, however, that countersuggestible subjects were never under these conditions found to be in a state of kind $B(1)$ but were always found in a state of kind $B(0)$; thus, the theory could not be proved false by this method. In that case, we might try a different system of transmitting information, which I call code X. If the subject is found in a state of kind $B(0)$, the signal S_1 will be sent as a means of transmitting the information that T predicts that on receipt of the signal the subject will bring about $\overline{M}_a$—in other words, will not bring about M_a. The scientist tells subjects this code before examining them. The scientist then examines them and sends signal S_1 to such as are found in $B(0)$. They will then know that T predicts of them that they will bring about $\overline{M}_a$. Being countersuggestible, some of them bring about M_a and so show the theory to be false.

Since every brain state is either of kind $B(1)$ or of kind $B(0)$, T could only fail to be shown false by use of one or other of these methods if the very process of informing subjects of the code, of which kind of brain state they would be in if the signal S_1 were to be sent, would cause them not to be in a brain state of that kind. That is, the sensory stimuli (the impinging on the subject's eardrums of certain airwaves, or on the eyes of certain light waves) causing a subject to have a belief that a certain code will be used to signal the predictions of T about the subject's behavior on receipt of the signal, if he is found in a brain state of a certain kind, will cause the subject never to be in a brain state of that kind. This would hold whether the information was transmitted orally or in writing and in whatever language. And not just for the two simple codes described so far, but for all of an infinite number of codes that could be used to signal to subjects the predictions of T about their behavior on receipt of the prediction. Consider a marginally more sophisticated system of information transmission that I call code Y. This system uses two digits: the digit 1 displayed on a screen, causing the stimulus S_1 to be sent along the subject's optic nerve; and the digit 2, causing the stimulus S_2 to be sent along the subject's optic nerve. Adopt the following system of labeling kinds of brain states. As before, call brain states $B(1)$ if, according to T, when the subject receives S_1 the subject will bring about M_a, the arm movement described earlier. Of the remaining states, call those states B(2), which are such that, according to T, when the subject receives S_2, the subject will bring about M_a. Call all other states B(0). If the subject is informed of the coding and then found in a brain state either of kind B(1) or of kind B(2), the scientist can send such signals as will enable the subject to defeat the predictions of the theory. If T is to be true, it must be that the very process of informing the subject of this method of coding will produce a brain state other than one that can be utilized to send the subject information about that brain state—that is, a brain state of kind B(0). And so on for infinitely many methods of coding.

Codes can easily be devised that allow an informative signal to be sent if the subject is found in any brain state other than a very small proportion of possible brain states. Consider the effect of S_1 (the sensory input caused by displaying digit 1 on the screen) on the subject, causing or not causing M_a. Either the majority of the subject's brain states will be such that, according to T, when receiving S_1, the subject will bring about M_a; or the majority will be such that, according to T, if the subject receives S_1, the subject will bring about $\overline{M}_a$. Label states of the majority class states of kind B(1), and inform the subject that if found in any state of kind B(1), the subject will be sent S_1. Now consider the remaining states—those of the minority class. Either the majority of those brain states are such that, according to T, if the subject receives S_2 (the sensory input caused by displaying digit 2 on the screen) the subject will bring about M_a; or they are such that, according to T, if the subject receives S_2, the subject will bring about $\overline{M}_a$. Label states of the majority subclass among this minority class states of kind B(2), and inform the subject that if found in any state of kind B(2), the subject will be sent S_2. Continuing in this way with different signals S_3, S_4, S_5, and so forth, we can soon reduce to a very small proportion of the total the number of unlabeled brain states—ones that are such that if the subject is found in them, we do not have a signal whereby we can convey to the subject the predictions of T about the subject's behavior on receipt of the signal. Indeed, if the total number of brain states is finite, all brain states could be labeled in this way. However, there is a limit on the viability of too complicated a code, provided by the ability of subjects to hold in memory the rules of too complicated a code—a limit no doubt itself arising from the size and construction of subjects' brains. Yet the point made in the first sentence of this paragraph remains: that there are very many simple codes that allow an informative signal to be sent to the subject if the subject is found in any of the vast majority of possible brain states, and the signal is informative in the sense of telling the subject of the predictions of T about the subject's behavior on receipt of the signal.

It follows that if there is to be a true deterministic theory of the above type, if T is to be true, then informing a subject by any means whatever of any code whatever for transmitting to the subject information about the predictions of T about the subject's behavior on receipt of the informative signal will put the subject in one of a very small proportion of possible brain states where the code has no signal for this purpose.

So what we are being asked by the determinist to believe is that the brain-belief links are of this very peculiar character, which prevent the acquisition by a human of true beliefs of a certain sort—namely, any true beliefs about any well-supported predictions about the human's future behavior that coincide with the predictions of a certain theory T, by any language or any method of coding—despite the fact that, in general, the human brain is so constructed that it can cause the acquisition of all sorts of other kinds of belief, including any belief of any other kind that any other human tries to convey to its subject. This feature of a belief acquisition system for beliefs of a certain kind would make such a system complicated (perverse, perhaps one should say) and one of a very small proportion of logically possible belief acquisition systems.

This can be seen by considering the brain state-belief laws on their own. Successfully informing a subject that a certain code will be used to transmit information to the subject does, of course, limit the number of that subject's possible brain states; they now all have to include a part that will sustain the belief that the code will be used. The subject's future brain states have to include a part that is such that it gives rise to the belief K that the code will be used. But there is no particular reason, if we consider just the brain state-belief laws, why every brain state that included that part should be such that it lies inside the narrow range for which the code provides no signal for signaling to the subject which brain state is present. Why should informing the subject that code W is to be used automatically confine subjects to brain states of kind $B(0)$—in other words, states picked out by what T predicts will be the effect of S_1 upon them, that it will cause $\overline{M}_a$? There are so many logically possible brain state-belief laws that incorporate that information in other ways, and so on through all the vast number of possible codes. Granted that brain state-belief laws are deterministic, there is no reason a priori why they should have this very perverse character. It is very unlikely a priori that deterministic brain state-belief laws should belong to this narrow and complex class.

If we had reason to suppose that the laws governing brain-belief links were created by a being who wished to prevent us from acquiring certain sorts of knowledge—for example, a Cartesian evil demon—then we would have reason to believe that the links are of this kind. Or if we had prior reason for supposing brain state-purpose laws to be deterministic (and so there to be a true deterministic theory such as T), we would have reason to believe the brain state-belief laws to be of this narrow kind (for that is a necessary condition of the former being deterministic). But, we have noted, the situation is that on all the normal scientific evidence (which we considered in section III) we have no prior reason for supposing brain state-purpose laws to be deterministic. The consideration that these can only be deterministic if the brain state-belief laws are of a narrow and complex class, which a priori is unlikely (in view of the vastly larger class of different and simpler brain state-belief laws), counts against the brain state-purpose laws being deterministic. If it is equally likely that an A is B and that it is not B, and it is shown that is can only be not-B under very unusual and complex and so a priori unlikely conditions, the final judgment (the posterior probability) must be that it is likely that it is B.

The determinist is committed to holding that before ever there were humans or other conscious beings, there were deterministic natural laws such that if there evolved agents with brains of a certain construction, they would have beliefs of certain kinds—yet laws with the qualification already built in that there were certain beliefs that agents could not acquire, by any means, however hard anyone tried to give them to them. Nature, as it were, already foresaw the evolution of countersuggestible subjects and was determined to defeat their best endeavors. A more likely story is that there were available one or two different routes by which beliefs would be produced, deterministic and indeterministic. Natural selection favored a deterministic route but not of the narrow kind that prevented agents from acquiring beliefs of the stated type. There were also available one or two different routes by which purposes would be produced by brain states, deterministic and indeterministic. Natural selection favored the evolution of organisms whose purposes were produced by a nondeterministic mechanism because of the evolutionary advantages that would be possessed by organisms who tried to defeat the predictions of predators and those who would enslave them—the forecasts of experts and commands of authority! This very important characteristic of humans (their readiness to test the theories of the world put forward by others) that I have called countersuggestibility could have evolved *either* via deterministic laws, including some very complex and perverse brain state-belief laws; or via indeterministic brain state-purpose laws. The probabilities suggested by the evidence summarized in section III favor, I claim, the latter supposition. In this case, anything known by anyone can be conveyed to a subject, including the predictions of any theory T about the subject's behavior; but the subject will always be able to show T false, for *any* theory T.

I conclude that, given my two assumptions, human countersuggestibility is strong evidence of indeterminism in the production of purposes and so intentional actions because if would only be compatible with determinism on the assumption of an a priori very unlikely mechanism for the production of beliefs. Of course, subsequent scientific inquiry could prove me wrong; but the above, I suggest, is where the evidence points at present.

Notes

1. The present paper is the last of many versions. I am most grateful to Mary Hesse, Peter van Inwagen, John Lucas, and Donald Mackay for their helpful criticism of previous versions.

2. An agent may do one action X by doing another one Y in the sense that the agent does Y naturally—not by following a recipe—whereas the agent does X by following the recipe "do Y." In such a case, Y is teleologically more basic that X. Alternatively, the agent may do X by doing Y in the sense of doing Y intentionally in certain circumstances, with Y having certain effects; and of doing Y intentionally, knowing those to be the circumstances and effects that constitute doing X intentionally. In such a case, Y is causally more basic that X. Normally, the teleologically more basic is also causally more basic, and conversely. These seem to be the two main kinds of basic action among the narrower kinds distinguished by Annette Baier ("The Search for Basic Actions," *American Philosophical Quarterly* 8 (1971): 161-70). My concern is with causal basicness. I understand by a basic action an action than which no other is causally more basic; and by a mediated action, an action than which some other action is causally more basic.

Some philosophers consider that a mediated action is the same action as the basic action that generates it: my insulting you is the same action as my saying, "You are a fool"; these are simply two descriptions of the same action. (See, e.g., D. Davidson's "Agency" in his *Essays on Actions and Events* [Oxford, 1980].) Other philosophers hold that these are two distinct actions. I have adopted the latter way of talking, but nothing for my purposes depends on this issue. Anyone who prefers the former way of talking will need to rephrase some of my points in obvious ways—for example, the "result" of the basic action as the "result" of the action "under its basic-act description."

3. Some philosophers of the past have denied that there is any intentional action common to success and failure in performing a basic action. However, majority philosophical opinion today is against them; in agreement with that opinion, I write as I do in the above paragraph. For anyone who wishes to question what I have written, it could be phrased as a further assumption and the consequences of the paper derived from my other assumptions together with this one.

4. When the agent has the belief that not merely will performing the basic action achieve performing the mediated action but that performing no other basic action will do that, then, given that belief, the agent's purposing to perform the mediated action involves (has within it, as part of the agent's plan) the purposing to perform the basic action. When the agent believes that performing the basic action will achieve performing the mediated action but that performing some other basic action will also achieve performing the mediated action, there is (on this assumption) an additional element of purposing involved in causing the result of the basic action. The total purposing is not just to perform the mediated action, but also to perform it by a certain route. The total purposing in the context of the belief that the mediated action will be performed by the performance of the basic action (that the route in question is a possible route) causes the result of the basic action.

5. See, for example, David Lewis, "Radical Interpretation," *Synthese* 27 (1974): 331-44.

6. On this point, see my *The Existence of God* (Oxford, 1979), 170ff.

Free Will and the Structure of Motivation

DAVID SHATZ

Probably the most conspicuous of recent developments with regard to the free will problem has been the proliferation of 'hierarchical' accounts of free action and free will.[1] Such accounts begin by noting a salient feature of human beings, namely, their ability to form and assume higher-level motivational stances— preferences or desires about what preferences or desires to have, or about what preferences or desires should be effective in motivating action.[2] What these theories then maintain is that an action is done freely provided that the agent's preferences or desires are integrated in a certain way. Specifically, the efficacious lower-level motivational elements in his or her motivational structure must be in accord with, and perhaps under control of, the higher-level elements in that structure. Of course, preferences and desires are not the only motivational elements that can be featured in such an account; one can also highlight, with varying degrees of plausibility, wants, decisions, choices, or willings.

For the most part, advocates of hierarchical accounts see themselves as continuators or rehabilitators of classical compatibilism. In this paper, I want to examine some lines of thought that encourage this perspective. I hope to show that these lines of thought are mistaken and that classical compatibilism generates only an attenuated and problematic hierarchical account; the core of this account, moreover, was long ago articulated by Moore. At the end of the paper I offer a more general assessment of the prospects for a viable compatibilism.

I

Classical compatibilism teaches that a person S does action A freely provided that, in doing A, S is acting in accordance with and because of his motivation—he is doing as he wants, prefers, chooses, wills, decides, tries, or intends with respect to A and because he so wants, prefers, chooses, wills, decides, tries, or intends. In addition, most compatibilists stipulate that the following must be the case: if the agent were to have had a different motivation, he or she would have acted in accordance with that motivation. I stress that this position represents *classical* compatibilism.[3] There is a broader, generic sense of the term in which a position is compatibilist provided only that its conditions for free action do not include one specifying or implying that the agent's motivation is uncaused. Thus, if someone were to unpack 'S does A freely' as 'S does A without experiencing guilt, resentment, or conflict', his view would qualify as a version of generic compatibilism. My interest, however, is in classical compatibilism, which ties free action to action in accordance with the agent's actual and counterfactual motivation.

Notoriously, this account falls short of providing sufficient conditions for free action. The agent's behavior might be the product of a compulsion, mania, phobia, or addiction; or it might result from the implantation of wants, intentions, and so forth by others through hypnosis, brainwashing, psychosurgery, injection of drugs, or other forms of manipulation. Again, the agent may be coerced: as Hobbes noticed (*Leviathan,* X), a person who, at the point of a gun, hands over his billfold, *does* act as he wants. In the circumstances, after all, he chooses to submit to the threat, and nothing impedes him from carrying out that choice. Finally, on the assumption that some behavior of infants and nonhuman animals is to be explained by their having certain motivations (wants and beliefs), such creatures would have to be said to act freely given a compatibilist account framed in terms of wants (though not one framed in terms of, say, choices). In each of these instances, the agent acts in accordance with its motivation; furthermore, the agent would have done a different action had the motivational elements been different. Yet the relevant acts are unfree.

Hierarchical accounts propose to handle problem cases of the first type (compulsions, phobias, addictions) by locating some point of conflict between higher- and lower-level motivational elements. To make this more precise, it will be helpful to create a taxonomy of hierarchical accounts by noting certain distinctions.

(1) The higher-level desire may be either a desire not to have the lower-level desire or a desire not to have that desire be effective (what Frankfurt calls a higher-level volition).[4]

The difference between the two kinds of higher-level desires is brought out by Frankfurt's example of a psychotherapist who, to understand his patients' motivational structures, wants to have cravings like theirs (say, for certain drugs) but does not want these desires to be effective in action (1971, 9). Acting on either kind of unwanted desire might make for unfreedom.

(2) One theory (call it a simple accord theory) might require, for free

action, that the agent has a higher-level want or volition that merely accords with the agent's lower-level want or volition; whereas another theory might require, more stringently, that the higher- and lower-level elements be related to each other in some special way. One element, for instance, might be required to cause, explain, or provide a reason for the other. A different theory, however, would require neither accord nor accord plus some causal, explanatory, or reason-giving relation, but, rather, only the absence of discord. On a theory that requires accord or accord plus some appropriate relation, an agent who performs an action but has no higher-level attitude at all towards the motivational factors that produced it would not be acting freely; but on a theory that required only absence of discord, the agent would be. The differences between simple accord, accord-plus, and absence-of-discord theories are of some importance in the arguments to follow.

On typical accord theories, addicts or compulsives who approve of their first-level desires act freely. Accord theorists, however, may be perfectly willing to endorse this result; indeed, they may consider the distinction between willing (= free) and unwilling (= unfree) addicts, phobics, and compulsives to be a fruitful one. (Cf. Frankfurt 1971, 19-20, and 1975, 119; Neely 1974; Locke 1975, 100. Note, however, Locke and Frankfurt's distinction between conditions of freedom and conditions of responsibility.) It should also be noted that an accord theorist may want to require both accord and absence of discord. This would allow us to treat as unfree those cases in which an agent has both conflicting higher-level desires and parallel conflicting lower-level desires, each of which is thus endorsed by a higher-level desire. (See Slote 1980. Cf. Frankfurt 1971, 16; Locke 1975, 100-101.)

(3) A theory might require not only accord or accord plus an appropriate relation but also accord (or accord plus the relation) in counterfactual situations. Consider an addict who approves of her lower-level desire for a drug and of its being effective in action, but who would have and act on this desire even if her second-level stance were one of disapproval (cf. Frankfurt 1971, 19-20; Locke 1975, 103-104). On an accord model, she would be acting freely; on a counterfactualized model, she would not. These two models mirror a distinction one can make between two versions of simple compatibilism: one that requires only accord between motivation and behavior (or accord plus a relation) in the actual situation, another that requires, in addition, accord or accord-plus in counterfactual situations.[5] It is tempting to think that some candidates for the 'relation' (notably 'because') tend to generate a counterfactual condition as well, but this is not clear. Even if B happens because of A, it may be the case that had A not occurred, C would have and would have caused B.

(4) Some hierarchical theories may impose the hierarchical condition as a means of completing the conditions of free action; that is, the conjunction of the hierarchical condition with the standard conditions of compa-

tibilism will be claimed to generate necessary and sufficient conditions of free action. Others will take the hierarchical condition as but one additional necessary one, or will use it to generate only a set of sufficient conditions.

(5) Finally, hierarchical accounts may be differentiated from one another depending on what sort of motivational element they highlight (desires, choices, willings, decisions, etc.).

My presentation will not require any favored formulation of the hierarchical account as regards the specification of motivational elements. Except where it is significant to point out the virtues of other formulations, I will work with a theory couched in terms of 'wants', 'desires', or 'preferences', and I will take the hierarchical theorist to be advancing necessary and sufficient conditions. I will allow occasional shifts of terminology; it is not that no significant differences exist among various terms for motivational elements, but only that, for my purposes, these differences will not be relevant.

I plan to concentrate on counterexamples of the first type (phobias, compulsions, addictions). Nevertheless, it is worth noting that our other problem cases appear tractable once we allow a bit more play in our formulation of the hierarchical condition. Consider the subject of a hypnotic spell or the victim of a brainwashing. He may (a) occurrently disapprove of the specific desire implanted through the manipulative technique; (b) disapprove, in general, of desires induced in that way; or, at least, (c) *resent* having his desires so induced (Levin 1979, 249-52). In case (a), the conflict he undergoes is clear. In cases (b) and (c), it is less clear: after all, the subject or victim may not know that the desire in question was induced in one of the ways he disapproves of or would resent, and hence he will experience no conflict. Nevertheless, the relevant intuitions might be explained by a hierarchical theorist using a counterfactual formulation of the hierarchical condition. What makes the behavior unfree in these cases, a compatibilist may say, is that the agent would disapprove of the desire (higher-level stance) or resent its being induced if he had more facts (about the way it originated). Indeed, as Jerry Samet pointed out to me, a counterfactual, dispositional account of the attitudinal ascriptions in (b) and (c) may be the only account that even makes sense of these ascriptions.

It may appear that appeal to a subjunctive constraint is superfluous in this context; a condition of interlevel accord will suffice to block these cases since the manipulated agent does not have an approving higher-level desire. However, this response is aborted by the widely noted possibility of externally implanting higher-level motivational elements that accord with lower-level elements. An accord requirement is thus not enough to solve the problem (see, e.g., Locke 1975, 104-6; Slote 1980, 149-51).

What about cases involving coercion? Here, a hierarchical theorist might resort to the implausible move of counting coerced actions as free (see

Neely 1974, 35, 50; Frankfurt 1975, 113-17, 122-24). The theorist has two other options, however. The theorist may argue that the agent "minds acting from" the motive he or she acts on, and is for that reason not acting freely (Dworkin 1970; cf. Frankfurt 1975, 113-14). Or the theorist may attribute to the victim an ambivalence: the victim has not only a second-level desire that the first-level desire to capitulate be effective, but also (taken in by thoughts of heroism) a second-level desire that the desire to resist be efficacious. Since the desire to resist is not efficacious, the action if unfree (Slote 1980).

Turning, finally, to lower animals and infants: though they experience no conflict, these creatures are blessed in this way only because they cannot approve of their desires either. Their lack of conflict traces to their inability to satisfy any requirement of hierarchical agreement. For that reason, they are not the sort of beings who can act freely or unfreely.

But why should the presence of interlevel conflict lead to unfreedom? And even if conflict generates unfreedom, does whatever motivating argument is given for this absence-of-discord condition also dictate an accord, or accord-plus, requirement? Hierarchical theorists who see themselves in the classical compatibilist tradition have given scant attention to such questions, despite the fact that we should expect any constraints added to those set down by classical compatibilism to fit into the leading ideas and insights of that viewpoint. In what follows, I will consider three basic arguments that purport to fill this gap: the argument from tranquility, the argument from externality, and the argument from control. I will comment briefly on the first two, and then extensively on the third.

II

The argument from tranquility maintains that the fact of conflict per se makes for unfreedom because freedom requires tranquility (see Neely 1974, 39; cf. Slote 1980, 140, n.9). But if this were so, then not only interlevel conflict but even conflict at the first level should result in unfreedom; conflicts at the first level also impede the attainment of tranquility—in fact, they do so in a more obvious way, as they tend to be more intense and preoccupying than interlevel (hierarchical) tensions. Yet cases of conflicting wants are often regarded as paradigms of free choice and action (see, e.g., Nozick 1981, chap. 4). Of course, it may be replied that conflicting first-level desires need not conflict occurrently but only dispositionally; hence they need not impair tranquility (this suggestion was made by Jerry Samet). But the same could then be said for interlevel conflicts, in which case the tranquility argument collapses anyway.

Moreover, hierarchical accounts do not typically require the extirpation of one of two conflicting first-level desires. The agent acts freely provided she wants to have the desire she acts on and/or wants it to be effective in action—regardless of whether the conflicting first-level desire continues to exist. (We may want to add that the agent has no conflicting second-level desire that this first-level desire not win out; see Slote 1980). Thus, the tranquility condition would be violated even in cases of free action.

Hierarchical theorists are likely to respond that I have failed to distinguish two sorts of conflict. In one, it is just a contingent matter, an accident of circumstance, that the two desires cannot be jointly satisfied; I am "conflicted" as to whether to take a train or a bus, or whether to go to the concert or the movie. Here, one resolves the conflict by ordering the desires—making one first choice, the other second choice. In the other sort of conflict, however, to elect to satisfy one desire entails *rejecting* the competing desire, perhaps labeling it as bad or ignoble; further, there is a sense in which the desires necessarily conflict (see Frankfurt 1976, 248-51; Slote 1980, 140; Taylor 1976). The compatibilist claim will be that only conflict of the second type interferes with freedom. Against this, I would claim that the distinction between the types is not at all clear;[6] that from the point of view of tranquility, the distinction should be irrelevant; and that not even conflict of the second type interferes with freedom. As many libertarians have emphasized in their talk about moral struggle, if I give charity and 'endorse' this desire to give, or to submit to duty, and 'reject' my miserly feelings, the persistence of those miserly feelings does not make the act less free; nor do I act unfreely if the situation is reversed (i.e., I don't give but have impulses to give). And in any case, what if I want to be conflicted at the first level because I want temptation and would not be tranquil without a struggle against it? Some would go so far as to say that the act is truly free *only* if there is a struggle.

These criticisms do not preclude one's claiming that if someone *acts* on a rejected desire, that person for that reason acts unfreely; but this is to go beyond the claim that conflict alone generates unfreedom. The latter claim makes it difficult to see why the *rejected* desire must be the one acted on in order to generate unfreedom.

Perhaps it will be said that, although the rejected desire can persist, it will then be external to the person; hence, the *person* is not conflicted, and his or her action is free even though a conflicting *desire* persists (Frankfurt 1976, 250). But this appeal to externality is a different strategy from the appeal to tranquility, and the characterization of externality is, as we will see, no easy task. Moreover, if conflict is the crucial issue, then, given the idea that the rejected desire is external and that hence *I* am not conflicted, it follows that even if I act on the *rejected* external desire (which conflicts with both a first- and a second-level desire), I act freely (since *I* am not conflicted); hierarchical theorists deny that.

In any event, the view that conflict per se is what makes for unfreedom would not furnish an account for cases of hypnosis, in which the agent's conflict is but a counterfactual one and need not impair tranquility. Contra

Slote, furthermore, my intuition is that victims of coercion act unfreely even when they entertain no visions of defiance and heroism but instead act out of unmitigated fear or calculated prudence. In addition, infants, the mentally defective, and nonhuman animals are not conflicted, yet they do not act freely. Although we should recall the response that only in a creature capable of discord is absence of discord significant, the fact is that these creatures prima facie enjoy a tranquil state of mind.

Thus, the tranquility constraint does not block all cases we need to block. Not only is absence of conflict not necessary for free action but its conjunction with the other conditions of classical compatibilism does not yield a set of sufficient conditions. And, finally, the tranquility condition has no evident connection to classical compatibilism and may be at odds with it.[7] For the tranquility condition should allow that someone all of whose desires were frustrated by external obstacles is a free agent if he retains his tranquility, whereas classical compatibilism would seem committed to denying this since the frustrated action would not even be performed. In other words, the tranquility constraint grows out of concern with the phenomenology of a free *agent;* classical compatibilism suggests a very different theory of a free agent—a free agent is one who performs free actions. The distinction between a free agent and a free action will surface again later.

III

I turn next to the externality argument. What this argument maintains is that, for a compatibilist, you are free if and only if you are able to act on *your* wants and desires. If you act on desires that are alien or external to you, you do not satisfy the compatibilist criterion.[8] Now the wants on which a compulsive, phobic, or addict acts are not hers but are alien to her. As such, they become like external obstacles to the realization of her true desires.

The externality argument faces two problems. First, it cannot be vindicated without a fairly determinate theory of personality—a theory according to which the "real you" is the "higher-level you" or those first-level elements approved by this "higher-level you"; or, more conservatively, a theory in which desires whose origin lies in unconscious conflict are not "the real you" (Macklin 1976). The basic difficulty for such theories has been articulated by Irving Thalberg (1978, esp. 223-25; 1983), who notes that, on a psychoanalytic understanding of personality, compulsive desires and the like are not alien.[9] Moreover, certain attitudes—regret about having a bad lower-level desire, feeling that having it diminishes one's self-image, wishing that one had a different sort of personality—make little sense if the first-level desires in question are not part of the self (see Berofsky 1980 and 1983). The 'true self' criterion appears still more problematic when one realizes that addictive or phobic bits of behavior may be associated, in some instances, with other traits of personality and that second-level desires can be formed casually and unreflectively; in the latter case, they are not a reliable barometer of one's 'true' desires (cf. Berofsky 1980).

Second, the externality argument seems misguided. For to the extent that the efficacious desire is looked upon as an external force, the behavior it produces should cease to be regarded as an act, as a product of agency. A person carried away by the wind does not act. Granted, 'he accidentally *did A*' is a legitimate way of describing cases where the agent did not intentionally do anything; nevertheless, it is clear that addicts, compulsives, and phobics act in a stronger sense. Addicts and phobics, in fact, may conceive and implement elaborate plans to satisfy their cravings or avert consequences they fear. Perhaps the compatibilist can find a way of characterizing 'externality' that allows an external force to cause actions of this kind. But it is far from obvious what that characterization might be.

Perhaps what the compatibilist wants to say is that, although the relevant desires are in some sense the agent's, only those desires and beliefs that are part of a person's *character* are to be thought of as producing free actions. But this narrows unduly the range of free actions. Transient or whimsical desires and aversions, loves and fears—these are not related in any evident sense to character. Yet actions produced by such 'forces' would appear to be free. Moreover, as noted, there is no assurance that phobias and addictions are not related to traits of character.

To escape these objections to the externality argument, compatibilists might concede that first-level desires are part of the self; their contention would be that for an action to be free it must issue from a particular part of the self, a part that reflects what the agent wants most. But since all desires, lower and higher level, would seem to derive from a single part of the personality,[10] compatibilists are well advised to argue that free actions come from a different part of the self altogether—say, the 'rational' faculty. Gary Watson (1975) suggests, for example, that free action is action in accordance with and because of *valuation* (cool, reflective, evaluative judgments) and not action in accordance with and because of *desire*. This account does not really fall within my characterization of 'hierarchical' theories (it is not founded on distinctions of levels within desires), and I think it has some advantages and some disadvantages when compared with such theories. Be that as it may, the account prima facie needs independent motivation. For why are one's valuings the important thing? Isn't that because Watson is assuming a debatable theory of personality? Also, what if the agent doesn't desire to be moved by valuings but rather by first-level desires, 'identifying' more with those; (see David Zimmerman 1981, 362-63)?[11] What if the agent doesn't value being moved by value but values being moved by desire? What if he or she values being moved only by *uncaused* desires? In what sense do the valuings reflect what the agent 'really' or 'most' wants? Until such queries are answered, Thalberg's challenge remains.[12]

IV

A natural way for a hierarchical theorist working within the framework of classical compatibilism to motivate the idea that hierarchical conflicts lead to unfreedom is to argue that such conflicts signal a lack of control. There are two ways in which an agent who satisfies the conditions of classical compatibilism might be said to have control over his behavior. First, his behavior is produced by his wants, beliefs, choices, desires, preferences, reasons, or whatever; second, had he been motivated differently, the behavior would have been different. What he wants makes a difference to what he does. "A man is in control to just the extent that what he wants makes a difference to how things go" (Levin 1979, 238).

Critics of compatibilism maintain that satisfaction of these conditions is not a sufficient condition for control because the agent may not have control over what motivational elements he has. First, his wants may be produced by factors outside him; second, "some conditions would prevent a person from choosing to do something but would not prevent him from performing the action if he did choose to do so" (Lehrer 1980, 189). In other words, we can always ask "whether the person could have chosen other than he did" (ibid., 190). To this the hierarchical compatibilist's response is to tighten the conditions of free action so as to ensure that the agent controls his motivational structure in precisely the way that his first-level motivational structure controlled his behavior in the original, unrefined account.

This strategy is illustrated by Keith Lehrer's and Harry Frankfurt's presentations of their hierarchical accounts (Lehrer 1980, Frankfurt 1971). After noting the second objection quoted above, Lehrer maintains that the hierarchical account furnishes a reply to the objection:

> If... we substitute 'choose to do A' for 'A' to determine whether the person could have done A, we get the result that the person could have chosen to do A if and only if he would have chosen to do A if he had chosen to choose to do A. (Pp. 190-91)

Since compulsives, for example, violate this condition, their actions are unfree; others who satisfy the condition act freely. (Lehrer's own account is phrased in terms of 'preferences', not 'choices'.) Lehrer also stipulates that 'S has a hierarchy of preferences'.

The kind of control envisaged for the counterfactual situation (if S were to prefer to prefer... he would prefer...) would appear to be of a direct, internal kind. Otherwise, a compulsive who prefers to prefer otherwise would 'prefer otherwise'—he would wind up with the preference he prefers by undergoing a long process of therapy. Lehrer notes independent reason to stipulate that the relevant control must be internal. He cites Peter van Inwagen's counterexample of a person who would prefer that p if he preferred to prefer it, but only because he would in those circumstances be manipulated externally to prefer that p; to block this case, Lehrer suggests adding a clause that rules out external causation (193, n. 3). Admittedly, the internal/external and direct/indirect distinctions are somewhat fuzzy, but their general intent should be clear.

Lehrer's account calls to mind Moore's celebrated remark: "By saying that we could have chosen to do it, we may merely mean that we should have so chosen if we had chosen to make the choice" (1965, 93). Moore's emphasis on 'choice' as opposed to wants may be questionable, since 'wanting to want' is more intelligible than 'choosing to choose' (Lehrer 191; Van Inwagen 1983, 116). Nevertheless, viewed with Moore in mind, the imposition of a counterfactual hierarchical constraint hardly seems a novel chapter in the history of compatibilism.

Lehrer advances hierarchical conditions only as sufficient conditions for 'S could have done otherwise'; he acknowledges that "we may wish to say of a person whose preferences contain some conflict at some level that he could have performed the action nonetheless" (191). I would like to consider, however, a view stronger than Lehrer's: namely, that hierarchical accounts give necessary and sufficient conditions. For it is the claim of necessity that needs to be protected if we are to understand why the compulsive is not free (we were told that the compulsive violates a necessary condition). Let it be understood, then, that I am considering the view of Lehrer in a stronger form than he endorses.

That the hierarchical account is motivated by reference to the standard compatibilist analysis is suggested by Frankfurt as well. Frankfurt urges that we mark a distinction between freedom of action and freedom of the will, and then he explains:

> Now freedom of action is (roughly, at least) the freedom to do what one wants to do. Analogously then the statement that a person enjoys freedom of the will means (also roughly) that he is free to want what he wants to want. More precisely it means that he is free to will what he wants to will or to have the will he wants. Just as the question about the freedom of an agent's action has to do with whether it is the action he wants to perform, so the question about the freedom of his will has to do with whether it is the will he wants to have. (1971, 15)

Once again, the analysis of free will is made to run on parallel tracks with the analysis of free action. Here, however, Frankfurt stresses not counterfactual control but rather the accord between actual higher-level wants and actual efficacious lower-level wants.[13] Moreover, he does not explicitly require a relation between the levels. But if the important factor is (as we are now suggesting) control, that relation must be required. One other observation. Given the control argument, it is not enough that S's first-level desire accords with his high*est*-level desire if at intermediate levels there are conflicting desires. Like the tranquility argument, and unlike the externality argument, the control argument takes dissonance at *any* two levels to destroy freedom (cf. n. 10).

The question before us, then, is whether the hierarchical account can be motivated in the way suggested by Frankfurt and Lehrer. What I will argue is that, within a classical compatibilist framework, no hierarchical condition of actual control—no condition stipulating that first-level wants must be produced by higher-level ones—can be justified. Consequently, classical compatibilism generates, at best, an absence-of-discord theory and a condition of counterfactual control. This theory, I argue, does not move much beyond Moore; moreover, the condition of counterfactual control is too easily satisfied in some cases and proves too stringent in others.

V

The basic claim of the control argument is that on compatibilist principles the will of the compulsive or addict is unfree. This claim may be exploited in two ways. First, the compatibilist might urge that there is a confusion in our intuitions about cases involving inner compulsions or addictions. In such cases, the actions are in fact free; only the will is not, and people confuse intuitions about the will with intuitions about action. On this view, unfreedom of the will behind an action does not make the action produced by that will unfree. Presumably, also, if S wills to will to do A and wills to do A, but does not will to will to will to do A (i.e., if S does not have the second-order will he wants at the third level), the first-order will is still free. Unfreedom at level $n + 1$ will not, on this way of looking at things, result in unfreedom at level n.

It is clear that this is not Lehrer's position; rather, Lehrer accepts the incompatibilist contention that the compulsive's actions are unfree. One way to ground this contention within a hierarchical framework is to endorse condition F:

> (F) For an action to be free, it must be produced by a free will, i.e., a free act of willing.

Assuming, perhaps generously, that willing is an act and that 'freely wills' is analyzed in a way that parallels 'freely acts', we can infer:

> (G) For S to do A freely, there must be freedom all the way up. If at any level S has an unfree want (or preference), that unfreedom makes all wantings at lower levels, and any resultant actions, unfree.

I reiterate that Lehrer himself does not propose necessary conditions like (F) and (G).

Conditions (F) and (G) contrast with a weaker one, namely:

(H) For *S* freely to do *A* or freely to will to do *A, S* must be able to will otherwise; i.e., it must be the case that if *S* were to will to will otherwise, he would will otherwise without external causation of this lower-level will, and so on all the way up.

Condition (H) does not entail that *S*'s will was produced by a will to will. Hence it does not require that *S*'s will is 'free' according to the conditions of classical compatibilism. It sets down a requirement of counterfactual control rather than of actual control. (A condition still weaker than (H) may be obtained by deleting the phrase 'and so on all the way up', but this condition is too weak to do the job of blocking an infinite series of questions of the form 'but could he have willed otherwise'?)

An incompatibilist critic may accept these conditions; however, whereas for the incompatibilist, what makes the compulsive's will unfree is his inability to will otherwise simpliciter, for the compatibilist it is either the fact that his will is not the result of what he wants to will, or the fact that he cannot will otherwise *by* willing to will otherwise.

Let us begin with conditions (F) and (G). The requirement that the agent's will be free all the way up obviously threatens to generate a regress. For at each level *n, S* is required to have a free will; but to have a free will at level *n, S* must have a free will at level *n* + 1, and so on ad infinitum. I want to examine three possible responses to this problem; only the second should be associated with Lehrer's actual position.

(1) "The regress exists but is not vicious; for in point of fact, it is quite plausible that, in those cases in which he acts freely, a person has controlling preferences of this sort all the way up" (cf. Lehrer 1980, 193; Frankfurt 1971, 16-17). Clearly, though, the cited claim is not plausible. One way to make it at least somewhat plausible is to hold following Lehrer, that indifference, too, is an attitude: if *S* freely prefers *K* at level *n*, then *S* must either prefer to have that preference or must be indifferent (193). To be indifferent is to not have a preference—but "not in the way in which a river does not have a preference." Rather, indifference is a "primitive," and a condition of being indifferent in the relevant sense is that "one might have had a preference." Once indifference is allowed to count as an attitude that, for purposes of ascertaining the freedom of an action, is as good as a preference, perhaps there is no empirical barrier to the claim that people have preferences all the way up. For beginning at a certain level, people are indifferent all the rest of the way up.

However, there is a difficulty with taking the line set forth in response (1) when one is operating within a classical compatibilist framework. The difficulty becomes clear when we consider the following contrasting response to the regress problem, articulated by David Zimmerman:

It is no part of this program [the classical compatibilist program] to claim that we are always free 'to please as we please as we please'. . . . Precisely because he concedes the truth of determinism the compatibilist is perfectly willing to acknowledge that even where a desire is free, there is some point in the motivational hierarchy where the higher-order desire playing the crucial endorsing role is itself an unwilled, unendorsed part of the agent's motivational equipment, to be explained in terms of non-motivational causes. . . .

. . . . There is no regress because non-compulsiveness does not require endorsement by some higher-level volition (actual or hypothetical). . . . All that is necessary is that there be no still higher-order volition with which [the desire at a given level] is in conflict.

One implication of this weaker condition is that human beings are wantons with respect to their highest-order non-compulsive, but unendorsed, desires, but this should not bother a compatibilist either, for his aim is to give a naturalist account of personhood, and in order to give such an account . . . it is enough that human beings be capable of entertaining desires up to some reasonably high order, not that they be capable of doing it up all the way up the hierarchy. (1981, 359)

Infinite motivational structures are of course not likely to find a place in 'naturalistic accounts of personhood', even if Lehrer has made headway towards showing that such structures are possible. In any case, there is a more fundamental difficulty for response (1) that is exposed by Zimmerman's response: namely, that there is nothing compatibilist about response (1). It is not just that, within classical compatibilism, there is no motivation for requiring higher-level attitudes—even of indifference—at any level, let alone every level, as response (1) does; worse, response (1) precludes the possibility of external causation of the will because it places all motivational elements under internal control.[14] Now it may be suggested that what is determined externally is that the lower-level desire accords with the higher (Frankfurt 1971, 20); but this move invites Van Inwagen-style counterexamples, in which the accord is guaranteed by external forces.

(2) "The motivational hierarchy is not infinite as response (1) claimed. Rather, the regress stops at the highest level of attitude, be that attitude preference or indifference. This highest-level attitude can be externally caused, however, without interfering with freedom." I suspect that Lehrer would use this reply were he defending a set of necessary conditions. But using the reply entails giving up conditions (F) and (G). For the agent loses by this response the first type of control—namely, that S's attitudes at each level are controlled by his attitudes at the next level; for this is plainly not true of whatever attitude is at the highest level. S's indifference, for example, is not controlled by a higher attitude; so his indifference is not freely willed; but then

the preference at the level beneath the indifference will not be controlled by a freely willed attitude. To make this point we need not even resort to dramatic possibilities, such as the indifference being implanted by brain-washing, hypnosis, drugs, and the like. Even without such illustrations, it is clear that *any* external cause of the highest-level preference violates (F) and (G).

There is yet another problem when indifference is the highest-level attitude. For indifference does not control a preference in the way that a preference controls an action or an n-level preference controls a preference at level $n - 1$. The 'control' here is entirely negative; that is, 'control' is being exercised by the absence of a specific preference. In classical compatibilism, an agent has positive control—his attitudes cause his actions. Indifference, however, does not cause a preference. So the attitude 'controlled' by indifference is not 'freely willed'. Again, therefore, (F) and (G) must go.

But once (F) and (G) are thrown out, why require a 'free preference' at any level? Why should, say, the first-level desire have to be produced by a second-level desire? (I will soon take a stronger stance—namely, that this sort of control is not present even in the case of higher-level preferences 'controlling' lower ones.) In accepting (F) and (G), we assumed that the agent is required to have some higher-level attitude if he is to act freely. It now appears that we must drop that assumption.

(3) "Drop the requirement that S have a hierarchy of preferences. S has control if (i) his first-level attitudes produce his actions; (ii) he has counter-factual control over his attitudes all the way up—if he would prefer a different first-level preference, he would have it, and so on." Essentially, this is an absence-of-discord theory (a la Zimmerman) combined with a condition of counterfactual control—which is pretty much the view that can be built up out of Moore. Interlevel discord, on this view, destroys freedom, but only because discord betrays a lack of *counterfactual* control. It would further seem that where S does have higher-level preferences, these need only accord with the lower ones and need not produce or sustain them.

This response is open to several criticisms. First, it implies that, if S's first-level attitudes are externally implanted, and hence are intuitively un-free, S will still have to be said to act freely provided he would change those attitudes by willing to do so. Thus, if the implanted hypnotic suggestion is: you will want to open the window unless you will want not to want to, in which case you will not want to, the action is free. Whether (3) can survive this objection depends on whether the hierarchical theorist's treatment of cases of external implantation (sketched in section I), or any other method of differentiating external causes that destroy freedom from external causes that do not, is adequate. I will not explore that question here; still, it is worth noting that, to the extent that hierarchical theories appeared to turn back the question by putting the agent on internal control, the fact that the question arises after all diminishes the attractiveness of the theory.

More generally, absence-of-discord theories will not be able to rule out free actions by nonhuman animals and human infants, mental defectives, and so forth. It may well be true of such creatures that they have counterfactual control: if they had higher-level preferences, they would have the preferred lower-level preferences. It is just that they do not have higher-level preferences. In other words, the original difficulty—that 'could have done otherwise' is satisfied too easily—applies as well to 'could have willed otherwise'.

No doubt, the compatibilist response to this will be to add a proviso: that free actions are the domain of creatures who have the capacity for higher-level attitudes (recall Lehrer's constraint: the agent 'might have had a preference'). However, the only difference between, on the one hand, creatures who have the capacity but don't exercise it (viz., human beings who are in fact indifferent) and, on the other hand, creatures who lack the capacity, is that the former but not the latter are properly characterized as indifferent. But in criticizing response (2), I argued that the requirement of indifference at the level above the highest level at which the agent has preferences is not well motivated. Response (3) was initiated in recognition of this fact. Hence, there should be no damage in the contention that "there is some point in the motivational hierarchy" where a *lower*-level desire "is itself an unwilled, unendorsed part of the agent's motivational equipment" (David Zimmerman's phrases cited earlier in this chapter). But this being so, why should there be a distinction between creatures with a capacity for higher-level preferences and creatures without such a capacity, as long as neither exhibits discord and both have efficacious first-level wants? (Cf., however, Frankfurt 1971, 14). It will not do to say that only if a creature is capable of discord is the *absence* of discord significant. For on the suggestion we are considering, discord itself is significant only because it betrays a lack of counterfactual control. Our problem is that infants, animals, and the mentally defective do not lack counterfactual control, as defined thus far.

The whole strategy, furthermore, seems misguided. The compatibilist maintains that infants, defectives, and nonhuman animals lack the capacity for higher-level preferences. Now, if they lack this capacity, they presumably cannot control their preferences. By condition (H), then, they cannot will otherwise, even at the *first* level. But is it not easy to have the intuition that they *can* have different first-level wills (though not necessarily because they would if they so willed)? Admittedly, it is strange for an incompatibilist to lodge this objection. If these creatures *can* will otherwise, shouldn't they be said to act freely? But this rejoinder works only on the level of a tu quoque. It does not make the hierarchical account in version (3) more plausible. Furthermore, there is nothing blocking an incompatibilist from imposing additional conditions, including hierarchical ones of the sort supposed in response (1), to account for the unfreedom of these creatures. The compatibilist, we have seen, does not have that option.

Let me note, parenthetically, that the proper analysis of "capacity" is far from evident. In what sense do the mentally defective or nonhuman animals not have the capacity for higher-level preferences? Is this equivalent to: it is false that they 'might have had a (higher-level) preference'? No. There seems to be a sense in which someone who is mentally defective 'might have had a higher-level preference' if there were some simple surgical procedure or pill that would have made the person normal; certainly that person's situation is different from, say, that of a rock. On the other hand, consider a normal adult who *in fact* has no higher-level preferences. If determinism is true, this fact is nomically determined; so there is a sense in which the adult could not have had a higher-level preference. At this point, one might submit a conditional analysis of 'they can have a higher-level preference (though they do not)'; one will treat preferences as analogous to actions, which seems to be what our compatibilist did in motivating a condition of counterfactual control. But then the sense in which creatures 'cannot' have a higher-level attitude must be that given by the compatibilist account of what an agent can do; specifically, they 'can't' have such attitudes in the sense that the following is false: if they were to prefer to have a higher-level preference, they would. But that condition is not met even in the case of normal adult human beings. Given actual indifference at level n, we cannot ensure our having a preference at level n just by preferring to have a preference. In other words, the notion of 'could have had a preference' itself must be explicated. If having a preference is analyzable in a way analogous to doing an action, 'could have' must be explicated by means of a conditional analysis, at least if one is a compatibilist; if it is not thus analyzable—is not treated as actions are—then it seems inappropriate to characterize the situation as one of counterfactual *control*. Also, on the assumption of determinism, one might at least initially argue that nobody who in fact has no higher-level preference regarding a particular action could have had one.

These reflections do not show that the compatibilist is wrong that infants, mentally defective humans, and nonhuman animals lack the capacity for higher-level preferences. Clearly they do lack that capacity. What the reflections show, rather, is that the notion of a capacity is not readily explicated in terms of "might have" and the like. That point taken by itself does not block the compatibilist from requiring the capacity for higher-level preferences as a condition of free action. What I have questioned, however, is why this condition should be imposed given the compatibilist program as outlined by Zimmerman. It is clear, in any case, that without the condition, the compatibilist must concede counterfactual control and free action to infants, the mentally defective, and nonhuman animals.

More generally, the compatibilist's stress on the significance of counterfactual control seems excessive. (Some of what I am about to say generates worries about conditional analyses of ability that are independent of hierarchical accounts.) Suppose I am thrown against a wall by an unexpected wind. I may have counterfactual control here: if I wanted not to be thrown, I would not have been thrown (I would have girded myself); if I wanted to want not to be thrown, I would have wanted not to be thrown; and so on all the way up. This sort of counterfactual control, I think, counts for little because the behavior was not produced by my wants at all. Now the only difference between this case and the case where an agent does an *action* over which he has counterfactual control is that in the latter case his wants produce the action. But that alone ex hypothesi does not make for control; after all, compulsives have *that* sort of control. Indeed, they have that sort of control plus one bit of counterfactual control—different attitude, different action. It is fair to ask: if counterfactual control over behavior does not confer control in the wind example, why should counterfactual control over motivation confer control in the case of the person whose first-level wants produce his action? Did we not start with the fact, evident from the case of the compulsive, that production by wants, even in conjunction with one bit of counterfactual control, does not ensure control? Perhaps the existence or nonexistence of counterfactual control is a barometer of an agent's being free *with respect* to some *alternative* action that he does not perform; it need not bear directly on whether S is doing A freely now (cf. Frankfurt 1975, 118). Whether this view is correct will depend, in part, on intuitions about 'Lockean cases' in which a person decides to do A but lacks counterfactual control because he or she could not act in accordance with a contrary motivation (cf. Frankfurt 1969). Of course, skepticism about the relevance of counterfactual control cannot be put forward by incompatibilists without impugning their own stress on 'could have done otherwise'; but, here again, we have only a tu quoque. Furthermore, incompatibilists do not have to understand 'could have done otherwise' in a way that *forces* them to say that the person thrown against the wall could have done otherwise. For incompatibilists, external causation of the act might deprive the agent of the ability to do otherwise. Whether ultimately plausible or not, this option is at least available.

The condition of counterfactual control is suspect for another reason. Consider the conditional: 'if S were to will to will otherwise, he would will otherwise'. On a possible-worlds reading of counterfactuals, a person could violate this condition yet still act freely. For in some cases, the nearest possible worlds in which S wills to will otherwise are worlds in which he does not will otherwise; yet it would be outlandish to say that S is not free. An example suggested in conversation by Robert Hambourger makes the point. Imagine a man who indulges his appetite for ice cream and right now has no reason to will that he will otherwise—he is in perfect health, looks svelte, and so forth. It may be that the nearest possible world in which he wills to will otherwise is a world in which he would have this will as the result of reading some literature by religious ascetics; but in such a world, although he might give credence to this literature, he would be weak willed and eat anyway. Surely the fact that in that world he would indulge should not affect whether he eats freely now! In fact, imagine that the two nearest possible worlds in which he would will to will otherwise are $W1$, a world in which his doctor tells him to lose weight, and $W2$, a world in which he reads the religious literature. Imagine that in $W1$ he abstains but in $W2$ he is weak-willed. Whether he is free depends on which world is closer. Imagine that on Monday, $W1$ is closer (his doctor is about to send him a reminder, but no journal the man reads has considered printing ascetic material), whereas on Tuesday, $W2$ is closer (the doctor's reminder was thrown out by mistake at the post office, and a journal is now considering an ascetic's article). So the agent indulges freely on Monday and unfreely on Tuesday, and for reasons that are as extraneous as could be (remember, the person's doctor need not be set to chide him, and no publisher needs to be considering ascetic material—these are just the closest possible scenarios in which he wills to will something else). As we will see, problems of this sort affect other compatibilist accounts that require some sort of counterfactual responsiveness.

It is clear that hierarchical theorists owe us an interpretation of their crucial counterfactuals and a brief in favor of the significance of counterfactual control. It is not my *main* purpose to show that these cannot be provided; perhaps with a bit more work they can. My aim, rather, is to show that even if these could be furnished, we would get, a best, an absence-of-discord requirement, and that requirement itself would be grounded in an iterated version of counterfactual control. Thus, the only viable version of a hierarchical account that can be generated from classical compatibilism is the one familiar from Moore. The more robust requirement that the agent's motivational structure be produced by internal attitudinal factors would appear to be available only to an incompatibilist. Whether the theory can prove viable in the hands of incompatibilists will depend on how well incompatibilists can cope with the regress argument.

VI

It remains for us to consider the version of the control argument according to which the agent's actions in the problem cases are free but his or her willings are not. Presumably, the will is said to be free when it satisfies the conditions set down in the standard compatibilist analysis of free action. Hence an agent wills freely if and only if (i) he wills as he wants and because he so wants, and perhaps (ii) he would will otherwise were he to will to will otherwise, without any external intervention. This formulation immediately raises the specter of an externally implanted want producing a 'free' want at the level below. Even apart from this, however, it can be shown that the proposed analysis of 'S freely wills (wants, prefers, etc.) to do A' cannot be made to run on parallel tracks with the compatibilist account of '*S* freely does *A*'.

For the parallel to be sustained, the compatibilist will have to avoid a simple accord theory. For *S* to freely act or freely will at a given level, it is not enough that *S* wants or prefers so to act or will; *S* must do as he wants because he so wants. Otherwise, actions would count as free even when there is no explanatory connection between *S*'s want and *S*'s action, or where the connection is deviant (cf. Davidson 1973). Now whether reasons are causes or are not causes, this much seems clear: the 'because' clause must give the reason why *S* acts as he does. (cf. Blumenfeld 1972, 426-29).

But if for *S* freely to do *A* by virtue of his having certain wants and beliefs, those wants and beliefs must constitute the reason he does *A*, then, for *S* freely to want to do *A* by virtue of his having certain higher-level wants, those higher-level wants must constitute the reason he wants to do *A* (in conjunction with a belief that having the lower-level want will lead to satisfaction of the higher). But this condition is rarely satisfied. *S*'s reason for wanting to do *A* will refer to some fact about *A*, even if that fact is just that he wants to do *A* for its own sake; that *S* wants to want to do *A* is not his reason for doing *A*. Often, my reasons for wanting to do *A* and my reasons for wanting to want to do *A* will be identical, but neither is typically the reason for the other (cf. Darwall 1983, 92; Watson 1975, 219).

It may appear that I have mixed up two senses of 'want': wanting to do *A*, and wanting *x* (which want is satisfied by doing *A*). The charge would be that my wanting to do *A* is never my reason for doing *A*; my reason is that doing *A* will lead to *x*—better, my reason is my wanting *x* and my believing that doing *A* will lead to *x*. But this observation is of no help to the compatibilist. For my reason for wanting to do *A* is not that, by wanting to do *A*, I will bring about something else that is described by the content of a second-level want. Hence the parallel to action collapses anyway.

There may be ways for a compatibilist to avoid the claim that higher-level wants are the reason for lower-level ones. In particular, recent work on the explanation of action suggests that it is too crude to regard wants and beliefs as reasons; reasons, it is said, are better identified with 'dicta' (Darwall 1983) or 'belief contents' (Bond 1983, 16). Consider the following kind of view: often, when an agent does an action for a reason, there is also some desire (and belief) that explains the action; however, the desire (and belief) explain the action only in the broad sense in which a prejudice, tendency to mimic, or physiological condition explains an action (Darwall, chaps. 2-3; Darwall rejects the view that such a desire is always there). By formulating matters this way, the hierarchical theorist avoids claiming that wants per se function as reasons and hence that higher-level wants must function as reasons. The control exerted by higher-level elements over lower-level ones is the control of cause over effect, not the control of a reason over what it explains.

But is S's having the higher-level want a cause of his having the lower-level one? In some cases, notably those in which an agent's current desires are the result of a regimen that rid him or her of a previous desire or inculcated this one, the answer appears to be yes. In others, though, the second-level want is the effect, not the cause, of what transpires at the first level. Often we find ourselves with first-order wants implanted by genetic endowment, environmental influence, or God, and then find ourselves having second-level desires to have those first-level desires.[15] If one takes these desires as free (to be sure, on the present suggestion, the fact that the actions they explain are free does not entail that the *desires* are), we have a counter-example to the hierarchical theorist. Moreover, if S, after careful deliberation, arrives at a desire to do A, but this desire is not caused by a higher-level desire (though S may *have* such a desire), we would hardly declare the desire unfree on those grounds alone. And even in seemingly favorable cases (the inculcation of a desire by means of a regimen), it seems more correct to take the higher-level attitudes as explaining S's undertaking the regimen, and his undertaking the regimen as explaining his acquiring or losing the desire, than to take the higher-level attitudes as explaining his acquiring or losing the desire (cf. Jeffrey 1974, 378-79).

Perhaps the second-level desire will be said to be a necessary condition for the first-level desire. However, it is intelligible to suppose that, if S were not to have the higher-level want, he would still have the lower-level want. The situation may be such that he will want one thing or the other; whichever he wants, his having a higher-level want will not be a necessary condition of his wanting that thing.

A compatibilist might demur here and draw a parallel to the case of the willing addict—an addict who approves of the addiction but who would take the drug anyway, even if he or she didn't approve. Compatibilists could regard this agent's will as unfree; they might therefore argue that if S would have the lower-level want without having the higher-level want, his lower-level want is not free. But we must distinguish two cases: (i) S has lower-level desire D and would have it even if he wanted not to have it; (ii) S has D and would have D even if he had no higher-level desire with respect to D, but would not have D if he desired not to have it. Even if compatibilists are right to deny freedom in case (i), they would be wrong to do so in case (ii); and in case (ii), the higher-level want is not a necessary condition of the lower.

In short, to model freedom of the will on freedom of action, a compatibilist must ascribe to second-level wants a causal or explanatory hegemony over first-level wants that they do not in fact enjoy, or that at least does not seem necessary for freely willing. Insofar as this suggests that a free desire need not be produced or sustained by a higher-level desire, it suggests that if accord is necessary at all for free desire, it is for reasons that have nothing to do with classical compatibilism. Why, though, *do* accord and discord seem to be significant in assessing the freedom of a desire? One answer may be that a desire arrived at by cool, deliberate reflection is likely to be endorsed by a higher-level desire; hence, although production by reflection or valuation is what is crucial to freedom, accord is a sign that the desire is free, albeit not that which makes it free (cf. Watson 1975, 219; David Zimmerman 1981, 363-65). From this perspective, the control argument has things exactly backwards: the higher-level want should be produced by the lower one or by whatever valuations produce the lower one.

This is not entirely satisfactory. For an agent who does not want to be moved by his or her reflections and valuations, but is anyway, *might* be thought of as unfree, ostensibly in virtue of this rather peculiar sort of discord. Adapting a point made by Zimmerman (363) (who favors hierarchical accounts), opponents of hierarchical accounts might explain this intuition by embracing a kind of internalism, arguing that such discord signals a misreading of the valuation. Alternatively, they might want to grant some significance to counterfactual control and to take the presence of discord as indicative of an absence of such control. But another answer is possible— namely, that a distinction needs to be drawn between what is required for an action or desire to be free, and what is required for an agent to be free in doing that action or having the desire. The latter requires tranquility; for that reason, discord is relevant. On this view, all the cases of conflict cited in our treatment of the tranquility argument are cases in which the agent is unfree, but not necessarily the action. So, too, the person who acts according to reason but does not desire to could be viewed as an unfree agent performing a free action. Admittedly, these suggestions about the relevance of accord and discord need to be fleshed out; they do suggest, however, that hierarchical accounts might be defensible as theories of a free agent (here I am indebted to Sidney Morgenbesser). Be that as it may, it seems unlikely that in a theory of free *action,* higher-level wants will have to control lower-level ones in the manner suggested by the control argument. At best, no more than a counterfactual constraint on 'free desire' can be generated by classical compatibilism.[16] And even this constraint is suspect; for in the counterfactual situation, the agent lacks the relevant sort of control for the same reason that he or she lacks it in the actual situation: the 'because' relation is not exemplified in the right way.

VII

In arguing against hierarchical accounts of free will, I have not argued against compatibilism per se; rather, I have argued that one theory that purports to protect compatibilism against a standard group of counterexamples has no rationale within classical compatibilism. To draw some more general conclusions about the viability of compatibilism, I would like briefly to consider other compatibilist responses to the problem cases and in that way discern the direction in which a compatibilist theory will have to go if it is to work.

One group of responses is what might be dubbed "counterfactual responsiveness" theories. In the most popular version of this view, a free action must be "reason-sensitive" (the phrase is Levin's [1979, chap. 8]). The behavior in question must be modifiable by the influence of rational considerations; the agent must be "open to rational persuasion" (Glover 1970, 98. See also Davis 1979, 114ff.; Fingarette 1972; MacIntyre 1957; and Neely 1974). Generally, advocates of this approach do not maintain that the behavior must be modifiable in the face of *objectively* rational considerations; their claim is, rather, that in the case of free action, if the agent were presented with considerations that he himself, subjectively, were to regard as rational considerations for not doing A, he would not do A.[17] Such a claim would appear to be an analogue of the claim of counterfactual control we encountered earlier. Here what is required is not counterfactual control by desire, but counterfactual control by reasons.[18]

Two kinds of problems beset such views. One is that they lack motivation. To supply motivation, advocates of the reason-sensitivity criterion would have to show either that (i) a reason—insensitive desire is alien or external; or that (ii) reason-insensitivity shows that the action is not *explained* by reasons either;[19] or that (iii) 'he would do otherwise if presented with (subjectively) good reasons' gives a good account of 'he could have done otherwise'. None of these arguments is persuasive, in my view, though I do not have the space to show this here.

The second problem is that compulsive, addictive, or phobic behavior does seem to be modifiable under the influence of rational considerations, in at least three ways. First, there is therapy. Second, the agent might discover that he has some facts wrong—for example, the syringe contains water, not drugs. (Notice that even hypnotized subjects may modify their behavior if they learn they were hypnotized.) Third, suppose the agent were to become "rationally persuaded" that by giving in to his compulsion, addiction, or phobia, he will, here and now, lose his life. Surely it is intelligible to suppose that (i) he would modify his behavior under these circumstances, yet (ii) his behavior in the actual world is compulsive. (The same might apply in cases of hypnosis.)

In response to the third of these possibilities, a compatibilist might argue that as long as there could be *some* (subjectively) rational considerations that an agent would not respond to, this fact suffices to make the behavior count as compulsive, addictive, or phobic; and surely we can suppose that this same agent who would respond to the prospect of imminent death would not respond to, say, a threat to property or family, or the prospect of deterioration in health or of a prison sentence. But this revised condition makes an awful lot of behavior compulsive. Note that we have not stipulated that there must actually be 'reasons around' against engaging in the behavior, or some fact that the agent would take to generate a good reason for refraining; rather, the test bids us to imagine what would happen if there were such reasons. Suppose that I find myself in a lean and supple state and reach for a large helping of a hot fudge sundae. And suppose that in actual fact there are no other rational considerations that count against my taking this step—perhaps I even need to gain weight. On the present suggestion, my behavior counts as compulsive provided that were there (subjectively) rational considerations against engaging in the behavior, and I were presented with these considerations, I would persist in the behavior nonetheless. Imagine, then, a possible world in which there is some subjectively rational consideration to which I would not be responsive (e.g., a world in which I am obese) because I *would be* weak willed. (I may in general be weak-willed.) Surely my action here and now—taking the ice cream—is no less free for that reason. Even if Gary Watson is right that akratic actions are unfree (Watson 1977), it hardly follows that right now I am not eating the ice cream freely. The fact that in other, counterfactual circumstances, my action would qualify as akratic hardly establishes that it is akratic in the present circumstances. Right now, I do not judge that eating is detrimental to my interests; my desires right now are in perfect accord with my valuations; so eating is neither akratic nor unfree. At best, how I would respond in the counterfactual circumstances is a measure of the strength of my desire, my general powers of self-control, and the extent to which my judgments, in general or in cases of this sort, influence my motivational structure (though we may even suppose that in a world in which I would have the subjectively good reasons, I might have more intense desires, less self-control, etc.). But it is not an index of whether I am now acting unfreely. For many pleasurable actions, there may be some counterfactual point at which the agent would do the action purely out of weakness of will. But that should not result in such actions' being unfree; for the weakness of will is not implicated in the explanation of the action in the actual world.

Perhaps the compatibilist will suggest that a free action is one that is modifiable by *all* coercive incentives—incentives it would be altogether unreasonable for any rational person not to act on (see Gert and Duggan 1979)—and *some* noncoercive incentives. In my ice cream example, there must be *some* noncoercive incentives that would make me stop, and *no* coercive incentives that would not. I am not sure whether this will work. Suppose that in point of fact there are no noncoercive or coercive incentives against my doing what I'm doing; and I am doing it right now with perfect rationality. But imagine further that I would ignore all noncoercive incentives and some coercive ones (e.g., I might defy a gun to my head, out of resentment) were they present. Do I act freely? On the one hand, we might look at the production of the action, and its production was by reasons; if we are compatibilists, that would lead us to declare the action free and reject the reason-sensitivity criterion. On the other hand, we might take the un-modifiability of the behavior, at least in those cases where the un-modifiability cannot be traced to resentment over the very presence of a coercive incentive (e.g., a gun to my head), as an indication that rational reflection is not playing the role it seems to be, that my reasons are just rationalizations for behavior that really does not issue from reflection. But within classical compatibilism, this second perspective is hard to sustain. For in one sense my behavior is governed by reasons: my desire to bring about a certain state of affairs (eating ice cream, say) together with appropri-ate beliefs about what certain movements will achieve (cf. n. 19). What is true is that various reflective reasons—reasons having to do with whether to have the desire, with the rationality of the desire itself—are probably not doing the work they appear to be doing. But within classical compatibilism, it seems difficult to assign importance to reflection on the desire without gener-ating a requirement that an agent's desire be rationalized all the way up, thus excluding external causation; at the least, a compatibilist would owe us a more suitable conception of what counts as a rationalized action.

Thus, a classical compatibilist will have a hard time rejecting my coun-terexample without submitting a revised view of what counts as rational behavior. By the same token, the compatibilist will have to exclude, from the sphere of 'reason-sensitive' behavior, behavior that is sensitive to reason only in the following weak sense: that if I desired not to do the action and believed that by movements a, b, c I would not do it, I would not do it. Explaining why such actions are unfree was, after all, the original difficulty facing the compatibilist conception of counterfactual control. Free action cannot be required to display sensitivity to reason without a more suitable conception of reason.

In addition, it is not clear that the rational unmodifiability of the agent's behavior is more than a symptom, a test, of unmodifiability simplici-ter, something that must be *explained* by the agent's inability to do otherwise (see Berofsky 1973, 333, and Greenspan 1978, 229, n. 8). If that is so, focus on *reason*-insensitivity will be blocking out what is really important about insensitivity to coercive incentives. Depending on what this 'really impor-tant' factor turns out to be, the result may or may not be damaging to compatibilism. I leave this as an area for further inquiry.

Let us turn to an alternative compatibilist approach. In this approach, an agent acts freely provided that he acts as he would prefer to act "were he to consider all relevant information in a dispassionate way," "were he to be reflectively aware, in an imaginatively vivid way, of all facts regarding prop-erties that are internal to the thing preferred" (Darwall 1983, 93, 99).[20] Let us refer to a preference that the agent would have were he 'reflectively aware', and so on, as a C-informed (counterfactually informed) preference. At times,

C-informedness is invoked as a criterion for the authenticity of a desire, at times as a criterion of its rationality (cf. Brandt 1979). Either formulation might appear to help a compatibilist motivate the condition of C-informedness; for a free action, according to a compatibilist, must result from the influence of an agent's true preferences and must be rational.

But whether a desire is rational for an agent, or authentically his, should depend on facts about the actual situation, not on what would be the case in some counterfactual situation. The fact that my preference for cigarettes is not C-informed should not dictate that I do not authentically want to smoke now, when I am ignorant of potential health hazards; and if I have some foolish reason now for desisting from smoking, the fact I would desist were I fully informed does not make my current aversion rational. Nor can C-informedness be redefined in terms of what the agent would want were he to reflect in the right way on facts he has now. Imagine that S is now in the grips of a severe phobia; but were he to reflect on what he knows or believes now, he would want to avoid the same thing.[21] His current fear is not ipso facto rational. Neither should it be authentically his; for if the precedence given to reflection is rooted in the idea that reflective wants are more authentic (what other idea would give reflection precedence?), then whether he authentically wants to avoid that thing should depend on whether the aversion was *actually* produced by reflection (cf. Shope 1978).[22]

Sidney Morgenbesser has noted one other difficulty (in conversation). If I were to reflect fully I might conclude that I have no philosophical basis for wanting to maximize expected utility; yet my current preferences and desires are no less rational for that. Apparently, some restriction is needed that will limit the effect of the counterfactual reflection to considerations about the value of the thing preferred.

VIII

Significantly, all three of the accounts we have considered—the hierarchical account, the reason-sensitivity criterion, and the criterion of C-informedness—have encountered at least prima facie difficulties owing to their use of counterfactual conditionals. Initially, it would seem that whether an action is free hinges in great part, and (depending on one's views about the significance of counterfactual control or responsiveness), possibly in toto, on how the action was produced. Hierarchical theories began with the recognition that the standard framework of classical compatibilism, which emphasizes production by first-level wants and beliefs, gives an inadequate set of constraints on production; but we have seen that, so long as one stays roughly within the view of free action as getting what you want because you want it, as well as within the assumption that free will is compatible with external causation, one will not be able to squeeze out of classical compatibilism a hierarchical account that proffers a defensible set of constraints on production. It is this fact that pushes compatibilists in the direction of counterfactualized conditions and that forces them to let compatibilism stand or fall with the adequacy of those conditions.

As several of my remarks may have suggested, I have some sympathy with a particular view of production: the view that free action is action that is produced by and accords with reflection or 'valuation'. Whether *this* account can be developed within a compatibilist framework depends, however, on the answers to many questions. How much reflection is needed? Must one reflect on the value of reflection? How large a role can nonrational causes play in producing or sustaining reflection? How much freedom do we actually have on such a view? Can we salvage a fair share of the everyday free actions with which classical compatibilism credits us? Since few actions are produced *solely* by reflection, should we speak only of degrees of freedom? And, finally, if reflection is the crucial ingredient, what deeper theory accounts for this? Will it be a theory of personality? A theory of agency? A theory of explanation by reasons? Will that deeper theory be compatible with the thesis that nonrational causes can produce free action even of the highest degree? Will it bring us back to theories of agent-causation? These are questions for another time. But in light of the failure of recent compatibilist theories to exhibit a deeper motivation and to see fully the need for a condition of actual as opposed to counterfactual control, there is some significance in the recognition that these are the right questions to ask before affirming the compatibilist viewpoint.[23]

Notes

1. Among the numerous advocates of theories of this kind, or at least aspects of it, are Alston 1977; Davis 1979; Dworkin 1970, 1976; Frankfurt, esp. 1971 and 1975, but also 1973, 1976, 1982; Jeffrey 1974; Körner 1973; Lehrer 1980; Levin 1979, chap. 7; Neely 1974; Schiffer 1976; Taylor 1976; Watson 1975, 1977; Young 1979, 1980a, 1980b; and David Zimmerman 1981. The link between hierarchical accounts and compatibilism is made out most explicitly by Davis, Lehrer, Levin, Neely, Watson, Young, and Zimmerman. Frankfurt 1971, p. 20, notes that his account is neutral with respect to determinism, but precisely for that reason it is not neutral with respect to compatibilism.

2. Are such higher-level stances unique to human beings? Here we might distinguish higher-level stances towards one's own lower-level stances from higher-level stances toward lower- (or higher-) level stances in another creature's motivational structure. Dennett (1976, 179ff.) produces an example that suggests that nonhuman animals are capable of at least the second. Cf. Frankfurt 1971, 11, n. 5.

3. Technically, one should take care not to confuse classical compatibilism with soft determinism. The soft determinist takes a stand on determinism (by affirming it), whereas the compatibilist does not. A compatibilist who is not a determinist might restrict the role of causation in action to the causal connection between reasons and actions; indeterminism may be present with respect to causation of motivational elements. In point of fact, however, virtually all compatibilists appear to be (soft) determinists. Cf. David Zimmerman's (1981) depiction of the 'compatibilist program' in the quotation in section V below. My discussion follows the common assumption that compatibilists are determinists.

I have overlooked some complications in my formulation of compatibilism. For instance, a person who tries but fails to run a four-minute mile acts freely; yet if the motivation is described as "to run a four-minute mile," the person has not acted in accordance with motivation. (This example was suggested by Jerry Samet.) I do not think that the needed modifications will affect my main line of argument.

4. One might say that the agent must act on the desire that has for him highest priority (Neely 1974). I take this view to be close enough to the 'effective in volition' formulation to obviate my treating it separately.

The term 'want' is, of course, ambiguous. In one sense, it is tautologous that an agent does what he or she 'wants', whereas in another sense, an agent may do what he or she does not want to do. I hope that the reader will be able to tell from each context which sense I intend. For clarification, see Frankfurt 1971, 7-10. It may be interesting to locate parallel ambiguities at the second level—does the ambiguity carry over?

5. David Zimmerman (1981) calls these the 'satisfaction' and 'avoidability' models respectively; in the satisfaction model he adds the condition that "it is not the case that he performs the action only because he could not have done otherwise." However, Zimmerman overlooks the need for a 'because' clause in the satisfaction model and hence the claim, which in fact I reject, that the satisfaction model collapses into the avoidability model. Cf. Fischer 1982. I have trouble making sense of a 'simple accord' counterfactual (the 'if-then' seems to imply a relation), but I include it in my exposition for the sake of symmetry.

6. Far more can be said by way of characterizing types of conflict than I can undertake here. See, for example, Körner's (1973) distinctions between opposition, discordance, and incongruence. After this paper was completed, I read Schick's (1984) insightful discussion of conflict, struggle, commitment, and related notions (140ff.), which likewise suggests the need for a more complex account.

7. Slote (1980) sees interlevel conflict as irrationality, but he does not specify the operative sense of 'irrational'. It does not appear to be practical irrationality: the agent is not wanting to do A as a (poor) means of achieving his end of not wanting to do A. His irrationality may seem analogous to that of the akrates. It seems to me, however, that in the absence of a guarantee that higher-level desires reflect practical judgments, the akrates problem as conceived in a *hierarchical* account of akrasia is not so much irrationality as lack of control. Slote's idea is more profitably developed, I think, in the kind of framework proposed by Watson (1975). The connection between the relevant sense of rationality and classical compatibilism would need to be spelled out.

8. Whatever the plausibility of 'alienness' accounts with respect to S *does not freely do A*, 'alienness' accounts of S *is not responsible for doing A* are problematic. For if the fact a motivating desire is alien were to excuse S from responsibility, S could deliberately make certain of his desires alien (for instance, by taking a drug) for the purpose of evading responsibility. The best way to patch up such defects is to introduce indexes. Thus, we might say that S is responsible for doing A at $t2$ if there is some earlier time $t1$ such that at $t1$ S was able to avoid doing A at $t2$. An alternative approach is to insist that S is responsible only for his action A' at $t1$ (the action of making certain desires alien) but not for A (done at $t2$). On the first view, S would be responsible for doing A even though he did not freely do A. Thus, the link between responsibility and freedom is severed and replaced with a link between responsibility and avoidability. I will bracket this whole issue, but I wish to note relevant discussions in Audi 1974; Dworkin 1982; Frankfurt 1975, 122-25; Locke 1975; and Michael Zimmerman 1982.

9. Hierarchical theorists sometimes acknowledge this problem, but they do little by way of solving it. Neely (1974), while formulating pointedly a Freudian position ("the influence of what Plato called the rational element (superego) is . . . an alien intrusion into the self, thrust upon it from outside by parental training and social pressures" [42]) makes no headway towards establishing the superiority of the Platonic one and, in any case, casts his own view in terms of higher-level *desires*. And Watson (1975, 218) asks, against Frankfurt, "what gives these

[higher-level] volitions any special relation to 'oneself' ", but he does not answer satisfactorily the parallel question of what vindicates his Platonic picture as against the Humean one he contrasts it with.

10. Watson voices a trenchant criticism of those who take second-level desires as more authentic than first: "Since second-order volitions are themselves simply desires, to add them to the context of conflict is just to increase the number of contenders; it is not to give a special place to any of those in contention. The agent may not care which of the second-order desires wins out" (1975, 218). Cf. Frankfurt 1971, p. 13, n. 6, and p. 15.

There is some ambiguity in hierarchical theories as to whether *all* levels must be in accord with the lowest or whether it suffices if the *highest* accords with the lowest. If the latter, there is clearly no presumption that the higher the level, the more authentic it is. But that calls into question the significance of the high*est* with respect to authenticity.

11. David Zimmerman (1981, 362-63) points to Dostoevsky's Underground Man and to Augustine: "Give me continence and chastity, but not yet." Zimmerman maintains that a person can act freely even if valuation conflicts with desire, though he notes the possibility that valuation is partly constituted by higher-level desires. It also remains to be seen whether it is the fact of hierarchical accord between desires that accounts for freedom in the cases Zimmerman cites. Cf. the end of section VI below, where these examples are treated differently.

12. Some writers take the touchstone of authenticity to be some sort of subjective identification (see Bergmann 1977). Which desires are authentic is determined by what picture of self the agent adopts—Dostoevskian, Platonic, Aristotelian, and so forth. On this view, if one's actions are in fact determined (even perhaps, if one merely believes this), those actions will be free if one is a compatibilist and unfree if one is an incompatibilist because the latter will not identify with caused desires whereas the former will. Bergmann seems to acquiesce in this conclusion (236-38), but I find it quite odd. Free will and determinism turn out to be compatible only for one who thinks antecedently that they are compatible. Cf., however, the related thesis in Cummins 1979; cf. also Levin 1979, 252.

Coherence with other desires is another attractive criterion of authenticity (cf. Feinberg 1970). However, it is too much to expect positive coherence, as people's interests are many, varied, and mutually independent (cf. Berofsky 1980, 45); a redefinition in terms of absence of conflict with other desires would entail that one of a pair of conflicting desires is always alien, which is too extreme. Moreover, either of the pair seems eligible for selection as the authentic one. Finally, the criterion may prove circular, since the desire must cohere with other (authentic) desires *of that person*. For a fuller treatment of alienness, see Penelhum 1971 and 1979. In any event, the coherence criterion is not a hierarchical one.

13. John Martin Fischer has reminded me that Frankfurt (e.g., 1971, 18-20) requires counterfactual control only for having free will and freedom of action, not for acting freely. These distinctions are important in describing Frankfurt's view accurately, but my purposes are served by considering an idealized view that requires free action both actual and counterfactual control of attitudes and then seeing which elements of this view can be defended and which must be modified or rejected.

14. If the agent exhibits an infinite motivational structure, even the claim that hierarchical accounts generate sufficient conditions of free action will not really be a compatibilist claim. For the sufficient conditions articulated will preclude external determination of the will. This is not true of response (2).

15. It should be noted that when incompatibilists adduce such examples, they are being a bit disingenuous. For incompatibilists (even libertarians) will be likely to regard such 'determined' desires as productive only of unfree actions, and as unfree. Nevertheless, compatibilists, who pride themselves on paying attention to 'ordinary' uses of *free,* might be disposed to take such actions and desires as free; and so the argument works in an ad hominem way.

Compare Schiffer (1976), who argues that such first-level desires would not generate second-level desires at all. Grandy and Darwall (1979) criticize Schiffer in a way congenial to my views.

16. I have said little directly about the extensional adequacy of hierarchical accounts, and indeed it may be argued that if the theory correctly captures intuitions it is worthy of acceptance even if it lacks a deeper motivation. It is therefore not out of place to note ways in which the theory is prima facie inadequate even extensionally.

The version that requires that the agent want to have the want he acts on will have trouble with motivating appetites and needs that are discomfiting (cf. again Schiffer 1976, Grandy and Darwall 1979). It will also have trouble with the myriad cases in which I am indifferent as to what wants I have—ranging from my wanting to watch television (do I want to want to watch?) to cases of 'choice without preference'. (Cf. Ullmann-Margalit and Morgenbesser 1977). Cf. Levin 1979, 231, and my earlier remarks about absence-of-discord theories.

Next, with respect to the requirement that I must want the want to be effective, two interpretations of the requirement are possible: (i) I want desire $D1$ to be effective rather than $D2$; (ii) I want $D1$ to be effective rather than be frustrated by an external impediment. Formulation (i) cannot handle cases of indifference—for example, I want to answer the phone rather than continue reading, and freely answer the phone; but I don't necessarily want this want and not the other to be efficacious. And formulation (ii) does not explain the plight of the compulsive, who does not want an external impediment to interfere; obstructions would heighten the anxiety.

Another difficulty for hierarchical views is that it follows from them that a person who is able to resist a desire D but does not want to have D or does not want it to be effective is not free (cf. Slote 1980, 147-48). That seems wrong: resistibility should make for freedom. Akrasia seems to be a case in point, and indeed hierarchical views (as well as views like Watson's, 1975) have trouble distinguishing akrasia from compulsion. Cf. Watson's subtly argued response (1977) and Young's critique (1980a, 41-43); see also Hill (1984). Some of the problems just raised might be mitigated by emphasizing *degrees* of freedom, or by drawing a distinction between freedom and a more stringent concept, autonomy. I have to leave such suggestions aside, however.

17. The primary reason for attending to subjectively rational considerations rather than objectively rational ones is stated by Neely (1974, 47): if an agent were claimed to be acting unfreely because he does not respond to objectively rational considerations, then Socrates did not freely remain in prison if Crito's arguments are sound. A more general reason for favoring the 'subjective' formulation arises from the Humean tradition. See Williams (1979), who holds that nothing can be a reason for S to do A or to have desire D unless it can be linked to S's beliefs and desires. On this view, the notion of an 'objectively rational' consideration is incoherent if taken to mean a consideration that is not related to the agent's beliefs or desires. Cf. Bond 1983 and Darwall 1983. It is not clear to me how immediately a reason must be linkable to S's desires according to the Humeans in this debate. If the link must be immediate, the condition is too strong. If it need not be immediate, it is not clear what sort of considerations are not linkable in the required way. I must bracket this issue along with two others: how we can know whether someone really recognizes a given set of considerations as rational, given that those considerations do not modify the behavior; and whether reason-sensitivity is necessary for responsibility in light of the sorts of cases adduced in n. 8.

18. This is reminiscent of the ingenious thesis propounded by Wolf (1980), but it contains a subjectivist twist.

19. Cummins 1980, sect. 6, considers and rejects a similar argument regarding culpability; his objection does not affect the present argument regarding free action. What is wrong with the argument in our context is that the behavior of compulsives, addicts, and so forth *can* be given an explanation in terms of reasons such as the satisfaction of desire or relief from anxiety, as argued by Frankfurt 1978, 161; Greenspan 1978; and Watson 1977, 337, n. 20 [cf. Ayer 1954]. Such allegedly reason-insensitive yet rationally motivated behavior itself serves to defeat the principle that, if a piece of behavior is not alterable by rational considerations, it is not explained by reasons or motivations. The compatibilist cannot belittle such 'explanation by reasons' by

requiring that the motivating desire itself be rationalized, for that would deprive us of many free actions (e.g., drinking Coke) and would invite a requirement that a free action be rationalized all the way up. A classical compatibilist should not care whether a motivating desire-belief complex has its origin in reasons or in other causes. Note also that the fact that a piece of behavior (a twitch, say) is modifiable under the influence of rational considerations does not entail that it is explained by reasons.

20. Darwall is not discussing compatibilism and draws no implications concerning it. I am merely trying to bring his views to bear on our present context.

21. Actually, this case needs to be better described. After all, if the fear is genuinely phobic, the agent's *current* reflective judgment must be that the situation need *not* be avoided. The case as described displays incoherence by assuming that the agent would *reflectively* want to *avoid* it. I would therefore specify that the agent's judgment (that the object need not be avoided) is based on a mistaken assessment of evidence due either to assigning undue weight to certain facts, or to judging in the heat of the moment. Upon optimal reflection, he or she would want to avoid the situation.

22. One area of comparison between the version of compatibilism just dismissed and classical compatibilism lies in their assessments of the relevance of ignorance. On the 'C-informedness' criterion, ignorance per se is no obstacle to free action. But in classical compatibilism as well, there seems to no place for ignorance among sufficient conditions of unfreedom. This causes trouble for the idea that freedom entails responsibility, since (excusable!) ignorance is an excusing condition. However, it seems to me that ignorance does not generate unfreedom, and so I take the fact it does excuse as still another reason (alongside of, say, negligence) for questioning the link between freedom and responsibility. Cf. David Zimmerman, 363-65.

23. In writing this paper I have profited immensely from comments by Bernard Berofsky, John Martin Fischer, Robert Hambourger, Sidney Morgenbesser, Jerry Samet, and George Sher.

References

Alston, William. 1977. "Self-Intervention and the Structure of Motivation." In *The Self: Philosophical and Psychological Issues,* edited by T. Mischel, 65-102. Oxford.

Audi, Robert. 1974. "Moral Responsibility, Freedom, and Compulsion." *American Philosophical Quarterly* 11:1-14.

Ayer, A. J. 1954. "Freedom and Necessity." In *Philosophical Essays,* 271-84. London.

Bergmann, Frithof. 1977. *On Being Free.* Notre Dame.

Berofsky, Bernard. 1973. Review of Jonathan Glover's *Responsibility. Journal of Philosophy* 70:331-34.

Berofsky, Bernard. 1980. "The Irrelevance of Morality to Freedom." In *Action and Responsibility,* edited by M. Bradie and M. Brand, 38-47. Applied Philosophy Program, Bowling Green State University.

Berofsky, Bernard. 1983. "Autonomy." In *How Many Questions: Essays in Honor of Sidney Morgenbesser,* edited by L. Cauman, I. Levi, C. Parsons, and R. Schwartz, 301-20. Indianapolis.

Blumenfeld, David. 1972. "Free Action and Unconscious Motivation." *Monist* 56:426-43.

Bond, E. J. 1983. *Reason and Value.* Cambridge.

Brandt, Richard. 1979. *A Theory of the Good and the Right.* Oxford.

Cummins, Robert. 1979. "Could Have Done Otherwise." *The Personalist,* 60: 411-14.

Cummins, Robert. 1980. "Culpability and Mental Disorder." *Canadian Journal of Philosophy* 10:207-32.

Darwall, Stephen. 1983. *Impartial Reason.* Ithaca, N.Y.

Davidson, Donald. 1973. "Freedom to Act." In *Essays on Freedom of Action,* edited by T. Honderich, 139-56. London.

Davis, Lawrence. 1979. *Theory of Action*. Englewood Cliffs, N.J..

Dennett, Daniel. 1976. "Conditions of Personhood." In *The Identities of Persons,* edited by A. O. Rorty, 175-96. Berkeley.

Dworkin, Gerald. 1970. "Acting Freely." *Nous* 4: 367-83.

Dworkin, Gerald. 1976. "Autonomy and Behavior Control." *Hastings Center Report* 6:23-28.

Dworkin, Gerald. 1982. "Reply to MacIntyre's 'How Moral Agents Became Ghosts' ". *Synthese* 53: 313-18.

Feinberg, Joel. 1970. "What Is So Special about Mental Illness?" In *Doing and Deserving,* 272-92. Princeton, N.J.

Fingarette, Herbert. 1972. *The Meaning of Criminal Insanity*. Berkeley.

Fischer, John. 1982. "Responsibility and Control." *Journal of Philosophy* 79:24-40.

Frankfurt, Harry. 1969. "Alternate Possibilities and Moral Responsibility." *Journal of Philosophy* 66: 829-39.

Frankfurt, Harry. 1971. "Freedom of the Will and the Concept of a Person." *Journal of Philosophy* 68: 5-20.

Frankfurt, Harry. 1973. "Coercion and Moral Responsibility." In *Essays on Freedom of Action,* edited by T. Honderich, 65-86. London.

Frankfurt, Harry. 1975. "Three Concepts of Free Action II." *Proceedings of the Aristotelian Society,* suppl. vol. 49: 113-25.

Frankfurt, Harry. 1976. "Identification and Externality." In *The Identities of Persons,* edited by A. O. Rorty, 239-52. Berkeley.

Frankfurt, Harry. 1978. "The Problem of Action." *American Philosophical Quarterly* 15:157-64.

Frankfurt, Harry. 1982. "The Importance of What We Care About." *Synthese* 53:257-72.

Gert, Bernard, and Duggan, Timothy. 1979. "Free Will as the Ability to Will." *Nous* 13:197-217.

Glover, Jonathan. 1970. *Responsibility*. New York.

Grandy, Richard, and Darwall, Stephen. 1979. "On Schiffer's Desires." *Southern Journal of Philosophy* 17: 193-98.

Greenspan, Patricia. 1978. "Behavior Control and Freedom of Action." *Philosophical Review* 87:225-40.

Hill, Christopher S. 1984. "Watsonian Freedom and Freedom of the Will." *Australian Journal of Philosophy* 62: 294-98.

Jeffrey, Richard. 1974. "Preference among Preferences." *Journal of Philosophy* 71:377-91.

Körner, Stephen. 1973. "Rational Choice." *Proceedings of the Aristotelian Society* 47: 1-17.

Lehrer, Keith. 1980. "Preferences, Conditionals, and Freedom." In *Time and Cause,* edited by P. van Inwagen, 187-201. Dordrecht.

Levin, Michael. 1979. *Metaphysics and the Mind-Body Problem*. Oxford.

Locke, Don. 1974. "Reasons, Wants, and Causes." *American Philosophical Quarterly* 11: 169-79.

Locke, Don. 1975. "Three Concepts of Free Action I." *Proceedings of the Aristotelian Society,* suppl. vol. 49: 95-112.

MacIntyre, Alasdair. 1957. "Determinism." *Mind* 56: 28-41.

Macklin, Ruth. 1976. "A Psychoanalytic Model for Human Freedom and Rationality." *Psychoanalytic Quarterly* 45: 430-54.

Moore, G. E. 1965. *Ethics*. New York.

Neely, Wright. 1974. "Freedom and Desire." *Philosophical Review* 83: 32-54.

Nozick, Robert. 1981. *Philosophical Explanations*. Cambridge, Mass.

Penelhum, Terence. 1971. "The Importance of Self-Identity." *Journal of Philosophy* 68: 667-78.

Penelhum, Terence. 1979. "Human Nature and External Desires." *Monist* 62: 304-19.

Schick, Frederick. 1984. *Having Reasons*. Princeton, N.J.

Schiffer, Stephen. 1976. "A Paradox of Desire." *American Philosophical Quarterly* 13: 195-203.

Shope, Robert. 1978. "Rawls, Brandt, and the Definition of Rational Desires." *Canadian Journal of Philosophy* 8: 329-40.

Slote, Michael. 1980. "Understanding Free Will." *Journal of Philosophy* 67: 136-51.

Taylor, Charles. 1976. "Responsibility for Self." In *The Identities of Persons,* edited by A. O. Rorty, 281-99. Berkeley.

Thalberg, Irving. 1978. "Hierarchical Analyses of Unfree Action." *Canadian Journal of Philosophy* 8: 211-26.

Thalberg, Irving. 1983. "The Problem of 'Alien Desires'." In *Misconceptions of Mind and Freedom,* 93-125. Lanham, Md.

Ullmann-Margalit, Edna, and Morgenbesser, Sidney. 1977. "Picking and Choosing." *Social Research* 44: 757-85.

Van Inwagen, Peter. 1983. *An Essay on Free Will.* Oxford.

Watson, Gary. 1975. "Free Agency." *Journal of Philosophy* 72: 205-19.

Watson, Gary. 1977. "Skepticism about Weakness of Will." *Philosophical Review* 86: 316-39.

Williams, Bernard. 1979. "Internal and External Reasons." In *Rational Action,* edited by R. Harrison, 17-28. Cambridge.

Wolf, Susan. 1980. "Asymmetrical Freedom." *Journal of Philosophy* 77: 151-66.

Young, Robert. 1979. "Compatibilism and Conditioning." *Nous* 13: 361-78.

Young, Robert. 1980a. "Autonomy and the 'Inner Self.'" *American Philosophical Quarterly* 17: 35-43.

Young, Robert. 1980b. "Autonomy and Socialization." *Mind* 89: 565-76.

Zimmerman, David. 1981. "Hierarchical Motivation and Freedom of the Will." *Pacific Philosophical Quarterly* 62: 354-68.

Zimmerman, Michael. 1982. "Moral Responsibility, Freedom, and Alternate Possibilities." *Pacific Philosophical Quarterly* 63: 243-54.

Cartesian Interaction

MARK BEDAU

A priori considerations convinced Descartes that mind and body are fundamentally distinct substances: mind is essentially conscious, and body is essentially extended.[1] Everyday experience convinced him that mind and body causally interact. These convictions taken together I will call *Cartesian interaction*. Cartesian interaction has attracted widespread criticism. Much of this criticism has focused on the *causal connection* that it requires between mind and body. It is often thought that the fundamental difference between their natures rules out the possibility of any causal connection between them. How could something conscious possibly causally interact with something extended? In fact, it is sometimes thought that Descartes himself was moved by this objection. In this paper I will argue that Descartes had no sympathy for this objection but, rather, made a response to it that was fair, appropriate, and plausible; indeed, this response should carry weight with today's critics of Cartesian interaction. Throughout I will assume, for the sake of argument, that mind and body are essentially distinct Cartesian substances; for the position I want to defend is that there is no incoherence in the idea that essentially distinct Cartesian substances interact.

I

There are three sorts of reasons why Descartes might be thought to have admitted that it is inconceivable that distinct substances interact. In this section I will consider these three reasons and reject them.

Descartes's thesis that distinct substances interact has recently been claimed to conflict with Descartes's own position on causation.[2] This claim relies on an interesting and novel interpretation of Descartes's causal adequacy principle that a cause must already contain that which it brings about in its effect. The principle is interpreted so as to restrict what *kinds* or *categories* of substance can interact; in particular, it is interpreted so as to imply that a cause must be able to possess the same sort of modification as it brings about in its effect.[3] Since a thing's nature determines what sort of modifications it can possess, if this interpretation is accepted, then, in the words of one critic, "as Descartes himself sees the causal situation, one substance cannot produce a modification in another substance which is of an entirely different nature.[4] This conclusion does indeed conflict with Cartesian interaction between mind and body.[5]

The category interpretation is striking in part just because it is inconsistent with Cartesian interaction. Indeed, this feature initially makes one suspect that the category interpretation must be incorrect. Descartes is well known for having thought that mind and body, although essentially distinct, causally interact (in sensation, emotion, and willful action, for example). So, it is hard to believe that Descartes would have thought that causes and effects must be the same kind of substance in order to interact. It is no surprise, then, that Descartes's causal principle supports another interpretation, according to which it is taken as a remark about *degrees* or *amounts* of reality. Indeed, this could be called the traditional interpretation. It implies only that a cause must contain *at least as much reality* as it brings about in its effect. Descartes provides precious little information about how one is to think about degrees of reality,[6] but he does sketch this much of a picture: things are arrayed on an ordinal scale corresponding to their degree of reality: "reality admits of more and less."[7] Infinite and independent substance (God) tops this scale, with finite and dependent substance below; and below all this fall accidents or modes.[8] If there were such things as so-called real qualities or incomplete substances, these would fall on the scale between finite (complete) substances and their modes.[9] A thing's position on the scale corresponds to the rule that its position is lower than the position of anything else without which it cannot exist.[10] Now, how Cartesian interaction fares under the degree interpretation depends on the relative degree of reality of mind and body. Although Descartes's picture of degrees of reality is sketchy, it is definite on the point that mind and body both are finite and dependent substance. Thus, they have the same degree of reality.[11] Therefore, since the degree interpretation prohibits only those causes that would have less reality than their effects, it does not conflict with Cartesian interaction.

Which view of causation did Descartes hold, then?[12] There is not space for a full discussion of this issue, but, nevertheless, it is implausible on the face of it that Descartes accepted the category interpretation.[13] Descartes often used language that explicitly invokes the idea of degrees of reality;[14] the passages in which he appeals to his causal adequacy principle without explicitly mentioning degrees of reality occur in contexts in which he does make other explicit references to degrees of reality;[15] and he nowhere explicitly rules out the degree interpretation. Furthermore, Descartes often addresses this issue and states that the category difference between mind and body does not bar them from interacting. He said, for example, that, "there is no necessity for it [i.e., the mind] itself to be a body although it has the power of moving body,"[16] and that

> the perplexity involved in these questions [about how things with different natures can interact] arises entirely from a false supposition that can by no means be proved, viz., that if the soul and body are two substances of divers nature, that prevents them from being capable of acting on one another.[17]

So, on the face of it, it is implausible to use Descartes's causal adequacy principle to ground the claim that Descartes would have been sympathetic to criticism of Cartesian interaction.

Another influential reason for thinking that Descartes would have been sympathetic to criticism of Cartesian interaction is that, as critics have been quick to point out,[18] Descartes's own words can sound like the denial that distinct kinds of substance can interact. Descartes comes closest to saying this in a widely quoted passage from *The Principles of Philosophy,* where he says:

> We can very well conceive how the movement of one body can be caused by that of another, and diversified by the size, figure, and situation of its parts, but *we can in nowise understand how these same things (viz., size, figure and motion) can produce something entirely different in nature from themselves, . . .*[19]

(I shall henceforth refer to this as the *different-natures passage.*) This passage also occupies a central position in the support for the category interpretation of Descartes's causal adequacy principle. After all, isn't Descartes stating, in the most explicit language, that "causal interaction between very different kinds of things is inconceivable"?[20] Thus, we must examine this passage with special care.

When views about the inconceivability of interaction between different kinds of substance are attributed to Descartes, it is important to distinguish two very different theses.[21] Descartes should have been embarrassed if he ever said:

(T) It is inconceivable *that* distinct kinds of substance interact.

But there is no direct evidence that Descartes ever believed (T). He never states (T), nor does he state anything that obviously entails (T). It might seem that Descartes believed (T) because of his statements on a (different but) similar thesis:

(H) It is inconceivable *how* distinct kinds of substance interact.

Descartes did believe (H), and the different-natures passage is one of the places where he clearly expresses his belief in (H). But nothing, I shall argue, in the different-natures passage suggests that he believed in (T).

To begin with, notice that Descartes's own words in the different-natures passage are closer to (H) than (T). He says that we can conceive *how (quo pacto)* movement in a body causes movement in another body but we cannot conceive *how (quo pacto)* it can cause something of an entirely different nature from movement in a body. All Descartes is saying is that, although we can grasp the means by which bodies interact (to wit, push-pull mechanical action), the means by which totally different substances interact—not questioning whether they do interact—simply escapes us.

Secondly, the immediate context of this passage illustrates Descartes's deep conviction that different kinds of substance do interact. In the sentence that follows the quoted passage, Descartes says: "We know *that* the mind is of such a nature that the diverse motions of body suffice to produce in it all the diverse sensations that it has. . . ."[22] The principle in which the different-natures passage occurs opens by stating that local motions of nerves "excite in us" feelings and sensations, and the immediately preceding principle states that "our mind is of such a nature that the motions which are in body are alone sufficient to cause it to have all sorts of thoughts. . . ."[23] It requires us to attribute a flagrant inconsistency to Descartes to read him as asserting in the same breath that interaction between different kinds of substance is impossible.

Finally, (H) is precisely what Descartes needs in the argument in which the passage occurs. Principle 198 is part of an extended discussion about sensation. The different-natures passage functions in the principle as one premise in an argument for the conclusion that we know of the objective flavors, colors, and so forth, of bodies only as secondary qualities; we have no reason to think that the phenomenal flavors and colors that we sense are actually in external bodies. The role of the passage in this argument is to undercut the scholastic picture of sensation according to which our senses reveal to us the substantial forms and real qualities in objects, and one consideration against the scholastic picture is that we cannot understand *how* it would happen. Descartes does not go on to conclude that it is inconceivable *that* substantial forms and real qualities cause motions in bodies. He concludes only that our senses provide no evidence that substantial forms or real qualities exist in the external world. The argument presented in Principle 198 is as follows: All our sensations are caused by motions in our sensory apparatus. But what features of external objects cause these motions? They might be caused by other local motions in external bodies. This suggestion is perfectly intelligible, for "we can very well conceive how" various motions in one body could cause various motions in another. So we know that local motions in external bodies are the kind of thing that could produce our sensations. Furthermore, in some cases, such as when we rub our eyes, we know for a fact that the cause is nothing but certain local motions in external objects. On the other hand, the scholastic suggestion that substantial forms and real qualities set our senses in motion is mysterious at best. So, what is certain is that we can conclude nothing about the properties of the external objects—whether they be local motions or something else—that cause us to experience colors, smells, tastes, *except* that they have the power to set our sensory apparatus in motion in such a way that we end up having sensations.

So, in the different-natures passage Descartes does claim (H) that it is inconceivable *how* certain things with distinct natures interact. But this is far from admitting (T) that it is inconceivable *that* things with distinct natures interact. Therefore, Descartes's point in the different-natures passage does not support the category interpretation.

There is one more possible reason for thinking that Descartes might have been sympathetic to the idea that there is a problem with Cartesian interaction. That mind and body are essentially distinct is the truth, thought Descartes, but not the whole truth; in addition, he thought, mind and body are *united* in a special way.[24] He went on to concoct some rather mysterious and puzzling views about the union between mind and body, and some think that he was driven to these puzzling views in an attempt to solve a problem that he otherwise had to face about how essentially distinct mind and body interact.[25] If true, this too might indirectly support the category interpretation, for Descartes's adherence to it would be a plausible explanation of why he would be troubled by essentially distinct substances interacting.

Mind-body union presents a fascinating and intricate puzzle, which I shall not attempt fully to unravel. Although mind-body union is closely connected with Cartesian interaction,[26] it would not serve as a solution to a problem about how essentially distinct substances could interact. First of all, it is unsuited to solve problems arising from the essential distinctness of mind and body, as Descartes would have been aware. The existence of mind-body union does not alter the fact that mind alone and body alone are essentially distinct substances. Even when insisting that mind and body are united, Descartes never denies that mind and body are separable, essentially different substances.[27] Even if mind-body union is itself a substance (as Descartes sometimes seems to suggest),[28] this would not collapse Descartes's ontology from two things (mind and body) to one (mind-body union); rather, it would expand it to three things: mind, body, and mind-body union. Mind-body union is somehow involved in causal connections between mind and body, but the mind and the body that interact are still essentially distinct. So the doctrine of mind-body union makes it no less true that essentially distinct mind and body interact along classic Cartesian lines.[29] Furthermore, Descartes never suggests that God-mind union and God-body union would be required to give God the means to create mind and body;[30] and he mentions that angels could be causally connected by remote control with robot like bodies and yet not be *united* with these bodies.[31] Although the doctrine of mind-body union seems to be a response to *some* issue involving Cartesian interaction,[32] that issue is not likely to be the impossibility of essentially distinct substances interacting.

II

Even if Descartes himself did not worry about Cartesian interaction, many believe that he was not entitled to be so untroubled about the utter inconceivability of *how* mind interacts with body. So far the search for the means by which mind and body interact has produced singularly meager results, but the worry about the coherence of Cartesian interaction stems from something deeper than this. What is so troubling is that we do not know where to begin to look for the means of their interaction, and we have no reason to be confident that this situation will ever improve. We seem unable to find even the first indication of how something essentially *conscious* could be causally connected with something essentially *extended*. This makes it seem unreasonable to hope of *ever* being able to conceive *how* Cartesian mind and body interact. And, if we have no hope of ever conceiving *how* they interact, shouldn't we deny that they do interact?[33] In other words, since (H) it is inconceivable *how* conscious mind and extended body interact, it follows that (T) it is inconceivable *that* they interact. The heart of the worry, then, is that Descartes was wrong to deny that (H) entails (T).

Descartes was well aware of this objection, and he typically responded to it in a certain way.[34] In this section I shall argue that he successfully put his finger on the weakness in this objection, even if his philosophical methodology led him to restrict his response unnecessarily. Then I shall explore how the spirit of Descartes's response might be pursued today.

The strongest way to reply to the objection would be to produce an uncontroversial actual case of some Cartesian substance *A* causing a modification in a substance *B*, even though how *A* does this to *B* is no more conceivable than how minds interact with bodies. There is a case of this form that most of Descartes's contemporaries should have accepted. Many of Descartes's contemporaries did not doubt *that* God created mind and body; but it would have verged on heresy for them to think that they could know *how* God, in his infinite wisdom and power, brought this about.[35] Since people disagree about what actually causes what, it might be difficult to find a case of the appropriate sort that *everyone* agrees is an actual case of interaction.[36]

How else, then, can Descartes defend Cartesian interaction? The objection relies on the following inference pattern: if it is inconceivable how *A* causes modifications in *B*, then *A* does not cause modifications in *B*, or, at least, it is unreasonable to think that it does. To undermine this sort of inference, it would suffice to describe a *hypothetical* case in which *A* causes a modification in *B* despite the fact that how this happens is no more conceivable than Cartesian interaction.[37]

But a critic of Cartesian interaction might stubbornly refuse to accept even these hypothetical cases. "Even these cases," the objector might complain, "beg my question. If I accept your hypothesis that it is inconceivable how *A* causes modifications in *B*, then I cannot grant the rest of your hypothesis that *A* causes modifications in *B*. Your hypothetical cases are exactly the sort of situation that I deny is possible."

One could still argue against someone who stubbornly objects in this way by adopting a *dialectical* strategy. One would start by asking what sorts of things the *objector* thinks are causally connected; then, with any luck, one can show that the objector is also committed to things being causally connected in a way that turns out to be no more comprehensible than the way in which mind and body are connected. That is, the Cartesian's belief in mind-body interaction could be shown to be no less comprehensible than the anti-Cartesian's belief in some other sort of causal connection. This is exactly the sort of reply that Descartes made to his critics, at least to those who subscribed to the scholastic doctrine of real accidents or qualities.

Descartes's responses take the following form: First he points out that his critics believe, for example, *that* accidents can cause changes in body;[38] then he claims that none of them can any better conceive *how* accidents accomplish this than they (or the Cartesian, at least) can conceive how mind and body interact; finally, he concludes, by parity of reasoning, that any difficulty there might be in conceiving how mind and body interact is no bar to their interaction. Descartes made this sort of argument a number of times, two typical instances of which are the following.[39] In a letter to Hyperaspistes, after saying that mind acts on body, Descartes continues with this remark:

> This is no harder for us to understand than it is for those who believe in accidents to understand how they act on corporeal substances while belonging to a wholly different category.[40]

In a letter to Arnauld written seven years later, Descartes again asserts that the incorporeal mind can "set the body in motion." He considers this "one of those self-evident things which we only make obscure when we try to explain them in terms of others." Nevertheless he offers a "simile" to provide some help in conveying what happens when mind and body interact:

> Most philosophers, who think that the heaviness of a stone is a real quality distinct from the stone, think they understand clearly enough

how [*quo pacto*] this quality can impel the stone towards the center of the earth . . . . [I]t is no harder for us to understand how [*quomodo*] the mind moves the body, than it is for them to understand how [*quomodo*] such heaviness moves a stone downwards.[41]

Notice that in these passages Descartes stops short of claiming that it *is* inconceivable how accidents act on bodies, just as he does not concede that mind-body interaction is inconceivable. Compare Locke's opinion about a similar matter. Locke wrote to the Bishop of Worcester that he could not conceive any way that bodies act on one another except through contact.

But I am since convinced by the judicious Mr. Newton's incomparable book, that it is too bold a presumption to limit God's power, in this point by my narrow conceptions. The gravitation of matter towards matter by ways inconceivable to me, is not only a demonstration that God can, if he pleases, put into bodies, powers and ways of operation, above what can be derived from our idea of body, or can be explained by what we know of matter, but also an unquestionable and everywhere visible instance, that he has done so.[42]

Locke here admits that something inconceivable is nevertheless true. Descartes's method of doubt, his unwillingness to accept anything that he could not clearly and distinctly perceive, discourages him from adopting a like attitude. What he will admit is that it is no harder for him to understand how the mind moves the body than it is for his critics to understand how accidents act on bodies. He equivocates, though, about whether in fact one can conceive how minds move bodies.[43]

It might help to highlight the nature of the dialectical response if we consider Descartes's criticism of the traditional scholastic explanation of natural phenomena. The scholastics explained natural phenomena like falling objects by appealing to real accidents like heaviness. One might suspect that Descartes's criticism of the scholastics is inconsistent with the defense of Cartesian interaction that I have attributed to him. After all, didn't Descartes criticize the scholastic doctrine on the ground that it was inconceivable how real accidents could cause the natural phenomena attributed to them? But to make this objection is to misunderstand the *dialectical* aspect of Descartes's defense. The defense is dialectical because it is not necessary for Descartes himself to accept the conceivability of accidents causing natural phenomena; it is sufficient if his interlocutors accept this. For if his interlocutors accept this, then Descartes can go on to point out that their acceptance of this is inconsistent with their objection to his acceptance of Cartesian interaction.

If Descartes had been less wedded to his method of doubt, he might have employed the dialectical strategy slightly differently. He might have admitted that we can conceive neither how mind and body interact nor how accidents act on bodies. Unless one is adhering to the strict method of suspending judgment about everything that one cannot clearly and distinctly perceive, the inconceivability of mind-body interaction is no reason to doubt that mind and body interact, just as Descartes's scholastic critics would not give up their belief that accidents act on bodies merely because they could not conceive how it happens. To use Locke's words, isn't it too bold a presumption to limit God's (or nature's) power by our narrow conceptions? Pressing the objection against Cartesian interaction smacks of epistemological hubris. What's so special about our minds that we must be able to grasp the means of every causal connection?[44]

Descartes's strategy for defending Cartesian interaction might seem outdated. What a contemporary Cartesian needs is an example of a causal connection that is no better understood than is mind-body interaction. Consider the following example: We all know *that* magnets can pick up tacks, but what do we know about *how* they pick up tacks? The average person knows something like this: magnets have the ability to attract iron objects like tacks, and when a magnet is close enough so that its attraction on the tack overcomes the force of gravity, then the magnet pulls the tack up to it and holds it there. Those of us who would give this sort of explanation assume that magnets have the ability to attract iron without having any idea *how* they have this ability. All we can say is that "they just *do;* that's the kind of thing that a magnet is." What is relevant here is that, even though the average person has no particular idea how magnets pull on tacks, still that person does not in the least doubt that this is what they do. Why should Descartes's scientifically sophisticated critics doubt, then, that conscious mind and extended body interact? True, they cannot conceive how mind and body interact, but they cannot conceive any better how magnets pull on tacks; and that does not stop them from being convinced that magnets work.

The case of the magnet and the tack is not odd or exceptional. Essentially the same points could be made if the magnet and tack example were replaced with a gravitation example or an example involving repulsion between like-charged bodies. The common feature of these cases is that one body acts on another body even though they have no physical contact; they all involve action at a distance. We seem to have no difficulty conceiving how one body can affect another when they have contact,[45] whereas it is a mystery how bodies act at a distance. Nevertheless, they seem to do just that. We seem to have no reason to doubt that action at a distance occurs (in magnetic and gravitational phenomena, for example) even though we understand how it happens no better than we understand how minds act on bodies.

It might be thought that I am not giving Descartes's contemporary critics enough credit for being scientifically sophisticated. Even if the average person does not know how magnets move tacks, there are experts (e.g., physicists) who do, whose job it is (among other things) to figure out just this sort of thing. We need not worry about not understanding how magnets work because we know that there are experts who know how magnets work.[46] But there are no experts who could tell us how mind interacts with body. So, the problem of how mind and body interact remains.

There are two responses I want to make to this objection. First, the availability of experts on magnets is a historical contingency the benefits of which we today happen to be lucky enough to enjoy. However, through most of history there were no experts on magnets and no adequate theory of magnetism. Nevertheless, there was never any doubt that magnetic phenomena existed, mysterious though they were. In a similar fashion, at present we have no adequate theory of mind-body interaction, yet we do commonly speak and think in terms of just such interaction. Unless we are given good reason to believe that the lack of experts on Cartesian interaction is not merely another historical contingency, then our present lack of such experts is no reason to question Cartesian interaction.

Second, and more important, it is not clear that in the final analysis the existence of experts on magnetism creates a relevant disanalogy with Cartesian interaction. All causal explanations, even those given by experts, must eventually stop at a fundamental claim or law that itself is not explained. In electromagnetic dynamics, the explanation might stop at the fundamental claim that electromagnetic fields just *can*, by their nature, exert a force on ferrous matter. Or the explanation might stop with the claims that oppositely charged particles just *do* attract one another and that electrons and nuclei just *are* held together by the "weak" force. What brings the explanation to a stop might be simply the limitations of our understanding. Or, it might be that there is nothing more, nothing "deeper" about the phenomenon in question for us to understand. It might be, for example, that oppositely charged particles attract one another not in virtue of some further fact about them but simply because of their nature—that is just the kind of thing that they are. No expert can explain everything about a given phenomenon; something is always left over without its own further explanation. So the lack of experts on mind-body interaction is not evidence that mind-body interaction is any less possible or plausible than a magnet's ability to attract tacks or than the ability of oppositely charged particles to attract each other.[47]

Someone might think that my scientific examples of action at a distance fail to mirror a relevant feature of Cartesian interaction, a feature that Descartes's scholastic examples succeed in mirroring. The worry about how mind and body interact is thought somehow to stem from the vast difference in the essences of mind and body. Magnets and tacks, gravitating masses, charged particles, on the other hand, all these have the *same* essence: they are all physical, extended bodies. Now, it is true that the examples involving action at a distance are disanalogous in the alleged respect. However, this disanalogy is irrelevant. The vast difference in the essences of mind and body is not *in and of itself* a reason to question whether they do interact. Rather, this vast difference is taken as support for the claim that (H) mind-body interaction is inconceivable, and it's (H) that makes Descartes's critics worry whether mind and body *do* interact. Therefore, to undercut this worry, or at least to redirect it, it would suffice to show that the inability to conceive how something happens is not in and of itself good reason to doubt that it happens. So, the examples of action at a distance between two bodies are appropriate to allay the worry about Cartesian interaction.

Nevertheless, there are other scientific examples of causal connections between things that have quite different natures. Some of these examples naturally come up for consideration in response to a certain reservation about the examples of action at a distance. It might be thought that there are no genuine cases of action at a distance, on the grounds that each case of apparent action at a distance involves a force-field as an intermediary, and no distance separates the force-field and the bodies on which it acts. Notice that, if we have this reservation, then we have tacitly accepted a case of a causal connection between things with quite different natures: the magnetic field and the tack, or the gravitational field and the apple. Surely the magnetic field has a quite different nature from the tack, as does the gravitational field from the apple. Yet the field acts on the body. The question that we need to consider is whether we can conceive *how* these force-fields act on bodies; in particular, is there some sense in which we can conceive this any better than we can conceive how minds act on bodies? The answer, surely, is no. We have no idea how gravity, for example, pulls, how it gets its grip on the apple. All we can say is that it just *does;* that's the kind of thing that gravity is. So Descartes's strategy for defending Cartesian interaction can be deployed with up-to-date examples in which cause and effect are fundamentally distinct kinds of things.[48]

This last example might seem to involve a cheat. Although force-fields indeed are different from bodies, they seem to be significantly *more* like bodies than minds are. In particular, they seem to be *physical* in some sense in which minds are not. If true, this might weaken Descartes's defense of Cartesian interaction. It might be thought that this shared physicality of mass and force-field gives us *some* understanding of how they interact, a kind of understanding that we lack for how mind and body interact. This would block Descartes's dialectical defense, for it would no longer be true that Cartesian interaction is as well understood (in all relevant respects) as gravitation or magnetism.

Descartes himself considered a version of this objection, in which real qualities were claimed to be physical in some crucial sense, and he worked out the beginnings of an adequate response to it. No doubt there is something right about the claim that gravitational fields, for example, are physical. But exactly what does their physicality amount to? First, are they physical in the same sense in which ordinary physical objects—sticks and stones, tables and chairs, atoms and galaxies—are? It's not completely clear what the physicality of ordinary physical objects amounts to, but it seems to involve something like being solid, occupying a spatial location from which other physical objects are excluded, and perhaps having a mass. Descartes characterized ordinary physical objects in a variety of ways (in addition to his famous identification of them with things that are extended). He said that ordinary physical objects consist of "whatever is made up of the substance called body"[49] or "what has the nature of body."[50] The extension of the really physical is "determined to a definite place, from which it excludes all other bodily extension;"[51] "impenetrability can be shown to belong to the essence of extension and not to that of anything else."[52]

It should be clear that gravitation and other fields (and real qualities) are not examples of physical objects in this primary (Cartesian) sense. They do not occupy space from which other physical objects are excluded; they have no mass; they are not "made up of the substance called body."[53] Nevertheless, they might be said to be physical in a secondary sense, in virtue of being able directly to affect (or be affected by) things that are physical in the primary sense. Descartes gave a variety of characterizations of what it is to be physical secondarily, among which are these:[54] the secondarily physical is "whatever belongs to a body, even though not of the same nature as body;"[55] it is "anything that can in any way affect a body."[56] Descartes said that he conceived of the secondarily physical "as powers or forces, which although they can act upon extended substances, are not themselves extended."[57] There is a correlative derivative sense in which things that are physical secondarily might be said to be located; for example, we think of magnetic fields as being located in the area around the magnet. Of course, this way of being "located" is quite different from the way in which primarily physical objects are located. First of all, other physical objects can occupy exactly the same location that a field does. Second, it would seem that a field's location is "extrinsic" in that it depends on the "intrinsic" location of primarily physical bodies. That is, the cash value of a field's being located somewhere is that it has the potential of directly affecting ordinary physical objects that are located at that same place. Things that are secondarily physical might analogously be said to have a quantity, in those cases in which their ability to affect ordinary physical objects can be assessed in quantitative terms.

Therefore, there is a sense in which force-fields are physical. But this does not make it unfair or misleading to try to defend Cartesian interaction by pointing to its analogy with the action of force-fields on bodies. For minds, although not primarily physical, of course, are physical secondarily; that is, they have the ability directly to affect things that are primarily physical. As Descartes said, "That the mind, which is incorporeal, can set the body in motion—this is something which is shown to us—by the surest and plainest everyday experience."[58]

The upshot of this is that there is no relevant disanalogy established yet between mind and force-fields like gravity. Neither mind nor gravity is primarily physical, and both are secondarily physical. The "physicality" that gravity shares with bodies is also shared by minds, so the "physicality" of gravity does not make gravity-body causation any less problematic than mind-body interaction.[59] Therefore, defending Cartesian interaction by appealing to the analogy with gravity-body causation has not been shown to involve a cheat.

Descartes investigated non primary senses of "physical" no further. But there is at least one more sense in which things might be said to be physical, a sense in which, at least for Descartes himself, the mind is *not* physical whereas force-fields are. It was Descartes's conviction that minds could exist apart from bodies.[60] A mind was not by its nature required to be connected with bodies. Force-fields, on the other hand, by their nature cannot exist apart from bodies. In this sense, force-fields are necessarily part of the physical order. This leaves room for a criticism of Cartesian interaction still to be mounted. In the remainder of this paper, I briefly consider such a criticism.

III

Cartesian interaction is the conjunction of two claims about mind and body: that they interact and that each has its well-known Cartesian essence. I have not attempted to prove that Cartesian interaction is true, but I have tried to defend it, in two respects. First, the mere fact that mind is essentially conscious and nonextended, and body extended and nonconscious, is not sufficient grounds for concluding that they do not interact. Second, our inability to conceive *how* they interact is not sufficient grounds for concluding that they do not interact. So, the familiar objection to Cartesian interaction that conscious mind and extended body could never interact is simply not well founded.

In conclusion, I want to sketch another problem with Cartesian interaction, to which Descartes also had a response, though one that is less satisfactory. This last problem is not unrelated to the common objection to Cartesian interaction that I have been considering up to now; in fact, it might be that an unarticulated awareness of this problem has helped make the common objection so popular. Up to now I have been arguing (what Descartes argues) that nothing *prevents* something conscious and nonextended from interacting with something nonconscious and extended. The point I want to make now is that nothing in what Descartes has told us about mind and body can *explain* their ability to interact. Although Cartesian interaction is *conceivable*, it still is not *explainable*. It might help to bring out my point if we consider an analogy. What minimally is required to explain the ability of opium to put people to sleep? Consider two different hypothetical situations.

In the first, all we know about opium is that it has a certain characteristic color, odor, and taste; that it is produced from certain poppies, and so on. In the second, we know one additional property of opium—it has a *virtus dormitiva*. Now, on analogy with the case of Cartesian interaction, in both of these two situations it is *conceivable* that opium has the ability to put people to sleep. In the first situation, though, there is nothing in what we know about opium that would enable us to explain this ability, whereas in the second situation we do know something that would explain this ability— its *virtus dormitiva*. Admittedly, this explanation is not very illuminating; in fact, it has long been used as a parody of an explanation. Nevertheless, there is a difference between having an unilluminating explanation and having no explanation at all. The crucial feature of the second situation that renders it explanatory is that we can point to something in the nature of opium as the source of its ability to put people to sleep.

Now, if mind and body can interact, this too must hold in virtue of something about them that enables them to interact. It is not that there must be some underlying, "deeper" fact about minds and bodies that explains their ability to interact. They might interact simply in virtue of being the kinds of things that they are. The point is this: if minds and bodies can interact simply because of being the kinds of things that they are, then they must not be merely what Decartes thought they were. Their respective consciousness and extendedness is insufficient to account for their ability to interact.

It is often thought that Cartesian interaction is flawed because it claims too much: its two theses taken separately are consistent, but they become inconsistent or incoherent or inconceivable when taken together. The truth, I think, is that Cartesian interaction does not claim enough: its two theses taken together are consistent but incomplete. A thing's nature is supposed to explain its basic capacities. So if mind and body have the capacity to interact, as they do according to Cartesian interaction, then their natures must include more than what Cartesian interaction allows.

It might be thought that Descartes would not have found this explanatory gap troubling. He seems to have thought that *something* enables mind and body to interact, but not something about *them*. Their capacity to interact does not come from their own "internal" natures but from their relation to a third thing. God created mind and body and *He* is what enables them to interact even though they are essentially distinct, even though they can (indeed, according to Descartes and his contemporaries, usually do) exist apart from each other. So, far from being a "basic capacity," it is an *accident* that mind and body interact.[61] So, it should be no surprise, Descartes might have thought, that the natures of mind and body contain nothing that explains their capacity to interact.

This dismissal of the explanatory gap will not appeal to Cartesians who are unhappy viewing mind-body interaction as an accident. Furthermore, even if one *does* believe that it is only an act of God that enables mind and body to interact, one is still required to say what it is that God has done to them in virtue of which they are able to interact. It is clear that Descartes takes this requirement seriously. His lifelong correspondence with Princess Elizabeth began when she asked "how man's soul, being only a thinking substance, can determine animal spirits so as to cause voluntary actions?" He acknowledged in his reply that she had put her finger on an important and relevant issue.

> I may truly say that the question you ask is the one which may most properly be put to me in view of my published writings. *There are two facts about the human soul on which depend all the things that we can know of its nature. The first is that it thinks, the second is that it is united to the body and can act and be acted on along with it.* About the second I have said hardly anything; I have tried only to make the first well understood. For my principal aim was to prove the distinction between soul and body, and to this end only the first was useful, and the second might have been harmful.[62]

Descartes seems to be acknowledging here that there is more to the fundamental nature of a person's mind than that it thinks or is conscious. By nature, every person's mind is also united to a body with which it interacts, and the mind's consciousness cannot explain this union.[63] It is not difficult to reconcile these remarks with Descartes's view that it is an accident that mind and body interact. Although the mind and body that God made are not required to be united, nevertheless, when a mind and body are the mind and body of a person, God sees to it that they are of a nature so as to be united. One might put this by saying that it is the nature of a person's mind and body to be united (at least, as long as the person lives). With the notion of mind-body union in hand, Descartes thinks he has an explanation of the capacity of a person's mind and body to interact.[64] Unfortunately, his deployment of this idea is not well worked out and suffers from some fundamental difficulties.[65] For example, it is unclear whether union is an attribute that a person's distinct mind and body share or whether the union of a person's mind and body is some distinct third sort of substance.[66] Descartes's struggles on this topic lead him into notorious difficulties.[67] But perhaps most troubling of all is the difficulty of seeing how the introduction of mind-body union will *illuminate* the capacity of mind and body to interact. The appeal to something like mind-body union is exactly the right type of move to make to plug the explanatory gap in Cartesian interaction, but it is not an illuminating instance of that type. It seems to provide no better an explanation of Cartesian interaction than the *virtus dormitiva* does of opium's ability to put people to sleep.[68] This is not to say that it is impossible for Cartesians to provide a *good* explanation of mind-body interaction, any more than it is impossible for those who believe in hidden powers to provide a good explanation of opium's power to put people to sleep. But Cartesians must deepen their understanding of the nature of mind and body before they will have more than a superficial understanding of how mind and body interact.

Notes

1. I am pleased to acknowledge my indebtedness to all those who helped me at various stages of this work, including especially George Bealer, Hugo Bedau, Janet Broughton, Alan Code, Tim Monroe, George Myro, and Allan Silverman.

2. This claim was made at least a decade ago, when Daisie Radner argued that interaction between Cartesian mind and body conflicts with Descartes's causal views. Broughton raises substantially the same criticism (forthcoming, 4-8); and Wilson, who cites Broughton in a note, alludes to this criticism (1978, 215).

3. Radner uses this sort of language. Broughton expresses the same point with somewhat different language, claiming that Descartes's causal principle means (among other things) that "a cause must be characterized by the same property that comes to characterize its effect" (forthcoming, 2).

4. Radner 1971, 161.

5. Descartes said that "after the idea we have of God, which is very different from all those we have of created things, I do not know of any other pair of ideas in nature which are as different as these two [body and mind]" (K 109: AT iii 419). See also HR ii 212: AT vii 358.

6. Curley attempts to piece together Descartes's views about degrees of reality (1978, 129-32).

7. HR ii 71: AT vii 185. Ideas are arrayed on a parallel scale according to their degree of representative reality (HR i 162: AT vii 41).

8. HR ii 56: AT vii 165-66; HR ii 71: AT vii 41.

9. HR ii 71: AT vii 185.

10. K 115-16: AT iii 429. Kenny points out (1961, 134) that the reason modes cannot exist without substances differs from the reason finite substances cannot exist without infinite substances.

11. Descartes sometimes suggests that body (*res extensa*) is not finite but indefinite and unlimited. (See, e.g., Wilson's discussion of this point [1978, 167].) However, when a mind interacts with a body, it interacts only with a small part of the sum total of all body, and this part will be finite; so when a mind and a body interact, they each have the same degree of reality. (Actually, things might not be quite this simple, for if a finite part of an infinite substance is not itself a substance but a mode, then a human body has less reality than the human mind associated with it. But Descartes may have ways around this problem.)

12. The only explicit supporters of the category interpretation that I know of are Radner and Broughton. The majority of the secondary literature does not explicitly compare the degree and category interpretations but advocates the degree interpretation without seriously considering any alternative. See Keeling 1968, 117-18; Kenny 1961, 133; *The Essential Descartes,* xx-xxi; Wilson 1978, 105, 122, and 137ff.; Curley 1978, 129ff.; and Williams 1978, 135ff. Loeb (1981, 140-143) does specifically discuss the competing interpretations of Descartes's causal principle, and he concludes that the causal principle does not conflict with Cartesian interaction. His arguments overlap a bit with those that I give.

13. Broughton (forthcoming) vigorously argues that Descartes accepted the category interpretation as a fundamental principle of natural change; but I would dispute most of her arguments, some of which I reject below. The most likely places in which Descartes might have been influenced by something like the category interpretation are in some remarks about innate ideas

and perhaps in his formulation of the argument for the existence of the external world in the *Meditations*. But, as far as I can tell, in these passages he gives no evidence of acknowledging that there is a problem in thinking that different kinds of substances interact.

14. See, for example, HR i 162-63: AT vii 40-41; HR ii 33-34: AT vii 133-34; HR ii 56: AT vii 165.

15. The contexts in which he appeals to the causal adequacy principle without explicitly invoking degrees of reality are the three passages referred to in the previous footnote.

16. K 239: AT v 270.

17. HR ii 132: AT ix-1 213. See also K 112: AT iii 424-25; K 235f: AT v 221-23; K 210: AT iv 603f: K 239: AT v 270; K 249: AT v 342; K 257: AT v 403f; K 139: AT iii 667; and *Descartes' Conversation with Burman,* 16-17.

18. For example, Kenny (1961), Radner (1971), and Broughton (forthcoming).

19. HR i 295: AT viii-1 322; emphasis added.

20. Broughton (forthcoming), 5.

21. Kenny clearly distinguishes these claims on p. 222.

22. HR i 295, my emphasis: AT viii-1 321. This indirect speech uses the Latin accusative + infinitive construction, which is seldom, if ever, used to express indirect "how" questions.

23. HR i 294: AT viii-1 320.

24. Passages in which Descartes discusses mind-body union are too numerous to review here. One especially well-known passage is in the sixth Meditation where Descartes says, "I am not only lodged in my body as a pilot in a vessel, but . . . I am very closely united to it, and so to speak so intermingled with it that I seem to compose with it one whole" (HR i 192: AT vii 81).

25. For example, Radner (1971), Mattern (1978), Broughton and Mattern (1978), and Broughton (forthcoming). Louis Loeb disagrees (1981, 139-140).

26. One of Descartes's most detailed comments about mind-body union is a direct reply to Princess Elizabeth's question "how man's soul, being only a thinking substance, can determine animal spirits so as to cause voluntary actions" (*The Essential Descartes,* 373). In the famous "pilot in a vessel" passage (HR i 192: AT vii 81), mind-body union is introduced to explain certain features of the interaction between mind and body. He also suggests that our knowledge of mind-body interaction depends on the sensations that are made possible by mind being united with body (K 256: AT v 402; see also K 128: AT iii 493).

27. See, for example, HR i 244: AT viii-1 29; and HR ii 102-3: AT vii 228. Mattern discusses this point.

28. For example, see K 142: AT iii 693.

29. In fact, it might be best to think of mind-body union in terms of the existence of some special kind of causal relation between mind and body (e.g., a causal relation that *differs from* the causal relation that connects a pilot and his ship). Beck (1965, 266-68) and Loeb (1981, 130-31) develop this position.

30. His silence on this score might result from the distinctive manner in which God is a cause. (See HR i 229: AT viii-1 14 and HR ii 34: AT vii 137). Note, however, that in one passage Descartes explicitly avoids the suggestion that God is a world-union united to matter (K 257: AT v 404).

31. K 127-128: AT iii 493. Descartes at K 256: AT v 402 shows that he is a bit unsure about what relation angels could have with bodies.

32. Descartes acknowledges that the doctrine of mind-body union is a response to some hitherto *unanswered question* about mind-body interaction. (See HR ii 132: AT ix-1 213 and K 137: AT iii 664-65.) At the end of this paper, I explain what I take that question to be. Note that Descartes does *not* acknowledge that mind-body union is a response to a problem, a difficulty or an objection to Cartesian interaction.

33. A host of objections have been inspired by this worry. Princess Elizabeth expressed her uneasiness on this point to Descartes (*The Essential Descartes,* 373-74: AT iii 661; *The Essential*

Descartes, 376-77: AT iii 684), and Burman also questioned Descartes on this point (*Descartes' Conversation with Burman,* 28). It bothered Gassendi, who wondered, "How can the corporeal have anything in common with the incorporeal?" (HR ii 202: AT ix 213). The attempt to allay this worry helped generate a diverse family of post-Cartesian philosophies, ranging from the occasionalism of De La Forge, Cordemoy, and Malebranche to the preestablished harmony of Geulinex and Leibniz and the monism of Spinoza (Keeling 1968, 219-20; Beck 1965, 269; Williams 1978, 287f.; Radner 1971, 170; Doney 1967, 41f.; *The Essential Descartes,* xxxi; and Broughton [forthcoming], 3). The popularity of this sort of objection has shown no sign of abating. Contemporary philosophy of mind began when Ryle diagnosed the inconceivability of mind-body interaction as the result of a "category mistake" (Ryle 1949, 16) bred of the philosopher's "paramechanical myth" (19). Anthony Kenny, a generation later, said that "the properties of the two kinds of substances [mind and body] seem to place them in such diverse categories that it is impossible for them to interact" (1961, 223). Margaret Wilson has expressed this worry especially clearly (*The Essential Descartes,* xxix-xxx). Bernard Williams has voiced this worry in the last half decade, (1978, 287-88), and John Searle took this worry quite seriously and devoted a chapter of his recent book to address it (1983, 264ff; Searle addresses this worry as it applies to his own non-Cartesian picture of mind-body interaction).

34. Beck (1965, 269-76) and Loeb (1981, 136-40) also attempt to explain how Descartes responded to this objection. They both (correctly) emphasize his tendency to dismiss the objection; but they omit any mention of (what below I call) his 1982; dialectical strategy for responding to the objection. R. C. Richardson (1982, a paper that came to my attention after I had finished my work) interprets Descartes's response in a way that is similar to mine (although we differ on various details), but he too does not bring out the dialectical nature of Descartes's response.

35. Descartes seems to be making something like this argument in a letter to More (K 252: AT v 347). For more on our ignorance of God's attributes, see HR i 229: AT viii-1 14 and HR ii 34: AT vii 137.

36. Later in this section, I speculate about contemporary examples of actual but perhaps inconceivable causal connections.

37. To most of us today, one such hypothetical case would have A be God and the world be B; most of us are willing to grant at least that *if* God created the world, then He did it in a manner opaque to us.

38. Perhaps Descartes's response misrepresents the scholastic doctrine of accidents as mistakenly treating accidents as *substances* and as mistakenly treating accidents as *efficient causes* of changes in bodies. But Descartes could find another example and keep his argumentative strategy the same.

39. See also K 139: AT iii 667. I do not mean to suggest that Descartes's responses to this objection always took exactly this form. Descartes deploys a slightly different sort of strategy when replying to the atomist Gassendi (HR ii 132: AT ix-1 213).

40. K 112: AT iii 424; see also HR ii 131-32: AT ix-1 213.

41. K 235-36: AT v 222-23.

42. Second Reply to Bishop of Worcester (1698), *Works of John Locke,* 1768, I, 754; quoted in Hesse 1961, 166-67.

43. Compare K 138-39: AT iii 665-67 and K 252: AT v 347 with K 235: AT v 221-22.

44. Hilary Putnam reminds us that what is inconceivable (at one time in history) can still be true. For example, on the assumption that "our world is Riemannian in the large," the statement that one cannot return to the place from which one started by traveling in a straight line in space in a constant direction, although literally inconceivable (at least before the conceptual revolution), is true (1975, xiv-xv).

45. The attempt to avoid action at a distance in explanations of phenomena like magnetism and gravitation exercised corpuscular philosopher-physicists from Descartes onward. (It is somewhat ironic that Descartes himself so firmly insisted on the need to avoid action at a

distance.) See Hesse for a thorough treatment of the historical vicissitudes of the doctrine of action at a distance.

46. This attitude reflects a sociological fact that might be called the *division of epistemic labor,* analogous to Putnam's division of linguistic labor. See Putnam 1975, 227-29.

47. One might object that fundamental psychophysical laws differ in important respects from the laws at which purely physical explanations stop. First, psychophysical laws usually have exceptions; they are true only if qualified with *ceteris paribus* clauses. Purely physical laws, on the other hand, need no such qualifications. Second, fundamental psychophysical laws are much less general and unified than fundamental physical laws. For example, a few general laws suffice to explain all magnetic phenomena, whereas a long (possibly open-ended) list of relatively specific laws are required to explain all sensory phenomena. Unfortunately, I must forbear any attempt to discuss these issues here. I thank Corby Collins for reminding me of the relevance of this issue.

48. This example assumes that force-fields and bodies genuinely are causally related, but this is controversial. An alternative view is that force-fields are not themselves causally efficacious but rather *explain* in what way the bodies cause each other to gravitate. On this view, we would be able to appeal to the original examples of action at a distance to defend Cartesian interaction.

49. K 112: AT iii 424-25.

50. K 236: AT v 223.

51. K 143: AT iii 694.

52. K 249: AT v 342. See also K 239: AT v 270.

53. One might think that gravitational fields are not primarily physical for the same sort of reason that motion is not primarily physical; that is, roughly, because they are properties rather than substances. If this is so, however, then it is implausible to think of fields as being causally efficacious in themselves; phenomena involving fields would involve genuine action at a distance. So, the issue of the physicality of fields would not arise.

54. Descartes at one point proposed what is in effect a "focal meaning" account of the concept of being physical or extended (K 239: AT v 270). See Owen (1960, 169) for an explanation of focal meaning.

55. K 236: AT v 223.

56. K 112: AT iii 424.

57. K 239: AT v 270.

58. K 235: AT v 222.

59. Descartes made exactly this kind of point to Arnauld. See K 236: AT v 223.

60. See, for example, HR i 190: AT vii 78.

61. Descartes stated exactly this position when he advised Regius how to reply to orthodox scholastic critics at Utrecht. See K 121: AT iii 460. Other passages in which Descartes suggests this view are HR ii 257: AT vii 445; K 124-25: AT iii 477-78; HR i 244: AT viii-1 29, HR i 190: AT vii 78.

62. K 137: AT iii 664-65; my emphasis.

63. In his next letter to Elizabeth, Descartes remarks, apparently with approval, that

everyone feels that he is a single person with both body and thought so related *by nature* that the thought can move the body and feel the things which happen to it. (K 142: AT iii 694; my emphasis)

64. Descartes shows that he thinks mind-body union explains mind-body interaction in the following passages: K 138: AT iii 665; HR ii 132: AT ix-1 213; K 235 : AT v 222; K 210: AT iv 603f; K 257: AT v 404.

65. In some passages, it seems that Descartes uses mind-body union to account not for the mere fact that a person's mind and body interact but for the particular quality of the sensations that people have. See K 256: AT v 402; K 127: AT iii 493; HR ii 291: AT viii-1 317; HR i 255: AT viii-1 41f.

66. For one of the many attempts to sort out Descartes's views on mind-body union, see Broughton and Mattern (1978).

67. See, for example, K 142: AT iii 693. Mattern (1978) discusses this passage.

68. Descartes sometimes suggests that mind-body union is a "simple notion" that, if we sufficiently reflect on it, can be seen to explain Cartesian interaction. See K 138f: AT iii 665f. But this is simply to beg the question in Descartes's favor, and it is not likely to be very convincing.

References

Oeuvres de Descartes. 1897-1913. Edited by Charles Adam and Paul Tannery. 12 vols. and Supplement. Paris. Cited as AT, with volume number in lower case roman numerals: e.g., AT vii.

The Essential Descartes. 1969. Edited with an introduction by Margaret D. Wilson. New York.

Descartes: Philosophical Letters. 1970. Edited by Anthony Kenny. Oxford. Cited as K.

The Philosophical Works of Descartes. 1972. Edited and translated by Elizabeth Haldane and G. R. T. Ross. 2 vol. Cambridge. Cited as HR i and HR ii.

Descartes' Conversation with Burman. 1976. Translated with introduction and commentary by John Cottingham. Oxford.

Beck, L. J. 1965. *The Metaphysics of Descartes.* Oxford.

Broughton, Janet. 1977. "Descartes's Rejection of the Scholastic Picture of Physical Change." In *Aspects of Natural Change in Descartes's Philosophy,* 13-61. Ph.D dissertation, Princeton University.

Broughton, Janet. "Adequate Causes and Natural Changes." In a Festshrift for Marjory Grene, edited by Michael Wedin, Alan Donagan, and Anthony Perovich. Boston Studies in the Philosophy of Science. Forthcoming.

Broughton, Janet, and Ruth Mattern. 1978. "Reinterpreting Descartes on the Notion of the Union of Mind and Body." *Journal of the History of Philosophy.* 16: 23-31.

Curley, E. M. 1978. *Decartes against the Skeptics.* Cambridge, Mass.

Doney, Willis. 1967. "Cartesianism." In *The Encyclopedia of Philosophy,* edited by Paul Edwards, vol. 2, 37-42. New York.

Hesse, Mary B. 1961. *Forces and Fields.* New York.

Keeling, S. V. 1968. *Descartes.* 2d ed. London.

Kenny, Anthony. 1961. *Descartes: A Study of His Philosophy.* New York.

Loeb, Louis E. 1981. *From Descartes to Hume.* Ithaca, N.Y.

Mattern, Ruth. 1978. "Descartes's Correspondence with Elizabeth: Conceiving Both the Union and Distinctness of Mind and Body." In *Descartes: Critical and Interpretive Essays,* edited by Michael Hooker, 212-22. Baltimore.

Owen, G. E. L. 1960. "Logic and Mathematics in Some Early Works of Aristotle." In *Aristotle and Plato in the Mid-Fourth Century,* edited by I. Düring and G. E. L. Owen, 163-90. Göteborg.

Putnam, Hilary. 1975. *Mind, Language and Reality. Philosophical Papers, vol. 2.* Cambridge.

Radner, Daisie. 1971. "Descartes' Notion of the Union of Mind and Body." *Journal of the History of Philosophy* 9: 159-70.

Richardson, R. C. 1982. "The 'Scandal' of Cartesian Interaction." *Mind* 91:20-37.

Ryle, Gilbert. 1949. *The Concept of Mind.* New York.

Searle, John R. 1983. *Intentionality: An Essay in the Philosophy of Mind.* Cambridge.

Williams, Bernard. 1978. *Descartes: The Project of Pure Inquiry.* London.

Wilson, Margaret Dauler. 1978. *Descartes.* Boston.

'I Think': Some Reflections on Kant's Paralogisms

JAY F. ROSENBERG

The representation 'I think' lies at the heart of the problematic of apperception. It is also the nerve center of Descartes' *cogito* argument. Only from the 'I think', only from the *cogito,* claims Descartes, can we demonstrate the cogency of a belief in the very existence of the world as such. More significantly, however, Descartes claims that we can also derive from this 'I think' a clear and certain knowledge of the *self* as such—of the essence or nature of this 'I' which thinks. The *cogito* alone is to supply the whole answer to the questions of apperceptive consciousness—the questions of self-awareness and of self-knowledge. A claim this bold deserves close and careful scrutiny.

One key passage occurs midway through the Second Meditation. Having concluded that he knows with certainty at least that *he* exists—"[The] statement 'I am, I exist' is necessarily true every time it is uttered by me or conceived in my mind" (MED, 17)[1]—Descartes proceeds to inquire into his nature, that is, to ask what *kind* of entity this 'I' which thinks is, of whose existence he is indubitably certain:

> But what then am I? A thing that thinks. What is that? A thing that doubts, understands, affirms, denies, wills, refuses, and which also imagines and knows.
>
> It is truly no small matter if all of these things pertain to me. But why should they not pertain to me. Is it not I who now doubt almost everything, I who nevertheless understand something, I who affirm that this one thing is true, I who deny other things, I who desire to know more things, I who wish not to be deceived, I who imagine many things against my will, I who take note of many things as if coming from the senses? (MED, 19-20)

"I am . . . a true thing and truly existing [*res vera et vere existens*], "Descartes sums up, "but what kind of thing? I have said it already: a thing that thinks." *Sum res cogitans.*

A "res cogitans," we may conclude from these passages, is in the first instance a one in contrast to a many—one thinker in contrast to many thoughts (*cogitationes*). These thoughts, Descartes tells us, "pertain to" the 'I'. Equivalently, the 'I' "has" them. The thinking 'I' or self, then, insofar as it is a "res cogitans," is the *single* haver of many thoughts.

There is, however, a manifest problem about this thinking 'I' or self: It is not in the world. This observation is, in fact, crucial to Descartes' self-proclaimed success in his search for certainty. What Descartes thought he had discovered was that whatever is ostensibly in the world—any object among objects—can coherently be thought as illusion, coherently be supposed *not* actually to exist. The thinking self, however, the *subject* who can thus freely think the objects of its ostensible encounters as illusory, is immune to such "hyperbolic" doubt. As Descartes suggests, "the world" might, it seems, be nothing but the fabrication of a demonic deceiver; and yet, for all that, the experiencing self may still exist—indeed, *must* still exist, if he is to be deceived, to doubt, to be convinced, or even (as Descartes puts it) to think anything at all. This self, therefore, cannot itself also be something *in* the world, as an object among objects. How, then, is it to be known?

It is precisely this Cartesian observation which Kant is echoing in his repeated remark that the representation of the 'I' is not intuitive.

> [The] identity of the subject, of which I can be conscious in all my representations, does not concern any intuition of the subject, whereby it is given as object . . . . (B408; cf. A350, B412-13)

'Intuition' (*Anschauung*) is Kant's term for a singular cognition, a representation of a 'this'. Kant distinguishes sharply, (as his predecessors did not) between such singular cognitive representations (*Erkenntnisse*) and mere sensations (*Empfindungen*), which "relate solely to the subject as the modifications of its state" (A320-B376). Intuitions, that is, are "thoughts" in the fullest intentional sense of the term. They are thoughts of individuals *as* individuals, as 'this' es. In consequence, as Kant sees it, intuitions are already conceptually structured.[2] They already (somehow) embody "the logical form of a judgment," and they arise (somehow) from operations of the "understanding":

> The same function which gives unity to the various representations *in a judgment* also gives unity to the mere synthesis of various representations *in an intuition* . . . . The same understanding, through the same operations by which in concepts . . . it produced the logical form of a judgment, also introduces a transcendental content into its representations, by means of the synthetic unity of the manifold in intuition in general. (A79-B104-5)

To put the point in a more contemporary terminology, what Kant is saying is that "perceptual takings"—the "subject terms" of perceptual judgments—already embody "the logical form of a judgment" insofar as they are all necessarily takings *as* or takings *to be*. A representation of an individual as an individual, in other words, is not the representation of a "bare" 'this' but always and necessarily the representation of a 'this-*such*'—'this fierce growling bear', 'this red brick', 'this tall blond man', and so on. The observation that the representation of the 'I', the self-qua-subject, is not intuitive thus amounts to the observation that the representation of the 'I' is *not* the representation of a 'this-such'. The self does not enter into our experience as the subject term of any perceptual judgment. The self, in short, is not *encounterable*.

Hume, we recall, concluded from this nonencounterability of the self as a this-such that the 'I' is not a thing (*res*) at all.[3] According to Hume, the identity which we ascribe to the self across time is spurious—that is, the 'I' is not a continuant—and its unity is only the "virtual" unity of a series, sequence, set, or collection of variously related items. To the extent that the 'I' is something (*alquid*), then, it is not a thing (*res*) but rather a composite of ontologically more-basic entities (ideas and impressions) which is not strictly identical across time.

Descartes obviously would demur. On his account, the identity of the self is precisely the identity of a continuant, the identity of a single perduring *substance*. The 'I' of the Cartesian *cogito* is itself ontologically basic—the single "*unhad* haver" of many thoughts—and in no sense a composite of parts. The manifold of thoughts "pertain to" the 'I', but they do not compose or constitute it. For Descartes, that is, the self is also "simple." It is a unitary simple substance, strictly identical across time.

Descartes' argument for this view, to the extent that his remarks suggest one, is straightforward. If I think *X* and I think *Y,* for example, it seems to follow directly that the 'I' who thinks *X* is (strictly) identical to the 'I' who thinks *Y*. Descartes, that is, apparently reasons essentially as follows:

(1) I think *X and* I think *Y.*

(2) Ergo, the 'I' that thinks *X* = the 'I' that thinks *Y*.

Now to a certain extent Kant is here in essential agreement with Descartes. Sentence (2), indeed, formulates what Kant calls "the *analytic* unity of apperception," and it forms one of the keystones of his notorious "Transcendental Deduction of the Categories." Where Kant parts company with Decartes, however, is in his insistence that the inference of (2) from (1) is not an unconditionally valid immediate formal inference, but something akin to an enthymeme. It has, that is, a *presupposition*. This presupposition, in fact, is precisely what Kant calls "the *synthetic* unity of apperception."

[The] thoroughgoing identity of the apperception of a manifold which is given in intuition contains a synthesis of representations, and is possible only through the consciousness of this synthesis. For the empirical consciousness, which accompanies different representations, is in itself diverse and without relation to the identity of the subject. That relation comes about, not simply through my accompanying each representation with consciousness, but only in so far as I *conjoin* one representation with another, and am conscious of the synthesis of them. Only in so far, therefore, as I can unite a manifold of given representations in *one consciousness,* is it possible for me to represent to myself the *identity of the consciousness in these representations.* In other words, the *analytic* unity of apperception is possible only under the presupposition of a certain *synthetic* unity. (B133)

The "empirical consciousness, which accompanies different representations" of which Kant here speaks is simply the direct, experiential or perceptual, "object-level" consciousness of X and of $Y,$ of "things in the world." The Cartesian premise (1), then, is precisely what results from "accompanying *each* representation with consciousness"—that is, by ascending *severally* from the "object-level" to corresponding metarepresentations: I think (that) $X,$ and I think (that) $Y.$ What Kant is insisting upon in this passage is that this sort of "ascent" alone does not yet induce any real relation over the *represented* items X and $Y,$ and that *therefore* neither does it induce any real relation over their represent*ings*.

Consider, as an analogy, a situation in which we are observing the flow of traffic on a busy street. At one time of day we notice an Alfa Romeo driving by; later our attention is caught by a passing Bentley. One thing which we might do, then, is to "ascend" from representations (perceptions) of these passing automobiles to representations (thoughts) of their drivers. We might conclude, for instance, that, on the given day:

(1′) Someone drove an Alfa Romeo, and someone drove a Bentley.

It is obvious, however, that we would *not* be entitled to conclude, simply on the basis of (1'), that:

(2′) the driver of the Alfa Romeo = the driver of the Bentley.

Here we are dealing with what is literally an enthymeme. What we would need to do in order to justify the conclusion (2') would be somehow to arrive at *independent* knowledge of the identities of the respective drivers. We might, for example, stop each of the cars and observe or question their drivers, examine their licenses, take fingerprints, and so on. We might, in other words, gather the evidence which we need in order to apply some "test" or appeal to some "criterion" of personal identity. Only on the basis of such independent evidence could we in principle be warranted in concluding that the two drivers were, in fact, one *person.*

It is just such gathering of independent evidence, however, that we *cannot* carry out in the case of the original inference of (2) from (1). As Kant points out, the unity of apperception is an *original* unity:[4]

> ... that self-consciousness which, while generating the representation '*I think*' (a representation which must be capable of accompanying all other representations, and which in all consciousness is one and the same), cannot itself be derived from any further representation. (B132)

We cannot, that is, arrive at the "analytic unity of apperception"—at identity statement (2)—by applying "tests" or appealing to "criteria of personal identity" for various 'I's of which we somehow severally have *independent* knowledge. The reason, simply, is that there is and can be no such "independent knowledge" of any 'I', any self-qua-subject. No such 'I' is, even in principle, an object of possible encounter. On this point Kant is in full agreement with both Descartes and Hume. There is no experience of the 'I', no intuitional awareness of the self as a this-such, to which we could appeal as an ostensible *source* of "independent evidence" regarding identity. It is simply not there "in the world" to be "observed" or "interrogated." Our experience yields nothing to which we could relevantly *apply* tests or criteria of personal identity.

What Kant concludes, then, is that Descartes is entitled to infer (2) from (1) only on the condition that a certain *presupposition* is satisfied, on the condition that it is also *possible* to "unite the manifold of given representations in *one consciousness*"—that is, possible to have the (meta-) thought:

(3) I think $(X + Y)$,

a thought in which the represent*eds* X and Y are first brought into relation to *one another* (caught up in a "synthesis") and in which the resulting "unity" $X + Y$ (the "synthesized manifold") is ascribed to "one consciousness" in the sense of being thought within the scope of a *single* 'I think'.

> The thought that the representations given in intuition one and all belong to me, is therefore equivalent to the thought that I unite them in one self-consciousness, or can at least so unite them; and although this thought is not itself the consciousness of the *synthesis* of the representations, it presupposes the possibility of that synthesis. In other words, only in so far as I can grasp the manifold of the representations in one consciousness, do I call them one and all *mine*. For otherwise, I should have as many-colored and diverse a self as I have representations of which I am conscious to myself. Synthetic unity of the manifold of intuitions ... is thus the ground of the identity of apperception itself .... (B134)

The *validity* of the Cartesian inference of (2) from (1), that is, presupposes (and, in fact, is equivalent to) the possible *truth* of (3).

What renders Kant's alternative solution to the problem of validating the Cartesian inference of (2) from (1) necessary is the fact that the thinking self is not an object of encounter and that the unity of apperception must thus be, in the specified sense, an original unity. That Kant's proposed solution is sufficient can be made clear by examining a structurally parallel solution to our analogy of cars and drivers. We began there, we recall, with the premise

(1′) Someone drove an Alfa Romeo and someone drove a Bentley

and wished legitimately to arrive at the conclusion that

(2′) the driver of the Alfa Romeo = the driver of the Bentley.

The first solution, which appealed to tests or criteria of personal identity, treated the inference of (2') from (1') as a literal enthymeme. It required additional premises having roughly the form:

The driver of the Alfa has characteristics A, B, C . . .

and

The driver of the Bentley has characteristics A, B, C . . .

(e.g., driver's license #*nnnn*, such-and-such fingerprint patterns) together with a "criterial" truth or (if we are applying a "test" rather than appealing to "criteria") a "lawful" generalization to the effect that

If P1 has characteristics A, B, C . . . and P2 has characteristics A, B, C . . ., then P1 is the same person as P2 (i.e., P1 = P2).

The Kantian solution, on the other hand, makes recourse to a single *presupposition* which takes, in the case of our example, roughly this form:

(3′) Someone drove (an Alfa Romeo *and then later* a Bentley),

in which the two automobiles are represented as themselves, so to speak, combined into a single "complex" entity—call it an "automotive dyad"—which is then taken as the object of a *single* (temporally spread-out) act of driving. If we pretend for the moment that such an automotive "synthesis" makes sense, it is clear enough that the possible truth of (3') alone would be logically sufficient for the truth of (2'), and thus for the validity of the inference of (2') from (1').[5]

The analogy here, of course, is merely formal. Our representational resources, that is, do not in fact include the concept of an "automotive dyad" as a candidate specification for the object of an act of driving. For us, (3') simply abbreviates:

(3″) Someone drove an Alfa Romeo and then later *he* drove a Bentley,

and, for us, (2') is in fact prior in the order of knowing to (3″). More generally, indeed, in such "third-person" cases, our entitlement to assert such compound propositions as (3") *always* rests, if only implicitly, on our entitlement to assert such identities as (2'), and this, in turn, rests upon at least the possibility of "independent knowledge" of the two drivers—that is, the possibility of an appeal to some test or criteria of personal identity in the style of the first, non-Kantian, solution.

Kant's special genius, however, lay in his recognition that, in *"first -person"* cases, this order of epistemic priorities must be reversed. The "analytic unity of apperception" represented by the '=' in (2) *presupposes* the possibility of awarenesses of the modes of synthesis or combination of representeds abbreviated by the '+' in (3). Since there is no multiply-encounterable intuitable 'I' to which anything like a test or criterion for personal identity might, even in principle, be applied, we cannot treat such Cartesian inferences as that of (2) from (1) as literally enthymematic. The *only* way to legitimate such identities as (2) is by appeal to the possibility of truths of the form (3), themselves knowable *prior to and independently of* the desired identities.

This anti-Cartesian conclusion is exactly analogous to a key thesis regarding time which Kant presses against Hume: that the representation of a sequence is not a sequence of representations. In order to represent a manifold *as* temporally sequential, Kant argues, what is needed is that the temporal relationships ostensibly obtaining among the represented items (events or occurrences) themselves be represented. As the famous examples of the house and the ship (A190 = B235ff.) illustrate, "*every* apprehension of an event is . . . a perception that follows upon another perception"(A192 = B237). The sequence of representations

(I see) the foundation of a house *and then*
(I see) the roof of the house

is not, in respect of its own temporal discursiveness, in any way different from the sequence of representations

(I see) a ship opposite the dock *and then*
(I see) the ship opposite a tree.

Both are so far mere sequences of representations, but neither is yet, on that account alone, the representation of a sequence. In order to represent a temporal sequence, it is necessary that the objects of successive acts of apprehension be *themselves* "synthesized" or "combined" into the unitary object of a single possible act of apprehension:

(I see): (a ship opposite the dock *and then* opposite a tree).

Only the possibility of such a synthesis of intuit*eds*—a synthesis in which the represent*eds* (ship-opposite-dock and ship-opposite-tree) are brought into relation to one another to constitute a "composite" object for a single act of representing—allows the representation of a temporal sequence *as* a sequence.

Temporality, then, is one possible mode of synthesis or combination among representeds. Spatiality, of course, is another, and indeed is already implicit in the example of the ship, for the ship and the dock or the ship and the tree are themselves manifolds, caught up into unitary syntheses through representations of a relation of (spatial) adjacency.

Most significantly, however, a third and fundamental mode of synthesis or combination among representeds is also implicit in these examples: the mode of synthesis which manifests itself in multiple references to *one* house or *one* ship. Here the original "manifold of representations" is composed of multiple "views" or "glimpses" of the house or the ship, and this manifold is "synthesized" precisely in that these diverse views or glimpses are *thought* as views or glimpses of a *single* house or ship, i.e., as encounters with one and the same *object*. "An *object* is that in the concept of which the manifold of a given intuition is united" (B137).

Ships and houses are but two sorts of objects. The concept of an object in general, in turn, is precisely what is specified by Kant's Categories: the concept of a perduring spatio-temporal substance in reciprocal causal interaction with other such substances. It is important to realize that the (epistemic) notion of the *concept* of an object (the notion of an object-concept) is, for Kant, prior in the order of understanding to the (ontological) notion of an object per se. Kant is an inheritor of the Terminist tradition represented in medieval logic by, for example, Ockham; and he regards such "categorial" ontological terms as 'object' not as "first-level" descriptive predicates but rather as "forms of judgment," *metaconceptual* classificatory predicates which sort descriptive terms according to their functional roles, their most general semantic and epistemic powers. ("These supposedly transcendental predicates of *things* are, in fact, nothing but logical requirements and criteria of all *knowledge* of things in general ..." [B114]). The pure categories specify the generic concept of an object—in other words, what it is (functionally speaking) for a concept to be an object-concept; the schematized categories sketch out the specific (but not yet determinate) concept of an object-situated-in-space-and-time.

The ostensible "metaphysical/ontological" predicate 'is an object' is thus, for Kant, in essence *defined* in terms of the "semantic/epistemic" predicate 'is the concept of an object' ('is an object-concept'), itself applied *to* concepts (i.e., to aspects of representings). This metaconceptual notion of an object-concept, in turn, is then elucidated in terms of the *synthesizing role* of such concepts in experience, that is, in terms of their function as principles of unity under which an intuited manifold can be thought and thereby "combined" into a single (intentional) object of a possible act of representing.

The key to Kant's Transcendental Deduction lies in his recognition that a command of such modes of synthesis or combination is a condition of the very possibility of *apperceptive* consciousness as well. The "analytic" unity of apperception:

(2) the 'I' that thinks X = the 'I' that thinks Y

presupposes the possibility of the "synthetic" unity of apperception:

(3) I think $(X + Y)$,

and thus presupposes as well space, time, and the Categories (object-concepts), precisely *as* the modes of combination or synthesis by means of which the represented (intuiteds) X and Y can be thought as united into a single possible (intentional) object of a single act of apprehension (or, more generally, of representation).

> The original and necessary consciousness of the identity of the self is thus at the same time a consciousness of an equally necessary unity of the synthesis of all appearances according to concepts, that is, according to rules, which not only make them necessarily reproducible but also in doing so determine an object for their intuition, that is, the concept of something wherein they are necessarily interconnected. For the mind could never think its identity in the manifoldness of its representations, and indeed think this identity *a priori,* if it did not have before its eyes the identity of its act, whereby it subordinates all synthesis of apprehension ... to a transcendental unity, thereby rendering possible their interconnection according to *a priori* rules. (A108)

It is the requirement that truths of the form (3) be knowable prior to and independently of identities of the form (2), therefore, which yields the possibility of a priori knowledge of objects—that is, of an a priori general, metaconceptual description of every system of ("first-level") descriptive concepts which is possible for such passive, apperceptive, temporally discursive intelligences as we are. A central thesis of the first *Critique,* however, is that, although a great deal can thus be known a priori about possible objects of experience—about 'this-suches'—there is nothing at all which can analogously be known a priori about the subject of experience, about (as Kant puts it) "this I or he or it (the thing) which thinks" (A346 = B404).

At this point, then, Kant parts company with both Descartes and Hume, for both Descartes and Hume hold that one *can* know something a priori about the self, about, so to speak, the "ontological status" of the subject of experiences. As we have already remarked, Descartes believed that we can know a priori that the self is a substance; Hume, in contrast, that we can know a priori that the self is *not* a substance. Kant, however, can consistently accept neither of these conclusions, for Kant allows no a priori knowledge outside the boundaries of possible experience, and, since the self is not intuitable, neither is it experienceable. The "I" is the subject of all experience, but it is the object of none. If either Hume or Descartes were right, then, a key thesis of Kant's critical philosophy would be irredeemably undermined.

> Indeed, it would be a great stumbling-block, or rather would be the one unanswerable objection, to our whole critique, if there were a possibility of proving *a priori* that all thinking beings are in themselves simple substances, and that consequently . . . personality is inseparable from them, and that they are conscious of their existence as separate and distinct from all matter. For by such procedure we should have taken a step beyond the world of sense, and have entered into the field of noumena. . . . (B409)

What Kant consistently concludes, therefore, is that we can have no a priori knowledge of the self—and he proceeds to examine and criticize arguments to the contrary, arguments which, he attempts to demonstrate, are one and all "paralogisms."

As we have seen, Kant insists, contrary to Hume, that the diachronic *identity* ascribed to the self in the "analytic unity of apperception" is unavoidable.

> It must be possible for the 'I think' to accompany all my representations; for otherwise something would be represented in me which could not be thought at all, and that is equivalent to saying that the representation would be impossible, or at least would be nothing to me. (B131-32)
> This principle of the necessary unity of apperception is itself, indeed, an identical, and therefore analytic, proposition . . . . (B135)

Hume's official view—that I "mistake" an orderly series of resembling and contiguous "impressions and ideas" for a diachronic continuant self—is thus open to the immediate objection that Hume here in fact *presupposes* just that unitary self which he hopes to eschew, for, in order even to formulate his view, Hume must posit a single 'I' *who*, qua subject, thus mis-takes a series for a continuant. Nor will it do to reply that this mis-taking is simply another "idea" in the series of ideas and impressions, for that reply merely opens the question: "In *which* series of ideas and impressions?", to which the only possible answer seems to be: "In the series composed of *my* ideas and impressions." For what impressions and ideas could *I* mistake for a continuant self (for *my*self) if not *my* impressions and ideas?

To put the point in a less contentious and more contemporary way, what Kant in effect recognizes is that 'idea' and 'impression'—or, more generally, 'representation' and 'thought'—are "verbal nouns." They are, that is, nominalizations of verbs ('to represent', 'to think'), and the concept of *someone's* thinking or representing (sensing, ideating) is logically prior to the concept of *a* thought or representation (someone's "having" a thought/idea/impression) in the same way that, for example, the concept of someone's smiling is prior to the concept of a smile (someone's "wearing" a smile).[6] That there are no "unhad" ideas or impressions—that thoughts require a "thinker" or a subject—is thus not, in Kant's eyes, a problematic or debatable claim, but rather a trivial, analytic proposition, akin to the proposition that any smile is necessarily someone's smile. The representation of an 'I' as the single, simple "haver" of many thoughts (as the subject of ideas and impressions) is thus an inevitable analytic correlate of the representation of thoughts, ideas, or impressions per se, in the same way that the representation of a "smiler" is an inevitable analytic correlate of the representation of smiles per se.

Kant, then, sides with Descartes to the extent that he agrees that the *representation* of the self-qua-subject, of the 'I', is—and is necessarily—single, simple, and substantial. As Kant puts it,

the bare apperception, 'I', is *in concept* substance, *in concept* simple, etc.; and in this sense all those psychological doctrines are unquestionably true. (A400; my emphases)

Contrary to Descartes, however, Kant goes on to insist that it does *not* follow from these necessary truths (that the self is "in concept" simple, "in concept" substance, etc.) that the self *is* ("in itself") simple, substance, etc. Such necessary truths concerning the *representation* of the subject of experience, in fact, yield no conclusions at all concerning the *nature* of that subject, the nature of the 'I'. For Kant immediately continues:

Yet this does not give us that knowledge of the soul for which we are seeking. For since none of these predicates are valid of intuition, they cannot have any consequences which are applicable to objects of experience, and are therefore entirely void. The concept of substance does not teach me that the soul endures by itself, nor that it is a part of outer intuitions which cannot itself be divided into parts, and cannot therefore arise or perish by any natural alterations. (A400)

On the face of it, Kant's insistence that we can derive no a priori knowledge of the subject of experience from necessary truths regarding the representation of such a subject appears paradoxical. For is it not a central thesis of the critical philosophy that we *can* derive a priori knowledge regarding objects of (possible) experience from necessary truths regarding the representations of such (intentional) objects—from necessary metaconceptual truths regarding object-*concepts?* Why, then, should the situation vis-à-vis the subject be in this respect crucially different?

Well, in a certain sense, the situation is *not* crucially different. From the standpoint of his "transcendental idealism," that is, Kant in fact *endorses* the Cartesian picture of the self—as phenomenon:

> If then we ask, whether it follows that in the doctrine of the soul dualism alone is tenable, we must answer: 'Yes, certainly; but dualism only in the empirical sense'. That is to say, in the connection of experience matter, as substance in the (field of) appearance is really given to outer sense, just as the thinking 'I', also as substance in the (field of) appearance, is given to inner sense. Further, appearances in both fields must be connected with each other according to the rules which this category introduces into that connection of our outer as well as of our inner perceptions whereby they constitute one experience. (A379)

The Cartesian picture becomes fallacious, on Kant's view, only when it is offered as a defensible account of the "noumenal" self or soul, just as the category of substance cannot be legitimately extended from "phenomenal" objects of outer sense to "things (as they are) in themselves."

> Neither the *transcendental object* which underlies outer appearances nor that which underlies inner intuition, is in itself either matter or a thinking being, but a ground (to us unknown) of the appearances which supply to us the empirical concept of the former as well as of the latter mode of existence. (A379)

Otherwise put, both the notion of a "transcendental object" and the notion of a "transcendental subject" are purely "formal" notions, adverting in the first instance to *modes* of representation, functionally conceived. The "pure concept of a transcendental object," Kant tells us, "cannot contain any determinate intuition and refers only to that unity which must be met with in any manifold of knowledge which stands in relation to an object" (A109). Analogously, "through the 'I', I always entertain the thought of an absolute, but logical, unity of the subject (simplicity). It does not, however, follow that I thereby know the actual simplicity of my subject" (A356). Or, again: "The identity of the consciousness of myself at different times is . . . only a formal condition of my thoughts and their coherence, and in no way proves the numerical identity of my subject." (A363).[7]

> *Modi* of self-consciousness in thought are not by themselves concepts of objects (categories), but are mere functions which do not give thought an object to be known, and accordingly do not give even myself as object. (B406-7)

From the standpoint of "transcendental idealism," then, the "noumenal" self and the "noumenal" world are strictly parallel. We can have knowledge neither of "transcendental objects" nor of the "transcendental subject." The way in which, for Kant, the possibility of a priori knowledge of objects diverges from the (im)possibility of a priori knowledge of subjects manifests itself not in his "transcendental idealism" but in his "empirical realism." The objects of which we *can* have a priori knowledge are not "noumenal" objects ("things in themselves") but rather objects of (possible) experience, "phenomenal" objects. We might, then, expect Kant to hold analogously that, although we can have no knowledge of the "noumenal" self (the self as it is "in itself"), we *can* have a priori knowledge of the "phenomenal" self, that self which is the subject of possible experiences. It is just this thesis, however, which Kant is concerned to reject in his discussion of the "Paralogisms of Pure Reason."

Our *ostensible* a priori knowledge of the self-qua-subject arises, according to Descartes, immediately from the *cogito*. The text 'I think', given to me as a certain premise in the meditative *cogito* argument, in other words, supposedly forms the basis of a putative "science of pure reason"—Kant calls it variously "pure" or "rational" or "transcendental" psychology—which ostensibly yields an a priori knowledge of the subject of experience as a single, simple, continuant substance (from which, further, the immateriality, incorruptibility, and personality of the self=soul, and ultimately its immortality as well, supposedly can be logically derived).

As we have seen, Kant apparently agrees with Descartes that the *representation* of the self, the 'I', is necessarily the *representation* of a unitary "unhad haver" of many thoughts, existing continuously across time. The disputed conclusion, however—that the subject of experiences *is* a single, simple, continuant substance—seems to be a direct consequence of this concession. Kant formulates the ostensible demonstration in an exemplary syllogism:

> That which cannot be thought otherwise than as subject does not exist otherwise than as subject, and is therefore substance.
>
> A thinking being, considered merely as such, cannot be thought otherwise than as subject.
>
> Therefore it exists also only as subject, that is, as substance. (B410-11; cf. A348)

The simplicity and diachronic identity of the self lend themselves to parallel reasonings:

> That which cannot be thought otherwise than as unitary (identical across time) does not exist otherwise than as unitary (identical across time), and is therefore simple (a continuant).
>
> A thinking being, considered merely as such, cannot be thought otherwise than as unitary (identical across time).
>
> Therefore it exists also only as unitary (identical across time), that is, as simple (a continuant). (Cf. A352, A361)

Such syllogisms, claims Kant, are fallacious *"per sophisma figurae dictionis,"* by reason of an ambiguous middle term. In the footnote in which we find perhaps the clearest assertion of this thesis, Kant tells us:

'Thought' is taken in the two premisses in totally different senses: in the major premiss, as relating to an object in general and therefore to an object as it may be given in intuition; in the minor premiss, only as it consists in relation to self-consciousness . . . . In the former premiss we are speaking of *things* which cannot be thought otherwise than as subjects; but in the latter premiss we speak not of *things* but of *thought* (abstraction being made from all objects) in which the 'I' always serves as the subject of consciousness. The conclusion cannot, therefore, be 'I cannot exist otherwise than as subject', but merely, 'In thinking my existence, I cannot employ myself, save as subject of the judgment'. (B411-12)

It is safe to say, I would conjecture, that it is not immediately clear what Kant is up to here. What we need to do, in fact, is to disentangle Kant's insight here—for insight there is—from the general apparatus of his critical philosophy.

That the 'I' cannot be thought otherwise than as a (logical) subject, as unitary (noncomposite), and as identical across time are themselves consequences of small supplementary arguments scattered throughout Kant's text. The "substantiality" of the self, for example—that the 'I' is, as Kant puts it, an "absolute subject" (A348)—is supported not only by appeal to the anti-Humean points which we examined above, but by various "Sartrean" considerations as well.[8] The notion of the self-qua-subject, that is, is necessarily the notion of something *other than* the determinations (thoughts, representations) which are ascribed *to* it. A self is always "not this, not that," but is also always manifesting a (directed, intentional) "consciousness *of* this or that." The 'I' is necessarily thought of as a one over against the many thoughts which are *its* thoughts—as a "haver" of thoughts which is not itself "had." The self, in other words, cannot be identified with any represent*ed* nor severally with any represent*ing* (i.e., any of *its* representings). Hume's strategy was to attempt to identify the self with its representings (impressions and ideas) *collectively*—but, as we have noted, the fact that the relevant collection of ideas and impressions can be picked out, even in principle, only by means of a specification of the *subject* to whom they are correctly ascribable, renders this strategy untenable. We concluded with Kant, therefore, that "Everyone must . . . necessarily regard himself as substance, and thought as only accidents of his being, determinations of his state (A349)."

Analogously, we cannot represent the "parts" of a thought—say, its logical subject and predicate—as distributed among different "parts" of an ostensibly composite self. This is a further consequence of the fact that 'representation', 'thought', and the like are "verbal nouns." The verb 'to think', we remarked, is prior to the noun 'a thought' in the sense that the form

   X has the thought that S is P

is, in essence, a long-winded, "nominalized," way of saying

   X thinks that S is P,

just as "Mary wore a warm, seductive smile" is a long-winded way of saying "Mary smiled warmly and seductively." But the verb 'to think' ('to represent', etc.) takes only a single logical subject as its correlative. Attempting to distribute the "parts" of a thought among different logical subjects, in other words, would be analogous to attempting to distribute the warmth and the seductiveness of Mary's smile among different logical subjects. Smiling-warmly-and-seductively is a single act of smiling (one *way* of smiling) and thus logically presupposes a single agent. Similarly, thinking-that-S-is-P is a single act of thinking (one way of thinking), and thus also logically presupposes a single agent. Kant puts it this way:

> For suppose it be the composite that thinks: then every part of it would be a part of the thought, and only all of them taken together would contain the whole thought. But this cannot be consistently maintained. For representations (for instance, the single words of a verse), distributed among different beings, never make up a whole thought (a verse), and it is therefore impossible that a thought should inhere in what is essentially composite. (A352)

That someone thinks that S is P, in short, cannot mean that one thing thinks of S and another thing thinks that something is P.

Finally, we cannot represent the identity of the 'I' as the "virtual identity" of a diachronic series of items, for it is only by virture of being ascribed to one self that *this* diachronic manifold of representings is constituted *as* a series. The series in question, that is, is just the (temporal) series (composed) of *my* representings. The "virtual identity" of the series qua series *presupposes* the ascription of its several members to a single logical subject, thought as strictly self-identical across time, and therefore can neither be substituted for such diachronic identity (a la Hume), nor supply an independent premise from which the strict diachronic identity of that subject might be inferred. Or, to quote Kant again:

> I refer each and all of my successive determinations to the numerically identical self, and do so throughout time . . . . This being so, the personality of the soul has to be regarded not as inferred but as a completely identical proposition of self-consciousness in time . . . . For it really says nothing more than that in the whole time in which I am conscious

of myself. I am conscious of this time as belonging to the unity of myself; and it comes to the same whether I say that this whole time is in me, as individual unity, or that I am to be found as numerically identical in all this time. (A362)

What is important to note about such supplementary supporting reflections is that each of them initially delivers a conclusion about what the representation 'I' *cannot* be. The 'I' is other than whatever it represents, and thus is (necessarily) *not* representable as an aspect or determination of anything else (i.e., of any "ontologically more basic" *representable*). The thinking self is (necessarily) *not* representable as a composite or system of (more basic) entities to which "parts" of its activity could be ascribed. And, since ascription to a single 'I' is the only way in which a diachronic series of items suitable to serve as a candidate for Humean "identification" with the self could be "collected" in the first place, this self is also (necessarily) *not* representable as a series or sequence of other items.

We have, in other words, a family of essentially *negative* minor premises concerning the representation of the 'I': Insofar as it is thought merely as the subject of thoughts and experiences (of representings),

the 'I' is not representable as an aspect or determination of any other item;

the 'I' is not representable as a system or composite of any other items;

and

the 'I' is not representable as a series or sequence of any other items.

The corresponding major premises of the syllogisms of "rational psychology," in contrast, are essentially *positive* in import:

Whatever is necessarily represented only as a logical subject (vs. as a predicable) is substance.

Whatever is necessarily represented only as unitary (vs. as composite) is simple.

Whatever is necessarily represented only as identical across time (vs. as a series) is a continuant.

On the face of it, this looks like a difference which makes no difference. Assuming that representation as (logical) subject and as predicable exhaust all the possibilities for the self's being represented *at all,* what, after all, is the difference between saying that

The self is necessarily not representable as a predicable of any logical subject

and saying that

The self is necessarily represented only as a logical subject of predicables

At this juncture, Kant proceeds to make two points, although he does not clearly distinguish them from one another. The first point is this: Even if there is *no* difference between these two formulations of the minor premise, and thus even if it does follow that the self (the 'I') is necessarily represented as a (single, simple) logical subject, we could *not* validly conclude that the self *is* a single, "ontologically basic" item—in other words, a simple (indivisible) substance. The inference from

X is necessarily *represented as* φ

and

Whatever is φ is (necessarily) ψ

to

X is (necessarily) ψ,

in short, is simply invalid.

It is this point which lies at the center of Kant's field of vision when he is anxious to defuse (from the standpoint of his "transcendental idealism") Cartesian conclusions about what the self is *"in itself"*—to make room, in other words, for the Spinozistic view that extension and thought are "in themselves" (as having "formal being") indeed aspects or determinations of something ontologically more basic (two *modes* of one substance: *Deus sive Natura*):

> The something which underlies the outer appearances and which so affects our sense that it obtains the representations of space, matter, shape, etc., may yet, when viewed as noumenon (or better, as transcendental object), be at the same time the subject of our thoughts. (A358)

The (speculative) hypothesis that

> the substance which in relation to our outer sense possesses extension is in itself the possessor of thoughts, and that these thoughts can by means of its own inner sense be consciously represented,

insists Kant, is *not* rendered false or unintelligible by the observations concerning the *representation* 'I' which he has conceded. And if such a hypothesis could acquire the epistemic status of something known (as, of course, given Kant's strictures regarding knowledge of "things in themselves," it cannot),

> what in one relation is entitled corporeal would in another relation be at the same time a thinking being. . . . Accordingly, the thesis that only souls (as particular kinds of substances) think, would have to be given

up; and we should have to fall back on the common expression that men think. . . . (A359-60)

(Here one should think of the Strawsonian thesis that the concept of a person is "logically primitive", the concept of something to which both "M-predicates"—extension—and "P-predicates"—thought—can correctly be ascribed.)[9]

Another analogy will help bring out Kant's point here. Consider *teams*. A team, surely, is a complex entity. It consists of its members; the members constitute the team. The *representation* of a team, however, is unitary and simple. It is a commonplace, for instance, that an assertion to the effect that one team, *X*, played and defeated another team, *Y*, cannot be "analyzed" or "reduced" to any statements about "more basic" entities—about, for example, the members or players of the two teams. Team-*talk*, that is, is not analyzable into member-*talk*. It is an autonomous discourse. The claim that team *X* defeated team *Y* on such-and-such a date is not equivalent to any claim, however complex, about the activities (running, throwing, hitting, kicking) of the members of those teams on that date.

Indeed, proper predicables of teams and proper predicables of players in the vast majority of cases simply do not overlap at all. Of a team, for example, but not of a player, one can correctly say that it won, lost, or tied a game. Conversely, of a player, but not of a team, one can correctly say that she ran, threw, kicked, or caught. The discourses are distinct.

Now, *within team discourse,* a team is necessarily represented as a single, simple, logical subject—of *team*-predicables, We may also say, with Kant and the tradition, that whatever *is* (in itself) a single, simple, logical subject is (necessarily)—from the "ontological point of view"—a simple, indivisible substance. But, of course, from the *ontological* point of view, a team is not such a simple substance but rather a composite of "more basic" entities, of players. The necessary truth about the unity and simplicity of *representations* of teams (within team-talk, vis-à-vis team-predicables), in short, neither contradicts nor renders unintelligible the "ontological" claim that teams are not per se simple indivisible substances. The point is a straightforward one: team-talk is not an "ontological" mode of discourse. It has no ontological import.

Kant's first point, then, can be formulated similarly: (first-person) 'I'-talk is not an "ontological" mode of discourse. It has no ontological (or, as Kant puts it, "transcendental") import. From the truth that the representation of the self is necessarily unitary and simple *within 'I'-discourse,* nothing at all follows about the nature of the self per se (from the ontological or "transcendental" point of view).

This team analogy helps us understand Kant's views on the diachronic identity of the self as well. Teams can and do outlive their members. Babe

Ruth and Mickey Mantle both played for the New York Yankees. They were both members of the *same* team. But the member-team relation is itself temporally conditioned—a player is a member of a team *at a time*—and no player who was a member of the Yankees when Ruth was a member was also a contemporary of Mantle. The diachronic identity of a team, in short, is not the diachronic identity of a continuant substance—nor does it presuppose the perdurance of its "ontologically more basic" constituents, its members, from year to year. In Kantian terms, the diachronic identity of a team is only a "logical identity." And so too, concludes Kant, *might* be the diachronic identity of the self, the 'I':

> The identity of the consciousness of myself at different times is . . . only a formal condition of my thoughts and their coherence, and in no way proves the numerical identity of my subject. Despite the logical identity of the 'I', such a change may have occurred in it as does not allow the retention of its identity, and yet we may ascribe to it the same-sounding 'I', which in every different state, even in one involving change of the subject, might still retain the thought of the preceding subject and so hand it over to the subsequent subject. (A363)

(As the win/loss record of the Yankees during Ruth's era was in fact "retained" and "handed over" to the Yankees during Mantle's era.)

Kant's *second* point, which he does not clearly distinguish from this first point, concerns the fact that there is indeed an important difference between positive and negative premises. In particular, argues Kant, we must be careful to distinguish between claims of the form

(E) X is (necessarily) not represented as ϕ

and those of the form

(P) X is (necessarily) represented as not-ϕ.

It is this point which lies at the center of Kant's field of vision when he is anxious to defuse (from the standpoint of his "empirical realism") Cartesian conclusions about the separateness or distinctness of mind (soul) and matter (body), and specifically when he undertakes to demonstrate that the ostensible problem of soul-body "interaction"—Kant himself calls it "communion"—is a pseudo-problem.

The problem of "communion" arises for Descartes, Kant argues, precisely because Descartes commits the fallacy of moving inferentially from a true *exclusionary* premise of the form (E) to a false *predicational* premise of the form (P). This inferential move occurs quite casually, in fact—in the transition from the *cogito* argumentation of the Second Meditation to the arguments for the distinctness of mind and matter and the existence of the mind or soul as a separate and immaterial substance in the Sixth.

In the Second Meditation, Descartes in effect argues that, although the self is necessarily represented as the single thinker of many thoughts (and is thus, as Kant would put it, "in concept" a unitary, simple, substantial continuant), the self is *not* "in concept" material. I cannot represent myself except as thinking, claims Descartes, but I can represent myself as thinking without representing *anything* corporeal. He thus arrives both at a predicational conclusion:

The self is (necessarily) represented as thinking

and at an exclusionary conclusion:

The self is (necessarily) *not* represented as extended.

Or, more precisely, the representation of the self as thinking is not, as such, a representation of anything *as* extended.

As this point in the Second Meditation, however, Descartes explicitly leaves open the further question of whether this self which thinks, although not represented as extended, might not nevertheless *be* something extended (a corporeal substance in space):

> But perhaps it is the case that nevertheless, these very [corporeal] things which I take to be nothing (because I am ignorant of them) [consonant with the method of "systematic doubt"] in reality do not differ from that self which I know. This I do not know. I shall not quarrel about it right now; I can make a judgment only regarding things which are known to me. (MED, 19)

Descartes here recognizes, in other words, that from the mere fact that the bare representation of the self as thinking is not, as such, a representation of anything as extended, it no more follows that the self is not extended than, for example, it follows from the fact that the bare representation of Descartes as a philosopher is not a representation of anything as French, that Descartes is not French. Given only the *cogito* argumentation of the Second Meditation, then, the possibility remains that the self which (necessarily) thinks is, in point of fact, a *body* which thinks, a thinking corporeal substance.[10]

Only in the Sixth Meditation does Descartes believe he is prepared to advance an argument for the "real distinctness" of mind and body. To this end, he proposes to apply the "method of clear and distinct ideas" which he has developed and defended in the intervening text. To apply this method, of course, Descartes requires premises which assert that he is in fact in *possession* of certain "clear and distinct" ideas. For the ideas of body (corporeal substance) and of himself (a thinking thing) which he needs in order to begin, then, Descartes ostensibly reaches back to the results arrived at in the Second Meditation. On that basis, in fact, he advances *two* claims:

(B) I have a distinct idea of a body—insofar as it is merely an extended thing, and not a thing which thinks

and

(S) I have a clear and distinct idea of myself—insofar as I am a thing that thinks and not an extended thing. (MED, 49)

Premise (B) is relatively unproblematic for our purposes. We evidently can and do have an idea (perhaps even a "clear and distinct" idea) of such *mere* bodies as stones—in other words, of nonthinking, spatially-extended chunks of material. But just where has Descartes established his claim to possess the "clear and distinct idea of self" which he ascribes to himself in premise (S)? For premise (S) is, logically speaking, a conjunction. It incorporates two subsidiary claims:

(St) I (clearly and distinctly) represent myself as thinking,

and

(Se) I (clearly and distinctly) represent myself as not-extended.

We have seen the claim (St) before, in the Second Meditation:

The self is necesssarily represented as thinking.

But what we had in the Second Meditation was *not* the predicational premise (Se), roughly:

The self is necessarily represented as nonextended,

but only the *exclusionary* premise:

The representation of the self as thinking is not, as such, the representation of anything as extended,

which, at best, amounts to:

The self is necessarily *not* represented as extended.

Descartes, in other words, has evidently inferred from the exclusionary premise

(nSe) (Necessarily) the self is *not* represented as extended,

the predicational conclusion that

(Sne) (Necessarily) the self *is* represented as *not*-extended.[11]

But *that* inference, insists Kant, is already fallacious!

Kant's point here is a logical one, concerning this predicative "form of judgment" in general—concerning singular predications. The logical function of attributing a predicate to a subject (of predication) in a judgment is (as Strawson, for example, has argued at length) "decomposable" into two sub-functions: "referring" and "characterizing," or, less technically, "picking something out" and "saying something about it." In Kantian terms, a "given" subject is "thought under" some concept. Now where the subject of predication is "independently identifiable" in the sense that we can "pick it out" in a way which does not *presuppose* the predicative judgment at issue—where, for example, we are dealing with an intuitable subject, in Kant's sense of the term, and thus can "pick it out" as an object of sensory encounter, as a "this-such"—the inferential passage from an exclusionary to a predicational judgment is unproblematic. For instance, from

Air is not represented as colored,

we are legitimately entitled to infer

Air is represented as colorless,

for air is "intuitively," sensorily, encounterable (as a heavy wind is sufficient to remind us) and thus can be "picked out" as a subject of potential predications in ways which do not presuppose any judgments regarding its *visual* sensible qualities.[12]

The inference from an exclusionary to a predicational judgment becomes problematic, however—indeed, fallacious—when the ostensible subject of predication is not in this way an object of possible "intuitive" encounter, where there is no way of "picking out" or "independently identifying" this ostensible "subject" apart from its ostensible "predicables." But precisely this is what happens when the ostensible subject of predication is supposed to be the *self!* As Kant repeatedly stresses—and, as we have seen, as Descartes necessarily agrees—the self is not "intuitable."

Descartes' error, argues Kant, lies in treating the *formal* "unity of consciousness," which is a necessary condition of the possibility of any experience at all, *as if* it were itself an object of such experience, an "independently identifiable" intuitable object-of-encounter.

The unity of consciousness, which underlies the categories, is here mistaken for an intuition of the subject as object, and the category of substance is then applied to it. But this unity is only unity in *thought,* by which alone no object is given, and to which, therefore, the category of substance, which always presupposes a given *intuition,* cannot be applied. Consequently, this subject cannot be known. The subject of the categories cannot by thinking the categories acquire a concept of itself as an object of the categories. (B421-22)

What Kant recognizes, to put the point differently, is that the logical function of ascribing many thoughts to one subject is distinct from the logical function of attributing many properties to one object. The abstract and formal notion of the "logical subject" of a judgment or proposition, in fact, blurs over precisely the crucial distinction which needs here to be observed. The 'I' which is the subject *of experiences* (E-subject) is not, as such, a subject *of predicates* (P-subject). Despite the formal parallelism of the one-versus-many pattern, the way in which one 'I' "collects" many thoughts or experiences ("its" thoughts and experiences, those which it "has") is nevertheless functionally, and thus logically, radically different from the way in which one object "collects" many properties ("its" properties, those which it "exemplifies").

What Kant is saying, in essence, is that judgments of the form:

I think that-p

(the schema of Descartes' *cogito)* do not have the "logical form" of a relation: *xRy.* Not only is the self not an object, "its" thoughts and experiences (awarenesses, representations) are *also* not objects. Descartes' error lay precisely in his "hypostatizing" both the self and its thoughts (*cogitationes)* as objects of reference and predication.

> [All] controversy in regard to the nature of the thinking being and its connection with the corporeal world is merely a result of filling the gap where knowledge is wholly lacking to us with paralogisms of reason, treating our thoughts as things and hypostatising them. (A395)

Kant's third, and deepest, point, then—the insight which underlies and supports his claims concerning the nonequivalence of exclusionary and predicational judgments—is that the term 'I' which occurs in self-ascriptions is not a "referring expression": " . . . the 'I' is merely the consciousness of my thought" (B413). Representations of oneself as an E-subject, as a subject of thoughts and experiences, are not representations of a P-subject, a subject predicates, *at all.* Self-ascriptions are neither singular predications nor relational propositions.

> By such statements we are not . . . enabled to know what kind of an object it [the self] is, but only to recognize that if it be considered in itself, and therefore apart from any relation to the outer senses, these predicates of outer appearance cannot be assigned to it. (A358-59)

Since the self is not "given" as a this-such (an object of encounter) in the manner of "intuitable" objects, and thus not "independently identifiable" or "pickable out" as a potential subject of many predications, the *only* way to "identify" the self is *as* the subject (the E-subject) of "its" thoughts and experiences. What Kant recognizes, however, is that this mode of "picking out" is in the end only a *pseudo*identification. For, as we noted earlier in our remarks on Hume, the relevant assemblage of thoughts and experiences, the ones *to which* we ostensibly appeal in the putative process of "picking out" the self as a P-subject, can *themselves* be "identified" only *as* "its" thoughts and experiences, that is, in a way which presupposes the identity of the unitary E-subject. It follows, then, that the 'I' cannot be *picked out* at all. The representation 'I' thus remains, as Kant insists, "completely empty."

> [We] cannot even say that this is a concept, but only that it is a bare consciousness which accompanies all concepts. Through this I or he or it (the thing) which thinks, nothing further is represented than a transcendental subject of thoughts $= X$. It is known only through the thoughts which are its predicates, and of it, apart from them, we cannot have any concept whatsoever, but can only revolve in a perpetual circle, since any judgment upon it has always already made use of its representation. And the reason why this inconvenience is inseparably bound up with it, is that consciousness in itself is not a representation distinguishing a particular object, but a form of representation in general. . . . (A346 = B404)

Curiously enough, it follows, inter alia, that Descartes is not even entitled to his positive predicational premise (St)

> I clearly and distinctly represent myself as thinking

to the extent that Descartes' notion of a "clear and distinct idea" is simply and unreflectively supposed to correspond to the form of a singular predication (the attribution of a property to a P-subject) or to the positing in judgment of a relation among P-subjects.

The schema of an instance of the Cartesian *cogito* formula:

> I think that -p,

does not have the logical form of a relational claim (xRy) which Descartes implicitly attributes to it. Neither 'I' nor 'that-p' here functions logically as a P-subject, a singular term which (functionally viewed) picks out or identifies a subject of possible predications. It follows in turn, however, that Descartes' *res cogitans* formula:

> I am a thinking thing

is only a pseudoinstantiation of the "this-such" schematism for identification necessarily applicable to genuine objects of experience. There are no judgments of the form

> This thinking thing is ϕ

logically parallel to judgments of the form of, for instance,

> This black bear is dangerous.

'Thing' (*res*) does not indicate a kind of "this"—as, for example, 'bear' indicates a kind of "this"—but rather adverts to this-suches (to objects qua Kantian/Aristotelian substances) as enformed contents *tout ensemble*. And 'thinking' (*cogitans*) is not a predicable determination of a kind of "this"—as, for example, is 'black'—but at best gestures only at the availability of awarenesses as objects *of* awarenesses, that is, at the possibility of reflective *meta* representations of one's own representations *as* representations.[13]

Kant's first point was that the inference from the premise that the 'I' of the 'I think' is necessarily a grammatical substantive to the conclusion that the I (the self) is necessarily an ontological substance is fallacious or "paralogistic." His second point was that, even supposing the 'I' of the 'I think' to be a proper grammatical substantive, we could legitimately attribute categorial predicates to the I (the self) only negatively, in an exclusionary way, for the self is not an (intuitable) object of possible encounter and thus not independently identifiable or "pickable out" as a logical subject (a P-subject). (Cf. here, again, B132.) Kant's third point, however, is that the 'I' of the Cartesian 'I think' is not a proper grammatical substantive *at all*. The term 'I' is not a P-subject, a "referring expression." It is merely a *"dummy* substantive," and the 'think' of the Cartesian 'I think' is correspondingly merely a "dummy verb." The representational form 'I think that-' rather performs *as a unit* the logical (representational) *function* of "bracketing" within instances of the *cogito* schema ('I think that-p') the representation which follows that form, thereby representing that representation *as* a representation— that is, adverting to the mode of metarepresentation as a possible mode of awareness or consciousness.

The Cartesian form 'I think that-', as it occurs in "meditative" or introspective self-ascriptions, in other words, is basically nothing more nor less than a form of *quoting*. The collection of thoughts and experiences which "belong" to the self—which are *"mine"*—consists simply of those awarenesses of which I directly *can be aware*. They are "collected" (ascribed to one and the same E-subject) precisely *in that* they are potential contents of *my meta-awarenesses*. But, as Kant had the special genius to recognize, this way of "collecting" a many (of thoughts, vs. one thinker) is fundamentally different from the "predicational" way of "collecting" a many (of properties, vs. one object). The logical function of ascribing many representations to one E-subject is a different logical function from that of attributing many properties to one p-subject. And that is the deepest lesson of Kant's Paralogisms.

The problematic of apperception arises from the realization that the self, the 'I', is not "in the world." The self is the subject of every experience, but the object of none. How, then, are self-awareness and self-knowledge even *possible?*

What Kant shows us is that in the very posing of this problem we have been taking something for granted. We have been taking for granted that self-ascriptions are singular predications or relational judgments. We have been taking for granted, that is, that *self*-consciousness is awareness or consciousness *of a self* (of oneself) in the same way—logically and functionally—

that object-consciousness is awareness or consciousness *of an object*—in traditional terminology, that self-consciousness is a special case of "directed" or "thetic" or "intentional" consciousness. We have been supposing, in short, that singular predication—"picking something out" and "saying something about it"—is the correct logical paradigm for self-ascription and, in particular, that 'I' is a "referring expression," a representational element which functions *logically* as a proper name functions, to "pick out" or identify a P-subject to which predicables can be attributed.

What Kant saw, and argued, was that just this presupposition is false. Reasoning which is based upon it is thus from ground up fallacious—and this is true not only of those *positive* reasonings by means of which Descartes, for example, proposed to arrive at substantive theses concerning the nature or essence of the self, but equally true of those *critical* reasonings in virtue of which self-awareness and self-knowledge come to be represented as *problematic* in the first place. To "solve the problem of apperception," then, we must turn our attentions elsewhere. What is needed is not some unique and mysterious form of nonempirical or nonintentional consciousness but a proper appreciation of the global structures of our *ordinary* empirical awareness and the diverse modes of our *actual* intentional representations, an appreciation of the *sort* of "unity of consciousness" which is ours. For what we *should* learn from Kant is that this is the ultimate and proper locus of that uniqueness in virtue of which we *are,* in the end, self-conscious beings, the sort of beings who, alone, can pose "the problem of apperception."[14]

Notes

1. Page references to Descartes' *Meditations* (shown as MED) are to the translation by Donald A. Cress (Indianapolis, 1979), which happened to be handy. Citations from Kant are taken from the Kemp Smith translation of *Critique of Pure Reason* (London, 1958).

2. In accepting this interpretation, I thus align myself with Wilfrid Sellars ("Some Remarks on Kant's Theory of Experience", *Journal of Philosophy* 64 (1967): 633-60). Jonathan Bennett has explicitly criticized (in *Kant's Dialectic* [London, 1974], 30-31) this Sellarsian reading on the grounds that Kant allows that there can be "intuition without thought" (citing A111), but I do not think Bennett's critique holds up. Kant's reference to "intuition without thought" here is counterfactual (indeed, one might even say, "counter-transcendental") and should be understood as an instance of the same sort of speculative play as his occasional adversions to "intellectual intuition" (B xl, B68, B72, B159, B307). The remark on A111 that, *were* empirical concepts not based on a transcendental ground of unity, "appearances might, indeed, constitute intuition without thought" no more shows that *our* intuitions are nonconceptual items, or even that "intuition without thought" is *possible,* than the remark on B149 that "if we suppose an object of a *non-sensible* intuition to be given, we can indeed represent it through all the predicates which are implied in the presupposition that it has none of the characteristics proper to sensible intuition" shows that *our* intuitions are non-sensible, or even that "non-sensible intuitions" are possible.

3. *A Treatise of Human Nature,* I, iv, 6 (Clarendon Press, 1896).

4. The translation here departs from Kemp Smith's in accepting Goldschmidt's reading 'abgeleitet' ("derived from") in place of 'begleitet' ("accompanied by"). See the German edition of *Kritik der reinen Vernunft,* edited by Raymund Schmidt (Hamburg, 1956), 141b.

5. A more intuitive analogy might be this: Inspecting his stocks, the night chef in a delicatessen discovers that he needs to replenish the corned beef, the Swiss cheese, and the sauerkraut. "Ascending" from representations of these comestibles to representations of their consumers, he concludes that, during the day:

(1D) Someone ate some corned beef, and someone ate some Swiss cheese, and someone ate some sauerkraut.

He would certainly not be entitled to conclude on this basis alone, however, that:

(2D) The corned beef eater = the Swiss cheese eater = the sauerkraut eater.

The inference becomes immediately valid, however, when an astonished waiter informs the chef that:

(3D) Someone ate six *Ruben sandwiches,*

for a Ruben sandwich is precisely a "synthesis" of corned beef, Swiss cheese, and sauerkraut (on rye). Statement (3D), that is, has the (Kantian) form:

Someone ate (corned beef + Swiss cheese + sauerkraut)

in which the three comestibles are represented as themselves combined into a single "complex" entity which is then taken as the object of a *single* act of consumption.

6. For a further development of this theme, see my *Thinking Clearly about Death* (Englewood Cliffs, N.J., 1983), sects, 0.3, 2.1, and 2.2. The most explicit Kantian statement of the point occurs at A355: "Thus the renowned psychological proof is founded merely on the indivisible unity of a representation, which governs only the verb in its relation to a person."

7. Kant's *phenomenal* Cartesianism is thus compatible with all sorts of contemporary post-Kantian views regarding the ontological status of the self and its thought. The self "in itself," in other words, can very well turn out to be, for example, a *biological organism,* composed of a multiplicity of individual molecules in constant flux and alteration, with its thoughts (representings) *functional states* of that organism.

8. See my "Apperception and Sartre's 'Pre-Reflective Cogito'," *American Philosophical Quarterly* 18 (1981): 255-60, for a fuller exposition of these points.

9. See P. F. Strawson's "Persons" in *Minnesota Studies in the Philosophy of Science* (Minneapolis, 1956) and the discussion in *Individuals* (London, 1959).

10. The possibility is at least still open in the Fourth Meditation:

But now I not only know that I, insofar as I am a thing that thinks, exist, but also that, having observed some ideas of corporeal nature, I might question whether the thinking nature that is in me—or rather that I am—is something different from this corporeal nature, or whether both natures are the same thing. And I presume that no consideration has as yet occurred to my mind which convinces me of the one more than the other. (MED, 38)

11. The move appears to be made in one key sentence (MED, 49) in which Descartes commits something like a modal fallacy:

[From] the fact that I know that I exist, and that meanwhile I judge that nothing else clearly belongs to my nature or essence except that I am a thing that thinks, I rightly conclude that my essence consists in this alone: that I am a thing that thinks.

What Descartes seems to be doing is moving from:

(a) Nothing clearly belongs to my essence but thinking

(an exclusionary claim) to:

(b) Clearly nothing belongs to my essence but thinking,

(a predicational claim); an move akin to that from:

(a′) Nothing necessarily exists but God

to:

(b′) Necessarily nothing exists but God,

which even Descartes *should* find objectionable. But what Descartes needs for his "separateness" argument is precisely the unjustified claim that he has a clear (and distinct) idea of himself as thinking and *non*extended (i.e., that it is clear that extension does *not* belong to his essence), which corresponds to (b) here, not the perhaps-justified claim that he has a clear idea of himself as thinking but not a *clear* idea of himself as extended (or as anything else *but* thinking), which is the sense of (a).

12. It's not clear that Kant is right about the validity of inferences of predicational conclusions from exclusionary premises when the subject of predication *is* intuitable. For example, from:

I do not see the hen as having exactly sixteen speckles

I evidently cannot conclude that:

I see the hen as *not* having exactly sixteen speckles,

even though the speckled hen is, presumably, as intuitable as one could wish, and "pickable out" as a subject of potential predications in myriad ways. The inference of the predicational from the exclusionary, then, may be even *more* problematic than Kant takes it to be—but that, of course, offers no aid and comfort to Descartes.

13. See my *One World and Our Knowledge of It* (Dordrecht, 1980) chap. 3, for further elaboration of these themes.

14. Research for this paper—part of a longer study, *The Thinking Self,* in progress—was supported during academic year 1982-83 by a fellowship from the Alexander von Humboldt Foundation (Bonn-Bad Godesberg, West Germany) to whom thanks are gratefully extended. Thanks are also due my student Tom Powell for enlightening discussions and insightful objections to earlier drafts of the essay.

Concepts of Mind

GODFREY VESEY

P L. Heath says of the term 'concept' that it is "essentially a dummy . expression or variable, whose meaning is assignable only in the context of a theory, and cannot be independently assigned."[1] Philosophers use a good many terms of which the same might be said. Examples are 'cause', 'substance', and 'matter'. The term 'mind', however, might seem to be different. To talk of a person's mind is to talk of that person's capacity for thought, and "thought is a word that covers everything that exists in us in such a way that we are immediately conscious of it."[2] So we are in an exceptionally privileged position to assign a meaning to the word 'mind'; we do not have to bother about theories. But the concept of mind that involves the concept of thought as that of which we are immediately conscious is itself one that exists in a context of theory. In fact, it has a background of theorizing, and counter-theorizing, that goes back at least as far as Plato. I shall begin by investigating this background. What is the theory, or what are the theories, that provide the context for Plato's use of the term 'mind'?

It seems to me that there are several theories and that the most significant, for subsequent developments, are the theory that things are ordered, that the ultimate explanation of things is in terms of purposes or ends; the theory that there is a realm of what is eternally existent, a realm of which the prime inhabitants are mathematical, and especially geometrical; and the theory that, in addition to sensible things, there are intelligible things. Plato combines these three different theories into one theory, his theory of Forms.[3] He does not expound the theory systematically, and commentators sometimes lose sight of one or more of the constituent theories in it. A common omission is any reference to what Plato says is "the origin of the designation *intelligible*,"[4] so perhaps that would be the best place to begin.

THE SENSIBLE AND THE INTELLIGIBLE

Plato introduces the concept of the intelligible by reference to a notion he got from Heraclitus, the notion that there are 'opposites', such as the beautiful and the ugly, the great and the small, the just and the unjust, and so on, and that anything we sense, if it has one of a pair of opposites, also has the other. A maiden is beautiful, by comparison with an ape, but also ugly, by comparison with a god.[5] A finger is both great and small: my second finger, for example, is both great, by comparison with my little finger, and small, by comparison with my middle finger. The problem, as Plato sees it, is that "perception no more manifests one thing than its contrary."[6] In the case of my finger, "sight saw the great and the small ... not separated but confounded." Hence "the sensation yields nothing that can be trusted," and "the intelligence is compelled to contemplate the great and the small, not thus confounded but as distinct entities, in the opposite way from sensation." And this, Plato says, is the origin of the designation 'intelligible' for the great in itself, separate from the small (and the small in itself, separate from the great), and of the contrary designation, 'visible', for the finger, in which the great and the small are confounded.

Despite Plato's assertion that this is the origin of the designation 'intelligible' for one of a pair of opposites, in itself, the question remains why he uses the word 'intelligible'. The great, in itself, is *thought*. But what does this mean? The answer is provided elsewhere, where he is discussing justice.[7] What is thought about the just, the beautiful, the great, and so forth, is what their nature is, how they are defined.

Plato has in mind a particular sort of definition. First, he rejects the sort of definition that consists simply in listing the things we call by a certain name, such as, in the case of 'just', acts of telling the truth and acts of returning what has been borrowed. The definition Plato is after expresses the essense of a thing. Take the case of shape. It is no good saying that shape is round, square, or triangular. Shape is "that in which a solid terminates."[8] That is its essence. Geometrical concepts, in particular, lend themselves to such definitions. A circle, for example, is "the thing which has everywhere equal distances between its extremities and its centre."[9] The way Plato puts it is to say that there is "one ideal form" by which things are what they are. In the case of holiness, for example, "there is one ideal form by which unholy things are all unholy, and by which all holy things are holy."[10]

Second, it is not the case that we simply get together and agree on a definition of this sort. The definition is something to be *known*, not something to be arbitrarily decided upon.[11] Plato might be said to hold that there are real (i.e., not merely conventional) definitions to which our use of names would conform if they were used correctly, in something like the same way as there are facts to which our sentences correspond if they are true. He is opposed to the view of some Sophists that there is not "any principle of correctness in names other than convention and agreement."[12]

Thus far, Plato's theory might seem to be limited in its application to opposites like the great and the small, the beautiful and the ugly, and so on. The intelligence is compelled to contemplate the great by itself because in the object of sense, the finger, it is confounded with the small. But the finger, as such, it would seem, is not confounded with its opposite, the non-finger. So it seems reasonable to say that sensation is adequate for the judgment that the object is a finger. In fact, Plato says as much in the passage I quoted from, above.[13] But it seems reasonable only because our standpoint, in considering the matter, has been one located in time. From the standpoint of eternity even the finger is confounded with its opposite, the non-finger, since fingers come into being and pass away. And the same is true of everything sensible. Nothing sensible remains eternally the same. Only the intelligible Form is constant and invariable. So, taking the standpoint of eternity, we must treat being a finger, or a man, or a horse, as we treat being great or small, beautiful or ugly, and so on. From the standpoint of eternity, no character whatsoever is exhibited in a sensible thing unconfounded with its opposite.[14]

But why should Plato take the standpoint of eternity? It is here that the second theory, the theory that there is a realm of what is eternally existent, comes in. Plato thought that knowledge differs from true opinion in having a different sort of object. Given that there is a realm of the eternal, it seemed to him obvious that it is in that realm that the objects of knowledge are to be found. So if there is knowledge with respect to fingers, men, and horses it will not directly concern the fingers, men, and horses that, or who, are here today and gone tomorrow. It will concern the Forms of finger, etc.—the "self-existent ideas unperceived by sense, and apprehended only by the mind."[15]

THE RECOLLECTION DOCTRINE

The above theory, which is based on the reflection that opposites are confounded in sensible things, is developed by Plato in a number of ways. One development is to meet an epistemological problem. Sensation sees opposites confounded in sensible things. For example, sight sees the great and the small confounded in the thing that is temporarily a finger. Now, for even this to be possible it must be possible for the opposites to be contemplated as distinct entities. Without having contemplated greatness in itself, which is intelligible not sensible, we could not have even the sensation-mediated opinion that something is great. Before sensing anything as having such-and-such a character, we must have known the character in itself. For example, to see someone as tall we must have known tallness in itself, that is, the intelligible tallness to know which is to know the real nature of tallness.[16] But we have had sight, hearing, and so on, from the moment of birth. So it looks as though we must have contemplated intelligible tallness *before* birth.[17]

Instead of treating this as a reductio ad absurdum of his theory, Plato uses it in support of one of the beliefs of the Pythagoreans, the belief that the soul exists before birth.[18] After birth, the soul's awareness of things is by the bodily senses; and the body acts as an impediment to attaining truth and clear thinking.[19] But before birth, the soul is unembodied. It is purely intellectual. So, if the prenatal soul is in a position to contemplate the Forms at all, it can contemplate them without impediment, in their self-existent, unconfounded purity. And Plato holds that the prenatal soul *is* in a position to contemplate the Forms. It inhabits the same realm of eternal truths as they do. But if the prenatal soul can know the Forms then so can the postnatal— by recollection.[20]

Plato does not represent recollection of the Forms as being easy. We have to be brought to recollect them. It is a process in which both the presence to us of sensible things and dialectical reasoning[21] play a part. It is beyond most people. As Plato puts it, "every man may be said to share in true opinion, but mind is the attribute of the gods and of very few men."[22] He believes it to be the attribute of so few men, in fact, that he represents the search for the real definitions, in his dialogues, as rarely, if ever, succeeding.

IMPERFECT COPIES IN AN INCOMPREHENSIBLE RECEPTACLE

Another development of Plato's theory is intended to explain, first, how sensible things are related to Forms (i.e., how that in which the great is confounded with the small is related to the great in itself); second, how it is that there can be many sensible things with the same character (i.e., many things in which the great is confounded with the small). In brief, Plato's answer to the first question is that sensible things are 'imperfect copies' of Forms.[23] Now, copies require a receptacle, for the copies to be in or on.[24] Plato's answer to the second question is that the receptacle for the copies is extended; it is space. A divine craftsman, the 'demiurge', copies the Forms in different parts of space (and, presumably, at different times). Hence there can be many sensible things that are (imperfect) copies of one Form. Plato seems not to have been very happy with either of his answers. He says that the receptacle is "an invisible and formless being which receives all things and in some mysterious way partakes of the intelligible, and is most incomprehensible."[25] And space, he says, "is apprehended, when all sense is absent, by a kind of spurious reason, and is hardly real."[26]

When a philosopher's theorizing leads him to talk of something being "most incomprehensible" and "hardly real," it may seem to be time to rethink the theory, so as to avoid such unacceptable consequences. In the *Republic,* as we have seen, Plato says that "perception no more manifests one thing than its contrary" (for example, it no more manifests the great than the small) and that there must therefore be something (for example, the great in itself) that is intelligible as opposed to sensible. These are the thoughts that lead, ultimately, to the unwelcome consequences. If we ignore them, does Plato give expression to other thoughts that suggest a more acceptable theory? It is arguable that he does. In the *Meno,* he expresses the view that all the virtues "have some common character which makes them virtues"[27]; and there is a passage in *Parmenides*[28] that could be quoted in support of this being the thought that lies behind the theory of Forms. Parmenides asks: "How do you feel about this? I imagine your ground for believing in a single form in each case is this. When it seems that a number of things are large, there seems, I suppose, to be a certain single character which is the same when you look at them all; hence you think that largeness is a single thing." And Socrates replies: "True."

But if belief in Plato's theory of Forms is belief that "largeness is a single thing," and if this means no more than that large things all have the same character (they are all large), then it is hard to understand, first, why it should be called a theory rather than a platitude, and, second, why Plato should say that largeness exists apart from large things. Aristotle, who omitted all reference to opposites being confounded in sensible things from his account of Plato's theory, had to think of some other ground for Plato holding that the character, or 'universal' as Aristotle called it, exists apart. He found it in an aspect of Plato's theory that he himself accepted, the notion that definitions are eternally true. According to Aristotle, Plato held that the eternally true definition must be a definition of something that exists apart because it "could not be a definition of any sensible thing, as they were always changing."[29] It was to solving the problem of how the definition can be eternally true and yet refer to perishable individual things, and not to Plato's problem about the nature of the 'receptacle', that Aristotle turned his attention. (See "Aristotle's Reaction to Plato," below).

TELEOLOGY IN PLATO'S THEORY OF FORMS

In the *Republic,* books VI and VII, Plato advances the theory that there is one supreme Form, the Form of the Good. He gives it a role in the apprehension of the other Forms comparable to that of the sun in the apprehension of the visible things. It "gives their truth to the objects of knowledge and the power of knowing to the knower" and so is "the cause of knowledge, and of truth in so far as known."[30] Although Plato calls it an idea (i.e., a Form), it is not like other Forms. Just as "the sun not only furnishes to visibles the power of visibility but also provides for their generation and growth and nurture though it is not itself generation," so "the objects of knowledge not only receive from the presence of the good their being known, but their very existence and essence is derived to them from it, though the good itself is not essence but still transcends essence in dignity and surpassing power."[31] The ultimate aim of the philosopher is to attain the apprehension of this supreme reality. When the philosopher "attempts through discourse or reason and apart from all perceptions of sense to find his way to the very essence of each thing and does not desist till he apprehends by thought itself the nature of the good in itself, he arrives at the limit of the intelligible."[32]

This can be viewed as the way that occurred to Plato whereby his theory of Forms could be developed so as to gratify Socrates' taste for explanation in terms of what is best for anything, the end it *ought* to have. In the *Phaedo,* Socrates describes the theory of Forms as a "makeshift approach to the problem of causation."[33] It is makeshift because it is not teleological. It ceases to be makeshift when Plato, in the *Republic,* develops the theory by subordinating the individual Forms to the Form of the Good. In virtue of this development of the theory, the individual Forms are revealed as covertly teleological, though the revelation is only for the most advanced philosophers, being "at the limit of the intelligible."

Plato describes Socrates' thoughts on causation as follows. As a youth, Socrates had "an extraordinary passion for that branch of learning which is called natural science."[34] He was constantly puzzling over such questions as whether it is when heat and cold produce fermentation that living creatures are bred.[35] But it was only when he heard someone reading from a book by Anaxagoras, asserting that it is mind that produces order and is the cause of everything, that he felt he had found an authority on causation after his own heart. If mind is the cause of everything, then mind "arranges each individual thing in the way that is best for it."[36] And in that case there is "only one thing for a man to consider, with regard both to himself and to anything else, namely the best and highest good."[37]

What this means with regard to himself is clear. In the case of his sitting there, submitting to whatever penalty Athens orders, the one thing to be considered is that he thinks it more right and honorable to do so than to run away. He scorns any supposed explanation in terms of his body being composed of bones and sinews, and the sinews contracting and relaxing, so that his limbs can bend, so that he can be seated. "Fancy being unable to distinguish between the cause of a thing and the condition without which it could not be a cause!"[38]

But in the case of such things as the earth keeping its place in the heavens, it is not clear what the teleological explanation is. Most people neither look for, nor believe in, "a power which keeps things disposed at any given moment in the best possible way."[39] And Socrates himself has to admit defeat: "For my part, I should be delighted to learn about the workings of such a cause from anyone, but since I have been denied knowledge of it, and have been unable either to discover it myself or to learn about it from another, I have worked out my own makeshift approach to the problem of causation."[40]

PLATO'S USE OF THE TERM 'MIND'

I have, so far, been answering the question "What is the theory, or what are the theories, that provide the context for Plato's use of the term 'mind'?" The question that naturally follows an answer to it is: "So how does Plato use the term mind?" The answer is that he uses it in two different ways.

First, Plato uses the term 'mind' in such a way that to have mind is to have knowledge, knowledge being of what is eternal. In this use of the term, "mind is the attribute of the gods and of very few men."[41] Moreover, it is far easier for a disembodied soul to have it, than an embodied one. The philosopher, approaching death, is consoled with the reflection that "if we are ever to have pure knowledge of anything, we must get rid of the body and contemplate things by themselves with the soul by itself. . . . [T]he wisdom which we desire and upon which we profess to have set our hearts will be attainable only when we are dead, and not in our lifetime."[42]

Secondly, Plato uses the term 'mind' for that which supposedly "sets everything in order and arranges each individual thing in the way that is best for it."[43]

If there is a connection between the two uses, it is that the highest knowledge is knowledge of the Form of the Good.

ARISTOTLE'S REACTION TO PLATO

Let us recall what Plato's problem was. It was that "perception no more manifests one thing than its contrary." The great and the small are confounded in the finger. From the point of view of eternity, even the finger is confounded with the non-finger. Nothing is unconfoundedly manifested in the sensible world. So, knowledge being of eternal truths, if we are to know what the great is, or what a finger is, we must employ some mode of contemplation other than sensation, namely intelligence. There must be the opposites in themselves, for us to know the nature of. But from birth, our awareness of things has been by sensation. And so on. That was Plato's problem.

Aristotle misrepresented Plato's problem by omitting all reference to opposites being confounded in sensible things. He represented it as the problem that the eternally true definition "could not be a definition of any sensible thing, as they were always changing." His solution to this problem involved a doctrine of primary and secondary substance.[44] Individual sensible things, such as an individual person or horse, are the primary substances that go to make up the world. But there are also *kinds* of individuals. More-over, there are different sorts of kinds. Some kinds are natural kinds. In saying of an individual that she is a human, I am referring her to a natural kind. Human is the species to which she belongs. I am not referring her to a natural kind if I say she is a good runner. *Runner* is not a species. The distinction between natural and nonnatural kinds is in terms of the facts of generation. The offspring of a person who is a good runner is necessarily a person but not necessarily a good runner. Similarly with plant life. If you planted a bed and the rotting wood acquired the power to send up a shoot it would not be a little bed that came up, but a little tree of the same kind as that from which you got the wood. These natural kinds, Aristotle says, are substance in a secondary sense. What are 'always changing' are individual sensible things. What are definable, with eternally true definitions, are the natural kinds to which they belong.

Aristotle's use of the word 'form' can be explained in terms of the bed. What was planted was made of wood. That was its 'matter'. And it had the form, bed, since that was the kind of thing made out of the wood, on this occasion.

This being what is meant by the 'form' of an object, there is not room for Plato's problem about a receptacle. Aristotle's 'forms' are not Platonic 'Forms' that need to be copied onto a receptacle that "in some mysterious way partakes of the intelligible." Sensible things, made of such-and-such a matter and with such-and-such a form, occupy a place; but there is no call for place to "partake of the intelligible" in some mysterious way. By taking individual sensible things to be substances, Aristotle solved his version of Plato's problem, while ignoring Plato's own version.

ARISTOTLE'S USE OF THE TERM 'MIND'

Aristotle uses the notions of form and matter, notions that he develops in his reaction to Plato, in his accounts of sense perception and mind. In sense perception, the sense or sense organ,[45] receives the sensible form without the matter. When someone puts his hand in hot water, for example, his hand becomes hot, but it does not become water. Only the sensible form, the quality of heat, is taken in. The matter of the sense organ is such that it can take in only certain forms. For example, the eye can take in colors, but not sounds.

Mind, on the other hand, is not limited in its objects, and so cannot itself be a combination of matter and form. Before it thinks, it is not actually any real thing; but potentially it is "whatever is thinkable."[46]

This way of putting it rather suggests that Artistotle equates thinking with forms being in the mind. But he distinguishes between mind as passive and mind as active and says that although mind as passive "is what it is by virtue of becoming all things," mind as active "is what it is by virtue of making all things."[47] The only clue he gives to his meaning is metaphorical. Active mind "is a sort of positive state like light; for in a sense light makes potential colours into actual colours." Mind as active is immortal and eternal. We cannot remember its former activity because mind as passive is destructible.

These are very puzzling sayings. Some of them are reminiscent of Plato. Perhaps they are puzzling to us because our philosophical position is one in which knowledge is the possession of individuals. For Aristotle there is knowledge in the individual, but also knowledge in the universe; and he seems to think of the former as being, in some respect, a share of the latter. We partake of the eternal and divine (and nonindividual) to the extent that we have knowledge.

ARISTOTLE'S TELEOLOGY, AND SCIENCE AS THE INTUITION OF ESSENCES

If what Aristotle says about the knowing mind is reminiscent of Plato, so is what he says about the cause of order in things. Like the Platonic Socrates, Aristotle admired Anaxagoras. When Anaxagoras said that "reason was present—as in animals, so throughout nature—as the cause of order and of all arrangement," Aristotle said, "he seemed like a sober man in contrast with the random talk of his predecessors."[48] But Aristotle's way of making teleology supreme was not Plato's. The Platonic Socrates had drawn the line at a direct teleological explanation of such things as the earth keeping its place in the heavens and had resorted to his "makeshift approach," the theory of Forms. It was only through the Forms being subordinated to the Form of the Good that teleology came back into the picture. But Aristotle looked for direct teleological explanations even in astronomy: "The fact is that we are inclined to think of the stars as mere bodies or units, occurring in a certain order but completely lifeless; whereas we ought to think of them as partaking of life and initiative. Once we do this, the events will no longer seem surprising."[49]

But teleological causation, Aristotle holds, is most evident among those things that are subject to generation: "The causes concerned in the generation of the works of nature are, as we see, more than one. There is the final cause and there is the motor cause. Now we must decide which of these two causes comes first, which second. Plainly, however, that cause is the first which we call the final one. For this is the Reason, and the Reason forms the starting-point, alike in the works of art and in works of nature."[50]

In the case of a work of nature such as an acorn, what Aristotle calls 'the Reason' is its having an end, an oak tree, towards which it develops in accord with its nature as a member of the species, oak. That is the acorn's specific end. But Aristotle had, also, a conception of a general end for all things: all things strive to partake in the eternal and divine.[51] How far they can achieve this end depends on their nature. A plant, which possesses the power of reproduction but not that of thinking, tries to achieve the end of partaking in what is eternal and divine in the only way open to it, namely, by continuing its existence in something of its own kind.

Aristotle thinks of natural science as being, like mathematics, demonstrative. "We suppose ourselves to possess unqualified scientific knowledge of a thing, as opposed to knowing it in the accidental way in which the sophist knows, when we think that we know the cause on which the fact depends, as the cause of that fact and of no other, and, further, that the fact could not be other than it is."[52] Such demonstration calls for premises of a certain character. "Assuming then that my thesis as to the nature of scientific knowing is correct, the premises of demonstrated knowledge must be true, primary, immediate, better-known than and prior to the conclusion, which is further related to them as effect to cause. Unless these conditions are satisfied, the basic truths will not be 'appropriate' to the conclusion."[53] Furthermore, "since the object of pure scientific knowledge cannot be other than it is, the truth obtained by demonstrative knowledge will be necessary. And since demonstrative knowledge is only present when we have a demonstration, it follows that demonstration is an inference from necessary premises."[54]

In the case of the biological sciences, the 'necessary premisses', or 'basic truths', will be about the 'essences' of the various natural kinds. In some respects, Aristotle's 'essences' are like Plato's 'Forms'. They are intelligible in the sense of having definitions, and the definitions are real, not nominal. Knowledge of them cannot itself be by demonstration. That would mean an infinite regress.[55] How, then, is such knowledge to be attained? Plato had said that knowledge of the Forms is recollection of what was known before birth. Aristotle rejects this as a solution of his problem.[56] The essences of the natural kinds are known by intellectual intuition, but it is an intuition that is somehow developed from sense perception. Precisely how this happens is not made clear. Aristotle's account is in terms of a simile: "It is like a rout in battle stopped by first one man making a stand and then another, until the original formation has been restored."[57] But it is not clear how the simile is to be interpreted.

DESCARTES'S MATHEMATIZATION OF NATURE

In the seventeenth century, the Aristotelian conception of science was rejected by, among others, Galileo and Descartes.

In place of the Aristotelian scientific methodology, based on there being things of fixed natural kinds whose changes were to be explained teleologically in terms of inbuilt ends, Galileo advocated a new methodology in which only what Aristotle called 'local motion' (changes in the place of things over time) counts for explanatory purposes, and the manner of such motion is described in exclusively mathematical terms. This revolution in scientific methodology meant a fundamental reassessment of our position vis-á-vis the world as an object of knowledge. Instead of being privileged to have an intellectual insight into the essences of things of various natural kinds, in a world that is much as it appears to ordinary sense perception, we now have to rely on our ability to detect regularities in the movements of atoms of matter in a world that is different from that which appears to sense perception in that it really possesses only those features that are amenable to mathematical treatment.

Galileo's publications of greatest philosophical interest are *The Assayer* (1623), in which he ridicules the Aristotelian philosophy and expounds the new scientific method, including a distinction between primary and secondary qualities; and the *Dialogue Concerning the Two Chief World Systems— Ptolemaic and Copernican* (1632). When it was realized that the *Dialogue* was in fact a defense of the Copernican system, Galileo was prosecuted for heresy and spent the last eight years of his life under house arrest.

Despite the philosophical interest of his works, Galileo was not primarily a philosopher. He would have rejected, as not answerable by the scientist as such, the question why the book of nature is, as he put it, "written in the mathematical language." It was enough that God had chosen so to write it. Descartes, on the other hand, was primarily a philosopher, and he was keen to justify the new scientific methodology with a new, non-Aristotelian physics. At the same time he did not want to suffer Galileo's fate. As a result it is not immediately obvious to an uninformed reader of, say, Descartes's *Meditations,* how different his principles are from those of Aristotle. To Marin Mersenne, the compiler of the *Objections to the Meditations,* he wrote on 28 January 1641: "I may tell you, between ourselves, that these six *Meditations* contain all the foundations of my *Physics.* But please do not tell people, for that might make it harder for supporters of Aristotle to approve them. I hope that readers will gradually get used to my principles, and recognize their truth, before they notice that they destroy the principles of Aristotle."[58]

In place of Aristotle's hypothesis that there are sensible things of a multitude of different natural kinds, each having its own substantial form, Descartes advanced the hypothesis that the things we apprehend as sensible really differ in only a single respect, namely in respect of their spatial extension. What is more, even to talk of a bodily thing having an extension is incorrect, for "space or internal place and the corporeal substance which is contained in it are not different otherwise than in the mode in which they are conceived by us."[59] This hypothesis, taken in conjunction with the assumption that physical space is Euclidean, and with analytical or coordinate geometry (which shows how spatial relations can be expressed numerically), constituted Descartes's physics a mathematization of nature. The Pythagoreans, finding there to be a numerical basis for musical concordances, wished to find a numerical basis for all natural phenomena. Descartes's physics is a gratification of just such a wish. What he called "the objection of objections" to his principles was that "the mathematical extension, which I take as the basal principle of my Physics, is nothing but my thought, and that it has and can have no subsistence outside of my mind, being merely an abstraction that I form from a physical body."[60] About this objection, Descartes remarked, philosophically: "I have something substantial wherewith to console myself, inasmuch as my critics here conjoin my Physics with pure Mathematics, which it is my deepest wish my Physics should resemble."[61] In short, the book of nature is written in the mathematical language because extension is the essence of matter, and the extension that is the essence of matter is the extension of pure mathematics. Incidentally, the contrast with Plato's conception of space could hardly be greater. Plato had said that the receptacle for the Forms, space, "is apprehended, when all sense is absent, by a kind of spurious reason, and is hardly real." By being mathematized, space had changed from being "apprehended by a kind of spurious reason" to being that of which our ideas are as clear and distinct as our ideas of anything.

It is worth noting that in one respect, Descartes's conception of science is very like Aristotle's. Aristotle said the proper object of unqualified scientific knowledge is something that cannot be other than it is. In a letter to Mersenne (11 March 1640), Descartes remarked: "I would think I knew nothing in Physics if I could only say how things could be, without proving that they could not be otherwise." But unlike Aristotle, he was able to add: "This is perfectly possible once one has reduced everything to laws of mathematics."

DESCARTES'S JUSTIFICATION OF A CRITERION OF TRUTH: THE COGITO

A major problem for Descartes was that of how we can know that the only properties things possess are mathematical ones. What is the criterion for a true judgment in such matters, and what is the justification for our accepting it as a criterion? The issue of a criterion had been prominent in the philosophy of the Stoics and had been discussed by Sextus Empiricus in his *Outlines of Pyrrhonism* (early third century). The writings of Sextus were translated into Latin in the sixteenth century and influenced Montaigne, whose principal philosophical work, *Apology for Raimond Sebond,* was published in a collection of essays in 1588. One of Montaigne's main contentions was that of scepticism about the possibility of knowledge in general. Possibly influenced by Montaigne, Descartes, in his *Meditations,* presented his philosophy in the context of an answer to scepticism about our having a criterion for judging what is true, rather than as an alternative physics to that of Aristotle. When he does say something that is flatly against Aristotelianism, such as that "the species of cause termed final finds no useful employment in physical things," he is careful to give, as his reason for saying it, something with which the ecclesiastics could hardly disagree—namely, that "the nature of God is ... immense, incomprehensible, and infinite."[62]

Descartes's chosen criterion of what can safely be accepted as true was that it should be clearly and distinctly perceived. There was a long tradition of the truths of mathematics being regarded as clearly and distinctly perceived, but also a tradition, nearly as long, of challenging the choice of any criterion. Descartes saw his problem as being that of meeting this challenge. He could meet it, he thought, by finding some proposition that no one could possibly doubt and about which people could see that the only reason why they could not doubt it was that they perceived it clearly and distinctly.[63] What proposition he found to fill this crucial role would be most unlikely to occur to anyone whose only knowledge of Descartes was his mathematization of nature. It has nothing whatsoever to do with either mathematics or physical things. It is, as will be well known to all readers of this paper, the proposition "I think, therefore I am."[64] Perhaps Descartes got it from St. Augustine,[65] but the use to which he put it, as a justification for using clear and distinct perception as a criterion of truth, was his own.

Descartes's choice of this proposition, together with an argument based on what can be and what cannot be doubted, led to his holding that the mind is a substance distinct from the body, the essence of the mind-substance being that it thinks and the essence of the body-substance being that it is extended.

THE WAY OF IDEAS: MALEBRANCHE, DESCARTES, AND LOCKE

The remark that the essence of the mind is that it thinks invites the question, "And what is thinking?" Descartes uses the term very widely. Thought, he says, "is a word that covers everything that exists in us in such a way that we are immediately conscious of it."[66] For example, it covers not only understanding but also sensing.[67] Another term Descartes uses is 'idea'. Idea, he says, "is a word by which I understand the form of any thought, that form by the immediate awareness of which I am conscious of that said thought."[68] Ideas, accordingly, come into his accounts both of understanding and of sense perception. He cannot say anything, understanding what he says, "without that very fact making it certain that I possess the idea of that which these words signify."[69] And he cannot perceive anything without envisaging the appropriate ideas—ideas of pain, color, sound and the like. They are envisaged, he says, on the occasion of certain corporeal movements, but they have no likeness to the corporeal movements.[70]

It is natural to ask whether Descartes's 'ideas' are better understood as descendants of Plato's 'Forms', those "self-existent ideas unperceived by sense, and apprehended only by the mind," or of the 'forms' that Aristotle supposed the sense organ to take on when there is sense perception. One of Malebranche's uses of the term 'idea' was clearly Platonic. Malebranche greatly admired St. Augustine, and in the Christian Neoplatonism of Augustine, Plato's Forms had become archetypal ideas in the mind of God.[71] Malebranche held that human minds have their 'place' in God's mind, and so share in His ideas. (This was the doctrine of 'seeing all things in God' that Berkeley found incomprehensible.)[72] Malebranche was a contemporary of Descartes. One might reasonably expect contemporaries to mean the same when they use a term in a specialist sense.

But to draw the conclusion that Descartes's 'ideas' are better understood as descendants of Plato's 'Forms' than of Aristotle's 'forms' is to ignore a significant feature of Descartes's 'ideas'. He conceived of ideas as having what he called "objective reality."[73] An idea's objective reality corresponds to the "actual reality" of whatever the idea is of. It is an idea's being *of* something that distinguishes it from a Platonic Form. Plato's Forms are not thoughts of things.[74] But are Aristotle's forms, in so far as they exist in the mind, of things? I am not sure. As I said earlier, I find Aristotle's remarks on this subject very puzzling. Perhaps it would be safer to say that Descartes's 'ideas' are descendants of Aquinas's 'forms', and leave it to others to argue about whether Aquinas correctly understood Aristotle. Anthony Kenny says that "according to Aquinas, when I think of redness, what makes my thought be a thought of redness is the form of redness."[75] If he is right about Aquinas, and if I am right about Descartes, Descartes is like Aquinas in thinking of ideas as being essentially of, or about, things. To use the technical term, they are characterized by 'intentionality'.

Before moving on to Locke, mention must be made of another meaning that Malebranche gave to the term 'idea'. He argued that the mind cannot perceive objects external to it (at a distance from it) by themselves, since they are not present to it; and he concluded that there must be an intermediary object that *is* present to it: "our mind's immediate object when it sees the sun, for example, is not the sun, but something that is intimately joined to our soul, and this is what I call an *idea.*"[76] He thought that everyone would agree with him that "we do not perceive objects external to us by themselves,"[77] but, of course, not everyone did agree. Antoine Arnauld, for example, accused him of trading on the equivocality of the word 'presence'. It does not follow, Arnauld said, from something's not having 'local presence' (i.e., spatial presence) that it does not have 'objective presence' (i.e., presence as an object of consciousness).[78]

Just how Locke conceived of 'ideas' in the *Essay* is not clear. Are they descendants of Plato's Forms or of Aristotle's forms, or are they essentially representative of material things (needed either because material things are not 'present' or because material things do not really have the qualities we sense them as having)? If when Locke wrote the *Essay* he had already had the thoughts that went into his *Examination of Malebranche's Doctrine,* then the first possibility can be ruled out. The second possibility seems more plausible. Locke calls ideas "materials of thinking,"[79] which suggests that he thinks of them as being of, or about, things. But he also writes as if ideas are caused in us as pain is caused by something indigestible entering the stomach.[80] And it is arguable that pain is not of, or about, something. It is, we might say, a sensation, not a concept. Perhaps Locke did not mean that ideas *are* sensations, but that they *come from* sensations. He calls sensation the "source of most of the ideas we have."[81] I have a sensation of redness on looking at red things, and this is the source of my idea of redness. But what is 'a sensation of redness'? Is it a feeling I get when my eyes are bloodshot, or is it my perceiving something as red? If the former, then the sensation of redness could arise from looking at black and white television too long, and has nothing to do with things, other than eyes, being red.[82] If the latter, then to have the sensation I must already have the concept, so the sensation could not be the source of the concept.

THE INVISIBILITY AND SAMENESS OF 'IDEAS'

Descartes defines 'thought' as "everything that exists in us in such a way that we are immediately conscious of it."[83] The 'us' and the 'we' in this definition refer to the individual person. One person cannot be immediately conscious of another person's thoughts. As Locke put it, "man, though he have great variety of thoughts, and such from which others as well as himself might receive profit and delight, yet they are all within his own breast, invisible and hidden from others, nor can of themselves be made to appear."[84] To make them appear, Locke continues, "it was necessary that man should find out some external sensible signs, whereof those invisible ideas, which his thoughts are made up of, might be made known to others."[85] The 'external sensible signs' are words. Words stand for "the ideas in the mind of him that uses them," and the end of speech is that a speaker's words 'may make known his ideas to the hearer.'[86]

But there is a problem. In the ordinary, nontechnical use of the word 'idea', it makes sense to talk of two people having, or not having, the same idea of something: for example, the same idea of democracy or the same idea of discipline. If two people come from very different backgrounds, they may have very different ideas. Locke acknowledges this. He says such things as that "unless a man's words excite the same ideas in the hearer which he makes them stand for in speaking, he does not speak intelligibly."[87] "The chief end of language in communication being to be understood, words serve not well for that end . . . when any word does not excite in the hearer the same idea which it stands for in the mind of the speaker."[88] This is a truism in the ordinary use of 'idea', but what does it mean when the word 'idea' is used for something produced in someone in the way in which pain is produced in the stomach by indigestible food?

The solution, of course, is that 'the same idea' in Locke's remarks, means 'similar ideas'. This, however, invites a further question. If a person's ideas are invisible to everyone but himself, how can two people's ideas be known to be similar?

Locke does not answer this question directly, but an answer can be abstracted from what he says about ideas not being false[89], and being real[90]. One man could not know another man's ideas to be similar to his own because "one man's mind could not pass into another man's body" to perceive the appearances produced by the other man's sense organs. But it does not matter if the ideas themselves are not similar. All that matters is that each man's ideas should "have a conformity with the real being and existence of things." In the case of simple ideas, such as the ideas of whiteness, coldness and pain, this is guaranteed by the ideas being produced by the things that have 'real being and existence'. In other words, I can speak intelligibly to you, using the word 'white', because you have an idea that, even if it is what I would call an idea of blackness if I could perceive it, is like mine in being produced by the same things, such as snow, these things having 'real being and existence'.

The phrase 'real being and existence' has a metaphysical flavor. What theory lies behind it? The complete sentence is: "By *real ideas,* I mean such as have a foundation in nature; such as have a conformity with the real being and existence of things, or with their archetypes." The word 'archetypes' is a clue. Plato's Forms were traditionally referred to as 'archetypes'. Is there some point of resemblance between Locke and Plato?

If there is, it is likely to be of a very abstract nature. In philosophy, the most abstract ideas (in the ordinary senses of 'abstract' and 'idea') concern what may broadly be termed 'the relation of thought and reality'. Does Locke have a theory of the relation of thought and reality that is, despite the differences between them, like Plato's theory? Plato held that a word, such as 'large', is used correctly if it is used in conformity with the real definition of largeness. Correctness is not just a matter of convention and agreement, a nominal definition. There is an intelligible Form for our thought to conform to. In such conformity lies the harmony of thought and reality.

It seems to me that this very abstract idea about the harmony of thought and reality is shared by Locke, the difference being that Locke holds an empiricist version of the theory whereas Plato, of course, held a rationalist version. Whereas the extralinguistic realities for Plato are intelligible Forms, for Locke they are things with powers to produce ideas, or sensations, of whiteness, coldness, pain, and so on, in us.

Some support for the notion that Locke actually had Plato in mind in what he said about the reality of ideas is provided by the following passage:

> I would not here be thought to forget, much less to deny, that nature, in the production of things, makes several of them alike: there is nothing more obvious, especially in the races of animals, and all things propagated by seed. But yet I think we may say the *sorting* of them under names *is the workmanship of the understanding, taking occasion, from the similitude* it observes amongst them, to make abstract general ideas, and set them up in the mind, with names annexed to them, as patterns or forms (for in that sense the word form has a very proper signification), to which, as particular things existing are found to agree, so they come to be of that species, have that denomination, or are put into that *classis*.[91]

The phrase in parenthesis is, I take it, Lock's way of implying that his version of thought/reality realism is vastly to be preferred to Plato's version.

The proposition 'Nature makes things alike' may be given a quite innocuous, nontheoretical interpretation. Nature makes many white things and hence there are many things that resemble one another in being white. Or it may be interpreted as a realist theory that another philosopher might wish to oppose. One way of opposing it is to go to the opposite extreme, as John Stuart Mill did. He said that "resemblance is evidently a feeling; a state of consciousness of the observer."[92] The trouble with this way of opposing Lockean realism is that it invites the objection that one person's feelings are as good as another. Feelings cannot be said to be correct or incorrect. On the other hand, a person's use of the word 'white' can be said to be correct or incorrect. ("What you call 'white men' are really various shades of pink.") Locke and Mill, between them, open the way for a radical rethink of the thought/reality question, one that neither makes mind a mirror of reality, nor reality a mirror of mind.

REJECTING LOCKE'S WAY OF IDEAS, AND EMPIRICISM, BUT RETAINING REALISM

Locke, like Hobbes,[93] writes as if there are three things: mental propositions, unspoken verbal propositions, and spoken verbal propositions.[94] He holds (1) that verbal propositions are meaningful in virtue of there being mental propositions; (2) that the elements of mental propositions are ideas; (3) that some ideas, at least, are real, meaning that they "have a conformity with the real being and existence of things, or with their archetypes"; and (4) that simple ideas, such as those of whiteness and coldness, are real, or have a "steady correspondence" with the distinct constitutions of real beings, such as snow, because "they are constantly produced by them."

It is possible for a philosopher not to follow Locke's way of ideas, and not to be an empiricist, and yet to hold some form of metaphysical language-reality realism. Plato is an example of such a philosopher. But we do not have to go back to ancient Greek philosophy for an example. Wittgenstein's *Tractatus Logico-Philosophicus* combines a rejection of the notion that thinking is possible without language[95] with acceptance of the realist doctrine that, besides the reality that justifies us in saying something (that is, what we say is true), there is a reality that justifies the very language in which we say it.[96] Locke explained the harmony of language and reality causally: ideas, which give language meaning, are produced by the constitutions of real beings. This was his empiricism. Unlike Russell, whose logical atomism is in the tradition of Locke, Hume, and Mill, Wittgenstein did not propound his realist philosophy of language in the interests of empiricism. Rather, he was struck with the thoughts that for a proposition to say something, it must be "a picture of reality" (were it not a picture, then one would not be able to understand a proposition that one had not previously encountered); and that a proposition, being a picture, must have a sense that is definite. What is pictured cannot be indefinite. It is this that generates the demand for the 'simple objects' of the *Tractatus*.[97] Wittgenstein even says things, such as that the simple objects constitute the substance of the world, substance being "the fixed, the existent," as opposed to "the changing, the variable" configurations of simple objects,[98] which suggests that his nonempiricist logical atomism might interestingly be compared, and contrasted, with Plato's theory of Forms.

INTELLIGIBILITY WITHOUT REALISM, AND IMPLICATIONS FOR THE CONCEPT OF MIND

Locke and the later Wittgenstein agree in holding that what are intelligible (or, occasionally, unintelligible) are the things other people say, whereas Plato held that what are intelligible are primarily things in the realm of the eternally existent: the objects of mathematics and the Forms. But Locke and the later Wittgenstein disagree about the conditions of the intelligibility of the things other people say.

Locke analyzes intelligibility in terms of having ideas, things that are, as he puts it, "invisible" to other people. Because ideas are invisible to others, we have to use signs for them—words. But there is no natural connection between words and ideas. We make words stand for ideas "by a perfectly arbitrary imposition."[99] Ultimately, the only reasons we have for thinking that our hearers know what we mean are the convictions (a) that our hearers' ideas, no matter what they may be like in themselves, do, like our own, correspond to the reality of the things that produced them; and (b) that there is a resemblance *in nature* (i.e., not just in our apprehension of nature) between the things that produced our hearers' ideas and the things that produced our own. These convictions are a matter of faith, faith that God would not have ordained otherwise. Like some other seventeenth-century philosophers, Locke habitually invoked God when he had no other explanation for something.[100]

In his later philosophy, Wittgenstein, like Locke, uses the term 'arbitrary'. He says that the rules of grammar are arbitrary. But for Wittgenstein, unlike for Locke, the arbitrariness is not rendered unimportant by our conviction of the truth of language/reality realism. On the contray, the remark that the rules of grammar are arbitrary is *directed against* the possibility of a realist justification, a justification "constructed on the model of justifying a sentence by pointing to what verifies it."[101] For the later Wittgenstein, unlike for Locke and the earlier Wittgenstein, intelligibility does not require there to be a reality other than that which consists in what we say being true.

What does it require? Understanding Wittgenstein's answer to this question involves making a distinction that Locke did not make, between a sensation and a concept. Although the word 'concept' was used in the seventeenth century in something approaching its modern meaning, it was not, to the best of my knowledge, used by Locke. He may even be said not to have had the concept of concept. He used the terms 'sensation', 'idea', and 'conception', but almost interchangeably. Ideas of sickness and pain are sensations of sickness and pain,[102] and conceptions are either ideas[103] or various ideas collected into complex ones.[104] Locke does not distinguish between a conception of pain and a sensation of pain as Wittgenstein distinguishes between the concept of pain and a sensation of pain.

For someone who does *not* distinguish between concepts and sensations, the answer to such a question as "How does a person learn the meaning of the word pain?" has to be something like "He has a sensation of pain, and names it pain." For someone who *does* distinguish between concepts and sensations, the way is open for thinking of acquiring a concept as acquiring a capacity to use a word as the rest of us use it. The question "How does a person learn the meaning of the word pain?" can then be answered as Wittgenstein answers it. He writes: "Here is one possibility: words are connected with the primitive, the natural, expressions of the sensation and used in their place. A child has hurt himself and he cries; and then adults talk to him and teach him exclamations and, later, sentences. They teach the child new pain-behaviour.[105] Roughly, acquiring linguistic pain behavior is acquiring the concept of pain.

So what does acquiring the concept require? It requires that the person who is to acquire the concept share with the teachers what Wittgenstein calls a "form of life"—in this case, the form of life that consists in expressing pains by crying and reacting in certain ways to people who cry. There must be this agreement in form of life for the word 'pain' to have the common meaning it has. The bodily sensation of pain may be said to be in a person's mind, but "the concept of pain is characterized by its particular function in our life."[106] The essential thing about *the mind* may be said to be that it is *private* (at least in the sense that whereas the third-person psychological proposition 'He is in pain' is to be verified by observation, the first-person one 'I am in pain' is not)[107]; but the *concept of mind* is characterized by its function in our *public* life. Instead of mutual intelligibility being ultimately dependent on God, as with Locke, it is dependent on our sharing the same form of life. For someone who has come to see this, the concept of mind has changed. It has changed because the context has changed. The context has changed from being that of metaphysics and theology to being that of natural history.

MIND AND MECHANISM IN PSYCHOLOGY

The thesis of this paper has been that the meaning of the term 'mind' is assignable only in the context of a theory. I have conducted a selective survey of the meanings philosophers have assigned to the term from Plato to Wittgenstein. In conclusion, I shall say something about the recent reintroduction of the term in psychology. But before doing so, I need to give a brief outline of the historical context, beginning with Locke's introduction of the expression 'the association of ideas'.

The association of ideas, in the philosophy of Locke, who was the first to use the expression, is a connection of ideas that is "wholly owing to chance and circumstance."[108] Locke contrasted ideas associated in this way with those that have "a natural correspondence and connection with one another." It is the task of our reason to trace natural connections. But unnatural ones can be understood only as a chance product of our physiology: "Custom settles habits of thinking in the understanding, as well as of determining in the will, and of motions in the body: all which seem to be but trains of motion in the animal spirits, which, once set a-going, continue in the same steps they have been used to."[109]

Locke neither thought it worthwhile to list the ways in which ideas come to be associated, nor gave the association of ideas any useful role to play in how everyone's mind works. In these respects, Hume is in sharp contrast with Locke. Hume lists three principles of association: contiguity, resemblance (which Locke regarded as a natural connection, since resemblance of ideas is the result of nature making things alike), and causation. Whereas Locke disparaged the association of ideas as a chance affair and concentrated on how *dissimilar* associations in different people make the opinions, reasonings, and actions of other people seem odd and extravagant,

Hume contrasted ideas being associated in accordance with universal principles with their being joined by chance, and used the universality of the principles of association to explain how it is that different people make *similar* associations. He was particularly concerned with simple ideas being associated to form complex ones. It is because, in general, different people associate the same simple ideas to form the same complex ones that "languages so nearly correspond to each other." Thus, whereas the association of ideas is an uncontroversial afterthought in Locke's philosophy, in Hume's it is a central tenet in the controversial theory that simple ideas, othewise "entirely loose and unconnected," are combined to form complex ones. Hume likened the association of ideas in his account of the workings of the mind to Newton's gravitational attraction in his account of the workings of the physical world: "here is a kind of ATTRACTION, which in the mental world will be found to have as extraordinary effects as in the natural."[110]

Hume had recourse to physiology only to explain what he regarded as mistakes in the association of ideas. His theory was that when the mind desires to survey a particular idea, it dispatches the animal spirits into that region of the brain in which the idea is located, so as to excite it; but the animal spirits naturally wobble about a bit and may fall into an adjacent trace, thus exciting some other idea than the one intended.

Unlike Hume, David Hartley in his *Observations on Man, His Frame, His Duty and His Expectations* developed a systematic psychophysiology in which the association of ideas in the mind was presented as the effect of vibrations in the nervous system. He was no less hopeful than Hume about the usefulness of the doctrine. James Mill, in *The Analysis of the Human Mind,* undertook the task of pursuing and perfecting the doctrine. But John Stuart Mill abandoned any hope of analysis, holding the properties of mental compounds not to be deducible from the properties of the alleged sensory elements.

The severest philosophical criticism of associationism in the nineteenth century was that of F. H. Bradley. He accepted as a psychological fact the association of ideas in the ordinary, nontechnical sense of 'idea'; but he dismissed the notion, common to Hume, Hartley, and James Mill, that 'simple ideas' can be associated. A simple idea "exists only for a moment." The notion that it can recur, as is implied in the doctrine that simple ideas can be associated to form complex ones, should be repudiated, he said, as one of the "touching beliefs of a pious legend."[111] But it was the seemingly unresolvable dispute among psychologists themselves—for example, about whether there is imageless thought—that led to disenchantment with introspectionist psychology. Observations of animal behavior, begun in the late nineteenth century to test Darwin's theory of the continuity between animals and humans, were yielding results on which investigators could agree. Some of the theories could be tested under laboratory conditions. There seemed to be a strong case for using the same observational methods in the study of humans as had proved fruitful in the study of animals.

Oddly enough, it was Descartes who paved the way for a methodological-ly different sort of psychology from that of the introspectionists. He had supposed there to be two quite different ways in which bodily movements might be caused. First, 'animal spirits' reaching the brain through sensory channels may automatically be 'reflected' into motor channels, producing what we call 'involuntary' movements. Second, the soul, by willing, can make the part of the brain with which it is united move in the way requisite for producing the bodily movement aimed at in the volition. Such a move-ment is said to be 'voluntary'.

This 'reflex' explanation of involuntary movements was taken a stage further by Pavlov, who found that digestive secretions take place in a dog not only in response to food, but also in response to what he called a 'psychic stimulus' such as the sound of the rattling of dishes in the preparation of food.

This suggested to behaviorist psychologists an analogue of the associa-tion of ideas in introspectionist psychology. Instead of acquired associations of ideas, there are acquired associations of physical stimuli and behavioral responses. The implication was obvious. If Descartes could be shown to be wrong about some movements having a mental cause, then the new S-R (stimulus-response) associationism would provide just what was needed to put psychology on an equal footing with even the most deterministic and mechanistic of the natural sciences. A contemporary of Darwin, T. H. Hux-ley, had shown the way, declaring the individual human being to be a con-scious automaton, and saying that "the feeling we call volition is not the cause of a voluntary act, but the symbol of that state of the brain which is the immediate cause of the act."[112] Mind, the province of the introspection-ist, could be explained away as an 'epiphenomenon'. In this spirit, the best-known pioneer of behaviorism, J. B. Watson, held thinking to be identical with movements in the brain and larynx, emotions to be implicit visceral reactions, and both to be amenable to Pavlovian conditioning.

Pavlovian conditioning is a method whereby something an animal does automatically (e.g., salivating) as a reflex response to something (food) is made to occur in response to something else (e.g., a sound). There is also a method whereby an animal can be got to do again something it does voluntarily (e.g., a cat pulling a piece of string, or a rat pressing a lever) by rewarding it (e.g., releasing it from a cage, or giving it food). The second method was used by E. L. Thorndike in his investigation of learning in animals and later by B. F. Skinner, who called it 'operant conditioning' because it is based on the animal operating on its environment in some way. Thorndike found that in a problem-solving situation such as that of having to escape from a maze, the animal would indulge in what he called 'trial and error' behavior. If some particular 'try' was successful, the animal would tend to repeat it. Thorndike would then say that the tendency to repeat it had been 'stamped-in' as a result of its effectiveness. If learning could be explained by reference to 'the law of effect', then there would be no need to invoke something not open to public observation, 'insight'. For a time it seemed as if the notions of trial and error learning, and of conditioning, would give the behaviorists all they needed.

But sooner or later, behaviorists had to explain what they meant by 'behavior'. Is the assumption justified that how someone behaves is always analyzable in terms of smallscale bodily movements? A turning point was the publication of E. C. Tolman's *Purposive Behaviour in Animals and Man* in 1932.[113] Tolman distinguished between what he called 'molecular' and 'molar' behavior. Molecular behavior is the bodily motions studied by the physiologist. Molar behavior is the behavior studied by the psychologist. Some behaviorists had tried to deduce molar behavior from molecular. Tolman held such a deduction to be impossible; molar behavior has descriptive and defining properties that make it irreducible to molecular behavior. It is essentially purposive.

Tolman was ahead of his time. In the 1950s, behaviorism as a methodology of psychology was criticized by philosophers on the grounds that it ignores the distinction between an *event,* such as a reflex response to a stimulus, and an *action.* An event is to be explained in terms of what has made it happen, such as the tap below the knee that makes the knee jerk up. An action, on the other hand, may be explained, to someone acquainted with a social practice of some sort, in terms of its role in that practice. For example, one may explain the action of someone raising her arm by saying that she is voting to go on strike. This serves as an explanation for someone acquainted with such human institutions as organized labor, withdrawal of labor, and so on. If psychologists debar themselves from talking the language of human institutions, it may be because they mistakenly assume that they thereby protect psychology's right to be regarded as a science. The assumption is that only explanations that have a cause-effect or stimulus-response format are properly scientific. This, in brief, was the substance of the philosophers' critique of the sort of behaviorism advocated by Skinner. It is hardly surprising that Skinner, who is no mean fighter, should respond to the stimulus by declaring 'linguistic behavior' to be explicable in terms of conditioning.

But psychologists who followed Tolman in talking of purposive behavior were helped by what was happening elsewhere. Machines were being invented whose 'behavior' positively invited description in precisely the mentalistic terms the behaviorists shunned. Machines were invented, for example, to track the flight of an enemy aircraft, to store the information obtained by such tracking, to forecast the aircraft's probable position at a future time, to make corrections to that forecast as further information became available, and to aim a gun at the position the aircraft was expected to reach, with the purpose of shooting it down. The fact that one could describe the machine's behavior in terms of information, forecasting, correction, expectation, and purpose was seen as being entirely consistent with the machine itself being describable in exclusively physicalistic terms (wires carrying electric currents, and so on). If mentalistic terms can be used to describe a machine's behavior without having to postulate a nonmaterial substance somehow interacting with the machine, why should they not be used, similarly, to describe human behavior? Why should psychologists be deterred, by a false antithesis of mechanism and teleology, from describing human actions in terms that have meaning in virtue of human concerns? Some psychologists talked of mind having come back into psychology on the back of the machine[114] and joked about anthropomorphism in human psychology.

Precisely what concept of mind has returned to psychology I am not sure. With human beings, it is not just that we can describe their behavior in purposive terms ("Socrates sitting there, submitting to whatever penalty Athens orders"). We treat them as responsible for their behavior. This is part of our treating them as having minds. What I am not sure about is whether treating people as responsible for their behavior has any place in psychology. In psychotherapy, yes. But in psychology?

Notes

1. P. L. Heath, "Concept," in *The Encyclopedia of Philosophy* (New York, 1967), vol. 2, edited by Paul Edwards 178.

2. *Philosophical Works of Descartes,* translated by E. S. Haldane and G. R. T. Ross (Cambridge, 1911), II, 52.

3. Or 'theory of ideas'. The word 'Form' is preferable in view of the use of the word 'idea' by Locke and others. It is spelled with a capital 'F' to distinguish Plato's 'Forms' from Aristotle's 'forms'.

4. Plato, *Republic* VII, 524c. Where I quote from Plato, I use the translations in *The Collected Dialogues of Plato,* edited by Edith Hamilton and Huntington Cairns (New York, 1961).

5. *Greater Hippias,* 289a-d.

6. *Republic* VII, 523c.

7. *Republic* I, 331c-d.

8. *Meno,* 76a.

9. *Letters* VII, 342c.

10. *Euthyphro,* 6c-7a.

11. I take it that the view quoted in *Cratylus,* 383a, that names "are natural and not conventional—not a portion of the human voice which men agree to use—but that there is a truth or correctness in them, which is the same for Hellenes as for barbarians," although ostensibly about names like 'Cratylus', is intended also to be about names like 'holy' and 'just'.

12. *Cratylus,* 384d.

13. *Republic* VII, 523b.

14. I am indebted to G. E. L. Owen for this account of the relevance of sensible things changing. Owen says that the point that "all predicates are incomplete in their earthly applica-

tions, for all apply at one time and not at another," is expressly made in *Symposium*, 210e-211a, and that the principle that could suggest it is enunciated in *Republic* IV, 436b (G. E. L. Owen, "A Proof in the *Peri Ideon*," in *Studies in Plato's Metaphysics*, edited by R. E. Allen (London, 1965), 307).

15. *Timaeus*, 51d.

16. *Phaedo*, 65d.

17. *Ibid.*, 75c. In the translation in Hamilton and Cairns, tallness in itself is called 'absolute tallness', equality in itself is called 'absolute equality', and so on. In the case of equality, but hardly in the case of tallness, 'absolute' could be taken to mean 'exact', with the idea that two sensible things, such as two sticks, cannot be exactly equal since there is no theoretical limit to the degree of accuracy with which sticks are measured; whereas equality in arithmetic cannot be inexact, since arithmetical calculations do not involve measurement, and so must be perfect equality. And this may give rise to the idea that what Plato is getting at is that the perfect equality in arithmetic somehow sets a standard for sensible equality, in something like the way in which the standard meter sets a standard for the meters we measure. Not only are these ideas confused in themselves, they have nothing to do with the two fundamental assumptions of Plato's theory of Forms—namely, that opposites exist not only confounded in sensible things but also separate in themselves, and that in themselves they are intelligible, or have real definitions that we can, in theory, know.

18. Plato's goal in the *Phaedo* is, of course, to prove that the soul exists not only before birth, but also after death. Cf. *Meno*, 81b.

19. *Phaedo*, 66a.

20. Plato expounds his doctrine of recollection in terms of an example from geometry (*Meno*, 81a-86c). This is permissible since the truths of geometry are like the Forms in being eternal (*Republic* VII, 527b).

21. The dialectician is "the man who is able to exact an account of the essence of each thing" (*Republic* VII, 534b).

22. *Timaeus*, 51e.

23. *Phaedo*, 75b.

24. *Timaeus*, 49a.

25. *Ibid.*, 51a-b.

26. *Ibid.*, 52b-c.

27. *Meno*, 72c.

28. *Parmenides*, 131e-132a. Cf. *Republic* X, 596a.

29. Aristotle, *Metaphysics*, bk. 1, chap. 6, 987a 29 to 987b 13. Cf. *Metaphysics*, bk. 13, chap. 4, 1078b 13-32. Where I quote from Aristotle, I use the translations in *The Basic Works of Aristotle*, edited by Richard McKeon, (New York, 1941), except for a quotation from *De Caelo* (see n. 49).

30. *Republic* VI, 508e.

31. Ibid., 509b.

32. *Republic* VII, 532a.

33. *Phaedo*, 99c.

34. Ibid., 96a.

35. Ibid., 96b.

36. Ibid., 97c.

37. Ibid., 97d.

38. Ibid., 99b.

39. Ibid.

40. Ibid., 99c.

41. *Timaeus*, 51d.

42. *Phaedo*, 66d-e.

43. *Phaedo,* 97c.

44. *Categories,* chap. 5.

45. *De Anima,* bk. 2, chap. 12, 424a 17; bk. 3, chap. 2, 425 b 24. Aristotle seems to identify 'sense' with 'sense organ'.

46. Ibid., bk. 3, chap. 4, 429 b 30.

47. Ibid., bk. 3, chap. 5, 430 a 15.

48. *Metaphysics,* bk. 1, chap. 3, 984 b 15.

49. *De Caelo,* bk. 2, chap. 12, 292 a 18; from *De Caelo,* translated by W. K. C. Guthrie (London, 1960).

50. *De Partibus Animalium,* bk. 1, chap. 1, 639 b 12-16.

51. *De Anima,* bk. 2, chap. 4, 415b.

52. *Posterior Analytics,* bk. 1, chap. 2, 71 b 9.

53. Ibid., 71 b 20.

54. Ibid., chap. 4, 73 a 21.

55. Ibid., chap. 3, 72 b 23.

56. *Posterior Analytics,* bk. 2, chap. 19, 99 b 26.

57. Ibid., 100a 11.

58. *Descartes: Philosophical Letters,* translated and edited by Anthony Kenny (Oxford, 1970), 94.

59. *Philosophical Works of Descartes,* translated by E. S. Haldane and G. R. T. Ross (Cambridge, 1911), vol. 1, 259. (Subsequent references to this text will take the form HR I 259.)

60. HR II 131.

61. Ibid. On Descartes's conjunction of physics with pure mathematics, see Gerd Buchdahl, *Metaphysics and the Philosophy of Science* (Cambridge, 1969), 115, 117.

62. HR 173.

63. HR I 158.

64. HR I 101.

65. HR II 80, 96.

66. HR II 52.

67. HR I 222.

68. HR II 52.

69. Ibid.

70. HR I 443.

71. *De Diversis Quaestionibus,* LXXXIII, question 46.

72. *Principles of Human Knowledge* (1710), I, 148.

73. HR I 162.

74. *Parmenides,* 132b.

75. Anthony Kenny, "Aquinas: Intentionality," in *Philosophy through Its Past,* edited by Ted Honderich (London, 1984), 82.

76. *Search after Truth,* translated by T. M. Lennon and P. J. Olscamp (Ohio, 1980), III ii 1.

77. Ibid.

78. *Concerning True and False Ideas* (1683), chap. 8.

79. *Essay* (1690), II i 2.

80. *Essay,* II viii 18.

81. *Essay,* II i 3.

82. Thomas Reid remarked that "though all philosophers agree that in seeing colour there is sensation, it is not easy to persuade the vulgar that in seeing a coloured body, where the light is not too strong, nor the eye inflamed, they have any sensation or feeling at all" (*Essays* (1785), II, 18).

83. HR II 52.

84. *Essay,* III ii 1.

85. Ibid.

86. *Essay,* III ii 2.

87. *Essay,* III ii 8.

88. *Essay,* III ix 4.

89. *Essay,* II xxxii 15.

90. *Essay,* II xxx 1-2.

91. *Essay,* III iii 13.

92. *System of Logic* (1843), I iii 11.

93. *Leviathan* (1651), chap. IV.

94. Just as Hobbes distinguishes between 'mental discourse' and 'verbal discourse', so Locke distinguishes between 'mental propositions' and 'verbal propositions'. If we wonder why it is not generally recognized that there are, besides verbal propositions, mental ones, an explanation is ready to hand: "It is very difficult to treat of them asunder. Because it is unavoidable, in treating of mental propositions, to make use of words; and then the instances given of mental propositions cease immediately to be barely mental, and become verbal" (*Essay,* IV v 3).

95. *Tractatus Logico-Philosophicus* (London, 1922), 4.

96. This is how Wittgenstein characterizes the realism of the *Tractatus* in his later philosophy. See *Philosophical Investigations* (Oxford, 1953), I 402, 428-29.

97. *Tractatus,* 3.23, and *Notebooks 1914-1916* (Oxford, 1969), 63 ("The demand for simple things *is* the demand for definiteness of sense"). In the *Investigations,* Wittgenstein rejects, along with the picture theory, the notion that there cannot be sense without definiteness of sense (I 91-115, esp. 99).

98. *Tractatus,* 2.021, 2.0271.

99. *Essay,* III ii 7.

100. See *Essay,* II xxvii 13, IV iii 28.

101. *Zettel* (Oxford, 1967), 331.

102. *Essay,* II vii 18.

103. *Essay,* III ii 2.

104. *Essay.* III v 7.

105. *Philosophical Investigations,* I 244.

106. *Zettel,* 532.

107. Ibid. 472.

108. *Essay,* 4th ed., II xxxiii 5.

109. *Essay,* II xxxiii 6.

110. *Treatise of Human Nature* (1739), I i 4.

111. *Principles of Logic* (London, 1883), bk. 2, part 2, chap. 1.

112. "On the Hypothesis that Animals Are Automata, and Its History," in *Collected Essays* (London, 1898), vol. 1.

113. New York.

114. For example, George Miller. See J. Miller, *States of Mind: Conversations with Psychological Investigators* (London, 1983), 26.

Other Minds after Twenty Years

BRUCE AUNE

About twenty years ago, the problem of other minds was a fashionable topic in analytical philosophy. The most influential strategy for resolving it was neo-Wittgensteinian, a key theme being that "an inner process stands in need of outward criteria."[1] This strategy seemed promising as a means of frustrating the skeptic, but it brought one uncomfortably close to the absurdity of analytical behaviorism. Today, Wittgenstein's philosophy is out of fashion and the problem of other minds is rarely discussed. My aim in this paper is to reconsider the problem in the light of recent developments in the philosophy of mind and language.

The problem of other minds as it was understood in the 1960s was largely a problem about feelings, pain being a favorite topic of discussion. Although pains are dubious examples of mental states, at least if intentionality is a mark of the mental, the epistemic problem I want to discuss is focused on them, and I shall therefore be concerned with them here. To tie my remarks more closely to the proper subject of other minds and to come to terms with problems that were not on the agenda twenty years ago, I shall also be concerned with the more complicated concept of belief. An alternative title for my paper might be "Feeling and Belief."

As everyone knows, the traditional problem about the feelings of others arises from just a few basic convictions. To begin with, we are directly aware of our own feelings, which we know to occur within us. If other people have feelings, their feelings are not open to our view: we can know of their existence only by some kind of inference. But there are just two kinds of inference: deductive and inductive. If an inference from P to Q is deductively valid, it is impossible for Q to be false when P is true. Obviously, this kind of inference cannot show us that other people have feelings, for everything we can observe about other people—everything we can detect in their behavior and external circumstances—is logically consistent with their not having any feelings at all. Thus, we can know that others have feelings only by some inductive inference. Yet an inductive inference is ultimately based on a generalization from experience, and we have no experience of the supposed feelings of others. Induction, therefore, is apparently as useless here as deduction. What is to be done?

Although this line of reasoning involves a particularly crude conception of inductive inference, the criticism it received twenty years ago was focused on two different points. One was that we cannot presume to know what a feeling is "merely from our own case."[2] When we use an expression like "in pain" or "feels pain," we are not speaking a private language; we are using expressions that we have learned in a social context and that we have applied, from the very beginning, to others as well as to ourselves. The other point was a development of the first one: the words we apply to feelings are governed by socially accepted criteria.[3] Such criteria connect terms for feelings with terms for observable behavior, and they provide the basis for ascribing feelings to others. The connection between pain and pain behavior is not, therefore, merely contingent and known inductively. There is a "conceptual connection" between the inner and the outer, and this connection provides the basis for our conclusions about the sensory experiences of others.

The development of this last point is not very credible at a time when the doctrine of analytic truth is out of fashion, but it deserves to be rejected for a deeper reason. Consider the term "lunatic." In its original sense this term *meant* "a person whose madness has a lunar cause." In this sense of the term, there is conceptual connection between lunacy and the moon, one reflected in the conceptual truth that x is a lunatic just in case x's madness is caused by the moon. But if, in fact, the moon does not cause a kind of madness—as we now believe—there is no factual basis for applying the word "lunatic" to any person and, therefore, for using the world in its original sense. The same holds true for words such as "feels pain" or "is dizzy." Even if we allow that there are "conceptual truths" involving such words—truths that relate certain inner states to outer criteria—there must be some factual basis for their use. We must, that is, have some empirical assurance that words involving such an assumed connection between inner and outer apply to something real. This assurance, being empirical, cannot be ascertained by mere conceptual analysis; it can be ascertained only inductively.

When Strawson discussed the problem of other minds in his book *Individuals,* he remarked that the skeptic wants to drive a wedge between the inner and the outer but that concepts such as depression "span" the relevant "gap."[4] Given such concepts, we must allow, he said, that observable behavior provides "logically adequate criteria" for the existence (or occurrence) of such experiences as depression. To refuse to accept such criteria is, as he put it, to refuse to accept the "structure of the language" in which we speak of a person's mental or sensory states. It is clear that, as a resolution to the problem about other persons' sensory experiences, this maneuver gets us nowhere, for it does not come to terms with the question whether words such as "depression" apply to anything real. In everyday life we may accept the presumed assumptions associated with words such as "depression" just as uncritically as people once accepted the causal hypothesis associated with the word "lunatic." But the rational credentials of these assumptions remain in question; they are, one might say, the frog at the bottom of the beer mug labeled "the problem of other minds."

As I see it, this last problem about criteria can be resolved only by an adequate theory of induction or experimental inference, one that does justice to the kind of reasoning common in theoretical science.[5] I shall pursue this subject a little later; I now want to say something about the other Wittgensteinian assumption that was thought to undermine the traditional problem about the other minds—the assumption, namely, that we learn to describe our feelings in a social context and that we do not learn what feelings are merely from our own case.

Perhaps the first thing to say about this assumption is that it can actually be granted by a philosopher who is worried about our knowledge of other people's experiences. The key point is that feelings, if they exist, have relational as well as nonrelational properties. Pains are generally believed to result from cuts, burns, and stubbed toes; they are also believed to result in characteristic forms of behavior. Even a skeptic can allow that we learn to identify these supposed causes and effects of pain in a social context. In reply to the claim that such causes and effects are incorporated into the concept of pain as relational properties of a typical feeling of pain, the skeptic can insist that we need some rational assurance that such properties are, in particular cases, actually attached to an appropriate inner state; and this assurance cannot be supplied by a mere verbal convention. Although I am not a skeptic, I have already made this point in commenting on alleged "outer criteria" for inner states. We may have to learn from others that this or that is thought to be a relational property of a certain inner state; but even if there is a conceptual connection between inner state and outer (or relational) property, we still need some rational assurance that such conceptual connections have a foundation in fact—in a corresponding natural regularity.

Wittgenstein, in his famous private-language argument, maintained that we do not merely learn of what I have called the extrinsic properties of feelings in a social context; he claimed that everything we know about our feelings has its sourse in such a context.[6] We might suppose that we learn the intrinsic qualities of our feelings by mere inspection, but this supposition, he said, is incorrect. It is true that, when we are linguistically sophisticated, we can identify our feelings in words without attending to their external cause or effects. Yet our ability to do this is the result of training by others, and our confidence that the words we use are reliably correlated with appropriate feelings ultimately depends, Wittgenstein thought, on the corroborative testimony of others. Without the possibility of such corroboration we could draw no tenable distinction, he added, between correctly describing our feelings and merely thinking that we describe them correctly.

Wittgenstein's insistence on the social basis for subjective reports goes too far, however. We may require some assurance that our use of a common language agrees with the practice of others, but the individual judgments we make do not always require the possibility of an external corroborative check. As linguists emphasize, people who have learned a language not only have the ability to produce and understand countless sentences containing, for them and others, novel combinations of words; they also have the ability to describe novel objects in novel ways—using, if necessary, old predicates in new or extended senses. If such a speaker is presented with a special "object" to which other speakers lack access, there is no good reason to suppose that the description he or she confidently produces is any less reliable than the description of a less special object. In fact, the general linguistic competence of such a speaker provides an inductively plausible basis for the assumption that such a description, at least when candidly made and intelligently elaborated, is reliable or correct.

Opponents of Wittgenstein typically urge that the first-person reports in which such descriptions are included have a more secure basis than I am tacitly allowing here. According to some philosophers, such reports are, in fact, "incorrigible."[7] They support their view by insisting that psychological states are "self-presenting" or that it "makes no sense" to say a person could be wrong about being in such a state.[8] But these claims are fundamentally defective. The key consideration is this: A psychological state S is one thing, and a verbal report R is something entirely different. The assertion "If R is made, S occurs" is not, therefore, logically true. To argue that the conditional, though not logically true, is nevertheless analytic is tantamount to arguing that the gap between S and R can be adequately bridged by conceptual means. But this maneuver is, as I have shown, useless, since a conceptual bridge can be relied on only if it has a foundation in fact. In this case, the required fact is that reports like R are reliably associated with states like S. Such a fact, being patently empirical and also general, can be ascertained only by some inductive means.

Although the arguments supporting the view that psychological reports are infallibly true or incorrigible are seriously defective, there must be some basis for the widespread belief that such reports cannot err. Surely, it is absurd to suppose that everyone who holds the belief would subscribe to the reasoning I have just rejected. I think there is such a basis: it consists of a tacit inductive generalization. The inference is not a very strong one, but it accounts for the conviction in point.

Consider the case of pain. Most people who consider the matter will agree that, if we feel pain, we cannot fail to know what it is like. The claim is a very general one, and it is brought to mind only in the context of a philosophical discussion. What usually happens in such a discussion, at least in my experience, is something like this. People will imagine or recall some typical experience of being in pain and then ask themselves, "Could one have an experience *like this* and not know it?" Considering the unpleasant character of the experience and the way it (as it were) calls attention to itself, they say, "No one could possibly have such an experience and not know it." There is no surveying of possible cases here; there is immediate conviction. The conviction is a generalization, of course, and it is supported by a single case. The reasoning tacitly involved is, therefore, an instance of inductive generalization.

The claim that all sensory experiences yield infallible knowledge seems to be based, for most people, on a further generalization from a variety of experiences—from feeling pain, hearing the blast of a trumpet, seeing red, and so forth. This further generalization is weaker than the first one, for second thoughts intrude in many cases. If you hear a sound whose tone is C-sharp, must you realize that it is C-sharp? No. If you are visually aware of a spotty expanse, must you know how many spots you "see"? No. If you have a sinus headache, must you know that it feels like a sinus headache? No. Second thoughts of this kind bring out one important point: Knowing that an experience is like this or like that involves a comparison that, for some this's and that's, can easily be mistaken. Sensory knowledge is infallible, at best, only when special, minimal comparisons are involved.

Although the inferences I have spoken of account for a natural conviction about the certainty of some first-person reports, they also provide some evidence (at least) that the natural conviction is true. It is often said that inductive inferences of the kind I have described are inherently weak, involving an insufficiently varied evidence class. The force of such claims is easily exaggerated, however. For one thing, the pains one might recall or imagine in the sort of case I have described may be allowed to be typical of one's own experience, and a generalization from a typical case is much stronger than one drawn from a special case. For another thing, the epistemological conclusion one arrives at concerns another's experience only in a hypothetical way. The idea is that if anyone has an experience like *this,* he or she could not fail to know what it is like (given a minimal parameter of likeness). This idea does not imply that anyone else ever has an experience "like this."

Together with the inductively plausible assumption that sophisticated speakers can describe novel objects in reliable ways, the reasoning I have just described provides, as I see it, the only tenable basis for the common philosophical idea that sensory reports are "privileged." The favored epistemic status of such reports does not rest on some kind of convention; not only does no such convention exist, but even if one did exist, it could not guarantee a connection between distinct existents. The idea that such a connection can be known by some kind of a priori intuition is equally unwarranted. A priori intuitions may conceivably have some validity in mathematics, but it is anachronistic to suppose that they can inform us about the reliability of a psychological mechanism—the one underlying first-person reports. Apart from this, the authority of psychological reports obviously varies with the language used and the comparisons made; as I mentioned earlier, the authority of a report is greatest when it involves minimal comparisons—a notion that is exceedingly difficult to capture in general terms. It seems obvious to me that the evidence supporting claims about privileged access to one's feelings is not only limited and inductive, but it can be expected to change with the development of scientific knowledge.

Pains are generally called sensory "states," but this terminology deserves more thought than it usually gets. Our talk of states of things is based on our subject-predicate discourse: we apply predicates to a thing, and some of these predicates are said to describe the thing's "state." If we say "That iron rod is hot," we use "hot" to describe the rod's thermal state; if we say "Jones is in pain," we use "in pain" to describe Jones's sensory state. Although in describing Jones this way we are treating him as a unitary subject, we know that he is a complex thing—on one level of analysis, a system of living cells. We also know that his sensory state is, in some sense, a state of his nervous system; but we do not know, at least at the present time, just what this state involves. We lack a detailed knowledge of what it is and of how, exactly, it is related to the state of his brain that gives rise to the verbal report "I am in pain." The knowledge we lack here is philosophically important because it may affect what we shall want to say in problem cases that, as matters stand now, are hard to settle. People "hurt" in athletic contests may report feeling no pain even though they have been limping or clutching a damaged hand. Our usual evidence conflicts in such cases, the limping at odds with the report; a better knowledge of the physiology of pain may allow us to describe them with greater confidence or less dogmatism.

The claims I have made support the following picture. Although we learn to identify and describe sensory experiences in a social context, our most secure convictions about the sensory states of others are rationally defensible only on some kind of inductive grounds: an appeal to "outer" criteria ultimately requires empirical support. The inductive reasoning we can use to support our convictions here is, no doubt, fundamentally the same in basic structure as that by which "theoretical" hypotheses are supported in science. (But more on this in a moment.) As we master our language, we become capable of indentifying and describing our own feelings. Our access to our own feelings is direct in the sense that, when we wish to identify or describe them, appropriate words quickly come to mind. Such words often take the form of "reports" and they are, to some extent, privileged, though they are not "incorrigible." Their degree of reliability can be estimated only indirectly—by comparing them with other evidence bearing upon the occurrence of the states they indicate (such as our nonverbal behavior) and by taking into account the sort of comparisons we are tacitly making, the general reliability of our verbal habits, our apparent mental clarity or confusion, and so on.

I would like to be able to give a precise account of the kind of inductive reasoning by which statements about feelings are appropriately defended, but the subject is excessively complicated. Philosophers of science used to offer a fairly simple model of hypothetico-deductive (or HD) inference, one in which statements about unobservables are confirmed by statements about observables. This simple model is energetically disputed today,[9] but its application to the problem of other minds always seemed questionable in post-Wittgensteinian discussions. The trouble is that, epistemically speaking, one's own feelings are neither fish nor fowl from one's own point of view—that is, neither standard observables nor standard unobservables. The HD model seemed appropriate for the case of others; but when doubts are raised about one's own "inner identifications" (as they were by Wittgenstein), the model seemed utterly inappropriate and unhelpful.

About twenty years ago, I decided that the logic of scientific inference is obfuscated rather than illuminated by an emphasis on the distinction between observables and unobservables.[10] I was led to this view by the following considerations. In scientific investigation and even everyday life, observation claims are not always accepted uncritically. When they are evaluated, four sorts of things are ideally taken into account: the character of the observer, the means of observation, the nature of the object supposedly observed, and the circumstances under which the observation occurs. Clearly, all four are important for sound observations, and all four should be considered when an observation claim is evaluated. Yet these factors all involve theoretical components. The conclusion to be drawn from this is: Every observation claim must ultimately be evaluated by some background theory or theories.

The background theories relevant here cannot be purely metaphysical because they concern specific forms of observation, the actual character of observers, particular facts about the conditions of observation, and the like. Thus, although we may, in practice, speak of testing theoretical claims by observational data, such testing is merely conditional: the claims may be credible, or probable, to a certain degree given the data, but the acceptability and even the interpretation of the data are dependent on a further level of theory.[11] When this further level of theory is made explicit, we find that we are actually relating theory to theory, and the credibility of a particular claim is ultimately owing to the character of our total theoretical structure.

This holist view of empirical confirmation is helpful for thinking about the problem of other minds. The claim that another person feels pain may be highly credible given (a) a certain conception (or tacit commonsense theory) of pain and (b) certain observations of that person's behavior and circumstances. But this conception of pain and the assumptions tacitly made in accepting the observations are also subject to critical evaluation in the light of total theory. This total theory is crucial for the interpretation and evaluation of our first-person reports, when we confidently affirm "I feel pain." The vaunted asymmetry in first- and other-person psychological statements appears somewhat superficial at this level. Given a significant degree of linguistic maturity and the formation of appropriate habits, candid verbal responses such as "I feel pain" are about as reliable (as apt to be true in the mouth of a normal speaker) as a comparable utterance of "That is red" or "That's a dog." Yet the background considerations relevant to the interpretation and evaluation of such reports are closely related to—they are part of the same theoretical system as—the background considerations relevant to the interpretation and evaluation of "She feels pain." As I mentioned earlier, some of these background considerations may be altered as we learn more about the neurophysiology of sensory distress and of our ability to monitor our sensory experiences.

The basic claims I have been making about sensory states such as pain also apply to cognitive states, or attitudes, such as believing and desiring. These latter states raise special problems, however. A belief that p is generally said to involve a relation to a proposition, and a satisfactory philosophical account of belief as a cognitive state must come to terms with the supposed relation and the so-called propositional object. As I indicated at the beginning of this paper, my remarks on cognitive states will be restricted to the special case of belief.

As I see it, a good way to get a handle on the concept of believing that p is to begin with the notion of saying something. Viewed in a highly general way, saying something is a verbal act, one accomplished by making an utterance. If we know the words Jones uttered on a certain occasion, we can describe him as saying what he did in a direct way by saying, for example, "Jones said 'Snow is white'." In this case, we convey what Jones said by giving the words he uttered. It is, however, possible to describe what someone said in a less direct way by employing the device of indirect quotation, as in "Jones said that snow is white" or "Jones said that he would come tomorrow." In indirect quotation we do not claim to be giving the words the speaker actually used, though we might actually do so. Our aim, generally speaking, is to display words in our that-clause that are related to the speaker's words in a special way. In some cases, the words we display are a translation of the speaker's words; in other cases, they are what might be called a "differently indexed equivalent" to those words. If yesterday Jones actually said, "I will come tomorrow," we can report what he said by using the words "He said that he would come today." Indirect discourse is, however, a very flexible device; in some cases, we feel entitled to use words that agree with those of the speaker only in denotation, as when we say "He said he would come Friday"—using "Friday" in place of his "a week from today."

Believing something is, of course, very different from saying or even thinking something, for you can believe that snow is white even when you are asleep. Still, as Peirce and Ramsey emphasized, a belief is something on which one is prepared to act—the strength of the belief being shown by the risks one will take in thus acting.[12] To be sure, a belief in this last sense is something believed; thus the idea is more accurately expressed by saying that one who actually believes that p is prepared to act on the "proposition" that p (given a certain parameter of risk). The idea I want to develop here is that acting on a proposition is acting on some mental formula and that the propositional clause in the context "S believes that p" can reasonably be understood as an indirect quotation of the formula on which the subject, if truly described as believing that p, is prepared to act. The first step in developing this idea is to explain what is reasonably meant in speaking of action on a formula.

As I argued in my book *Reason and Action,* the most general thing one can say about acting on a formula F is this: S acts on F in doing A just when S does A as the result of a line of practical reasoning that psychologically explains his doing A and that contains the formula F as a premise or tacit premise.[13] Thus, if Jones in shooting Smith's dog acted on the idea (or formula) that wolves should be exterminated, then Jones's action is psychologically explainable by reference to a line of practical reasoning in which this idea or formula occurred as a premise or tacit premise. Ideally, practical reasoning leads to action by generating a decision that the action carries out. Such reasoning need not be valid, for fallacious reasoning can lead to action just as well as valid reasoning. It must, however, actually take place if it provides an acceptable explantion of a person's action.

If believing something can usefully be characterized by a formula on which the believer is prepared to act, the notion of acting on the formula must be adequately describable in terms other than "a formula the person accepts or believes." This can be done. The premises or verbal formulas involved in a person's reasoning may be mere suppositions or assumptions, but the ones that lead her to act (particularly in the face of some risk) are the ones that characterize a belief that she has. Disbelief that p is characterized by an unwillingness to act (or make decisions) on the basis of reasoning in which a formula indirectly quoted by "p" is a significant premise. Thus, if we are confident that someone acts as a result of reasoning in which a formula indirectly quotable by "p" actually occurs, we can confidently say that the person believes that p.

Two important questions arise at this point: What can we mean in speaking of covert (or unobservable) reasoning in which a formula F is featured? And how can we know, or provide a reasonable defense for the idea, that such reasoning actually takes place on this or that occasion? These are difficult questions that require delicate answers; here I can only try to say enough to make my general position intuitively plausible.

From one point of view, the concept of silent or covert reasoning is, as Sellars argued nearly thirty years ago, a common sense theoretical concept.[14] We conceive of such reasoning as a sequence of covert acts that is formally analogous to a sequence of utterances having the structure of an argument, that is, having various premises and a conclusion. The covert acts may be called "acts of thought"; they have the semantical properties of assertions, which are utterances with (roughly) sense, reference, and assertive force.[15] We normally conceive of thoughts as mental occurrences that can be overtly "expressed" in assertions. The notion of expression here is clearly metaphorical, suggesting that an utterance is a thought pressed out of the mind or head; but this suggestion can be eliminated if we think of expression merely as a relation between thought and utterance characterized (on first approximation) as follows: For every utterance u, there is an E-correlate t that has the same semantical properties, that is a causal factor in the production of u when u is an assertion, and that is governed by a set of habits on the part of the thinker-speaker that are analogous to his inferential-observational habits with respect to u.

This last sentence can be elaborated into a surprising powerful theory. Consider the matter of semantical properties. If an utterance u is true just when p, then the thought E-related to u, $E(u)$, is also true just when p. Furthermore, if u implies u', then $E(u)$ implies $E(u')$; and if u is true just when p is true and q is true, then $E(u)$ is true just when $E(p)$ is true and $E(q)$ is true. As for the relevant verbal habits, if the speaker-thinker S has the habit of inferring q from $\sim p$ and $(p \vee q)$, S also has the habit of inferring $E(q)$ from $E(\sim p)$ and $E(p \vee q)$. Again, if S has the habit (or propensity) of responding to red objects with the utterance "That's red" (given a certain mental set), S will also have the habit (given a related set) of responding to red objects with the thought E("That's red"). The importance of these habits is obvious: they permit us to provide psychological explanations for a large range of S's behavior. If S behaves in a way that requires some calculation—some weighing of information, as in a chess game—we can work out plausible psychological explanations for such behavior. Such explanations can be defended, or supported, in a variety of ways, but more on this in a moment.

I said above that the concept of covert reasoning is, from one point of view, a common sense theoretical concept. This point of view is, obviously, that of the other person. When we reflect on our own thinking, we do not regard it as something merely theoretical. Normally, we can simply say what we are thinking—no inferring is required. Even so, our thoughts do not (at least usually) have a phenomenal character: they are not present to our consciousness as a feeling is. This does not limit our ability to avow what we are thinking about, nor does it prevent us from vividly remembering what we thought about on this or that occasion. We do, of course, encounter some problems in avowing our thoughts. One such problem is owing to the fact that, when we are thinking, we are generally thinking about some other subject—something other than our own thinking. When, therefore, we begin to think about our current thinking, we mentally change the subject and thus have to remember what we were thinking. Usually we can do this, but our memory of what we were thinking is no better—in fact, it is sometimes worse—than our memory of what we were saying. One reason we have trouble recalling our thoughts is that we think (or process information) so quickly. Speaking and writing seem to slow us down mentally and help us keep better track of what we are doing. But the difficulty of monitoring our silent thoughts should not make us skeptical about their existence. On most days I spend the morning hours by myself, thinking out the lectures I shall give in the afternoon. Some of the words I later utter actually came to mind in these early hours.

If we think of an observation statement as Feyerabend once did— roughly, as a contingent singular statement that is quickly decidable with a minimum of inference[16]—then statements about our present and very recent thoughts will be, for us, observation statements. But this terminological decision has very little epistemological significance. In fact, as I emphasized when I discussed sensory states, the acceptability and even the proper interpretation of an observation statement (and this holds for observation statements in Feyerabend's sense) are always conditional on some background theory. If a person sincerely says, "I was just thinking of Socrates' criticism of Polemarchus," we are generally entitled to accept her remark as true—but we do so only on the assumption that the speaker knows the language and that an appropriate connection has been established between her spontaneous reports about her thoughts and the cognitive states, or acts, that they represent. The commonsense theory of thoughts to which others tacitly appeal in ascribing this or that thought to me supplies the basic framework, the background theory, by reference to which my avowals are interpreted and assessed.

Earlier, I remarked that the psychological explanations we might offer for a person's behavior can be defended, or supported, in a variety of ways; but I did not back up my remark with any details. One way of obtaining favorable evidence is to ask the person whether he reasoned as we say he did. Of course, his words are not absolutely conclusive evidence: he might be a liar, he might be confused, he might suffer from self-deception, or he may have forgotten why he acted as he did. Sometimes the best corroboration we can offer is fairly high level: a person with that information, those aims, and that character is bound to reason in somewhat the way we say he reasoned. To be sure, we may be wrong here; but sometimes the explanations we offer can be defended only on grounds of general plausibility. It goes without saying that in such cases we should take our explanations with a grain of salt. Certainty is not always possible, particularly in psychological matters. When it can be attained, it always based, at least tacitly, on holistic considerations and some background theory.

As in the case of reports about sensory experiences, it is often said that people's reports about their beliefs are highly privileged; in fact, some philosophers insist that beliefs are "self-presenting states" and that belief reports, at least when candidly made, are inherently credible.[17] This view strikes me as naive. Self-deception is ubiquitous in everyday life, and people who are deceived about their personality or character are usually deceived about many of their beliefs. For many people, beliefs seem to define the person: having the right religious, political, or professional beliefs (on how, for example, to "do" philosophy) is very important for being a certain kind of person and for belonging to a certain group. Avowing this or that belief is thus, for many, an expression of group identity and may have little relation to their actual conduct. Jones may be convinced, for example, that he values each person "as an end in himself," yet treat people with indifference or contempt; and Smith may shirk challenges after avowing that meeting them is what makes her life worthwhile. The point is not just that people may be deceived about, or unwilling to accept, the kind of people they actually are; they may be unwilling to acknowledge—to express in words—the beliefs on which they frequently act. Their self-esteem often seems to require the thought, "I am not just a good person; I actually believe what I am supposed to believe."

When I discussed sensory experiences, I remarked that we can expect to learn more about them as our knowledge of neurophysiology increases. Does an analogous point hold for beliefs and other propositional attitudes? I think yes. Although beliefs are understood as cognitive "states" of single subjects, persons, these subjects are complex objects whose brains are enormously complex molecular structures. The information storage and processing associated with the "state" of believing and the process of inferring are still badly understood; and our conception of believing and inferring is bound to be improved when we understand what goes on in the brain of a person when these conceptions are truly applicable to him or her. If believing that p is associated with a certain means or mode of storing information, our knowledge of the relevant neural mechanism may make it easier for us to understand how self-deception occurs and what its limits are.

I want to conclude this paper with some observations on a problem that is raised for belief by Quine's thesis of translational indeterminacy.[18] If, as I have suggested, the propositional clause in a true sentence of the form "S

believes that *p*" is an indirect quotation of a formula on which the subject is prepared to act, and if the formula is conceived of as, roughly, a mental counterpart to some utterance (or assertion) that the subject might use to express it, then to describe someone as believing that *p* is implicitly to interpret an utterance she might produce. If, further, the interpretation of an utterance is subject to the indeterminacy that Quine emphasized, the interpretation of a given belief is subject to a similar indeterminacy. Yet if this is so, the concept of belief is a very peculiar—perhaps even an anomalous—empirical concept. One might wonder whether, in attributing a particular belief to someone, one is actually making an empirical claim at all.

To resolve the puzzlement that arises from this issue, one should bear in mind certain points about indirect quotation. When we quote someone's words indirectly, we display words of our own that are semantic counterparts, at least, of the words he used. Such counterparts need not, as wholes, be synonymous with, or good translations of, the speaker's words; but they are more than just material equivalents of his words: usually, they contain parts that are translational equivalents of some of his words. In some cases, of course, the words we display are, as wholes, translational equivalents for his words; to explore the bearing of Quine's thesis on the subject of belief, we can suppose that all cases are like this.

According to Quine, a scheme of translation for a system of verbal behavior *V* (another person's language) is provided by a manual that correlates recurrent segments of *V* with words of a home language *L*. An appropriate correlation is based on various constraints; but no matter how carefully the constraints are specified, more than one such correlation is always possible for *V* and *L*. Different correlations meeting the relevant constraints yield different translation manuals, no one of which is any more correct than the others. If we have adopted a particular manual *M* for *V* and *L*, we may say that a certain utterance belonging to *V* is correctly translated by an expression *E* of *L*: the translation is correct relative to *M*. If no such manual is specified, the notion of a translation of *E* is indeterminate. Absolutely speaking, there is no such thing as a correct or incorrect translation of *E*.

Suppose that Quine is wholly correct about translation as, in main lines, I think he is.[19] It remains true that, if we adopt a manual *m* for another person's language or system or verbal behavior, we ideally base our acceptance of *m* on observable regularities in that behavior. If the manual is an acceptable one, the regularities we observe are characteristic of the relevant behavior, and the manual is applicable to that behavior only so long as these regularities occur. Although some of these regularities are largely phonetical, allowing us to identify recurrent utterances, others fall into three important groups; in Wilfrid Sellars's suggestive terminology, they are word-word, world-word, and word-world regularities.[20] The first sort is exemplified in the inferences a person draws; the second sort is exemplified in observation reports; and the third sort is exemplified in decisions to act. I call attention to these regularities because we commonly appeal to them when we attempt to explain someone's behavior by reference to his or her beliefs, intentions, and related practical reasoning.

If equally acceptable but significantly different manuals of translation are possible for V and a home language L, then different word-word, world-word, and word-world regularities of a suitable complexity must be discernible in V. How is this possible? The answer is given by Quine in his defense of the indeterminacy thesis. For my present purposes, it is perhaps sufficient to say that, according to Quine, different "segmentations" of V are possible—and different objects or semantical values can be assigned to these various segments. If, according to a manual m, u is an utterance that, by virture of an appropriate semantical interpretation, is acceptably translated by "Snow is white," then u-utterances must bear a systematic relation to snow and to white things. If a different translation for u is equally acceptable (relative to a different but equally acceptable manual), then u-utterances must also be systematically related to objects of a different sort—perhaps to snow-stages and white-stuff-stages. The crucial point is that, if the thesis of translational indeterminacy is correct, the regularities needed to justify these different translation manuals must actually exist.

Suppose, now, that I attribute to another person the belief that snow is white. In doing this, I am in effect claiming that she is prepared to act on a formula that I translate by "Snow is white." Even if other translations for what I single out as the relevant formula are possible, it does not follow that that formula—that "mental" occurrence—is not real or that, if it is real, it is not associated with habits that are reasonably interpreted as pertaining to snow. The analogy between thought and utterance is instructive here. Just as the reality of an utterance is not undermined by the fact that it can, in principle, be "segmented" and interpreted in different ways, so the reality of a thought or mental formula is not undermined by the fact that it can be conceptually segmented and interpreted in different ways. The point can be generalized: Just as the thesis of translational indeterminacy does not undermine the reality of the word-word, word-world, and world-word regularities associated with what are, according to a certain acceptable manual, assertions that snow is white, so the thesis does not undermine the reality of the regularities assumed by the claim that a person has a propensity to act on (to reason in accordance with) what is, according to a certain commonsense theory, a certain thought or formula. In particular, the thesis does not undermine the reality of the mental regularities to which we refer in explaining a person's behavior by reference to her beliefs and intentions.

Philosophers who object to "metaphysical realism" often suppose that, if the words we use or the conceptions we employ are humanly invented tools and not mere labels that we attach to an antecedently distinguished "ready-made world," then our words or conceptions do not correspond to "real" objects.[21] This supposition is, I believe, a mistake. As Leibniz put the point in his *Nouveaux essais,* "No matter what rules men make to goven how things are named and what entitlements go with names, provided that the system of rules is orderly (that is, interconnected and intelligible) it will be founded in reality"; and "whatever we truthfully distinguish or compare is also distinguished or made alike by nature."[22] If the world *is such* that it is truly describable by a system of concepts *C,* then it really contains the things or sorts of things that those concepts describe; if it is also truly described by a different system of concepts *C*,* it really contains other thngs or sorts of things as well. Generally speaking, objects may be singled out in reality for different purposes and from different points of view; yet if they are singled out, they must be there to be singled out. This does not in any way imply that reality, in itself, is indeterminate. Quite the contrary: reality is perfectly determinate, but its determinateness consists in its *being such* that determinate concepts apply to it.

My principle claim in this paper is that the traditional problems about other minds cannot be resolved by the analytical strategies popular twenty years ago. Insofar as they are epistemological problems about the feelings and beliefs of others, they are ultimately problems about inductive inference and, in the case of belief, about inductive inference and verbal interpretation. As such, these problems do not presuppose a special subject, the philosophy of mind; they are, broadly speaking, problems of applied logic and semantics.

Notes

1. See Norman Malcolm's influential essay, "Knowledge of Other Minds," in his *Knowledge and Certainty* (Englewood Cliffs, N.J., 1963), 130-40.

2. See ibid., 136f.

3. On this see Malcolm, "Review of Wittgenstein's *Philosophical Investigations,"* in *Knowledge and Certainty,* 96-129

4. See P. F. Strawson, *Individuals* (London, 1959), 106-11.

5. I use Hume's term "experiental inference" faute de mieux. The term "induction" often has the narrow sense of "inductive generalization," but the nondeductive or "ampliative" inferences common in science are not restricted to mere generalizations from experience. In what follows, I shall use "induction" in a broad sense to include all inferences of this ampliative kind.

6. See Ludwig Wittgenstein, *Philosophical Investigations,* translated by G. E. M. Anscombe (Oxford, 1953), sect. 243-308 and passim.

7. See Malcolm, "Direct Perception," in *Knowledge and Certainty,* 91.

8. See Roderick Chisholm, *Theory of Knowledge,* 2d ed. (Englewood Cliffs, N.J., 1977), 26, 33.

9. See Wesley Salmon, *The Foundations of Scientific Inference* (Pittsburgh, 1967), 108-32 and 142ff; Clark Glymour, *Theory and Evidence* (Princeton, 1980), chap. 1-4; and John Earman, ed., *Testing Scientific Theories: Minnesota Studies in the Philosophy of Science,* vol. 10 (Minneapolis, 1983).

10. See the concluding remarks in my *Knowledge, Mind, and Nature* (New York, 1967), 263-69.

11. Bayes's Theorem provides a natural pattern for this kind of testing; see Salmon, *Foundations of Scientific Inference*.

12. See C. S. Peirce, "How To Make Our Ideas Clear," in *Charles S. Peirce: Selected Writings*, edited by Philip P. Weiner, (New York, 1958), 112-36; and Frank P. Ramsey, "Truth and Probability," in his *The Foundations of Mathematics* (London, 1931), 156-98.

13. See *Reason and Action* (Dordrecht, 1978), chap. 2. By a "tacit" premise, I mean a premise one reasons "in accordance with." Jones reasons in accordance with "All whales are mammals" when he infers "This is a mammal" from "This is a whale," "That is a mammal" from "That is a whale," and so on. His tacit premise in such reasoning is, then, "All whales are mammals."

14. See Wilfrid Sellars, "Empiricism and the Philosophy of Mind," in *Minnesota Studies in the Philosophy of Science*, vol. I, edited by Herbert Feigl and Michael Scriven (Minneapolis, 1956), 253-329.

15. See Michael Dummett, "What Is a Theory of Meaning? (II)," in *Truth and Meaning*, edited by Gareth Evans and J. M. McDowell (Oxford, 1976), 67-139.

16. Paul Feyerabend, "An Attempt at a Realistic Interpretation of Experience," *Proceedings of the Aristotelian Society* 58 (1958): 143-17.

17. See Chisholm, *Theory of Knowledge*.

18. See W. V. O. Quine, *Word and Object* (Cambridge, Mass., 1960), chap. 2; and "Ontological Relativity," in his *Ontological Relativity and Other Essays* (New York, 1969), 26-68.

19. I discuss Quine's argument for translational indeterminacy in "Quine on Translation and Reference," *Philosophical Studies* 27 (1975): 221-236.

20. See Wilfrid Sellars, "Some Reflections on Language Games," in his *Science, Perception, and Reality* (New York, 1964), 321-50.

21. See Hilary Putnam, *Reason, Truth, and History* (Cambridge, 1981), chap. 3. The metaphsyical realism I defend here differs from the metaphysical realism Putnam attacks is one important way: his version of the thesis involves the claim that there is "exactly one true and complete description of 'the way the world is' " (see p. 49). I cannot see why a serious metaphysical realist—one holding that objects of successful reference really exist—should want to make this dubious claim.

22. See G. W. Leibniz, *New Essays on the Human Understanding*, translated by Peter Remnant and Jonathan Bennett (Cambridge, 1981), 310f.

Troubles with Fodor's Nativism

JERRY SAMET

If one thing is clear, it is that the classical doctrine [of innate ideas] is not. That doctrine is in fact a set of variations on a theme whose identity is obscure and doubtful; on a number of topics, even in the work of a single philosopher, the doctrine exhibits a bewildering tendency to fluctuate between one alternative and another. Indeed, the overall impression it conveys is itself ambiguous in a characteristically philosophical way: it seems at one moment a daring and almost incredible hypothesis, and at the next a resounding platitude.[1]

Nativists have traditionally been able to provoke empiricists quite easily. The Cartesian claim that there are innate ideas brought a sharp response from John Locke three hundred years ago, and Noam Chomsky's recent attempts to find support for the doctrine in the facts about language acquisition have drawn similar strong responses from such present-day sympathizers of Locke's as Nelson Goodman.[2] Empiricists have generally held nativism to be a pernicious doctrine; when it comes to innate ideas, any are already too many.

More recently, however, the feuding has settled down and (for the most part) cooler heads have prevailed. For one thing, it's become much more difficult for nativists to provoke empiricists. Quine has stated quite explicitly that the behaviorist is "knowingly and cheerfully up to his neck in innate mechanisms," and Quine is about as staunch as they come.[3] Of course, there is a difference between innate ideas and innate mechanisms, and it would be a serious mistake to take Quine's remark as a capitulation to nativists. It's more that the whole shape of the debate has changed. We've come to a better understanding of what nativists and empiricists could possibly be arguing about. Everyone agrees that learning requires that something be innate— even tabulas have some innate structure. The disagreement revolves around issues concerning what sorts of things are innate: are there innate concepts, ideas, truths, and so forth, or are there only innate mechanisms that mediate the acquisition of concepts, ideas, and truths? Are the innate structures tailored to specific domains of knowledge or are they general, second-order learning strategies? Empiricists have leaned to the second alternative on each of these questions, whereas nativists have tried to make the case for the first.

Part of our better understanding of this traditional dispute involves the realization that its resolution awaits empirical results in psychology. Philosophers may have a vested theoretical interest in the results coming out one way or another, but it doesn't seem that philosophers can settle these questions. It's the psychologists who have to formulate systematically what our knowledge in a particular domain comes to, determine what sorts of experiences are in fact required to attain this knowledge, and try to figure out what sorts of mental structures could take us from the experience to the knowledge. This is the strategy espoused, at least in principle, by the British empiricists and articulated again by Chomsky as the nativist plan of research. It seems to be the only way to go about settling the issues. In recent years, nativists have pointed to the poverty of the stimulus in various domains of knowledge, and they have tried to build the case for nativism piece by piece.[4]

In a number of recent publications, Jerry Fodor has argued that whatever the results of this piecemeal approach to innate principles and knowledge, there is an overlooked argument that shows that our concepts are all innate.[5] His defense of this view is complicated; as I read it, it involves two separate arguments. The first is more or less conceptual and tries to show that even on a generous reading, classical empiricist models of concept acquisition are committed to the innateness of primitive concepts (which empiricists typically identify as a subset of our sensory concepts). Fodor thinks that a natural move for empiricists at this point is to try to salvage what they can by developing a theory of concept learning for at least our complex concepts. Such a theory would try to establish that all our complex concepts are constructable out of the primitive sensory concepts. Fodor's second argument, which is more or less empirical, is supposed to show that this move fails because the psychological evidence tells against any constructability thesis. The net effect is that empiricists are wrong in thinking we learn concepts from experience; in fact, all our concepts are innate. In place of the empiricist picture of concepts learned from experience, Fodor offers a concept-triggering model. The concepts are all there, waiting patiently, as it were, for the right experience to bring them into cognitive play. This is, as Fodor likes to say, 'strong stuff', and it seems designed (in part) to renew the feud. It certainly seems audacious enough to provoke the empiricist once again.

I am generally sympathetic to nativism, and I suspect that some limited form of concept-nativism is in fact correct—that is, *some* of our concepts *are* innate. What I want to challenge here is Fodor's argument for a more radical view. There are a number of points where I think the empiricist can develop strong counterarguments. The bulk of this paper is concerned with outlining some of these counterarguments and the possible nativist rejoinders. I must say at the outset, however, that I do agree with Fodor's analysis of the confusions in some empiricist models of concept acquisition, and I think that many of his positive suggestions about how we come to have concepts can help advance our understanding of conceptual development. So despite the fact that Fodor's conclusion is unwarranted, his argument does force us to reexamine the empiricist program and provide a better articulation of the options available to the empiricist. There is no question but that his work has invigorated the debate. This paper is part of a larger project; here I consider only one part of Fodor's argument—namely, the claim that the empiricist must grant the innateness of our primitive sensory concepts.[6] In the first section I present Fodor's argument to this effect. In the second section I develop an empiricist defense against Fordor's argument. In the next section I sketch three arguments within the nativist tradition that might be marshaled to reinforce Fodor's original attack. My view is that such supporting arguments are inconclusive and underdeveloped at best. In the concluding section I discuss what I take to be deep, underlying tensions in our ordinary ways of thinking about concepts, and I briefly consider how these tensions affect the empiricist-nativist debate in general and Fodor's arguments in particular.

FODOR'S ARGUMENT

According to Fodor, empiricist psychologists (and philosophers) face a dilemma. If their idea of what should count as paradigmatic cases of concept learning is taken seriously, then it can be shown that their own theories commit them to a nativism of sensory concepts. If we don't take their model seriously, then they are left without any support for their antinativist claims. In either case, they pose no real alternative to nativists. We begin by looking at Fodor's version of the 'best empiricist model'.

This is how Fodor describes the typical empiricist concept-learning experiment.

You arrive in the experimental environment. The experimenter says to you something like "I have here a pack of stimulus cards. Each stimulus card displays a colored geometrical figure. There are some red triangles, there are some green squares, ... and so on. Now some of these cards are flurg and some are non-flurg and (for convenience) every card is either flurg or non-flurg. Your job is to figure out which cards are which.

And I am here to help you. For, though I will not tell you which ones the flurg cards are, still I will let you examine any card you like and guess whether it is flurg. And I will tell you if your guess is right." (PSIC 266)

The subject continues to make guesses about specific cards until she 'reaches criterion', that is, correctly classifies each card. The theory proposed to explain the subject's behavior is that she (consciously or unconsciously) formulates hypotheses of the form 'x is flurg iff . . .' and tests them against the evidence she gets until she arrives at an unrefuted hypothesis. On this view, "the mechanisms of concept learning are realizations of some species of inductive logic" (PSIC 267). That is, the subject must have an ordered set of hypotheses that she uses in formulating guesses, she must have a way to determine which hypotheses are ruled out by a particular response, and so on.

But now consider: if in midtask we can formulate a hypothesis using a predicate cointensional with 'flurg', then don't we have the concept flurg already? The concept flurg *is just that concept* expressed by such a complex predicate. But this means that even the concepts that are, *ex hypothesis,* learned, are employed at an earlier stage in the cognitive process that culminates in their being successfully learned.

This is a very simple argument with a very strong conclusion. It purports to show that the empiricist model presupposes that for every concept C that is 'identified' by the subject in this sort of task, the subject must have already had C in her conceptual repertoire. If this task is taken as a paradigmatic case of concept learning, then it means that all learned concepts are available for use before they are learned. But this either makes no sense or it means that even learned concepts are in some sense innate. Either way, the nativist is vindicated.

Although this is the conclusion Fodor will ultimately argue for, he doesn't expect to get it from this argument all by itself. He grants that the empiricist might respond in this way: the fact that the concept flurg is already available for hypothesis formation doesn't show that we 'have' the concept before the concept-learning situation. To really have a concept is not merely to have it available for such hypothesis projections, but to be able to employ it in a wide range of cognitive tasks. This, the empiricist will claim, is the essence of learning, and it doesn't happen until the subject reaches criterion and can identify new cards as flurg. So, this argument only restates Edgley's 'resounding platitude' that the empiricist can happily grant: that we potentially have the concepts we learn before we learn them.

Whatever the merits of this response, and however we determine what it 'really' means to have a concept, Fodor correctly points out that it assumes that at least *some* concepts must be innate. This is so because the empiricist's model presupposes that the subject engaged in the learning is keeping track of the flurginess or lack of flurginess of the stimuli as she goes along—her record keeping is of the form 'second blue square is non-flurg' (notice that 'flurg' and 'non-flurg' are not really used here, only mentioned). Without this sort of record keeping, the subject will regularly project hypotheses that are incompatible with what she has already found out about flurginess. But this means that we must (really) already have concepts like second, blue, and square or there will be no way to collect an evidential base. So for every concept C that is learned (given this paradigm of concept learning), there must be some set of concepts ($C1 \ldots Cn$) that are already available. If we follow this back far enough, we come to some set of concepts S that is available before any learning has occurred. Since the traditional empiricist line has been to take primitive sensory concepts as the building blocks in conceptual development, the empiricist must grant that these primitive sensory concepts could not be learned, but must be innate.

Fodor's argument threatens to turn the tables on the empiricist. The empiricist ends up claiming that we are *rational* cognitive agents when it comes to concept acquisition, and the nativist takes us to be *arational*, passive subjects. For the empiricist, concept acquisition is inductive learning—it is a mental act; for the nativist it is a matter of triggering—a mental event and no more.

A REPLY TO FODOR

Let's begin by seeing what the empiricist must grant to Fodor. As I indicated in the introduction, I think that Fodor is right in challenging the viability of the experimental paradigm under consideration as a case of concept learning. The empiricist seems trapped on the horns of a second dilemma. If (really) acquiring the concept flurg involves supplementing the set of categories the subject has for experiencing the world—getting her to approach the world with an eye for flurginess, so to speak—then the experiment fails to teach the concept. Most subjects will forget about the flurg/non-flurg distinction as soon as the experiment ends. If the learning is only the ability to sort the flurg things from the non-flurg things, the subject clearly has had this ability all along; she just didn't understand the term 'flurg'—she didn't know which of her already present sorting abilities she was supposed to use. Either way one looks at it, this is not a good paradigm for concept learning. What then are we to make of the experiment?

Broadly speaking, the intention of the experiment is to probe the ability of subjects to form equivalence classes of nonidentical stimuli. The question is how we master particular classification schemes, and the general answer is that we discriminate certain readily identifiable attributes and use them as a basis for our guesses. But calling this *concept learning* involves a failure to distinguish between concept identification and concept acquisition. The former, which is what goes on in the experiment, is like playing the game Twenty Questions—we have to guess who or what someone is thinking about. Clearly, one cannot learn about *new* people or things in successfully playing this game (except incidentally). You can only win if you are already familiar with what you're trying to guess. Similarly, the experimenter provides hints as to which concept he has in mind, and the subject has to use these hints to figure out which of the concepts she already has available is the one the experimenter has in mind. But this, to use another analogy, is like getting hints as to how many jelly beans there are in a jar: unless one is already acquainted with the range of possible answers (the positive integers), there is little chance of making the right guess.

Fodor argues that if the empiricist accepts this point, as I think he should, then he must give up the hypothesis generation and testing model as an account of the original acquisition of our sensory concepts. If he also grants that the generate-and-test models are the only models of learning that we have, then he must next give up the claim that sensory concepts are learned. But if he is willing to concede that sensory concepts are not learned, then how does he differ from the nativist? As Fodor sees it, "Both sides assume that primitive concepts are, in a certain sense, unlearned, indeed that they are, in a certain sense, innate" (PSIC 275). I want to discuss what I think are other ways to see it. As I see it, the empiricist can resist Fodor's line of reasoning here in three ways: he can defend the generate-and-test model as a model of concept learning; he can give up the generate-and-test model but claim that this is not the only model of learning available; or he can give up the generate-and-test model as well as the idea that concepts are learned from experience, but argue that these concessions do not establish nativism. That is, he can resist Fodor's inference (in the passage above) from 'unlearned' to 'innate'. All three lines are worth exploring; I will take up the first two elsewhere,[7] but here I consider only the third. I will argue that although the empiricist may have to admit that sensory concepts are not learned (on Fodor's interpretation of learning), such an admission does *not* imply that sensory concepts are innate.

To see why this is so we need to look at Fodor's notion of learning. Although we use the term 'learn' rather loosely in ordinary talk—to learn that *p* is simply to come to know that *p*—there is a distinction to be made between those cases in which we figure out *p* on the basis of some systematic thought process (conscious or unconscious) and those cases that don't involve such processes. Fodor assumes that there are causal stories to be told about both sorts of knowledge acquisition, but he distinguishes between the 'rational-causal' processes that underlie real learning and the 'brute-causal' processes that underlie the other cases. This is at best a rough dividing line; but in the extreme cases, the distinction is clear enough. If a student acquires a knowledge of first-order logic in class, we presume that the mental processes involved instantiate some sort of inductive logic—one deserves the credit for having learned it. If one could come by the same body of knowledge by ingesting a pill, then we might not assume that the same sorts of processes played any role. Again, although we might colloquially say that Holmes learned the identity of the murderer from the clues and Watson learned it from Holmes, there is obviously a significant difference between the sorts of processes involved.

What I think is not at *all* obvious is how the fact that our concepts are unlearned is supposed to support the claim that they are innate. Fodor sometimes speaks as if there is an immediate inference from 'unlearned' to 'innate':

> In any theory of the modification of concepts available to us there is no such thing as a concept being invented. It is obviously also true that there must be *some* sense in which our conceptual repertoire is responsive to our experiences, including the experiences of the species in doing things like inventing mathematics. What that implies, it seems to me, is that a theory of the conceptual plasticity of organisms must be a theory of how the environment selects among the innately specified concepts. *It is not a theory of how you acquire concepts, but a theory of how the environment determines which parts of the conceptual mechanism in principle available to you are in fact exploited.* (LL 151)

On the view I'm suggesting, the empiricist can happily grant that (sensory)[8] concepts are not invented—they are not the product of our intellectual initiative or imaginative powers. But he can reject the conclusion that Fodor wants to draw: that concept acquisition is a matter of the environment 'exploiting' individual pieces of an innate network of concepts.

Consider this sort of counterexample (using the biological metaphor many contemporary nativists favor). Children get infections in the course of development. These are not invented or learned; they are as brute-causal as anything can be. At the same time, these infections are dependent on environmental factors. We can even adapt Fodor's claim about the conceptual mechanism and say that the environment determines which parts of the 'infection repertoire' in principle available to the child are in fact exploited. Despite this parallel, it doesn't seem correct to say that infections are physiologically innate in any way: that the environmental stimuli only trigger the infections that are already latently there. Being 'in principle available' is not the same as being innate. The nativist must provide a further argument to show that the concept case is significantly different from the infection case.

What the empiricist has to elaborate is how concepts get into the mind if it's *not* a matter of inductive learning or the triggering of innate material. The obvious alternative is the one that adapts the infection story to concept acquisition. Roughly put, it says that if we go out into the world with our sensory channels kept open we 'catch' (sensory) concepts. This, in fact, is very close to the traditional empiricist conception of the matter. Now it might seem at first that this is no alternative at all—it is not a theory that tells us *how* interaction with the world eventuates in our coming to have concepts; 'catch' seems an empty metaphor without a theory of the 'catching' process to fill it out. But my empiricist should not be thought of as evading the need for a theory of 'concept catching'. He is claiming that there is no mentalistic (cognitivist, rational-causal, etc.) theory to be had, although there could be such a mentalistic or information-processing characterization of what it is that is caught. All we can say about concept acquisition is that there are input-output regularities of a certain sort, and we might develop a neurophysiological theory to explain these regularities. What the empiricist should deny is that there is any *mental* process that eventuates in sensory concepts; we don't 'think them up' or 'figure them out'. They are simply recorded in us as a result of our interaction with the world.

This talk of input-output regularities sans any mentalistic theory of internal processes will sound very much like behaviorism (generally: antimentalism) rearing its head again. To be fair to Fodor, at an early stage in the presentation of his argument (PSIC 258-59) he makes it clear that he only wants to challenge 'classical' empiricists who are committed to mentalism and the representational theory of mind (whatever the differences are between these two positions will not matter in this context). If the empiricist is ready to drop back into a behaviorist stance, Fodor grants that his arguments won't go through. But he obviously thinks that to force one's opponent into this stance is to win the point; behaviorism, as Dennett has remarked, is a cliff that you push your opponents off of. Let us assume for the sake of argument that Fodor is right to write off behaviorism as a serious candidate for a comprehensive psychological theory. If the choice were between nativism and behaviorism, we would opt for nativism. But I want to argue that this is a false choice. The empiricist position I've been developing *is* 'classical' (on Fodor's sense of the term). The problem is that Fodor fails to consider seriously the possibility that behaviorism, though generally wrong, is right about the acquisition of sensory concepts. My empiricist is *not* a behaviorist; he need not take concepts to be dispositions to overt behavior—he can even agree with Fodor that they are mental entities manipulated in cognitive processing (this is what allows him to meet Fodor's criteria as a 'classical empiricist'). Concepts can be internal mental representations that are part of a language of thought. Furthermore, he can reject completely behaviorist accounts of the acquisition of beliefs about the world, and so forth, and claim that not only are they not to be understood dispositionally, but that for them there may be no discoverable schedules of reinforcement. All my empiricist claims is that the negative behaviorist point about the acquisition of concepts is correct—in other words, there is no mentalistic story to be told about this process.

It might look as if my empiricist is left with a patchwork theory—a nonmentalistic view about concept acquisition tacked on to an otherwise mentalistic psychology. But it is a mistake to think of this as theoretically awkward. In the first place, nativists who agree with Fodor end up adopting just the same sort of hybrid theory: brute-causal accounts for concept acquisition (triggering) and rational-causal, information-processing accounts for thought and the propositional attitudes. What's more important, however, is that only a hybrid theory makes any *intuitive* sense. Intuitively, concepts are the building blocks of thought. But this means that they are prior to thoughts in just the way that bricks are prior to brick walls: you need the bricks before you start to build. The claim that we can't learn concepts—if it's taken (a la Fodor) to mean that we can't use our rational thought processes to figure out our concepts—now begins to sound like a resounding platitude. "Of course," we want to say, "if thinking is a matter of manipulating concepts, then we can't use thought to derive our original concepts. Bricklayers build *with* bricks, but they don't build the bricks themselves." The empiricist is simply saying that the fact that we don't 'think up' our concepts does not imply that they were there all along innately, just waiting to be triggered. Consider the apprentice bricklayer's parallel conclusion that the bricks on his new job site were always there, just waiting for him to come along with his mortar and his trowel.

Perhaps Fodor's point is that it's precisely this very commonsensical insight—that acquiring concepts can't be like learning facts—that somehow escaped empiricist thinkers. Such a claim is extremely farfetched. Perhaps some empirical psychologists have missed it, but there is little reason to think that traditional empiricists were committed to anything like a rational-causal conception of concept acquisition. I don't want to get into detailed questions of historical exegesis here,[9] but it seems to me that Fodor has misconstrued the basic motivation of empiricists—at least of empiricists like Hume. Such empiricists are *not* primarily committed to the view that our epistemic holdings are all the result of learning (construed as hypothetico-inductive rational activity). What they are really out to establish is that our contact with the external world is the *source* of all that we know. The method of acquisition is not as critical as the source. Of course, empiricists have had to provide a theory about the method of acquisition in order to make their views about the source of our knowledge at all plausible. And in providing such theories, some empiricists have mistakenly committed themselves to hypothetico-inductive models of concept acquisition. So Fodor is right in arguing that whatever the merits of these models as explanations of, say, Holmes's learning which of the suspects is in fact the murderer, they have no explanatory value as a theory of how we acquire concepts. But this result is not inimical to empiricism; it only challenges the scope of the hypothetico-inductivist versions. Hume would happily grant Fodor's argument against concept learning, and not feel his empiricism was at all jeopardized. To take one of Hume's examples: the fact that we know the taste of wine and the Laplander does not has nothing to do with the application of our rational faculties to anything at all. It is simply a matter of exposure. That I have a concept of a centaur whereas my neighbor has never entertained such fancies is again not to be credited to my inductive powers, but to the play of my imagination.

THREE NATIVIST RESPONSES

I've claimed that the nativist needs to provide some argument to bridge the gap between 'unlearned' and 'innate' and thereby rule out infection-type accounts of concept acquisition. Fodor, as far as I can make out, does not explicitly provide such arguments, and he sometimes leaves the impression that he thinks no such arguments are needed.[10] Setting Fodor aside for the moment, I think that the nativist literature does have some resources that can be called on here. In this section I want to briefly lay out three very general sorts of arguments that nativists have appealed to that might be adapted to close this gap. I then consider how an empiricist might reply to each of them.

The Poverty of the Stimulus Argument can be traced back to Plato, and it has surfaced regularly in nativist writings ever since. In the *Phaedo,* Plato argues that the fact that we have the concept of equality, which serves as an approachable but never reached standard for judging the (near) equalities we encounter in everyday life, is proof that our concept of equality could not be copied or derived from the not-exactly-equalities we experience.[11] The argument form has been revived by Chomsky and used to support his views about the innate basis of language acquisition. He cashes out the argument in terms of the underdetermination of theory by evidence. The primary linguistic data that we're exposed to radically underdetermines the knowledge that we in fact acquire in the course of normal language learning. The conclusion drawn is that innate factors play a substantive role in getting us to the correct generalizations.[12] Both versions of the argument threaten the empiricist view of concepts as unlearned but still environment based. For many of our concepts, at least, the environment provides us only with a bad sample—inadequate as a source of our concept.

The Irrelevance of the Stimulus Argument, applied to sensation and perceptual experience, can be found in this passage from Descartes:

> For nothing reaches our mind from external objects through the organs of sense beyond certain corporeal movements. . . . [B]ut even these movements and the figures which arise from them are conceived by us

in the shape they assume in the organs of sense. . . . So much the more must the ideas of pain, color, sound, and the like be innate. . . . For they have no likeness to the corporeal movement.[13]

Descartes seems to be distinguishing here between the external object, the corporeal movement in the organ of sense that the external object gives rise to, and our ideas and conceptions. One claim he makes here is that all three are different. To this is tacked on a familiar and powerful point: the pain is not in the fire and communicated to us by contact. In fact, there is no pain in the environment we are exposed to—it's all in us. All that the environment does to us is create internal motions. But our concepts are not just concepts of motion. We have concepts of color, shape, and so on. So there is an incommensurability between stimulus and concept.

This argument is usually not distinguished from its predecessor, but it differs in at least one crucial respect. The claim of the poverty of the stimulus argument is that the objects we experience (i.e., the *distal* stimuli) fall short of the precision of our concepts. This incommensurability argument claims that our representational repertoire could not be derived from our causal contact with external objects, that the *proximal* stimuli could not be the *sources* of our concepts. Here the argument seems to rest on the physiological theory of sensation and sense perception that Descartes accepts and an assumption akin to Fodor's methodological solipsism. Perceptual contact with the world, on this view, comes about as a result of the fact that the minute motions of external objects cause corresponding motions in our organs of sense. But our concepts are not of motions in our sense organs. They are concepts of physical entities with physical properties. It's as if the conduits of sensation are not wide enough to carry the information needed to form a conception of the external object. But we *do* have such conceptions. So the source must be internal, not external.

The Uniformity of Competence Argument is one of a flurry of arguments used by Chomsky to support the view that language learning depends heavily on an innate component.[14] Chomsky's idea is that the primary linguistic data—the evidence we get about the structure of our language—varies greatly from individual to individual. We hear different sets of sentences and nonsentences, and the explicit instruction and correction we receive is far from uniform. But despite this variance, we all end up knowing the same language/grammar. If learning were a matter of applying some generalized inductive procedure to our sample, then we should expect that the stages of development and the generalizations we arrive at would vary more. Applied to our domain of concept acquisition, the claim would be that if our experience was really the source for concepts, then we should expect the idiosyncrasies of our experience to show up at the conceptual level. But despite the differences in our experiences, our concepts are very similar—for one thing, we understand each other. On Fodor's triggering model this can be explained by the fact that experience only serves to trigger innate concepts, and we all share the same set of innate concepts. The empiricist, it could be argued, is not able to deal with these facts about conceptual convergence.

I think that these arguments are worth developing in more detail; here I only indicate why I think they're inconclusive. Let us begin with the uniformity of competence argument. The first thing to note is that Chomsky's original claim is presented as a *special* feature of the language case, a singularity that suggests that we are dealing with a domain of competence that depends on a significant innate endowment. As such, it is supposed to work in tandem with a number of other considerations—that children learn language at a period when they cannot learn anything else of such complexity, that the acquisition depends only minimally on general intelligence, that acquiring a language after the critical period has passed is especially difficult, and so on. What is not at all obvious is that these considerations transfer to the general case of concept acquisition. The empiricist could argue that whatever we think of Chomsky's claim about the uniformity of linguistic knowledge, there is no reason to assume that our conceptual repertoires are in fact uniform.[15] It is often assumed that such a uniformity is a prerequisite of successful communication, but I know of no convincing argument for this view.

I'm not sure what to make of the irrelevance of the stimulus argument. Consider the way a camera works. As it stands, Descartes's reasoning would seem to imply that the environment is not really the source of the camera's output. By parity of reasoning, we should say that what really happens is that the environmental stimulus triggers an innate image. The 'stimulus' affects the internals of the camera only as rays of light; but the output is not in fact rays of light, but a photograph. The camera, therefore, does not 'conceive' the original in the shape it assumes in its 'organs of sense'; so it must work by having some innate material triggered. To return to one of our earlier analogies, this is tantamount to saying that the environment is not the source of our infections since there are no infections in the environment—only bacteria and viruses. It is no doubt true that infections are a matter of environment-organism interaction, but the environment provides more than a wake-up call to the latent infections in us.[16]

There is another perspective on Descartes's claim that we might adopt. We might see him as simply saying that concepts are psychological entities; they are ontologically *mental* entities. There are no concepts in the world that give rise to our concepts. The point then would be that concepts are *not* like splinters, but *are* like infections. This is a reasonable point, but one that empiricists have recognized.[17] What should be clear is that it does *not* support Fodor's triggering conception. To take one last analogy: programs, *construed as electrical patterns or arrays of O's and 1's,* begin their existence in a computer. Be that as it may, it doesn't follow that all the programs are innate in the machine and that the programmer's typing merely triggers what's already there. And this is so despite the fact that every possible program that is representable in the machine can in principle be determined from the structure of the machine itself. In some respects, modern computers *are* 'triggered systems', but this has to do with specific prior programming. My claim is only that we need a further argument to the effect that our acquisition of sensory concepts is a matter of such specific preprogramming.

Finally, we come to the poverty of the stimulus argument. As I observed at the start, this form of argument is the bread-and-butter strategy of the nativist's research program, and I have no reason to question its general soundness. The issue is whether a *specific* argument of this type can be constructed in the case of (sensory) concept acquisition. The argument would have to show that concepts are not 'impressed' on us from the outside because our experiences fall short of our concepts in some clearly specifiable way. Let's look briefly at both of the versions of the argument that we mentioned earlier—the *Phaedo* version and Chomsky's version.

Recall that Chomsky's use of the argument depends on the familiar underdetermination of theoretical generalizations by evidence statements. Of course, it's not the underdetermination itself that helps support the innateness hypothesis, but the fact that we all manage to *overcome* this underdetermination and converge on a/the 'correct' theory. (In this form, the argument is a close cousin of the uniformity of competence argument discussed above.) How, we must ask, does this argument carry over from the domain of language acquisition to the domain of concept acquisition? One natural way to look at the language case, granting for the sake of argument Chomsky's nativist interpretation of the data, is to see the language learner as equipped with a set of innate constraints on the hypotheses that the learner will come up with in the course of acquisition. The analogous position in the case of *concept* acquisition would be an innate set of constraints on the sorts of concepts we might develop.[18] A view very close to this—but applied to percepts instead of concepts—was developed by Gestalt psychologists like Koffka.[19] Their argument begins with the same observations Plato uses: we naturally perceive things as near squares, almost-straight lines, and so on, not as exact quadrangles or curves of a specific type. This prompts a search for the general principles that could account for this sort of idealization or 'perceptual organization'. But this is a far cry from the claim that sensory concepts are innate. Constraints on concepts are not concepts. We have again arrived at a nativist position that is acceptable to, and indeed espoused by, empiricists.[20]

The second version of the argument, from the *Phaedo,* seems more appropriate to the domain under discussion. In contrast to the Gestaltist search for general principles/constraints, Plato posits concept-specific, innate endowments (for reasons mainly having to do with his theory of Forms).[21] Furthermore, he also makes use of something like triggering to explain the activation of the innate material. For Plato, the crucial feature of the comparison is that the perceived instances 'fall short' of the concept. It is this 'falling short', what Plato refers to as the "inferiority" of the perceptual objects, that motivates his nativist claim. Our concepts *transcend* the world of experience, so they must have their source outside that world (in the Forms that we have innately represented). The basis of the empiricist response should be, and has been, that the transcendence is illusory. There is a sense in which the empiricist can admit that there is a qualitative 'gap' between concepts and objects. But to make his case, the nativist first has to show that even in the case of sensory concepts, this gap is not a matter of concept formation by 'abstraction'. That is, to show that we're talking about a *positive* innate contribution over and above what the environment provides, and not merely some process of subtraction. Second, even if we grant this much, the nativist has to explain how this sort of view supports the ascription of a *completely* innate conceptual repertoire that's only triggered by experience. Why accept more than an innate *contribution* to concept construction—a contribution compatible with a substantive *environmental* contribution?

COMMON SENSE AND CONCEPTS

To this point, I've been concerned with the dialectic of possible arguments and counterarguments prompted by Fodor's claim that even the empiricist must admit that primitive sensory concepts are innate. I've said nothing, however, about a more fundamental question—namely, 'what *are* concepts?' This evasiveness is very much in keeping with the tradition. The whole rationalist-empiricist debate over innate 'ideas' has always been much more focused on the innateness and less concerned with specifying precisely what it is that's supposed to have this property. 'Ideas' in 'innate ideas' functions as a variable. I noted at the outset that part of our 'new understanding' of the controversy involves the realization that this is a crucial question that must be addressed directly,[22] but Hume too suspected that the failure to be clear on this matter robbed the debate of much of its significance.[23] I want to suggest in this section that two different tensions in our ordinary common-sense conception of concepts—in the 'folk psychology' of concepts—might be at the root of some of the confusion in the debate. Fodor says explicitly that his interest is only in the innateness of concepts, not beliefs, traits, and so on. But the fact that we can agree that we're talking about the innateness of *concepts* does not guarantee that we know what we're talking about.

Consider again the analogy discussed earlier, of concepts as the building blocks of thought. It is very natural to think of concepts in this way; as the counterparts of *terms*. Terms, we say, express concepts, a concept gives the meaning of a term, it fixes the extension of a term, it is what a term contributes to the semantics of larger complexes of which it is a part, and so on. Many of these assumptions have come under sharp philosophical attack in recent years, but the idea that concepts are term-sized has survived intact. We have a concept of *bread,* but no concept *that Tuesday it rained.* Our ordinary view is that when we combine concepts in the right sorts of ways, we get the that-clauses that express the contents of thoughts. In cognitive science, we say that the concepts are the counterparts of mental words and the thoughts are the counterparts of mental sentences. This is the undergirding for the building-block metaphor; and I've argued that, in this light, Fodor's argument about the *nonlearnability* of primitive (sensory) concepts is obviously correct. We can't have any psychological complexes before we have the psychological primitives out of which they are constituted. So, among other things, we can't begin to think unless we have the concepts required to put thoughts together. If learning is a form of thinking, then we can't learn our primitive concepts.

This is all well and good, except for the fact that there is another way of thinking about concepts that seems at odds with all this. On this approach, to have a concept is not to have a *term-sized* item—a mental word—but rather to have a complex, interconnected body of knowledge. That is, something like a *paragraph-sized* item—a set of mental sentences or propositions. To have the concept of a bachelor is to know that bachelors are humans, that they are male, and so on. These propositions are not just contingently associated with the concept; many seem to be *constitutive* of the concept. If S doesn't know that humans are biological organisms, then (on this approach) he doesn't have the concept of a bachelor. Again, we're talking about (the philosophical expression of) a commonsense picture that has come under severe philosophical attack. But the idea of concepts as sets of propositions remains part of our way of thinking.

There is a second tension that I think is relevant to the nativist's argument. This has to do with the *role* folk psychology assigns to concepts. Sometimes we think of concepts as playing a sort of Kantian role. They make our experience of a world possible. That experience is the effect of our applying concepts (or: of concepts being applied) to an inherently unparsed stimulus array—to the busy, bustling, blooming confusion of sensation. Because we have concepts, our experience is organized, coherent, and regular. If we didn't have them, we wouldn't experience anything at all. In this sense, they are *preexperiential;* they are logically prior to experience.

But again, there is another way we think about concepts that seems at odds with the Kantian role. On this natural way of thinking, experience provides us with a perceptual data-base—a set of potential evidence statements—and concepts are what we come up with in trying to come to terms with these deliverances of experience. As before, there are a number of philosophical issues raised by this conception of concepts having to do with the proposed line between the theoretical and the observational. But on this view, concepts are the sorts of things that we actively fashion. They form the bases of the theories about the world that we create. In this guise, they are *postexperiential* constructs. To take one relevant application, it seems clear that the empiricist concept-learning paradigm that Fodor attacks as being inadequate as a comprehensive theory is based on this notion of a concept as a postexperiential construct.

There is a systematic tie between the poles of these respective tensions. To the extent that one construes concepts as preexperiential categories, one is likely to see them as terms under which particulars can fall. The concept in this way is the extension determiner, or at least it determines what the organism chunks together as repeated tokens of a type. On the other hand, when we think about grasping concepts quâ postexperiential product of directed intellectual activity, we are thinking of concepts as sets of beliefs or as a body of knowledge.

We can see how the first tension comes out in Fodor's positive views about concepts. Most of his discussion fits the conception of concepts as *terms* in the language of thought, as mental representations that can combine to form propositions. These representations are all innate and are triggered by experience. We also have an innate combinatorial mechanism that can concatenate these concepts to form truth-bearing mental representations (among other things). Crudely put, experience triggers more and more of these mental words so that we can think more and more thoughts. In discussing conceptual growth, Fodor provides interesting reasons for the view that the triggered concepts are ordered—planted at various depths in a seedbed, as it were—so that our concepts become available to us (partially) on the basis of an internal schedule. Such a supposition would explain why it is that children don't get the concept imperialism before they get the concept of a government triggered. Imperialism is 'buried deeper' than government, and it cannot be triggered except (perhaps) via the concept of a government. Fodor suggests that the concepts closest to the surface—the first to be triggered—are the concepts of midsized objects in our environment. All this fits the concepts-as-terms construal quite well. But consider the following parenthetical comment:

> It might be held that you can't, in point of logic, have the concept BACHELOR unless you have the belief that bachelors are unmarried. If this is true, then the question whether the concept bachelor is innate willy nilly involves the question whether the belief that bachelors are unmarried is. (PSIC 257-58)

But *how* could this be true on Fodor's construal of concepts? The belief that bachelors are unmarried involves the concepts bachelor and unmarried. It follows from this that one cannot have the concept bachelor before one has the concept unmarried. So there are two possibilities: either they are triggered simultaneously (along with the belief that all bachelors are unmarried), or unmarried is triggered first. In either case, it is difficult to see how this is supposed to square with the thrust of Fodor's point about innate orderings. He says, for instance, that children acquire the concept dog before they get the concept of an animal (PSIC 311). But surely, if any concept is constituted by any belief, the belief that dogs are animals is constitutive of the concept dog.[24]

I don't take this to be a serious objection to Fodor's general argument. But I think it does indicate the sorts of tensions between these different conceptions. The view that there is some 'logical' connection between the concept bachelor and the belief that all bachelors are unmarried (and this logical connection will presumably extend from unmarried to married to sexuality and contract and gender and on and on) seems to me not to fit well with the view of concepts as individually triggered that dominates Fodor's discussion. But the problem is not specifically Fodor's—it is common sense that allows us to make *both* of the following claims: (1) To know that all bachelors are unmarried one must *first* have the concept bachelor, and (2) one doesn't have the concept bachelor unless one knows that all bachelors are unmarried.

The second tension makes itself felt in discussions about the relation of concepts and language, concepts and consciousness, concepts and animals, and so on. Typically, when developmental psychologists talk about concepts, they have the *preexperiential* notion in mind. When psychologists contend that a one-year-old infant already has a concept of number, they mean that the child has something—perhaps only an identification procedure—that allows the child to react differentially to groups of two, to groups of three, and so on. When philosophers say, as they often do, that psychologists are confused about concepts, it's usually the postexperiential conception that they have in mind. They mean that it is premature to ascribe to the one-year-old the knowledge structures one would need to understand what a number is. This seems to me to be a brute sociological fact about the meeting point of these two disciplines. But what it indicates, among other things, is that this tension is not just a dividing line between two groups of concepts—say, the observational and theoretical. That line certainly needs to be drawn, but here we are talking about two construals of one and the same concept: the concept of number. These construals are compatible, but because we have one phrase— 'the concept of number'—referring to both, discussion is often at cross-purposes.

Given this jumble of ideas that underlies our commonsense conception of concept, one is led to wonder again whether Hume's diagnosis was correct.[25] One is tempted to reconstruct at least part of the debate in roughly this way. Each side begins with an essential insight. The nativist's contribution is that there must be preexperiential concepts—let's call them categories—or else there would be no experience.[26] The empiricist insight is that what makes our knowledge of the world (to the extent that we have knowledge at all) *knowledge,* is the fact that we construct true theories of the world that we test against the empirical evidence. Perhaps the deep disagreement is no more than the record of overreaching on the part of both parties?

Let me end this section by admitting that I haven't made any attempt to solve the problems I've raised here, and I've indulged in some very broad speculation. But I suspect that we are lulled into a false sense of security by the fact that we have a single word in English—'concept'—that embraces these different, and perhaps incompatible, senses. At the very least, this all suggests that there may be very different sorts of concepts, and we can't just assume that we will have a single theory that gives a uniform account for them all.[27]

CONCLUSION

The original seventeenth- and eighteenth-century debates over innate ideas had their place in a much broader set of metaphysical concerns. At issue were such questions as the foundations of morality and religion and the proper understanding of the relationship of God, humanity, and the world. In Plato, the doctrine of innate ideas served as a lemma in one proof of the immortality of the soul. I want to conclude by considering the bigger picture within which Fodor's nativism might finds *its* place. There are really two familiar and incompatible pictures that I want to consider. One can read Fodor's radical nativism as supporting a metaphysical conception of ourselves as very specifically fashioned for the world we inhabit. From the subtle changes that things cause in us, we come to have a rich conception of what those things are. We can 'decipher' these subtle effects because nature has provided us with a built-in key: namely, the innate concepts that correspond to these changes. This would be an 'optimistic' frame for Fodor's nativism. It is optimistic in that it takes the triggered concepts to somehow accurately represent the triggering world. Our concepts are not *merely* caused by the world; they accurately reflect it.

The second view is more pessimistic. It acknowledges the possibility that although the world that triggers our concepts might vary indefinitely, we remain trapped within the range of our innate endowment. We have only a limited spectrum of conceptual responses; we are not indefinitely flexible; we do not necessarily have the resources to accurately represent the variety that's out there in the world. Since triggering is presumably a many-to-one relation, such potential variety might be forced to conform to our innate range. On this second view, our innate endowment is something of a liability.

I think that both pictures are interesting and philosophically attractive. They both raise deep questions about realism, concepts, and human nature. I have argued, however, that they both can be resisted by the resourceful empiricist.[28]

Notes

1. Roy Edgley, "Innate Ideas," in *Knowledge and Necessity,* Royal Institute of Philosophy Lectures, vol. 3, 1968-69 (London, 1970).

2. See "The Epistemological Argument," Goodman's contribution to Symposium on Innate Ideas; reprinted in *The Philosophy of Language,* edited by J. Searle (Oxford, 1971), 140-44.

3. W. V. Quine, "Linguistics and Philosophy," in *Language and Philosophy,* edited by S. Hoor (New York, 1969), 96.

4. See, for example, E. S. Spelke, "Perception of Unity, Persistence, and Identity: Thoughts on Infants' Conceptions of Objects," in *Neonate Cognition,* edited by J. Mehler (in press); and D. Starkey, E. S. Spelke, and R. Gelman, "Number Competence in Infants: Sensitivity to Numeric Invariance and Numeric Change," paper presented at the International Conference of Infant Studies, New Haven, Conn., April 1980.

5. Fodor has developed the nativist argument in *The Language of Thought* (LT), (New York, 1975); "The Present Status of the Innateness Controversy" (PSIC), in *Representations* (Cambridge, Mass., 1981); and his contributions throughout *Language and Learning* (LL), edited by M. Piattelli-Palmarini (Cambridge, Mass., 1980).

6. I discuss related issues in three papers in preparation: "In Defense of Learning" (with Alan Zaitchik), "Nativism and Prototypes," and "Concepts of Concepts."

7. See "In Defense of Learning."

8. Unless the context indicates otherwise, by 'concepts' I'll mean primitive sensory concepts.

9. "In Defense of Learning" contains a discussion of some of the historical complications.

10. The discussion in LL suffers because the existence of this gap in the argument is not addressed directly.

11. *Phaedo,* 73b-76a, in *Plato: Five Dialogues,* translated by G. M. A. Grube (Indianapolis, 1981).

12. The general argument can be found in many of Chomsky's writings. See, for instance, *Reflections on Language* (New York, 1975), chap. 1.

13. "Notes against a Certain Program," in *The Essential Descartes,* edited by M. Wilson (New York, 1969), 371.

14. This argument can be found in Noam Chomsky, "Recent Contributions to the Theory of Innate Ideas," in Searle, ed., *Philosophy of Language,* 122.

15. One appeal of prototype theories of concepts is that they allow for the idiosyncracy of an individual's concepts but still steer clear of any sort of subjectivism of meaning or truth. For an assessment of Fodor's critique of prototype theories, see my "Nativism and Prototypes."

16. We might note in passing that although Hobbes seems to have held the same sort of physiological theory of sensation as did Descartes, Hobbes rejects the inference from the fact that all that gets to our organs of sense are 'motions' to a triggering of innate ideas theory of sensation/perception.

17. Hume seems to be assuming something like this in claiming that "all our impressions are innate, and our ideas not innate." See *Enquiry Concerning Human Understanding,* 3d ed., edited by L. A. Selby-Bigge (Oxford, 1975), p. 22n.

18. See F. C. Keil, "Constraints on Knowledge and Cognitive Development," *Psychological Review* 88 (1981): 197-227.

19. See, for example, Kurt Koffka, *Principles of Gestalt Psychology* (New York, 1963).

20. Quine's notion of a quality space can be construed as an innate set of constraints on possible percepts.

21. A second relevant contrast is that the Gestaltist point seems to be about the relation of the distal stimulus to the percept; Plato is talking about the relation of the percept to the concept.

22. See, for instance, J. L. Mackie, "The Possibility of Innate Knowledge," Meeting of the Aristotelian Society, May 1970.

23. In discussing the adversaries in the innate ideas controversy, Hume says: "The terms, which they employed, were not chosen with such caution, nor so exactly defined, as to prevent all mistakes about their doctrine. For what is meant by *innate?* . . . Again, the word *idea*, seems to be commonly taken in a very loose sense, by Locke and others . . ." (Enquiry, p. 22n).

24. *If* any belief is constitutive; see Hilary Putnam's "The Meaning of Meaning," in *Language, Mind, and Knowledge*, edited by K. Gunderson (Minneapolis, 1975).

25. See note 23.

26. One might hypothesize that these categories are preexperiential but not innate. That is, that they develop in the infant as a result of the early sensory irradiation.

27. These issues are discussed at greater length in my "Concepts of Concepts."

28. I've benefited greatly in writing this paper from discussions with Eli Hirsch, Alan Zaitchik, Deborah Zaitchik, David Shatz, Ray Jackendoff and Owen Flanagan.

Solipsistic Semantics

ERNEST LEPORE AND BARRY LOEWER

In a famous passage of the *Meditations,* Descartes writes:

At this moment it does indeed seem to me that it is with eyes awake that I am looking at this paper; that this head which I move is not asleep, that it is deliberately and of set purpose that I extend my hand and perceive it .... But in thinking over this I remind myself that on many occasions I have been deceived by similar illusions, and in dwelling on this reflection I see so manifestly that there are no certain indications by which we may clearly distinguish wakefulness from sleep that I am lost in astonishment. And my astonishment is such that it is almost capable of persuading me that I now dream.[1]

In his skeptical arguments, Descartes is claiming not merely that it is possible that all his thoughts about the world are false but that it is possible for him to have these very thoughts and that they be false. It is possible that he is dreaming that there is a world outside his mind though none exists. Descartes's radical skepticism also involves his view that he can know the contents of his thoughts, even though he knows nothing of the world, or knows even if there is a world. On the Cartesian picture, the content of a thought is a property intrinsic to the thought and conceptually independent of any individuals outside the mind.[2]

Semantics for a system of mental representation assigns to each mental representation a meaning or content. The assignment can take a number of forms, for example, a truth theory, an assignment of Fregean senses, or even an image theory. We will say that semantics is *solipsistic* (hereafter *SS* for "solipsistic semantics") if in assigning meanings to representations it does not presuppose the existence of any mental or physical individuals other than the thinker and his thoughts. This characterization needs to be sharpened. There are at least two ways in which an assignment of meanings to representations may presuppose the existence of individuals. One is for the semantics to *interpret* a representation by assigning as its meaning some individual other than the thinker and his representations. For example, semantics that interprets a proper name as directly referring to an actually existing individual implies that the reference of the name exists or did exist. The other sort of presupposition is a bit more difficult to specify.

Given a language *L* and an interpretation for *L,* we can ask the question, In virtue of what does *L* have that interpretation? For an interpretation of mental representations, the question is, What is it about the representations, their structures and other intrinsic properties, their interactions with each other, with the thinker's physical and social environment, and so forth, in virtue of which they have that interpretation? We will call a theory that answers this question for a language *L* with interpretation *I* a *theory of meaning* for *L.* It is important to distinguish the question a theory of meaning is supposed to answer from the question of what events happen to cause a representation to have a particular interpretation. The distinction is parallel to two ways of understanding the question, What makes a good man good? One question is, What causes a man to be good? (or how can we make a man good?). The other question is, What kinds of facts make a good man good? The second question is a conceptual or metaphysical question about the nature of goodness. It is this kind of question concerning meaning that a theory of meaning attempts to answer.

An example of a theory of meaning that does not presuppose the existence of individuals other than the thinker and his thoughts are certain "picture" or "image" theories of meaning.[3] On this view, thoughts are mental images whose representational powers are determined by intrinsic features of the image, for example, its phenomenal color and shape. The image refers to whatever resembles it, but it has the meaning it does entirely in virtue of its intrinsic features. An example of a theory of meaning that does presuppose the existence of individuals external to the thinker is Kripke's causal theory of names. A name means what it does in virtue of bearing a certain causal relation to its bearer. As we pointed out, Kripke's interpretation is also nonsolipsistic since it interprets a name as meaning its bearer. It may be that the correct theory of meaning for some kinds of expressions is solipsistic whereas the correct theory of meaning for other kinds is nonsolipsistic. It is plausible that the mental counterparts of logical constants possess the meanings they do in virtue of their functional roles and that functional role is solipsistic. *SS* for *L* requires that neither the interpretation nor the theory of meaning for *L* presuppose the existence of individuals external to the thinker.

A theory of meaning and interpretation for *L* may be solipsistic even though *L* contains terms that *purport* to refer to individuals external to the thinker. This is just the sort of possibility Descartes envisaged. The central idea of *SS* is that the determinants of the meanings of one's mental representations are entirely within oneself. A doctrine closely related to *SS* is that if two of a person's mental representations have the same or different meanings, then it will be possible for him to determine that they have the same or different meanings by introspection alone. We will call this doctrine "transparency." Given the accessibility of one's mental representations to consciousness, transparency is entailed by there being *SS* for mental representations.

In this paper we will examine Cartesian and more contemporary motivations for the view that there must be *SS* for mental representations. We will discuss some well known arguments that show that various kinds of natural language expressions can possess nonsolipsistic semantics. An apparent consequence of this is that when sentences containing such expressions are used to specify thoughts, as in attributions of propositional attitudes, the thoughts are characterized nonsolipsistically. We argue that semantics for English is so thoroughly nonsolipsistic that even if thoughts have *SS* their contents cannot be expressed in English. We then argue that the most plausible theories of meaning for mental representations are also nonsolipsistic. Our discussion results in an apparent dilemma. On the one hand, there are the Cartesian intuitions and other motivations for thinking that thoughts possess *SS*. On the other hand, there are the arguments that seem to show that given our usual ways of characterizing thought contents, their semantics is nonsolipsistic. We conclude with some tentative remarks on how these two views might be reconciled.

Descartes is not alone in his advocacy of *SS*. Hume remarks that "to form the idea of an object and to form an idea is the same thing; the reference of the idea to an object being an extraneous denomination, of which in itself it bears no mark or character."[4] Hume is saying that the interpretation of his ideas is solipsistic since one can have an idea of an object even though the object fails to exist. Hume's image theory of meaning is also solipsistic since it locates the representational powers of an idea in its intrinsic features. Frege also seems to endorse *SS*.

> Let us just imagine that we have convinced ourselves, contrary to our former opinion, that the name Odysseus, as it occurs in the Odyssey does designate a man after all. Would this mean that sentences containing the name "Odysseus" expressed different thoughts? I think not. The thoughts would strictly remain the same; they would only be transposed from the realm of fiction to that of truth. So the object designated by a proper name seems to be quite inessential to the thought-content of a sentence which contains it.[5]

Frege is saying that the name "Odysseus" has the sense it has whether or not Odysseus exists. His account is that to understand the name is to grasp its sense. Although he doesn't say much about what it is to grasp a sense, his view seems to be that the grasping of senses is a matter strictly between the mind and the realm of senses. It requires the existence of no physical or mental individuals (senses are neither mental nor physical) other than the thinker and his thoughts. Frege also holds "transparency." He frequently uses it to establish that two expressions have different senses. Since one can grasp the senses of "Hesperus" and "Phosphorus" without realizing that they have the same reference, it follows, according to Frege, that they have different senses.

Descartes and Frege were dualists. On their accounts, the mind possesses an intrinsic and unexplained power to represent the world. There are also physicalist versions of *SS*. Physicalism will attempt to account for semantic facts in terms of physical properties and laws. A physicalist who endorses *SS* for mental representations thinks that the physical facts that determine the meanings of thoughts involve only intrinsic physical properties of the thinker's body. One can express this view with the claim that the semantic properties of a thinker's mental representations *supervene* on intrinsic physical (e.g., neurophysiological) states of his body.[6]

Physicalistic *SS* can make for strange bedfellows. Two prominent contemporary proponents are John Searle and Jerry Fodor, who agree on little else in the philosophy of psychology.[7] Searle expresses *SS* as follows:

> If I were a brain in a vat I could have exactly the same mental states I have now; it's just that most of them would be false. . . . The operation of the brain is causally sufficient for intentionality. It is the operation of the brain and not the impact of the outside world that matters for the content of our internal states. [BBS 452]

> I think in the relevant sense that meanings are precisely in the head— there is nowhere else for them to be. [Int 200]

Searle's view is that the causal operations of the brain are sufficient (and perhaps necessary) to produce thoughts with their contents.

Fodor's version of *SS* is different from Searle's. Fodor advocates (whereas Searle rejects) the "computational theory of mind" (hereafter, *CTM*). According to Fodor, mental processes are analogous to the operations of a computer. For example, when one forms an intention to, say, go to a certain Chinese restaurant for dinner, one's mind (brain) engages in computational processes involving the manipulations of various mental representations. Fodor argues how a great deal of theorizing in cognitive psychology presupposes *CTM*. He also argues that *CTM* provides plausible explanations of various features of mental states and processes (e.g., the opacity of belief). Fodor argues that *CTM* is committed to the following "formality condition":[8] if psychological states (processes, etc.) have the same computational characteristics, then they must be the same psychological state (process, etc.). Fodor also maintains that psychological states (or an important subset of them) are characterized in terms of their contents. It follows from this and the formality condition that, if states are computationally the same, then they have the same contents (or rather are composed of representations with the same contents). In other words, thought contents supervene on computational features of thought. Since computational features, whatever they might be, supervene on intrinsic physical features, it follows that thought contents supervene on physical features. In this way Fodor seems committed to there being SS for mental representations.

Fodor's view is more complicated than we have so far indicated. Referring to considerations that we will soon discuss, he observes that our normal attributions of belief violate the formality condition. But he thinks that they come close to satisfying it. He writes that "taxonomy with respect to content may be compatible with the formality conditions plus or minus a bit."[9] The suggestion is that even if our usual scheme of belief attributions assigns contents nonsolipsistically, it is close enough so that with a little tinkering, we can construct SS for mental representations.

Fodor's reasons for thinking that there exists SS for mental representations are mainly theoretical. He holds that modern cognitive theory requires it. SS also has a powerful intuitive appeal. The intuitions that underlie SS are supported by the Cartesian thought experiment. One can imagine each of his thoughts about the external world being false, even the thought that there is an external world, whereas the thoughts themselves remain the same. So it might seem that thoughts have the contents they do independently of any individuals that are extrinsic to them. Furthermore, although one might be mistaken about the meanings of words in one's public language, it seems absurd to think that one might be mistaken about the meanings of one's own thoughts. Descartes beautifully expresses this line of thought.

> Now ideas considered in themselves and not referred to something else, cannot strictly be false; whether I imagine a she-goat or a chimera, it is not less true that I imagine one than the other. ... The chief and commonest error that is to be found in this field consists in my taking ideas within myself to have similarity or conformity to some external object; for if I were to consider them as mere modes of my own consciousness, and did not refer them to anything else, they could give me hardly any occasion of error.[10]

Despite the cognitivist's arguments and the Cartesian's intuitions, the very possibility of SS is called into question by recent developments in the philosophy of language and mind associated primarily with work by Kripke, Kaplan, Putnam, and Bruge. Taken as a whole, this work apparently shows the inadequacy of the Fregean account of meaning. Because of the close connection between Frege's theory and *SS*, these developments have a bearing on the possibility of *SS* for thought.

Saul Kripke's work on names was the spearhead of the attack against the Fregean accounts.[11] According to Frege, a name—for example, "Aristotle"—expresses a sense that, as it happens, picks out a certain referent (Aristotle). If things had turned out differently, the same sense might have picked out someone else or nothing at all. Kripke argues that Frege is wrong. A name does not express a sense but, instead, *directly* refers to its bearer. In terms of the apparatus of possible world semantics, a name refers to its bearer at every possible world. A term that expresses a sense—for example, a definite description—may refer to different individuals at different worlds. According to Kripke, the reference of a use of a name is determined by a causal chain that begins with a baptism of the bearer with the name. Someone who hears the name "Aristotle" used by a competent speaker can himself use it to refer to Aristotle even if the information that he associates with "Aristotle" is insufficient to determine Aristotle (e.g., he is a Greek philosopher) or even if the information is uniquely true of someone else (e.g., he is the greatest Greek playwright).

How is Kripke's account of the meaning of names relevant to the semantics for mental representations? It is natural to assume that when someone is reported as thinking the thought that Aristotle was wise, he is said to have a thought whose content is the same as the content of "Aristotle is wise." His mental representation contains a constituent that directly refers to Aristotle. These semantics are nonsolipsistic in both ways discussed earlier. The interpretation of "Aristotle" is Aristotle himself and so involves an individual other than the thinker and his thoughts. Also, Kripke's account of what determines the interpretation of a name requires that its bearer exist at the time of baptism. So Kripke's theory of meaning for names is nonsolipsistic. We also note that "transparency" fails for Kripke's semantics. Someone might use the names "Hesperus" and "Phosphorus" which, according to Kripke, have the same interpretation, and yet have no way of discovering by introspection that they have the same interpretation. Meaning, according to Kripke, is not entirely in the head.

Kripke's direct reference account of names is superior to Frege's sense theory in a number of ways. However, there are problems with the account that seem to support the view that names also must have a solipsistic interpretation that is relevant when they are used in contexts ascribing thoughts. If names are rigid designators, then since "Tully" and "Cicero" designate the same man, the thought that Tully was an orator and the thought that Cicero was an orator are thoughts with the same interpretation. But it seems possible to believe one without believing the other.[12] If believing that *p* is to be explained (as in Fodor) as tokening a mental representation that means that

p, then it seems that the mental representations corresponding to "Tully was an orator" and "Cicero was an orator" must have different interpretations.[13] Another perhaps even more serious problem is that it certainly seems possible to think that Homer was a Greek even though it turns out that Homer never existed. But on the direct reference account, if Homer never existed, "Homer was a Greek" would fail to express any proposition.[14] It was precisely consideration of these problems that led Frege to postulate senses as the meanings of names. It is essential to his solution to the problems that whether a sense determines a reference or whether two senses determine the same reference is irrelevant to the grasping of senses. This suggests that semantics for names that is adequate for propositional attitude contexts will also interpret them as expressing senses.

David Kaplan has proposed semantics for indexical sentences that is nonsolipsistic.[15] According to Kaplan, when Arabella utters the sentence "She is a spy," pointing at Barbarella, she asserts a proposition that is essentially about Barbarella. This proposition actually contains Barbarella as a constituent. If it turns out that Arabella is not pointing at anyone, then, on Kaplan's view, her utterance simply fails to express a proposition. It is clear that Kaplan's semantics interprets indexical utterances nonsolipsistically.

Suppose that when Arbella utters "She is a spy," she expresses a thought that has the same interpretation as her utterance. On Kaplan's account, this thought would contain a constituent that directly refers to Barbarella. According to this account, if Arabella and her neurophysiological twin point respectively at Barbarella and Twin Barbarella and each utters "She is a spy," they are thinking different thoughts. So the interpretations of mental representations containing indexicals do not supervene on neurophysiological states.[16]

Even if indexical thoughts have nonsolipsistic interpretations, there also seems to be a need to associate solipsistic interpretations with them. From Arabella's point of view, she is thinking the same thought when she utters "She is a spy," whether or not she is pointing at anyone. If thoughts are individuated in terms of their causal consequences for behavior, then it makes no difference whether or not Arabella is pointing at Barbarella, her twin, or is just hallucinating. Kaplan's distinction between the character of an indexical sentence and the proposition expressed by an utterance of the sentence may provide the ingredients for a solipsistic interpretation of indexical thoughts. Character is a function from contexts of utterance to propositions. For example, the character of "I am in Ann Arbor" uttered by Arabella at time t yields the proposition that Arabella is in Ann Arbor at t. This proposition contains Arabella himself as well as Ann Arbor and t as constituents. Semantics that assigns this proposition to indexical thoughts is clearly nonsolipsistic. But semantics that assigns to the thought its character might be compatible with *SS*. Arabella can have the character of "She is a spy" in mind, even though she is pointing to no one. Arabella and her twin have the same character in mind.

Character is not sufficiently robust to characterize the semantics of mental representation in all cases.[17] This can be seen in the following situation. Arabella is looking at two TV screens. One shows Barbarella from the front, the other from the back. Arabella doesn't realize this. She thinks twice "She is a spy." It is intuitively clear that her two thoughts are different even though they share character and express the same proposition. Searle develops an account of indexicals that distinguishes the two thoughts. His view is that the content of Arabella's thought is something like [the (female) person who is causing *this* visual experience is a spy].[18] One way of understanding Searle's view is that the proposition expressed by this thought contains the visual experience as a constituent. Searle's semantics is apparently solipsistic since the interpretation of the thought requires the existence of nothing other than Arabella and her mental contents.

Hilary Putnam first introduced twin arguments (like the one used above) to show that natural kind terms, expressions like "water," "gold," "tiger," and so forth, have nonsolipsistic meanings.[19] Arabella and Twin Arabella are neurophysiologically identical. They inhabit, respectively, Earth and Twin Earth, which are identical except that the stuff called "water" on Earth is composed of H_2O molecules, whereas the stuff called "water" on Twin Earth is composed of XYZ molecules. We also suppose that the time is before chemistry has been discovered so that no one on Earth or Twin Earth can distinguish H_2O from XYZ. According to Putnam, Arabella's word "water" refers to H_2O, whereas Twin Arabella's word "water" refers to XYZ. A version of the causal theory of reference explains these reference relations. Roughly, Arabella's use of "water" refers to H_2O because her use is a link in a causal chain that begins with original dubbings of samples of H_2O. Arabella's use refers to anything that belongs to the same natural kind as the original samples. Since XYZ is not the same natural kind as H_2O, Arabella's tokens of "water" do not refer to XYZ, even though Arabella cannot distinguish the two kinds. If she were miraculously transported to the shores of the Twin Pacific on Twin Earth and said "Water, water, everywhere," she would be wrong.

When Arabella and Twin Arabella think the thoughts each would express by uttering "Water is wet," they think different thoughts. Arabella's thought is true iff H_2O is wet, whereas her twin's thought is true iff XYZ is wet. It follows that their thought contents do not supervene on their neurophysiologies. Furthermore, on Putnam's causal account of how "water" gets its meaning, Arabella could not think her thought unless she was on the receiving end of a causal chain that originates with an event involving H_2O. Putnam's interpretation of and theory of meaning for natural kind terms are squarely nonsolipsistic.[20]

Putnam's positive account is that the meaning of a natural kind term consists of a number of components. One is the reference of the term, in our example, H_2O. A second component he calls "stereotype." It consists of the information that competent speakers associate with water, for example, that it quenches thirst, fills oceans, and so forth. Putnam gives the impression that this component is entirely within the mind. This suggests the possibility that Arabella's mental representation corresponding to "water is wet" may have two interpretations: a nonsolipsistic interpretation that includes H_2O, and a Fregean solipsistic interpretation as in [the stuff that quenches thirst, fills oceans, and so forth, is wet]. We will pursue this idea later.

Tyler Burge pushes a variant of the Twin Earth parables that also shows that the meanings of certain expressions are determined by factors external to the thinker.[21] Burge imagines an English speaker who does not know that arthritis is specifically a condition of the joints, although most of her beliefs concerning arthritis are true. She utters "I have arthritis in my thigh." According to Burge, her utterance means that she has arthritis (in our sense) in her thigh. His reason for claiming this is that Arabella will defer to members of her linguistic community should they correct her. When corrected, she will say that her utterance was false. Burge then considers this woman's twin, who speaks Twin English, which is like English, except that in it, "arthritis" refers to inflammations of the thigh as well as of the joints. Her twin's utterance is true. On the assumption that the thought expressed by an utterance has the same interpretation as the utterance, Arabella and her twin think different thoughts even though they are neurophysiologically identical. [This we take to be Putnam's early view.]

It is interesting to compare Burge's and Putnam's arguments. Putnam's argument applies to natural kind terms. Burge's argument can apparently be applied to any expression, even to adjectives, adverbs, and logical connectives. If Putnam is correct, then the interpretation of a natural kind term includes the reference of the term—for example, the substance water. If water never existed, we couldn't think that water is wet anymore than we could think that Aristotle is wise if Aristotle never existed. Burge's argument has no such conclusion. The term "arthritis" might have been introduced by description and there might never have been cases of the disease.[22] Putnam and Burge have nonsolipsistic theories of meaning, but they emphasize different ways in which meaning is determined. Putnam emphasizes the causal connections between the tokening of an expression and a dubbing of a natural kind. Burge emphasizes the role that one's linguistic community has in determining the meanings of one's words. Of course, it may be that both Putnam and Burge are correct and that an adequate theory of meaning for English will include reference to both causal chains and community practices.

The arguments that we have quickly canvassed purport to show that certain expressions and representations have nonsolipsistic semantics. In each case, the arguments show that these representations have meanings that they could not have unless certain individuals other than a thinker and her thoughts exist. How might the view that thought possesses *SS* be defended against these arguments? One strategy is to fight battles on each front, arguing that Kripke is mistaken about names, Putnam mistaken about natural kind terms, and so forth. This is the strategy pursued by Searle. The other strategy is to admit defeat on the fronts but then to circle the wagons around the mind and defend the possibility of constructing a characterization of meaning that is solipsistic. This is the strategy pursued by Fodor and the one that we will follow. Still, we can make use of Searle's accounts by taking his views about the correct semantics of English expressions as suggestions for how to construct *SS*.

Fodor's strategy is to associate with each mental representation a narrow and a wide content.[23] The arguments of Kripke, Putnam, et. al., are taken to show that wide content does not supervene on the thinker's body. But narrow content is supposed to supervene on the thinker's body, including states of his brain and sense organs, and therefore is a version of physicalistic *SS*. The problem is to construct an appropriate notion of narrow content.

When he wrote MS, Fodor seemed to think that it would not be all that difficult to construct *SS* for mental representations that could play an explanatory role in cognitive psychology. After discussing some of the antisolipsistic considerations we have reviewed, he remarks:

> To summarize: transparent taxonomy is patently incompatible with the formality condition: whereas taxonomy in respect of content *may* be compatible with the formality condition, plus or minus a bit. That taxonomy in respect of content *is* compatible with the formality condition, plus or minus a bit, is perhaps *the* basic idea of modern cognitive theory [emphasis in the original].[24]

Fodor is claiming that if we stick to opaque, as opposed to transparent, interpretations of mental representations, we will come close to semantics that conforms to the formality condition, that is, to *SS*. But it seems to us that the construction of *SS* that can be used in cognitive theory is a much more formidable, perhaps an impossible, task. In the remainder of this paper we will consider reasons why this is so.

What are the adequacy conditions that a characterization of narrow content must satisfy? Since it is solipsistic, it will assign the same contents to Arabella's and her twin's thoughts "Water is wet" and also assign the same contents to the thoughts of the woman and her twin in Burge's story. It will assign different contents to the thoughts expressed by "Cicero was bald" and "Tully was bald" when the thinker does not believe that Cicero = Tully. The characterization of narrow content should serve the needs of cognitive theory. Fodor seems to understand this requirement so that propositional attitudes interpreted narrowly will yield rationalizing explanations of action (when the actions themselves are described narrowly). Folk psychological theory, according to Fodor, contains generalizations like the following: when an individual believes that his obtaining water requires that he raise his hand and he wants it to be the case that he obtains water, then he will, ceterius paribus, raise his hand. This generalization does not apply to Twin Earthlings because they do not have beliefs about water. This is due to the fact that belief content is characterized widely in the generalization. Fodor suggests that cognitive theory will contain refinements of such generalizations which apply on Earth and Twin Earth. So a requirement on narrow content ascriptions is that it should be employable in such generalizations. In MS, Fodor held that the appropriate notion of content satisfies the formality condition and so supervenes on neurophysiological states. In more recent writings, he seems to hold that narrow content supervenes on bodily states or perhaps on boldily states together with a specification of inputs to the organism's perceptual systems.[25] If the inputs are characterized in ways that make reference to no individuals external to the organism's body, then the characterization is still a version of *SS*. One final requirement on narrow content is for there to be a plausible theory of meaning that is solipsistic and that accounts for how representations obtain their contents.

What form will *SS* take? One currently fashionable answer is provided by "conceptual role theories" (*CRT*).[26] A *CRT* for a person's language of thought characterizes the meaning of a mental representation in terms of its causal or inferential role in relating stimuli, behavior, and the tokening of other mental representations. The characterization is a version of *SS* only if representations, behavior, and stimuli are described in ways that make no reference to individuals external to the thinker's body. We have discussed *CRTs* elsewhere and argued that characterization of *CR* is not itself a characterization of content.[27] For present purposes it is sufficient to point out that a characterization of *CR* does not yield appropriate complements to put into "believes that . . ." and other propositional attitude contexts. But we need such expressions of content if we are to construct rationalizing explanations of behavior of the sort that Fodor wants to capture in cognitive psychology. It should also be clear that *CR* does not provide a characterization of content suitable for expressing Cartesian skepticism. Descartes was not claiming that all his thoughts might be false even if they have the same conceptual role they actually have. They could have the same conceptual role and yet be about quite different things. So we have to look elsewhere for a specification of narrow content.

We know of two other proposals for constructing narrow content or *SS* for linguistic and mental representations. One we will call the "indexicalist strategy." It involves interpreting thoughts indexically in a way that is supposed to presuppose no individual external to the thinker. We will call the second approach the "phenomenological strategy." It involves finding a collection of expressions that have SS and constructing interpretations for thoughts from these expressions. The approach is called "phenomenological" since the nonlogical vocabulary of these interpretations consists of "observation" terms that are supposed to describe how things seem or how they appear. In a number of recent papers, Fodor has employed both proposals to construct a characterization of narrow content. But we will argue that the prospects for success are poor. We will discuss the phenomenological strategy first.

The phenomenological strategy applied to proper names suggests that a name is interpreted as expressing a sense that the thinker associates with the name. For example, the thought that Aristotle was Greek might be interpreted as having the content that the author of the *Metaphysics* was Greek (or some similar content that can be expressed without using the proper name "Aristotle"). The phenomenological strategy might be applied in the following way to natural kind terms. Although Arabella and Twin Arabella refer to different things when they utter "Water is wet," it may be that they associate the same stereotype with "water." This suggests that the stereotype has a solipsistic interpretation. The idea is that the thoughts of both twins can be interpreted phenomenologically as having a content like [the liquid that people drink, fills oceans, and so forth, is wet].

However, the interpretations that we associated with "Aristotle was Greek" and "Water is wet" are certainly not completely solipsistic. The description "The author of the *Metaphysics*" contains another proper name and so we do not yet have a solipsistic interpretation. And even if the name were replaced by a description, the question would arise whether the predicates that occur in the description can be given solipsistic interpretations. This question also arises when we consider the stereotypes associated with kind terms. The suggestion was that the solipsistic interpretation of "Water is wet" is that the liquid that people drink, fills oceans, and so forth, is wet. It is clear that the content of this stereotype is not sufficiently narrow to be solipsistic. The expressions "oceans" and "people" have different meanings for Arabella and Twin Arbella. For Arabella, "people" refers to Earthlings, whereas for Twin Arabella it refers to Twin Earthlings. The same point applies to "oceans" and "liquid" and perhaps to other concepts in the stereotype. By imagining suitable differences between Earth and Twin Earth, while keeping constant the ways things seem to the twins, it looks as though Twin Earth arguments will succeed in showing that no natural kind term has SS. It might be suggested that those expressions that describe the ways things seem, the truly phenomenological expressions, are immune from the Twin Earth arguments. Are there any such predicates in English? The best candidates are "observation terms," for example, "red," "round," and "bitter."

If these do not have *SS*, it is difficult to see how the phenomenological can be made to work.

As we already pointed out, the argument Burge gave to show that the meaning of "arthritis" depends on features external to the thinker, specifically, community usage, applies to any natural language expression. If these arguments are correct, they show that even predicates like "is red" do not have *SS*. However, it seems that we can imagine a language that is like English except that the deferential practices on which Burge's arguments rely are absent. For this reason we will give another argument that shows that the semantics of observation terms is nonsolipsistic. Suppose that on Twin Earth those things that are red on earth (blood, ripe tomatoes, boiled lobsters—or rather their counterparts on Twin Earth) are green. So, if an earthling visited Twin Earth, she would correctly think that the things that Twin Earthlings call "boiled lobsters" are green. However, the Twin Earthlings are born with color-inverting lenses so that when looking at what they call "a lobster," they experience the same kind of sensations (are in the same brain states) that Earthlings experience when looking at boiled lobsters. Suppose, as usual, that Arabella and her twin are neurophysiologically type identical and that each utters "Roses are red." The things the Twin Earthlings call "roses" are actually green.

How should we translate Twin Arabella's word "red" into English? Her utterances of "That's a red one" are typically caused by things that are green. When she says "I am looking for a red dress," she is satisfied when she finds a green one. So we have every reason to suppose that her word "red" means green. If we translate her word "red" by our word "red," the result would be that we would interpret Twin Arabella as being pervasively mistaken about the colors of things. This is certainly intolerable. It is much more plausible to translate her "red" by our "green." This translation interprets that Arabella and Twin Arabella are thinking different thoughts when each says to herself "That's a red one," even though they are in neurophysiologically identical states and they are experiencing the same qualia.[28]

Fodor might reply that Arabella and her twin are really in identical bodily states since the twin's color-inverting glasses count as part of her body. In his most recent discussions of narrow content, Fodor characterizes narrow content so that it supervenes on the states of an organism's brain and transducers.[29] Plausibly, the color-inverting lenses are part of the twin's visual system. This reply can be deflected with some more science fiction. We suppose that on Twin Earth a substance in the atmosphere changes light from red to green and vice versa soon after it is reflected. In the revised story, Arabella and her twin are in identical brain and transducer states although one is thinking that's a red one while the other is thinking that's a green one.[30]

The second approach that the solipsistic semanticist can take is the indexicalist strategy. An indexical sentence has both a content and a character. The character is a function from contexts to contents. So when Arabella and Twin Arabella each utter "She is a spy," their utterances have different contents (one utterance is about Barbarella, the other about twin Barbarella) but the same character. Character may be solipsistic even if content is not. So if we can associate an indexical interpretation with each mental representation, we might yet succeed in constructing SS for thought. But we doubt that this can be carried out. Exactly what indexical interpretation can be given to "Water is wet"? Fodor suggests that "perhaps 'water' means something like 'the local, transparent, potable, dolphin-torn, gong tormented . . . stuff one sails on.'"[31] The reference to its being local provides the indexicality. Arabella and her twin may mean the same by "water" and yet refer to different substances because they inhabit different contexts. But the obvious problem with this suggestion is that this paraphrase contains expressions that are interpreted nonsolipsistically.

Searle suggests an interpretation for "water" that may seem to avoid this problem. He says that " 'water' is defined indexically as whatever is identical in structure with the stuff causing *this* visual experience."[32] But this suggestion faces a couple of difficulties. First, it is not clear that "stuff" and "causing" or even "visual experience" have nonsolipsistic semantics. Second, the expression does not uniquely refer. There are many things and events causing *this visual experience*. One of the causes is the pattern of neuron firing in the optic nerves. We could exclude this by adding "the external liquid stuff causing . . . ," but now we are faced with the problem that "external liquid" does not have SS.

There is another way to pursue the indexicalist strategy.[33] Think of Arabella's entire environment, including its history, as a context. Her sentence "Water is wet" can be interpreted as expressing a character that maps that context onto the content that H_2O is wet. Twin Arabella's sentence expresses the same character, which maps her different context onto the content that XYZ is wet. It is clear that character construed in this way supervenes on neurophysiology. But it cannot serve as a specification of narrow content. At most, the account provides sufficient conditions for when two individuals' thoughts have the same meaning, and then, only when the two are neurophysiologically identical. If two people are not neurophysiologically identical, then the account says nothing concerning whether structurally similar representations possess the same or different characters. Nor does this characterization of meaning as character yield appropriate specifications of content that can follow "believes that." As Fodor, who suggests this proposal, says, "First it is one thing to have a criterion for the intentional identity of thoughts; it is quite another to be able to say what the intention of a thought is."[34] It is the latter that we need if we want to employ narrow content in the rationalizing explanations of cognitive psychology.

The preceding considerations show that it is not easy to construct SS.

The usual, nonsolipsistic interpretation of thoughts misses being solipsistic by a great deal more than "plus or minus a bit." There is no solipsistic part of English out of which solipsistic interpretations of thought can be constructed. But this doesn't show that SS is impossible. It shows only that our language is so thoroughly nonsolipsistic that it doesn't contain the resources to construct nonsolipsistic semantics. Perhaps mental representations have SS that cannot be expressed in English. However, we will argue that the most plausible theories of meaning for mental representations rule out SS. Since Fodor himself advocates a version of this theory of meaning, our argument will be, to a certain degree, an ad hominem one.[35]

The account that Fodor favors is a development of Fred Dretske's views. According to Dretske, the content of a mental representation is determined by its informational origins.[36] To consider the simplest kind of case, suppose that a mental structure can either be in state Y or state N and that under certain "normal conditions," it is in Y when the organism is looking at a fly but in N when the organism is not looking at a fly. Then the mental structure carries the information that there is a fly in view when conditions are normal. Fodor endorses an account of this kind although he substitutes certain epistemically ideal conditions for normal conditions.[37]

Although there are substantial difficulties with Dretske's and Fodor's proposals, it is the most promising.[38] Here we only want to show that if we take this account seriously, then either it results in nonsolipsistic semantics or it leads to SS that interprets one's mental states as being about one's own nervous system. First, observe that on a plausible understanding of "normal" and "ideal," Fodor's theory of meaning is already nonsolipsistic. Normal and ideal conditions are such in virtue of the evolutionary history of an organism. If the organism had evolved in different circumstances, different conditions might count as normal or ideal. Let's ignore this problem for a moment. Suppose that a frog's mental state carries the information that a fly is in view. Clearly it carries this information only because of its interactions with its environment. Change the environment, and the frog's neural state will carry different information, for example, that a moving BB is in view. The obvious reply to this point is to say that the frog's neural state was designed by evolutionary pressures to carry information about the presence of flies not BBs. But the proponent of SS cannot avail himself of such considerations because the self-assigned task is to construct meaning from ingredients that are entirely within the head. Neurophysiologically identical organisms might have evolved in different environments and so their neural states might carry different information. If we are to use a Dretskean theory of meaning to support a solipsistic interpretation of the frog's mental representations, then we will have to find something for these representations to carry information about that is immune from the kind of environmental tinkering used in the Twin Earth stories. But it would seem that all that can remain constant under these environmental changes is the working of the frog's nervous system itself. There will be some covariation between states Y and N and certain patterns of irradiation on the frog's eyes. So we can solipsistically interpret Y as having the content that a certain pattern of occular irradiation is occurring. If we adopt a Dretskean theory of meaning, then the only interpretations consistent with SS interpret an organism's thoughts as being about its own nervous system.

A proponent of SS holds that, although thoughts and ideas purport to refer to the external world, their meanings are entirely a product of mental activity. Originally, he may have thought that the semantics for all the expressions of our language is solipsistic. But the considerations advanced by Kripke, Putnam, and Kaplan show that vast portions of natural language have interpretations that are incompatible with SS. This showed that our usual ways of individuating the contents of mental representations are also nonsolipsistic. We considered a response that granted the points made by Kripke, et al., but attempted to construct solipsistic interpretations out of the fragment of language that remained solipsistic. We argued that this strategy is unlikely to succeed because almost all natural language expressions, even observation terms, have nonsolipsistic semantics. The prospects for constructing SS for thought seem even bleaker when we reflect on the difficulty of providing a plausible account about what makes it the case that a thought has the content it has that is compatible with solipsism. If an informational answer to this question of the sort suggested by Dretske and Fodor is correct, then a language with SS is a language that is solipsistic in another way. In it one can refer only to oneself and one's mental states. Solipsism with respect to sense results in solipsism with respect to reference.[39]

If the view that thought possesses SS is not plausible, what are the consequences for cognitive theory and for our Cartesian intuitions? With respect to cognitive theory, there seem to be two alternatives. The first, recommended by Stich, is to abandon the use of propositional attitude explanations in cognitive theory.[40] The second, recommended by Burge, is to accept the fact that propositional attitudes do not supervene on bodily states and to argue that this in no way counts against their explanatory ability.[41] We cannot enter into this debate here. But we do want to make a few remarks concerning the Cartesian intuitions that seem to provide such strong support for there being SS for thought.

The Cartesian observes that it is possible for all his thoughts about the external physical world to have the contents they have even if there is no external world. If this is correct, then thought-world interactions cannot be an essential determinant of the contents of thoughts. It follows that thought has SS. The first point to make about this argument is that at most it shows that it is *epistemically* possible for the Cartesian that he has the thoughts he actually has even if there is no external world. The argument is similar to other Cartesian arguments that show that it is epistemically possible for a mental event or state to exist even though no physical events or states exist. But epistemic possibility is not the same as metaphysical or conceptual possibility and only these would establish the need for *SS*. However, we must admit that our arguments do not establish that *SS* is not possible. At most we have shown that plausible theories of meaning are nonsolipsistic.

There is a related intuition that may lead the Cartesian into thinking that thought must have *SS*. It is the observation that one can know the contents of one's thoughts without engaging in any empirical investigation. When considering another person, we might be persuaded that his thoughts have the contents they have in virtue of interactions with his environment, his linguistic community, and so forth. But I can know the contents of my own thoughts without evidence and, in particular, without knowing much about these matters. Since I can know the contents of my thoughts without investigating the world outside myself, it is tempting to conclude that these contents must be determined by events entirely within myself. We have here a real and, we think, quite deep tension. The tension between nonsolipsistic theories of meaning and the Cartesian intuitions would be relieved somewhat if it could be shown that there is no genuine conflict between the claim that we know our own thought contents without evidence and the claim that those thought contents are determined by matters external to us about which we may have no knowledge.

We would like to show that even though a mental representation R has the content it has in virtue of matters external to the thinker, he might still know R's content without evidence. We tentatively offer the following account. Let us suppose that A grasps the concept *water*. We cannot give necessary and sufficient conditions for grasping this concept but something like the following story seems plausible. To grasp the concept *water* is to have a mental representation that plays a certain kind of functional role in one's thought and that is related in an appropriate way to H_2O.[42] Suppose that A thinks the thought that water is wet. What is required of A in order that he know what his thought means? If it is required that he knows that water is H_2O, then it must be admitted that he does not know what his thought means. But this requirement is not plausible and does not follow from the fact that A grasps the concept. Now suppose that A grasps the concept *is true* and has a way of referring to his thoughts, say by quoting them. A's thought ["Water is wet" is true iff water is wet] will then express his knowledge of the content of his thought "Water is wet." And A will know that this thought is true simply in virtue of grasping the concepts of *truth, quotation, water,* and *is wet.* Suppose that A had lived on Twin Earth. In that case, his concept would be different since it would refer to XYZ. However, he could know the content of his thought "Water is wet" since he knows the truth conditions. He would express this knowledge by saying " 'Water is wet' is true iff water is wet."

It might be objected that in our example A does not know that "Water is wet" is true iff water is wet but only that the representation " 'Water is wet' is true iff water is wet" is true.[43] The source of the objection is this. Suppose that B knows how quotation works in English, knows the disquotational effect of "is true," and is able to recognize grammatical sentences of English but knows nothing else about English. B will be in a position to recognize English sentences of the form " 'Water is wet' is true iff water is wet" as true. But this is not the same as knowing the truth conditions of "Water is wet."[44] Someone could recognize this sentence as true and yet not know what it means. The objection is that A is in the same position with regard to his thoughts as B is with respect to English. Our reply is that there is an important difference between the two cases. We assumed that A had the ability to think that water is wet on the basis of there being a mental representation that plays a certain conceptual role in his thinking and its playing this role in a particular environment. The sentence "Water is wet" does not play the appropriate functional role in B's thought that it would if B understood "Water is wet." But A's thought "Water is wet" does play the appropriate role; it must if it is to be the thought that water is wet. If this is correct, then we can see how the meaning of a person's thoughts can depend on matters external to him and yet how he can be in a position to know the meaning of a thought without appealing to these external matters.[45]

Notes

1. René Descartes, *The Philosophical Works of Descartes,* vol. 1, translated and edited by Elizabeth S. Haldane and G. R. T. Ross (Cambridge, 1967), 146.

2. Some qualification is needed here. Descartes did think that some of our ideas were not conceptually independent of anything outside the mind, for example, our idea of God and of infinity.

3. The view that ideas are images and that images represent by picturing was held by Locke. See his *Essay Concerning Human Understanding,* bks. 2 and 3.

4. David Hume, *A Treatise on Human Nature,* edited by Selby-Bigge (Oxford, 1888), 20.

5. Gottlob Frege, *Posthumous Writings,* edited by H. Hermes (Berkeley, 1979), 191.

6. A property P supervenes on properties $Q1, Q2, \ldots$, if and only if it is metaphysically impossible for two individuals to differ with respect to P without differing with respect to some of the Qs. For a discussion of supervenience, see Jagewon Kim, "Concepts of Supervenience," *Philosophy and Phenomenological Research* 45 (1984): 153-76.

7. John Searle, "Minds, Brains, and Programs," *The Behavioral and Brain Sciences* 3 (1980), and *Intentionality* (Cambridge, 1983). Hereafter these works are indicated by BBS and INT. Jerry Fodor, "Methodological Solipsism Considered as a Research Strategy in Cognitive Psychology," *Representations* (Cambridge, Mass., 1980), 225-56. Hereafter MS.

8. MS 229.

9. MS 250.

10. René Descartes, *Descartes' Philosophical Writings,* translated and edited by E. Anscombe and P. Geach (New York, 1971), 78.

11. Saul A. Kripke, *Naming and Necessity* (Cambridge, Mass., 1980). Kripke does not commit himself to the view that there is a causal relation between the token of a name and its bearer, although others have made this claim.

12. Saul Kripke, "A Puzzle about Belief," *Meaning and Use,* edited by A. Margalit (Dordrecht, 1976), 239-83.

13. Kripke can avoid this objection by abandoning transparency.

14. Kripke's non*SS* requires either that we cannot have such thoughts or that the mental representation corresponding to "Homer" is not a directly referring expression.

15. David Kaplan, "Demonstratives," unpublished manuscript, 1977.

16. One might infer from this nonsupervenience that Kaplan holds a non*SS* theory of meaning. However, compare note 18. Supervenience fails and yet *SS* obtains. Nothing in Kaplan's writings tells whether he is or is not a non*SS* theorist of meaning about indexicals. We also note that transparency fails for him. Arabella may be looking in a mirror, pointing unwittingly at herself, and think what she would express by "I am tall" and "She is tall," not knowing these express the same proposition.

17. Actually, we think something much stronger than this. In our "Dual Aspect Semantics," forthcoming, we argue that, at best, character provides a method for individuating thoughts, not for identifying or ascribing them.

18. John Searle, INT: 203. Interestingly, on Searle's account Arabella and her twin are having thoughts with different contents since each refers to her own visual experience. So even though Arabella and Twin Arabella are in type identical neurophysiological states, they can have solipsistic thoughts with different contents. This shows that we cannot always argue from the fact that two individuals in type identical neurophysiological states have thoughts with different contents to the conclusion that the thoughts are nonsolipsistic.

19. Hilary Putnam, "The Meaning of 'Meaning'," in *Mind, Language, and Reality,* vol. 2 (Cambridge, 1975) 215-71.

20. Putnam also abandons transparency. The thoughts expressed by "Water is wet" and "H_2O is wet" are the same, but surely one need not recognize them as such.

21. Tyler Burge, "Individualism and the Mental," *Midwest Studies* 4 (1979): 73-121.

22. This suggests we could have a language with a non*SS* theory of meaning but with *SS* interpretations.

23. Jerry Fodor, "Narrow Content and Meaning Holism," unpublished manuscript.

24. Jerry Fodor, MS 240.

25. Jerry Fodor, "Narrow Content and Meaning Holism."

26. See, for example, Brian Loar, *Mind and Meaning,* (Cambridge, 1981), Colin McGinn, "The Structure of Content," *Thought and Object,* edited by A. Woodfield (Oxford, 1982), 215-71, and Hartry Field, "Logic, Meaning, and Conceptual Role," *Journal of Philosophy* 7 (1977): 379-409.

27. See Ernest LePore and Barry Loewer, "Dual Aspect Semantics," forthcoming.

28. We do not mean just that we lack epistemic warrant in translating her word "red" as our word "red" but that it would be an error to do so.

29. Jerry Fodor, "Narrow Content and Meaning Holism."

30. Fodor's strategy suggests a fourth semanticist. One might be a *SS* theorist of meaning but have non*SS* interpretations. This depends on several things. First, it is important to see that Fodor is not offering a theory of meaning here. The phenomenological approach is a strategy for ascertaining which thoughts an individual can entertain without looking outside the organism's physical structure. If this strategy succeeded, one might be inclined to infer that there is a *SS* theory of meaning for mental representations. However, Fodor has not given us one. He is not here telling us *in virtue* of what do mental representations have the contents they do. He is telling us only how to discern these contents. Second, Fodor is not a phenomenalist. He does not claim that phenomenological properties are in the head. This is no problem for him. Qua cognitive psychologist, his concern is only that he need not look outside the organism to discern its psychology. However, that these properties exist outside the organism does not commit Fodor to non*SS* interpretations. This depends on his ontological view about properties. If properties are universals, abstract entities, then his interpretations are *SS*. If phenomenologi-

cal properties are sets of physical objects, then his interpretations presuppose the existence of physical entities outside the organism, and he is therefore committed to non*SS* interpretations.

31. Jerry Fodor, "Banish Discontent," unpublished manuscript.

32. John Searle, INT: 203.

33. A view like this one is developed by Stephen White in "Partial Character and the Language of Thought," *Pacific Philosophical Quarterly* 63 (1982): 37-65.

34. Jerry Fodor, "Banish Discontent."

35. We are not claiming that Fodor ever intended Dretske's informational theory of meaning to be a *solipsistic* theory of meaning of these representations. However, this is the only kind of theory of meaning that Fodor has presented for mental representations.

36. Fred Dretske, *Knowledge and the Flow of Information* (Cambridge, Mass., 1981), chaps. 10 and 11.

37. Jerry Fodor, "Psychosemantics," unpublished manuscript.

38. Informational accounts of content are discussed by Barry Loewer in "Information and Content," *Synthese,* forthcoming.

39. This is not necessarily a criticism. Someone might simply swallow the idea that all our thoughts are about our own mental states in order to keep meaning in the head. But Fodor cannot if he is to provide rationalizing explanations of the sort discussed above. No matter how narrowly we describe Arabella's and Twin Arabella's behavior, we will not be able to construct a cognitive psychology that issues in rationalizations of their behavior if we limit these twins to having thoughts only about their own brain states.

40. See Steven Stich, *From Folk Psychology to Cognitive Science* (Cambridge, Mass., 1983).

41. Tyler Burge, "Individualism and Psychology," read at Sloan Conference, M.I.T., 1984.

42. This kind of account of concepts is developed by Colin McGinn in "The Structure of Content," *Thought and Object,* edited by A. Woodfield (Oxford, 1981).

43. This objection was made in conversation by Paul Boghossian, who is unpersuaded by our reply.

44. Much is made of this distinction in Barry Loewer and Ernest LePore, "Translational Semantics," *Synthese,* 1980.

45. We would like to thank Paul Boghossian, Donald Davidson, Umberto Eco, Peter Klein, Hilary Putnam, Steven Shiffer, and Bas van Fraassen for discussion on earlier drafts of this paper.

Earlier versions of this paper were read at the Universities of Alberta, Calgary, Oklahoma, Michigan, Central Michigan, Regina, and the Florence Center for the History and Philosophy of Science. We would like to thank all the members of these various philosophy departments for their helpful suggestions and criticisms.

Advertisement for a Semantics for Psychology

NED BLOCK

Meaning is notoriously vague. So, it should not be surprising that se-manticists (those who study meaning) have had somewhat different purposes in mind, and thus have sharpened the ordinary concept of meaning in somewhat different ways. It is a curious and unfortunate fact that semanticists typically tell us little about what aspects of meaning they are and are not attempting to deal with. One is given little guidance as to what extent "rival" research programs actually disagree.

My purpose here is to advocate an approach to semantics relevant to the foundations of psychology, or, rather, one approach to one branch of psychology, namely cognitive science. I shall be talking in terms of some of the leading ideas of cognitive science, most importantly the representational theory of mind, aspects of which will be sketched as they become relevant.[1] The representalist doctrine that my argument depends on is that thoughts are structured entities. I know this will be a sticking point for some readers, so I will say a bit more about what this comes to, and I will compare my position with related positions that reject it.

My strategy will be to begin with some desiderata. These desiderata vary along many dimensions: how central they are to meaning, how psychologically oriented they are, how controversial they are. I will argue that one approach to semantics (not to keep you in suspense—conceptual role semantics) promises to handle such desiderata better than the others that I know about. Though I think my desiderata yield a coherent picture of a psychologically relevant semantics, they are not intended to be pretheoretically obvious; rather, they were chosen to flatter the theory I have in mind. I will *not* be arguing that semantic theories that fail to satisfy these desiderata are thereby defective; there are distinct—and equally legitimate—questions about meaning that a semantic theory can seek to answer.

The view that I am advertising is a variant on the functionalism familiar in the philosophy of mind. However, I will not be attempting to counter the objections that have been raised to that view (except briefly, and in passing). My bet is that looking at functionalism from the point of view of meaning (rather than mentality) and with an eye to its fertility and power rather than its weaknesses will provide a rationale for working on its problems.

DESIDERATA

Desideratum 1: Explain the relation between meaning and reference/truth. This is the least psychological of all my desiderata. The details of what I have in mind will be discussed when I say how conceptual role semantics promises to explain the relation between meaning and truth.

Desideratum 2: Explain what makes meaningful expressions meaningful. What is it about 'cat' in virtue of which it has the meaning it has? What is the difference between 'cat' and 'glurg' in virtue of which the former has meaning and the latter does not? (And so on, for types of expressions other than words.)

Desideratum 3: Explain the relativity of meaning to representational system. This desideratum is arguably just a special case of the preceding one, but I think it is worth mentioning and discussing separately. As we all know, one linguistic item—for example, a sound or linguistic expression—can have different meanings in different languages. For example, many vocabulary items have different meanings in the dialects of English spoken in North America and England, as in 'trailer' and 'bathroom'.

But the significance of this relativity of meaning to system of representation goes deeper than such examples suggest. One way to see this is to note that whole semantic (and syntactic) *categories* are relative to system of representation. Ink marks that function as a picture in your tribe may function as a word in mine. Further, within the category of pictures, representations are understood differently in different cultures.[2] Finally, syntactic category is relative in the same way. Handwriting, for example, differs in different school systems. Perhaps the ink marks that are regarded as an 'A' in Edinburgh are regarded as an 'H' in Chicago. Is there some common explanation of the relativity to representational system of both semantic and syntactic categories?

Desideratum 4: Explain compositionality. The meaning of a sentence is in some sense a function of the meanings of the words in it (plus the syntax of the sentence). What, exactly, is the relation between the semantic values of sentences and words? Is one more basic than the other? Another question arises once we have fixed on an answer to these questions—namely, why is it that the semantic value of a sentence has whatever relation it has to the semantic values of its parts?

Desideratum 5: Fit in with an account of the relation between meaning and mind/brain. Why should one expect (or at least hope for) a *semantic* theory to fit into an account of the relation between meaning and mind or brain? Because it would be surprising if the nature of meaning (what meaning *is*) were utterly irrelevant to explaining what it is to grasp or understand meanings, and how grasping meanings can have physical effects. At least, one can imagine differences between x and y that make for a difference between what it is to grasp x and y. For example, understanding x may require skills or recognitional abilities, whereas understanding y may require only propositional knowledge.

I said "mind *or* brain," but in fact I will focus on the brain. And in discussing this matter, I will simply adopt a form of materialism (the "token" identity thesis—that each particular mental occurrence is a physical occurrence).

What is supposed to be in need of explanation about the relation of meaning to the brain? Well, one obvious question is: what is it for the brain to grasp meanings, and how is it that the brain's grasp of meanings has effects on the world? Meanings are (at least apparently) nonphysical abstract objects. And the relation between a brain and the meanings it grasps does not seem to be like the relation between a metal bar and the number of degrees Celsius that is its temperature—a case in which there are proposals about how a change in the value of the temperature can cause, say, expansion of the bar (see Field 1980). Yet the difference between a brain that grasps a certain meaning and a brain that does not makes for a difference in the causal properties of that brain. A brain that grasps the meaning of 'transmogrify' can win a quiz show for its owner, transporting the two of them to a hotel in the Catskills. We need an account of how such a relation between a brain and a meaning can make a causal difference.

Desideratum 6: Illuminate the relation between autonomous and inherited meaning. If there are representations in the brain, as the representational theory of the mind contends, then there is an obvious distinction to be made between them and other representations—for instance, representations on this page (Searle, 1980a; Haugeland, 1980). The representations on the page must be read or heard to be understood, but not so for the representations in the brain. The representations on the page require for their understanding *translation,* or at least *transliteration* into the language of thought; the representations in the brain (some of them, at any rate) require no such translation or transliteration. Let us say that the representations that require no translation or transliteration have *antonomous* meaning, where as the ones that do require translation or transliteration have *inherited* meaning.

Different views of meaning have quite different consequences for the issue of what a semantic theory could hope to say about either type of meaning. On Searle's view, for example, the most a semantic theory could say about this matter is to give an account of how inherited meaning (*observer-relative* meaning, in his terminology) is inherited from autonomous meaning (*intrinsic meaning,* in his terminology). Explaining autonomous meaning itself, in his view, is simply outside the scope of semantics. The most we can say by way of giving an account of autonomous meaning, according to Searle, is that it arises from the causal powers of the human brain and would arise from any other object (e.g., a machine) that has "equivalent causal powers."

Despite the panoply of views on this matter, there are a few questions whose interest should be agreed on by all who accept the distinction between autonomous and inherited meaning to begin with. The main questions are: What are autonomous and inherited meaning? What is the relation between autonomous and inherited meaning? For example, are they just two different types of meaning, neither of which is derivative from or reducible to the other?[3]

A related question is how a representation with autonomous meaning can mean the same as a representation with inherited meaning. Many philosophers would disparage such a question because of skepticism about synonymy. But it is not clear that those who accept it are caught in the Quinean quicksand. That depends on whether the notion of meaning used in cognitive science must carry with it commitment to *truths* of meaning, and hence commitment to a priori truth.[4]

Desideratum 7: Explain the connections between knowing, learning, and using an expression, and the expression's meaning. Obviously, there is a close connection between *the meaning of a word,* on the one hand, and *what we know when we know or understand a word* and *what we learn when we learn a word,* on the other hand. Indeed, it is intuitively plausible that these italicized descriptions have the same referent (though it would be a mistake to adhere dogmatically to this pretheoretic intuition).

Further, one who has learned an expression (and therefore knows it) automatically has a capacity to use it correctly; also, evidence of correct usage is evidence for knowing the meaning. A psychologically relevant theory of meaning ought to illuminate the connections between knowing/understanding/learning and usage, on the one hand, and meaning on the other.

Desideratum 8: Explain why different aspects of meaning are relevant in different ways to the determination of reference and to psychological explanation. One can distinguish between two aspects of meaning that are relevant to psychological explanation in quite different ways. One type of case involves indexicals, for example:

(1) I am in danger of being run over.
(2) Ned Block is in danger of being run over.

Consider the difference between the beliefs I would express by uttering (1), as compared with (2). Believing (2) cannot be guaranteed to have the same life-saving effect on my behavior as believing (1), since I may not know I am Ned Block (I may think I am Napoleon).[5] So there is an important difference between (1) and (2) with respect to causation (and therefore causal explanation) of behavior.

This observation is one motivation for a familiar way of thinking about meaning and belief content in which, when you and I have beliefs expressed by our (respective) utterances of (1), we have beliefs with the same content. This is the way of individuating in which two lunatics who say "I am Napoleon" have the *same delusion*. Corresponding to this way of individuating belief content, we have a way of individuating meanings in which the meanings of the two lunatics' sentence tokens are the same. This is the way of individuating meanings of tokens that is geared toward sentence types, and thus seems most natural for linguistics—since it makes the meaning of a sentence a function of the meanings of the words in the sentence (plus syntax). Notice that on this way of individuating, utterances of (1) and (2) by me have *different* meanings and standardly express beliefs with *different* contents. Again, this way of individuating is natural for linguistics, since no reasonable dictionary would give 'I' and 'Ned Block' the same entry.

Nonetheless, (1), said by me, and (2) express the same proposition, according to a familiar way of individuating propositions. In a familiar sense of 'meaning' in which two sentence tokens have the same meaning just in case they express the same proposition, (1), said by me, and (2) have the same meaning. If we individuate contents of beliefs as we individuate the propositions believed, the belief I express by (1) would have the same content as the belief I express by (2). Further, the belief I express by (1) would have different content from the belief you express by (1); similarly, the meaning of my utterance of (1) would be different from your utterance of (1).

Call the former scheme of individuation *narrow* individuation and the latter *wide* individuation (cf. Kaplan's different distinction between character and content). Wide individuation groups token sentences together if they attribute the same properties to the same individuals, whereas narrow individuation groups sentence tokens together if they attribute the same properties using the same descriptions of individuals—irrespective of whether the individuals referred to are the same. In other words, narrow individuation abstracts from the question of (i.e., ignores) whether the same individuals are involved and depends instead on how the individuals are referred to.[6] (Note that the question of how individuals are referred to is quite different from the question of how the referrer thinks of the referent. For example, two uses of (1) have the same narrow meaning (in my sense of the phrase) even if one user thinks he's Napoleon while the other thinks he's Wittgenstein.)

One can think of narrow and wide individuation as specifying different aspects of meaning, narrow and wide meaning. (I am not saying that narrow and wide meaning are *kinds* of meaning, but only aspects or perhaps only *determinants* of meaning.) Narrow meaning is "in the head," in the sense of this phrase in which it indicates supervenience on physical constitution,[7] and narrow meaning captures the semantic aspect of what is in common to utterances of (e.g.) (1) by different people. Wide meaning, by contrast, depends on what individuals outside the head are referred to, so wide meaning is not "in the head." The type of individuation that gives rise to the concept of narrow meaning also gives rise to a corresponding concept of narrow belief content. Two utterances have the same narrow meaning just in case the beliefs they express have the same narrow content.

Note that despite the misleading terminology, wide meaning does not *include* narrow meaning. Utterances of (1) (by me) and (2) have the same wide meaning but not the same narrow meaning.[8]

Narrow meaning/content and wide meaning/content are relevant to psychological explanation in quite different ways. For one thing, the narrow meaning of a sentence believed is more informative about the mental state of the believer. Thus narrow meaning (and narrow content) is better suited to predicting and explaining what someone decides or does, so long as information about the external world is ignored. Thus, if you and I both have a belief we would express with (1), one can explain and predict our sudden glances at nearby vehicles and our (respective) decisions to leap to the side. Wide meanings are less suited to this type of prediction and explanation, because they "leave out" information about the way one refers to oneself. Since the wide meaning of (1) said by me and (2) are the same, if you are told I believe a sentence with this wide meaning (i.e., the wide meaning common to my [1] and [2], you know that I believe that something—me, as it happens, but you aren't told that I know it's me—is in danger of being run over. Thus, information is omitted, since you aren't told how I conceive of the thing in danger. On the other hand, you do know that I believe that something is in danger, so you do have *some* information about my mental state.

From what I have just said, it would seem that narrow meaning includes everything relevant to psychological explanation that wide meaning does, and more. But wide meaning may be more useful for predicting in one respect: to the extent that there are nomological relations between the world and what people think and do, wide meaning will allow predicting what they think and do without information about how they see things. Suppose, for example, that people tend to avoid wide open spaces, no matter how they describe these spaces to themselves. Then knowing that Fred is choosing whether to go via an open space or a city street, one would be in a position to predict Fred's choice, even though one does not know whether Fred describes the open space to himself as 'that', or as 'Copley Square'.

Narrow meaning has another kind of theoretical import: it determines a function from expressions and contexts of utterance onto referents and truth values.[9] When you and I utter 'I' in (1), there is something we share, some semantic aspect of the word 'I' that in your context maps your token onto you and in my context maps my token onto me.

Let me guard against some misunderstandings. First, as I already indicated, the narrow meaning of 'I' does not include one's conception of oneself. Second, although I have said that there is a shared semantic aspect of 'I' relevant to explaining behavior and a shared semantic aspect relevant to determining a function from context to referent, I do not suggest that these shared semantic aspects are exactly the same. It is an open question whether they are the same, and hence whether 'narrow meaning', as I am using the term, picks out a single thing. On the theory I will be arguing for, the semantic aspect that determines the function from context to referent (and truth value) turns out to be a *part* of the semantic aspect that plays a part in explaining behavior. Thus the latter semantic aspect does *both* jobs. Hence, I will use 'narrow meaning/content' as uniquely referring to the more inclusive semantic aspect. I do want to note, though, that this way of talking carries a strong theoretical commitment. Finally, the narrow/wide distinction as I have described it so far applies to tokens, not types. However, there is an obvious extension to (nonindexical) types.

I will now pause to say what the considerations raised in this section so far have to do with a semantics for psychology. First, a semantics for psychology should have something to say about what the distinction between narrow and wide meaning comes to and, ideally, should give accounts of what the two aspects of meaning are. Second, the theory ought to say why it is that narrow and wide meanings are distinctively relevant to the explanation and prediction of psychological facts (including behavior). Third, the theory ought to give an account of narrow meaning that explains how it is that it determines a function from the context of utterance to reference and truth value.

I have been talking so far about the meaning of sentences with indexicals, but the points I have been making can be extended to names and, more controversially, to natural kind terms. Consider Teen (of Earth) and her twin on Twin Earth, Teen$_{te}$. The two are particle-for-particle duplicates who have had exactly the same histories of surface stimulations. In various different versions of the story, we are to imagine various differences in their worlds outside the sphere of what has impinged on them. For now, let us suppose their environments are exactly the same, except, of course, that the individuals on the two worlds are distinct—Teen's hero is Michael Jackson, whereas Teen$_{te}$'s hero is a distinct but indistinguishable (except spatiotemporally) personage. Teen and Teen$_{te}$ each have the thought they would express with:

*Mofiee wrde/ti
This distinatin
name Putnam
iont the or Fodor one.*

(3) Michael Jackson struts.

Once again, we can distinguish between two ways of individuating thought contents, and also the meanings of the sentences thought. On one, the narrow scheme, we can talk of Teen and Teen$_{te}$ as having the same thought, and we can talk of them as uttering sentences with the same meaning. If they would both sincerely say "Michael Jackson has supernatural powers," they share the same delusion. This is narrow meaning and narrow content. Alternatively, we can regard the meanings and thought contents as distinct simply in virtue of the fact that Teen is referring to Michael Jackson and Teen$_{te}$ is referring to Michael Jackson$_{te}$. This is wide meaning and content.

This illustrates same narrow/different wide meaning and content. The case of same wide/different narrow meaning (the case analogous to [1] and [2] above uttered by the same person) is illustrated by 'Cicero orates' and 'Tully orates'. The principles of individuation in these name cases are the same as in the indexical cases, though their motivation is in one respect weaker because it is controversial whether names even *have* meanings. Also, the nomological connection between names and behavior is not as simple as that between 'I' and behavior.

There are two basic facts on which the narrow/wide distinction is based. One is that how you represent something that you refer to can affect your psychological states and behavior. So if you know that Cicero orates and you don't know that Cicero = Tully, you are not in a position to make use of the fact that Tully orates. The second basic fact is that there is more to semantics than what is "in the head." The contents of the head of a person who asserts (3), together with the fact that Michael Jackson struts, are *not enough to determine whether (3) is true or false,* since the truth value depends as well on who 'Michael Jackson' refers to. Imagine that though Michael Jackson is an excellent strutter, his twin cannot strut; the strutting ascribed to his twin by Twin Earth teenagers is actually done by a stuntman. Then utterances of (3) on Twin Earth differ in truth value from utterances of (3) on Earth, despite no relevant differences between teenage heads on the two planets, and despite it being just as much a fact on Twin Earth as on Earth that Michael Jackson struts. (If this seems mysterious to you, note that in the last sentence, I used 'Michael Jackson' as it is used in my language community—Should I talk someone else's language?—and the language community on Twin Earth uses the same expression to refer to a different person.) *Since the truth value of a sentence is determined by the totality of semantic facts, plus the relevant facts about the world, there is more to the totality of semantic facts about the sentence than is in the speaker's head. The "extra" semantic facts are about what the referring terms in the sentence refer to.*[10] But even though there are semantic differences between Teen's and Teen$_{te}$'s utterance of and thinking of (3), there are important similarities as well—and this is the main point of this section—that give rise to notions of aspects of content and meaning (narrow content and meaning) *that are shared by Teen and Teen$_{te}$* and that explain similarities in their (for example) fantasy life and ticket-buying behavior and that determine the function from their different contexts to their different referents.

As in the idexical case, wide meaning and content are not well suited to explaining change of mental state and behavior. The wide meaning of 'Water is wet' (in English—not Twin English) is the same as that of 'H$_2$O is wet', despite the potentially different effects of believeing these sentences on mental states and on behavior. Further, as Kripke's Pierre example reveals (Kripke 1979), if one's conception of translation is overly referential (allowing 'London' to translate 'Londres' inside belief contexts), one is faced with situations in which one is forced to ascribe contradictory beliefs that are no fault of the believer.[11] In addition, what is shared by Teen and Teen$_{te}$ also determines that one is referring to Michael Jackson, whereas the other is referring to Michael Jackson's twin. What is shared determines a function from context to reference. Had Teen been raised on Twin Earth, she would have been molecule for molecule the same as she actually is (ignoring quantum indeterminacy), but her token of 'Michael Jackson' would have referred to Michael Jackson's twin.[12]

The reader may wonder why I have gone on about this desideratum (on the narrow/wide distinction) at such length. (And I'm not finished yet!) The version of conceptual role semantics that I will be defending characterizes *narrow* meaning in terms of conceptual role. There is another version (Harman 1982) that has no truck with narrow content or meaning. Harman's conceptual roles involve perceptual and behavioral interactions with what is seen and manipulated, that is, objects in the world, whereas my conceptual roles stop at the skin. (So if you don't like all this narrow this and narrow that, you can still appreciate the previous desiderata as motivating a Harmanian version of conceptual role semantics.) I prefer my version, and I am trying to spell out part of the motivation for it.[13] (I will say more about Harman's alternative shortly.)

Consider Putnam's original Twin Earth story. My doppelgänger (again, a physical duplicate)[14] uses 'water' to refer to XYZ. Suppose, along with Putnam, that XYZ is *not* a type of water. Further, we may add into the story ideas developed by Burge (Burge 1979) that show the differences in how our different language communities use words can determine differences in the meanings of our words, even when they do not result in differences in stimuli impinging on our surfaces. Suppose my twin and I both say to ourselves:

> My pants are on fire. But luckily I am standing in front of a swimming pool filled with water. Water, thank God, puts out fires.

If Burge and Putnam are right (and I am inclined to agree with them), there are substantial semantic differences between my twin's and my meanings and thought contents because of the differences in physical and social environment. Nonetheless—and here, again, is the crucial idea behind my advocacy of narrow meaning and content—*there is some aspect of meaning in common to what he says and what I say (or at least a common partial determinant of meaning), and this common semantic aspect of what we say provides part of a common explanation of why we both jump into our respective pools.* And if current ideas about the representational theory of mind are right, narrow meaning and content will be usable to state nomological generalizations relating thought, decision, and action.

Further, had my twin grown up in my context, his token of 'water' would refer to H_2O rather than XYZ. Thus, as before, it seems that there is some common semantic aspect of our terms that operates in my case to map my context onto H_2O, and in his case to map his context onto XYZ.

The reader may have noticed my shift to the natural extension I described of the narrow/wide distinction from tokens to types. Since 'Cicero' and 'Tully' are standardly used to refer to the same person, we can regard the sentence types 'Cicero orates' and 'Tully orates' as having the same wide meaning. Likewise for 'water' (as used in English as opposed to Twin English) and 'H_2O'.

Let us say that a propositional attitude or meaning ascription is individualistic if it is supervenient on the physical state of the individual's body, where physical state is specified nonintentionally and independently of physical and social conditions obtaining outside the body.[15] I believe that there is an important individualistic scheme of individuation of beliefs, belief contents, and the meanings of the sentences believed. There is a strong element of individualistic individuation in ordinary thought, but its main home lies in scientific thinking about the mind, especially in contemporary cognitive science. I also agree with Burge and Putnam that there is an important nonindividualistic scheme of individuation in ordinary thought. No incompatability yet.

But Putnam, Burge, and others have also argued against individualistic individuation. Putnam's conclusion (1983) is based on an argument that it is impossible to come up with identity conditions on content or meaning, individualistically considered. I don't have identity conditions to offer, but I am inclined to regard this not as an insurmountable obstacle but as an issue to be dissolved by theory construction. My guess is that a scientific conception of meaning should do away with the crude dichotomy of same/different meaning in favor of a multidimensional gradient of similarity of meaning.[16] After all, substitution of a continuum for a dichotomy is how Bayesian decision theory avoids a host of difficulties—for example, the paradox of the preface—by moving from the crude pigeonholes of *believes/doesn't believe* to degrees of belief.[17]

Burge (1984) is arguing mainly against "pan-individualism," the claim that *all* propositional-attitude individuation in psychology is individualistic. However, I am not advocating this doctrine but only the more limited claim that there is an important strain of individualistic individuation in psychology (and in commonsense discourse). Burge has doubts about this too, but the matter can only be settled by a detailed discussion of psychological practice.

Let me mention only one consideration. Psychology is often concerned with explaining psychological differences. The measure of these differences is *variance*.[18] For example, variance in intelligence and other mental attributes and states is ascribed to differences in genes and environment (and interactions of various sorts between these causal factors). Suppose we fill a tour bus with travelers, half from Twin Earth and half from Earth. The Earthlings believe that water is wet and prefer drinking water to gasoline, whereas the Twin Earthlings do not hve these propositional attitudes (because when they think about what they call 'water', they are not thinking about water—they have no term that refers to water). Suppose that the Earthlings and Twin Earthlings do not differ in relevant ways in genes or in the surface stimulation that has impinged on their bodies over their whole lives. Hence, in this population, differences in propositional attitudes cannot be attributed to environment (in the sense of surface stimulation) and genes (and their interactions): the differences in water attitudes are due to something that has nothing to do with differences in the genes or surface stimulations that have affected these people. An analysis of variance would have to attribute a large component of variance to differences in a factor that does not cause any differences in proteins, synaptic connections, or any other physicochemical feature of the body, as do differences in genes and surface stimulations. This would amount to a kind of action at a distance, and this would clearly go counter to the methodology of attribution of variance. (Note that this point could have been formulated in terms of Burge's point about the social nature of meaning rather than Twin Earth.)

I just argued for individualistic individuation of propositional attitude states—for example, beliefs. But there is a gap between individuating beliefs individualistically and individuating belief *contents* individualistically. One might hold that when you individuate belief individualistically, you still have belief of some strange sort; but that content, individualistically individuated, is like a president who is deposed—no longer a president (cf. Stich 1983). I propose to fill the gap as follows.

Where we have a relation, in certain types of cases we have individualistic properties of the related entities that could be said to ground the relation. If x hits y, y has some sort of consequent change in a bodily surface, perhaps a flattened nose, and x has the property of say, moving his fist forward. Of course, the same individualistic property can underlie many different relational properties, and some relations notoriously don't depend on individualistic properties—for example, 'to the left of'. When content is *non*individualistically individuated, it is individuated with respect to relations to the world (as in the Twin Earth case) and social practice (as in Burge's arthritis example).[19] There is a nonrelational aspect of propositional attitude content, the aspect "inside the head," that corresponds to content in the way that moving the fist corresponds to hitting. This nonrelational aspect of content is what I am calling narrow content. But is narrow content really content?[20]

I find much hostility among philosophers to the ideas of narrow content and narrow meaning. There are many reasons for this resistance that I accept as points of genuine controversy, and about which I am not at all confident about my position. But the worry just mentioned seems to me misplaced, at least as a criticism of conceptual role semantics. The criticism is that I have wrongly assumed that the aspect of meaning or content that is inside the head is something genuinely *semantic*. Jerry Fodor once accused me of a "fallacy of subtraction," that is, of assuming that if you take meaning or content and *subtract* its relation to the world and its social aspect, what you have left is something semantic.

There *is* such a thing as a fallacy of subtraction, of course. If you subtract the property of being colored from redness, you do not get colorless redness. But the issue with respect to conceptual role semantics is merely verbal. Nothing in my position requires me to regard narrow meaning and narrow content as (respectively) *kinds* of meaning and content. As mentioned earlier, I regard them as aspects of or as *determinants* of meaning and content. All that is required for my position is that what I am calling narrow meaning is a distinct feature of language, a characterization of which has something important to contribute to a total theory of meaning (e.g., as indicated in my desiderata). Similarly for narrow content.

Am I conceding that conceptual role semantics isn't really part of *semantics?* The first thing to be said about this question is that it is of very minor intellectual importance. It is a dispute about the border between disciplines; like so many of these disputes, it can be resolved only by a kind of ordinary language philosophy applied to technical terms like 'semantics' (or, worse, by university administrations). Ordinary language philosophy has its place in analyses of concepts that play a central role in ordinary human thought; but application of these techniques to technical terms, where stipulation is the order of the day, is not very illuminating. Nonetheless, I am as willing to quibble as the next person. The correct application of disciplinary terms depends in large part on developments in the disciplines. Often the pretheoretic ideas about the domain of the discipline are left far behind. If meaning indeed decomposes into two factors, then the study of the nature of these two factors belongs in the domain of semantics, even if one or both of them are quite different from meaning in any ordinary sense of the term.

To appeal to ordinary ideas about meaning to argue for excluding narrow meaning from the domain of semantics is like excluding electrons from the domain of the study of matter on the ground that they aren't "solid" and diffract like light.

Further, the role of narrow meaning in determining the function from context to reference and truth value seems especially deserving of the appellation 'semantic'. (I will argue in discussing Desideratum 1 below that narrow meaning—as specified by conceptual role semantics—does indeed determine this function.)

I will continue to talk, as I have, of narrow meaning and narrow content; but I won't mind if the reader prefers to reformulate, using phrases like 'narrow determinant of meaning'.

CONCEPTUAL ROLE SEMANTICS AND TWO-FACTOR THEORY

Conceptual role semantics is not among the more popular approaches, but it has the distinction of being the only approach (to my knowledge, at any rate) that has the potential to satisfy all these desiderata. The approach I have in mind has been suggested, independently, by both philosophers and cognitive scientists: by the former under the title "conceptual role semantics" and by the latter under the title "procedural semantics." (Oddly, these two groups do not refer to one another.) The doctrine has its roots in positivism and pragmatism and in the Wittgensteinian idea of meaning as use. Among philosophers, its recent revival is due mainly to Harman (following Sellars),[21] and Field.[22] Churchland, Loar, Lycan, McGinn, and Schiffer have also advocated versions of the view.[23] In cognitive science, the chief proponent has been Woods,[24] though Miller's and Johnson-Laird's[25] versions have been of interest. The version I like is a "two-factor theory" something like the one advocated by Field,[26] McGinn, (1982), and Loar (1982). (See also Lycan 1981.)

The idea of the two-factor version is that there are two components to meaning, a conceptual role component that is entirely "in the head" (this is narrow meaning)[27] and an external component that has to do with the relations between the representations in the head (with their internal conceptual roles) and the referents and/or truth conditions of these representations in the world. This two-factor approach derives from Putnam's argument (1975, 1979) that meaning could not both be "in the head" and also determine reference. It also takes heart from the Perry-Kaplan points about indexicals mentioned earlier (character and content are two "factors"). The two-factor approach can be regarded as making a conjunctive claim for each sentence: what its conceptual role is, and what its (say) truth conditions are.[28] I will refer to the *two-factor version* of conceptual role semantics as CRS, though perhaps it should be TFCRS to remind the reader of the two-factor nature of the theory.

For present purposes, the exact nature of the external factor does not matter. Those who are so inclined could suppose it to be elucidated by a causal theory of reference or by a theory of truth conditions. The internal factor, conceptual role, is a matter of the causal role of the expression in reasoning and deliberation and, in general, in the way the expression combines and interacts with other expressions so as to mediate between sensory inputs and behavioral outputs. A crucial component of a sentence's conceptual role is a matter of how it participates in inductive and deductive inferences. A word's conceptual role is a matter of its contribution to the role of sentences.[29]

For example, consider what would be involved for a symbol in the internal representational system, '$\rightarrow$', to express the material conditional. The '$\rightarrow$' in 'FELIX IS A CAT $\rightarrow$ FELIX IS AN ANIMAL'[30] expresses the material conditional if, for example, when the just quoted sentence interacts appropriately with:

> 'FELIX IS A CAT', the result is a tendency to inscribe 'FELIX IS AN ANIMAL' (other things equal, of course).
>
> 'FELIX IS NOT AN ANIMAL', the result is a tendency to prevent the inscription of 'FELIX IS A CAT', and a tendency to inscribe 'FELIX IS NOT A CAT'.
>
> 'IS FELIX AN ANIMAL?', the result is a tendency to initiate a search for 'FELIX IS A CAT'.

Conceptual role is *total causal role,* abstractly described. Consider, by way of analogy, the causal role of herring. They affect what they eat, what eats them, what sees them and runs away, and, of course, they causally interact with one another. Now abstract away from the total causal role of herring to their culinary role, by which I mean the causal relations involving them that have an effect on or are affected by human dining. Presumably, some of what affects herring and what they affect will not be part of their culinary role: for example, perhaps herring occasionally amuse penguins, and this activity has no culinary causes or effects. Similarly, elements of language have a total causal role, including, say, the effect of newsprint on whatever people wrap in it. Conceptual role abstracts away from all causal relations except the ones that mediate inferences, inductive or deductive, decision making, and the like.

A crucial question for CRS (*the* crucial question) is what counts as identity and difference of conceptual role. Clearly, there are many differences in reasoning that we do not want to count as relevant to meaning. For example, if you take longer than I do in reasoning from x to y, we do not necessarily want to see this as revealing a difference between your meanings of x and/or y and mine. Our reasoning processes may be the same in all inferentially important respects.

Further, CRS must face the familiar "collateral information" problem. Suppose you are prepared to infer from 'TIGER' to 'DANGEROUS', whereas I am not. Do our 'TIGER's have the same conceptual role or not? More significantly, what if we differ in inferring from 'TIGER' to 'ANIMAL'? Does the first difference differ in kind from the second?

CRS has less room to maneuver here than, say, Katzian semantics, since CRS cannot make use of an analytic/synthetic distinction. The problem is that if we make the inferences that define 'cat' just the putatively analytic ones (excluding, for example, the inference from 'cat' to 'is probably capable of purring'), we get a meaning for 'cat' that is the same as for 'dog'. (One could try to distinguish them by making use of the difference between the words themselves [e.g., the fact that 'is a cat' entails 'is not a dog'], but that would at best allow intrapersonal synonymy, not interpersonal synonomy. See Field 1978.) This is not a problem *within* Katzian semantics because Katzians appeal to primitive (undefined) elements of language in terms of which other elements are defined. (See Katz 1972.) The Katzian picture is that you can distinguish the meaning of 'dog' from 'cat' by appealing to the analytic truths that cats are feline (and not canine) and dogs are canine (and not feline), where 'feline' and 'canine' are primitive terms. This move is not available for CRS, since it has no truck with primitive terms: conceptual role is supposed to completely determine narrow meaning. (One qualification: it *is* possible to take conceptual role as a *part* of a theory of the narrow meaning of *part* of the language—the nonprimitive part—while appealing to some other conception of meaning of primitives; procedural semanticists sometimes sound as if they want to take *phenomenal* terms as primitives whose meaning is given by their "sensory content," while taking other terms as getting their meanings via their computational relations to one another and to the phenomenal terms as well [perhaps they see the phenomenal terms as "grounding" the functional structures]. It should be clear that this is a "mixed" conceptual role/phenomenalist theory and not a pure conceptual role theory.)

Without an analytic/synthetic distinction, we would, as I mentioned earlier, have to move to a scientific conception of meaning that does away with the crude dichotomy of same/different meaning in favor of a multidimensional gradient of similarity of meaning (hoping for results as good as those achieved by decision theory in moving from an all-or-nothing notion of belief to a graded notion).

If CRS is to be developed to the point where it can be evaluated seriously, definite proposals for individuating conceptual roles must be framed and investigated. One of the purposes of this paper is to try to make it plausible that CRS is worth pursuing.

What about the social dimension of meaning demonstrated in Burge (1979)? Two-factor theory *can* try to capture such phenomena in the referential factor. For example, perhaps the causal chain determining the reference of my use of 'arthritis' is mediated by the activities of people who know more about arthritis than I do. (See Boyd [1979] for an indication of how to knit the social aspect of meaning together with a causal theory of reference.) Alternatively, two-factor theory may have to expand to three-factor theory, allowing a distinct social factor to meaning. Since my mission is to compare the broad outlines of the view I am espousing with alternative points of view, I will not pursue the matter further (though later on I will take up the question of how the conceptual role factor is related to the referential factor).

It should be becoming clear that CRS as I am conceiving of it is so undeveloped as to be more of a framework for a theory than a theory. Why bother thinking about such a sketchy theory? I think that the current status of CRS is reminiscent of the "causal theory of reference." The root idea of causal theories of reference seems clearly relevant to central phenomena of reference, such as how one person can acquire the ability to refer to Napoleon from another person, even without acquiring many beliefs about Napoleon, and even if most of what he believes is false. Detailed versions of causal theories (Devitt 1981) have not commanded widespread agreement; nonetheless, since the only alternative theories of reference (e.g., the description theory) seem hopeless as accounts of the phenomena just mentioned, we are justified in supposing that the central ideas of the causal theory of reference will have to play a part in some way in any successful theory of reference. I intend the desiderata I've discussed to provide a similar rationale for supposing that the central ideas of CRS must somehow fit into our overall semantic picture.

I should mention that (as with the causal theory of reference) a two-factor conceptual role semantics has been set out in one precise version—that of Field (1977). Though Field's account is very suggestive, I will not adopt it, for a number of reasons. For one thing, Field's account is not quite a conceptual role account in the sense in which I have defined it, since his conceptual roles are not quite causal. Field defines conceptual role in terms of conditional probability. Two sentences have the same conceptual role if and only if they have the same conditional probability with respect to every other sentence. Though Field is not explicit about this, he obviously intends some kind of causal account in terms of the causal consequences of new evidence on degrees of belief. Harman (1982) criticizes Field's account on the ground that it does not allow for revision of belief. Harman's argument, apparently, is that Bayesians merely change their degree of belief rather than changing their mind. That is, Bayesians do not treat new evidence as dictating that they should reject claims they formerly accepted (or conversely), but rather that they should move from a .67 degree of belief in a claim to a .52

degree of belief. I don't find Harman's objection very persuasive; what corresponds to change of mind in the Bayesian perspective just *is* change of degree of belief. The Bayesians reject change of mind in favor of change of degree of belief; this is a theoretical disagreement that is not settled by insisting. However, a version of Harman's conclusion seems quite likely right, but for another reason: in seeing change of mind entirely in terms of change in degree of belief via conditionalization (or generalized conditionalization), the Bayesian perspective (like the logical empiricist views that are concerned with justification rather than discovery) cannot model the kind of change of mind that involves the generation of new hypotheses (this point is most convincing with regard to new hypotheses that involve new ideas). Its not that the Bayesian perspective is in any way incompatible with the generation of new hypotheses, but rather that on the Bayesian account of reasoning, new hypotheses must be treated as "given" via some non-Bayesian process, and so the Bayesian account is importantly incomplete. Conceptual role includes the kind of reasoning in which one infers from evidence against one's hypothesis to an obvious variant deploying a revised version of an old idea, and this cannot be captured wholly within a Bayesian framework.

Even ignoring this matter, Field's account highlights a choice that must be made by CRS theorists, one that has had no discussion (as far as I know): namely, should conceptual role be understood in ideal or normative terms, or should it be tied to what people actually do? As Harman (forthcoming) points out (in another context), accounts of reasoning that involve change of degree of belief by conditionalizing on evidence require keeping track of astronomical numbers of conditional probabilities. (Harman calculates that a billion are needed for thirty evidence propositions.) So any Bayesian account would have to be very far removed from actual reasoning. However, if we opt against such idealization, must we stick so close to actual practice as to include in conceptual role well-known fallacious reasoning strategies, such as the gamblers' fallacy?[31]

I prefer not to comment on this matter, in part because I'm not sure what to say and in part because I am trying to stay away from controversies *within* conceptual role semantics, because the points I want to make can be made on the basis of a version of the doctrine that contains very little in the way of details.

Calling the causal roles CRS appeals to 'conceptual' or 'inferential' shouldn't mislead anyone into supposing that the theory's description of them can appeal to their meanings—that would defeat the point of reductionist theories. The project of giving a nonsemantic (and nonintentional) description of these roles is certainly daunting, but the reader would do well to note that it is no more daunting than the programs of various popular philosophical theories. For example, the causal theory of reference, taken as a reductionist proposal (as in Devitt's but not in Kripke's versions) has the same sort of charge. And, a rather similar charge falls on "traditional" non-representational functionalism (e.g., as in Lewis's or Putnam's versions), where the causal roles of propositional attitude states are to be described in nonintentional and nonsemantic terms.

Representationalists differ in how important they think the role of English expressions are in reasoning, deliberation, and so forth. At one end of the spectrum, we have the view that English is *the* language of thought (for English speakers). Near the other end, we have those who, more influenced by cognitive psychology, have tended to see reasoning in English as the tip of an iceberg whose main mass is computation in an internal language common to speakers of English and Walburi.[32] On the latter view, the narrow meaning of English expressions is derivative from the narrow meanings of expressions in the internal language. (The dependency would, however, be the other way around for the referential component of meaning, since it is English expressions that are more directly related to the world.) I will not be concerned with this and a number of other disputes that can occur *within* the framework of conceptual role semantics.

In what follows, I shall be quite relaxed about this issue of the role of English in thinking. Sometimes, I will take English to be the language of thought. However, when it is convenient, I will assume that English is used only for communication and that *all* thought is in a language that does not overlap with English, mentalese. When on this latter tack, I will also assume that mechanisms of language production and language understanding establish a *standard association* between English and mentalese expressions. When a speaker formulates a message using 'CAT', language—production mechanisms map 'CAT' onto 'cat'; and when the hearer understands 'cat', the language—understanding mechanisms map it onto 'CAT'.

This standard-association notion can be used to construct a way of individuating conceptual roles in which English expressions have the conceptual roles of the mentalese expressions with which they are standardly associated. Suppose I am told that Felix is a cat and am asked about Felix's weight. I answer "Felix weighs more than .01 grams." I suggest we start with the following simple mechanistic picture. When I hear "Felix is a cat," language-understanding mechanisms produce "FELIX IS A CAT." Reasoning mechanisms produce "FELIX WEIGHS MORE THAN .01 GRAMS," and language-production mechanisms result in the utterance of "Felix weighs more than .01 grams." Now an English sentence and its internal standard associate certainly hve different causal properties. For example, one is visible or audible (normally) without neurophysiological techniques. But we can individuate conceptual roles so as to give them the *same* conceptual roles, simply by (1) taking the relevant causal properties of English expressions as the ones that are mediated by their causal interactions with their standard associates and (2) abstracting away from the mechanisms that effect the standard association. Then any cause or effect of 'cat' will, for purposes of individuation of conceptual roles, be regarded as the same as a cause or an effect of 'CAT'.

An analogy: Consider a computer in which numbers are entered and displayed in ordinary decimal notation, but in which all computation is actually done in binary notation. The way the computer works is that there are mechanisms that transform the '3 + 4' you enter on the keyboard into an internal expression we can represent as '+ (11,100)'. This is a translation, of course, but we can talk about it without describing it as such, by describing it in terms of the mechanism that computes the function. Internal computational mechanisms operate on this expression, yielding another expression, '111', which is transformed by the translation mechanisms into a '7' displayed on the screen. Now the process by which '3 + 4' yields '7' is exactly the same as the process by which '+ (11,100)' yields '111', except for the two translation steps. So if we (1) ignore causes and effects of decimal digits other than those mediated by their interactions with binary digits in the innards of the machine and (2) abstract away from the translation steps, we can regard the decimal and corresponding binary expressions as having the same computational roles.

Thus, one can speak of the conceptual roles of English expressions, even when adopting the view that internal computation is entirely in mentalese. This will seem strange if your picture of English tokens is inert expressions in dusty books, as compared with the dynamic properties of the internal representations in which all thought is actually conducted. So remember that I am adverting to what the English expressions do when seen or heard.

Let me try to clarify what I am trying to do with the notion of standard association by mentioning some caveats.

(1) The English language is of course a social object. In speaking of the conceptual roles of English expressions, I do not intend a theory of that social object. Conceptual role, you will recall, is meant to capture narrow meaning. Indeed, since causal roles differ from person to person, CRS deals with *idiolect* narrow meaning rather than public language narrow meaning.

(2) The existence of the mechanisms that effect the standard association is an empirical question (though, as Stich [1983, p. 80] argues, something like this idea seems to be part of commonsense psychology). I appeal to empirical work on the "language module"—see Fodor (1983b). Were the empirical assumption to turn out false, a conceptual role theory of (the narrow meaning of) external language could still be given (in terms of the causal interactions between external and internal language), but what would be lost would be the plausibility of a conceptual role theory in which for almost any external expression, one could expect an internal expression with the same narrow meaning. So as to have my empirical eggs in one basket, let me include the assumption of a language module under the rubric of "representationalism."

(3) In order for the notion of standard association to be usable to define conceptual roles, it must be characterizable nonsemantically and nonintentionally. But doesn't this idea founder on obvious facts about the devious road from thought to language, for example, that people lie? The point of my appeal to the language module is that it works (once engaged) without the intervention of any intentional states. Of course, it is used by us in a variety of ways, since we have many purposes in using language. The language module works the same in lying and truth telling; the difference is to be found in the mentalese message. Perhaps confusion would be avoided if one focuses on the use of language, not in communication, but in thinking out loud or in internal soliloquies.

(4) Language production may have to bear more of the burden in characterizing standard association than language perception, since the latter encounters complications with indexicals and the like. When one hears "I'm sick," one doesn't represent it the way one would represent one's own first person thought.

(5) Despite the convention I've adopted of writing mentalese as English in capitals, nothing in the CRS position requires that a sentence spoken have the same meaning as that sentence thought. One can make sense of the idea that in speech one uses the English word 'chase' to mean what one means in thought by the English word 'CHAIR'. Imagine yourself moving to a place where they speak a dialect of English that differs from yours in exchanging the meanings of these two words. If you continue to think in your old dialect but talk in the new one, you would be in the described situation. Consider two quite different scenarios. In one, the new situation never effects a change in your language production/perception module. In communicating, you consciously adjust your words, but in thinking out loud, you talk as before. In the other scenario, the module changes so as to adjust to the external shift. In the former case, standard association will be normal. In the latter, 'chair' will be standardly associated with 'CHASE', and the conceptual role of 'chair' will derive from 'CHASE'-thoughts (involving trying to catch rather than sitting). 'Chair' will have the same conceptual role as 'CHASE'. Neither scenario provides any problem for the view of conceptual role of external language that I sketched. Schiffer and Loar have emphasized that if there is an internal language, a sentence spoken need not have the same meaning as the same sentence thought, but they have been led to conclude that if a language of thought hypothesis is true, it is reasonable to deploy two quite different types of theories of meaning—one for internal language, one for external language. Their concern with external language is with meaning in public language, whereas mine is with narrow meaning in idiolect, so there is no direct conflict. Still, I want to emphasize that a conclusion analogous to theirs for idiolect narrow meaning is mistaken. (See Loar 1981; Schiffer 1981.) This matter will come up again in the section below on what makes meaningful expressions meaningful.

One final point of clarification: Though I am advocating CRS, I am far from a true believer. My position is that CRS can do enough for us (as indicated by the desiderata it satisfies) to motivate working it out in detail and searching for solutions to its problems.

Perhaps this is the place to mention why I am willing to advocate a version of functionalism despite my arguments against functionalism in Block (1978). First, I am impressed by the questions this particular version of functionalism (apparently) can answer. Second, I am now willing to settle for (and I think there is some value in) a theory that is chauvinist in the sense that it does not characterize meaning or intentionality in general, but only *human* meaning or intentionality. Third, the arguments I gave for the conclusion that functionalism is liberal (in the sense that it overascribes mental properties, e.g., to groups of people organized appropriately) were strongest against functionalist theories of *experiential* mental states. I am now inclined to regard intentional mental states as a natural kind for which a functionalist theory may be OK, even though it is not acceptable for experiential states. Indeed, if the domain of CRS is a natural kind, then so is the domain of intentional mental phenomena.

Ironically, this concession to functionalism may make my position harder to defend against thoroughgoing functionalists, since it may commit me to the possibility of intentionality—even intentional states with the same sort of intentional content as ours—without experience. Perhaps I would be committed to the possibility of "zombies," whose beliefs are the same as ours (including beliefs to the effect that they are in pain), but who have no real pains (only "ersatz" pains that are functionally like pain but lack qualitative content). Then I would have to confront the arguments against this possibility in Shoemaker (1984, chaps. 9 and 14). (On my view, pain, for example, is actually a composite state consisting of a nonfunctional qualitative state together with a functional state. Since the qualitative state can be neurophysiologically—but not functionally—characterized, I regard the full account of the mental as part functional, part physiological.) Finally, I believe many of the other arguments that have been advanced against functionalism in its various forms to be defective (see my argument below against Searle).

Two Factors or One Factor?

The version of CRS I have been talking about is a "two-factor" version, in which the conceptual role factor is meant to capture the aspect (or determinant) of meaning "inside the head," whereas the other is meant to capture the referential and social dimensions of meaning.

As I mentioned earlier, Gilbert Harman has been advocating a different version of conceptual role semantics. Harman's version makes do with *one* factor, namely, conceptual role. How does he do without the referential and social factors? By making his one factor reach out into the world of referents and into the practices of the linguistic community. I have been talking about conceptual roles along lines common in functionalist writing in philosophy of mind. These conceptual roles stop roughly at the skin. Outputs are conceived of in terms of bodily movements or, according to the more scientifically minded, in terms of outputs of, say, the motor cortex (allowing for thoughts in disembodied brains). Inputs are conceived of in terms of the proximal stimuli or in terms of outputs of sensory transducers. By contrast, here is Harman on the subject.

> Conceptual role semantics does not involve a "solipsistic" theory of the content of thoughts. There is no suggestion that content depends only on functional relations among thoughts and concepts, such as the role a particular concept plays in inference. (Field, 1977, misses this point.) Also relevant are functional relations to the external world in connection with perception, on the one hand, and action on the other. What makes something the concept red is in part the way in which the concept is involved in the perception of red objects in the external world. What makes something the concept of danger is in part the way in which the concept is involved in thoughts that affect action in certain ways.[33]

One might speak of Harman's conceptual roles as "long-armed," as opposed to the "short-armed" conceptual roles of the two-factor theorist.

My objection to Harman, in brief, is that I don't see how he can handle the phenomena one would ordinarily think of as being in the purview of a theory of reference without extending his account to the point where it is equivalent to the two-factor account.

The point emerges as one looks at Harman's responses to problems that are dealt with by familiar theories of reference. Consider a resident of Earth who travels to Twin Earth in a space ship. He lands in a body of XYZ; but, ignorant of the difference between Twin Earth and Earth, he radios home the message "Surrounded by water." At first glance, one would think that the Harmanian conceptual role of the traveler's word 'water' would at that moment involve a connection to XYZ, since that is what his perception and action is at that moment connected with. Then Harman would be committed to saying the traveler's message is true—in contrast with the Putnamian claim that his message is false because he is not surrounded by water (but rather twin water). Since Harman accepts the Putnam line, he deploys a notion of "normal context" (Harman 1973), the idea being that the traveler's conceptual role for 'water' is to be thought of as involving the substance he normally refers to using that word.

Another case Harman discusses is Putnam's elm/beech case. (You will recall that the question is how I can use 'elm' to refer to elms when what I know about elms is exactly the same as what I know about beeches (except for the names). Harman's solution is to include in *my* conceptual role for 'elm' its role in the minds of experts who actually know the difference.

It begins to look as if Harman is building into his long-arm conceptual roles devices that have usually been placed in the theory of reference. The point can be strengthened by a look at other phenomena that have concerned theories of reference, such as borrowed reference to things that do not now exist but did exist in the past. I can refer to Aristotle on the basis of overhearing your conversation about him, even if most of what I believe about Aristotle is false, because I misunderstood what you said. Will Harman deal with this by making his conceptual roles reach from one person to another, into the past, that is, making a causal relation between Aristotle and me— mediated by you, and your source of the word, and your source's source, etc.—part of the conceptual role of my use of 'Aristotle'? If not, how can Harman handle borrowed reference? If so, Harman certainly owes us a reason for thinking that the outside-the-body part of his long-arm conceptual roles differs from the referential factor of two-factor theory.[34] The burden of proof on Harman is especially pressing, given that it appears that one could easily transform a theory of the sort he advocates into a theory of the sort I have been advocating. If you take Harman's long-arm conceptual roles and "chop off" the portion of these roles outside the skin, you are left with my short-arm conceptual roles. If the outside-the-body part that is chopped off amounts to some familiar sort of theory of reference, then the difference between Harman's one-factor theory and two-factor theory is merely verbal.

Conceptual role semantics is often treated with derision because of failure to appreciate the option of a two-factor version, a failure that is as common among the proponents of the view as the opponents. Consider Fodor's critique (1978) of Johnson-Laird's version of conceptual role semantics. Johnson-Laird's version tended in his original article towards verificationism; that is, the roles of words he focused on were their roles in one specific kind of reasoning, namely verifying. Fodor correctly criticizes this verificationism.[35] But I want to focus on a different matter. Fodor objected that the meaning of 'Napoleon won the Battle of Waterloo' could not possibly consist in any sort of a set of procedures for manipulating internal symbols. That idea, he argued, embodies a use/mention fallacy.

> Suppose somebody said: 'Breakthrough! The semantic interpretation of "Did Napoleon win at Waterloo?" is: *find out whether the sentence "Napoleon won at Waterloo?" occurs in the volume with Dewey decimal number XXX, XXX in the 42nd St. Branch of the New York City Public Library'*. . . . " 'But', giggled Granny, 'if that was what 'Did Napoleon win at Waterloo?' meant, it wouldn't even be a question aobut *Napoleon*'. 'Aw, shucks', replied Tom Swift."[36]

Fodor's objection is that if meaning is identified with the causal interactions of elements of language, sentences would be about *language,* not the world.

My defence of Johnson-Laird should be obvious by now. Take the procedures that manipulate 'Napoleon', etc. (or, better, the whole conceptual roles of these words) as specifying *narrow* meaning. Fodor's argument would only be damaging to a theory that took conceptual role to specify what language is *about.* But if conceptual role specifies only narrow meaning, not reference or truth conditions, then Fodor's criticism misses the mark. Were Johnson-Laird to adopt a two-factor theory of the sort I have been advocating, he could answer Fodor by pointing out that the job of saying what language is about is to be handled by the referential component of the theory, not the narrow-meaning component.

A similar point applies to Dretske's rather colorful criticism of remarks by Churchland and Churchland, (1983).

> It sounds like magic: signifying something by multiplying sound and fury. Unless you put cream in you won't get ice cream out no matter how fast you turn the crank or how sophisticated the "processing." The cream, in the case of a cognitive system, is the *representational* role of those elements over which computations are performed. And the representational role of a structure is, I submit, a matter of how the elements of the system are related, not to one another, but to the external situations they "express."[37]

But the cream, according to two-factor theory, is conceptual role *together with* Dretske's representational role. Since CRS puts in Dretske's cream, plus *more,* there is no mystery about how you get ice cream out of it.

The same sort of point applies against criticisms of CRS that take the conceptual role component to task for not providing a *full* theory of meaning. Our judgments of sameness of meaning are controlled by a complex mix of conceptual role and referential (and perhaps other) considerations.[38]

Fodor (1985) points out that the concept of water can be shared by me and Blind Me. He says this presents problems for theories like CRS. He goes on to say:

> The obvious reply is that the properties of causal relations that make for sameness and difference of functional roles are very abstract indeed. Well, maybe; but there is an alternative proposal that seems a lot less strained. Namely that if Blind Me can share my concept of water, that's not because we both have mental representations with abstractly identical causal roles; rather, it's because we both have mental representations that are appropriately connected (causally, say) to *water.*[39]

But the two replies he gives aren't *incompatible alternatives;* CRS can adopt them both—though I think Fodor is right that the fact that the reference by me and Blind Me is to the same stuff is probably the main thing here. The point is that one cannot criticize a two-factor theory for not doing it all with one factor.

OVERVIEW

The rest of the paper is mainly concerned with showing how CRS satisfies the desiderata and with comparing CRS with other semantic theories in this regard. I will be talking about two quite different (but compatible) kinds of semantic theories: reductionist and nonreductionist. A reductionist semantic theory is one that characterizes the semantic in nonsemantic terms. A nonreductionist semantic theory is not one that is *anti*reductionist, but only one that does not have reductionist aims. These theories are mainly concerned with issues about constructions in particular languages, for example, why 'The temperature is rising' and 'The temperature is 70°' do not entail '70° is rising'. The nonreductionist theories I will mention are possible-worlds semantics, the model-theoretic aspect of situation semantics, Davidsonian semantics, and Katzian semantics. The reductionist theories are CRS; Gricean theories, by which I mean theories that explain the semantic in terms of the mental; and what I call "indicator" theories, those whose metaphor for the semantic is the relation between a thermometer and the temperature it indicates, or the relation between the number of rings on the stump and the age of the tree when cut down. These theories regard the nomological relation between the indicator and what it indicates as the prime semantic relation. In this camp I include views of Dretske, Stampe, Fodor, and one aspect of Barwise and Perry's position.

The reductionist/nonreductionist distinction as I have drawn it does not do justice to Davidson's views. The problem is *not* that Davidson's work on, for example, the logical form of action sentences makes him a nonreductionist, whereas his view about what meaning is makes him a reductionist. As I pointed out, the reductionist and nonreductionist enterprises are compatible, and there is nothing at all odd about one person contributing to both. The problem, rather, is that Davidson has views about what meaning is, thereby making it seem (misleadingly) that he is a reductionist, however, his views of what meaning is are clearly *not* reductionist. (See Davidson [1984, p. xiv], where he describes his project as explaining meaning in terms of truth.) A finer-grained classification would distinguish between (1a) reductionist and (1b) nonreductionist theories about what meaning is and distinguish both types of views of what meaning is from (2) the project of model-theoretic semantics, Davidson's work on action sentences, and the like. In labeling (1a) as reductionist and everything else as nonreductionist, I've unhappily lumped together (1b) and (2), but this is unimportant for my purposes, since I am ignoring (1b) theories.

Being reductionist in intent, CRS should not really be regarded as competing with the nonreductionist theories. Nonetheless, I shall be comparing CRS with these nonreductionist theories as regards the desiderata I have listed. To prevent misunderstanding, I want to emphasize that I am not attempting to criticize these nonreductionist theories. Rather, my purpose is to make it clear that they should not be seen as pursuing the same goals as the reductionist theories.

I will also be comparing CRS with the reductionist theories. These theories are in the same ball park as CRS, but most are not genuine competitors. Since CRS in the version I am promoting is a two-factor theory, it requires the partnership of a reductionist truth-conditional theory. Indicator semantics is a candidate. Another candidate that is both truth-conditional and reductionist is Field's interpretation (1972) of Tarski. I won't be discussing it because I know of no claims on its behalf that it is a full theory of meaning—indeed, Field views it as a candidate for the truth-conditional factor of a two-factor theory (see Field 1977). Though I do not regard indicator semantics as a real competitor, I will mention serious problems with the view.

The only circumstance in which the reductionist truth-conditional theories would be genuine competitors to CRS would be if one of them could satisfy a range of desiderata of the sort I've mentioned. I consider it no problem if they can contribute to *some* such desiderata, since there is often more than one way of explaining something. But if some truth-conditional reductionist theory could satisfy *all of them*, the need for the conceptual role component would be brought into question.

The only approach that remains as a genuine competitor is the Gricean approach. I shall not attempt to refute this approach (for one thing, as will appear, it has considerable similarity to mine). I mainly aim to block an argument that anyone who favors a functionalist approach to meaning should adopt some sort of Gricean view rather than CRS.

A brief guide to the semantic theories I will be mentioning: I lump the truth-conditional theories minus indicator semantics plus Katzian semantics together as nonreductionist. Gricean and indicator theories, by contrast, are reductionist.

```
                Situation semantics————  ⎞
                Davidsonian semantics———⎛—Truth
                Possible-worlds semantics——⎧——conditional
           ⎧—— Indicator semantics————  ⎠
Reductionist⎨———Gricean semantics
                Katzian semantics
```

As you can see, four of the six theories I will be contrasting with CRS are classifiable as truth-conditional. While CRS in the version I am adopting has a truth-conditional component, it will play little role in satisfying the desiderata. Thus it may seem that I am taking truth-conditional theories to task for not doing something that they were never intended to do. The rationale for the contrasts I will be making is that radical disagreement is so common with regard to matters semantic that there is little consensus about which semantic theories have which purposes. For each of the truth-conditional theories I will mention, claims have been made on its behalf in the direction of satisfying desiderata of the sort I've listed.

Representationalism

Before I go on to discuss how CRS satisfies the desiderata, I want to make sure my representationalism is not misunderstood. I am committed to complex reasoning being a process that involves the manipulation of symbolic structures. I am not committed to the idea that these symbolic structures are *independent* of representational states of mind, mental objects that are viewed by an inner eye. It is convenient to talk in terms of internal representations as if they were literally sentences in the brain (and I do talk this way), but this talk is, of course, metaphorical. My commitment will be satisfied if the representational states themselves constitute a combinatorial system; that is, if they are structured in a way that allows parts corresponding to words to be combined so as to constitute representational states corresponding to sentences.[40]

I am not committed to the manipulation of symbol structures being involved in *all* reasoning, since I want to allow for "primitive" reasonings out of which complex reasonings are built. (E.g., in some computers, multiplication is a symbolic process in that a multiplication problem is "decomposed" into a series of addition problems; but addition itself is not "decomposed" into another type of problem, but rather accomplished by a hardware device, a primitive processor, that contains no internal representations. If you ask how the computer multiplies, you get a representational answer; if you ask how it adds, you do not.) I am not committed to rules for reasoning being themselves represented. Such an assumption involves notorious paradoxes, and in computers we have examples of symbol manipulators many of whose symbol-manipulating "rules" are implicit in the way the hardware works (See Block 1983). I am not committed to any detailed thesis as to what the internal computations are like. For example, I am not committed to any such idea as that in computing '99 + 99 = 198' there is any internal analog of carrying a '1', or any such symbol manipulation of the sort a person might carry out in doing such a sum.

Further, the claim that we are symbol manipulators is intended as empirical and contingent. I find the idea perfectly intelligible and possible that we are "analog" computers whose internal activities involve no symbol manipulation at all. I make the representationalist assumption for two reasons: the most promising line of research in cognitive science is massively committed to representationalism, and it seems to be paying off; and I believe that there are an astronomical number of thoughts that people are capable of having. I would argue that the number of thinkable sentences thirty words long is greater than the number of particles in the universe. Consider the set of entertainable sentences of the following form: $n \times m = q$, where n and m are in the hundreds of billions range familiar from the national budget (twelve figures), and q is twice as long. Many of these sentences are not believable (e.g., nine hundred billion times itself $= 0$), but each is certainly thinkable. The number of distinct entertainable propositions of the form mentioned is on the order of forty-six digits long. An instructive comparison: the number of seconds since the beginning of time is only about eighteen digits long. I don't see what the mechanism could be by which a person can think any one of such a vast variety of thoughts without some sort of combinatorial system being involved. My representationalist assumption is in the spirit of Smart's claim that pain is a brain state: an empirically based thesis about what reasoning most likely is.

Of the semantic theories I will be contrasting with CRS, only Fodor's version of indicator semantics has a comparable representationalist assumption; nonetheless, I do not think that my representationalism ought to be seen as the key difference between the theory I am advocating and most of the other theories. For one thing, a denotational theory like Fodor's could be framed in terms of assent to English sentences instead of computational relations to internal sentences. Fodor is a sententialist in that he believes that propositional attitude states are relations to internal sentences. But the internal sentences have no privileged *semantic* role in his account. Also, there are nonrepresentationalist avenues towards the type of functionalist-based semantics I am advocating—for example, Loar's and Schiffer's version of the Gricean program. If CRS in the form in which I am advocating it were to meet serious empirical problems because of its representationalism, I would pursue a nonrepresentationalist version.

Question: If my basic commitment is to a functionalist theory of meaning, why don't I *now* adopt a nonrepresentationalist version of functionalism (e.g., the Loar-Schiffer program) instead of pursuing a program based on a risky empirical assumption (representationalism)? Answer: As I shall point out later, even if the Loar-Schiffer program works for natural language, if there is a language of thought not identical to natural language, their theory won't work for *it*. So *both* theories are subject to empirical risk. Theirs is inadequate if representationalism is true, whereas mine is wrong if representationalism is false.

SATISFYING THE DESIDERATA

In the rest of the paper, I shall be mainly concerned with showing how CRS satisfies the desiderata I sketched above and contrasting CRS's treatment with treatments possible for other approaches.

What Is the Relation between Meaning and Reference/Truth?

From the CRS perspective, what this question comes to is: what is the relation between the two factors? Are the two factors independent? Do they fit together in a coherent way?

I think the conceptual role factor is *primary* in that it determines the nature of the referential factor, but not vice versa. Suppose, for illustration, that one of the familiar versions of the causal theory of reference is true. What makes it true? Facts about how our language works—specifically, how it applies to counterfactual circumstances. Kripke convinces us that it is possible that Moses did not do any of the things the Bible said he did, but rather was an itinerant Egyptian fig merchant who spread stories about how he was found in the bulrushes, saw the burning bush, and so on. Kripke is convincing because we use names such as 'Moses' to refer to the person who bears the right causal relations to our uses of the name, even if he does not fit the descriptions we associate with the name. This is a fact about the conceptual role of names, one that can be ascertained in the armchair, just by thinking about intuitions about counterfactual circumstances.

Of course, our names could have functioned differently; for example, they could have functioned as the competing "cluster of descriptions" theory dictates. If that had been how names functioned, it too could have been ascertained by thinking of the right thought experiments, since it would be a fact purely about the internal conceptual role of names. For example, if 'Moses' functioned according to the cluster of descriptions theory, the intuition about Kripke's story dictated by the way names function would be "Oh, in that case Moses doesn't exist—there never was a Moses." What makes the cluster theory wrong is that that just isn't the intuition dictated by the function of our terms—the intuition, rather, is given by: "In that case, Moses wouldn't have done the things the Bible ascribes to him."

(Note that one cannot *identify* the intuition dictated by the function of names with the intuitions we actually have about cases, since there are all sorts of other factors that influence those intuitions. In the early days of the mind-body identity theory, many philosophers voiced the intuition that there was something semantically wrong with "I just drank a glass of H_2O." Presumably, they were influenced by the "oddity" of mixing scientific terms with mundane terms. Using intuitions to isolate facts about the function of names is not a simple matter.)

In short, what theory of reference is true is a fact about how referring terms function in our thought processes. This is an aspect of conceptual role. So it is the conceptual role of referring expressions that determines what theory of reference is true. Conclusion: the conceptual role factor determines the nature of the referential factor.

Note the crucial difference between saying that the conceptual role factor determines the nature of the referential factor and saying that the conceptual role factor determines reference. I hold the former, but not the latter. The two-factor theory is compatible with a variety of different mappings from a single conceptual role onto aspects of worlds. For example, a word with the conceptual role of our 'water' could map onto one substance here, another on Twin Earth, and another on Triplet Earth. What is in the head—conceptual role—determines the nature of reference without determining reference itself.

If what I've just argued is right, it is easy to see that conceptual role determines the function from context to reference and truth value. It is the referential factor (as described in a theory of reference) that determines that 'water' picks out H_2O on Earth, but XYZ on Twin Earth. For example, on a causal theory of reference, this will be held to be a matter of the causal relation to different liquids in the two contexts. But since the referential factor must take context into account in this way in order to dictate reference, it will determine the function from context to reference.

What Is the Connection between the Meaning of an Expression and Knowing or Learning Its Meaning?

CRS says meaning is conceptual role. If someone uses a word (or a word functions in her brain) that has the conceptual role of 'dog', then the word in question means the same as 'dog'. If a person's brain changes so as to cause a word to be used (by her or her brain) so as to have the conceptual role in question, then she has acquired the concept of a dog (unless she already has it); if the word in question is 'dog' itself or a mentalese standard associate of 'dog', and if the brain change is a case of learning, then she has learned the meaning of 'dog'. Also, CRS allows us to see why evidence for proper use of 'dog' is evidence for knowing the meaning of 'dog'. For a word to have proper use is for it to function in a certain way; hence someone whose word 'dog' functions appropriately thereby knows the meaning of dog; hence evidence of function can be evidence of knowing the word. Finally, CRS allows us to see how knowing meaning is related to our ability to use language. To know the meaning of an English word is for it to function in a certain way, and the obtaining of this function, together with certain psychological facts (e.g., about motivation) explains correct external usage.

The nonreductionist theories should not be regarded as aimed at answering the questions just discussed, but should nonreductionists disagree, they could give a kind of answer (in the metatheory, of course). A theory that postulates a type of semantic value V (e.g., truth conditions, situations, sets of possible worlds, markerese structures) can say that what it is to know or acquire the meaning of a sentence is to know or learn or acquire its V. But saying this only shifts the question to what it is to know or acquire V's. Consider the project of producing an account of what it is for 'cat' to acquire its semantic value in the child. If the semantic value is conceptual role, we can at least picture how the project would go. But what would the project be like—if not the same as the one we just pictured—for semantic values like truth conditions, situations, sets of possible worlds, or markerese structures (rather, senses expressed by these structures)? Davidsonians say that to know the meaning of 'Snow is white' is just to know that it is true iff snow is white. But, as Harman has pointed out, saying this just raises the issue of how one represents to oneself that snow is white. If one uses some sort of symbol structure (and how else is one supposed to do it?), the Davidsonian has only pushed the question back a step, for now we want a theory of the meaning of the symbol structure itself.

Further, there is an open question, on these nonreductionist semantic theories, as to how knowing a word's or a sentence's V could explain our ability to use the word or sentence appropriately. For example, suppose knowing the meaning of "The balloon burst" is knowing what situation it denotes. But how can knowledge of the denoted situation explain how we use the sentence appropriately?[41] Not that these questions could not be answered by the nonreductionist—for example, they could *adopt CRS*. The point is that the nonreductionist semantic theories I mentioned have no account of their own. (Of course, as I keep saying, this is not a *defect* of these theories.)

Another matter that distinguishes CRS from the nonreductionist theories (and the non-Gricean reductionist theories) is that CRS promises to give a semantic explanation of certain "principles of charity." Many philosophers of language imagine a "radical translation" or "radical interpretation" situation, in which one is trying to interpret utterances (typically, the problem is introduced with an anthropological situation, and then it is observed that the same issues arise in justifying the homophonic translation). As many philosophers have stressed, one must consider one's hypotheses about what the foreign terms mean together with hypotheses about the speakers' beliefs (and other propositional attitudes). It is the "simplicity" of the *total* theory that counts. Now it is often said that it is the *truth* of the alien beliefs that counts (Davidson sometimes says this); but this seems clearly wrong, in the absence of reason to believe that the alien has got things right. A better approach to principles of charity emphasizes coherence. Attribution of irrational belief cannot go on without limit; eventually, one loses one's grip on the content of what one has attributed. But this kind of charity can be explained by CRS. To understand the alien's beliefs, one has to appreciate their inferential roles (or rather, the inferential roles of the symbol structures that express them).

If the mismatch between the alien's inferential roles and our own is too great, there will be no way for us to translate what he says (cf. Loar 1982).

Further, to the extent that inferential role is normative (an issue within CRS, and therefore one I have avoided), there will be rationality constraints on what can sensibly be attributed. These rationality constraints are in no way a by-product of considerations about translation or about a mismatch of conceptual roles; rather, they are a matter of constraints on the conceptual roles that can possibly express concepts.

Let us return to the familiar claim that to know the meaning of a sentence is to know its truth conditions. In any sense in which this claim has substantial content, it is not at all obvious. For example, it is possible to imagine someone knowing the entire set of possible worlds in which a sentence is true without knowing what the sentence means. For the *way the person represents the set of possible worlds* may not capture its meaning. Perhaps it is possible to develop a canonical notation for representing possible worlds. In terms of such a notation, one could develop an ordering of possible worlds, and thus one might be able to exhibit a set of possible worlds via an arithmetical predicate that picks out the right numbers. But if one knows, say, that the prime-numbered possible worlds are the ones in which a sentence is true, does one thereby know its meaning? Further, even if no such ordering exists, one can imagine representing the possible worlds in which a sentence is true in a way that makes use of a motley of devices, different devices for different classes of worlds. Such a representation needn't capture what the worlds have in common in virtue of which they are the ones in which the sentence is true.[42]

Though it is not at all obvious that knowing truth conditions guarantees knowing meaning, the converse claim is more plausible. And, as Harman has pointed out,[43] CRS can explain this in the following way: normal users of language understand certain metalinguistic ideas, such as the disquotational use of 'true', and this is what gives them knowledge of truth conditions. The conceptual roles of 'true' and nonsemantic terms yield knowledge of biconditionals like " 'Snow is white' is true iff snow is white." But even if knowing meaning involves knowing truth conditions, one can hardly jump to the conclusion that knowing meaning *is* knowing truth conditions.

The fertility of the CRS account of learning can be illustrated by its solution to what might be tendentiously called Fodor's Paradox. Fodor's Paradox is posed by the following argument (Fodor 1975):

1. Learning the meaning of a word is a matter of hypothesis formation and testing.
2. When we learn a new English term (e.g., 'chase'), we can do so only by hypothesizing definitions in terms already known (including terms of the language of thought).

3. The history of attempts to define English terms "decompositional-ly" (e.g., 'try to catch') has been a dismal failure, and there are familiar Quinean considerations that explain why. This suggests that most English terms cannot be so defined.

4. Therefore, when a term like 'chase' is learned, it must be learned by hypothesizing a definition in terms of a *single* term of the language of thought, 'CHASE', which has the same meaning as 'chase'. In other words, the typical word-learning hypothesis has the form: 'chase' means 'CHASE'.

5. Therefore, for most terms of English, we grasp them only because they correspond to (indeed, are standardly associated with) innate terms of mentalese.

I call the argument a paradox because the conclusion is obviously unacceptable; the issue is which premise to give up. Why is the conclusion unacceptable? Could scientific concepts like 'meson' and 'enzyme', as well as technological ideas such as 'monitor', 'zipper', and 'transistor', be *individually* innate? If so, either evolution mysteriously foresaw the concepts needed for science and technology, or else progress in science and technology is possible only with respect to a highly arbitrary, accidentally prefigured vocabulary. Were this the case, one could expect that some accidental modification of some current technological device would produce a new and utterly unintelligible device that we could use the way a two-year-old uses a telephone while confused about whether it is a game in which daddy is somehow hiding inside the phone.

So what premise must go? The first premise is empirically plausible, justified, for example, by appeal to the type of errors children make. Also, hypothesis formation and testing is the only model of learning we have.

Much ink has been shed over the third premise. No doubt readers have made up their minds on the issue, and what I could say in a brief space here would be of no use at all. I shall confine myself to the remark that *if* it has been shown that there aren't many analytic decompositional definitions in natural languages,[44] that doesn't *show* that there aren't many decompositional definitions of natural-language terms in mentalese; but the burden of proof is on those who think mentalese differs from English in this respect.

The premise CRS militates against is 2. According to CRS, the way we learn a new English term needn't be a matter of definition at all. Rather, the CRS picture is that the term (or its newly formed mentalese standard associate) comes to have a certain function. To the extent that hypotheses are involved, they are hypotheses about how the term functions in thought, reasoning, problem solving, and so forth.

One way to see what the CRS proposal comes to is to reflect on how one learned the concepts of elementary physics, or anyway, how I did. When

I took my first physics course, I was confronted with quite a bit of new terminology all at once: 'energy', 'momentum', 'acceleration', 'mass', and the like. As should be no surprise to anyone who noted the failure of positivists to define theoretical terms in observation language, I never learned any definitions of these new terms in terms I already knew. Rather, what I learned was how to *use* the new terminology—I learned certain relations among the new terms themselves (e.g., the relation between force and mass, neither of which can be defined in old terms), some relations between the new terms and old terms, and, most importantly, how to generate the right numbers in answers to questions posed in the new terminology. This is just the sort of story a proponent of CRS should expect.[45]

Note that CRS is not a psychological theory. In particular, though it can tell us that Fodor's second premise *needn't* be true, it is compatible with its actually being true. For it is compatible with the CRS account that the way one learns to use a new term correctly is by linking it to a term one already has that functions appropriately.

Let me now raise a bogeyman that will come up repeatedly: psychologism. Am I just making the verbal maneuver of using 'semantics' to mean the study of the psychology of meaning, rather than the study of meaning proper? As pointed out in connection with the question of whether narrow meaning is genuine meaning, this question is a quibble. However, my answer is that although knowing is a mental state and learning is a mental process, it is not psychologism to suppose that a theory of what meaning *is* ought to be in some way relevant to what it is to know or learn meaning. For example, one can imagine quite different ideas of what good taste is (ranging from a form of knowing how to a form of knowing that) that would engender quite different ideas of what it is to learn good taste. Closer to home, consider the view that philosophy is conceptual analysis contrasted with the view that philosophy is a kind of history (in which heavy emphasis is placed on knowing the texts). These conceptions would lead to different ideas of what it is to learn philosophy.

But how is the idea that meaning is, say, truth conditions, supposed to be in any way relevant to what it is to learn or know meaning? (Unless truth conditions are identified with *verification conditions,* in which case we have a rather unattractive *special case* of CRS in which conceptual role is role in verifying.) The issue of what it is to learn or know truth conditions, or situation denoted, or associated semantic marker, or function from possible worlds to truth values is just as much in need of illumination from a theory like CRS as what it is to learn or know meaning.

I chose the desideratum about learning as the place to bring up the psychologism bogeyman first because this desideratum is perhaps the most psychological of the ones I mentioned; so it is this desideratum for which, if I am just changing the subject, it should be most apparent. My hope is that exposing the weakness of the psychologism charge here will allow me to pay less attention to it with regard to later desiderata.

What Makes Meaningful Expressions Meaningful?

I will use this section to lay out the basic ideas of the comparisons with the alternative theories, especially the reductionist competitors. So this will be a long section. According to CRS, what makes an expression meaningful is that it has a conceptual role of a certain type, one that we may call "appropriate." The difference between 'cat' and 'glurg' is that 'cat' has an appropriate conceptual role, whereas 'glurg' does not. What gives 'cat' the particular meaning that it has is its particular conceptual role. The difference between meaningful expressions with different meanings ('cat' and 'dog') is a conceptual role difference *within* the category of appropriate conceptual roles.[46]

The dominant perspectives in semantics—possible worlds semantics, situation semantics, and the approaches of Davidson and of Katz, can be used to give responses to my questions that look just as good at first glance. Suppose they say, for example, that what makes a meaningful sentence meaningful is that it has truth conditions, or a set of truth values in possible worlds, or an associated (sense expressed by a) markerese structure, or a denoted situation. But such answers just *put off* the semantic issue. For now we want to know what it is that makes for the difference— what it is in virtue of which there *is* a difference—between sentences that *have* and sentences that *lack* truth conditions, truth values in possible worlds, associated markerese structures, or denoted situations, and to these questions these non-reductionist perspectives have no answers.[47]

Of course, one can also ask of CRS what the difference is between sentences that have and sentences that lack conceptual roles. But CRS has an answer: certain causal properties. And if the questioner wants to know why sentences have the causal properties they do, again there are answers, at least in principle, to be sought, of the same sort that one would give to "Why do genes have the causal properties they have?"

What the difference comes down to is that CRS aims for a reductionist account, indeed, a naturalistic-reductionist account, in proposing to explain a semantic property in terms of a naturalistic, nonsemantic property: causation. CRS's reductionism and naturalism allow it to promise an answer to "What makes a meaningful expression meaningful?" The semantic approaches mentioned in the paragraph before last, being nonreductionist, cannot answer this question.

Although the dominant views in semantics should be regarded (in my view) as just not directed towards the sort of question typified by this desideratum, it should be noted that they often seem to be responding to much the same motivation that lies behind a naturalistic-reductionistic account. For instance, Davidsonians, though not reductionists, make much of the claim that a theory of the sort they favor will allow a deduction from a finite nonsemantic base of a specification of truth conditions for any indicative sentence.

On the whole, most of the standard approaches have been primarily concerned with the *relations* among meaning*s*, not the nature of meaning itself. For example, the standard approaches have been concerned with an aspect of compositionality: how the meanings of larger elements such as sentences are related to the meanings of smaller elements such as words. Another sort of issue motivating the standard theories is what we can tell about the logical form of "Sam ate with a fork" from the fact that if it is true, so is "Sam ate." Another issue (one that has been a stumbling block for possible-worlds semantics and one that situation semantics hopes to make progress on) is what the relation is between the semantic value of 'Grass is green' and 'John believes that grass is green'. But these questions can be and have been discussed without ever broaching the issue of what it is in virtue of which expressions have their meanings in the first place.

The main aim of most of the standard approaches to semantics has been to *correlate* meanings with certain objects, so that relations among meanings are mirrored by formal relations among the corresponding objects. These approaches have often been concerned with a purely *descriptive* project, a kind of "curve-fitting," not with explaining the nature of meaning.

The major tradition within this conception of semantics is well described in Barwise and Perry (1984).[48]

We have intuitions about the logical behavior of a certain class of sentences. With attitudes reports, these are largely intuitions about the phenomenon of "opacity": reluctance to substitute co-referential terms and the like. We codify these intuitions in a set of logical principles, and then semantics consists of finding a collection of plausible set-theoretic models that makes the logical principles come out correct. I think this is the traditional conception in semantics, and it is the setting for Montague Grammar, but it is what I would now call the thin conception of semantics.

As suggested earlier, the Barwise and Perry effort to produce a semantics that satisfies a richer, "thicker" conception of semantics can be seen as moving on two fronts: one involves model-theoretic ideas (e.g., the idea of a partial model), the other a kind of indicator semantics (discussed later in this section). Another aspect of the thickness that Barwise and Perry seek is to make semantics compatible with commonsense psychology, for example, to avoid the possible-worlds semantics problem that one would seem to believe everything logically equivalent to what one believes.[49]

Now Barwise and Perry (1984) have advocated a functionalist theory of propositional attitudes. Perhaps they (and some Davidsonians, Katzians, and possible-worlds semanticists) envision a two-stage process of semantic theorizing: first, a nonreductive account of meaning*s*, and second a reductive account aimed at desiderata something like the ones I have mentioned. Theorists in these traditions have not, however, put forward second-stage theories. I know of only two types of reductionist approaches to semantics other than CRS (and the causal theory of reference, which I am not discussing in any detail); after considering an objection, I shall sketch these approaches and their relation to CRS.

It may be objected that I have confused:

(i) In virtue of what is a particular token/ches/-noise an utterance of the English word 'chase' meaning, of course, 'try to catch')?

(ii) In virtue of what does the English word type 'chase' mean 'try to catch'?[50]

It may be said that (ii) has no nontrivial answer—it is part of what it *is* to be the English word 'chase' to mean what it does.[51] Asking (ii), on this view, is like asking what makes the number two even. If it weren't, it wouldn't be the number two. (Or: 'Two is even' is analytic.)

On the objector's view, the problem I raise does not *disappear,* but is rather transformed. Instead of asking what it is in virtue of which 'chase' means what it does, I must ask what it is in virtue of which a token is of the type *'chase' in English,* with the meaning that that word necessarily (?) has. Since the problem survives, I suppose that the real objection here is that the question I raise (being about a token) is really pragmatic rather than semantic.

Perhaps some perspective can be gained by contrasting the question about language with the question of why, in the American system of government, cabinet officers are approved by the Senate but presidential advisors are not? Here there seems little utility to seeing the American system of government as an abstract object that has this property necessarily (or analytically). It is not helpful to see the question as one about whether a certain token system is a token of the type "the American system of government." But is language more like a political institution or more like mathematics? This question won't get us very far. What issues belong in pragmatics as opposed to semantics is a matter to be settled by finding out which way of dividing up issues makes the most theoretical sense, not by consulting intuitions about whether language is more social than mathematical.

The important point against the objection is that it is a mistake to see the contrast the objector raises as hinging on the type/token distinction. This becomes especially obvious when one is reminded that the English language is in constant flux. 'Yuppie' has no meaning in English-1982, but it has a meaning in English-1985. And 'chase' may mean something different in English-1988 from what it does in English-1985. If a word's meaning is a necessary—though language-relative—property of the word, then (1) we must regard different dialects and language stages as in the relevant sense, different languages; and (2) we must recognize a sense of 'word type' in which word types are language specific. So we cannot speak of one word's different meanings in different dialects. But this is just a peculiar way of talking. As we have seen, there is a natural use of the notion of a word type in which we *can* speak of one word as having different meanings in different dialects (as is the case with 'yuppie'). So, deploying the notion of word type in the latter way, the question of why the word type 'chase' means 'try to catch' in English-1985 is not trivial.

The Reductionist Alternatives

There are two competing families of approaches to semantics that *are* reductionist,[52] and hence that *do* have genuine answers to the questions posed in the desiderata I've been talking about. One of them is the approach of reducing meaning to *mental content*. Call this type of approach "Gricean." The Gricean approach as developed by Grice himself, and later Schiffer, reduces speaker meaning to the content of speaker's intentions. For the speaker to mean such and such by what he says is for him to intend his utterance to affect the propositional attitudes of hearers in certain ways. Sentence meaning, on this theory, can be reduced to speaker meaning via a conventional correlation between sentences in the language and communicative intentions. This conventional correlation makes it practicable for a speaker to use certain sentences to produce certain effects in hearers.[53]

Searle has an approach that is Gricean in my sense, in which the intention isn't communicative but rather an intention to produce an object with certain "satisfaction conditions" (Searle 1983a). A rather different sort of Gricean approach was taken by Ramsey, who attempted to reduce the meaning of an item of language to the beliefs that would be expressed by that item.

Gricean approaches have been enveloped in controversies, none of which will be discussed here. Nor is this the place for a full-dress comparison between Gricean and conceptual role accounts. However, there are a few points of comparison that can be made rather briefly. Although I do not want to belittle the Gricean accomplishment, without a naturalistic account of the mental, the Gricean approach has little to contribute to the project I am discussing. One who is concerned with the questions I have been asking about meaning will be equally concerned with corresponding questions about intentional content. Consider, for example, the three questions involved in the desideratum currently being discussed:

1. What is it about a meaningful expression that makes it meaningful?
2. What is responsible for an expression's having the particular meaning it has?

3. What is the difference between expressions with different meanings in virtue of which they have different meanings?

The Gricean faces corresponding questions about intentional content, viz.:

1'. What is it about a contentful state that makes it contentful?
2'. What is responsible for a state's having the particular intentional content it has?
3'. What is the difference between states with different intentional contents in virtue of which they have their different contents?

In the light of this problem, Griceans have a number of options. First, they could simply regard intentional content as primitive—in other words, regard questions like 1', 2', and 3' as having no answers. For Griceans to take this line would be to give up on satisfying the desiderata I've been talking about. This is the nonnaturalistic option I mentioned. Another line would be to pursue some nonfunctionalist reductionist strategy, such as physiological reductionism. This is an unpromising tack (see Fodor 1974), and it is especially unattractive if one is interested in a semantics that might apply to the language use of an intelligent computer or computerlike machine, if we ever construct one.[54]

Another option is Searle's reduction of intentionality to *the brain or whatever has "equivalent causal powers."* The wild card of "equivalent causal powers" allows Searle to avoid the usual drawbacks of physiological reduction. For example, the theory is not chauvinist because it allows for the possibility that the control systems of intelligent machines can have causal powers equivalent to ours. However, the other side of the coin is that the theory is far from naturalistic. To say a machine has causal powers equivalent to those of the human brain is only to say that the machine has causal properties that result in intentionality. So Searle must either (1) regard intentionality as primitive, in which case he has not answered the questions I am talking about, or (2) he must give some nonintentional analysis of "equivalent causal powers." It is clear that Searle takes option (1). That is, he has no intention of giving a reductionist theory of intentionality, though he takes physicochemical properties of *each being* that has intentional states to cause that being's intentional states. (See Searle 1984.)

Searle repeatedly *says* that it is an empirical question whether a given machine has equivalent causal powers, but the careful reader discerns that it is an empirical question only in that the machine itself *will know* if it does indeed have equivalent causal powers.[55] The crux of the disagreement between Searle and me is not about whether a sapient and sentient machine will have to have innards with causal powers equivalent to those in us (we agree on this); the crux rather is whether some sort of functionalist thesis is true of us. For if intentionality can be characterized functionally, then *the way to make a machine with intentional states is to make a machine functionally equivalent to us—the equivalent causal powers of the machine's brain will come along for free.* Searle's argument against functionalism is his "Chinese room" argument, to be discussed briefly later in this paper.

There is one final "methodological" point to be made against Searle. One should not adopt his view without proper exploration of the alternatives, since if Searle's account is true, the sciences of mind and meaning would seem to be severely limited. In particular, it is hard to see how science (or philosophy) could ever tell us anything substantive about what the source of autonomous meaning or intentionality is.

Another Gricean option is that championed by Schiffer and Loar (and perhaps Grice): they couple the reduction of meaning to the mental with a functionalist reduction of the mental. A major difference between the functionalism-based Gricean theory and CRS is that the Gricean theory is not committed to any sort of representationalism, even of the weak sort that CRS is committed to (viz., that thoughts have recombinable ingredients). This difference between the Loar-Schiffer account and the CRS account is a disagreement about the empirical facts about how the mind works (or about how much philosophical ice such empirical facts cut), not about the functional source of meaning.[56] In sum, in one version Gricean theory is not a competitor to CRS; in another version, it is a competitor but has drawbacks; and in another version, it differs with respect to representationalism and, of course, the details of the Gricean reduction in terms of intentions, as well as the focus on public language meaning as opposed to idiolect narrow meaning.

I shall now turn to an argument by Loar (1981, chap. 9; 1983) against the sort of view I am advocating. As I understand it, Loar's argument is that a theory of meaning should not depend on a speculative psychological claim such as representationalism. So Loar advocates the Gricean reduction of external language to mentality (coupled with a functionalist reduction of the mental). If representationalism happens to be true, Loar favors what amounts to a conceptual role semantics theory of the internal language (though not external language). My objection is simple: if representationalism is false, CRS is certainly false. But if representationalism is true, Loar is stuck with an intention-based semantics for external language plus a conceptual role semantics for internal language—whereas CRS makes do with the latter type of semantics for *both* types of language. (Of course, Loar is concerned with public meaning rather than narrow idolect meaning, but this fact does not play any direct role in his argument.) So, if representationalism is true, the Loar-Schiffer account seems at a disadvantage.

Is there some way in which the Gricean account could be extended to internal language? Computation in internal symbol systems appears to be of a rather "automatic" sort which gains efficiency through inflexibility.[57] For example, if one memorizes a list of six letters, say 'UEKNMG', and one is asked whether 'E' is on the list, one does an "exhaustive" serial search, looking at all six letters, one by one, even if 'E' is the first letter in the list.[58] (This is one of the better tested results in all of cognitive psychology.) Is it at all plausible that one forms an *intention* to look at all the items, or to do an exhaustive serial search? Further, even if the uses of the internal system are intentional in some sense, surely the intentions are not intentions to *communicate,* as in the standard Gricean theories.

But what if the internal symbol system *is* English (that is, the same as whatever external language is spoken)? Can the Gricean then avoid the problem of the last paragraph by giving a theory of meaning for English, and simply postulating that sentences in the language of thought have the same meaning as in English? First, it is not at all obvious that the meaning of English as used in thought (if it is used in thought) is somehow derivative from its use in communication. Why not the other way around? Second, and more importantly, I have talked as if it is perfectly possible that English is the language of thought, but this is simply *not* in the cards. For one thing, external language is radically ambiguous, both syntactically and semantically. If there is no confusion in *thought* as between financial banks and river banks, then one word in the internal system presumably does not carry both meanings. And if someone says "I tire of visiting relatives," knowing full well whether relatives are visiting her or whether she is the visitor, then it is doubtful that the English sentence could be the vehicle of the thought. (But see Block and Bromberger 1980.) From what I've said thus far, one might suppose that the language of thought might be a kind of regimented English (e.g., syntactic trees with English terminal nodes, as suggested for part of the language of thought in Harman, [1970]). But, at most, some sort of regimented English could be *part* of the language of thought. (Indeed, although there is controversy over whether English is part of the language of thought, there is none over whether English is the *whole* of the language of thought.) For example, there is enormous evidence for representations in mental imagery (see Block 1983 for discussion and references to the literature); and it is quite out of the question that these representations are in English (none of the defenders of the view that the representations of imagery are languagelike have suggested such a thing). When one looks in any detail at what a languagelike representation would have to be to play the role of representations of imagery, this is obvious. Nor would any such suggestion be remotely sensible for the representations of early vision (see Marr 1982).

If English is part of the language of thought, it would seem especially peculiar to treat the semantics of that part of the language of thought so differently from the semantics of external English.

In sum, the Griceans cannot claim that their account is to be preferred to CRS on the ground that their account has no empirical vulnerability, since both accounts have an element of empirical vulnerability. Nonetheless, the choice between the two approaches seems mainly a matter of philosophical metatheory. If one wishes to insulate one's semantics from experimental falsification, while being willing to tolerate ad hoc addition of components to handle experimental discoveries, the Loar-Schiffer perspective is better. If one is interested in a semantics based on the best empirical theories extant, CRS is better.

There is a second family of reductionist approaches to semantics that could be claimed to satisfy my desiderata: what I called "indicator semantics." Dretske (1981) and Stampe (1977) have similar versions, which I believe have been refuted by Fodor (1984), who has his own version of the view (Fodor 1984, forthcoming). Barwise and Perry (1983) have a view that has affinities to that of Dretske and Stampe, which I will not be able to discuss in detail here.

Dretske and Stampe say what it is for a sentence S to have the content that T in terms of tokens of S carrying information about T; carrying information, in turn, is cashed in terms of a nomological relation between S's and T's (roughly, an S nomologically requires a T).[59] Fodor objects that if error is possible, then a non-T can cause a tokening of S; but then why should we regard T as the state of affairs with which S is nomologically correlated when S has a *better* correlation with the disjunctive state of affairs whose disjuncts are T and the non-T state that causes S? So it seems that, on the Dretske/Stampe view, error is not possible.

Barwise uses the type/token distinction to deal with this problem. Suppose Ed "says 'It is 4 p.m.' at 4:30. While we can truly report that *Ed means what he says,* we can also truly report that *Ed's statement does not mean that it is 4 p.m.*"[60] Barwise's claim is that 'means' is ambiguous: there is one sense appropriate to tokens, another to types. A false token does not convey the information (this is the sense of meaning appropriate to tokens) conventionally associated with the corresponding type. (What about false sentence types? According to Barwise and Perry, it is only tokens [e.g., utterances] of sentences that have truth values, not sentence types.)

But I don't see how Barwise and Perry propose to avoid Fodor's objection in giving an informational account of sentence type meaning. One often gets the impression that their theory is that the meaning of a sentence type is the information *normally conveyed* by tokens of it. But what could 'normally' come to here? This cannot be shorthand for information conveyed by *true uses,* since that would ruin any attempt to give an account of the semantic in nonsemantic terms. If 'normal' is some sort of appeal to what is usual, however, Fodor's problem stands in the way. The correlation between tokens of S and the disjunction of T and pseudo-T states of affairs (ones that mislead people into false assertions of S) will inevitably be better than the correlation between S and T itself. Indeed, it is not hard to think of sentences whose assertions are more often false than true (e.g., famous last words). If 'normal' is some sort of appeal to the conventional, Barwise and Perry owe us an account of how that is supposed to connect with information conveyed and how they expect to avoid an analysis of conventionality in terms of intentional notions (as in Lewis's analysis). If it is a teleological notion, my guess is that their account will succumb to the kind of criticism now to be raised against Fodor's own account. (I've been assuming that Barwise and Perry do aim for an account of meaning in nonsemantic and nonintentional terms. This conception seems to me to permeate Barwise and Perry (1983), though it is never explicitly announced. In recent conversations with Barwise and Perry, I gather that they do not take themselves to be aiming for an account of meaning that is reductionist in this sense.)

Fodor's own view attempts to captitalize on the very fact that torpedoes the Dretske-Stampe approach. The basic idea is that, in a sense, error is not possible. The aim of Fodor's theory is to give a naturalistic account of what it is in virtue of which a sentence has the truth condition it has—what *makes* a sentence have the truth condition that it has. Some examples of theories that are in the same ball park: (1) the British empiricist theory that what gives a mental representation its truth condition is *resemblance* between the representation and the state of affairs, (2) the Skinnerian theory that what makes T the truth condition of S is that T is the discriminative stimulus of S. These are both false doctrines, for well-known reasons, but they are nonetheless naturalistic.

Fodor's task is one that many writers have seen the need for. As Field (1972) pointed out, the Tarskian approach, on one construal, yields the truth conditions of sentences only by means of *lists* of the referents of singular terms and the denotations of predicates. ('Boston swelters' is shown to be true only because the object that is listed as the referent of 'Boston' is in the set that is listed as the denotation of 'swelters'.) However, serious suggestions for solving this problem are thin on the ground. The only remotely plausible views I know of are the indicator semantics approach (common to Fodor, Dretske/Stampe, and Barwise and Perry); and Tarski's approach, construed as in Field (1972), together with a naturalistic theory of reference such as the causal theory. (Field's construal of Tarski is as giving a way of reducing truth to primitive denotation.)

The heart of the theory is an account of the truth conditions for mental sentences.[61] The account makes use of the claim that believing is a computational relation between a person and a mental sentence. (This computational relation is described below as the sentence being in the "belief box.") The claim is that what it is for T to be the truth condition for a mental sentence M is:

(1) If the cognitive system is functioning as it is *supposed* to; and
(2) idealizing away from epistemic limitations, then M is in the "belief box" $\longleftrightarrow T$.

There are two "wheels" that drive this account: the teleological wheel, indicated by the 'supposed' in condition (1), and the epistemic idealization wheel. The idea behind Fodor's account is that there are cognitive mechanisms that are designed to put sentences in the belief box if and only if they are true. Error results when these mechanisms fail, or when epistemic conditions are less than ideal. Thus, if one can spell out the teleological notion and say what epistemically ideal conditions are in a naturalistic way, one will have a naturalistic theory of truth conditions.

There are serious problems with each of two "wheels." Let us begin with the epistemic idealization. One sees how it is supposed to go for cases of things that are too small to see, or happened too far away or too long ago. In these cases, what Fodor imagines we idealize away from is how big we are, where we are, or when we are. The idea is that if epistemically ideal conditions held, one's nose *would be rubbed in the truth* ; then mechanisms whose function it is to make one see the truth would take over, and one would indeed see the truth.

But what about statements to the effect that space is Riemannian, or that some quarks have charm, or even that one is in the presence of a magnetic field? Here, it is not enough to suppose one's nose is rubbed in the truth, for its no use having your nose rubbed in the facts—you have to come up with the right theory, too, and you have to know that it is the right theory. Imagine that in the long run the evidence converges on a Riemannian geometry for the universe The ideal scientific community will only believe in this claim if someone *thinks* of it. After all, it is quite intuitive to suppose that there is exactly one parallel to a given line at a given point, as Euclidean geometry tells us. No *series of measurements* can guarantee that anyone thinks of (or takes seriously, even if they think of) claiming that the Euclidean parallel postulate is false. To make a long story short, I don't see how such theoretical statements can be handled without in one way or another abandoning naturalism—for example, appealing to some sort of magical machinery or smuggling something semantic into the specification of the epistemic idealization. Suppose that whenever a "theoretical" property of the sort I just mentioned is raised, the Fodorean constructs an idealization in which humans have a perceptual detector that detects this property. Nothing semantic need be smuggled in with the description of these detectors: they say 'p' if and only if p. With such detectors, if your nose is rubbed in a fact, you will perceive it to obtain. But this response abandons naturalism. We have no idea how such detectors would work or even whether they are possible. Appealing to them is like saying: "Aha, what makes T the truth condition for M is that an omniscient wizard (i.e., one who believed 'p' if and only if p) would believe M if and only if T." You don't get a naturalistic account of truth conditions by appealing to the imaginary behavior of an imaginary being.

Idealizing often starts with something familiar and envisions a systematic change. So, in the last paragraph, we started with normal perceptual detectors and imagined them getting better and better (or, alternatively, more and more numerous). Another idea is to try envisioning systematic change in our theorizing mechanisms. Of course, we need a nonsemantic characterization of the ideal theorizing mechanisms. It won't do to say they find the *right* theory, since that is a semantic notion. Perhaps we can simply envision mechanisms that construct all possible theories and choose the simplest of them that is compatible with the data. The problems here are complex, and I can only hint at them. I would argue that on any formal notion of simplicity (e.g., one that involves counting symbols), it just is not true that the simplest theory is true. And even if the simplest theory were true, this assumption—which, of course, is a semantic assumption—would be part of the account. So, the account would not be naturalistic.[62] On the other hand, a *semantic* conception of simplicity (e.g., one that involves the concept of truth) won't be naturalistic either.

The second wheel driving Fodor's account is the idea that the cognitive system is *supposed* to function in a certain way. How is this teleological talk supposed to be understood? (Anyone who has read the current literature on teleology knows that promising suggestions are hard to find.)[63] Sometimes Fodor talks in terms of a notion of teleology provided by evolutionary theory. The cognitive system is supposed to function a certain way in that that is what evolution designed it to do.

One problem is that one cannot rely on evolution in such a simple way, since one can imagine a molecule-for-molecule duplicate of a baby who comes into being by chance and grows up in the normal way. Such a person would have language with the normal semantic properties, but no evolutionary "design."

Quite a different type of problem comes in through evolutionary theory itself. I think it is now quite generally accepted among evolutionary biologists that one cannot suppose that every phenotypic (i.e., actual) characteristic of an organism is an optimal design feature (in any nontrivial sense), given the environment.[64] To take a rather extreme case, for purposes of illustration, consider the phenomenon of "meiotic drive." Normally, each of a pair of genes has an equal chance of ending up in an offspring: if you have one blue-eye gene and one brown-eye gene, the chance that your child will get one of these from you is equal to the chance that it will get the other. But there are some known cases of genes—the mouse t-allele, for example—that beat out whatever gene they are paired to, thus propelling themselves into the next generation. Any such gene that does not have lethal effects on the phenotype is likely to spread in a population very quickly, even if it has suboptimal pheonotypic effects. The upshot is that there are known mechanisms (of which this is only one of many examples) that could have the effect of producing cognitive mechanisms that aim, to some extent, at properties of beliefs other than truth.[65]

One final point about Fodor's account. One peculiar fact about it is that it does not exploit the compositional structure of the language at all. (This is especially odd in view of the fact that Fodor's representationalism gives him objects in the belief box ripe for compositional exploitation.) In this respect, it is markedly inferior to Field's proposal (mentioned above), in which the truth conditions for sentences are built up out of naturalistic analyses of reference and denotation. This feature of Fodor's theory renders it vulnerable to the following problem (I am indebted here to Michael Bratman): If S and S' are nomologically correlated states of affairs, then on Fodor's analysis, any sentence that is mapped onto one of them will be mapped onto the other. Consider, for example, the correlated properties of electrical and thermal conductivity (whose correlation is expressed in the Wiedemann-Franz Law). Let us agree with Fodor that it is the function of the cognitive mechanisms to put 'The electrical conductivity is rising' in the belief box (in ideal epistemological circumstances) iff the electrical conductivity is rising. But since the right-hand side of this biconditional is true iff the thermal conductivity is rising, the left-hand side will be true iff the thermal conductivity is rising. So Fodor's theory will not distinguish between the semantic values of 'The thermal conductivity is rising' and 'The electrical conductivity is rising'. I don't see how such a problem can be dealt with without going to a compositional story (e.g., by adding a conceptual role component to the theory).[66]

Let me summarize. I've mentioned two types of reductionist theories—indicator semantics and Gricean semantics. (I've also mentioned the causal theory of reference, but I haven't compared it with CRS since it is not normally thought of as a full semantic theory. It—like indicator semantics—is a candidate for the referential-truth-conditional factor of a two-factor theory.) I've mentioned and endorsed Fodor's reason for thinking one version of indicator semantics won't work, and I've given some reasons to be dissatisfied with Fodor's theory. I've mentioned a few versions of Gricean theory, arguing that Searle's version isn't naturalistic (and so isn't a competitor to CRS); and I have countered an argument that the Grice-Schiffer-Loar version should be preferred to CRS because the former, unlike the latter, does not depend on what psychologists find out about mental representation.

Before I go on to the next desideratum, I shall very briefly consider an objection to the whole enterprise: I have been comparing a conceptual role theory of *narrow meaning* with theories that have conceptions of meaning that are quite different from narrow meaning (and also from one another's conceptions of meaning). Isn't this comparing apples, oranges, and mangoes?

Reply: (1) It would not change my points were I to switch from talk of narrow meaning to talk of meaning. Since meaning, on my view, is a pair of factors—the narrow meaning factor and the referential factor—to talk in terms of meaning would be to talk in terms of both factors of the two-factor account of meaning rather than just one of the factors (narrow meaning). After all, I chose the desiderata to exhibit strengths of the conceptual role factor of the two-factor theory, and I will be exercising the two-factor theory's right to introduce the referential factor where relevant. (2) It is true that different semantic theories differ in their conceptions of meaning, but that does not make comparison illegitimate. Vienna and New Delhi differ in their conception of dessert, but that won't stop me from preferring strudel to gulabja.

Why Is Meaning Relative to Representational System?

The CRS explanation of this relativity is simple. The conceptual role of a symbol is a matter of how it *functions* in a representational system (for this reason, conceptual role is sometimes called "functional role"). How a representation functions in a system depends, of course, on the system. If meaning is function, as CRS dictates, then meaning is system relative.

The nonreductionist semantic theories can, of course, be used to handle this phenomenon (in a nonexplanatory way) by assigning different semantic values to an expression when it manifestly has different semantic properties. Thus a sentence with 'trailer' in it would be assigned different situations, or truth conditions, or extensions in possible worlds or markerese representations, depending on whether the dialect is American English or English English. Once again, this is accommodation, not explanation. The difference between CRS and the nonreductionist theories is that conceptual roles are, by their nature, system relative because they are functional entities and the semantic values of the nonreductionist theories are not.

It is worth emphasizing how important a matter this is. It is a banal feature of languages that the shape or sound of a word does not determine its meaning. Indeed, this point is sometimes described as "trivial semantic conventionalism," to distinguish it from more interesting claims. If no semantic theory could explain such a fact, semantics would be in trouble.

Perhaps it is worth mentioning the psychologism allegation again. Am I just demanding that semantics answer a question that belongs in the domain of, say, the psychology of language? Pretheoretically, the fact that one linguistic element can have different meanings in different languages would seem to be a clearly semantic phenomenon. I would think that the burden of argument would be on anyone who wanted to argue otherwise.

So CRS can explain the general fact that meaning is relative to representational system. Also, as pointed out in the last section, it promises to explain *particular* meaning differences. Since the difference in meaning of 'trailer' in English English (in which it means: movie preview) and American English is a matter of differences in the causal properties of the term, it is in principle possible, according to CRS, to specify the factors that cause the difference in causal properties. By contrast, think of how a possible-worlds semanticist or a Katzian would go about explaining the difference. Nothing in such nonreductionist semantic theories would help.

The relativity of meaning to system of use is more fundamental to cognitive science than attention to examples such as 'trailer' indicates. Functional differences determine differences in the semantic (and syntactic) *categories* of representations—for example, the difference between the representational properties of *languagelike* and *picturelike* representations. This is especially important because there is reason to believe that many of our mental representations may actually be pictorial. None of the other semantic theories has a chance to explain the difference between the semantics of languagelike and picturelike representations.

Moreover, recall that syntactic category is as relative to system as semantic category. The relativity of syntactic category has the same explanation as the relativity of semantic category: syntax is functional too. If this isn't obvious, consider two processors that read English text: one reads odd-numbered characters, whereas the other reads even-numbered characters. One would read 'CDAOTG' as 'CAT', the other as 'DOG'. CRS allows a common explanation of an interesting fact—that both syntactic and semantic category are relative to system.

Further, CRS is important for avoiding misconceptions about concepts that are widespread in the psychological literature. The word 'concept' is used in psychology to denote a mental or physiological entity that expresses or represents a concept in the philosopher's sense of the term (in which concepts are abstract entities). The concept of a cat (in the psychologist's sense of the term) is a mental or physiological entity that expresses or represents cathood (much as the word 'cat' expresses or represents cathood). It is widely supposed in developmental psychology that mental images are probably children's concepts but that they could not be adult concepts. Piaget says:[67]

> The preconcepts of this level can be considered to be still half-way between the symbol and the concept proper.... [T]he preconcept involves the image and is partially determined by it, whereas the concept, precisely because of its generality, breaks away from the image....

Another example: Premack (1982) argues that whereas the concepts of many lower animals are pictorial, the concepts of primates must be in part languagelike because pictorial concepts cannot express certain abstract ideas. For example, chimps can "match to sample" not only in cases where the sample is red and the correct multiple choice item is red, but also where the sample is AA and the choices are AB, BC, and BB. Here the correct choice is BB, and the common property is being a pair whose members are identical.

According to Premack, this requires a nonimagistic concept because the sample and target do not "resemble" one another. Another issue where this mistake (Which mistake? See the next paragraph) sometimes comes in is the issue of whether there is a "third code" more abstract than either languagelike or picturelike codes. The mistaken reasoning is that we have a nonlanguagelike code but that it could not be pictorial because pictorial representations could not have the kind of generality required of a concept.[68]

The doctrine that picturelike representations won't do for general or adult or primate concepts involves a conceptual error, one for which CRS is a corrective. CRS tells us that to be a concept of, say, dog, a mental representation must function in a certain way. Obviously, you can't tell how a certain representation functions by confining your attention to the representation alone, or to its "resemblances" to things in the world. You must know something about how the processors that act on it treat it. Thus a pictorial representation can express quite an abstract property, so long as the processors that act on it ignore the right specificities. To take a venerable example, a picture of an equilateral triangle can serve to represent triangles in general so long as the processors that act on it ignore the equality of the sides and angles. Similarly, a picture of a set of twins *could* represent or express the concept of a pair whose members are identical.

Note that I am not just pointing out that Piaget and Premack are the victims of "resemblance" theories of pictorial representation. The error I am pointing to is more fundamental in the sense that it includes the resemblance-theory error, plus a failure to see the shape of a positive doctrine—namely, that how or what a representation represents is a matter of more than the intrinsic properties of the representation or simple relational properties like "resemblance"; in particular, it is a matter of a complex relational property: how the representation functions.

What Is the Relation between Meaning and Mind/Brain?

How does the brain confer meaning on its representations?[69] Answer: By conferring the right causal roles on the representations. What is it for a person to grasp the meaning of a word? Answer: For a person to grasp the meaning of a word is for the word (or its standard mentalese associate) to have a certain causal role in his or her brain. How can it be that a person grasping an abstract object can propel the person (and his or her brain) to Hawaii? Answer: The difference between grasping a meaning and not grasping it is a difference in the causal role of entities in the person's brain, and differences in such causal roles can make for differences in behavior and the rewards that are contingent on behavior.

As before, the nonreductionist semantic theories can give superficial answers to the desideratum question. How does the brain grasp meanings? By grasping truth conditions or a denoted situation or a markerese structure.

But the question of how the brain grasps truth conditions or denoted situations or markerese structures is just as pressing as the original question.[70]

What Is the Relation between Autonomous and Inherited Meaning?

Recall the distinction (made in Desideratum 6) between autonomous and inherited meaning. Inherited meanings, like those of the linguistic expressions on this page, require translation or transliteration into the language of thought of a reader or hearer for their understanding. Autonomous meaning, the kind of meaning of the elements of the language of thought itself, requires no reading or hearing and thus no translation or transliteration in order to be understood. The questions I raised were: What is autonomous meaning? What is inherited meaning? What is the relation between autonomous and inherited meaning? For example, is one reducible to the other? Or are they both manifestations of a single type of meaning? Or are they unrelated phenomena with only a superficial resemblance?

The CRS answers to the first two questions are simple: autonomous meaning is conceptual role—and so is inherited meaning. (You will recall that using the notion of standard association, one can individuate conceptual roles of English as their standard associates in the internal system.) Further, the conceptual roles of external language are inherited from those of internal language. So inherited meaning is (surprise!) inherited from autonomous meaning.

The nonreductionist semantic theories, by contrast, have little to say about these matters. They *can* say that 'cat' and 'CAT' have the same semantic values; but as far as I can see, none of them have conceptual resources adequate to spell out any reasonable characterizations of autonomous and inherited meaning or say anything about whether one is reducible to the other.

Psychologism again: Is CRS supposed to be better for the purposes of psychology simply because it *contains* some psychological claims? Autonomous and inherited meaning are two categories of meaning (maybe even basic categories). It would be a surprise—*which itself would need explaining* —if no good theory of the nature of meaning could illuminate the issues I have been discussing about the relation between these two categories.

Indeed, once one sees the distinction between autonomous and inherited meaning, it is reasonable to ask of any theory of meaning *which* type of meaning it is intended to speak to. CRS speaks to both. Indeed, CRS explicates the difference between autonomous and inherited meaning without giving up a *unified* account of the two types of meaning. English inscriptions and utterances affect one another (via their effects on internal language) so as to give English expressions conceptual roles; and these conceptual roles are (at least on the simplified model I discussed) dependent on the conceptual roles of internal expressions.

Thus far, I have said little about causal theories of reference. Such theories, if they can be made to work, potentially have more to say about the relation between autonomous and inherited meaning than nonreductionist theories such as possible-worlds semantics, situation semantics, Davidsonian semantics, and Katzian semantics, because they can say something about the similarities and differences between the causal chains leading to 'cat' and 'CAT' that explains the differences and similarities between the two representations. But causal theories of reference cannot capture the aspect of meaning inside the head.[71] For example, they cannot capture the aspect of sameness in meanings of the sentences of me and my twin on Twin Earth (despite the difference in our causal chains outside our heads). From the point of view of a causal theory of reference, 'Hesperus = Hesperus' and 'Hesperus = Phosphorus' have the same semantic value.[72] Further, the theory that I am promoting can appropriate whatever successes causal theories of reference may have. Recall that CRS in the version I favor is part of a two-factor theory, the external factor of which can adopt aspects of a causal theory of reference account. In sum, causal theories of reference cannot accomplish the task I have set; and whatever they can accomplish can be appropriated by the two-factor version of CRS.

One final advantage of the CRS approach to the distinction between autonomous and inherited meaning is that it allows a theoretical approach to Searle's "Chinese Room" argument. With apologies to those who have heard this too many times: we are to imagine a monolingual English speaker who is placed in a room in a robot's head. He has a large library of instructions in English (the program) that tells him to push certain buttons (controlling outputs of the body) or write certain notes to himself (thus changing the "internal state" of the system) depending on what input lights are on and what notes he has written to himself earlier. The man never understands any Chinese, but nonetheless the robot he controls "speaks" excellent Chinese. Searle argues that since the man never understands Chinese, and since the robot paraphernalia adds no understanding, what we have is a Chinese simulator with no genuine Chinese understanding.

The most penetrating criticisms have focused on what Searle—anticipating the challenge—calls the systems reply. The systems reply says that since the system as a whole—man + library + room + robot body and control system—has the information processing characteristic of an intelligent Chinese speaker, we should take the whole system as understanding Chinese, even though the homunculus inside does not. The critics insist that the whole system does understand Chinese. (See Dennett 1983.) Searle has a clever reply. He tells the critics to just imagine the paraphernalia of the "system" *internalized,* as follows. First, instead of having the homunculus consult a library (the program), let him *memorize* the whole library. Second, let him memorize his notes instead of writing them down. Finally, instead of having the homunculus inhabit a robot body, let him *use his own body.* That is, what we are to imagine in the new version is that the homunculus manipulates his own body in just the way he manipulated the robot body in the previous version. When he seems to be asking for the salt in Chinese, what he is really doing is thinking *in English* about what noises and gestures the program dictates that he should produce next.[73]

At this point, the issue seems to come down just to a matter of conflicting intuitions. The opponents say the man following the instructions does understand Chinese, Searle says he does not.[74] This is where CRS comes in. The trouble with the systems reply as so far discussed is that it contains no theoretical perspective on what it would be for the system's Chinese symbols to be meaningful for it in the way the symbols in the head of a normal Chinese speaker are meaningful for that person—it contains no perspective on autonomous meaning. CRS has an answer: what would give the symbols autonomous meaning is the right conceptual role. There is a complication that makes this point harder to see. Namely, there is a crucial ambiguity in Searle's statement of his examples. Is the robot system (and the later case in which the homunculus internalizes the program) supposed to be one in which the information processing of a normal Chinese speaker is *simulated*? Or is the information processing of a normal Chinese speaker actually *instantiated* or *emulated* in the system?[75] (I can simulate an Aristotelian physicist's information processing by figuring out what someone would think if, like Aristotle, he didn't distinguish average from instantaneous velocity; but I cannot instantiate or emulate this information processing—that is, have this type of information actually go on in me—because I cannot avoid seeing the distinction.) In the case of mere simulation, the information-processing point of view does not dictate that the system *does* understand anything. But in the emulation case—the one in which Chinese symbols are processed so that they have the same conceptual roles they have in a normal Chinese speaker.[76]—then CRS dictates that the robot does indeed understand Chinese. I think that what makes Searle's argument sound so convincing is that it is difficult to imagine a version of Searle's example that is a genuine instantiation or emulation rather than a mere simulation.[77] In sum, CRS allows one to see an important distinction that is not respected in the debate, and it gives those who are inclined toward functionalism a positive view about autonomous meaning so they can steer away from mere intuition-mongering.

What's the difference between Searle's argument and my argument in Block (1978)? To make a long story short, though our examples were similar, Searle's argument has a wider target, the symbol-manipulating view of the mind common in cognitive science. This view entails functionalism but is not entailed by it. My aim, by contrast, was mainly to argue that functional definitions constructed from commonsense psychology (by a Ramsification procedure) carried a burden of proof. I argued that nothing of any substance had been said in their favor, and there was some reason to doubt them. Desiderata like the ones mentioned in this paper can be used to satisfy this burden of proof—for intentional states but not experiential states.

Compositionality

The points to be made about compositionality are very similar to points already made, so I will be brief.

According to CRS, it is sentences (and perhaps larger chunks of discourse) that embody hypotheses, claims, arguments, and the like, not subsentential elements. So, according to CRS, the semantic values of words and other subsentential elements are a matter of their contributions to the conceptual roles of sentences and supersentential elements. The conceptual role of 'and', for example, derives from such facts as that a commitment to rejecting 'p' (in the absence of a commitment to accept 'p and q') can lead (in certain circumstances) to a commitment to rejecting 'p and q'. In this way, CRS explains why words have the conceptual roles they do by appeal to conceptual roles of sentences; thus the semantic values of words are seen to be a matter of their causal properties.

The nonreductionist theories do not and should not be regarded as aimed at this type of issue. They are concerned with what the relations among meanings of, say, words and sentences are, not with the issue of why those relations obtain.

What about indicator semantics and Gricean semantics? They, like CRS, take sentential and perhaps supersentential chunks as the basic semantic unit. And, like CRS, they can regard the meanings of words as their contributions to the semantic values of sentences. CRS has no advantage in this matter.

Narrow Meaning, Twin Earth, the Explanation of Behavior, and the Function from Context to Reference and Truth Conditions

The hard work of this section was done (or at any rate, attempted) in the desideratum on narrow meaning. I can be brief here, concentrating on objections and extensions.

What is narrow meaning? (Recall that CRS can do without the claim that narrow meaning is genuinely a kind of meaning, rather than a determinant of meaning.) Here, the comparison with the other theories looks quite different than with the other desiderata. CRS does have an answer—namely, conceptual role—and the other theories have no answer. But the other theories I've been mentioning are not *about* narrow meaning.

Why is narrow meaning relevant to the explanation of behavior, and why is it relevant in the same way for me and my twin? Taking the second question first: since my twin and I are physically identical, all of our representations have exactly the same internal causal roles, and hence the same narrow meanings. But why is narrow meaning relevant to the explanation of behavior in the first place? To have an internal representation with a certain narrow meaning is to have a representation with certain likely inferential antecedents and consequents. Hence, to ascribe a narrow meaning is to ascribe a syndrome of causes and effects, including, in some cases, behavioral effects (or at least impulses in motor-output neurons). The reason my twin and I both jump is that we have representations with conceptual roles that have, as part of their syndrome of effects, jumping behavior. The reason that wide meaning is not as relevant to the explanation of behavior as is narrow meaning is that differences in wide meaning that do not involve differences in narrow meaning (e.g., the difference between me and my twin) do not cause behavioral differences.[78]

The CRS explanation of behavior may seem circular, hence trivial. How can I characterize a meaning functionally, in part in terms of a tendency for representations that have it to cause jumping, and then turn around and explain jumping by appeal to a representation's having this meaning? This is an objection of a well-known sort to explanation in terms of functionally individuated entities, and it has a familiar sort of rebuttal. 'Gene' is defined functionally in Mendelian genetics, in part in terms of effects on, for instance, hair color. 'Reinforcement' is defined in operant-conditioning circles in part in terms of effects on, for instance, bar-pressing. How, then, can one turn around and explain blonde hair in terms of genes, or bar-pressing in terms of history of reinforcement? Part of the answer is that one is not talking about a *single* effect, postulated ad hoc, but rather a complex web of interacting effects. A sickle-cell gene yields sickle-cell anemia in one circumstance (when paired with another sickle-cell gene) but resistance to malaria in another. When one postulates a gene on the basis of one effect, one can obtain converging evidence for it from other effects; and these effects enrich the functional characterization. If you give a rat Burpee Rat Chow (at 80% body weight[79]) contingent on bar-pressing, the rat's bar-pressing response normally increases in strength (on a variety of measures). So it is said that the Burpee Rat Chow is a reinforcer. Part of what makes this a nonempty claim is that one can get the rat to do all sorts of other things using Burpee Rat Chow or other reinforcers.

Second, and more importantly, a functionally individuated entity can, in principle, be identified by independent (usually physicalistic) means and the mechanism of its causal connection to the effects described. For example, a gene identified functionally via the methods of Mendelian genetics can be identified as a clump of DNA via the methods of molecular genetics. And the mechanism by which the gene produces phenotypic characteristics can be described biochemically. Similarly, the mechanism by which Burpee Rat

Chow affects behavior can (presumably) be characterized biologically, or perhaps even psychologically (in terms of the rat's information processing).

The application of the first point to CRS is obvious, but the application of the second is more problematic. The problem has to do with the type-token relation for mental representations. The hope is that there will be a stable physical realization (at least over short stretches of time) of, say, the representation 'CAT', which of course will be identifiable only by its functional role. Then, in principle, one could trace the causal links between this representation and behavior, just as the biochemist can in principle trace the mechanism by which a gene affects the phenotype.[80]

Let us now turn briefly to the matter of the essential indexical. 'I am in the path of danger', and 'Ned Block is in the path of danger' can have systematically different conceptual roles, depending on whether I know I am Ned Block (rather than, say, Napoleon). 'I', used by a speaker, differs systematically from the speaker's own name in its conceptual role, even though they refer to the same thing. Hence CRS assigns them different narrow meanings. Thus the thought I express with 'I' (or its internal associate) is different in narrow content from the thought I would have expressed were my name to have replaced 'I'. Thus, narrow meaning, as articulated by CRS, can be used to explicate a notion of thought *state* distinct from thought *object* that will serve the purpose for which Perry suggested this distinction.[81]

Similar points apply to the examples using names and natural kind terms mentioned in the desideratum on this subject. 'Cicero struts' and 'Tully struts' have different conceptual roles; so despite the fact that they have identical wide meanings, we can see why believing these different sentences could have different effects on other mental states and behavior.[82]

Let us now turn again to the determination of the function from context to reference and truth value. I argued in the section on meaning and reference/truth that conceptual role does determine this function. Take 'I', for example. If someone says "I am in danger," one can infer that the speaker has said, of himself, that he is in danger. In general, it is part of the conceptual role of 'I' that it refers to the producer of the token of 'I' (except in contexts such as quotation). However, there are other aspects of conceptual role that are relevant to, say, explanation of behavior, but not to determination of the function from context to reference and truth value. For example, one can infer from "I entirely fill such and such a spatiotemporal volume" to "You do not occupy this volume." But this inference does not seem relevant to the determination of the aforementioned function. Similar points apply to other types of terms. One can infer from 'water' to 'colorless' (or, at least to 'colorless if pure'); but this has little or nothing to do with determination of reference. I would still be referring to the same liquid even if I were under the impression that in its pure state it has a bluish tinge to it. Indeed, it may be that the aspect of conceptual role that determines the function from context to reference is the same for all natural kind terms. My highly tentative conclusion is that the aspect of conceptual role that determines the function from context to reference and truth value is a small part of the conceptual roles relevant to the explanation of behavior and psychological state.

In conclusion: In this paper, I have not attempted to elaborate CRS, or supply any analyses of language from its perspective. Rather, I have tried to provide reason for suppressing the "put up or shut up" reflex that dogs talk of conceptual roles in the absence of identity conditions for them. My hope is that this theory will get more attention and that more detailed versions of it will allow us to evaluate its prospects better.[83]

Notes

1. Good sketches of the ideas of the representational theory of mind are to be found in Fodor (1981) and Lycan (1981). A more detailed treatment is provided in Pylyshyn (1984).

2. See Block (1983) for a discussion of this distinction and for references to the literature on this topic.

3. I hope my "inherited/autonomous" terminology won't make these questions seem trivial.

4. It is commitment to a priori truth (by which I mean truths for which there is no epistemic possibility of refutation) that really causes trouble for friends of analyticity—not our inability to come up with identity conditions for meaning. After all, no one has ever come up with satisfactory identity conditions for people or ships.

5. Perry (1977, 1979); Kaplan (unpublished).

6. A natural variant on the notion of narrow individuation that I described would require in addition that the same properties be attributed in the same way.

7. Note that the claim that narrow meaning is in the head, in this sense, is not incompatible with the idea that what it is for a word to have a certain narrow meaning is for it to express a concept, where concepts are taken to be abstract objects not locatable in space and time; in this respect, "in the head" is not an apt phrase.

8. Of course, one could define a referential notion of meaning that included narrow meaning and therefore better deserved to be called "wide." This would also result in a more intuitive treatment of vacuous reference. Since the main use I'll be making of the notion of wide meaning is to highlight narrow meaning, I'll stick with the simple definition I've introduced.

9. See Loar (1982), 279; White (1982); and Fodor (1985).

10. Cf. Field (1977).

11. This is a controversial reading of the lesson of Kripke's puzzle. I don't have the space here to describe either the puzzle or the conceptual role semantics solution.

12. White (1982) attempts to *define* a narrow meaning notion using such counterfactuals. But this seems misguided, since there is something shared by the twins *in virtue of which* the counterfactuals are true, and that seems a better candidate for narrow meaning.

13. See McGinn (1982), esp. 211-16, for arguments from the nature of representation to narrow content and meaning.

14. Ignore the problem that since we are made up largely of water, my twin and I can't be duplicates—fixes for this have been proposed by Putnam and Burge.

15. Burge (1979).

16. Actually, my position is that such a multidimensional gradient is needed for full-blooded narrow meaning, but not for the *part* of narrow meaning responsible for mapping contexts onto referents and truth conditions.

17. See Horwich (1982b). Here is the paradox of the preface: I write a book all of whose sentences I believe; nonetheless, I am sure that, being human, I have asserted at least one falsehood. Contradiction. Solution: I have a high degree of belief in each sentence in the book, but that is compatible with a high degree of belief in the falsity of their conjunction.

18. Variance is mean squared deviation from the mean.

19. Burge (1979). Burge constructs cases in which a man has a slight misunderstanding about how a word is used (e.g., he thinks you can have arthritis in the thigh). He then argues, persuasively, that a doppelgänger of this man in a language community in which 'arthritis' is standardly used to include rheumatoid inflammations of bones such as the thigh should not be regarded as meaning by 'arthritis' what we and our man mean by the word.

20. LePore and Loewer (1985) seem to object in this way to two-factor conceptual role semantics.

21. See Harman (1974, 1975, and 1982) and Sellars (1963, 1969, and 1974); see also Putnam (1979).

22. Field (1977, 1978).

23. See Churchland (1979), Loar (1981, 1982), Lycan (1981), McGinn (1982), and Schiffer (1981). Loar and Schiffer advocated conceptual role semantics only as a subsidiary semantic theory for the language of thought, if there happens to be one. The semantic theory they advocated for external language is a functionalized Gricean theory.

24. Woods (1977, 1978, and 1981).

25. Johnson-Laird (1977) and Miller and Johnson-Laird (1976).

26. Though in a paper given at the MIT Sloan Conference, 1984, Field suggests a view in which meaning and content are abandoned altogether. Field's 1977 and 1978 papers are quite skeptical about intersubjective comparisons of conceptual role—because of the collateral information problem. For that reason, he placed great weight on the referential component; recent skepticism about the referential component has led to skepticism about meaning and content altogether.

27. That is, the narrow aspect or determinant of meaning.

28. McGinn (1982) states the theory as assigning states of affairs to sentences. This leads LePore and Loewer (1985) to suppose that a two-factor theory must be more liberal than Davidsonian truth theory in allowing, in the external factor: 'Water is wet' is true $\leftrightarrow$ H_2O is wet. But a two-factor theorist *can* adopt Davidsonian truth theory for the external factor, even though demanding that the sentence on the right-hand side of the biconditional be a *translation* of the quoted sentence on the left-hand side is a stronger demand than necessary for the two-factor theorist.

29. For purposes of this discussion, I shall be ignoring pictorial internal representations.

30. Brain-writing, as everyone knows, is spelled in capital letters.

31. See Kahneman, Slovic, and Tversky (1982) and references therein for detailed studies of such fallacies.

32. Harman (1970) contrasts code-breaking views of language understanding with incorporation views. On the latter, understanding English is translation into a different language; whereas on the former, English is part of the language of thought (actually, a system of syntactic structures with English vocabulary items is part of the language of thought), so no translation is involved.

33. Harman (1982), 14.

34. See Loar (1982), 278-80, for a different slant on what is wrong with Harman's view. Loar takes the line that devices such as Harman's "normal context" and conceptual role in the minds of experts are ad hoc.

35. Johnson-Laird's reply (1978) to Fodor pretty much abandons this verificationist tendency in favor of a generalized conceptual role much like the idea I've been alluding to here.

36. Fodor (1978); reprinted in Fodor (1981), 211.

37. Dretske (1983), 88.

38. This is well argued by Stich (1983). (Although, as I think Sterelny (1985) shows, Stich deploys the wrong notion of "potential" in characterizing his functional roles.) Oddly, Stich considers mental representations, functionally individuated, without ever considering whether there is a distinction to be made between the aspect of functional role relevant to semantics and the aspect that might be called syntactic. (Indeed, these are in effect identified on p. 200.) This is a distinction we make with respect to English orthography. If someone writes the letter 'a' in an idiosyncratic way, we can identify it *functionally*, by the way it appears in words—e.g., it appears by itself, it appears in '*b*n*n*', in place of the asterisks, etc. At the same time, we can distinguish functionally between two uses of the same syntactic type, 'bank'.

39. Fodor (1985).

40. See Hills (1981), 18-19, for a dicussion of the two ways of talking about internal symbolism, and Harman (1973) for an application of the representational state version.

41. See Horwich (1982) for a discussion of this issue in another context.

42. Lycan (forthcoming) argues that God could tell us which worlds were the ones in which a sentence is true without telling us what the sentence means. I think he is right, but only for the reason mentioned in the text. God could indicate the possible worlds in a way that allows us to represent which ones they are without representing what they have in common in virtue of which they are the ones in which the sentence is true. See Lycan's paper for a discussion of indexicals and for references to the literature on this topic.

43. See also Loar (1982), 277.

44. This is Putnam's claim in an influential series of articles beginning with "The Analytic and the Synthetic" (1962); the few decompositional definitions he allows are those that, like 'bachelor = never-married adult male; involve a single "criterion." The idea is that the term 'bachelor' responds to only one "concern," and so there is no possibiiity that different concerns will "pull apart," creating a situation in which we will have to choose arbitrarily how the word is to apply. Putnam has also formulated a version of the argument given below against Fodor's innateness thesis.

45. Of course, it is not a particularly *new* story. Indeed, it is just what you would expect if you believed aspects of Quine and Kuhn, or if you accepted Lewis' "functional definition" story in "How to Define Theoretical Terms" (Lewis 1970). See Kuhn (1983) for semantic views quite close to those of conceptual role semantics.

46. I have heard it said that a conceptual role account of meaningfulness is much more plausible than a conceptual role account of particular meanings. This view is reminiscent of the cognitive theory of emotions that says that what makes a state an emotional state is a certain type of physiological arousal, but what makes such a state joy as opposed to anger is a difference in cognitive "overlay." The application of this idea to semantics cannot be evaluated in the absence of a suggestion as to what it is that accounts for the differences among meanings. Just one comment: in the case of experiential mental states, this type of view is less plausible than the reverse: that some sort of physiological state makes a state experiential, whereas functional *differences* are responsible for the difference between pain and the sensation of red.

47. These theories can often explain semantic defects in complex entities on the basis of the semantic properties of primitives. For example, Katzian semantics can explain why 'red idea' is semantically defective on the basis of the semantic values of 'red' and 'idea'. But Katzian semantics can give no answer to the question of what makes a primitive meaningful element meaningful. The Katzian accommodates the difference between 'red' and 'glub' by putting 'red' but not 'glub' in his dictionary. But it is not part of the theory to give an account of *why*.

48. This article is a jointly written pseudointerview in which the quoted material is put in Barwise's mouth (p. 51), but Perry continues the line of thought.

49. See Stalnaker (1984) for an attempt to solve this within the possible-worlds framework.

50. I derive this objection by analogy to a point made with regard to truth in Soames (1984), 426.

51. This may be Soames's view in the article mentioned in note 50, and I also see a tendency towards this view in Katz (1982), though Katz and Soames probably have different notions of necessity in mind.

52. Though, in the case of at least one version of the Gricean approach, not naturalistic.

53. See the statement of the theory in Schiffer (1982).

54. I used to think that the Fodor-Putnam multiple realizability arguments against physiological reductionism settled the matter. Their point, in essence, was that physiological reductionism was a chauvinist thesis in that, construed as a theory of the mind *simpliciter,* it would exclude intelligent machines or Martians. I now think that the best one is likely to get in the way of a theory of the mind will be a theory of the *human* mind. Such a theory will inevitably be chauvinist. The representational theory of mind that I am adopting here is a theory in that chauvinist tradition. What makes physiological reductionism look so bad is not simply that it is chauvinist—i.e., not just that there are merely *possible* creatures that share our intentional states without sharing our physiology—but rather that we do have promising theories of the human mind and that they are computational-representational (which is not to say that they are committed to the claim that the brain is a digital computer). If the scientific "essence" of intentional states is computational-representational, then it is not physiological—for the old multiple realizability reasons. So multiple realizability is the nub of the matter, but only because one chauvinist theory of the mind is multiply realizable in terms of another.

55. This comes through loud and clear in Searle (1980b).

56. Though in a draft of an article circulated in 1984, Schiffer rejects his earlier approach.

57. See Posner (1978) and Fodor (1982).

58. Sternberg (1969).

59. I can't possibly go into the details here. Dretske's view is couched in terms of the interesting notion of the *most specific information* that a tokening of a representation carries about a state of affairs.

60. Barwise (1984), 8.

61. The theory is sketched in Fodor (1983a, 1984) and expounded in detail in a widely circulated but as yet unpublished paper, "Psychosemantics" (see Loar [1983] for further comments on this paper), which Fodor is now saving for a book he is preparing of the same title. The reason I devote so much space to a largely unpublished account is that the problems with Fodor's account, together with Fodor's refutation of the Dretske-Stampe view, gives us an excellent picture of the type of problem faced by indicator semantics.

62. I am indebted to Paul Horwich here.

63. See, for example, the articles in the relevant section of Sober (1984).

64. There are disagreements about the *extent* of forces orthogonal to optimality. Lewontin and Gould, for example, are controversial in their insistence that the extent of such orthogonal forces is very great. (See their article in Sober [1984].) But this disagreement in the field should not obscure the important agreement mentioned in the text.

65. This issue can be discussed in terms quite distant from evolutionary biology. One example considered by Fodor is that when it comes to beliefs about poisons, false negatives are much more damaging than false positives. False positives ("This is a poison," said of something that is harmless) can cost you a meal, but false negatives can cost you your life. There are mechanisms in rats and even people that could perhaps be interpreted as inclining one to overattribute noxiousness to foods. Fodor insists that in such cases, one should *always* interpret the organisms as paying heed to low probabilities of very bad things rather than falsely ascribing high probabilities to the bad things. He sees this as a product of a principle of charity. The trouble with this reply is that this is not an a priori issue. If the mental sentence theory of belief is right, there is a difference between acting on a belief that *p* and acting on an estimate that, though *p* is unlikely, it would be terrible if true. Independent evidence could be marshalled in favor of one or another alternative. Further, even if Fodor's a priori assumption is right about our cognitive mechanisms, it is contingently right. If we come to understand how our cognitive

mechanisms work, perhaps we could build cognitive mechanisms that work otherwise. It would be a strange semantic theory that depends on such a highly contingent and perhaps quite alterable fact about the cognitive mechanisms that we happen to have. Such a semantic theory would not apply to robots who think, act, and talk almost exactly as we do, but, say, are built to overattribute poisonous qualities to foods on the basis of slim evidence. Will Fodor say we are barred by the logic of the concepts involved from building such a robot?

Another problem with Fodor's a prioristic method of handling these cases is that he is forced to adopt, ad hoc, *other* methods of handling other cases in which supposedly cognitive mechanisms don't aim at truth. In considering the possibility that our cognitive mechanisms are built to *repress* certain unpleasant truths, Fodor stipulates that such mechanisms are not cognitive. He is stuck with simply stipulating which mechanisms are cognitive and which are not.

66. There is a parallel problem in causal theories of reference that *seems* more tractable, but perhaps only because it is more familiar.

67. Quoted in Mandler (1983). On this issue as on many others, one finds glimmers of quite different views in Piaget. There are other passages where he seems to have some appreciation of the Berkeleyan point I make below. See also the discussion in Fodor (1975).

68. This is not the only argument for the third code. There are powerful empirical reasons for postulating a third code. See Potter, Valian, and Faulconer (1977) for both the good and the bad reasons for believing in a third code. Brison (n. d.) (1984) contains an excellent rebuttal of arguments for a third code that make this (and other) mistakes. See also Kolers and Brison (1984).

69. Recall that I am ignoring the mind, concentrating on the brain.

70. The issue of psychologism naturally comes up with respect to this issue, but I have already answered it a number of times.

71. Unless they include in their causal chains the causal roles inside the head, in which case they include CRS itself.

72. Field (1977), 390.

73. This example is similar to ones described in Block (1978, 1981).

74. See the replies in the issue of *Behavioral and Brain Sciences* in which Searle's article appeared and the interchange between Searle and Dennett in *New York Review of Books* (Searle 1983b; Dennett 1983).

75. See Block (1980, 1981).

76. At the appropriate level of abstraction, of course. In this case, as in others I have mentioned, identity of conceptual role is compatible with a variety of causal differences.

77. The only reply I've seen that contains a glimmer of the CRS reply is Haugeland's in the BBS issue just mentioned (Haugeland 1980).

78. Burge (1984) objects that this use of 'behavior' begs the question in favor of individualistic accounts, behavioral ascriptions often being nonindividualistic. I agree that ordinary behavior descriptions are nonindividualistic; I would argue along the lines suggested in Desideratum 8 that an important line of work in cognitive psychology *is* individualistic.

79. To make sure it is hungry—an explanation avoided by most of those who condition rats.

80. Actually, I think there is less of a problem here than meets the eye. Letters of the alphabet are individuated functionally—that is why we recognize shapes that we have never seen before as *A*'s. But what allows us to do this is some degree of stability in the shapes of other letters. It is hard to see how there could fail to be some analogous story about how the brain works—if representationalism is true.

81. This point is similar to the one made by Lycan (1981), (See also Dennett [1982].) However, Lycan somehow sees this point as an argument for the internal sentence story (the conceptual role semantics comes in almost incidentally). I talk about thoughts rather than beliefs because the representationalist story is more plausible for occurrent mental states. As

many commentators have pointed out, one can ascribe a belief if it follows in a simple way from what a person has explicitly thought, even if the belief ascribed has never actually occurred to the person. See Fodor (n.d.).

82. On Kripke's puzzle: since 'Londres' and 'London' have different conceptual roles, it is a mistake to accept Kripke's translation principle. In particular, from the fact that Pierre croit que Londres est jolie, we should not conclude that Pierre believes London is pretty—if the content of his belief is given by 'London is pretty'. Lycan (1981) and McGinn (1982) have interesting discussions of the conceptual role semantics response to Kripke's puzzle, but neither pinpoint the translation principle as the culprit.

83. I am grateful to the John Simon Guggenheim Memorial Foundation and the Center for the Study of Language and Information for support while writing this paper. I would like to thank Michael Bratman, Martin Davies, Hartry Field, Jerry Fodor, Gilbert Harman, Paul Horwich, David Israel, Phil Johnson-Laird, Jerry Katz, Brian Loar, Bill Lycan, and Georges Rey for their helpful comments on earlier drafts.

References

Barwise, John. 1984. *The Situation in Logic—I*. Technical report CSLI-84-2, Stanford University, March. Paper presented at International Congress on Logic and Philosophy of Science, Salzburg, July 1983.

Barwise, Jon, and John Perry. 1983. *Situations and Attitudes*. Cambridge, Mass.

Barwise, Jon, and John Perry. 1984. *Shifting Situations and Shaken Attitudes*. Research report CSLI-84-13, Stanford University, August. To appear as a reply to critics in a special issue of *Linguistics and Philosophy* devoted to situation semantics.

Block, Ned. 1978. "Troubles with Functionalism." In *Perception and Cognition: Issues in the Foundations of Psychology*, edited by C. W. Savage. Minneapolis.

Block, Ned. 1980. "What Intuitions about Homunculi Do Not Show." *Behavioral and Brain Sciences* 3: 425-26.

Block, Ned. 1981. "Psychologism and Behaviorism." *Philosophical Review* 90: 5-43.

Block, Ned. 1983. "Mental Pictures and Cognitive Science." *Philosophical Review* 92: 499-541. Reprinted in *The Philosophers' Annual* 6 (1984), edited by P. Grim et al.

Block, Ned, and Sylvain Bromberger. 1980. "States' Rights." *The Behavioral and Brain Sciences* 3.

Boyd, Richard. 1979. "Metaphor and Theory Change." In *Metaphor and Thought*, edited by Andrew Ortony. Cambridge.

Brison, Susan J. n.d. "Do We Think in Mentalese?" Forthcoming.

Burge, Tyler. 1979. "Individualism and the Mental." *Midwest Studies in Philosophy* 4:73-121.

Burge, Tyler. 1984. "Individualism and Psychology." Paper presented at Cognitive Science Conference, Massachusetts Institute of Technology. Stephen Stich and Ned Block were the respondents. This paper will appear in the Philosophical Review.

Churchland, Paul M. 1979. *Scientific Realism and the Plasticity of Mind*. Cambridge.

Churchland, P. M. and P. S. Churchland. 1983. "Content—Semantic and Information-Theoretic." *Behavioral and Brain Sciences* 6: 67-78.

Davidson, Donald. 1984. *Truth and Interpretation*. Oxford.

Dennett, Daniel C. 1982. "Beyond Belief." In *Thought and Object: Essays on Intentionality*, edited by Andrew Woodfield. Oxford.

Dennett, Dan. 1983. "The Myth of the Computer: An Exchange." *New York Review of Books* (June 14). This contains a letter from Dennett criticizing Searle (1983b).

Devitt, Michael. 1981. *Designation*. New York.

Dretske, Fred. 1981. *Knowledge and the Flow of Information*. Cambridge, Mass.

Dretske, Fred I. 1983. "Why Information?" *Behavioral and Brain Sciences* 6: 82-89. This is Dretske's reply to critics.

Field, Hartry. 1972. "Tarski's Theory of Truth." *Journal of Philosophy* 69: 347-75.

Field, Hartry. 1977. "Logic, Meaning, and Conceptual Role." *Journal of Philosophy* 74: 379-409.

Field, Hartry. 1978. "Mental Representation." *Erkentniss* 13: 9-61.

Field, Hartry. 1980. *Science without Numbers: A Defense of Nominalism.* Oxford.

Fodor, J. A. 1974. "Special Sciences." *Synthese* 28: 77-115. Reprinted as part of Fodor (1975) and in my *Readings in Philosophy of Psychology,* vol. 1.

Fodor, J. A. 1975. *The Language of Thought.* New York.

Fodor, J. A. 1978. "Tom Swift and His Procedural Grandmother." *Cognition* 6: 229-247.

Fodor, J. A. 1981. *RePresentations.* Cambridge, Mass.

Fodor, J. A. 1982. "Cognitive Science and the Twin-Earth Problem." *Notre Dame Journal of Formal Logic* 23: 98-118.

Fodor, J. A. 1983a. "A Reply to Brian Loar's 'Must Beliefs Be Sentences?' " In *PSA 1982,* vol. 2, edited by Peter Asquith and Thomas Nickles. Ann Arbor.

Fodor, J. A. 1983b. *The Modularity of Mind.* Cambridge, Mass.

Fodor, J. A. 1984. "Semantics, Wisconsin Style." *Synthese* 59: 1-20. This is primarily an attack on Dretske and Stampe, but it does contain a brief exposition of Fodor's own theory.

Fodor, J. A. 1985. "Banish DisContent." In *Proceedings of the 1984 Thyssen Conference,* edited by Jeremy Butterfield. Cambridge.

Fodor, J. A. n.d. *Psychosemantics.* Forthcoming.

Harman, Gilbert. 1970. "Language Learning." *Nous* 4: 33-43. Reprinted in *Readings in Philosophy of Psychology,* vol. 2, edited by Ned Block. Cambridge, Mass., 1981.

Harman, Gilbert. 1973. *Thought.* Princton, N.J.

Harman, Gilbert. 1974. "Meaning and Semantics." In *Semantics and Philosophy,* edited by M. K. Munitz and Peter Unger. New York.

Harman, Gilbert. 1975. "Language, Thought and Communication." In *Language, Mind and Knowledge,* edited by K. Gunderson.

Harman, Gilbert. 1982. "Conceptual Role Semantics." *Notre Dame Journal of Formal Logice,* 23: 242-56.

Haugeland, John. 1980. "Programs, Causal Powers, and Intentionality." *Behavioral and Brain Sciences* 3: 432-33.

Hills, David. 1981. "Mental Representations and Languages of Thought." In *Readings in Philosophy of Psychology,* vol. 2, edited by Ned Block. Cambridge, Mass.

Horwich, Paul. 1982a. "Three Forms of Realism." *Synthese* 51: 181-201.

Horwich, Paul. 1982b. *Probability and Evidence.* Cambridge.

Johnson-Laird, P. N. 1977. "Procedural Semantics." *Cognition* 5: 189-214.

Johnson-Laird, P. N. 1978. "What's Wrong with Grandma's Guide to Procedural Semantics: A Reply to Jerry Fodor." *Cognition* 6: 241-61.

Kahneman, D. P. Slovic, and A. Tversky. 1982. *Judgement under Uncertainty: Heuristics and Biases.* Cambridge.

Kaplan, David. n.d. "Demonstratives." Circulated in mimeograph form since 1977 and the subject of the 1980 John Locke Lectures.

Katz, Jerrold J. 1972. *Semantic Theory.* New York.

Katz, J. J. 1982. *Language and Other Abstract Objects.* Totowa, N.J.

Kolers, Paul A., and Susan J. Brison. 1984. "On Pictures, Words and Their Mental Representations." *Journal of Verbal Learning and Verbal Behavior* 23: 105-13.

Kripke, Saul. 1979. "A Puzzle about Belief." In *Meaning and Use,* edited by A. Margalit. Dordrecht.

Kuhn, Thomas S. 1983. "Commensurability, Comparability, Communicability," In *PSA 1982,* vol. 2, edited by Peter Asquith and Thomas Nickles. Ann Arbor.

LePore, E., and B. Loewer. 1985. "Dual Aspect Semantics." In a festschrift for Donald Davidson, edited by E. LePore. I sent the authors a number of criticisms of a draft of this paper; I have no idea whether the version to be published retains the points I criticize here.

Lewis, David. 1970. "How to Define Theoretical Terms." *Journal of Philosophy* 67: 427-46.
Loar, Brian. 1981. *Mind and Meaning.* Cambridge.
Loar, Brian. 1982. "Conceptual Role and Truth Conditions." *Notre Dame Journal of Formal Logic* 23: 272-83.
Loar, Brian. 1983. "Must Beliefs Be Sentences?" In *PSA 1982,* vol. 2, edited by Peter Asquith and Thomas Nickles. Ann Arbor.
Lycan, W. 1981. "Toward a Homuncular Theory of Believing." *Cognition and Brain Theory* 4:139-59.
Lycan, William G. "Semantic Competence and Truth Conditions." Unpublished manuscript.
Mandler, Jean M. 1983. "Representation." In *Cognitive Development,* edited by P. Mussen. Vol. 3 of *Manual of Child Psychology.* New York.
Marr, David. 1982. *Vision.* San Fransciso.
McGinn, Colin. 1982. "The Structure of Content." In *Thought and Object,* edited by Andrew Woodfield. Oxford.
Miller, G. A., and P. N. Johnson-Laird. 1976. *Language and Perception.* Cambridge, Mass.
Perry, John. 1977. "Frege on Demonstratives." *Philosophical Review* 86: 474-97.
Perry, J. 1979. "The Problem of the Essential Indexical." *Nous* 13: 3-21.
Posner, M. I. 1978. *Chronometric Explorations of Mind.* Hillsdale, N. J.
Potter, M. C., V. V. Valian, and B. A. Faulconer. 1977. "Representation of a Sentence and Its Pragmatic Implications: Verbal, Imagistic, or Abstract?" *Journal of Verbal Learning and Verbal Behavior* 16: 1-12.
Premack, David. 1983. "The Codes of Man and Beast." *Behavioral and Brain Sciences* 6: 125-37.
Putnam, Hilary. 1962. "The Analytic and the Synthetic." In *Mind, Language and Reality,* edited by Hilary Putnam. Cambridge.
Putnam, Hilary. 1975. "The Meaning of 'Meaning'." In *Language, Mind, and Knowledge,* edited by K. Gunderson. Minneapolis. Also in Putnam's *Mind, Language and Reality.*
Putnam, Hilary. 1979. "Reference and Understanding." In *Meaning and Use,* edited by Avishai Margalit. Dordrecht.
Putnam, Hilary. 1983. "Computational Psychology and Interpretation Theory." In *Realism and Reason,* edited by Hilary Putnam. Cambridge.
Pylyshyn, Zenon. 1984. *Computation and Cognition.* Cambridge, Mass.
Schiffer, Stephen. 1981. "Truth and the Theory of Content." In *Meaning and Understanding,* edited by H. Parret. Berlin.
Schiffer, Stephen. 1982. "Intention-Based Semantics." *Notre Dame Journal of Formal Logic,* 23: 119-59.
Searle, John. 1980a. "Minds, Brains and Programs." *Behavioral and Brain Sciences* 3: 417-24.
Searle, John. 1980b. Searle's reply to critics of "Minds, Brains, and Programs." *Behavioral and Brain Sciences* 3: 450-57.
Searle, John. 1983a. *Intentionality: An Essay in the Philosophy of Mind.* Cambridge.
Searle, John. 1983b. "The Myth of the Computer." *New York Review of Books* (June 14).
Searle, John. 1984. "Intentionality and Its Place in Nature." *Synthese* 61:3-16.
Sellars, Wilfrid. 1963. *Science, Perception and Reality.* London. See "Empiricism and the Philosophy of Mind" and "Some Reflections on Language Games."
Sellars, Wilfrid. 1969. "Language as Thought and as Communication." *Philosophy and Phenomenological Research* 29: 506-27.
Sellars, Wilfrid. 1974. "Meaning as Functional Classification." *Synthese* 27: 417-27.
Shoemaker, Sydney, 1984. *Identity, Cause, and Mind.* Cambridge.
Soames, Scott. 1984. "What Is a Theory of Truth?" *Journal of Philosophy* 81: 411-29.
Sober, Elliot. 1984. *Conceptual Issues in Evolutionary Biology.* Cambridge, Mass.
Stalnaker, Robert C. 1984. *Inquiry.* Cambridge, Mass.

Stampe, Dennis W. 1977. "Toward a Causal Theory of Linguistic Representation." *Midwest Studies in Philosophy* 2: 42-63.

Sterelny, Kim. "Is Semantics Necessary? Stephen Stich's Case Against Belief." Forthcoming. To appear in *The Australasian Journal of Philosophy.*

Sternberg, S. 1969. "Memory Scanning: Mental Processes Revealed by Reaction Time Experiments." *American Scientist* 57: 421-57.

Stich, Stephen. 1983. *The Case Against Belief.* Cambridge, Mass.

White, Stephen L. 1982. "Partial Character and the Language of Thought." *Pacific Philosophical Quarterly* 63: 347-65.

Woods, William. 1977. "Meaning and Machines." In *Proceedings of the International Conference on Computational Linguistics,* edited by A. Zampoli, Florence.

Woods, William. 1978. *Semantics and Quantification in Natural Language Question Answering.* Technical report 3687. Cambridge, Mass.

Woods, William. 1981. "Procedural Semantics as a Theory of Meaning." In *Elements of Discourse Understanding,* edited by A. Joshi, B. Webber, and I. Sag. Cambridge.

Contributors

Bruce Aune, Department of Philosophy, University of Massachusetts at Amherst

Lynne Rudder Baker, Department of Philosophy, Middlebury College

George Bealer, Department of Philosophy, Reed College

Mark Bedau, Department of Philosophy, Dartmouth College

Ned Block, Center for the Study of Language and Information, Stanford University, and Department of Linguistics and Philosophy, Massachusetts Institute of Technology

Myles Brand, Department of Philosophy, University of Arizona

Michael Bratman, Department of Philosophy, Stanford University

Curtis Brown, Department of Philosophy, Trinity University

Jerry A. Fodor, Department of Linguistics and Philosophy, Massachusetts Institute of Technology

Richard Foley, Department of Philosophy, University of Notre Dame

Jennifer Hornsby, Corpus Christi College, Oxford University

Robert Kraut, Department of Philosophy, Ohio State University

Igal Kvart, Department of Philosophy, The Hebrew University of Jerusalem

Ernest LePore, Department of Philosophy, Rutgers, The State University of New Jersey

Barry Loewer, Department of Philosophy, University of South Carolina

Hugh J. McCann, Department of Philosophy, Texas A&M University

Brian O'Shaughnessy, Department of Philosophy, King's College, London University

Amelie Oksenberg Rorty, Department of Philosophy, Boston University

Jay F. Rosenberg, Department of Philosophy, University of North Carolina at Chapel Hill

David M. Rosenthal, Department of Philosophy, City University of New York

Jerry Samet, Department of Philosophy and History of Ideas, Brandeis University

David Shatz, Department of Philosophy, Yeshiva University

Sydney Shoemaker, Sage School of Philosophy, Cornell University

Avrum Stroll, Department of Philosophy, University of California, San Diego

Richard Swinburne, Department of Philosophy, Oriel College, Oxford University

Peter Unger, Department of Philosophy, New York University

Godfrey Vesey, Department of Philosophy, The Open University, England

Eddy M. Zemach, Department of Philosophy, The Hebrew University of Jerusalem

Peter A. French is Lennox Distinguished Professor of Philosophy and chairman of the philosophy department at Trinity University in San Antonio, Texas. He has taught at the University of Minnesota, Morris, and has served as Distinguished Research Professor in the Center for the Study of Values at the University of Delaware. His books include *The Scope of Morality* (Minnesota, 1980), *Ethics in Government* (1982), and *Collective and Corporate Responsibility* (1984). **Theodore E. Uehling, Jr.,** is professor of philosophy at the University of Minnesota, Morris. He is the author of *The Notion of Form in Kant's Critique of Aesthetic Judgment* and articles on the philosophy of Kant. **Howard K. Wettstein** is associate professor of philosophy at the University of Notre Dame. He has taught at the University of Minnesota, Morris, and has served as a visiting associate professor of philosophy at the University of Iowa and Stanford University. Wettstein has published papers in the philosophy of language.